Microprocessor-Microcomputer Technology

Frederick F. Driscoll
Wentworth Institute of Technology

Boston, Massachusetts

To Peter, my firstborn

Breton Publishers
A Division of Wadsworth, Inc.

Library of Congress Cataloging in Publication Data

Driscoll, Frederick F., 1943–
Microprocessor/microcomputer technology.
Includes index.
1. Microprocessors. 2. Microcomputers.
I. Title.
QA76.5.D693 1983 001.64 82-9744
ISBN 0-534-01326-0

ISBN 0-534-01326-0

Printed in the United States of America
5 6 7 8 9–87 86 85

Microprocessor-Microcomputer Technology was prepared for publication by the following people:
Sponsoring editor: George J. Horesta
Production editor: Jean T. Peck
Art coordinator and interior designer: Ellie Connolly
Cover designer: Stephen Wm. Snider
Illustrations by: Atlantic Offset Company

Contents

Preface

Microcomputers have reached into almost every area of our lives, from business to home entertainment. They are used in diverse applications such as industrial control, scientific research, environmental protection, education, and medical equipment.

The heart of a microcomputer (μC), like any other computer, is its central processing unit (CPU). The CPU fetches and executes instructions, performs arithmetic and logical operations, and establishes timing waveforms needed to carry out instructions. In a μC, the central processing unit is the microprocessor (μP). Advances in integrated circuit technology have allowed semiconductor manufacturers to design the μP as a single integrated circuit (IC) housed in a 40-pin, dual-in-line package.

This book is an introduction to microcomputers and microprocessors. It presents the fundamental concepts of eight-bit μPs. After introducing the basic parts of μPs, the text describes three widely used μPs: 8080A, 6800, and 6502. Most users of μPs usually encounter at least one of these devices, and they cover a variety of μP designs. The 8080A's internal architecture differs significantly from that of either the 6800 or the 6502. Although the 6502 is closer to the 6800 and can use all of its peripheral chips, it is included because it has an "on board" clock generator circuit and is the CPU of some popular μC systems, such as the Apple and Pet computers.

Most students who take a μP or μC course have had a fundamental course in digital electronics. For the reader who has not had such a course or wishes to review some basic material, material on the binary number system is included in Appendix A. Therefore, this text can be used by nonelectronic majors who wish to study the fundamentals of μPs and μCs.

A student usually approaches a μP/μC text or course in one of several ways—to learn only the general concepts, to learn the general concepts and a specific μP, or to learn the general concepts and the differents among μPs. This text can be used by all three types of readers, because it deals with both fundamentals and specifics. A breakdown of the chapters is as follows:

General Chapters

1. Introduction and History of Digital Computers
2. Introduction to Microcomputers and Microprocessors
3. Use of Codes with Microcomputers
4. Microprocessor Software
5. Microprocessor Architecture and Instructions
15. Semiconductor Memories

17. Interface Devices
20. Automatic Testing System

Specific Chapters

6. 8080A Microprocessor Instruction Set
7. 8080A/8085/Z80 Programs
8. 8080A Microprocessor
9. 6800 Microprocessor Instruction Set
10. 6800 Programs
11. 6800 Microprocessor
12. 6502 Microprocessor Instruction Set
13. 6502 Programs
14. 6502 Microprocessor
16. Memory Chips and Organization
18. Programmable Peripheral Interface 8255A
19. Peripheral Interface Adapter 6821

For students interested only in general concepts, Chapters 1, 2, 3, 4, 5, 15, 17, and 20 should be referenced. Chapters 15 and 17 are "stand alone" chapters. For readers who want general knowledge and information about a specific μP, the general chapters and those that deal with a particular μP should be consulted. Each μP has three chapters of information. Chapters 6, 7, and 8 deal only with the 8080A; Chapters 9, 10, and 11 cover only the 6800; and Chapters 12, 13, and 14 deal only with the 6502.

The chapters that treat a μP's instruction set have a worked-out example for almost every type of instruction. Therefore, this text can be used for self-study because of the number of examples and the problems at the end of the chapters. The chapter following the instruction set for each μP uses the instructions in the most commonly used programs. The programs have also been chosen to use every type of instruction in a practical application. The third chapter that deals with a specific μP covers its hardware aspects, pin designation, clock signals, timing diagrams, interrupts, and so forth.

Since a μP is only one part of a μC system, memory and I/O devices are needed. Chapter 15 introduces the semiconductor memories most often used in μC systems. Chapter 16 deals with some of the popular memory devices and how they can be wired into a system.

Interface devices are in Chapter 17 to show the similarities that exist among these devices. One of the peripheral chips most often used in an 8080A system is the 8255A programmable peripheral interface. This device is covered in Chapter 18. The 6800 and 6502 μPs often use the 6821 peripheral interface adapter chip, covered in Chapter 19.

Chapter 20 describes a complete μC system that is designed to test printed circuit boards. The chapter illustrates a practical application of the material presented in the text. Both the hardware and software concepts of μPs are considered in Chapter 20 to show how a dedicated μC product is designed and built.

Special thanks go to Alexander Avtgis, department head of Electronic/Electrical Engineering Technology, and Professor Robert Coughlin, both of Wentworth Institute of Technology, who, as always, provided valuable assistance and support. Phyllis Wolff, of Wentworth, a proficient typist, also deserves praise for her contribution to the manuscript. I would also like to thank my colleagues Robert Villanucci, William Megow, John Marchand, Howard Noyes and Robert Carlson who built the μC system discussed in Chapter 20. Their time, energy, and expertise were the reasons for a successful product on the first try. Also, my appreciation is extended to Gary Boyington, Chemeketa Community College, Salem, Oregon; Ramesh Gaonkar, Onondaga Community College, Syracuse, New York; and David Hata, Portland Community College, Portland, Oregon, for reviewing the manuscript and offering many valuable suggestions. Finally, I thank my wife Jean for her cooperation, support, understanding, and patience in coping with my decision to write another textbook and for the hours of labor she contributed in the final preparation of the manuscript.

Introduction and History of Digital Computers

1.0 INTRODUCTION

As human beings, we are users of many tools. Sometimes we are almost helpless without them. Tools may increase the power of our muscles or senses or help us move around. We are always trying to make tools that work better for us by redesigning or rebuilding old ones and creating new ones for future needs.

In the past few decades, one tool has been developed that has greatly improved our ability to calculate, to store information, and to control processes or the environment. This tool is the electronic computer. It has helped us to increase our knowledge by performing in seconds calculations that otherwise may take hours, weeks, or even years to do by hand. Not only is the computer fast, but also it is accurate and can do tedious jobs without becoming bored. We are then spared the drudgery of making the same calculation over and over again. Computers are machines (or tools) that solve problems for people.

Computers come in all sizes, shapes, speeds, and costs. They can be divided into two classifications: (1) analog and (2) digital. This text concentrates on digital computers, but both types will be discussed briefly to show the difference between them.

1.1 CLASSIFICATION OF COMPUTERS

1.1.1 Analog Computers

Analog computers get their name from the word *analogy*, meaning similarity or likeness. In this type of computer, an electrical circuit is designed so that it behaves electrically as some other operating system behaves. Analog computers have been designed to simulate heat transfer, liquid flow, collision between two vehicles, engine control systems, process control systems, and so on.

The first step in using an analog computer is to develop a set of equations for the original system. The next step is to use electronic components to design and build an electrical circuit that conforms to the set of equations. In the analog computer, measured quantities, usually voltage, are caused to vary in the same way that the original system would vary. In addition to voltage changes, the computer's components (resistors, capacitors, amplifiers, and so on) may be adjusted to simulate changes in the original design. For example, an inductor simulates mass, a capacitor simulates elasticity, and a resistor simulates friction. Thus, the analog computer solves the problem and gives us an output like the output of the original system. However, the majority of computers are digital rather than analog because digital computers can solve more problems faster, more easily, and with greater flexibility.

1.1.2 Digital Computers

While an analog computer deals directly in measurable quantities (voltage, current, resistance, and so on), a digital computer deals in numbers. The term *digital* comes from the word *digit*, meaning a finger or toe, the unit humans probably used when they began counting. The numbers used in digital computers are 0 and 1, the numbers that make up the binary system. The binary system is used because electrical, magnetic, and mechanical devices that have only two states can be used to represent binary digits. For example, a lamp is either on or off.

Digital computers solve problems by carrying out instructions given to them. The set of instructions that solve a given problem is called a *program*. The person who writes such a set of instructions is referred to as a *programmer*. A digital computer is designed to recognize an instruction and to execute it. Programs are called *software*, while the electronic components and circuits that store and execute the instructions are called the computer's *hardware*. In this text, we will examine both the hardware and software of digital computers, but first we will discuss development.

1.2 HISTORY OF DIGITAL COMPUTERS

1.2.1 Calculating Machines

The electronic digital computer is a modern tool, developed in the last few decades. However, its history may well have its origins when people first began counting using their fingers or stones. Probably the earliest digital machine is the abacus, which has been used for over five thousand years. Figure 1–1 shows an abacus. This manual calculator is made up of a rectangular frame that supports a number of parallel rods. The rods represent a decimal place, ones, tens, hundreds, thousands, and so forth. On each rod is a

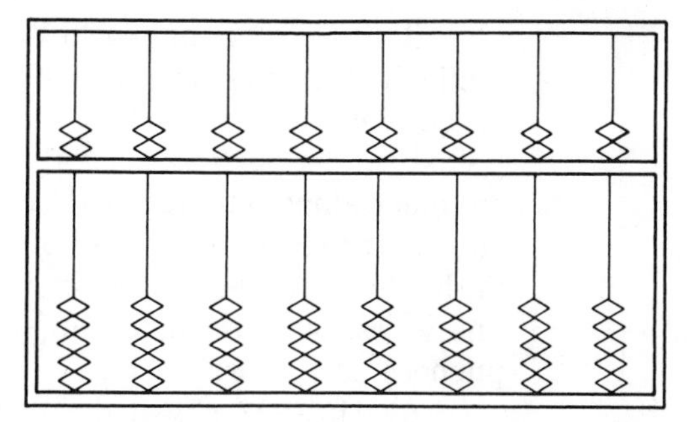

FIGURE 1–1 Chinese Abacus, a Manual Calculator Used for Thousands of Years

number of beads that move along the rod. An operator can move the beads to add, subtract, multiply, and divide, all by hand.

Mechanical devices did not appear until the 17th century. In 1642, Blaise Pascal, a mathematician, invented a desk calculator. This machine used gears to perform addition and subtraction. Multiplication and division could only be performed by repeated additions or subtractions. Pascal's machine was improved in 1671 by another mathematician, G.W. Liebnitz. Liebnitz designed a device that could do multiplication directly. Although his machine never became practical because of mechanical difficulties, it was improved in later years by other individuals.

The next major step toward today's computers came in 1833 when Charles Babbage, an English scientist and mathematician, designed a machine that he called an analytical engine. This machine was a forerunner to the modern computer. It had a program that was stored on punched cards in a section separate from the section that performed the arithmetic operations. Unfortunately, Babbage had a history of never fully completing a design, and this machine was no exception.

Between 1833 and 1930, most of the advances in the area of digital technology were with calculating machines. They were made faster and more capable of handling different applications. In 1920, the electric motor was added to calculators. Some machines of this period were called analyzers. They were designed to solve some specific problem such as a differential equation. Many analyzers of this period were mechanical machines.

1.2.2 Electromechanical Machines

In 1937, George Stibitz, a research mathematician at Bell Telephone Laboratories, built a binary arithmetic machine using relays, flashlight batteries, and bulbs. It is the first known machine that could do binary arithmetic. At first, it was seen as a curiosity by his colleagues and its potential was not immediately pursued. Stibitz also designed an electromagnetic calculator to multiply and divide complex numbers. This machine, known as the complex number calculator, had a high degree of reliability and was faster than comparable machines of the time. It was the first machine that could be used from a remote location.

Until the start of World War II, Bell Labs was not interested in pursuing the idea of a large-scale computer. But between 1939 and 1944, the U.S. Army asked Bell Labs to design five relay computers to aid in calculations for ballistics testing. The computers that resulted were highly reliable and had minimum downtime (breakdowns). They introduced two important new concepts: a program that could be entered by tape and floating point arithmetic. Both ideas are still used in today's computers. These computers, like the analyzers, were designed for a particular purpose. They are called special-purpose computers.

Also in 1937, Howard Aiken, an engineer, proposed building an automatic computing machine that would be controlled by a set of instructions. Each instruction would have its own code and the machine would perform one specific job according to the particular instruction code it was given. In addition to solving problems, the machine could produce either punched cards or typed pages. After being turned down by the Monroe Calculating Machine Company, Aiken was able to convince International Business Machines Corporation (IBM), with some financial support from the U.S. Navy and Harvard University, to build such a machine. The machine was completed in 1944 and was called the automatic sequence controlled calculator, better known as the Mark I. In the late 1940s, Aiken designed the Mark II, III, and IV. The Mark III was an all-electronic computer but it was not the first of its kind.

1.2.3 Electronic Computers

In 1943, John Mauchly and J. Presper Eckert teamed up to design an all-electronic computer. Mauchly had written an original proposal for such a computer in 1942 but it was rejected by the U.S. Army. By 1943, the situation had changed, and the Army needed a way to get more and faster ballistic calculations. A U.S. Army lieutenant and mathematician, Herman Goldstine, reworked Mauchly's proposal and presented it again. This time it was approved. The result was the electronic numerical integrator and computer, more commonly known as ENIAC I, which was completed in 1946.

In comparison to the Mark I, the ENIAC I was a thousand times faster and could perform five thousand additions or subtractions per second. With the exception of some input and output equipment (typewriters and printers), the ENIAC I was the first computer that operated using all-electronic components. However, it was a monster of a machine, containing 18,000 vacuum tubes. Modifying a program required hours of rewiring the electronic circuits.

In 1946, John von Neumann, a professor of mathematics at the Institute of Advanced Study at Princeton University, along with Herman Goldstine, and another colleague, Arthur Burks, wrote a paper describing a computer in which the program could be stored and changed without changing hardware. The first computer that worked from this principle was built by Maurice Wilkes, a computer scientist at Cambridge University. Eckert, Mauchly, and von Neumann also designed and built such a computer, but it was not completed until 1950 and was called the EDVAC I.

1.2.4 Commercial Computers

During the 1930s and 1940s, only a relatively small group of mathematicians and engineers was interested in computers. Computer applications were limited to special scientific projects that required a large number of calculations. Businesses saw little purpose for such machines and committed no money for research and development. In 1950, however, Eckert and Mauchly believed that computers could be sold for commercial purposes and therefore formed their own company, which was bought by Remington Rand. In 1951, the U.S. Bureau of the Census bought the first commercial computer from Remington Rand, the UNIVAC I (universal automatic computer).

During this time, von Neumann and Goldstine had returned to Princeton and were continuing to work on experimental computers. Computer architecture designed by von Neumann became the basis of many of today's computers.

In 1950, IBM began to design what it called the 701 scientific computer. Its success resulted in the company's design of the 702, intended for commercial uses.

Computers in the early 1950s were large and bulky machines. Advances in technology were needed to speed the progress of the computer industry.

1.2.5 Second-Generation Computers

Relay and vacuum-tube computers are considered to be the first generation of digital computers. The progress of computers using this technology would have been severely limited because of size, cost, and power consumption. But two separate inventions—the transistor and the magnetic core—helped significantly to promote the growth of the computer industry and to reduce the cost of individual computers. The transistor and the magnetic core reduced the size, weight, power consumption, and thus the cost of computers. The magnetic core also allowed the computer to keep and store a program when the power was turned off. Computers developed with this technology are considered to be second generation.

1.2.6 Third-Generation Computers

In the mid-1960s, semiconductor manufacturers were able to mass-produce a reliable package that contained ten to twenty transistors in the same area that had contained a single transistor. These packages are called *integrated circuits*, or ICs. This dense packaging allowed computer designers to build digital computers that were faster, more powerful, much smaller, and cost less than their predecessors. The market for these third-generation computers expanded and new uses were found for the machines. IC packages, or *chips*, are still used today and we will use some of them in this text. These first IC packages used in computers are called *small-scale integration*, or SSI, chips.

1.2.7 Fourth-Generation Computers

Just as the transistor was replaced by SSI chips in individual computers, the many functions of the SSI package have been replaced by newer and more complex ICs. These packages are classified as *medium-scale integration*, or MSI, and *large-scale integration*, or LSI, chips. The MSI package contains from twelve to two hundred devices, while the LSIs contain thousands or even tens of thousands of devices. Figure 1–2 shows a typical LSI chip housed in a 40-pin dual-in-line package (DIP).

The digital computers discussed in this text use this new technology and are called *microcomputers*. In comparison to the ENIAC I of the 1940s, these fourth-generation computers have more computing power, are twenty to fifty times faster, and are thousands of times more reliable. In addition, the newest digital computers cost less, occupy less space, and consume only the smallest fraction (less than 1/10,000th) of the power needed by earlier models.

1.2.8 LSI Applications

LSI chips have revolutionized military, industrial, and commercial computer designs. Traditional equipment is becoming "smart" and new designs are constantly emerging. An everyday example is the hand-held calculator. LSI chips have allowed manufacturers to cut the cost of the calculator while increasing its performance and number of functions. A few other commercial products using LSI chips are ovens, dishwashers, gas pumps, telephones, automobiles, video games, television sets, and navigation equipment. The potential use of LSI chips seems endless. In each case, the new electronic designs have reduced the size, weight, and power consumption of the circuitry it has replaced while improving reliability and performance.

The LSI chip that has spawned most of these new designs was designed in 1971 by Intel Corporation. It is the *microprocessor*—the central processing unit of a microcomputer. The revolution in microelectronics has brought about low-cost personal computers (microcomputers) with enough capacity to sup-

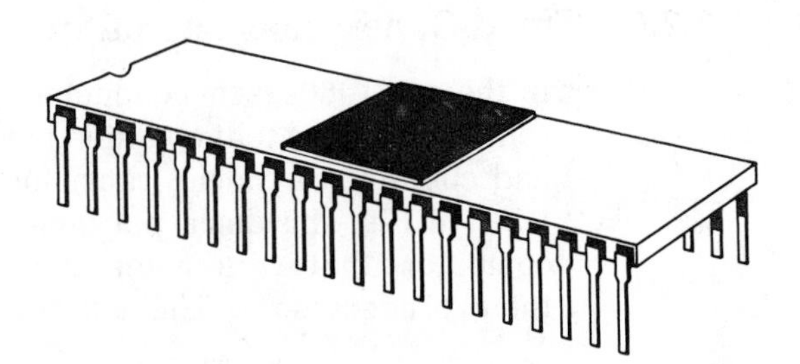

FIGURE 1–2 Typical LSI Chip Housed in 40-Pin Dual-in-Line Package (DIP)

port high-level computer languages and color graphic displays. In the following chapters, we will study microprocessors and other LSI chips that are used to build microcomputers.

1.3 SUMMARY

Computers can be classified as either analog or digital. This text deals only with the digital type—both hardware and software. Modern electronic computers have their origins in mechanical calculators of the 17th century. It was not until 1946 that an all electronic computer, ENIAC I, was first completed. This machine was designed for military applications. Computers for commercial purposes were introduced in the early 1950s. Transistors and magnetic cores helped significantly in reducing the size, weight, power consumption, and cost of computers. The next major steps in designing more efficient computers were taken in the mid-1960s when semiconductor manufacturers were able to mass-produce integrated circuits. These IC packages are classified as SSI, MSI, and LSI. Although a complete microcomputer system uses all three types of ICs, the principle components are the newer LSI chips. With the history of digital computers in mind, we are now ready to delve more deeply into the design and functions of microcomputers and their major element, the microprocessor.

PROBLEMS

1-1 Define computers.
1-2 List the two classifications of computers.
1-3 List some of the advantages of digital computers over analog computers.
1-4 Define programmer.
1-5 Define software and hardware.
1-6 What was the first all-electronic digital computer?
1-7 What two inventions in the 1950s reduced the size and cost of computers?
1-8 What is the principle component in fourth-generation computers?

Chapter 2

Introduction to Microcomputers and Microprocessors

2.0 INTRODUCTION

Today's digital computers fall into three categories: (1) large main-frame computers, (2) minicomputers, and (3) microcomputers. Some of the factors used to determine the category of a computer are physical size, speed, cost, and application.

The *large main-frame computers* are the fastest and most powerful—that is, they can handle a large number of instructions, and they can handle large amounts of data. Banks, insurance companies, and airlines are among the many users of large main-frame computers in which many operators have access to a common source of data. At an airline terminal, for example, airline personnel can check a reservation regardless of where the ticket was purchased or at which airport the passenger will board the airplane. Large main-frame computers are also used for inventory control, weather forecasting, and satellite calculations. The circuitry of large main-frame computers is the most complex; thus, these computers cost more than the other two types. They are designed for general purposes and can usually accept a large number of different programs.

Until the mid-1960s, most computers were of the large main-frame variety. Manufacturers then introduced computers that were slower, smaller, and designed for specific rather than general applications. These computers became known as *minicomputers*. At first, they were mainly used in laboratories and process control applications in industry. Then, the use of minicomputers grew considerably, primarily in small businesses. Minicomputers opened markets that needed computers but could not afford large main-frame machines. Both markets—large main-frame and minicomputer—are continuing to grow.

With fabrication processes that allowed tens of thousands of transistors to be placed in a single integrated circuit, semiconductor manufacturers were able to interconnect a few IC chips and design a new computer. These *microcomputers* are physically smaller than either main-frame computers or minicomputers. In most cases, they are slower and cost less too. In a few short years, microcomputers have carved their own share of the computer market. They are presently being used in machine and process control; in test, scientific, and medical equipment; in traffic control; in communications equipment; and in home appliance and entertainment devices. Although the major principles of all digital computers are the same, we shall concentrate our efforts in this text on the microcomputers—both their hardware and their software.

Thus far we have considered how computers are classified by size, speed, cost, and application. Another way of classifying computers is by their word length.

2.1 BIT, BYTE, AND WORD LENGTH

As previously mentioned, digital computers operate using numbers. The familiar decimal number system that we use every day is composed of 10 digits (0, 1, 2, 3, 4, 5, 6, 7, 8, and 9). However, digital computers use a different number system, the *binary system*. The binary system is composed of only two digits, (0 and 1). These two digits can be used in many combinations to express not only numbers but also letters, punctuation, special characters, and, even more importantly, computer instructions.

The major reason digital computers use the two digits 0 and 1 is that these digits can be represented by mechanical, magnetic, or electrical devices that have only two states. For example, a switch or relay can be either open or closed; a vacuum tube or transistor can be either off or on. The open or off state is the binary 1; the closed or on state is the binary 0. Although the binary digits 0 and 1 are commonly and easily used, keep in mind that these values in a number system are actually two different voltage levels inside the computer. In many digital computers, the binary digit 0 is a voltage range between 0 volts and 0.8 volts, while the binary digit 1 is a voltage range between 2.4 volts and 5 volts.

The term *binary digit* is used so often in digital work that it is commonly abbreviated to *bit*. An 8-bit pattern of binary numbers is called a *byte*. Figure 2–1 shows three different examples of 8-bit binary patterns.

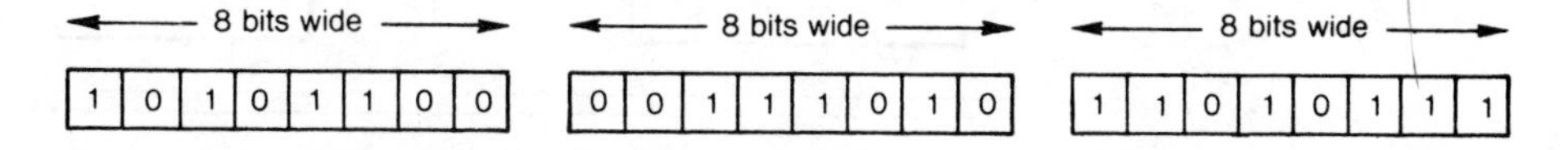

FIGURE 2–1 Examples of Eight-Bit Binary Patterns

TABLE 2–1 Comparison of Computer Word Lengths and Their Categories

Category	Number of Binary Digits								
Micro	1	4	8	12	16				
Mini				12	16	32	48		
Large							48	60	64

Most microcomputers on the market today "speak" in a digital language for which every *word* has the same number of digits. The word length or word size for many microcomputers is 8 bits. The word length describes the width of the binary pattern—that is, the number of bits—that is handled at once. Some computers (large main-frame, minis, and some micros) handle information in binary patterns other than 8 bits. Computers have been designed with word lengths from as small as one bit (these computers are usually called controllers) to as wide as 64 bits (large main-frame computers). The commonly used lengths are 1, 4, 8, 12, 16, 32, 48, 60, and 64. Table 2–1 shows a comparison of computer word lengths and their corresponding categories.

Microcomputer programs can occupy several thousand bytes of memory. In order to eliminate writing or referring to large numbers, the symbol K is often used; it stands for 1024. Thus,

1K byte = 1 × 1024 = 1,024 bytes
4K bytes = 4 × 1024 = 4,096 bytes
16K bytes = 16 × 1024 = 16,384 bytes
64K bytes = 64 × 1024 = 65,536 bytes

Note: The symbol k = 1000, but the symbol K = 1024.

2.2 MICROCOMPUTER ARCHITECTURE

A single-board microcomputer (μC) can be simplified into three major parts, as shown in Figure 2–2. They are: (1) central processing unit (CPU), which is the microprocessor (μP) chip; (2) input/output ports, which connect the μC to peripheral equipment; and (3) memory, which stores data and instructions.

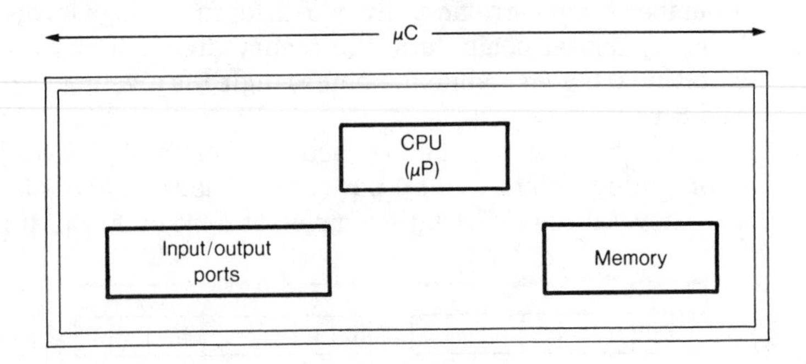

FIGURE 2–2 Main Parts of a Microcomputer (μC)

2.2.1 Input/Output Ports

A μC operator must have some way of communicating with the machine—that is, some way of entering a program and obtaining the result. The operator may use a keyboard, for example, to type in a request for information. The keyboard is connected to the μC through an input port, as shown in Figure 2-3. Input/output (I/O) ports are the parts of a computer that allow humans to communicate with it through *peripheral equipment* such as keyboards, cathode ray tubes (CRTs), card or paper tape readers, magnetic tapes, and magnetic disks.

The I/O port is an LSI chip that allows the computer either to communicate with humans or to control or be controlled by machines. It is often called a peripheral interface adaptor (PIA) device or a programmable peripheral interface (PPI) device. These chips can be programmed to act either as inputs to or outputs from the computer.

If the computer is being used in a process control application, then input devices called *transducers* (thermistors, thermocouples, and strain gages) are used. A transducer converts a physical analog quantity such as heat, light, or pressure into an electrical quantity. This quantity may have to be converted into a voltage or current that is usually very small. The voltage or current may first have to be amplified or otherwise processed before it is converted from an analog signal into a digital signal. For example, a thermocouple may be used as an input device to be connected with other circuitry to the I/O port, as shown in Figure 2-4. A thermocouple is used for measuring heat. Its signal, however, is small and usually requires amplification before being converted to a digital signal.

Output equipment used in process control applications may be meters, printers, or CRT displays. Other applications may have heaters, valves, relays, or solid-state switches (SCRs or triacs) as output devices to control even higher

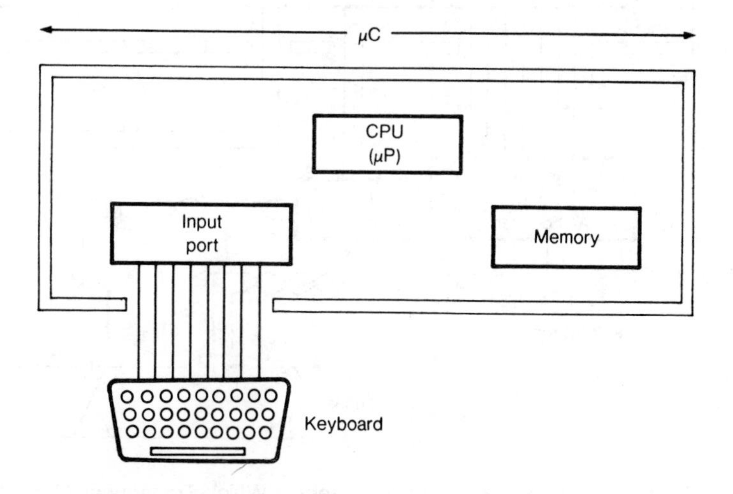

FIGURE 2-3 Keyboard Connected to μC through Input Port

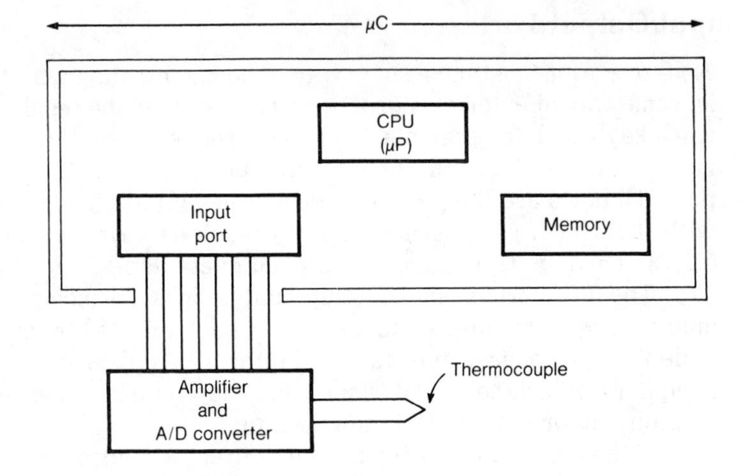

FIGURE 2-4 Thermocouple Used as Input Device to Be Connected with Other Circuitry to I/O Port

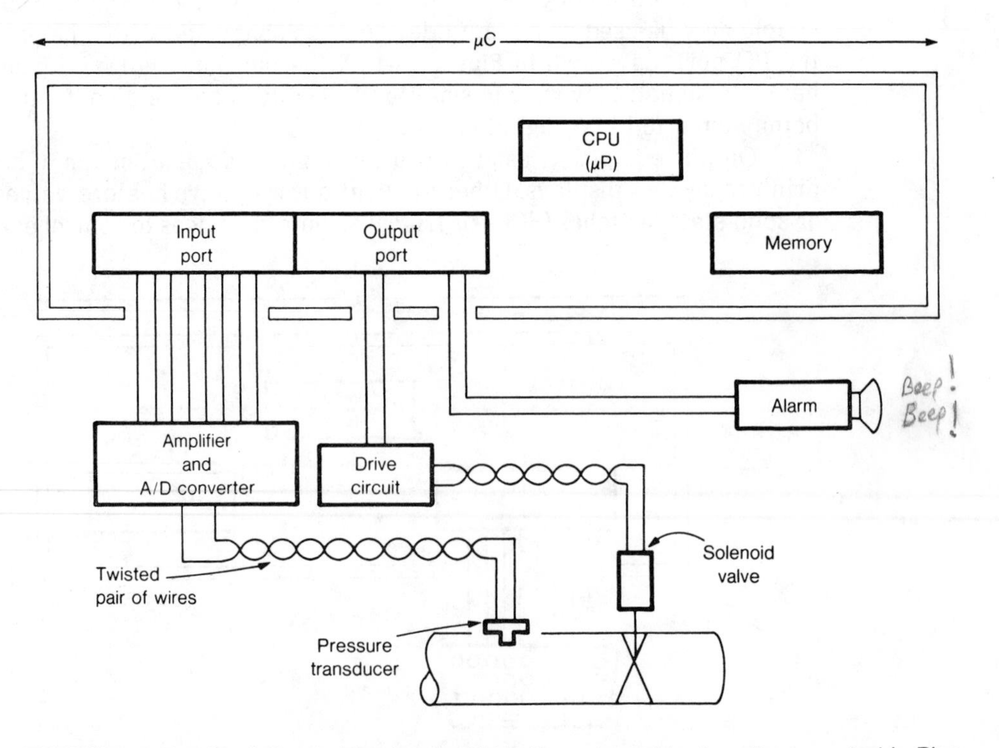

FIGURE 2-5 Feedback Control System in Which Transducer Monitors Pressure inside Pipe and Constantly Sends Back Data to μC

power devices such as motors that are required for operation of the process. Such systems are called *feedback control systems*. In Figure 2–5, for example, a feedback control system is shown in which the transducer monitors the pressure inside the pipe and constantly sends back data to the μC. A program is used to compare the data to a reference value stored in memory. If the pressure exceeds the reference, the μC sends out signals to close the valve and sound an alarm.

Peripheral equipment is usually slower than memory devices or the central processing unit. This equipment can cause the μC to waste time waiting for the equipment either to send or receive data. How peripheral equipment draws attention to itself when it wishes to communicate with the computer and how the computer responds will be discussed later. How the computer can perform many other tasks while it waits for a peripheral equipment instruction will also be considered later.

2.2.2 Memory

Memory is that portion of the computer that stores the program and the data until they are needed. It is easiest to think of memory as groups of storage cells. Each cell can store one bit of information, either a binary 0 or 1. For example, Figure 2–6 shows a group of 8 cells or bits storing a binary pattern that represents the letter P. As shown, a combination of 0s and 1s is needed to represent the letter P. Other letters or other types of information require other combinations. Most μCs store instructions and data in groups of 8 bits (one byte). To store more than one letter, we need more than one byte. Figure 2–7 shows what a portion of memory storing the word PENCIL would look like. Six bytes are required, one for each letter. The binary bits that are used to represent the letters will be studied in a later chapter.

We must store each letter in a known location so that we can retrieve it. Therefore, each byte stored in memory must have an address. For example,

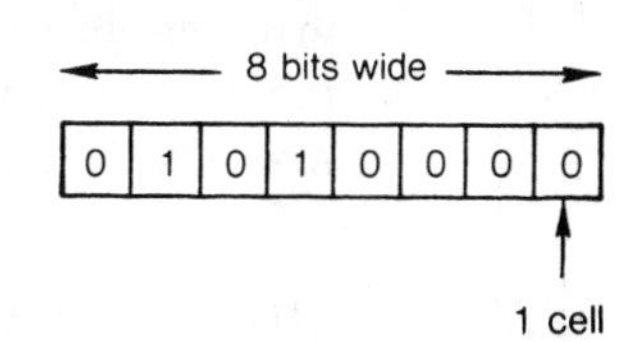

FIGURE 2–6 Letter P Stored in μC Memory as Eight-Bit Binary Pattern

P =	0	1	0	1	0	0	0	0
E =	0	1	0	0	0	1	0	1
N =	0	1	0	0	1	1	1	0
C =	0	1	0	0	0	0	1	1
I =	0	1	0	0	1	0	0	1
L =	0	1	0	0	1	1	0	0

FIGURE 2–7 Word PENCIL Stored in Memory as Six Binary Bit Patterns

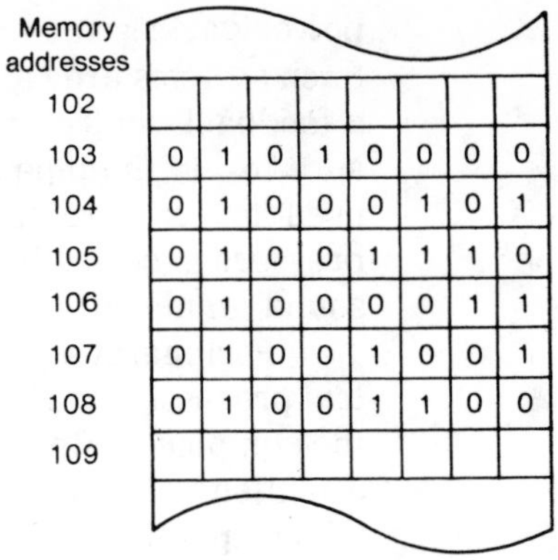

Memory addresses								
102								
103	0	1	0	1	0	0	0	0
104	0	1	0	0	0	1	0	1
105	0	1	0	0	1	1	1	0
106	0	1	0	0	0	0	1	1
107	0	1	0	0	1	0	0	1
108	0	1	0	0	1	1	0	0
109								

FIGURE 2-8 Binary Pattern for Word PENCIL Stored in Memory Locations 103 through 108

Figure 2-8 gives the memory addresses for each letter in the word PENCIL. In this example, this word has been stored in addresses 103 to 108. The μCs to be described later in this text are capable of having 65,536 addresses. The use of addresses lets the computer find quickly all information stored in memory. The terms *memory location* and *memory address* are sometimes used instead of *address*.

There are two types of memory: (1) volatile and (2) nonvolatile. A volatile memory is one that loses its information when the power is turned off. It is a temporary memory. A nonvolatile memory keeps its information when the power is turned off. It is permanent. Throughout this text, we will consider both types of memory and will see how each is used in a μC.

Although most μCs on the market today are capable of having 65,536 memory locations, not all systems use this much memory. Some of the applications we will examine require less than 100 memory locations while other applications require many more.

The nonvolatile memory chips to be discussed later are ROMs (read only memory), PROMs (programmable read only memories), EPROMs (erasable programmable read only memories), and EEROMs (electrical erasable read only memories). RAMs (random access memories), a type of volatile memory chip also known as read/write (R/W) memories, will also be described.

2.2.3 Central Processing Unit

The central processing unit (CPU) is the heart of a digital computer. It decodes the instructions, controls the other parts of the machine, performs the arithmetic operations, and in many cases contains some memory (volatile or nonvolatile or both). It is this section of the computer that took tens of thousands of vacuum tubes in the ENIAC I. In today's μCs, the CPU is a single integrated circuit—the microprocessor (μP). The reader may have heard the term *computer on a chip* used to describe the μP or may erroneously think that the terms *microprocessor* and *microcomputer* can be used interchangeably. Some of the confusion between these terms is probably caused by the fact that there are

LSI chips on the market that contain I/O lines, memory, and the CPU all in a single package. These devices are μCs that are best described by the term *single-chip microcomputers*. They are used in applications such as games, entertainment, household appliances, or other specialized or dedicated control purposes. In general, however, a μC is a system made up of a small number of LSI chips. The μP is one of these chips. (In some systems, the μP is more than one IC, because everything cannot be contained in a single package. This text covers only single-chip μPs because they are the most widely used.) Most μPs cost less than $20, and at this price it is understandable why they are so widely used.

In summary, then, the μP is the central processing unit of a μC. That is,

$$\mu C = \mu P + \text{memory} + I/O$$

and

$$\mu P = CPU$$

Now that we have examined the three major parts of a μC—I/O, memory, and CPU—we will see how they are connected to one another.

2.3 SYSTEM BUS

A bus is a wire (or wires) that connects the IC chips in the computer. On a printed circuit board, they are conductor patterns. Figure 2-9 shows an I/O port, memory, and a CPU connected to a system bus. A system bus is made up of three types of buses: (1) an address bus, (2) a data bus, and (3) a control bus. The *address bus* allows the CPU to address any memory location or I/O port. The *data bus* is used to transmit information (instructions or data) between the CPU and memory, between the CPU and an I/O port, or between memory and an

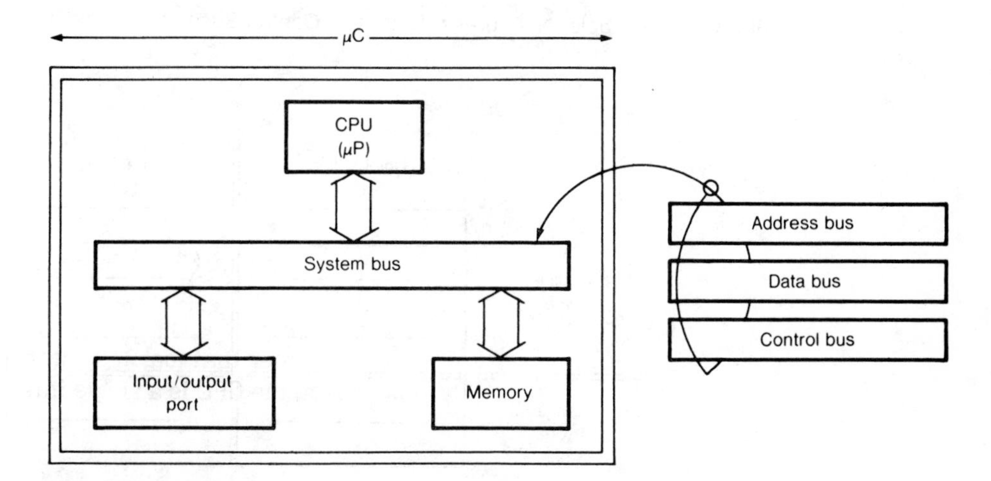

FIGURE 2-9 Major Parts of μC Connected to System Bus

I/O port. The *control bus* is used to transmit signals between devices that tell what is happening or should be happening. The job of the control bus is to keep everything running smoothly.

Circuit diagrams show a bus composed of more than one wire or conductor pattern as a wide double line or a single line with a slash through it. A single line with no slash indicates a single wire or conductor pattern. Figure 2–10 shows the three bus symbols used on circuit diagrams. The address and data buses are a set of parallel wires and are thus represented on circuit diagrams by the symbol given in either Figure 2–10A or Figure 2–10B. The control bus is made up of individual wires, and each control line is therefore represented by a single line as shown in Figure 2–10C.

Buses are either unidirectional or bidirectional. A unidirectional bus is one whose signals always travel in the same direction. A bidirectional bus is one in which the signals may travel in one direction at one time and in the opposite direction at another time. In circuit diagrams, arrows at the end of the bus symbols indicate which type of bus is being used. Figure 2–11 is a summary of the bus symbols used on μC diagrams.

The μC systems covered in this text have 16 address lines that are unidirectional, 8 data bus lines that are bidirectional, and 4 or 5 control lines. Most control lines are unidirectional, but some lines connected to I/O ports are bidirectional.

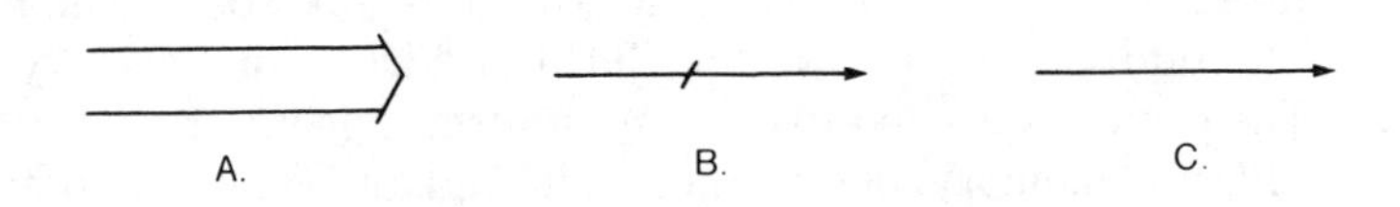

FIGURE 2–10 Symbols for Address, Data, and Control Buses Used on Circuit Diagrams

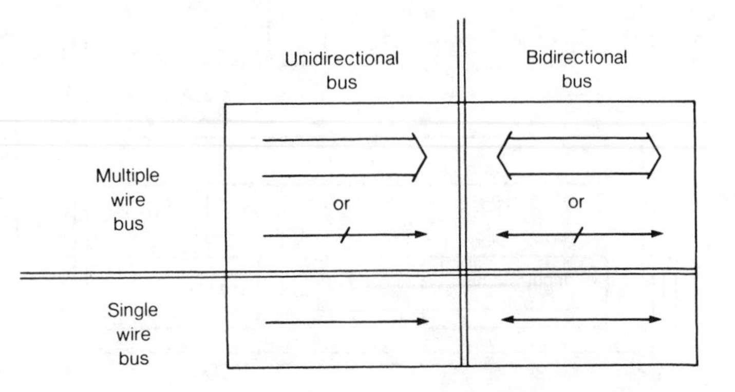

FIGURE 2–11 Summary of Bus Symbols Used on μC Diagrams

2.4 MICROPROCESSOR ARCHITECTURE

In Section 2.2, we described the μC as having three basic parts: I/O ports, memory, and the central processing unit. The central processing unit—that is, the μP—can be described as having four basic parts: (1) registers, (2) arithmetic and logic unit, (3) timing and control circuitry, and (4) decoding circuitry. Figure 2-12 shows these four basic parts.

A *register* is a storage location. The registers within the CPU are either 8 bits wide or 16 bits wide. The three most widely used registers, as shown in Figure 2-12, are the *accumulator* for general-purpose use plus the *program counter* and *instruction register* for specific use. The accumulator temporarily stores the results of an arithmetic or logic operation. The instruction register is used to store the instruction that the μP is currently operating on. The program counter stores the address of the next instruction to be operated on.

The *arithmetic and logic unit* (ALU) is that portion of the computer that actually works on the data. It performs the mathematical operations, addition and subtraction, and the logical operations, AND, OR, Exclusive OR, and complementing.

The *timing and control sections* control the internal operation of the CPU chip and are also connected to the control bus to control I/O ports and memory. A clock, part of the internal circuitry of the CPU in some μCs, sends out pulses that make the entire system work in an orderly manner. Clock pulses and circuitry are covered in later chapters.

The *decoding circuitry* of the CPU involves the process of *decoding*, by which a binary pattern is translated into an operation or sequence of operations. For example, if the binary pattern 10111001 means "add," the decoding circuitry will recognize it and send signals to all other parts of the μP to set its internal circuitry so that addition occurs.

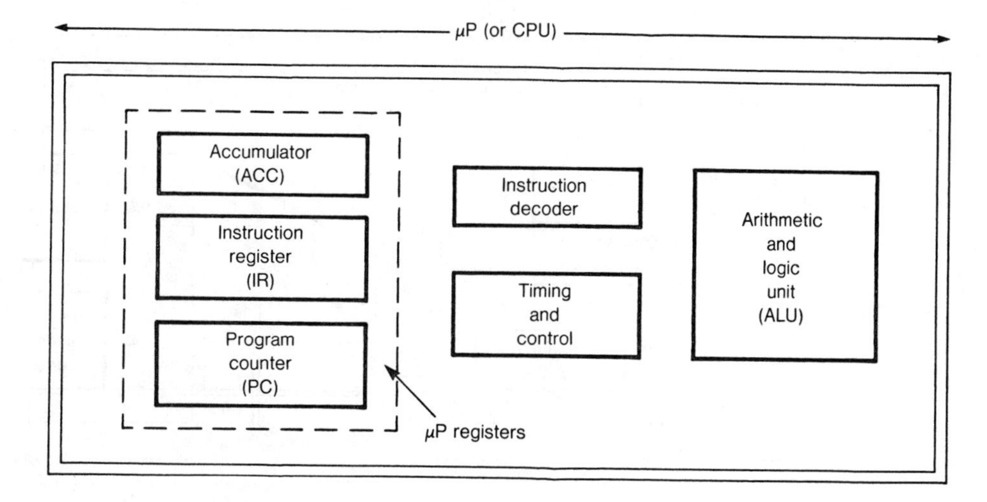

FIGURE 2-12 Four Basic Parts of a Microprocessor (μP)

2.5 PROGRAM EXECUTION

Assume that a computer program and data have been stored in memory and the program is ready to be executed. (In later chapters, we will discuss how the program and data got into memory.) When the computer operator presses the GO key (sometimes referred to as a run or start key), the following steps occur automatically:

1. The memory address of the first instruction of the program is loaded into the program counter (PC).
2. The PC places the memory address onto the address bus lines.
3. The address is sent to memory.
4. Memory decodes the address—that is, it finds the correct memory location.
5. Memory sends the instruction back to the μP over the data bus lines.
6. The instruction is placed in the instruction register (IR) inside the μP.
7. The μP decodes the instruction—that is, the instruction (by its binary pattern) tells the μP what to do.
8. The PC is incremented and the μP is now ready to receive the next piece of information, whether it is data or an instruction.

Figure 2-13 shows each of these steps, which cover the time from when the μP begins to send out an address until it sends out the next address. Steps 1 through 7 are accomplished in 0.5 to 5 microseconds (μs) because the manufacturer of the μP chip has designed into it the necessary steps to be carried out for each instruction.

Figure 2-14 shows another way to diagram the steps involved between the μP and memory. Steps 1 through 6 are referred to as the *fetch*, or read,

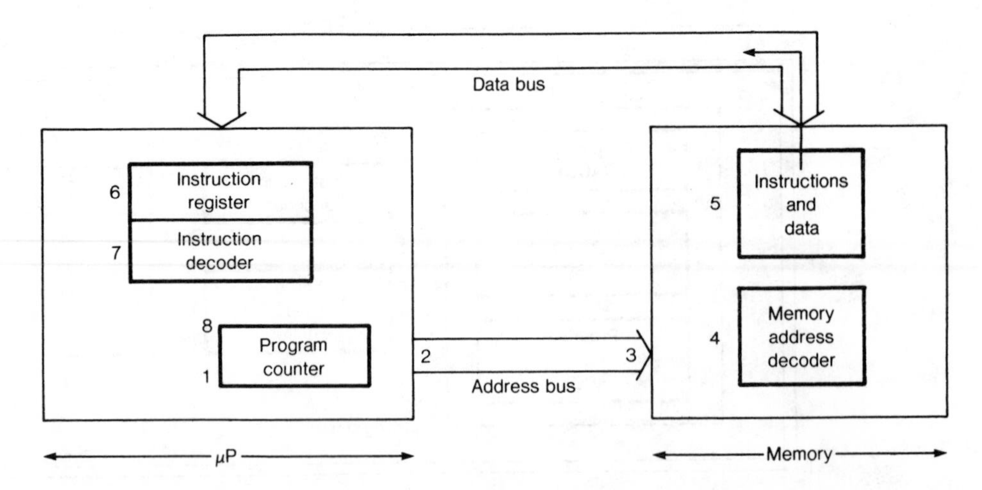

FIGURE 2-13 Steps Involved from Time μP Begins to Send Out an Address Until It Sends Out Next Address

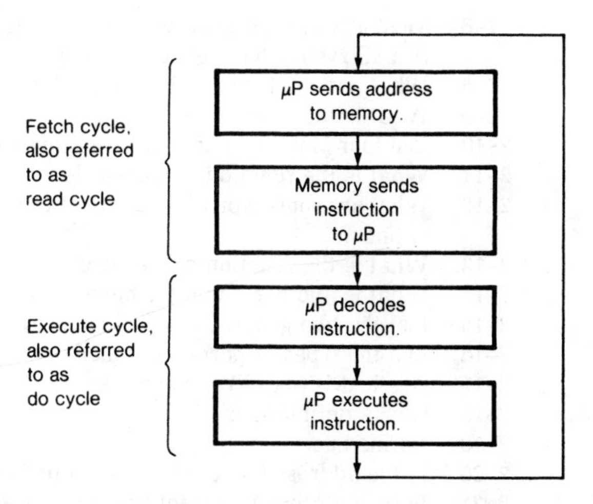

FIGURE 2–14 Block Diagram Summarizing Steps Involved between μP and Memory

cycle. Step 7 is the *execute*, or do, cycle. The fetch and execute cycles shown on the block diagram illustrate how a computer operates.

All 8 steps are repeated until the μP interprets a stop, or *halt*, instruction. Sometimes an instruction tells the μP to break the normal sequence and put a new address in the PC. This instruction is called a *jump* instruction, and we will examine applications that require such an instruction in Chapters 7, 10, and 13.

2.6 SUMMARY

This chapter introduced the terms bit, byte, and word and described how computer systems are classified according to word length. A microcomputer (μC) has three main parts: (1) input/output ports, (2) memory, and (3) the central processing unit (CPU), or microprocessor (μP). These parts are interconnected by a system bus—an address bus, a data bus, and a control bus. A brief example of how these buses are used to communicate information was given in Section 2.5. As we progress through this text, we will examine in detail the system bus and the μP architecture for three popular 8-bit μPs—the 8080A, the 6800, and the 6502. The internal architecture of a general-purpose μP was also described in this chapter. A μP has four basic parts: (1) registers, (2) arithmetic and logic unit, (3) timing and control circuitry, and (4) decoding circuitry. Before we go on to the basics of μC software, we need to consider codes, why they are needed, and how they are applied to μPs and μCs.

PROBLEMS

2–1 List the three major categories of digital computers.
2–2 List the types of companies that use large main-frame computers and minicomputers.
2–3 How many digits are there in the binary system?
2–4 What is the range of voltage for a logic 1 in most μCs?
2–5 Define bit and byte.

2-6 Most μCs are designed with word lengths of how many bits?
2-7 If a μC system has 48K of memory, what is the actual number of bytes?
2-8 What are the three major parts of a μC system?
2-9 What is the function of the I/O ports?
2-10 List four pieces of peripheral equipment that may be connected to a general-purpose μC.
2-11 What is the function of a transducer?
2-12 What are some typical pieces of output equipment that are used in process control applications?
2-13 What is the function of memory?
2-14 What is another name for memory location?
2-15 List the two general types of memory.
2-16 List the types of permanent memory chips that can be used in a μC.
2-17 Are RAMs and R/W memories used to define the same type of volatile memory?
2-18 Give a definition of μP.
2-19 Define bus.
2-20 Is the address bus unidirectional or bidirectional?
2-21 Is the data bus unidirectional or bidirectional?
2-22 List the four major parts of a central processing unit.
2-23 What is the name of the register that stores the results of the arithmetic and logic unit?
2-24 What is the name of the process by which a binary pattern is translated into an operation or sequence of operations?

Use of Codes with Microcomputers

3.0 INTRODUCTION

Digital computers operate using the binary system regardless of whether they are handling data or instructions. Data and instructions can be either numbers, words, punctuation, or special characters. We are all familiar with the decimal system and the English alphabet, but since digital circuits (hence, a computer) can only handle logic levels of 0 and 1, we have to learn a new "language," the binary system, and need to know how to convert from one system to the other.

Reading and writing binary patterns become very cumbersome, and it is easy to make a mistake. In particular, when binary patterns of 8 and 16 bits are used as they are on the μP data and address lines, mistakes can be constant. Therefore, to help reduce errors, we use codes. The codes most often used with μCs for grouping bits are the hexadecimal and octal codes. Other codes used with μCs are the BCD (Binary Coded Decimal) and ASCII (American Standard Code for Information Interchange) codes. Each of these codes is introduced in this chapter.

3.1 BINARY PATTERNS

As we know, the computer handles only binary bits, 0 and 1. Combinations of bits are used to form instructions that the computer can interpret or to form data for the computer to work on. The data may be numbers or letters. The computer has no trouble using the binary bits 0 and 1 because they represent two distinct voltage levels, but a column of binary 0s and 1s is very tiresome for a person to look at. It is quite easy to make an error if a column has to be copied. Columns of binary bits are difficult to understand and extremely time consuming to write or to enter as a program into the computer. It is sometimes difficult to distinguish between an instruction and data. For example, the following column of binary bits is meaningless without further interpretation or explanation:

00001100
10111100
00000010
00000000
10111001
00000101
01000000

Some of the questions we can ask about this binary column are: Is it a set of random instructions? Is it a program? Is it data? If it is a program, to which μP does it apply? (Instructions for one μP are meaningless for a different one.)

The first thing we can do to make it easier to write a column of binary digits is to use codes. Codes are a shorthand notation for a group of binary digits.

3.2 HEXADECIMAL CODE

One of the most widely used codes in μCs is the hexadecimal (or hex) code. The word *hexadecimal* means *sixteen*, which is the base of this system. It uses the digits 0 through 9 plus the letters A through F. Thus, the 16 hexadecimal symbols are as follows:

0 1 2 3 4 5 6 7 8 9 A B C D E F

Each hex symbol represents a group of 4 binary digits. Table 3–1 shows the relationship among the decimal, binary, and hexadecimal systems.

3.2.1 Binary to Hexadecimal Conversion

The reason that the hex system is popular in μCs is that data and memory addresses are easily grouped in blocks of 4 bits. For example, the data bus lines are 8 bits wide (one byte). Therefore, information on the data bus can be grouped in two blocks of 4 bits and then represented by two hexadecimal symbols. As an example, assume that the binary pattern 11001001 is obtained from the data bus. To convert it into its hexadecimal equivalent, we first split the binary pattern into two groups of 4 bits:

11001001 = 1100 1001

TABLE 3–1 Conversion Chart Showing Relationship among Decimal, Binary, and Hexadecimal Systems

Decimal	Binary	Hexadecimal
0	0000	0
1	0001	1
2	0010	2
3	0011	3
4	0100	4
5	0101	5
6	0110	6
7	0111	7
8	1000	8
9	1001	9
10	1010	A
11	1011	B
12	1100	C
13	1101	D
14	1110	E
15	1111	F

TABLE 3–2 Examples of Converting from Binary to Hexadecimal

Binary Pattern	Hex Equivalent
00001100	0C
10111100	BC
00000010	02
00000000	00
10111001	B9
00000101	05
01000000	40

Then, from Table 3–1, we find the hexadecimal symbol for each of the 4 bits:

1100 = C
1001 = 9

Therefore, $11001001_2 = C9_{16}$. The subscripts 2 and 16 indicate a binary number and a hexadecimal number, respectively. Sometimes, the word hex or the letter H is used instead of 16.

The column of binary bits shown in Section 3.1 is reproduced in Table 3–2 with the equivalent hex symbols. We can see how much easier the hex symbols are to look at and to check for mistakes. Keep in mind, however, that the computer only handles binary digits and that this code is for our convenience.

If the hexadecimal symbols are easier for us to use when there is an 8-bit binary pattern, we can quickly see the advantages when the binary pattern is

TABLE 3–3 Address Bus Lines in Decimal, Binary, and Hexadecimal

Decimal	Binary	Hexadecimal
0	00000000 00000000	0000
1	00000000 00000001	0001
2	00000000 00000010	0002
3	00000000 00000011	0003
•	•	•
•	•	•
•	•	•
65,533	11111111 11111101	FFFD
65,534	11111111 11111110	FFFE
65,535	11111111 11111111	FFFF

16 bits. This pattern occurs on the address bus lines. Sixteen lines of address bus can be represented by 4 hexadecimal symbols. For example, assume that the μP puts the following bit pattern onto the address bus:

1011000010101000

To find the hexadecimal equivalent, we first split the pattern into groups of 4 bits:

1011 0000 1010 1000

Then, we use Table 3–1 to obtain the equivalent hex symbol for each group of 4 bits:

1011 = B
0000 = 0
1010 = A
1000 = 8

Therefore, $1011000010101000_2 = B0A8_{16}$.

A μC with 16 address bus lines has $2^{16} = 65{,}536$ memory locations. The first location is 0; the last address is 65,535. Table 3–3 shows a few of the possible memory addresses that a μP can have.

3.2.2 Hexadecimal to Binary Conversion

A hexadecimal code is converted to its equivalent binary pattern by using Table 3–1. Each hex code is taken separately and converted to its binary equivalent. For example, to convert $9D_{16}$ to binary, from Table 3–1 we have:

9 = 1001
D = 1101

Therefore, $9D_{16} = 10011101_2$.

Similarly, we can convert the hex number 8F05 to binary by using Table 3–1:

8 = 1000
F = 1111
0 = 0000
5 = 0101

Then, $8F05_{16} = 1000111100000101_2$.

3.2.3 Counting in Hex

Table 3–1 shows the hex count from 0 through F. But now the question arises: What is the next count? As in the decimal and binary numbering systems, the first digit repeats to 0 and the next digit is incremented, as shown by the examples in Table 3–4. Since we will be using the hexadecimal system throughout this text, we should become familiar with this system and be able to count in hex.

3.3 MICROCOMPUTER MEMORY SPACE AND ALLOCATION

A μP that has 16 address bus lines can address 65,536 (2^{16} = 65,536) different memory locations. Table 3–3 summarizes this range in terms of decimal, binary, and hexadecimal digits. The 65,536 memory locations are called the *total memory space* in the μC. This space is divided into 256 pages labeled 00 to FF, as shown in Figure 3–1. In each page, there are 256 addresses. (As a check: 256 pages × 256 addresses per page = 65,536 addresses.)

The first two hex symbols of the address are its *page number*, while the last two hex symbols are the *line address* in that page. For example, consider the address $657A_{16}$: 65 is the page number, and 7A is the line in page 65. To summarize the interaction between the μP and memory: The μP puts onto the

TABLE 3–4 Examples of Counting in Hexadecimal

•	•	•	•
•	•	•	•
C	1C	9C	20FC
D	1D	9D	20FD
E	1E	9E	20FE
F	1F	9F	20FF
10	20	A0	2100
11	21	A1	2101
12	22	A2	2102
13	23	A3	2103
•	•	•	•
•	•	•	•
•	•	•	•

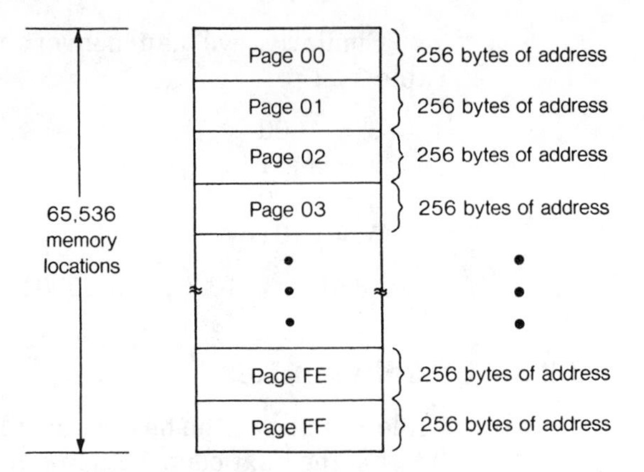

FIGURE 3–1 Total Memory Space of 65,536 Locations Divided into 256 Pages with 256 Addresses per Page

address bus lines a bit pattern whose hex equivalent is 657A. The memory chip or chips, and possibly external decoder chips, decode the pattern—that is, locate the address—and then send to the μP the data that is located at that address. In later chapters, we will investigate how the memory chips do their job.

Many applications do not require the μP to use all 65,536 memory locations. For example, assume that a μC application requires 1024 memory locations for data, 4096 memory locations for the main program, and 512 memory locations for input and output connections. This application thus requires only 5632 memory locations (1024 + 4096 + 512). In terms of pages, the memory locations are allocated as follows:

1024 memory locations = 4 pages
4096 memory locations = 16 pages
512 memory locations = 2 pages

Thus, a total of 22 pages is required.

One method of breaking the total memory space into pages for data, I/O, and the main program for this example is shown in Figure 3–2. The 1024 memory locations for the data have been allocated to the first 4 pages, whose hex addresses are 0000 to 03FF. The 512 locations needed for the I/O connections have been allocated to memory addresses 4000 to 41FF. The main program, which needs 4096 locations, has been given the 16 pages, F000 to FFFF. This example shows two unused portions of memory space that are available for future expansion. Later we will see what chips can be used for the data, I/O, and the main program. Note that the IC chips used for the I/O connections are assigned a memory address and are addressed by the μP as is any other memory location. This type of connection results in what is called *memory-mapped I/O*.

3.4 OCTAL CODE

Another code that is used by some μP manufacturers is the *octal* code. This code has 8 digits:

0 1 2 3 4 5 6 7

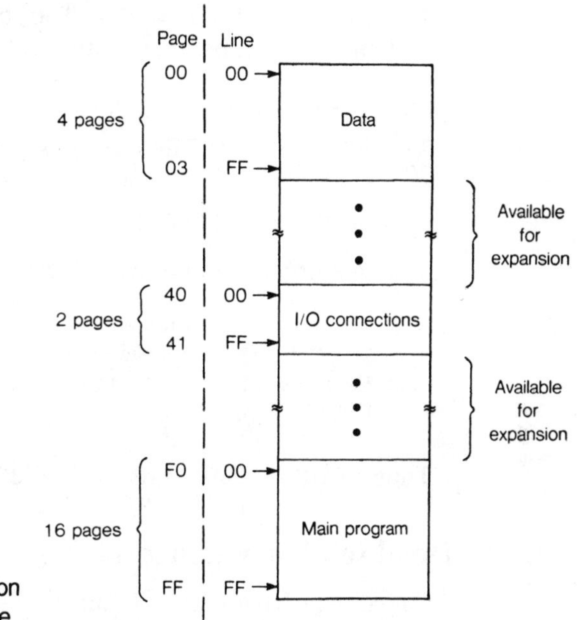

FIGURE 3-2 Typical μC Application That Breaks Up Total Memory Space

Table 3-5 shows the relationship among decimal, binary, and octal digits. From the table, we see that the octal and decimal number systems have similarities. However, only three binary bits are needed to form an octal digit.

3.4.1 Binary to Octal Conversion

Since most μPs have 8 lines for the data bus and 16 lines for the address bus, neither bus line may be divided evenly by 3. Therefore, to represent an 8-bit binary pattern by an octal code requires splitting the binary word into two groups of three bits and one group of two bits, starting at the right-hand, or least significant, bit. For example, to convert the binary word 11011100 to octal, we first group the bits as follows and then use Table 3-5:

Binary pattern	11	011	100
Octal equivalent	3	3	4

TABLE 3-5 Conversion Chart Showing Relationship among Decimal, Binary, and Octal Systems

Decimal	Binary	Octal
0	000	0
1	001	1
2	010	2
3	011	3
4	100	4
5	101	5
6	110	6
7	111	7

Therefore, $11011100_2 = 334_8$. The subscripts 2 and 8 indicate a binary number and an octal number, respectively.

To convert a binary address to its octal equivalent, we first break the binary pattern into two 8-bit patterns and then use the same procedure as before. For example, to find the octal representation of the address 0010111100011110, we first split the binary pattern into two groups:

00101111 00011110

Then we group the bits as follows and use Table 3–5:

	Group of 8 bits			Group of 8 bits		
Binary	00	101	111	00	011	110
Octal	0	5	7	0	3	6

Thus, $0010111100011110_2 = 057036_8$.

3.4.2 Octal to Binary Conversion

Conversion from octal to binary is simply the reverse of the process just described. Each octal digit is converted to its equivalent 3-bit binary pattern. The 8 possible octal digits are converted by using Table 3–5. For example, when we convert the octal number 021_8 to binary, the answer has to be represented by only 8 bits:

Octal	0	2	1
Binary	00	010	001

Hence, $021_8 = 00010001_2$.

As another example, let us convert 325_8 to its binary equivalent. We represent the answer in 8 bits:

Octal	3	2	5
Binary	11	010	101

Therefore, $325_8 = 11010101_2$.

3.4.3 Counting in Octal

As shown in Table 3–5, the highest octal digit is 7. Therefore, to count in octal, a digit is incremented from 0 to 7. Then the count repeats to 0 and the next higher digit is incremented by 1, as illustrated in the examples in Table 3–6.

3.4.4 Comparison of Hexadecimal and Octal Systems

The binary pattern used in Section 3.1 is repeated in Table 3–7 along with the equivalent hexadecimal and octal codes. As the columns in Table 3–7 and our previous examples show, the octal code requires more digits than the hex-

TABLE 3-6 Examples of Counting in Octal

•	•	•
•	•	•
•	•	•
5	45	775
6	46	776
7	47	777
10	50	1000
11	51	1001
12	52	1002
•	•	•
•	•	•
•	•	•

adecimal code. However, the octal code does not require the hexadecimal symbols A, B, C, D, E, or F, which at times can be confusing. Some manufacturers use the octal code and some use the hexadecimal code, so we need to know both and to be able to write the binary bit pattern regardless of which code is used.

We should also know how to convert from hex to octal and from octal to hex. Hex to octal conversion requires converting hex to binary first and then binary to octal. Octal to hex conversion is performed by going from octal to binary to hex.

3.5 OTHER CODES

Either the hexadecimal or the octal code is used to represent binary patterns on the data and address buses. These codes allow us to group bits so as to reduce human errors when we work with long strings of binary digits. Therefore, μP instructions are represented in one of these two codes.

Other codes are often used when information is going into or coming out of the μC through the I/O ports. Two of the codes widely used for this purpose are the BCD (Binary Coded Decimal) and ASCII (American Standard Code for Information Interchange) codes. The BCD code system is used only for numbers, while the ASCII code system is used for numbers, letters, punctuation

TABLE 3-7 Examples of Converting from Binary to Hex and Octal

Binary	Hex	Octal
00001100	0C	014
10111100	BC	274
00000010	02	002
00000000	00	000
10111001	B9	271
00000101	05	005
01000000	40	100

marks, and control characters. Since the terms BCD and ASCII are used in the next few chapters, the next two sections of this chapter cover the basic concepts of the two code systems.

3.6 BINARY CODED DECIMAL SYSTEM

The straight binary number system is based on positional weights (place value), as is the decimal system. For example, the decimal number 12 equals the binary number 1100. Although the μP handles straight binary numbers quite easily, we may not want to have to perform a binary to decimal conversion every time we want to know what the decimal number is. Also, the octal code only goes up to 7, and the hex code contains the letters A through F. Therefore, if the μC is to receive and display only decimal information, what we are looking for is a code that produces only the decimal digits 0 through 9. Such a code is the *Binary Coded Decimal System* (abbreviated BCD). Remember that the use of the octal and hex codes is different from the use of the BCD code.

3.6.1 Decimal to BCD Conversion

In the BCD system, each digit in a decimal number is represented by 4 binary bits. For example,

Decimal	4	3	2
BCD	0100	0011	0010

The reason that 4 binary bits are needed in the BCD system is that the decimal numbers 8 and 9 cannot be represented by 3 binary bits. That is, we run out of 3-bit binary combinations at 7 unless we add another digit. Thus,

Decimal	8	9
BCD	1000	1001

Table 3–8 shows the 4-bit BCD codes along with their decimal equivalents. Note that the binary numbers 1010, 1011, 1100, 1101, 1110, and 1111 are invalid BCD codes. We do not need these binary numbers because all the decimal numbers are already represented. These binary numbers would produce an error if they were used in the BCD system. Table 3–8 shows that only 10 of the possible 16 4-bit binary numbers are used. Other examples of decimal to BCD conversion are as follows:

12 = 0001 0010
47 = 0100 0111
63.5 = 0110 0011.0101

3.6.2 Comparison between BCD and Straight Binary

While the straight binary system is based on the position of the bits, the BCD system converts each decimal digit into a 4-bit binary number with weights used only within each 4-bit group. Therefore, the BCD code is also known as the

TABLE 3-8 Conversion Chart Showing Relationship between Decimal and BCD Systems

Decimal	BCD Code	
0	0000	Valid binary numbers
1	0001	
2	0010	
3	0011	
4	0100	
5	0101	
6	0110	
7	0111	
8	1000	
9	1001	
—	1010	Invalid binary numbers in BCD code
—	1011	
—	1100	
—	1101	
—	1110	
—	1111	

8-4-2-1 code, where 8, 4, 2, and 1 are the weights of each bit in a 4-bit group.

A BCD representation of a decimal number always requires more bits than a straight binary representation. For example, convert the number 240 to straight binary and to the BCD system and compare each result:

Straight binary $240_{10} = 11110000_2$
BCD $240_{10} = 0010 \quad 0100 \quad 0000$

The straight binary number requires only 8 bits, while the BCD representation requires 12 bits. Microprocessors are able to add and subtract in both straight binary and BCD. Although μPs can do both types of addition, straight binary is more efficient because it uses fewer bits. The disadvantage is that if the μP is making all of its calculations in straight binary, a program must be included to convert straight binary to BCD before the answer can be sent to a decimal display. If the μP is making all of its calculations in BCD, a conversion program is not necessary. The disadvantage with this method, however, is that more memory space is needed to store the data and execution of the program will be slower. In Chapter 13, we will study a conversion program.

3.7 ASCII CODE

Today's computers are more than just calculators. In addition to numbers, they must be able to store and process data such as letters, punctuation marks, and other special characters. The computer must be capable of receiving data from a keyboard, a teletype (TTY), paper tape, magnetic tape, other external storage equipment, or even another computer. The computer must also be able to send its data to equipment such as a printer, cathode ray tube (CRT), storage equipment, or another computer. A standard code is needed for a computer to communicate easily with peripheral equipment. One of the most commonly used alphanumeric standards is the *American Standard Code for Information Interchange* (ASCII). This code uses 7 bits, which produce 128 ($2^7 = 128$) possible alphanumeric codes. Figure 3–3 lists all 128 ASCII characters.

The ASCII codes can be grouped in three major blocks. The first 32 characters (columns 0 and 1 in Figure 3–3) are machine commands that control the hardware between the μC and the peripheral equipment. Machine commands are never printed in a message. They include such commands as start, stop, and carriage return.

The next major group includes columns 2, 3, 4, and 5 in Figure 3–3. These 64 characters include the 10 decimal numbers, the 26 uppercase letters, a blank or space (SP), and common punctuation marks and printed characters.

The remaining 32 characters are listed in columns 6 and 7 in Figure 3–3. They are the lowercase letters and little-used characters.

Although the ASCII code uses 7 bits, it can be represented by either the hexadecimal or octal code. Bit 8 is usually considered to be binary 0 when the

Bit numbers															
b_7 →								0	0	0	0	1	1	1	1
b_6 →								0	0	1	1	0	0	1	1
b_5 →								0	1	0	1	0	1	0	1
b_7 ↓	b_6 ↓	b_5 ↓	b_4 ↓	b_3 ↓	b_2 ↓	b_1 ↓	Column → / Row ↓	0	1	2	3	4	5	6	7
			0	0	0	0	0	NUL	DLE	SP	0	@	P	\	p
			0	0	0	1	1	SOH	DC1	!	1	A	Q	a	q
			0	0	1	0	2	STX	DC2	"	2	B	R	b	r
			0	0	1	1	3	ETX	DC3	#	3	C	S	c	s
			0	1	0	0	4	EOT	DC4	$	4	D	T	d	t
			0	1	0	1	5	ENQ	NAK	%	5	E	U	e	u
			0	1	1	0	6	ACK	SYN	&	6	F	V	f	v
			0	1	1	1	7	BEL	ETB	'	7	G	W	g	w
			1	0	0	0	8	BS	CAN	(	8	H	X	h	x
			1	0	0	1	9	HT	EM	)	9	I	Y	i	y
			1	0	1	0	A	LF	SUB	•	:	J	Z	j	z
			1	0	1	1	B	VT	ESC	+	;	K	[	k	{
			1	1	0	0	C	FF	FS	,	<	L	\	l	|
			1	1	0	1	D	CR	GS	-	=	M	]	m	}
			1	1	1	0	E	SO	RS	.	>	N	Λ	n	~
			1	1	1	1	F	SI	US	/	?	O	—	o	DEL

Columns 0–7: Hex code. Row (↑): Hex code. Columns 0–1: Machine commands; columns 2–5: Most often used; columns 6–7: Least often used.

FIGURE 3–3 7-Bit ASCII Codes

ASCII code is converted to either the hexadecimal or the octal code. Figure 3-3 includes the hexadecimal code. When using Figure 3-3 to convert codes, note that the high-order bit numbers 5, 6, and 7 are given across the top of the table, while the lower-order bit numbers 1, 2, 3, and 4 are given at the left of the table. Examples of several characters in the 7-bit ASCII code, the hexadecimal code, and the octal code are shown in Table 3-9.

A μC/printer application is shown in Figure 3-4. The μC is connected to a line printer by 7 lines. Stored in memory are 4 ASCII codes. Assume that a pro-

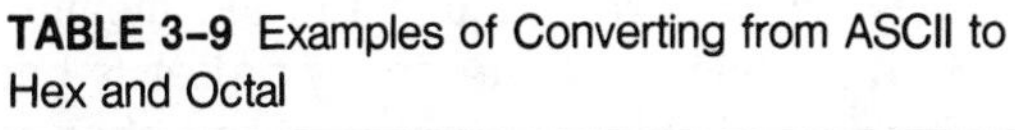

TABLE 3-9 Examples of Converting from ASCII to Hex and Octal

Character	7-Bit ASCII	Hex	Octal
A	1000001	41	101
D	1000100	44	104
S	1010011	53	123
1	0110001	31	061
9	0111001	39	071
+	0101011	2B	053
=	0111101	3D	075

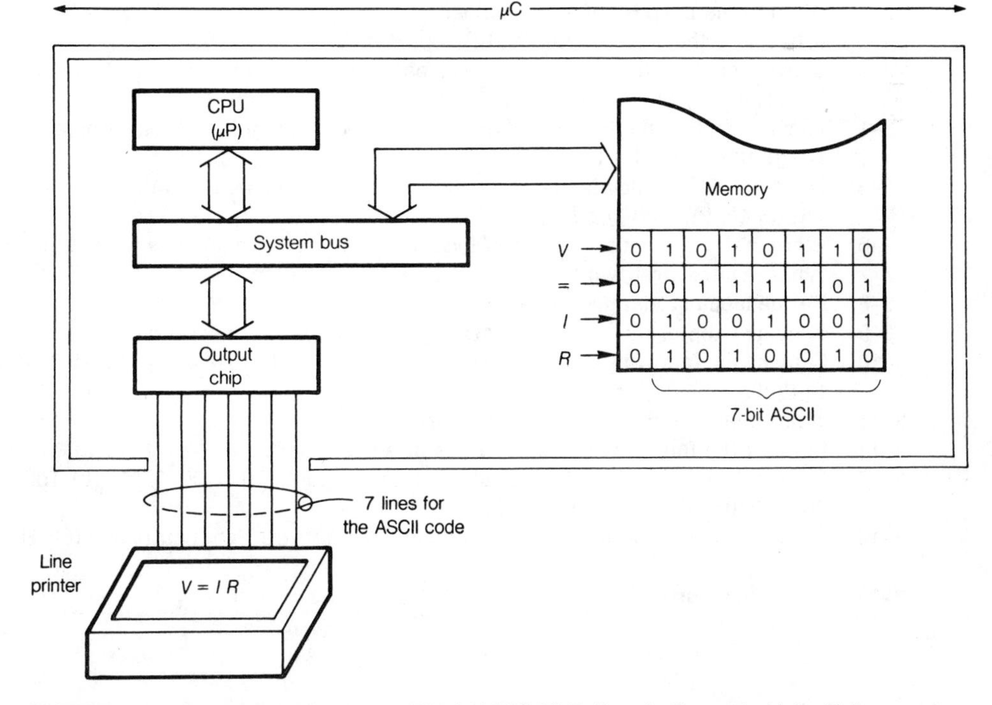

FIGURE 3-4 μC/Printer Application in Which ASCII Bit Pattern Is Converted into Alphanumeric Characters

gram takes each of these ASCII codes and sends them to the printer. As each binary pattern reaches the line printer, the device interprets it and prints one character. If each of these ASCII codes is sent to the line printer in sequence, the printer will type Ohm's law: $V = IR$. Thus, the ASCII binary patterns are a standard that allows any μC to be interfaced easily to any piece of peripheral equipment that needs to send or receive data or control signals.

3.8 SUMMARY

In a μC system, information is transferred among the μP, memory, and I/O devices as either 8-bit or 16-bit patterns. These binary patterns become awkward for humans to reproduce or check and increase the chance of error. Therefore, codes are needed. Each number or letter in a code represents a particular binary pattern. The codes most often used in μC systems are the hexadecimal and octal codes. In this chapter, these codes were applied to μPs and μCs, and examples were used to show how to convert between decimal, binary, hexadecimal, and octal. When a μC communicates with peripheral equipment such as keyboards, printers, plotters, CRT displays, and so forth, two other codes are often used, the ASCII and BCD codes.

PROBLEMS

3–1 What is the purpose of using codes?

3–2 What does the abbreviation ASCII represent?

3–3 Convert each of the following binary patterns into hexadecimal code: (a) 11000111, (b) 01101000, (c) 11110101, (d) 00111001, and (e) 10100100.

3–4 Convert each of the following hexadecimal codes into a binary pattern: (a) A9, (b) 17, (c) 4B, (d) 03FF, and (e) 17FA.

3–5 For each of the following hexadecimal codes, give the next hexadecimal value: (a) 19, (b) 7A, (c) 4F, (d) 10FF, and (e) 3FFF.

3–6 What is the maximum number of locations that a μP can address with 12 address lines?

3–7 What are the first two hex digits of an address called?

3–8 Define memory-mapped I/O.

3–9 Convert each of the binary patterns of Problem 3–3 into octal code.

3–10 Convert the following octal values into binary: (a) 301, (b) 064, (c) 125, (d) 043072, and (e) 114203.

3–11 What does the abbreviation BCD represent?

3–12 Convert the following decimal values into BCD: (a) 59, (b) 14, (c) 27, (d) 03, and (e) 88.

3–13 Convert the following BCD numbers into decimal: (a) 0100 0110, (b) 1001 1001, (c) 0010 0101, (d) 0110 1000, and (e) 0011 0000.

3–14 Convert each of the following decimal numbers into straight binary and into BCD: (a) 128, (b) 64, (c) 250, (d) 76, and (e) 32.

3–15 Write the word *microprocessor* in ASCII. Use hex code.

Microprocessor Software

4.0 INTRODUCTION

In Chapter 2, we saw that a μC consists of three major parts: the μP chip, I/O chip(s), and memory chip(s). These components, along with other digital and analog components, are needed to build a complete μC system. All of these devices together with the printed circuit board, power supply, keyboard, and so forth, are called the μC's *hardware*. What is accomplished by the hardware is controlled by the μC's *software* (the program). Microcomputer users often encounter the term *firmware*; it means both the hardware and software aspects of the μC. This and the next chapter will introduce the general principles of μC software and hardware. Chapters 6 through 14 deal specifically with the hardware and software aspects of three different μPs: the 8080A, the 6800, and the 6502.

Remember from Chapter 1 that a program is a sequence of instructions that solves a given problem. When the computer program "runs," each instruction directs the operation of the μP and the other digital circuits.

When a computer (large, mini, or micro) is being used, a change in a program usually does not require the programmer to change any components or wires (the computer's hardware). Therefore, the program is considered part of the computer's software. However, in some μC systems, a change in a program may require a change in one or more components. The following example illustrates this possibility. First, remember that a program is nothing more than a sequence of binary patterns. A change in a program is a change in one or more of the binary patterns. In a computer that has been designed for general use, a program change is made by the programmer through a keyboard. The change in the binary pattern itself occurs inside the computer and is not seen by the programmer. In a dedicated control application (where μCs are often used), the program may be stored in a PROM (programmable read only memory). A change in the program requires a new PROM to be programmed by removing the old PROM from the system, using a PROM programmer to "burn" the new program into a new PROM, and then inserting the new PROM back into the μC system. Even though a component (the PROM) was actually changed, the term *software* still applies to describe the change.

4.1 ASPECTS OF MICROPROCESSOR SOFTWARE

Many first-time computer users erroneously think that "computer software" refers only to the program or programs used. However, just as computer hardware is more than a few IC chips—it also includes timing, component layout, power supplies, and noise problems, for example—so software has aspects other than the program itself. Computer software includes the following steps: (1) defining the problem; (2) determining a logical solution to the problem; (3) writing the program; (4) loading, running, and debugging the program (very few programs work the first time); and (5) documenting all the steps.

4.1.1 Problem Definition

Problem definition may seem an obvious step, but it should not be considered lightly because it can make the remaining steps easier or more difficult. If hardware and software personnel work closely to define the problem, their jobs will each be easier. They will understand each other's role, and the final product can combine the best trade-off between hardware and software. At this step, the programmer must consider all the data that will be entered, all the major processes needed to process the data, and the desired output. The programmer should allow for design flexibility, which will almost certainly be needed. Time spent clarifying problems and making sure that the programmer understands all the specifications can avoid costly errors and delays later on. For example, if at the debugging stage it is found that the problem has not been defined correctly, then a considerable amount of time, effort, and money have been wasted in a product that does not work.

4.1.2 Logical Design

Once the problem is understood, a logical design can be created that solves the problem in the best and most efficient way. At this step, keep in mind the hardware constraints of the system such as memory space, clock frequency, number of inputs and outputs that have to be serviced, and so forth. For example, if a keyboard must be scanned every 40 milliseconds or a CRT display updated every second, then the programmer must keep these constraints in mind. During this development step, the design is broken into independent parts. Each part may be subdivided until there is enough detail to understand clearly what is to be accomplished by each subpart. The result is a step-by-step sequence for the computer to carry out. If the problem has been defined clearly, a logical design will result.

4.1.3 Programming

After we define the problem and develop a logical design, we know what types of programs are needed. For example, we will know if we need a multiplication program, division program, square root program, timing loop program, or some other program. For each program, a specific set of rules or steps must be carried out. A set of rules or steps to solve a specific programming problem is called an *algorithm*. Computer manufacturers keep a list of algorithms that have either been written by their own staff or that have been submitted to them by users. We cannot just choose an algorithm at random, however, because we must keep specific hardware constraints in mind. For example, if the μC system that we are using can contain only 8K bytes of memory, all the programming is confined to this amount of memory space.

4.1.4 Loading, Testing, and Debugging

After the program is written, it is loaded into the μC system. Loading may occur via a keyboard or, in a dedicated control system, the program may first be entered into an EPROM (this topic is covered in Chapters 15 and 16), which is then inserted into the μC. The program is run, and the system is tested. Since few programs run the way we wish the first time, debugging will probably be necessary. Changing the program, loading the program, testing it, and debugging it will have to be done several times before the final product is ready. After the μC system is operating the way it was intended, the program can be finalized. For large-volume production, we may wish to enter the program into a maskable ROM chip (this topic is also covered in Chapters 15 and 16).

4.1.5 Documentation

Throughout the design cycle, careful documentation of each step should be maintained. Documentation will guarantee that a design change will be remembered and will keep colleagues and supervisors informed at each point in the design. All too often documentation is left until the final product is designed, and many fine points are forgotten. Periodic documentation also avoids massive paperwork at the end of a project. Good documentation in one project can save a considerable amount of time in similar projects.

During all the steps of software design, then, we should constantly refine and document each step. All this documentation should be kept together and labeled. Documentation should always be presented clearly, but it does not have to be presented in the same way for each step. One documentation aid that is often used in trade journals, application notes, or other textbooks is a flowchart.

4.2 FLOWCHARTS

A *flowchart* is a graphical representation, or drawing, showing the logical sequence of a problem. Many times, a complex design or program can be described more easily by a flowchart than by a statement. The following flowchart symbols are most often used in μP documentation.

Flowpath Arrows: Flowpath arrows are lines with arrowheads that indicate the path or sequence the program follows. Some examples are shown in Figure 4–1.

Terminal Symbol: At the beginning and ending points in a program flowchart is an oblong symbol representing a terminal point. Words such as start, stop, end, halt, exit, and return are usually found within this symbol. There is only one flowpath arrow associated with a terminal symbol. The arrowhead is away from the terminal at the starting point and into the symbol at the ending point, as shown in the examples in Figure 4–2.

Process Symbol: The process symbol, sometimes called a *function box*, is a rectangle. Inside this box is a description of the operation the μP is to perform. A process symbol has two flowpath arrows associated with it—one entering and one leaving, as illustrated in Figure 4–3.

Decision Symbol: The power of any computer is its ability to make a decision. In hardware, decisionmaking is accomplished when the μP checks to "see" if a flip-flop is in the logic 1 or the logic 0 state. Depending on the state of the flip-flop, the answer to all decisions is either yes or no. In a flowchart, a decision symbol is a diamond shape. A decision symbol has three flowpath arrows associated with it—one entering and two leaving. The arrows leaving a decision symbol show the path for each condition. Examples are shown in Figure 4–4.

Connection Symbol: A connection symbol is a circle, and it indicates where there is entry from or exit to another part of the program. One use of a connection symbol is at the foot of a page when the flowchart is too long to fit on one page and must be continued on a second sheet. A connection symbol will also be shown at the beginning of the second sheet. In order to keep the proper page order, a letter or number is placed within the circle, as shown in the examples in Figure 4–5.

Input/Output Symbol: The I/O symbol is a parallelogram. It represents either input or output functions. For example, an input function such as when the μC reads data from a paper tape is shown on the flowchart by an I/O symbol. The symbol indicates where in the flowchart this input function happens. Likewise, an output function such as when the μC sends data to peripheral equipment is indicated by an I/O symbol. Note that on many μP

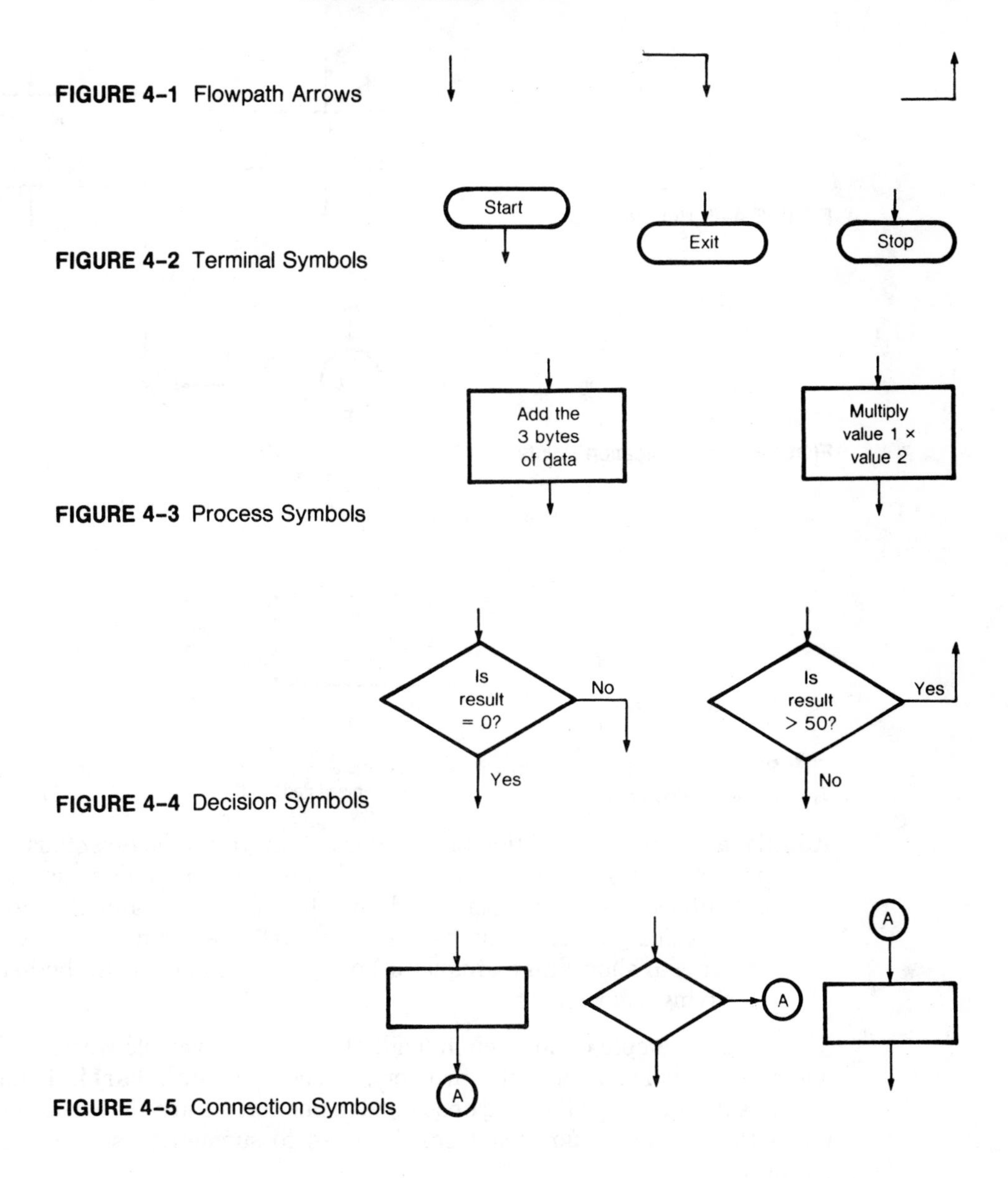

FIGURE 4–1 Flowpath Arrows

FIGURE 4–2 Terminal Symbols

FIGURE 4–3 Process Symbols

FIGURE 4–4 Decision Symbols

FIGURE 4–5 Connection Symbols

flowcharts there may be a rectangular box, the same as the one used for the process symbol, instead of a parallelogram for an I/O function. Figure 4–6 shows examples of I/O symbols.

Summation Point: A summation point is where two or more arrowheads come together. On some flowcharts, the symbol is a circle or a circle with a cross in it. Some μP flowcharts use no circles at all. Examples of summation points are presented in Figure 4–7.

Input data
from printer
Send first
line to
CRT display

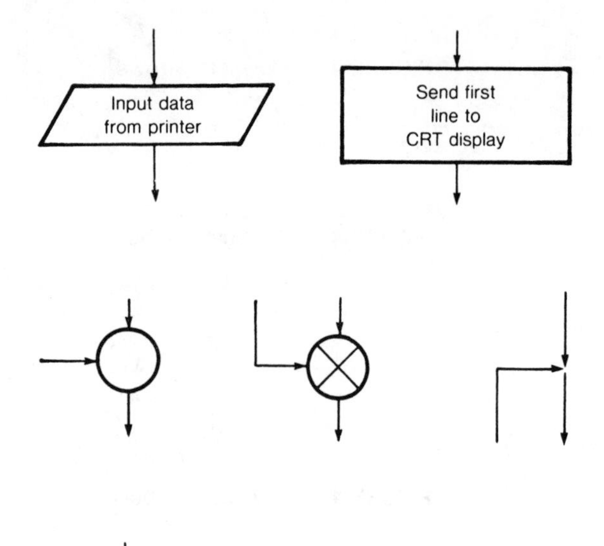

FIGURE 4–6 I/O Symbols

FIGURE 4–7 Summation Points

Multiply
value 1 x
value 2
Value 1 is a temperature
reading measured in °C

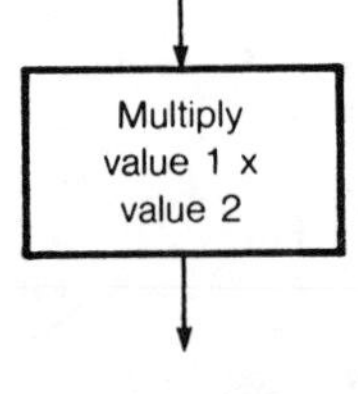

FIGURE 4–8 Programmer's Note That Clarifies Flowchart

Additional Notes: In addition to the information within the flowchart boxes, a programmer's notes are sometimes added for better documentation. A note allows the programmer and any other user at a later time to understand quickly what should happen at a particular point in the flowchart. Figure 4–8 shows an example of how additional notes can be helpful in clarifying a flowchart.

As an example of how the individual flowchart symbols work together to show the logical sequence of a problem, consider the flowchart in Figure 4–9. The μP software steps that are described in Section 4.1 are shown here in flowchart form. Thus, a flowchart can be used to summarize several pages of material.

4.3 PROGRAMMING LANGUAGE LEVELS

Computer programs are written in one of three language levels: (1) machine-level language (the lowest level), (2) assembly-level language (the middle level), or (3) high-level language (the highest level). Each level has its advantages and disadvantages and often the trade-off is between programming time and memory cost. In the following subsections, we examine these advantages and disadvantages.

4.3.1 Machine-Level Language

Machine-level language is the most basic, or lowest-level, programming language. With this language, the programmer "communicates" with the μC in binary.

Programming at this level is the most difficult because it is extremely tedious and can lead to a multitude of errors. Imagine the possibilities for error and time required to throw switches to enter a short program—one that contains only one hundred bytes of memory. Therefore, entering a program into memory using direct binary should be avoided if at all possible. Unless a person just interconnected some μC chips, he or she probably will not encounter this situation.

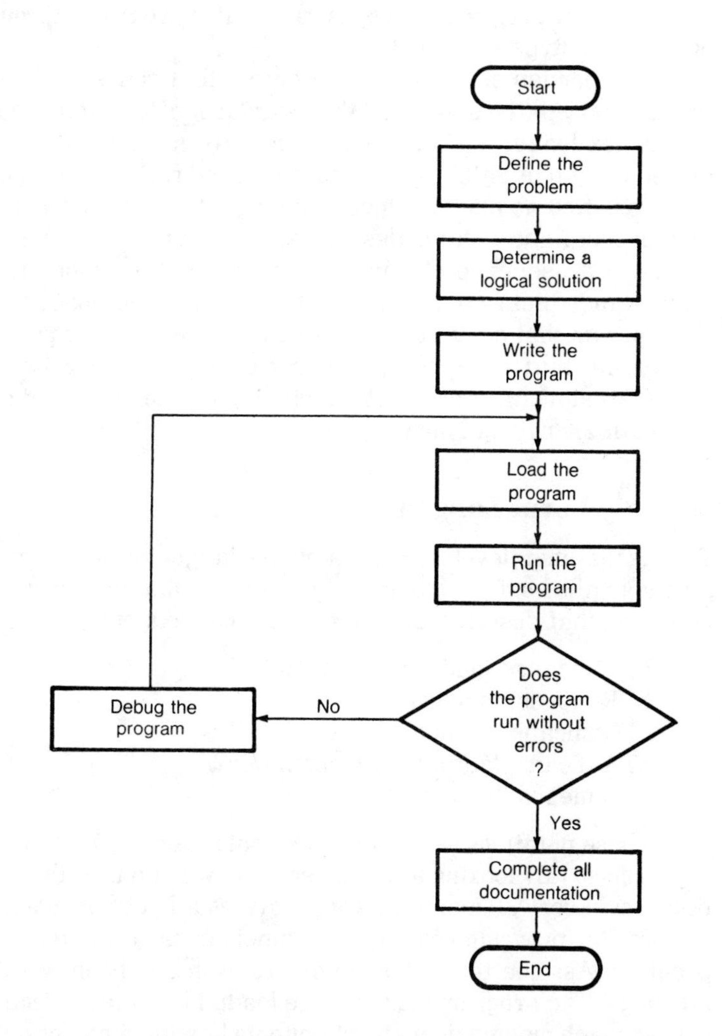

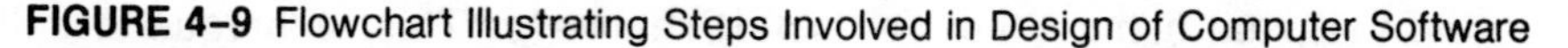
FIGURE 4–9 Flowchart Illustrating Steps Involved in Design of Computer Software

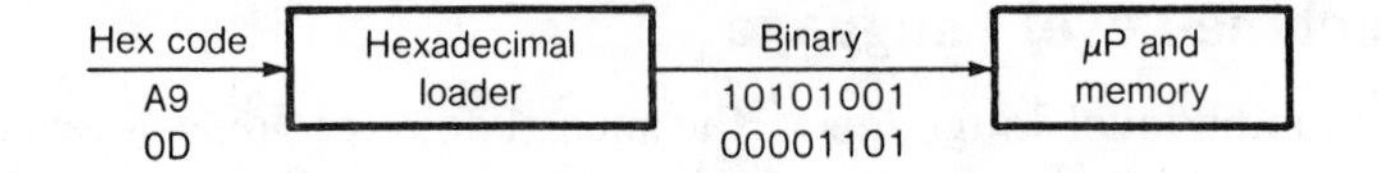

FIGURE 4–10 Hexadecimal Loader for Converting Hex Digits into a Binary Pattern

Most μC kits and some single-board computer systems include a PROM or ROM chip. This memory chip contains a monitor program. A *monitor program* is a program that gives the μC user some basic functions once power is applied. Some of these functions allow the user to load a program into RAM, execute, and debug it. Some μC manufacturers include in their monitor additional programs that allow storage and retrieval of a program from a tape cassette. The basic monitor program allows users to enter programs through a hexadecimal, octal, or teletype keyboard.

The portion of the monitor program that converts the hex (or octal) code into a binary pattern is called the *hexadecimal* (or *octal*) *loader*. An illustration of this hex loader is shown in Figure 4–10. Although the hex (or octal) loader makes the job of entering the program easier, it is still time consuming and is still classified as machine-level language. Remember from Chapter 3 that the hexadecimal and octal codes are easier to write and that it is easier to find errors in a sequence of hex or octal digits. Remember too that the μP only understands binary patterns. It is the hexadecimal loader portion of the monitor program that converts the hex code into the binary pattern. The monitor is a program that must be stored in memory and therefore requires memory space. Most monitor programs (including the hexadecimal or octal loader) use less than 2K bytes of memory.

4.3.2 Assembly-Level Language

The next-higher level of programming language is assembly language. This language allows a programmer to write a computer program using shorthand notations that describe the instruction. For example,

LDA means "load the accumulator"
EOR means "exclusive or"
CMP means "compare"
STA means "store the accumulator"
SUB means "subtract"

These notations are called *mnemonics* and are often referred to as "memory joggers." By looking at the mnemonic, we can usually tell what the instruction does. Every μP manufacturer provides a list of mnemonics for its product. A computer program written using mnemonics is called an *assembly language program*. Assume that a computer program has been written in an assembly language. The program must now be loaded into the μC. One way to load it is to convert each mnemonic instruction to its hexadecimal (or octal) code and enter the program using a hex (or octal) keyboard. This technique is called *hand*

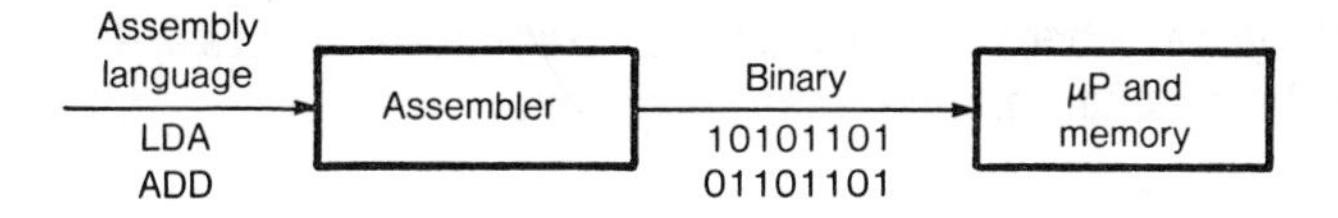

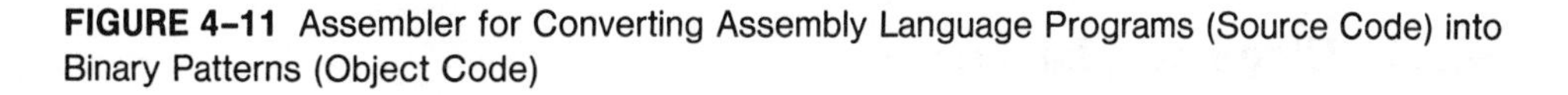
FIGURE 4–11 Assembler for Converting Assembly Language Programs (Source Code) into Binary Patterns (Object Code)

assembly. Although the hex (or octal) code is certainly easier to use than the binary code, it is still quite possible to make mistakes.

An easier way is to have the computer itself convert the mnemonics to binary patterns. A computer program that converts assembly language programs to binary patterns is called an *assembler*. In this method, the programmer uses a keyboard connected to the computer. Each instruction in the program is typed using the mnemonic notations and sent to the computer. Then the assembler takes over. When a program is written in either assembly or high-level language, it is called *source code*. Machine-level language is called *object code*. An assembler converts source code to object code, as shown in Figure 4–11. Most assemblers do more than just convert mnemonics to binary patterns. Many find the correct memory locations for different parts of the program, correct some programming errors, allow the programmer to assign labels to memory locations or to input and output devices, and allow the programmer to assign sections of memory for the main program and sections for temporary data.

An assembler, like a hexadecimal (or octal) loader, is a program and requires memory space. The more the assembler program can do, the more memory space it needs. The assembler translates each line of a program written in assembly language into one or more bytes of memory. A program that is 1000 lines of assembly language requires several thousand bytes of memory because each instruction in assembly language is converted into a μP instruction and each μP instruction requires either one, two, or three (some μPs have instructions that take four) bytes of memory.

Each assembly language program is written for a particular μP. Programs written for the Motorola 6800 μP are meaningless for the Intel 8080A μP. Therefore, assembly language programs are not portable (interchangeable). Many assembly language programs will not even run on different μPs made by the same manufacturer. For example, programs written for the Motorola 6800 are not guaranteed to run using the Motorola 6809 μP and vice versa. Programs written for the Intel 8080A μP will not run on Intel's 8086 μP.

To some degree, writing programs in assembly language is like writing programs in machine-level language. The programmer must have a working knowledge of the μC's hardware and know which instructions affect which components. The μP and many of the I/O devices have internal registers that are programmable. The μC programmer who uses either machine- or assembly-level language must understand both the hardware and software components. The programmer must know what data is stored in the registers and what flip-flops have been set or cleared. Otherwise, errors will occur and debugging will take a considerable amount of time.

4.3.3 High-Level Language

The next-higher computer software language is a high-level language. Some of the commonly used high-level languages associated with μCs are listed in Table 4–1.

As μC programs become longer and more sophisticated and are used in more data processing and problem solving applications, then high-level languages become more practical to use. In most cases, a program in a high-level language is approximately ten times faster and easier to write than a program in assembly language. This time is saved in actually writing the program. There is no additional time saved in the other software steps described in Section 4.1. In most high-level languages, an individual can tell from the statement what the program does, which is not true for machine or assembly languages.

Programs written in a high-level language are usually advertised as being portable. Thus, a FORTRAN program written for one computer should run on any other computer that has FORTRAN capability. Portability is not always guaranteed, however, and a user will have to learn each computer's idiosyncrasies. BASIC is one high-level language that seems to have so many different dialects that it can be frustrating for some users. If a program is indeed portable, a library of programs written for one computer can be used on another. The advantage is a tremendous saving in time for the programmer.

When a program is written in a high-level language, the programmer does not have to worry about the computer's internal registers, the bus structure, or any other hardware problems. In fact, the programmer need not know anything about how a computer works. However, high-level languages also have their disadvantages.

One major hurdle that has to be overcome is that the programmer has to learn the rules of the language and what can and cannot be done. If one rule is violated, the program will not run. Many high-level language programs have

TABLE 4–1 Commonly Used High-Level Languages

Acronym	Description	Major Use
FORTRAN	FORmula TRANslation	Mathematics and engineering
BASIC	Beginner's All-purpose Symbolic Instruction Code	General purpose and time sharing
COBOL	COmmon Business-Oriented Language	Business and management information
PASCAL	Blaise PASCAL (French mathematician)	Process control

internal error detection. When a rule is violated, the computer prints out an error message telling the programmer where and what kind of error has occurred.

We have previously mentioned trade-offs between ease of programming and memory space. High-level languages are easier to program but use more memory space. These languages must be converted from source code into object (machine) code before execution can take place. Two programs that do this conversion are compilers and interpreters.

4.4 TRANSLATORS

Assemblers, compilers, and interpreters are classified as *translators*. The difference between assemblers and translators is that when a program is written in assembly language it is the programmer who must keep track of the data contained in all the registers. When a high-level language is used, the compiler or interpreter does this job.

4.4.1 Compilers and Interpreters

Compilers are programs that translate a high-level language into a binary code, an assembly language, or an intermediate language sometimes called *pseudo code* or *P-code*. If the compiler generates the μP's binary pattern immediately, it is said to produce *real code*. If the compiler produces assembly language, then an assembler is needed for the final translation into machine language. Some compilers require as many as six passes through the program to complete all of the translation into the final machine language. This time constraint can easily make high-level languages and compilers unsuitable for real-time applications. (Real-time applications are applications that must be completed in the shortest possible time.)

Compilers are designed so that each statement of the program is read, analyzed, and stored (usually on a tape or disk) but *not* executed. After the compiler's translation from source code to object code is complete, the entire object code program is executed. As long as the object code program is stored, it is this program that is executed and the compiler does not have to be used again. Modern compilers can produce very efficient object code programs that can be executed relatively quickly.

Interpreters are programs that translate each high-level language statement into object code (machine-level language) immediately, and execute it before reading the next statement. When an interpreter receives a high-level instruction, it refers to a predefined sequence of machine instructions to execute the statement. These machine instructions are stored in the computer's memory. Unlike compilers, interpreters must translate each source statement every time the program is executed. As a comparison, an interpreter may execute a source program twenty times more slowly than a compiler can execute the same program.

Like assemblers, compilers and interpreters can do more than just translation. They can list error messages and other diagnostic information. Some μC manufacturers are including modified versions of FORTRAN, BASIC, COBOL, or PASCAL in their products. They are using either compilers or interpreters that fit into 8K to 32K of memory. Remember that the more a program is to do, the more bytes of memory are needed and the less memory is available to the programmer. The maximum amount of memory space for 8-bit μPs is 64K. A compiler that translates a high-level language program into a machine-level language program probably requires at least four times more memory space than the same program written in assembly language because high-level languages are made flexible and general enough for a wide range of problems. This flexibility produces a main disadvantage of high-level languages—longer machine-level programs. The trade-off is flexibility for memory space (programming time versus memory cost).

4.4.2 Cross-Compilers

Although μP and μC manufacturers provide high-level languages for their products, it is usually a modified form of a general high-level language. Some manufacturers use their own version of a high-level language, such as Motorola's MPL and Intel's PL/M. Remember that compilers and interpreters for a high-level language require a large amount of memory space and that this is a limitation in most μC systems. Because compilers do take a large amount of memory, many μC users use cross-compilers. A program is written in a high-level language; then it is entered into a large or mini computer, which generates a machine-level program for their μP. Therefore, their μC system does not have to have a compiler program contained in its memory. When a computer uses a compiler stored in its own memory, it is called a *self-compiler.* When it uses one in another computer, it is called a *cross-compiler.* Cross-compilers do have some disadvantages. A programmer must have access to a large computer or a minicomputer with a compiler program, and the programmer may have to wait for computer time. Waiting can be very aggravating in the middle of debugging a program.

Because many high-level languages are limited to a specific μP or have been modified for a particular μC system, the user does not gain the portability or extensive program libraries that are available in larger computers. However, high-level language programming is still easier than lower-level language programming. The μP application eventually becomes the prime factor in deciding which programming language is used.

4.5 LANGUAGE SELECTION

When we select a programming language, we may be limited to machine language because the only system available is a single-board computer that contains a monitor ROM and a hexadecimal or octal keyboard, and no additional development systems are available. If, however, the choice is between an assembly language and a high-level language, then we should be aware of the following trade-offs.

A major advantage of an assembly-level language over a high-level language is that the assembly-level language allows complete control of the steps that the μP will execute. This control, in turn, allows the programmer to minimize the number of programming steps, thus resulting in a μC system with the following benefits: (1) faster execution, (2) more data handling capability, (3) more accuracy, and (4) less hardware required. Let's consider each advantage.

Faster Execution: Some process or industrial control applications, military applications, and most communication applications require a μC to execute the program in the minimum amount of time. These applications are called real-time applications because every microsecond counts. In these applications, the result of the program is made available soon enough to influence or control the process. As we progress upward in language levels, it becomes easier to program and to understand what is happening in each program statement, but a high-level language requires more time to execute.

More Data Handling Capability: Assembly-level programming allows a program to be written in fewer possible steps. Thus, the amount of memory space required for the program is reduced, thereby saving more memory space for data. For example, a single-board computer (SBC) may only include 2K bytes of memory for the program. The more memory that is used for the program, the less is available for data. Exceeding the 2K limit at first may not seem to be a major disadvantage because the user may think that an additional memory board may simply be added to the SBC. Depending on the amount of memory added, however, the cost may be from a few hundred to several thousand dollars. Therefore, the number of units that are produced should determine whether the additional time spent on writing the program in assembly language is more cost effective than adding hardware.

More Accuracy: Programmers using assembly level language can include additional program steps so that more accuracy is obtained. With greater accuracy, a programmer may write a new algorithm or modify an existing one for the best solution to a problem.

Less Hardware Required: Programs can be optimized to require fewer memory chips in the system and thus result in a cost saving. Remember, however, it makes no sense to save a few bytes of memory space and not reduce the number of memory chips. For example, if the memory chip being used is 2K $\times$ 8, there are 2048 bytes of memory whether or not they are all used. It also makes no sense in low-volume applications to reduce the number of memory chips if the cost of the additional development time in programming is much greater than the saving in the memory chips. By using assembly-level language, it is possible to optimize the program and save memory space. This saving could lead to the following: (1) The entire system may be built on a single printed circuit board, or (2) the program may be designed onto a single-chip μC. Single-chip μCs are very attractive for low-cost, high-volume applications, such as electronic games and household appliances. Remember that many of the benefits mentioned can be offset by the additional programming time that is required.

In applications that require small to medium-size programs, need to control input/output devices, require limited data processing, and take into account memory cost as a factor, assembly language programs should be considered. Long programs, programs that contain a lot of data processing, or programs with a lot of computation and little input/output control are the best for high-level languages.

4.6 SUBROUTINES

Regardless of the language level used, most programs are written with one or more subroutines. A *subroutine* is a program written separately from the main program. The primary function of the subroutine is to solve a specific problem, such as a mathematical operation. As an example, if several places in the main program require multiplication, then instead of repeating the same multiplication program over and over and wasting valuable memory space, the programmer writes one multiplication program and stores it as a subroutine program. Then, whenever the multiplication operation is needed, the programmer inserts a *jump instruction* that causes the program sequence to change from the main program to the subroutine program. At the end of the subroutine program, the program sequence returns to the main program. Subroutines are extremely valuable programming tools whenever the same program is to be repeated or whenever the programmer wishes to break a larger program into more individual and manageable blocks.

Sometimes, subroutines have subroutines. This programming technique is referred to as *multilevel subroutines*, or *nesting*. Figure 4–12 shows flow lines for single and multilevel subroutines.

A *return instruction* is the last instruction in a subroutine program. It is this instruction that automatically brings the μP back to where it left off. In Figure 4–12A, there is only one subroutine program. Thus, the return instruction brings the μP back to the main program. However, in Figure 4–12B, which illustrates nested subroutines, the return instruction at the end of subroutine 2 brings the μP back to subroutine 1, not to the main program. It is the return instruction at the end of subroutine 1 that brings the μP back to the main program. Thus, the program returns to where it left off.

Every μP has instructions that allow it to jump to and return from a subroutine. Some μP manufacturers refer to their jump to subroutine instruction as a *call instruction* (the 8080A μP is one of these).

If used properly, subroutines are a valuable programming tool; if used incorrectly, they can be a waste of memory space and time and can be a nightmare to debug. Good documentation is a must to follow the sequence of events in subroutines.

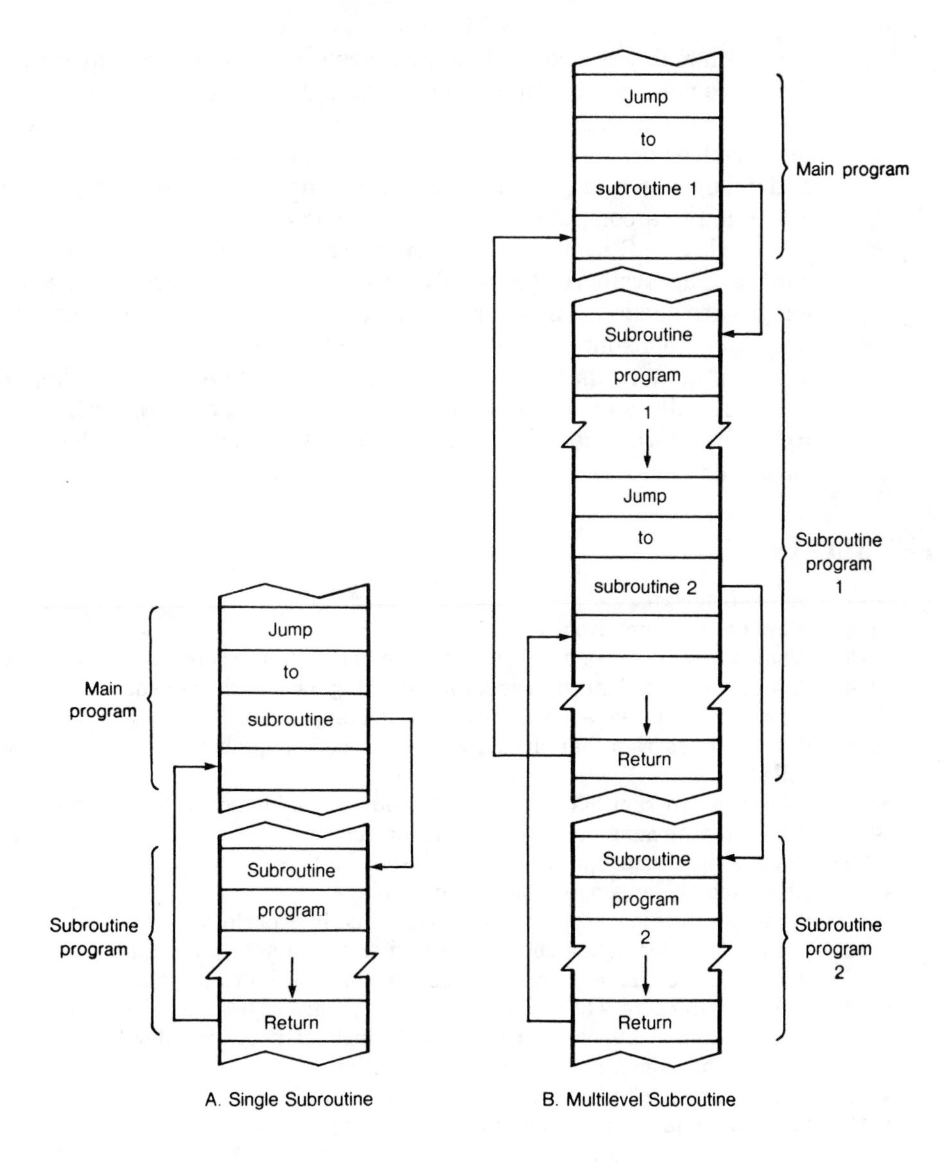

FIGURE 4–12 Program Sequence Using Single and Multilevel Subroutines

4.7 SUMMARY

This chapter introduced general rules of computer software that can be applied to any μP. First-time users often disregard the need for good software documentation and are troubled with problems later on, at which time they may not be able to pinpoint whether they have a hardware or software problem. In all probability, time will be wasted trying to track down a bug if the documentation is poor.

Although μPs are designed differently in both hardware and software, there are many similarities. This chapter discussed some of the similarities of computer software. One area of similarity regarding μP software is the process that involves problem definition; logical design; programming; loading, testing, and debugging; and documentation. One commonly used method of expressing a solution to a computer software problem is the flowchart.

Today's μC systems range from small single-boards to large multiuser, multitasking systems. To satisfy this μC range, different programming languages are needed. High-level languages use either a compiler or interpreter to translate from source code to object code. The application, cost, and μC size are some factors that are considered in choosing a programming language.

Regardless of which language level is used, most programs require subroutines. Subroutines eliminate the need for repeating an algorithm that occurs over and over again in a main program.

PROBLEMS

4–1 Define firmware.
4–2 What does computer software include?
4–3 What is a set of rules or steps to solve a specific programming problem called?
4–4 What is the graphical representation showing the logical sequence of a program called?
4–5 What are the three levels of programming languages?
4–6 What is a program that gives a μC user some basic functions once power is turned on called?
4–7 What is a program that converts hex code into a binary pattern called?
4–8 What programming language uses mnemonics?
4–9 What is the primary purpose of an assembler?
4–10 Are assembly language programs portable?
4–11 What is a difference between compilers and interpreters?
4–12 If a programmer uses a compiler stored on a computer other than the one that will run the object code, is the compiler a self-compiler or a cross-compiler?
4–13 List four advantages of assembly language programs over high-level language programs.
4–14 List three applications where assembly language programs should be considered.
4–15 What is the primary function of a subroutine?
4–16 What is another term for multilevel subroutines?
4–17 What is the last instruction of a subroutine?

Microprocessor Architecture and Instructions

5.0 INTRODUCTION

Computer software personnel, especially programmers using large and mini computers, often attempt to avoid the hardware aspects of the computer. However, the μC has forced hardware and software personnel to work together to produce useful dedicated products. To utilize fully the power of a μC, it is important to understand both its hardware and its software. Even if we use a general-purpose μC system along with a high-level language, an understanding of μP architecture and other components is helpful if the system is to be expanded. Like the large and mini computers, many general-purpose μC systems are designed so that peripheral equipment (such as keyboards, CRTs, floppy disks, and tape cassettes) is compatible and can be used to build a larger μC system. However, once we deviate from this compatibility and decide to add other I/O devices, then we must know about the μC's hardware, including the internal architecture of the μP. If we write programs in either machine-level or assembly-level language, we must keep track of what data is stored in which μP register. Many μCs are used in dedicated control applications, and the programs of these applications are often written in assembly language. Without a working knowledge of the μC's hardware, it is doubtful that we can fully understand a completed system or can build a useful μP product.

In previous chapters, the basic parts of a μC were introduced, but the μP's instructions and how the instructions affect the internal registers of the μP were not discussed. The internal architecture and instructions of each μP are different, but there are certain aspects that are common to most 8-bit μPs. This chapter introduces some of these common points. The next several chapters concentrate on the architecture and instructions specific to the 8080A, 6800, and 6502 μPs.

5.1 MICROPROCESSOR ARCHITECTURE

Section 2.4 introduced μP architecture in its four basic parts: (1) registers, (2) arithmetic and logic unit, (3) timing and control circuitry, and (4) decoding circuitry. The μP has been designed so that once a binary pattern representing an instruction is fetched from memory, the pattern is automatically placed in the μP's instruction register and decoded. The binary pattern establishes the μP's timing and control for the entire time the instruction is executed. Therefore, parts 3 and 4 of the μP are affected by the instruction. Parts 1 and 2 are used by the μP to operate on data or information.

All of the μP instructions together are called its *instruction set*. The programmer arranges instructions sequentially to solve a particular problem. The instructions allow the programmer to route data or information into or out of a μP register or into the arithmetic and logic unit (ALU). *Note:* The programmer usually does not have control of data coming out of the ALU because most of the time this data is sent directly to one particular μP register, the accumulator.

Each μP is unique in its architecture and its instructions. It is helpful, therefore, to visualize the basic internal architecture of a μP. A diagram, or programmer's model, of this internal architecture shows, for example, how many and what kind of registers there are. Figure 5-1A is a basic block diagram applicable to many 8-bit μPs. The dashed block indicates that other registers may be included in a μP. Figures 5-1B, 5-1C, and 5-1D show other registers that are included in the 8080A, 6800, and 6502 μPs, respectively. A brief description of the basic registers follows.

5.1.1 Accumulator

The *accumulator* (or accumulators in the case of the 6800 μP) is the most often used register. It is used to store data from memory or I/O and to send data to memory or an I/O device. It is also the register that is closely associated with the arithmetic and logic unit. In most μPs, when an addition or subtraction instruction is executed, one of the numbers comes from the accumulator. The result of the arithmetic operation is automatically stored in the accumulator. Sometimes the accumulator is simply referred to as the *A register*. The number of bits in the accumulator determines the μP's word size. The word size for an 8-bit μP is thus 8 bits.

5.1.2 Condition Code Register

The *condition code register* is 8 bits wide, although many μPs do not use all 8 bits. This register should be thought of as individual bits because the result of an instruction can either set or clear one or more of the bits. There are other instructions that can test each individual bit to see whether it is a logic 1 or a logic 0. Testing the bits allows the μP to make a decision. If the condition is true, the programmer may wish to execute one program. If the condition is false, the programmer may wish to execute a different program.

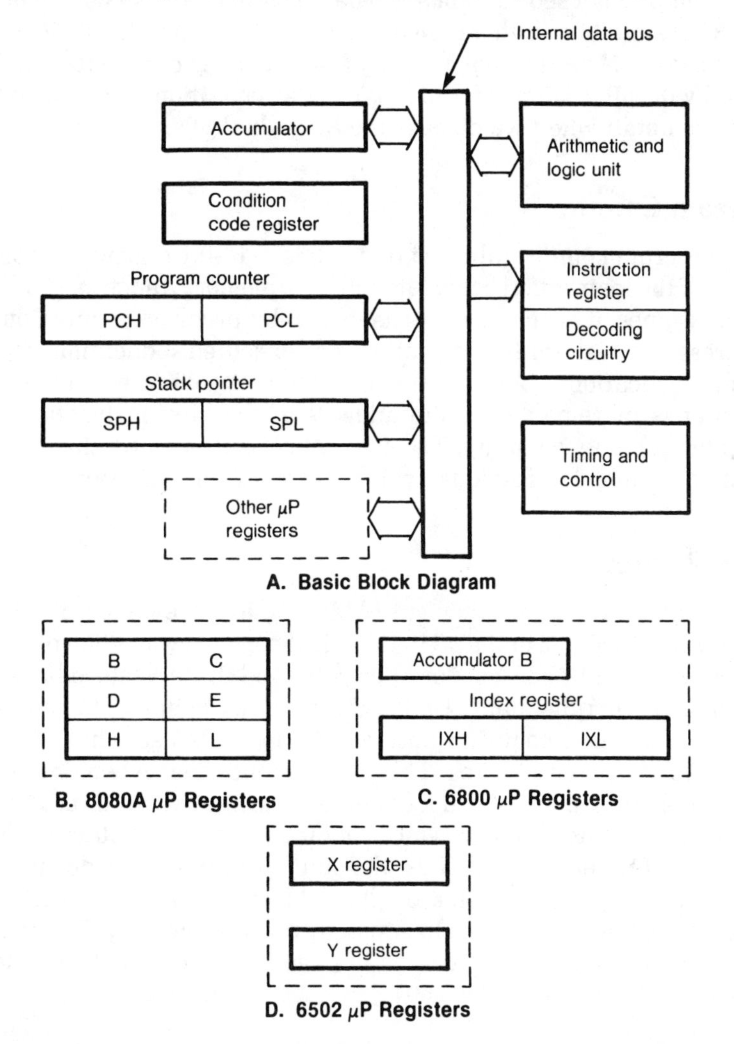

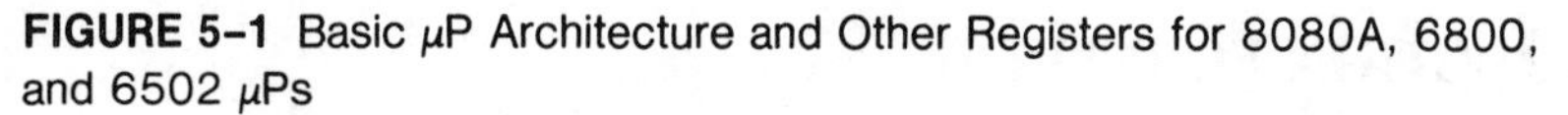

FIGURE 5-1 Basic μP Architecture and Other Registers for 8080A, 6800, and 6502 μPs

Although every μP has a condition code register, it is called different things in different μPs. Some of the names used for this register are *processor status word, processor status register, P register, status register, status word,* or *flag register*. An individual bit is referred to as a *flag bit*, a *status bit*, or a *flag*. Three of the most common flag bits are the carry flag, the zero flag, and the sign flag. The *zero flag* is used to indicate whether the result of an instruction is 0. The *carry flag* is used in the arithmetic operations of addition and subtraction to indicate whether or not there is a carry or a borrow, respectively. The *sign flag* is used to indicate whether a number is positive or negative. Of the 8 possible bits in this register, the 8080A uses 5, the 6800 uses 6, and the 6502 uses 7. Note that not all bits of this register can be tested. Some bits are used by the μP to keep track of a particular condition. Each flag bit is discussed in more detail when we discuss the individual μPs.

5.1.3 Program Counter

The *program counter* (abbreviated PC) is a 16-bit register. It contains the address of the instruction being fetched from memory. Since most 8-bit μPs have 16 address lines, it is necessary to have a 16-bit program counter, one bit for each address line. Generally, instructions are executed sequentially from successive memory locations. When one instruction is being executed, the program counter is incremented to the address of the next instruction. The program counter can only count up. The sequential order can be changed by the use of branch or jump instructions, which will be described later.

5.1.4 Stack Pointer

The *stack* is an area in memory (RAM) used to store temporary data. The *stack pointer* is a register in the μP that holds the memory location of the place on the stack where data can be stored or retrieved. Data is stored and retrieved sequentially from the stack. Unlike the program counter, the stack pointer is a register that can count up and down. Most μPs use what is called a "push down" and "pop up" stack. This name implies that when data is put onto the stack the stack pointer is decremented and that when data is retrieved from the stack the stack pointer is incremented. This type of stack is also referred to as *last in/first out* (LIFO). Thus, the stack pointer counts down to fill the stack and counts up as the stack empties. Most μPs have a 16-bit stack pointer. Therefore, the stack can be located any place in memory. The stack of the 6502 μP, however, can only be located in page 01; hence, the high byte of the stack pointer in the 6502 is always 01_{hex}.

5.2 INSTRUCTION FORMAT

Most μP instructions occupy either one, two, or three bytes of memory. (Some μPs have instruction words that occupy four bytes, but the 8080A, 6800, and

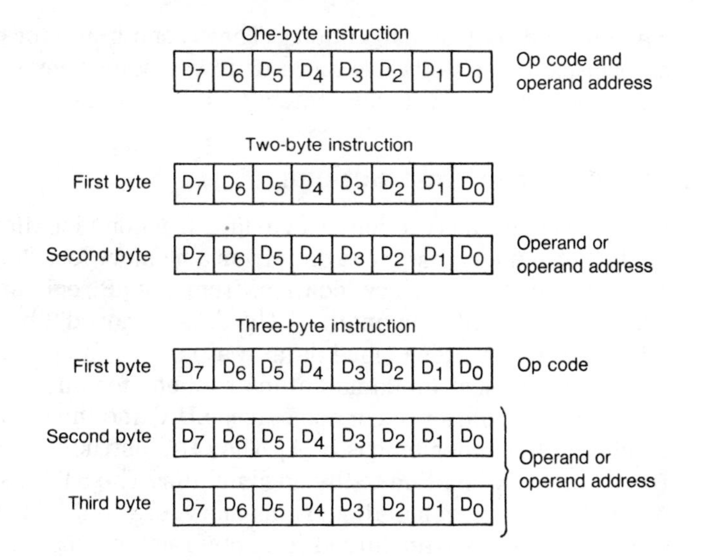

FIGURE 5-2 One-, Two-, and Three-Byte μP Instructions

6502 do not.) Because each byte is a line in memory, when an instruction word occupies more than one byte, it must be stored in successive memory locations. Figure 5-2 shows examples of one-, two-, and three-byte μP instructions.

All instruction words have two parts, the *op code* and the *operand*. "Op code" is short for "operation code." Sometimes the op code refers to the instructional code or type of instruction. This part of the instruction is decoded by the μP and "tells" the μP what to do. The operand is the data that is operated upon. In multibyte instructions, the first byte is the op code while the remaining byte or bytes are the operand (the data) or an address (the operand address) where the data can be found. In single-byte instructions, the op code and the operand address are contained in the one 8-bit pattern. In this type of instruction, the operand address is not a memory address but rather a μP register. Since μPs have only a few internal registers, the op code and the register where the action is to take place can be contained within 8 bits.

5.3 BASIC INSTRUCTION SET

Each μP has instructions that are unique to it. However, most μPs usually have the same basic set of instructions, although the machine codes will usually be different. In the next nine chapters, we will study the differences among a number of μPs and their instructions. But first let's consider the similarities in their instructions.

Instructions can be divided loosely into nine categories: (1) data movement instructions, (2) arithmetic instructions, (3) logical instructions, (4) compare and test instructions, (5) rotate and shift instructions, (6) program control instructions, (7) stack instructions, (8) input/output instructions, and (9) other machine and control instructions. (There is nothing sacred about the number of categories; other texts use more or fewer categories.) A description of what happens in each of the nine categories listed here follows.

5.3.1 Data Movement Instructions

Data movement instructions move data from one location to another. They include instructions that move data from a memory location to a μP register, from a μP register to a memory location, from one μP register to another, and from one memory location to another. The data is moved 8 bits at a time. Therefore, all of these operations move data in a parallel fashion.

The two most fundamental instructions for any μP are the instruction to load the accumulator (the mnemonic is LDA) and the instruction to store the accumulator (the mnemonic is STA). The LDA instruction transfers a byte of data from a memory location to the accumulator. The STA instruction transfers the contents of the accumulator to a memory location. It is important to remember that when data is transferred from one register to another, the information in the first register is *not* lost. The first register is called the *source*, and the second register is called the *destination*. After a data movement instruction is completed, the source and the destination registers both contain the same data. The only way to change the data in the first (source) register is to store new data in it. Figure 5-3 shows what happens when data is moved from a source register to a destination register. The data (72) from the source register is *not* lost; the data (15) that was originally in the destination register *is* lost.

Microprocessor instructions can be expressed by a symbolic notation. For example, the LDA instruction can be written as M→A. Some μP manufacturers use an arrow that points from left to right (the 6800 and 6502, for example, use this arrow), while other manufacturers use an arrow that points from right to left (the 8080A uses this arrow). In either case, the direction of the arrow is from the source to the destination. Examples of data movement instructions are given in Table 5-1. The instructions are shown in both mnemonic form and μP notation.

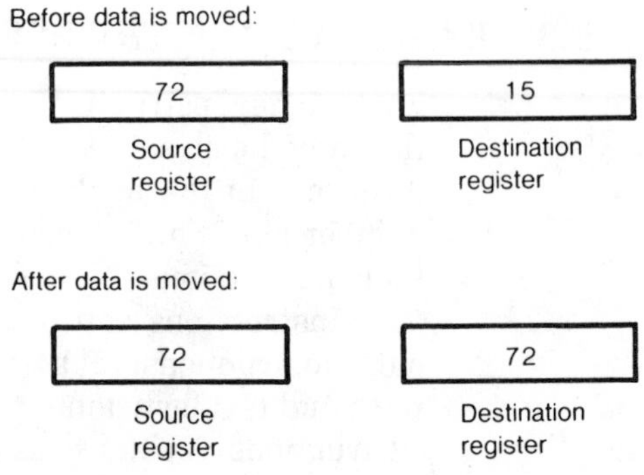

FIGURE 5-3 Source and Destination Registers before and after Data Movement Instruction

TABLE 5-1 Data Movement Instructions in Mnemonic Form and Symbolic Notation

Mnemonic	Description	μP Notation	Source	Destination
LDA	Load accumulator	M→A	Memory	Accumulator
LDX	Load X register	M→X	Memory	X register
STA	Store accumulator	A→M	Accumulator	Memory
STX	Store X register	X→M	X register	Memory
TAX	Transfer contents of accumulator to X register	A→X	Accumulator	X register
TXA	Transfer contents of X register to accumulator	X→A	X register	Accumulator

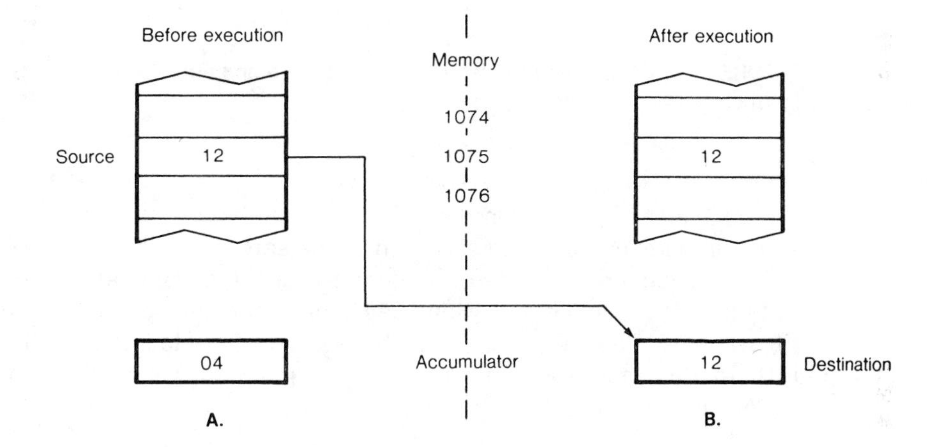

FIGURE 5-4 Memory and Register Contents before and after Execution of LDA Instruction

Load Instructions

An example of what happens when the μP executes an LDA instruction is shown in Figure 5-4. Figure 5-4A shows the situation before execution of the instruction. The contents of the accumulator are 04_{hex}, while the contents of memory location 1075_{hex} are 12_{hex}. After the LDA instruction is executed, 12_{hex} from memory location 1075_{hex} is loaded into the accumulator and 04_{hex} is lost, as shown in Figure 5-4B. In assembly language, the instruction is written as LDA 1075. Since other memory locations are not involved, their data is not transferred. Note that 12_{hex} in memory location 1075_{hex} has not been destroyed. In this example, memory location 1075_{hex} is the source and the accumulator is the destination.

Store Instructions

Figure 5-5 shows an example of what happens when the μP executes an STA instruction. In this example, the data in the accumulator is stored in memory location 1075_{hex}. In assembly language format, the instruction is STA 1075.

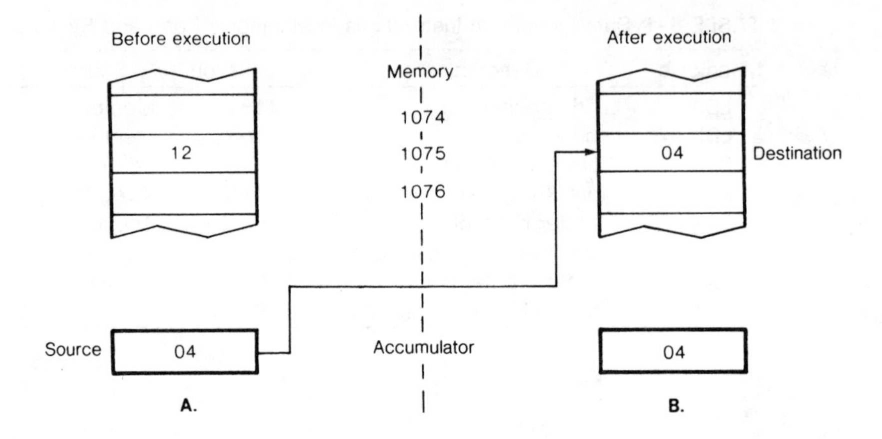

FIGURE 5-5 Memory and Register Contents before and after Execution of STA Instruction

Figure 5-5A shows the contents of the accumulator and memory before the instruction is executed. The situation is the same as in Figure 5-4A. After the STA instruction is executed, the contents of the accumulator are unchanged, but the data in memory location 1075_{hex} has been changed to 04_{hex}, as shown in Figure 5-5B. The value 12_{hex}, which was in memory location 1075_{hex}, has been lost. In this example, the accumulator is the source and memory location 1075_{hex} is the destination.

Transfer and Exchange Instructions

There are two types of instructions that move data between μP registers. The first type of instruction involves a transfer of data from one μP register to another. One register is the source and the other is the destination. The second type of instruction involves an exchange of data between two μP registers.

Figure 5-6 is an example of a register-to-register data transfer. The μP moves the contents of the accumulator into the B register. In μP notation, we can write A→B. Figure 5-6A shows two μP registers (the accumulator and the B register) and their contents. In this example, the accumulator is the source and the B register is the destination. When an instruction to transfer the accumulator to the B register is executed, the result is as shown in Figure 5-6B.

An example of a register-to-register data exchange is shown in Figure 5-7. Figure 5-7A shows the situation before the exchange instruction is executed, while Figure 5-7B shows the result after execution. For the registers shown in Figure 5-7, the notation is H↔D and L↔E. In this instruction, all registers are both sources and destinations. *Note:* The 8080A μP can exchange the contents of registers H and L with the contents of registers D and E. The 6800 and 6502 μPs do not have an exchange instruction.

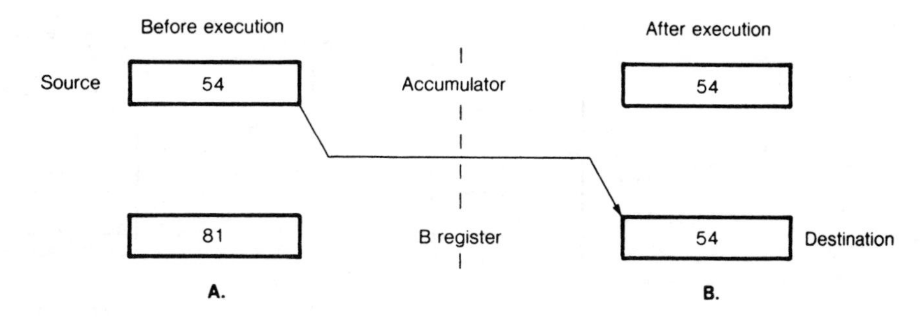

FIGURE 5–6 Register-to-Register Data Transfer (A→B)

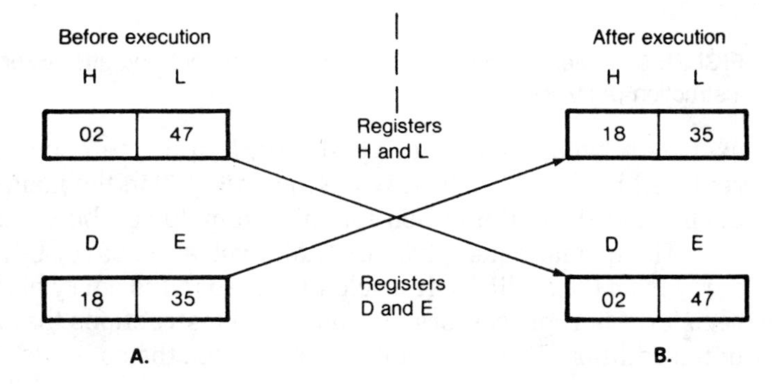

FIGURE 5–7 Register-to-Register Data Exchange (H↔D and L↔E)

5.3.2 Arithmetic Instructions

Arithmetic instructions use the arithmetic and logic unit (ALU). The basic arithmetic instructions are the add, subtract, increment (add 1 to a μP register or memory location), and decrement (subtract 1 from a μP register or memory location) instructions. The arithmetic instructions and other ALU instructions are often described as the most powerful instructions in a μP instruction set. These instructions allow the μP to compute and to manipulate data. Therefore, these instructions distinguish a computer from a collection of random logic circuits. The results of many of these ALU instructions are stored automatically in the accumulator.

Add Instruction

All 8-bit μPs are capable of adding two 8-bit numbers. Usually one number comes from the accumulator, while the other number comes either from a μP register or from memory. The result of the addition is automatically stored in the accumulator.

Figure 5–8A shows the contents of the accumulator and a memory location (FC41) before an add instruction is executed. Figure 5–8B shows the contents of the accumulator and the same memory location after the instruction is

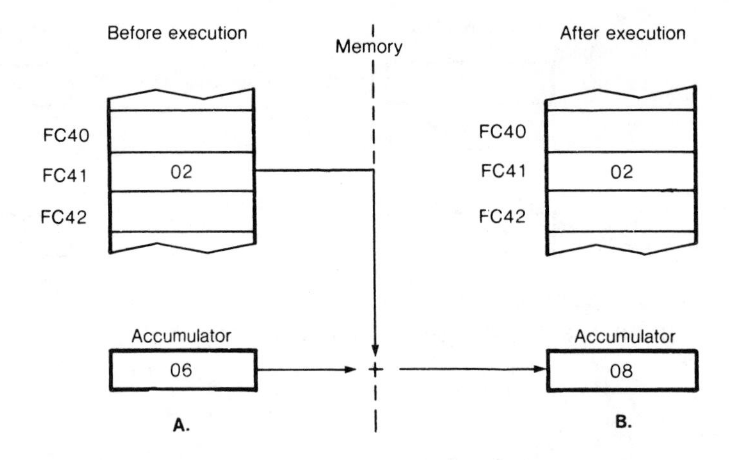

FIGURE 5-8 Memory and Register Contents before and after Execution of Add Instruction (A+M→A)

executed. Note that the original data (06) in the accumulator is lost and is replaced by the result (08), while the data (02) in the memory location remains unchanged. The μP notation for this example can be written as A + M→A.

The example just given did not involve the carry bit. If there should be a carry from the addition, it would be stored in the carry bit of the condition code register. Microprocessors also have add instructions that include the carry bit in the addition. This type of instruction adds the contents of the accumulator, a memory location (or another μP register), and the carry bit. The result is placed in the accumulator. The μP notation for this type of addition can be written as A + M + C→A.

Subtract Instruction

The subtract instruction, like the add instruction, is a fundamental μP instruction. This instruction involves subtracting data in a μP register or memory location from the contents of the accumulator. The result is automatically placed in the accumulator. The μP notation for this operation is A − M→A.

Figure 5-9A shows the same conditions as in Figure 5-8A, but now we will apply the subtract instruction. The data (02) at the memory location (FC41) is subtracted from the data (06) in the accumulator. After the subtract instruction is executed, the result (04) is stored in the accumulator, as shown in Figure 5-9B.

In all μPs, subtraction is done by 2's complement arithmetic. If the result is negative, the answer is in 2's complement form. For example, if the problem is 4 − 7 = −3, the answer, −3, in 2's complement form is 11111101 (binary) or FD (hexadecimal). Microprocessors have instructions that can check the logic state of bit 7, the most significant bit of the answer. If bit 7 is a logic 0, the answer is positive; if bit 7 is a logic 1, the answer is negative. Hence, a positive or negative answer can easily be determined.

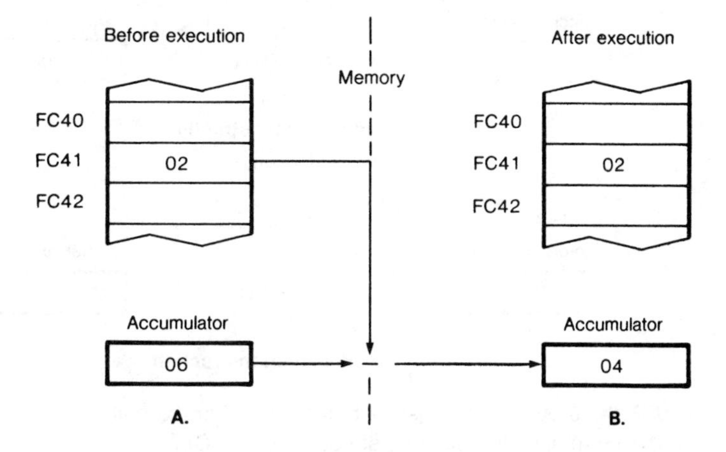

FIGURE 5-9 Memory and Register Contents before and after Execution of Subtract Instruction (A−M→A)

The carry bit is often referred to as the *borrow bit* when a subtract instruction is being executed. Some μPs, such as the 6502, have subtract instructions in which the borrow bit must be set to a logic 1 state before the subtract instruction is executed. Some μPs set the borrow bit in the condition code register to the logic 1 state to indicate a borrow, while other μPs clear this bit to the logic 0 state to indicate a borrow. Therefore, it is important always to check the instruction set given by the μP manufacturer.

Increment and Decrement Instructions

The increment and decrement instructions add 1 or subtract 1 from the contents of a μP register or from the contents of a memory location. The contents of a memory location are incremented (or decremented) in the following way: (1) The data in a memory location is moved from memory to the ALU, (2) the data is incremented (or decremented), and (3) the incremented (or decremented) data is transferred back to the original memory location. This type of instruction, which involves changing the contents of a memory location, is classified as a read/modify/write instruction. The number of steps involved in a read/modify/write instruction makes it one of the longest instructions that a μP has to execute.

Figures 5-10A and 5-10B show examples of an increment and a decrement instruction, respectively, and the contents of the registers before and after the instructions are executed. The μP notation for increment the accumulator is A + 1→A, and for decrement, it is A − 1→A.

Increment and decrement instructions produce a "roll-over" result. That is, if a register (or memory location) is all 1s and it is incremented, the result is all 0s and does not affect the carry flag. Likewise, if a register (or memory location) is all 0s and it is decremented, the result is all 1s and does not affect the carry flag.

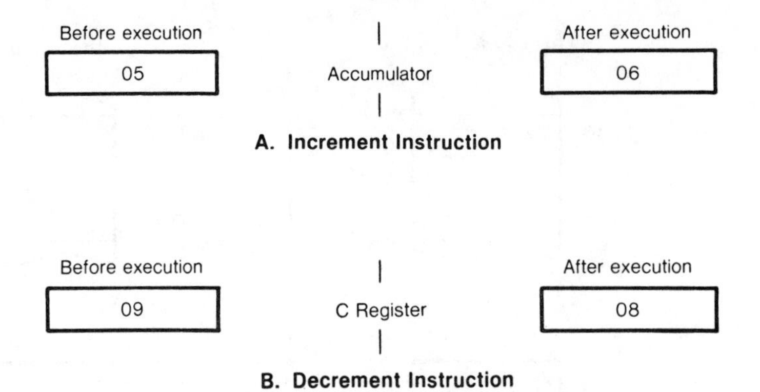

FIGURE 5-10 A and C Registers before and after Execution of Increment Instruction (A+1→A) and Decrement Instruction (C−1→C)

5.3.3 Logical Operations

The logical operations of AND, OR, and Exclusive OR are performed by the μP on 8 bits at a time. The contents of the accumulator and data from memory can be combined by the AND, OR, or Exclusive OR operations. Like the add and subtract instructions, these operations are performed in the ALU and the result is automatically placed in the accumulator. Different ways of writing logical operations in μP notation are shown in Table 5-2.

Figures 5-11A, 5-11B, and 5-11C show examples of logical AND, OR, and Exclusive OR instructions, respectively. The data has been written in the binary format so that it is easy to check the answers. *Note:* Some manufacturers use the + symbol to indicate both addition and logical OR. The user must be careful and know what operation is being executed each time the + symbol is used.

Complement instructions (both 1's and 2's complements) are logical operations. Some μPs do not include these instructions, some only have a 1's complement instruction, and others can do both operations. The reason that some μP instruction sets do not include complement instructions is that complementing can be done by using other instructions. For example, the 1's com-

TABLE 5-2 Symbolic Notation and Description of Logical Operations

Operation	μP Notation	Comments
AND	$A \bullet M \rightarrow A$ $A \wedge M \rightarrow A$	Contents of accumulator and memory location are ANDed together. Result is placed in accumulator.
OR	$A + M \rightarrow A$ $A \vee M \rightarrow A$	Contents of accumulator and memory location are ORed together. Result is placed in accumulator.
Exclusive OR	$A \oplus M \rightarrow A$ $A \veebar M \rightarrow A$	Contents of accumulator and memory location are Exclusive ORed together. Result is placed in accumulator.

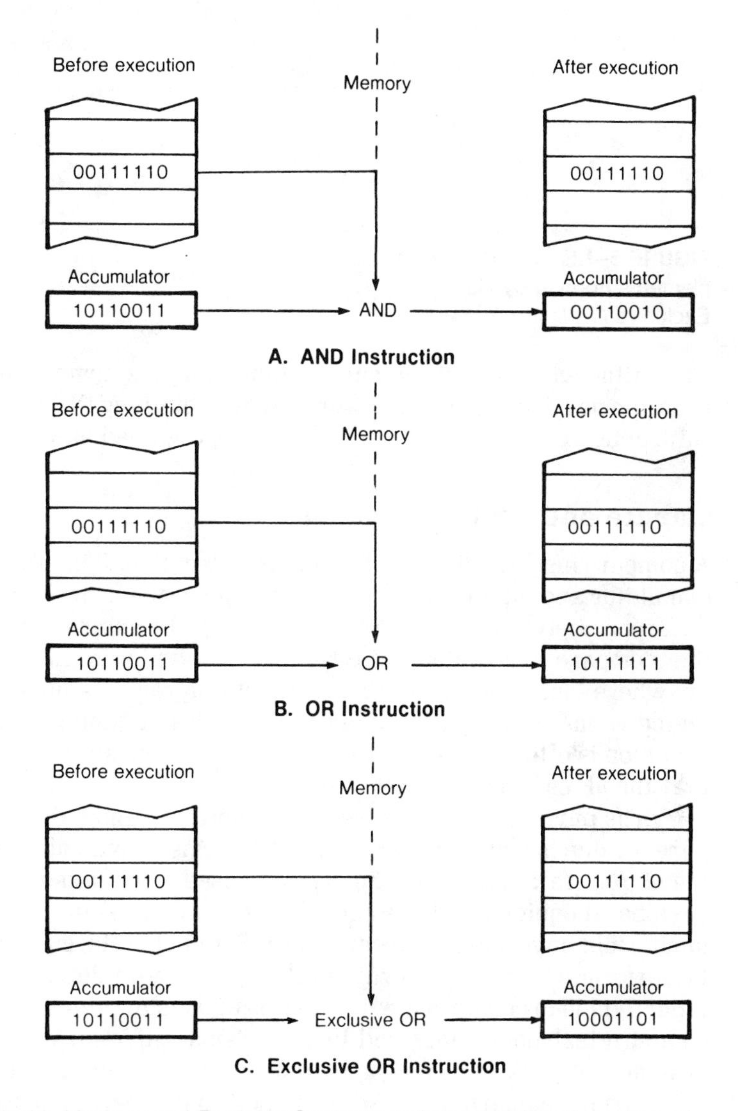

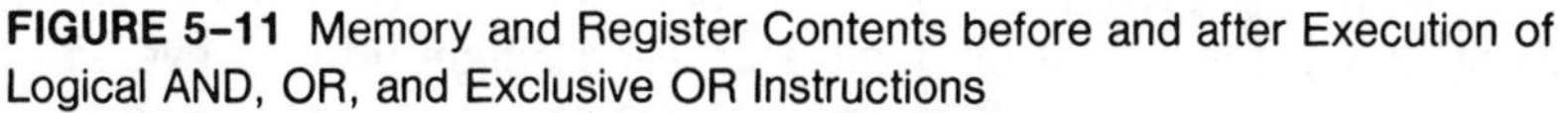

FIGURE 5-11 Memory and Register Contents before and after Execution of Logical AND, OR, and Exclusive OR Instructions

plement of a number can be formed by Exclusive ORing a register with all logic 1s. An example is shown in Figure 5-12A. The 2's complement of a number may be found by first obtaining the 1's complement and then incrementing it, as shown in Figure 5-12B. The term *complement* when used alone means 1's complement. The μP notation for the 1's complement of the accumulator is $\overline{A} \rightarrow A$.

The instruction set for the 6502 μP has neither complement instruction, and the 8080A μP has only a 1's complement instruction. The 6800 μP has instructions for doing both 1's and 2's complements.

A.		B.
11100110	← Accumulator →	11100110
11111111	← Exclusive OR with all 1's →	11111111
00011001	←1's complement→	00011001
	Increment →	00000001
	2's complement→	00011010

FIGURE 5-12 1's and 2's Complements Formed by Using Exclusive OR Instruction

Although μPs perform subtraction using 2's complement arithmetic, the programmer does not have to worry about obtaining the 2's complement. In the subtraction process, the 2's complement is obtained automatically by the ALU.

5.3.4 Compare and Test Instructions

A compare instruction is a subtraction instruction. It involves data from the accumulator and either data from another μP register or data from memory. The difference between a compare instruction and a subtract instruction is that for the compare instruction the result is not stored in the accumulator or anywhere else. Therefore, the accumulator remains unchanged. What is affected is one or more of the flag bits. The instruction following a compare instruction is often an instruction to check the logic state of a flag bit (or bits) so that the μP can decide what to do next.

The purpose of a compare instruction is to allow the programmer to compare a value in memory to a value in a μP register without changing the value of the μP register. This instruction is often used when data is being received from peripheral equipment. Let's consider an example. Data from peripheral equipment could have one of several values. For each different value, the program is to perform a different operation. A rapid way to determine the value of the input data is to compare it with a series of constants stored in memory. Use of a compare instruction followed by a decision-making instruction gives the programmer a quick and easy method of accomplishing this task.

Compare instructions are designed to compare bytes of data. If the programmer wishes to test the logic state of a single bit, however, there are two commonly used methods. The first is a *masking procedure*, and the second is a *bit-testing procedure.*

The masking procedure uses an AND instruction. The accumulator is ANDed with a byte of data that contains a logic 1 in the bit location (or locations) under test. If the bit being tested is not a logic 1, then the result of the AND operation is all 0s and the zero flag is set. The instruction following the AND instruction will be an instruction to check the zero flag, allowing the μP to decide what to do next. The disadvantage of this technique is that the contents of the accumulator are destroyed by the AND operation. Thus, the accumulator would have to be reloaded with the original data. To search a table for a single bit in a given position using a masking procedure would require extra programming and extra time for the instruction to be executed.

Figures 5-13 and 5-14 show bit 3 in the accumulator being tested using the masking technique. When the individual bit being checked is a logic 0, the result stored in the accumulator is zero and the Z flag is set. See Figure 5-13. When the individual bit being checked is a logic 1, the result stored in the accumulator is not zero and the Z flag is cleared. See Figure 5-14.

When data is being sent to or received from a peripheral device, the data often has to be modified by masking out either the least significant 4 bits or the most significant 4 bits. Figure 5-15 shows how the least significant 4 bits are

	Bit to be tested ↓	
Accumulator	10110100	
Memory	00001000	
Result is to be stored in accumulator.	00000000	←Since result is all logic 0s, Z flag will be set.

FIGURE 5-13 Testing Individual Bit (Logic 0) by Masking Using AND Instruction

	Bit to be tested ↓	
Accumulator	10111100	
Memory	00001000	
Result is to be stored in accumulator.	00001000	←Since result is *not* 0s, Z flag will be cleared.

FIGURE 5-14 Testing Individual Bit (Logic 1) by Masking Using AND Instruction

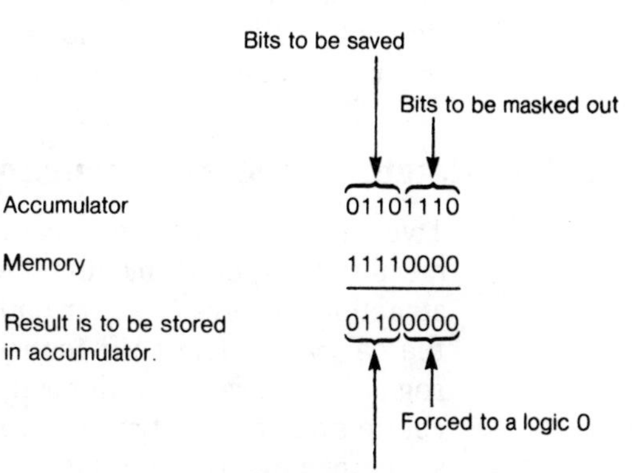

FIGURE 5-15 Testing Several Bits by Masking Using AND Instruction

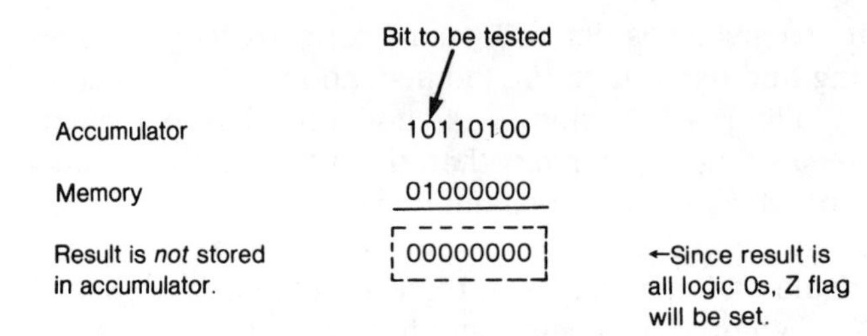

FIGURE 5–16 Testing Individual Bit (Logic 0) through Execution of Bit-Testing Instruction

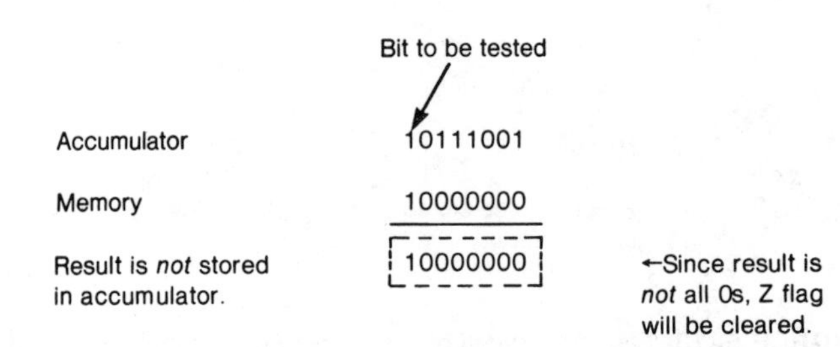

FIGURE 5–17 Testing Individual Bit (Logic 1) through Execution of Bit-Testing Instruction

masked out and the new result that is stored in the accumulator. In this figure, the Z flag is cleared because the result is not zero.

The second technique, the bit-testing procedure, also involves an AND operation, but the contents of the accumulator are not destroyed. Not all μPs have a bit-testing instruction, however, and in some of those that do, only some of the bits can be tested. Figures 5–16 and 5–17 show examples of the use of a bit-testing instruction. In Figure 5–16, the result is not stored in the accumulator, but the Z flag is set to a logic 1 because the result is zero. The result of Figure 5–17 causes the Z flag to be cleared to a logic 0 because the result is not zero. In most applications, the instruction that follows a bit-testing instruction is a conditional branch instruction. Branch instructions are program control instructions. They will be covered in Section 5.3.6.

5.3.5 Rotate and Shift Instructions

Two other instructions—rotate and shift—alter the data in a register or memory location by moving the present data either right or left one bit. Both instructions involve the carry bit. The rotate instructions rotate the data through the carry bit. The shift instructions do not move the carry bit back into the register. Figure 5–18 illustrates what happens to each bit during execution of rotate and shift instructions. *Note:* Rotate instructions save the data; shift instructions destroy the data.

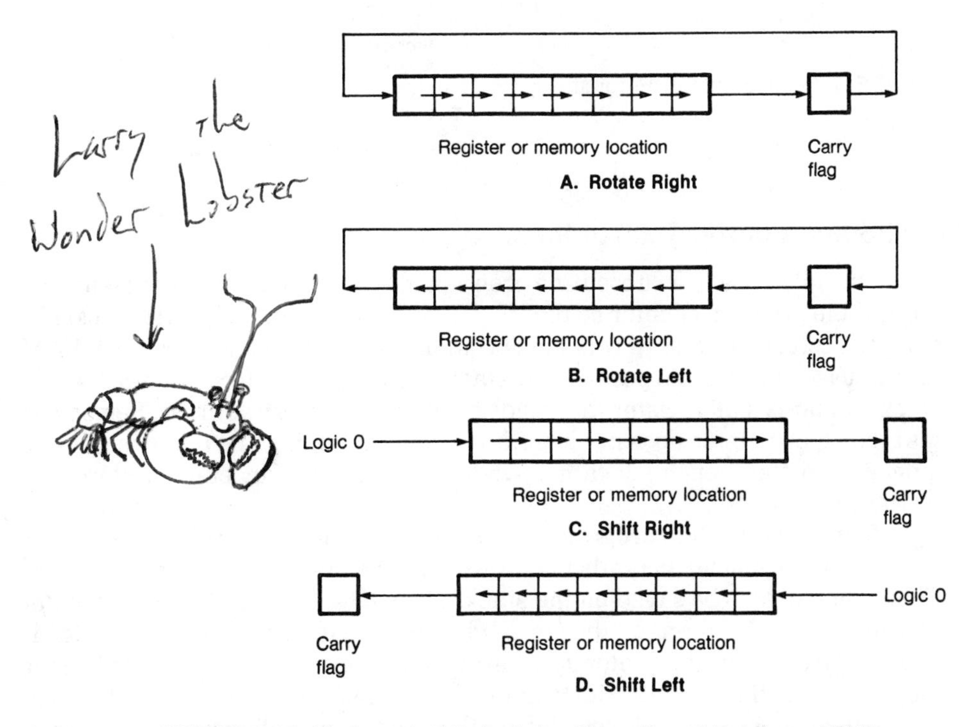

FIGURE 5–18 Movement of Data during Execution of Rotate and Shift Instructions

5.3.6 Program Control Instructions

Program control instructions change the contents of the program counter. The μP can then skip over a number of memory locations to execute a new program or go back to an old memory location and repeat a program.

Program control instructions are either *unconditional* or *conditional* instructions. When an unconditional instruction is executed, the program counter is always changed. For the program counter to be changed when a conditional instruction is executed, the state of a flag bit (or bits) must first be checked. If the condition is true (a yes answer), the program counter is changed. If the condition is false (a no answer), the program counter is not changed and the next instruction in the program sequence is fetched and executed.

One program control instruction is used to jump to a subroutine program, and another program control instruction is used to return from the subroutine to the main program or to the specific program that the user has left. Some of the program instructions that we will discuss in the next several chapters include the jump, call, branch, and return instructions. Figure 5–19 shows an example of the contents of the program counter before and after a jump instruction is executed. In this example, the μP executes a jump instruction telling it to go to memory location 8100. This instruction as written in assembly language is JMP 8100.

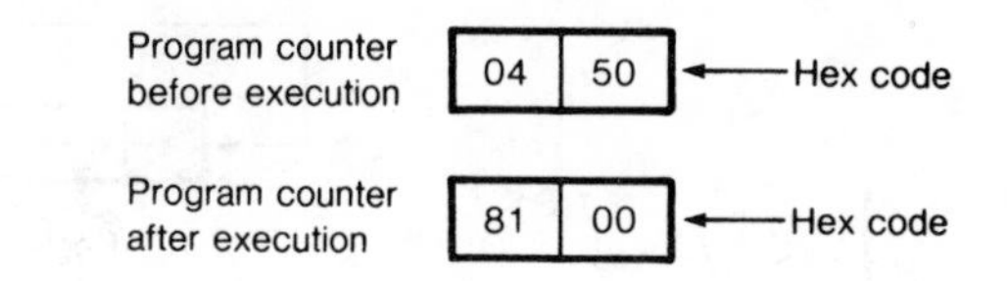

FIGURE 5-19 Contents of Program Counter before and after Execution of Jump Instruction

5.3.7 Stack/Stack Pointer Instructions

When the μP jumps to a subroutine program, the μP must store the present contents of the program counter so that the μP can know where to return. Most μPs store the return address in random access memory (RAM). The portion of RAM that is used for this purpose is the stack. As described in Section 5.1.4, the stack pointer is a μP register that holds the stack's memory address. Remember that the stack pointer does not hold the actual data but, as its name implies, is a pointer to the memory location where the actual data can be stored or retrieved.

Since a subroutine program will certainly use one or more of the μP registers, the programmer may also wish to save the contents of these registers. This data can also be saved on the stack. The contents of the program counter are automatically stored on the stack when a jump to subroutine instruction is executed. However, the contents of the other μP registers must be stored on the stack by inserting specific instructions to do this job. The instruction that stores the contents of a μP register on the stack is a push instruction. The instruction that retrieves the contents of a μP register from the stack is a pull or pop instruction. When a push instruction is executed for the 6800 or 6502 μPs, the contents of the μP register are stored on the stack and then the stack pointer is decremented by 1. Thus, the stack pointer is pointing to the *next* memory location where data can be saved. When a pull or pop instruction is executed by these μPs, the stack pointer is incremented by 1. Then this memory address is placed on the address bus and the data at that location is retrieved and moved to the proper μP register.

Some μP stack pointers work slightly differently. For example, the stack pointer of the 8080A μP does not point to the *next* memory location where data can be saved but rather to the *last* memory location where data has been saved. Therefore, when a push instruction is executed by the 8080A μP, the stack pointer is first decremented by 1 and this is the address where the data will be stored. When the 8080A μP executes a pull or pop instruction, the data stored at the memory address contained by the stack pointer is retrieved and sent to the μP register. Then the stack pointer is incremented by 1. The 8080A stores two bytes on the stack for each push instruction and retrieves two bytes for each pull instruction.

Figure 5-20 shows how a 6502 μP stores the contents of its program counter on the stack. In this example, a JSR EC00 instruction tells the 6502 μP to jump to a subroutine beginning at memory location EC00. Before going to location EC00, the μP saves the contents of the program counter (507A) on the stack. Some μPs, such as the 6800, interchange the two bytes of the program counter on the stack. The 8080A μP stores the data on the stack as shown in

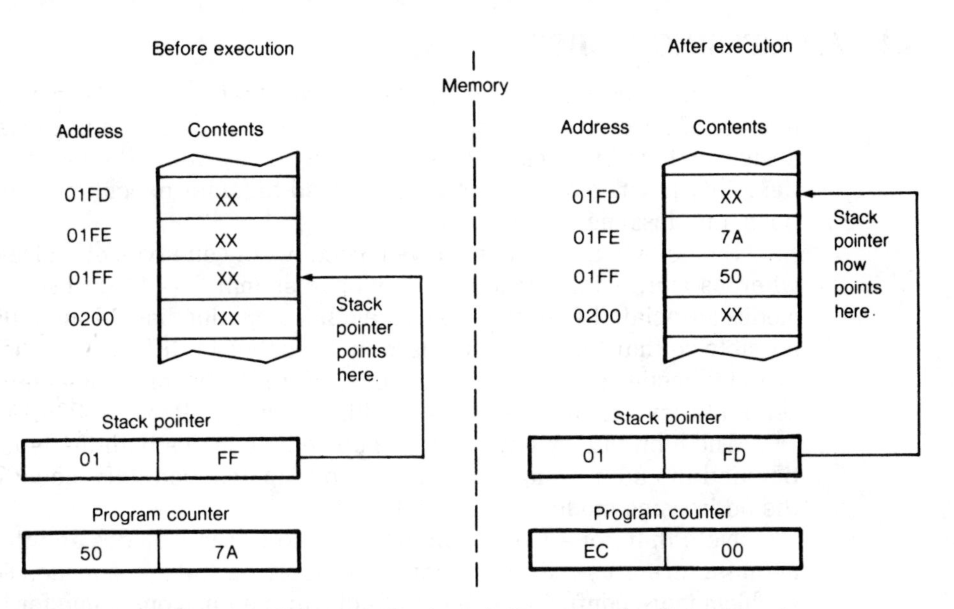

FIGURE 5–20 Memory and Register Contents before and after Execution of Stack/Stack Pointer Instruction

Figure 5–20, but the stack pointer would start at 0200 and end at 01FE. XX indicates any byte of data. Other examples will be examined in later chapters.

5.3.8 Input/Output Instructions

Input/output instructions deal specifically with controlling I/O devices. Microprocessors such as Intel's 8080A and 8085 and Zilog's Z–80 have I/O instructions. Other μPs, such as the Motorola 6800 and MOS Technology 6502, do not have specific I/O instructions. They deal with their I/O devices as with any memory location. This technique is called *memory-mapped I/O*. If a μP uses an I/O instruction to deal with an external device, the technique is called *isolated I/O*. Both techniques are covered in later chapters.

5.3.9 Other Microprocessor Instructions

Some instructions do not fall easily into any of the previous categories. These instructions are sometimes grouped together and referred to as special-purpose instructions, miscellaneous instructions, or other μP instructions. They include instructions such as enabling or disabling the μP's interrupt lines, clearing or setting the μP's flag bits, and allowing the μP to do binary arithmetic or BCD arithmetic. They also include instructions to halt or break the program sequence.

As we study different μPs, we will find that instructions do fall into one of the nine categories just discussed. Remember, some manufacturers use more categories and others use fewer, but it is only for our convenience that we group similar instructions.

5.4 ADDRESSING MODES

Microprocessor manufacturers design into their product's instruction set a number of different ways in which the μP can retrieve data from memory. This design feature involves *addressing modes*. They allow the programmer more flexibility to write a program that can lead to faster execution, simpler operations, and less memory space.

Single-byte instructions have basically only one type of addressing mode, whereas multibyte instructions may have as many as 11 different addressing modes associated with them. Thus, each instruction has as much flexibility as possible so that the μP can be used in a number of different applications. Addressing modes are an important part of a μP's architecture and instruction set, and they are often used as a selling point by μP manufacturers.

The 8-bit binary pattern of the op code includes both the type of instruction and the addressing mode. The type of instruction tells the μP what to do; the addressing mode tells the μP how to do it.

Note that not all μPs have the same addressing modes and that different manufacturers use different names to describe the same mode. To make the problem more confusing, one manufacturer may use one name for an addressing mode, while another manufacturer may use the same name for an entirely different addressing mode. These difficulties are illustrated in Table 5-3, in which each line is an equivalent addressing mode. Note that the addressing mode "Direct" means one thing to the 8080A user and something else to the 6800 user. Definitions and examples of each of the addressing modes follow.

TABLE 5-3 Addressing Modes for the 8080A, 6800, and 6502 Microprocessors

8080A	6800	6502
Register	Inherent[1]	Implied[1]
Immediate	Immediate	Immediate
Direct	Extended	Absolute
—	Direct	Zero page
—	Relative	Relative
—	Indexed[2]	Indexed[3]
		Absolute, X
		Absolute, Y
		Zero page, X
		Zero page, Y
Register Indirect	—	Memory indirect[4]
		Indirect
		Indexed indirect
		Indirect indexed

[1]This mode includes the accumulator addressing mode.

[2]The 6800 μP has one 16-bit index register.

[3]The 6502 μP has two 8-bit index registers.

[4]The 6502 μP has three types of indirect addressing modes. Each type is a memory indirect addressing mode.

5.4.1 Register/Inherent/Implied

The register/inherent/implied addressing modes apply to one-byte instructions. Both the op code and the operand address are contained in a single byte (8 bits). Examples are: clear a register, increment or decrement a register, clear or set the carry flip-flop, clear or set the interrupt flip-flop, and shift or rotate a register. When this type of instruction is decoded by the μP's instruction register, part of the 8 bits tells the μP what to do (op code) and the other part of the 8 bits tells the μP where to perform the instruction (operand address). The operand address for this instruction is always within the μP, such as an internal register or an internal flip-flop.

5.4.2 Immediate

An immediate addressing mode instruction is a two- (or three-) byte instruction. The first byte contains the op code and the register that will receive the data. The second (and third) byte is the data that is to be placed in that register. If the register is 8 bits wide, the instruction is two bytes. If the register is 16 bits wide, the instruction requires three bytes.

This type of addressing mode is used for quickly loading data into a register or performing arithmetic or logical operations using a known or fixed value. The bytes must be stored in successive memory locations. The symbol # is used quite often to indicate the immediate addressing mode.

For the immediate addressing mode LDA instruction shown in Figure 5-21, the data, 05_{hex}, is part of the instruction. It is contained in the second (and sometimes third) byte. Figure 5-21A shows the mnemonic and symbol for load the accumulator immediately. After the instruction is executed, 05_{hex} is placed in the accumulator, as shown in Figure 5-21B. The data (B2) in the accumulator is lost.

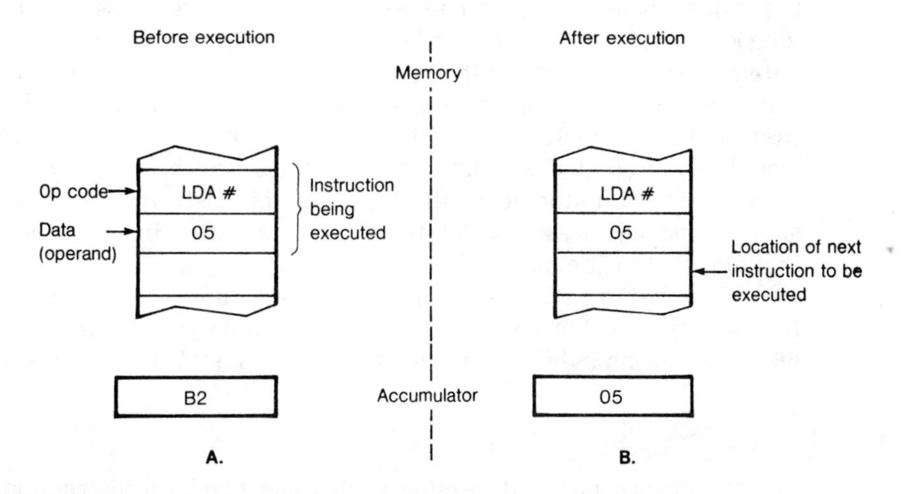

FIGURE 5-21 Memory and Register Contents before and after Execution of Immediate Addressing Mode LDA Instruction

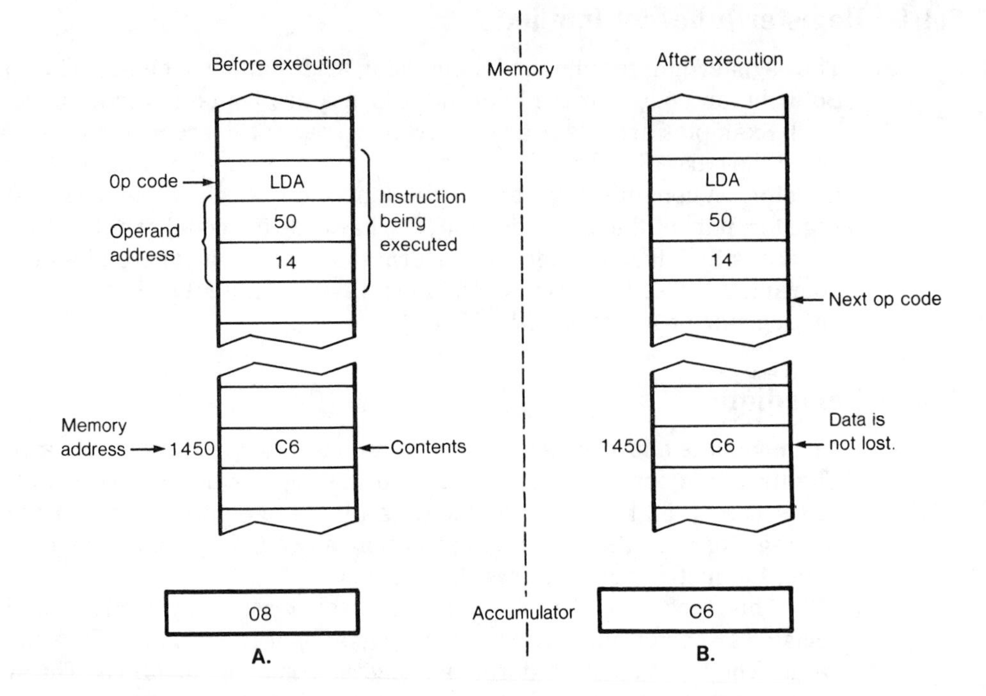

FIGURE 5–22 Memory and Register Contents before and after Execution of Direct/Extended/Absolute Addressing Mode LDA Instruction

5.4.3 Direct/Extended/Absolute

The direct/extended/absolute addressing mode instructions are three-byte instructions. The first byte is the op code, while the second and third bytes are the address where the data can be found (operand address). For the direct/extended/absolute addressing mode LDA instruction shown in Figure 5–22A, the data at memory location 1450 is moved into the accumulator when the μP executes an LDA 1450 instruction. The data (08) in the accumulator is lost. The first byte of the instruction is the address where the machine code for LDA would be stored. The second and third bytes are the memory address of the data to be put into the accumulator. When this instruction is executed, the μP goes to memory location 1450, finds the data that is in that memory location, and places it in the accumulator, as shown in Figure 5–22B.

Note that in some μPs, such as the 8080A and 6502, the second byte is the line address and the third byte is the page address. In other μPs, such as the 6800, the second byte is the page address and the third byte is the line address.

5.4.4 Direct/Zero Page

The direct/zero page addressing modes use two-byte instructions. The first byte is the op code, and the second byte is the line address. The page address is understood by the μP to be page zero. Figure 5–23 shows an example of an LDA

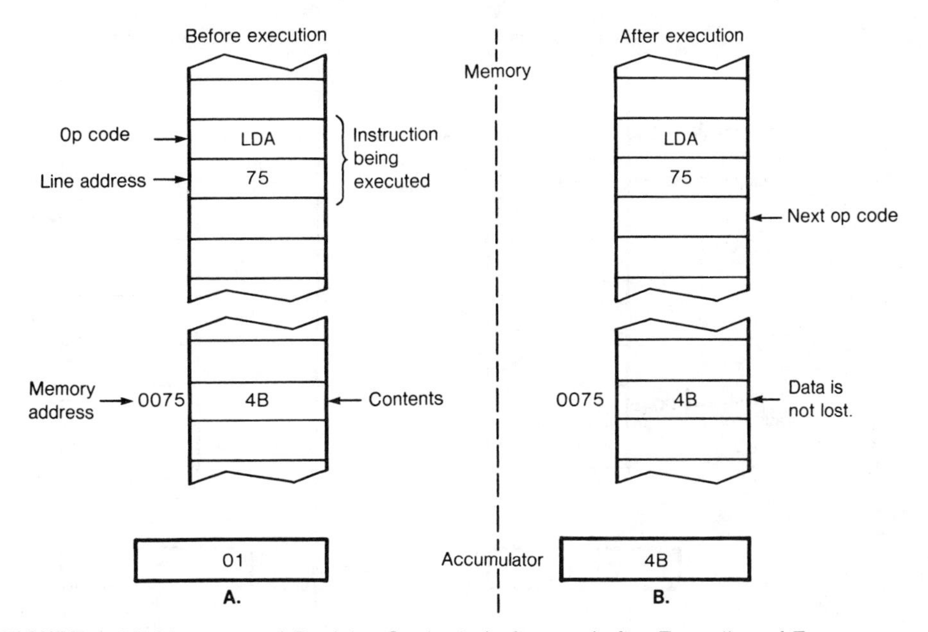

FIGURE 5–23 Memory and Register Contents before and after Execution of Zero Page Addressing Mode LDA Instruction

instruction using the zero page addressing mode. The accumulator is loaded with data from memory location 0075. The zero page address is understood by the μP when it decodes the instruction's op code. The previous data (01) in the accumulator is lost. Figure 5–24 shows an example of an STA instruction using the zero page addressing mode. The contents of the accumulator are stored in memory location 004E. The zero page address is understood by the μP when it decodes the instruction's op code. Any previous data (XX) in memory location 004E is lost. In the next two types of addressing modes to be discussed—relative and indexed—the final address, which is often called the *effective address*, must be calculated.

5.4.5 Relative

The relative addressing mode is used by the decision-making instructions for the 6800 and 6502 μPs. (The 8080A uses its direct addressing mode for its decision-making instructions.) These instructions check the condition of a flag bit and branch to a new instruction depending on the logic state of the flip-flop. Therefore, the relative addressing mode for the 6800 and 6502 μPs applies only to their branch instructions.

Relative addressing mode instructions use two bytes. The first byte is the op code. The second byte is called the *offset* or *displacement*. In this text, we use the term *offset*. If the branch is to be taken, then the offset is added to the program counter and the result is the final (or effective) address of the next instruction.

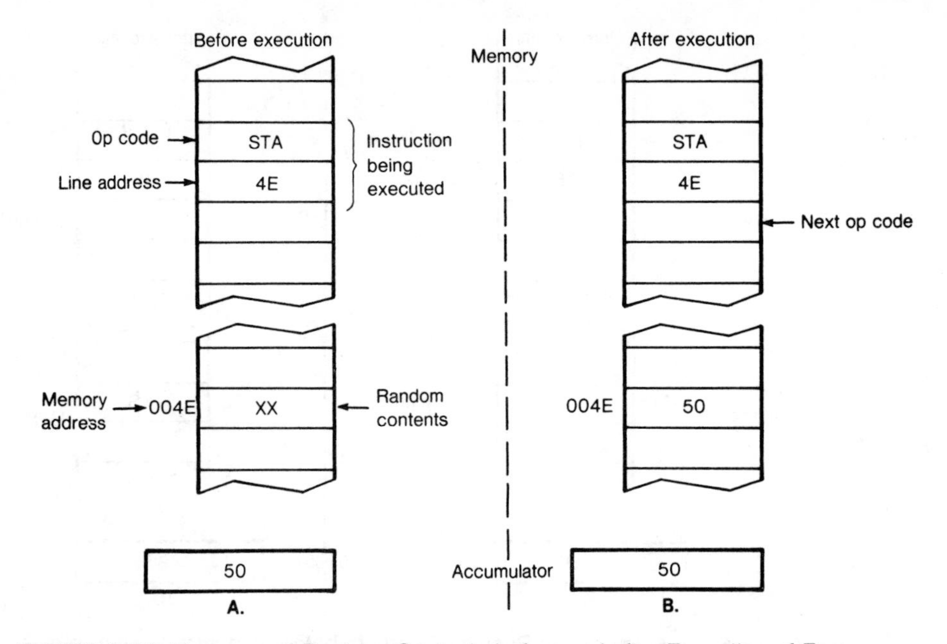

FIGURE 5-24 Memory and Register Contents before and after Execution of Zero Page Addressing Mode STA Instruction

Note: When the offset is added to the program counter, the result of the addition is placed back in the program counter so that the μP begins the program sequence from this new address. If the branch instruction is not taken, then the offset is not added to the program counter and the μP executes the next instruction in the program sequence.

Since the offset is the second byte of the instruction word, it has only 8 bits. Thus, the total range of addresses that can be added to the program counter is 256 ($2^8 = 256$). The range includes positive and negative offset values. This range allows the μP to branch forward and backward. All negative offset values are in 2's complement form. The maximum negative offset is −128 (1000 0000), while the maximum positive value is +127 (0111 1111). Although this range can be considered a limitation, it has been estimated that it satisfies 80% to 90% of branch applications.

Figure 5-25 shows an example of the relative addressing mode as applied to a branch instruction. If the branch is taken, the second byte (offset) of the instruction is added to the program counter as shown. If the branch is not taken, there is no addition and the program counter would be incremented to 7802.

5.4.6 Indexed

The indexed addressing mode also involves an addition to obtain the final (or effective) address. Microprocessors have a special register or registers for the purpose of indexing. The 6502 has two 8-bit index registers; the 6800 has one

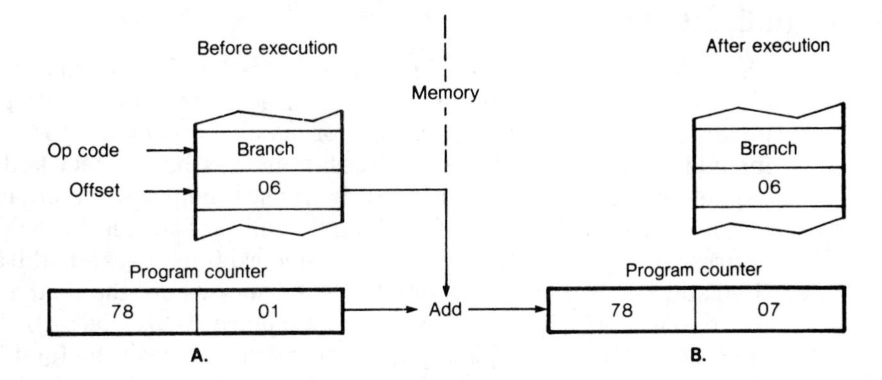

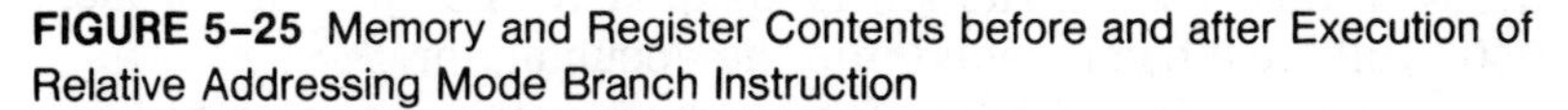
FIGURE 5-25 Memory and Register Contents before and after Execution of Relative Addressing Mode Branch Instruction

16-bit index register. The 8080A does not have this type of addressing mode. Unlike the other types of addressing modes, the indexed addressing mode cannot be used alone, but rather it increases the capabilities of an absolute or zero page addressing mode. For example, if an LDA instruction is using an absolute indexed addressing mode, the contents of the index register are added to the instruction's operand address. The result is the effective address where the data can be found. An example is shown in Figure 5-26. Here, the effective address (1607) is found by adding the instruction's operand address (1504) to the index register (0103). When this instruction is completed, the contents of memory location 1607 will have been moved into the accumulator.

If a μP has an index register, it also contains instructions that load, store, increment, decrement, or transfer data to or from the index register. Therefore, by controlling the contents of the index register with these instructions, the effective address can be controlled. The indexed addressing mode is especially useful in obtaining and operating on a list of data in sequential memory locations.

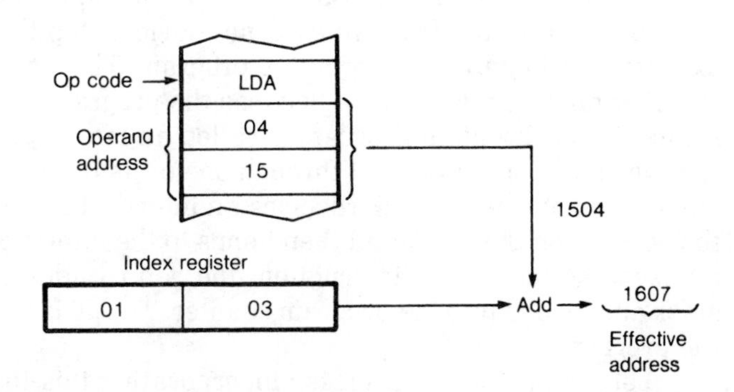

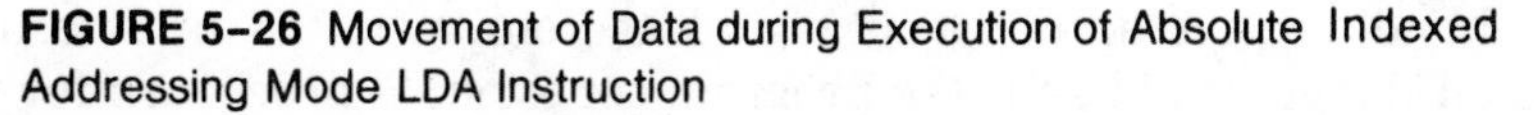
FIGURE 5-26 Movement of Data during Execution of Absolute Indexed Addressing Mode LDA Instruction

5.4.7 Indirect

The indirect addressing mode is an advanced addressing mode and is not included in many μP instruction sets. It is used quite often in data processing applications, and the μPs that are used primarily for control applications may not include it. Like the indexed addressing mode, the indirect addressing mode cannot be used alone, but rather it increases the power of either the absolute or zero page addressing mode. When the indirect addressing mode is used, the address associated with the instruction word (the operand address) is not the final address. Rather, it is a pointer to memory where the final address will be found. This principle is illustrated in Figure 5–27. Here, the instruction's operand address (5018) is a pointer to memory to find the final (effective) address. When this instruction is completed, the contents of memory location 0400 will have been loaded into the accumulator.

Some μPs (the 8080A, for example) use a register indirect addressing mode, while other μPs (the 6502) use a memory indirect addressing mode. The 6800 does not have this type of addressing mode. In register indirect, the contents of a μP register or registers contain the indirect address. In memory indirect, the indirect address is contained in two successive bytes of memory. As shown in Table 5–3, the 6502 μP has other indirect addressing modes that also use the index registers. More examples of these addressing modes are given in later chapters.

5.5 INTERRUPTS

Until now, we have seen the μP fetch and execute instructions in a program sequentially. The only method that has been described to change the program sequence is for the μP to execute either a jump or branch instruction. Both of these instructions are capable of changing the contents of the program counter and thus the program sequence. Sometimes the jump and branch instructions are used to allow the μP to execute a subroutine program. Since instructions belong to a μP's software, we can say that the program counter has been changed because of the software. Most μPs include a feature that allows the μP to recognize a signal from an external device, stop the program that is being executed, and jump to a subroutine program. The signal is called an *interrupt signal* or an *interrupt request* because the program has been stopped or interrupted. The subroutine program is called an *interrupt service routine.* The μP receives the interrupt signal through one of its IC pins. Figure 5–28 shows the steps that occur when a μP receives an interrupt request signal. The μP saves the address on the stack and then jumps to the interrupt subroutine. When the μP executes the return instruction, the return address is removed from the stack and loaded into the program counter. The μP is then able to continue with the program.

Let's consider a reason for incorporating this feature in the μP. If a μP could not receive an interrupt signal, the only way for an external device to signal the μP would be if the program contained a procedure for periodically

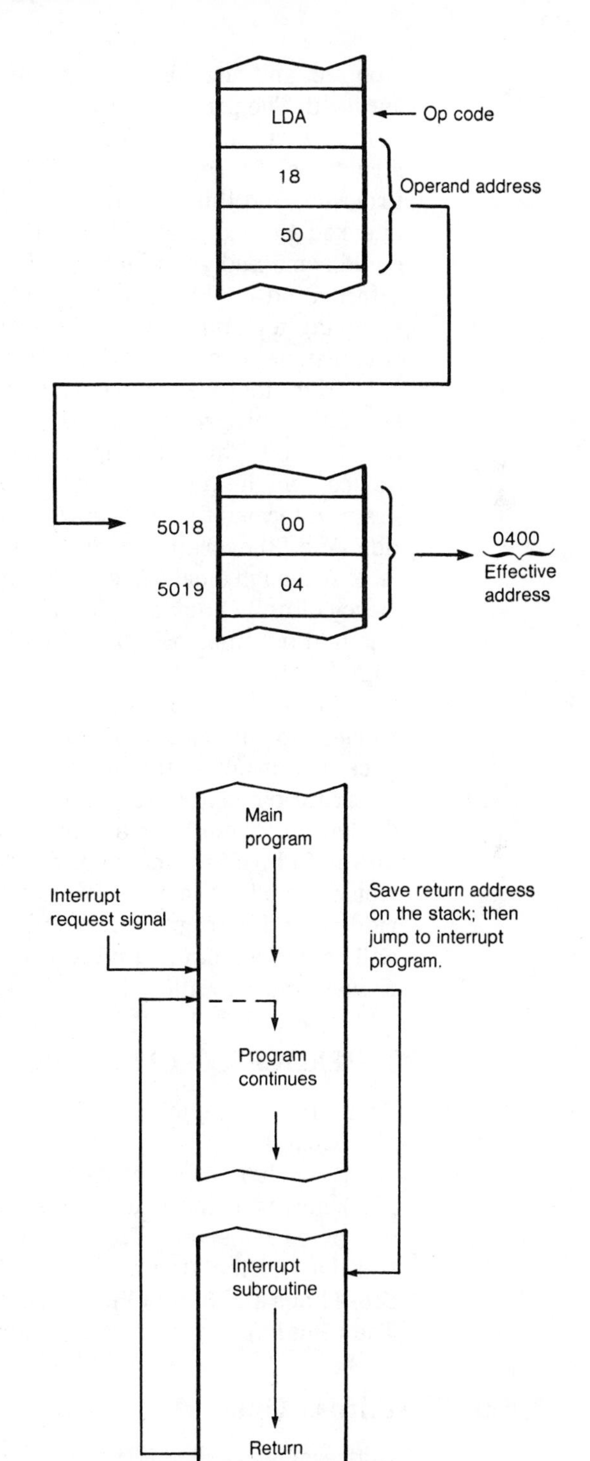

FIGURE 5-27 Memory Contents during Execution of Indirect Addressing Mode LDA Instruction

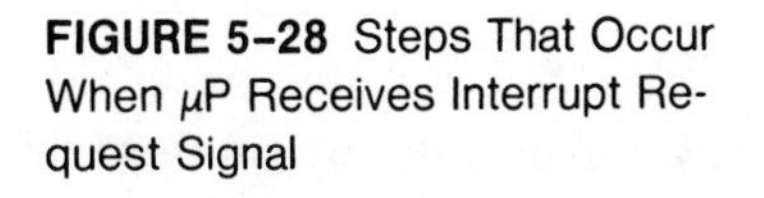

FIGURE 5-28 Steps That Occur When μP Receives Interrupt Request Signal

stopping and checking to see whether or not an external device needed to be serviced. The problem with this technique is that an external event usually occurs asynchronously. That is, the event is not timed with the μP's internal instructions. Therefore, in all likelihood, the event would not coincide with the program, and thus the event would not be sampled until the next time the μP checked the external device. What could happen is that the external event could come and go before the μP had time to check it. Thus, external data and information could be lost. In addition to the possibility of losing data, this sampling technique wastes memory space because the programmer must insert instructions telling the μP what to do and when to do it.

Manufacturers have built into the μP a hardware feature for calling a subroutine program, and this feature enables the μP to accept an interrupt request signal. This interrupt request signal transfers control of the μP to an I/O device, which, in turn, allows the programmer to write the most efficient program in terms of (1) recognizing an external signal, (2) faster program execution, and (3) overall memory space.

Although most μPs have an interrupt feature, the programmer is not at the mercy of an I/O device. Manufacturers also have included instructions to turn this feature on or off, thus allowing the μP to accept or not to accept an interrupt signal.

Some μPs, such as the 6800 and 6502, have two interrupt pins—*interrupt request* and *nonmaskable interrupt*. Signals on the interrupt request pin can be accepted or not at the programmer's discretion. A signal on the nonmaskable interrupt pin is always received by the μP. This pin would be connected to one device that would signal the μP only when there is an emergency, such as a power failure, an accident, or other catastrophe. In such a situation, the μP would jump to its nonmaskable interrupt service routine and could not be overridden by the programmer. Only a loss of power could stop it. Later chapters will show techniques that allow several I/O devices to use the same interrupt request pin and allow the μP to recognize each device.

5.6 MICROPROCESSOR PIN ASSIGNMENTS

There are many similarities in package style and pin functions among different μPs. Most 8-bit μPs are packaged in a 40-pin dual-in-line package like the one shown earlier in Figure 1–2. Some μPs are available in smaller packages (24 pins); however, these μPs do not have 16 address lines and they cannot address 64K bytes of memory. These smaller packages also do not contain all of the control lines of the 40-pin package. The 40-pin package usually contains 16 address lines and 8 data lines, which use a total of 24 pins of the 40-pin package. The remaining 16 pins are for power, control, and clock lines.

5.6.1 Address Lines

Address lines are unidirectional; that is, an address originates inside the μP, is placed on the address lines, and is sent to memory or to an I/O port. Most μP address lines are three state (logic 1, logic 0, or high impedance state). The 8080A and 6800 μPs have three-state address lines. The 6502 μP's address lines are only TTL; that is, this μP's address lines are not capable of going to the high impedance state. Except for the time that an address line could be going from a logic 0 to a logic 1 or vice versa, there is always a valid address on the 6502 address lines. In small systems, this could be an advantage because these systems probably do not require the address line to go to the high impedance state. At first glance, a two-state address line could be considered a disadvantage in larger systems because there are times when the address lines need to "float" (go to the high impedance condition). However, in larger systems, the address bus lines as well as the data bus lines and control lines usually require additional buffers. These buffers can be purchased to have three-state capability, and thus the μP itself does not need it.

5.6.2 Data Lines

The 8 data lines that make up the data bus are bidirectional. That is, information can be received from memory or an I/O device into the μP, or the μP can send data out to memory or an I/O device across these 8 lines. Data bus lines of all μPs are three state.

5.6.3 Power Supply Pins

Earlier μPs required three voltage levels, +12 V, +5 V and −5 V, in addition to ground. As technology improved, manufacturers were able to design a μP requiring only +5 V and ground, thus reducing requirements on the power supply and saving two pins for other purposes. The 8080A μP requires all three voltages and ground, while the 6800 and 6502 μPs require only +5 V and ground.

5.6.4 Clock Pins

Microprocessors are synchronous, sequential machines. The term *synchronous* means that all μP operations are controlled by a clock signal or signals. *Sequential* means that the operations are carried out one after the other in a logical order. The key to understanding a μP's synchronous, sequential operation is familiarity with its timing diagrams. The 8080A, the 6800, and the 6502 μPs, like most other 8-bit μPs, require two clock signals, as shown in Figure 5-29. These clock signals are known as ϕ_1 and ϕ_2 clock pulses. They are nonoverlapping pulse waveforms. The term *nonoverlapping* means that one clock pulse falls to a logic 0 before the other clock pulse rises to a logic 1. The overall cycle time is measured from the rising edge of a ϕ_1 pulse to the next rising edge of a ϕ_1 pulse. Thus, both clock pulses are never at a logic 1 at the same time. The reason is that the μP uses the rising and falling edge of a clock signal for different operations. For example, for one particular μP instruction, the rising edge of the ϕ_1 clock signal might place the contents of the program counter onto the address bus. The falling edge of the ϕ_1 clock signal might increment the program counter. The rising edge of the ϕ_2 clock signal might activate the input latch, and the falling edge of the ϕ_2 clock signal might latch the data coming into the μP. Thus, the nonoverlapping clock signals eliminate the problem of the μP trying to do two things at the same time. Some μPs require only a single-phase clock signal, while others require four clock signals.

Clock signals are generated either from a crystal or from an *RC* circuit. When stability is important, a crystal is needed. When stability is not of prime importance, as, for example, in games or household appliances, a low-cost *RC* circuit can be used.

Depending on the μP, the ϕ_1 and ϕ_2 clock signals are generated either internally or externally. If generation is internal, the μP manufacturer has designed a clock generating circuit into the μP chip itself. This circuit receives a single clock pulse from an external circuit (either crystal-controlled or *RC*-controlled) and generates the two-phase nonoverlapping clock signals. The 6502 is such a μP. External generation means that the two clock signals must be generated outside the μP. The 8080A and 6800 are two such μPs. In later chapters, we will examine each μP and its clock signals in more detail.

The 8080A, 6800, and 6502 μPs are dynamic devices. Thus, if power is lost or if the clock signals are too slow, then the data in the μP's internal registers is lost. Microprocessors also have a maximum clock frequency above which the μP cannot operate. The μP circuitry simply cannot respond to signals faster than the maximum clock frequency. Microprocessor manufacturers specify these limits as the minimum and maximum time of the clock signal, t_{cyc}, as shown in Figure 5–29. Since the manufacturer gives the limits in terms of time, the user has to calculate the frequency:

$$f = \frac{1}{t_{cyc}}$$

Table 5–4 shows that although the 6800 μP has a maximum clock frequency of 1.0 MHz, there are A and B versions with maximum frequency limits of 1.5 MHz and 2.0 MHz, respectively. Table 5–4 lists manufacturers' time specifica-

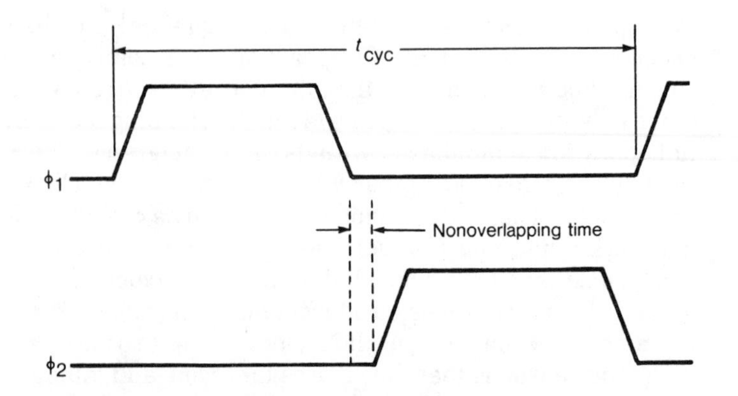

FIGURE 5–29 Two-Phase Nonoverlapping Clock Pulse

tions for the 8080A, 6800, and 6502 μPs. The minimum and maximum clock frequencies have been calculated and are also given in this table.

5.6.5 Control Lines

Control lines are the area in which there are the most differences among μPs. Section 5.5 discussed interrupt operations. We found that most μPs include at least one pin for an interrupt line and that some μPs, such as the 6800 and 6502, also have a nonmaskable interrupt line. Some newer μPs have three or more interrupt lines for design flexibility.

Read/Write Line

All μPs have a read/write line. Some μPs, such as the 6800 and 6502, designate this line as R/W. Other μPs, such as the 8080A, designate this line as $\overline{WR}$. The read/write line indicates whether the μP is going to read (receive) information from memory or an I/O device or write (send) information to memory or an I/O device. The terms *read* and *write*, regardless of where they are seen, always refer to the μP and not to what a memory chip or an I/O chip is doing. For example, a memory chip has a read/write pin, but the memory chip is not reading or writing data; the term refers to what the μP is doing. A logic 1 on the read/write line indicates that the μP is reading. A logic 0 on this line indicates that the μP is writing data. Figure 5-30 shows the direction that data is moving and the logic level of the read/write line. In Figure 5-30A, the R/W line is high and the μP is reading (receiving) data. In Figure 5-30B, the R/W line is low and the μP is writing (sending) data.

Reset Pin

All μPs have a pin assigned to be wired to the μC's reset line. When this line is brought to its active state, the μP resets itself. The active state for the 8080A is a logic 1. The active state for the 6800 and the 6502 is a logic 0. Once this line is activated, it overrides all other μP operations and the program counter is reset.

For the 8080A μP, the address 0000_{hex} is automatically loaded into the program counter and must be the starting address of the reset program. For the

TABLE 5-4 Summary of Cycle Times and Frequencies for the 8080A, 6800, and 6502 Microprocessors

	Cycle Time		Frequency	
μP	Min. (μs)	Max. (μs)	Min. (kHz)	Max. (MHz)
8080A	0.480	2.0	500	—
6800	1.000	10.0	100	1.0
68A00	0.666	10.0	100	1.5
68B00	0.500	10.0	100	2.0
6502	1.000	—	—	1.0
6502A	0.500	—	—	2.0
6502B	0.333	—	—	3.0

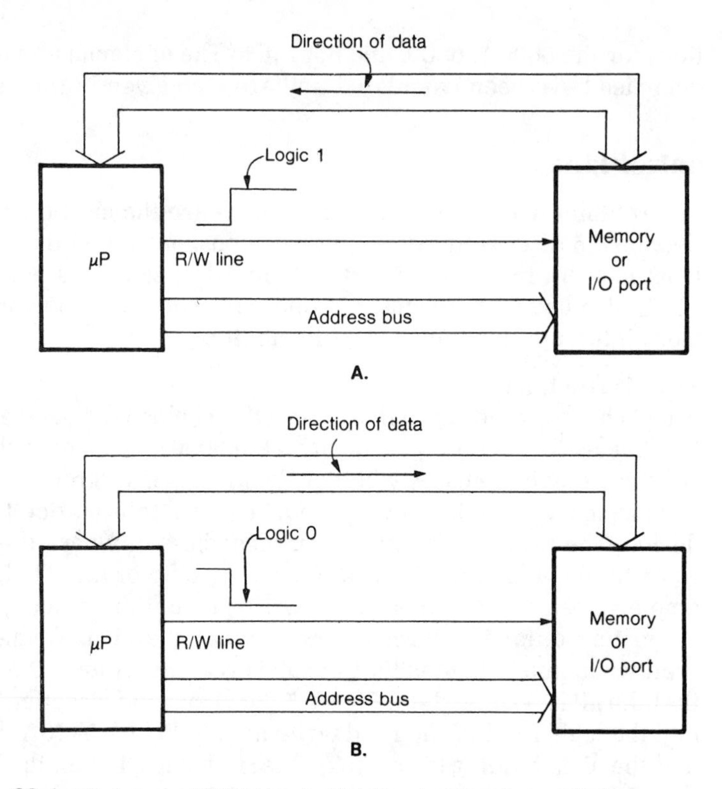

FIGURE 5-30 Logic Level of R/W Line in Relation to Direction of Data

6800 μP, the contents of locations FFFE and FFFF in memory will be loaded into the program counter, and the contents of these locations must contain the starting address of the reset program. For the 6502 μP, the contents of locations FFFC and FFFD in memory will be loaded into the program counter, and the contents of these locations must contain the starting address of the reset program.

Other Control Lines

As we discuss the individual μPs, we will look at several more control lines and their functions. For example, we will examine a pin that places the μP in a wait state—that is, stops the μP from fetching and executing any more instructions; a pin that indicates when a valid address is on the address bus; a pin that places the address bus or the data bus in its high impedance state; a pin that indicates when the μP is beginning to fetch a new instruction; and so forth.

5.7 SUMMARY

In this chapter, we focused on the similarities among μPs in their architecture, instructions, addressing modes, interrupt-handling capability, package style, and pin descriptions. First, we examined the four main architectural parts of a μP: (1) registers, (2) arithmetic and logic unit, (3) timing and control circuitry, and (4) decoding circuitry. A diagram, or programmer's model, illustrated these basic parts. Such a model can help a programmer visualize what happens when an instruction is executed.

Most instructions occupy either one, two, or three bytes of memory. Instructions have two parts, the op code and the operand or operand address. Although each μP has instructions that are unique to it, most μPs have the same basic instruction set. In this text, we have divided a μP instruction set into nine categories: (1) data movement, (2) arithmetic, (3) logical, (4) compare and test, (5) rotate and shift, (6) program control, (7) stack, (8) input/output, and (9) other machine and control instructions.

Addressing modes give an instruction flexibility by allowing the μP to read and write data in a number of different ways. In this chapter, we considered the following addressing modes: register/inherent/implied, immediate, direct/extended/absolute, direct/zero page, relative, indexed, and indirect.

In several sections of the chapter, we concentrated on the software similarities among μPs. We also examined some of the hardware similarities that exist among μPs, such as interrupt capability, address lines, data lines, control lines, clock pins, and power supply lines.

PROBLEMS

5-1 List the four basic parts of a μP.

5-2 In what register inside the μP is an instruction placed?

5-3 What does the term *instruction set* mean?

5-4 Does the 8080A μP have an index register?

5-5 Does each of the μPs described in this chapter have a stack pointer register?

5-6 How many accumulators does the 6800 μP have?

5-7 What are some of the other names used for the condition code register?

5-8 What are the three most common flag bits?

5-9 What does the abbreviation PC represent?

5-10 Define stack.

5-11 Is the program counter an up-down counter?

5-12 Is the stack pointer an up-down counter?

5-13 What are the two parts of an instruction?

5-14 What part of an instruction tells the μP what to do?

5-15 List the category the following instructions fall into: (a) transfer, (b) add, (c) subtract, (d) compare, (e) push, (f) load accumulator, (g) store accumulator, (h) jump, (i) branch, (j) move data one bit to the right, (k) ANDing, (l) ORing, and (m) clear carry flag.

5-16 If data is moved from the accumulator to memory location 0100, is the data lost in the accumulator?

5-17 Refer to Problem 5-16. Is the accumulator the source or the destination?

5-18 What is the purpose of load instructions?

5-19 What is the purpose of store instructions?

5-20 Given the following registers, show what happens for each operation: (a) transfer B to C, (b) transfer C to B, and (c) exchange B and C.

5-21 Are increment and decrement instructions arithmetic instructions?
5-22 What μP register automatically holds the result of an arithmetic or logical operation?
5-23 In the process of subtraction, what is the carry flag called?
5-24 If a register contains FF_{hex} and the register is incremented, what are the new contents in the register? Is the carry flag affected?
5-25 Can the 1's complement of a number be obtained by Exclusive ORing it with FF_{hex}?
5-26 What type of instruction usually follows a compare or test instruction?
5-27 What is the advantage of a compare instruction over a subtract instruction?
5-28 If you AND the following register with $0F_{hex}$, what is the result?

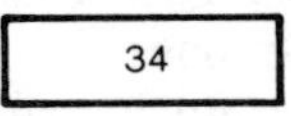

5-29 Refer to Problem 5-28. What is the result if a bit-testing instruction is used instead of the AND instruction?
5-30 What is the difference between a rotate instruction and a shift instruction?
5-31 What are the two classifications of program control instructions?
5-32 What is that portion of memory called that holds the contents of the program counter when the μP is executing a subroutine program?
5-33 What is the name of the μP register that holds a stack address?
5-34 What is the name of the instruction that stores the contents of a μP register on the stack?
5-35 What is the advantage of addressing modes?
5-36 Do all μPs have the same addressing modes?
5-37 If the first byte of an instruction is the op code and the second byte is data, what type of addressing mode is being used?
5-38 If the first byte of an instruction is an op code and the second and third bytes are an address, what type of addressing mode is being used?
5-39 What μP(s) has instructions that use the relative addressing mode?
5-40 What is the second byte of a relative addressing mode called?
5-41 What is one advantage in using a μP that can receive an interrupt request?
5-42 Can the programmer stop the μP from receiving (a) an interrupt request signal and (b) a nonmaskable interrupt signal?
5-43 In reference to clock signals, what does the term *nonoverlapping* mean?

8080A Microprocessor Instruction Set

6.0 INTRODUCTION

This chapter and the next two chapters deal specifically with the 8080A μP. This chapter covers its instruction set and shows examples of several types of instructions. The examples will help us understand and write assembly language programs using the 8080A μP. Chapter 7 combines the instructions in example programs. Chapter 8 deals primarily with hardware aspects of the 8080A μP, such as the function of each pin, some basic support chips, and timing diagrams. Later chapters show how the 8080A μP is connected to memory and how some of the more popular I/O devices associated with the 8080A work. Figure 6–1 shows the pin assignments for the 8080A μP and may be used for reference in this or the next chapter.

Before we study the instruction set, we should know about the internal architecture specific to the 8080A and its condition code register. The internal architecture will help us visualize what happens to data when each instruction is executed. That is, we can visualize where the data is, where it came from, and where it is going.

Since most of the instructions affect the condition code register, we must know what flag bits are in the 8080A μP and how they work. Remember, it is the flag bits that are checked by the μP and allow it to make a decision.

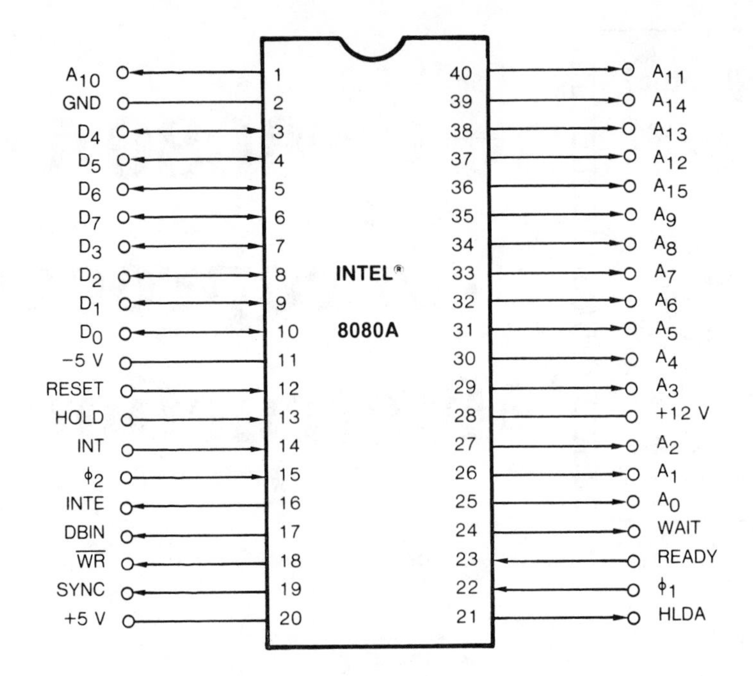

FIGURE 6-1 Pin Assignments for the 8080A μP (Redrawn from data sheet for 8080A microprocessor with permission. Intel Corporation, Santa Clara, CA)

6.1 8080A INTERNAL ARCHITECTURE

Figure 6–2 is a functional block diagram of the internal structure of the 8080A μP. It is more complete than the programmer's model presented in Chapter 5 because it shows the timing and control sections along with registers that are used by the μP for the internal execution of instructions not under the programmer's control. The *internal data bus* shown in Figure 6–2 is 8 bits wide and allows for the transfer of data among different parts of the μP. The registers shown in the register array section are similar to static RAMs. The registers that are under the programmer's control are the 16-bit program counter, the 16-bit stack pointer, and six 8-bit general-purpose registers (B, C, D, E, H, and L). These six general-purpose registers can be programmed as *individual registers* or in *pairs* as BC, DE, and HL. The first letter designates the high-order byte, and the second letter designates the low-order byte. Registers W and Z are temporary registers used by the μP during execution of an instruction and are not programmable.

The *program counter* maintains the memory address of the current program instruction. The program counter is incremented automatically during every instruction fetch.

The *stack pointer* maintains the address of the last-used stack location in memory. Since the stack pointer is 16 bits wide, the stack can be located in any portion of read/write memory. When data is put onto the stack, the stack pointer is first decremented by 1, and data is placed on the stack. After data is retrieved from the stack, the stack pointer is automatically incremented by 1.

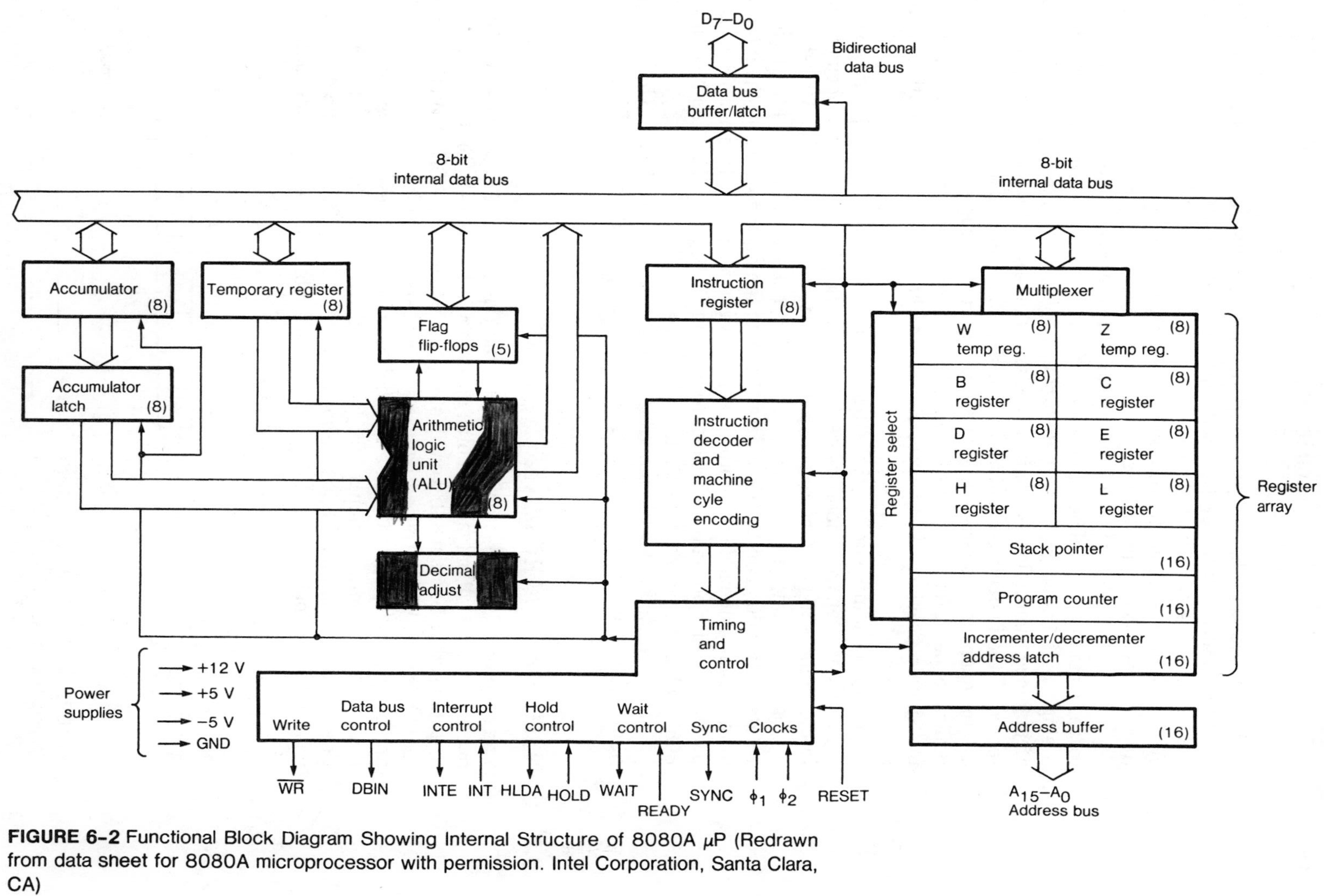

FIGURE 6–2 Functional Block Diagram Showing Internal Structure of 8080A μP (Redrawn from data sheet for 8080A microprocessor with permission. Intel Corporation, Santa Clara, CA)

The *data bus buffer/latch* circuitry isolates the μP's internal data bus from the external data bus. When the μP is receiving data, data from the external data bus is transferred to the internal data bus through this circuitry. When the μP is sending data, the data is loaded into the 8-bit latch, which, in turn, drives the output buffers.

When the μP fetches an instruction from memory, the op code is transferred from the internal data bus to the *instruction register*. If the instruction is a single-byte instruction, the entire byte is placed in this register. If the instruction is a multiple-byte instruction, only the first byte (the op code) is transferred to the instruction register. Remember that the remaining byte or bytes are the operand or operand address. The instruction register holds the op code while it is being decoded. The output of the decoder section combined with timing signals provides the control signals to the μP for the execution of the instruction.

As shown in Figure 6-2, the *arithmetic and logic unit* (ALU) has two 8-bit inputs—one from a temporary register and the other from the *accumulator latch*, which is also referred to as a *temporary accumulator*. The ALU also has a single input line from the carry flag. The result of an arithmetic, logic, or rotate instruction can be transferred back to the accumulator, to the internal data bus for placement in another register, or to a memory location. The result of ALU instructions may set or clear one or more flag bits. The flag bits for the 8080A μP are covered in Section 6.2.

Also associated with the ALU is a *decimal adjust block*. This feature allows the programmer to perform either binary addition or BCD addition.

6.2 CONDITION CODE REGISTER

The *condition code register*, also called the *flag register*, is 8 bits wide. However, the 8080A μP only uses 5 bits, as shown in Figure 6-3. Bits D_1, D_3 and D_5 are not used. In Section 6.9, we will study an instruction (PUSH PSW) that loads these bits with 1, 0, 0, respectively. As we will see in Section 6.8, bits D_0, D_2, D_6, and D_7 can be checked to decide whether to branch to a new program or to continue in the normal sequence. Bit D_4 is used by the μP during BCD addition. There is no branch instruction associated with bit D_4. Unless indicated otherwise, when an instruction affects a flag, it affects it in the following manner.

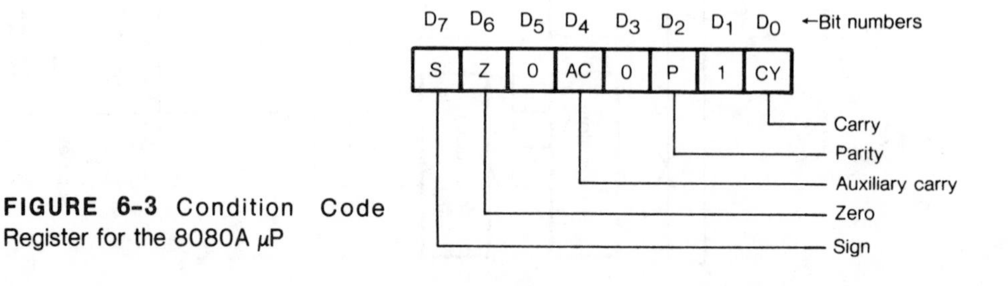

FIGURE 6-3 Condition Code Register for the 8080A μP

Zero Flag (Z Flag): If the result of an instruction is zero (that is, if each bit of a register or memory location is a logic 0), then Z = 1; otherwise, Z = 0. *Note:* When the result is 0, Z = 1. When the result is not 0, Z = 0. The reason is that the logic 1 state is the true state (a yes answer).

Sign Flag (S Flag): If the most significant bit of the result is a logic 1, then S = 1; otherwise, S = 0. If the result is from an instruction that applied to an 8-bit register, then the most significant bit is bit 7. If the result is from an instruction that applied to a register pair, then the most significant bit is bit 15.

Parity Flag (P Flag): If the result of an instruction is even parity, then P = 1; otherwise, P = 0 (indicating odd parity). Remember, even parity means that there is an even number of logic 1s in the result (zero is an even number). Odd parity means that there is an odd number of logic 1s in the result.

Carry Flag (CY Flag): If the result of an add instruction produces a carry from the most significant bit, then CY = 1; otherwise, CY = 0. If the result of a subtract instruction produces a borrow from the most significant bit, then CY = 1; otherwise, CY = 0.

Auxiliary Carry Flag (AC Flag): If an instruction causes a carry out of bit 3 and into bit 4 of the result, then AC = 1; otherwise, AC = 0. Although this bit is primarily used by the μP during BCD additions or increments, other instructions do affect this flag bit. This flag bit is automatically checked by the μP and not by a program instruction.

6.3 DATA MOVEMENT INSTRUCTIONS

The 8080A μP's data movement instructions can be divided into four categories: *move, load, store,* and *exchange* instructions. There are five move instructions, four load instructions, three store instructions, and two exchange instructions. The five move instructions include instructions that allow the μP to transfer data from one μP register to another. Since there are seven general-purpose registers (A, B, C, D, E, H, and L), the data movement instructions provide great flexibility to the user of the 8080A μP. Note that none of the data movement instructions affects any flag bits. Let's examine the instructions in each category.

6.3.1 Move Instructions

The five move instructions transfer data from a μP register or memory to another μP register or memory. The three MOV instructions are one-byte instructions; both the op code and the location are contained within 8 bits. The two MVI instructions use the immediate addressing mode and are two-byte instructions. The first byte is the op code; the second byte is the data that is being moved into a μP register or memory location. The term *register* (r) in the following move instructions refers to one of the μP's general-purpose registers. The symbol M refers to a memory location.

MOV r1, r2 Move Register

The contents of register 2 are moved to register 1. The source register is r2, and the destination register is r1. The contents of register 2 remain unchanged.

MOV r, M Move from Memory

The contents of the memory location whose address is in the H and L registers are moved to register r. The memory location is the source, and a μP register is the destination. When this instruction is to be executed, the H and L registers must already contain the memory location. The H register contains the page address, while the L register contains the line address.

MOV M, r Move to Memory

The contents of register r are moved to the memory location whose address is contained in the H and L registers. In this instruction, the μP register is the source, while a memory location is the destination.

The hexadecimal and octal codes for the three MOV instructions are given in Tables 6–1 and 6–2. To use either table, find the source location on the left-hand side. Follow that row over to the destination column, and read the hex or octal code. For example, suppose that we want to move the contents of register L to the accumulator (register A), and we want the hexadecimal op code. The L register is the source, and the accumulator is the destination. Find row L in Table 6–1, follow it over to column A, and read the hex code, 7D. This code is the instruction's op code that would be used in a program written in hex. This type of instruction would be written in a program as follows:

MOV A, B The contents of register B are moved to the accumulator.
MOV A, D The contents of register D are moved to the accumulator.

Note: In 8080A terminology, the source register is given last.

The two MVI instructions for all the 8080A μP's registers are listed in Table 6–3 with their op codes. The d8 expressions signify the 8 bits of data that

TABLE 6–1 8080A Microprocessor MOV Instructions in Hexadecimal Code

	Destination							
Source	B	C	D	E	H	L	M	A
B	40	48	50	58	60	68	70	78
C	41	49	51	59	61	69	71	79
D	42	4A	52	5A	62	6A	72	7A
E	43	4B	53	5B	63	6B	73	7B
H	44	4C	54	5C	64	6C	74	7C
L	45	4D	55	5D	65	6D	75	7D
M	46	4E	56	5E	66	6E	*	7E
A	47	4F	57	5F	67	6F	77	7F

*Hex code 76 is not a MOV instruction. It is the HLT instruction and is covered in Section 6.11.

TABLE 6-2 8080A Microprocessor MOV Instructions in Octal Code

	Destination							
Source	B	C	D	E	H	L	M	A
B	100	110	120	130	140	150	160	170
C	101	111	121	131	141	151	161	171
D	102	112	122	132	142	152	162	172
E	103	113	123	133	143	153	163	173
H	104	114	124	134	144	154	164	174
L	105	115	125	135	145	155	165	175
M	106	116	126	136	146	156	*	176
A	107	117	127	137	147	157	167	177

*Octal code 166 is not a MOV instruction. It is the HLT instruction and is covered in Section 6.11.

are contained in byte 2 of the instruction. Descriptions of how these instructions operate follow.

MVI r, data Move Immediate

The contents of byte 2 of the instruction are moved into one of the μP's registers.

MVI M, data Move to Memory Immediate

The contents of byte 2 of the instruction are moved to the memory location whose address is contained in the H and L registers.

The following examples show how the MVI instruction would be written in a program (the data is given in hex code):

MVI B, 42 Data 42 is moved into register B.
MVI D, 19 Data 19 is moved into register D.
MVI H, F0 Data F0 is moved into register H.
MVI A, 15 Data 15 is moved into the accumulator.

TABLE 6-3 8080A Microprocessor MVI Instructions with Their Op Codes

	Op Code	
Instruction	Hex	Octal
MVI B, d8	06	006
MVI C, d8	0E	016
MVI D, d8	16	026
MVI E, d8	1E	036
MVI H, d8	26	046
MVI L, d8	2E	056
MVI M, d8	36	066
MVI A, d8	3E	076

6.3.2 Load Instructions

The load instructions differ from the move instructions in that for a load instruction, either two registers are loaded by a single instruction or the accumulator is loaded by using the 8080A's direct or register indirect addressing modes. The four load instructions are listed in Table 6–4 with their op codes. Descriptions of how these instructions operate follow.

LDA addr **Load Accumulator Direct**

The contents of the memory location whose address is specified in bytes 2 and 3 of the instruction are moved into the accumulator. This instruction uses the direct addressing mode. The a16 expression shown in Table 6–4 represents two bytes of address information. In a program, this instruction would be written as follows:

LDA 021D The data at memory location 021D is put into the accumulator.

LDAX rp **Load Accumulator Indirect**

The contents of the memory location whose address is in a register pair (rp) are moved to the accumulator. *Note:* Only register pairs rp = B (registers B and C) or rp = D (registers D and E) may be used, as shown in Table 6–4. The first register is the page address, and the second is the line address. This instruction uses the register indirect addressing mode. Example 6–1 illustrates what happens in memory during execution of a LDAX D instruction.

LXI rp, data **Load Register Pair Immediate**

This instruction is a three-byte instruction. The first byte is the op code. Byte 2 of the instruction is moved into the low-order register (rl) of the register pair (rp). Byte 3 of the instruction is moved into the high-order register (rh) of the register pair (rp). The 8080A registers are paired as BC, DE, HL, and SP

TABLE 6–4 8080A Microprocessor Load Instructions with Their Op Codes

	Op Code		
Instruction	Hex	Octal	Example
LDA addr			
LDA a16	3A	072	
LDAX rp			
LDAX B	0A	012	
LDAX D	1A	032	6–1
LXI rp, data			
LXI B, d16	01	001	
LXI C, d16	11	021	
LXI H, d16	21	041	
LXI SP, d16	31	061	
LHLD addr			
LHLD a16	2A	052	

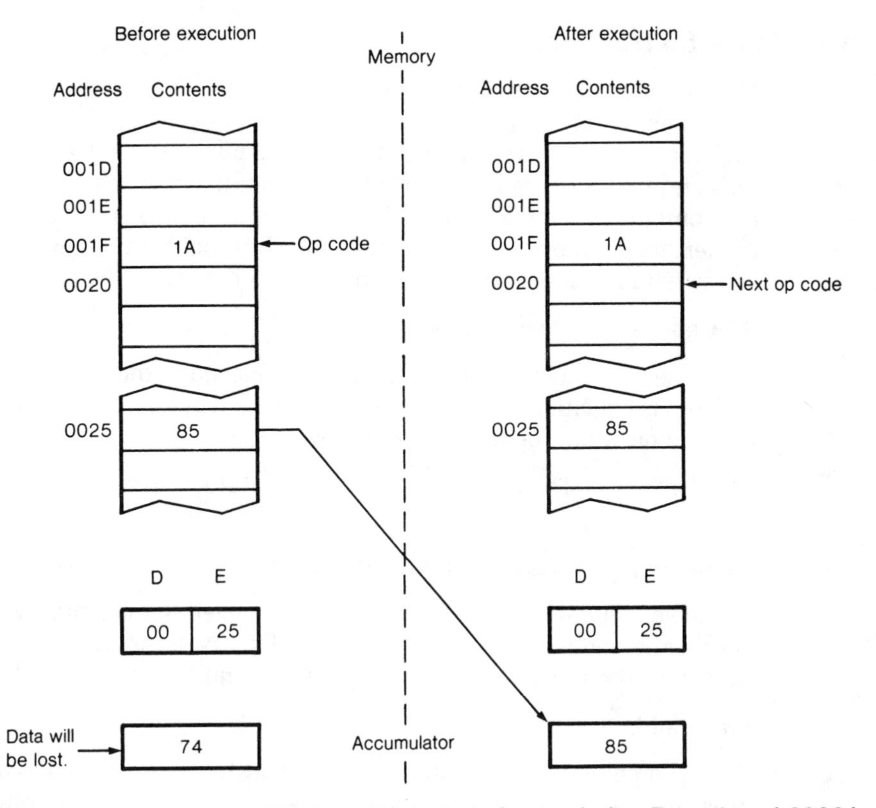

EXAMPLE 6–1 Memory and Register Contents before and after Execution of 8080A μP LDAX D Instruction

(stack pointer). When general-purpose registers are used as a register pair, the convention is to designate the pair by its first letter: B, D, or H. The stack pointer (SP) is not a general-purpose register. The d16 expressions in Table 6–4 represent two bytes of data following the op code. In a program, this instruction would be written as follows (all values are in hex code):

LXI B, 0815	Data 15 is put into register C. Data 08 is put into register B.
LXI SP, 0050	Data 50 is put into the low-order 8 bits of the SP. Data 00 is put into the high-order 8 bits of the SP.

LHLD addr **Load H and L Direct**

The contents of the memory location whose address is specified in bytes 2 and 3 of the instruction are moved to register L. The contents of the memory location at the next address are moved to register H. Again, the expression a16 shown in Table 6–4 represents two bytes of address information. A programming example follows:

LHLD 2570	The contents at memory location 2570 are put into the L register. The contents at memory location 2571 are put into the H register.

6.3.3 Store Instructions

The three store instructions differ from the move instructions in that they allow the accumulator to be transferred to memory by using either the direct or the register indirect addressing mode. There is also a store instruction that allows the H and L registers to be stored in consecutive memory locations. *Note:* Only the contents of the accumulator or of the H and L registers can be transferred to memory by these store instructions. Store instructions with their op codes are listed in Table 6-5. Each instruction is described below.

STA addr **Store Accumulator Direct**

The contents of the accumulator are moved to the memory location whose address is specified in bytes 2 and 3 of the instruction. In a program listing, this instruction would be written as follows:

STA 7431 The contents of the accumulator are stored at memory location 7431.

STAX rp **Store Accumulator Indirect**

The contents of the accumulator are moved to the memory location whose address is contained in a register pair (rp). *Note:* Only register pair rp = B (registers B and C) or rp = D (registers D and E) may be used.

SHLD addr **Store H and L Direct**

The contents of register L are moved to the memory location whose address is specified in bytes 2 and 3 of the instruction. The contents of register H are moved to the next memory location. A programming example follows:

SHLD 2F75 The contents of register L are placed in memory location 2F75. The contents of register H are placed in memory location 2F76.

6.3.4 Exchange Instructions

The 8080A μP has two exchange instructions. One of these involves the stack and is discussed in Section 6.9. The other exchange instruction is discussed here and is listed in Table 6-6 with its op codes.

TABLE 6-5 8080A Microprocessor Store Instructions with Their Op Codes

	Op Code	
Instruction	Hex	Octal
STA addr		
STA a16	32	062
STAX rp		
STAX B	02	002
STAX D	12	022
SHLD addr		
SHLD a16	22	042

TABLE 6–6 8080A Microprocessor Exchange Instruction with Op Codes

	Op Code	
Instruction	Hex	Octal
XCHG	EB	353
(XTHL)	(See Table 6–19.)	

XCHG Exchange H and L with D and E

The contents of register H are exchanged with the contents of register D, and the contents of register L are exchanged with the contents of register E. This instruction applies only to register pairs DE and HL. It is a register addressing mode instruction.

6.4 ARITHMETIC INSTRUCTIONS

The 8080A μP's arithmetic instructions can be divided into four categories: *add, subtract, increment,* and *decrement* instructions. Like most μPs, the 8080A gets one of the values for addition and subtraction from the accumulator. The other value can come either from a μP register or from memory. The result of any add or subtract instruction is automatically placed back in the accumulator. The increment and decrement instructions allow the programmer to add 1 or subtract 1 from a μP register, a memory location, or a register pair. Nineteen arithmetic instructions are covered in this section. Another instruction that allows the 8080A to add two numbers in BCD is covered in Section 6.11.

6.4.1 Add Instructions

The instruction set for the 8080A μP has seven add instructions. Four of these instructions do not include the carry flag in the addition. The remaining three instructions do include the carry flag in the addition. Unless indicated otherwise, all of the add instructions affect the zero, sign, parity, carry, and auxiliary carry flags, as described in Section 6.2. Add instructions with their op codes are listed in Table 6–7.

Add without Carry

In the four add instructions in which the carry flag is not included in the addition, the carry flag is not added to the least significant bits. The contents of a μP register or a memory location are added to the accumulator, and the result is automatically put in the accumulator. These four add instructions are described below.

ADD r Add Register

The contents of a μP register are added to the contents of the accumulator. The result is placed in the accumulator. *Note:* The accumulator can be added to itself.

TABLE 6–7 8080A Microprocessor Add Instructions with Their Op Codes

Instruction	Op Code Hex	Op Code Octal	Example
ADD r and ADD M			
ADD B	80	200	
ADD C	81	201	
ADD D	82	202	
ADD E	83	203	
ADD H	84	204	
ADD L	85	205	
ADD M	86	206	6–2
ADD A	87	207	
ADI data			
ADI d8	C6	306	
DAD rp			
DAD B	09	011	
DAD D	19	031	
DAD H	29	051	
DAD SP	39	071	
ADC r and ADC M			
ADC B	88	210	
ADC C	89	211	
ADC D	8A	212	
ADC E	8B	213	
ADC H	8C	214	
ADC L	8D	215	
ADC M	8E	216	6–3
ADC A	8F	217	
ACI data			
ACI d8	C7	307	

ADD M Add Memory

The contents of the memory location whose address is contained in the H and L registers are added to the contents of the accumulator. The result is placed in the accumulator. Example 6–2 shows what happens in the memory and the μP registers during execution of an ADD M instruction.

ADI data Add Immediate

This instruction is a two-byte instruction. The first byte is the op code; the second byte is the data. The contents of the second byte of the instruction are added to the contents of the accumulator. The result is placed in the accumulator. The carry bit is not included in the addition. The d8 expression shown in Table 6–7 represents 8 bits of data.

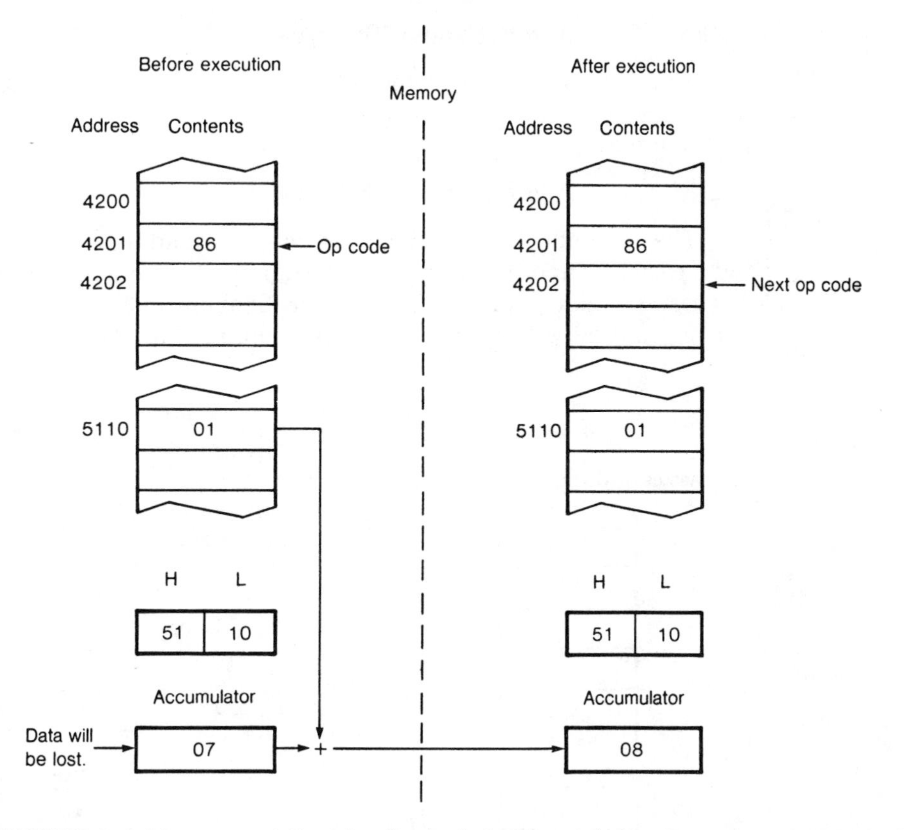

EXAMPLE 6–2 Memory and Register Contents before and after Execution of 8080A μP ADD M Instruction

DAD rp Add a Register Pair to H and L

The contents of a register pair (rp) are added to the register pair HL. The carry bit is not included in the addition. The result is placed in register pair HL. *Note:* The result of this addition only affects the carry flag. It is set (logic 1) if there is a carry out of the double-precision addition; otherwise, it is reset (logic 0). Note also that this instruction allows the HL register pair to be added to itself.

Add with Carry

In add instructions in which the carry bit is included in the addition, the carry flag is added to the least significant bits. *Note:* It is the logic state of the carry flag before the instruction is executed that is included in the addition. This instruction is used in multiprecision addition programs, which are discussed in Chapter 7.

ADC r Add Register with Carry

The contents of one of the μP's registers and the contents of the carry bit are added to the contents of the accumulator. The result is placed in the accumulator.

ADC M Add Memory with Carry

The contents of the memory location whose address is contained in the H and L registers and the contents of the carry bit are added to the accumulator. The result is placed in the accumulator. Example 6-3 shows what happens in memory and the μP registers during execution of an ADC M instruction.

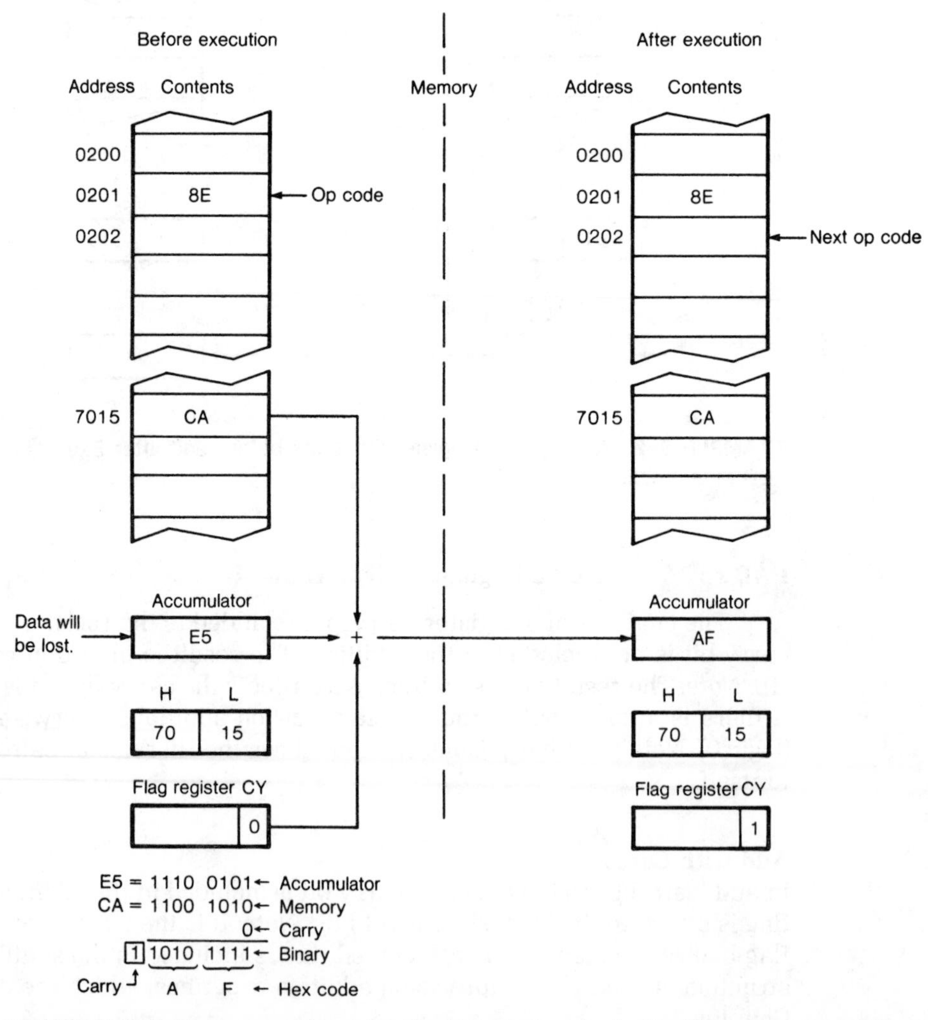

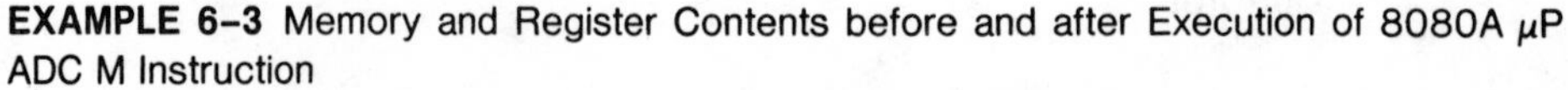

EXAMPLE 6-3 Memory and Register Contents before and after Execution of 8080A μP ADC M Instruction

ACI data **Add Immediate with Carry**

This instruction is a two-byte instruction. The first byte is the op code; the second byte is the data. The contents of the second byte of the instruction and the contents of the carry bit (CY) are added to the contents of the accumulator. The result is placed in the accumulator. As before, the d8 expression shown in Table 6-7 represents 8 bits of data.

6.4.2 Subtract Instructions

The 8080A μP has six subtract instructions. When the μP is performing subtraction, the carry bit is referred to as the *borrow bit*. These six instructions can be divided into two groups: subtraction *without* the borrow bit and subtraction *with* the borrow bit. All subtraction operations are performed using 2's complement arithmetic. The carry flag is set to a logic 1 if there is a borrow; otherwise, the carry flag is cleared to a logic 0. The other flag bits (Z, S, P, and AC) are affected as described in Section 6.2. Subtract instructions with their op codes are listed in Table 6-8.

TABLE 6-8 8080A Microprocessor Subtract Instructions with Their Op Codes

	Op Code		
Instruction	Hex	Octal	Example
SUB r and SUB M			
SUB B	90	220	6-4
SUB C	91	221	
SUB D	92	222	
SUB E	93	223	
SUB H	94	224	
SUB L	95	225	
SUB M	96	226	
SUB A	97	227	
SUI data			
SUI d8	D6	326	6-5
SBB r and SBB M			
SBB B	98	230	
SBB C	99	231	
SBB D	9A	232	
SBB E	9B	233	
SBB H	9C	234	
SBB L	9D	235	
SBB M	9E	236	6-6
SBB A	9F	237	
SBI data			
SBI d8	DE	336	

Subtract without Borrow

The three instructions described below subtract the contents of a μP register or a memory location from the accumulator. These instructions do not include the borrow bit, which means that the logic state of the carry flag is ignored during the subtraction. Of course, the result will either clear or set the carry bit.

SUB r **Subtract Register**

The contents of a μP register are subtracted from the contents of the accumulator. The result is placed in the accumulator. Example 6–4 illustrates what happens when a subtraction results in a negative answer. The program listing for this example would be SUB B.

SUB M **Subtract Memory**

The contents of the memory location whose address is contained in the H and L registers are subtracted from the contents of the accumulator. The result is placed in the accumulator.

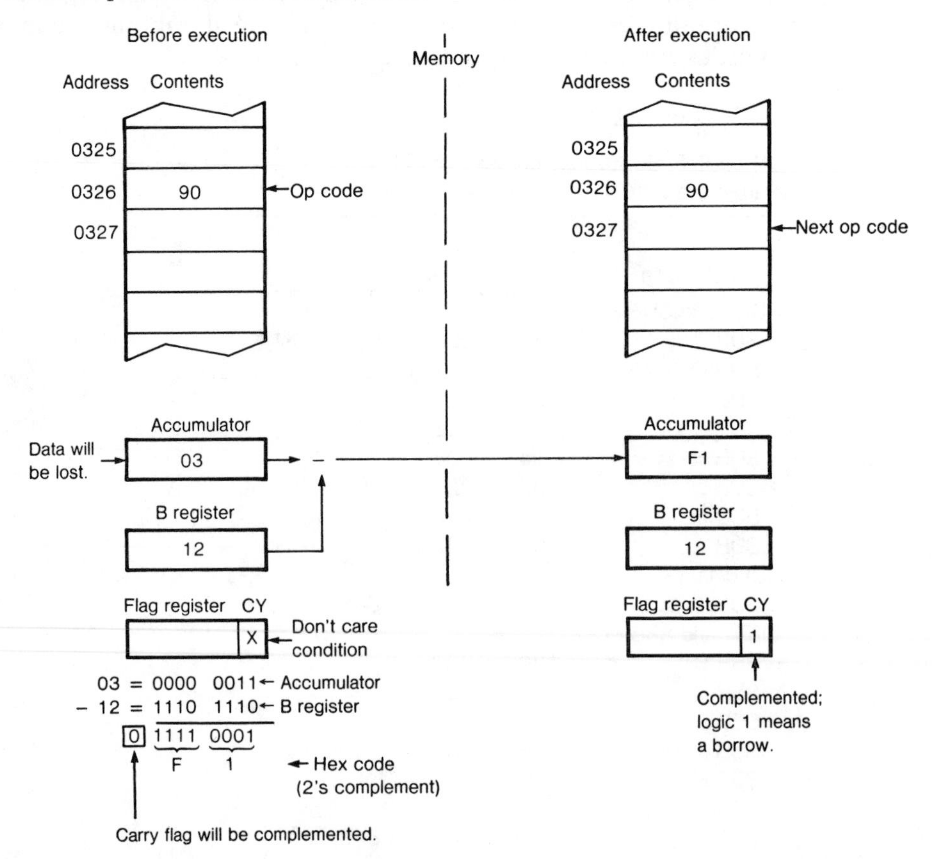

EXAMPLE 6–4 Memory and Register Contents before and after Execution of 8080A μP SUB B Instruction

SUI data Subtract Immediate

This instruction is a two-byte instruction. The first byte is the op code; the second byte is the data. The contents of the second byte of the instruction are subtracted from the contents of the accumulator. The result is placed in the accumulator. The d8 expression shown in Table 6-8 represents the 8 bits of data that will be subtracted from the accumulator. Example 6-5 shows what happens in memory and the μP register when a SUI d8 instruction is executed.

Subtract with Borrow

The three remaining subtract instructions, which are described below, subtract the contents of a μP register or memory location and the borrow bit (the carry flag) from the accumulator. The result is placed back in the accumulator. To check this subtraction, it is easier first to add the contents of the μP register to the carry flag and then obtain the 2's complement. Remember that all subtraction operations are performed by using 2's complement arithmetic.

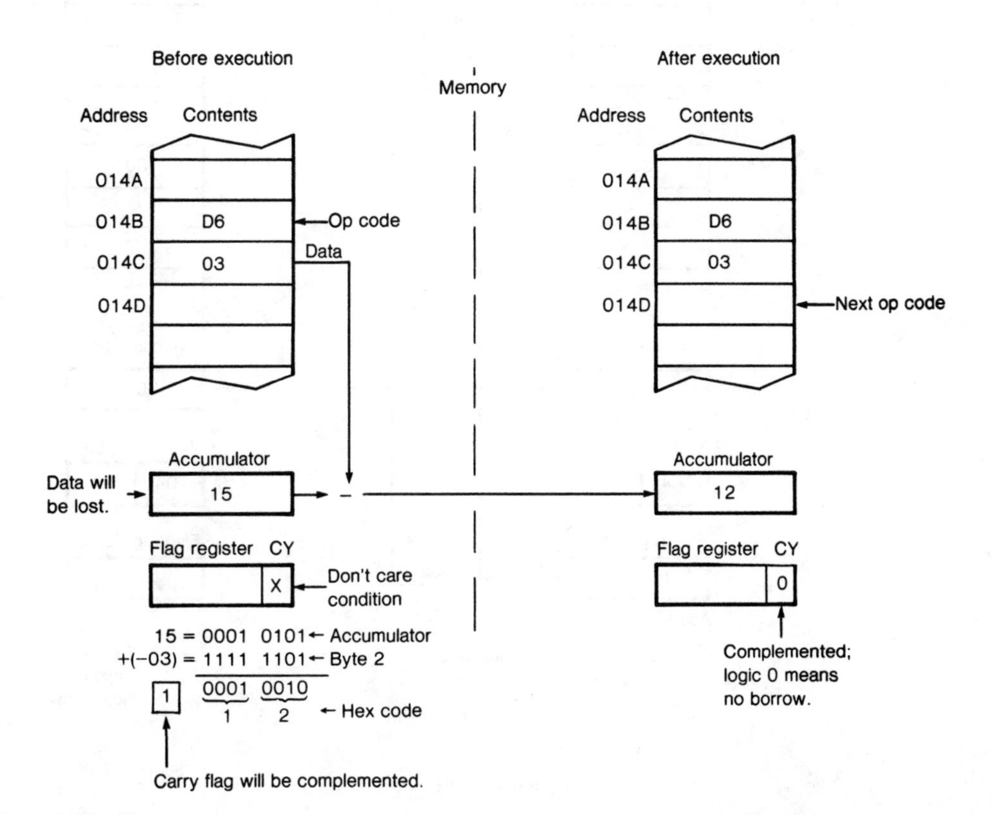

EXAMPLE 6-5 Memory and Register Contents before and after Execution of 8080A μP SUI Instruction

SBB r Subtract Register with Borrow

The contents of one of the μP registers and the contents of the carry (borrow) bit are both subtracted from the accumulator. The result is placed in the accumulator.

SBB M Subtract Memory with Borrow

The contents of the memory location whose address is contained in the H and L registers and the contents of the carry bit are both subtracted from the accumulator. The result is placed in the accumulator. Example 6-6 shows

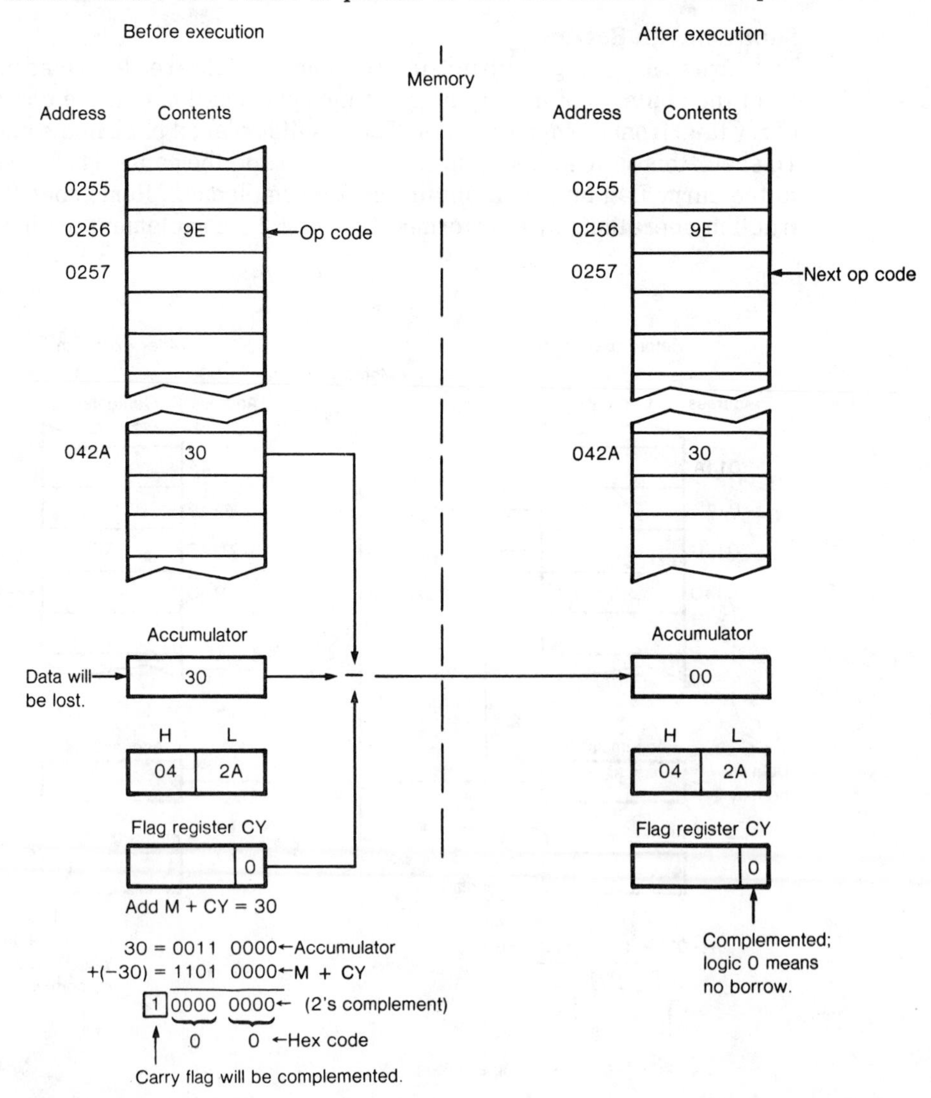

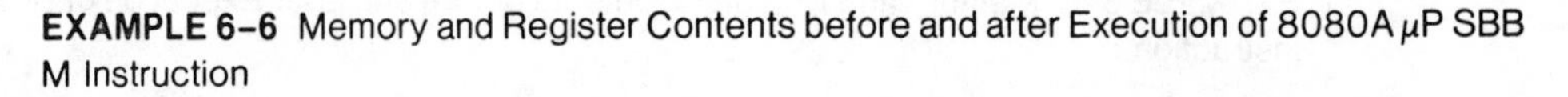
EXAMPLE 6-6 Memory and Register Contents before and after Execution of 8080A μP SBB M Instruction

what happens in memory and the μP registers when a SBB M instruction is executed.

SBI data **Subtract Immediate with Borrow**

This instruction is a two-byte instruction. The first byte is the op code; the second byte is the data. The contents of the second byte of the instruction and the contents of the carry bit are both subtracted from the accumulator. The result is placed in the accumulator. The d8 expression shown in Table 6–8 represents the second byte of the instruction that will be subtracted from the accumulator.

6.4.3 Increment Instructions

The 8080A μP has three increment instructions: (1) increment a μP register, (2) increment a memory location, or (3) increment a register pair. Increment instructions with their op codes are listed in Table 6–9. Each instruction is described below.

INR r **Increment Register**

The contents of a μP register are incremented by 1. All condition flags except CY are affected.

INR M **Increment Memory**

The contents of the memory location whose address is contained in the H and L registers are incremented by 1. All condition flags except CY are affected.

TABLE 6–9 8080A Microprocessor Increment Instructions with Their Op Codes

	Op Code		
Instruction	Hex	Octal	Example
INR r and INR M			
INR B	04	004	
INR C	0C	014	
INR D	14	024	
INR E	1C	034	
INR H	24	044	
INR L	2C	054	
INR M	34	064	
INR A	3C	074	
INX rp			
INX B	03	003	
INX D	13	023	6–7
INX H	23	043	
INX SP	33	063	

INX rp **Increment Register Pair**

The contents of a register pair (rp) are incremented by 1. *Note:* No flags are affected by this instruction. This instruction applies to four register pairs: BC, DE, HL, and SP. Example 6–7 shows what happens in memory and the μP register when an INX D instruction is executed.

6.4.4 Decrement Instructions

The 8080A also has three decrement instructions: (1) decrement a μP register, (2) decrement a memory location, or (3) decrement a register pair. Decrement instructions with their op codes are listed in Table 6–10. The instructions are described below.

DCR r **Decrement Register**

The contents of a μP register are decremented by 1. All condition flags except CY are affected.

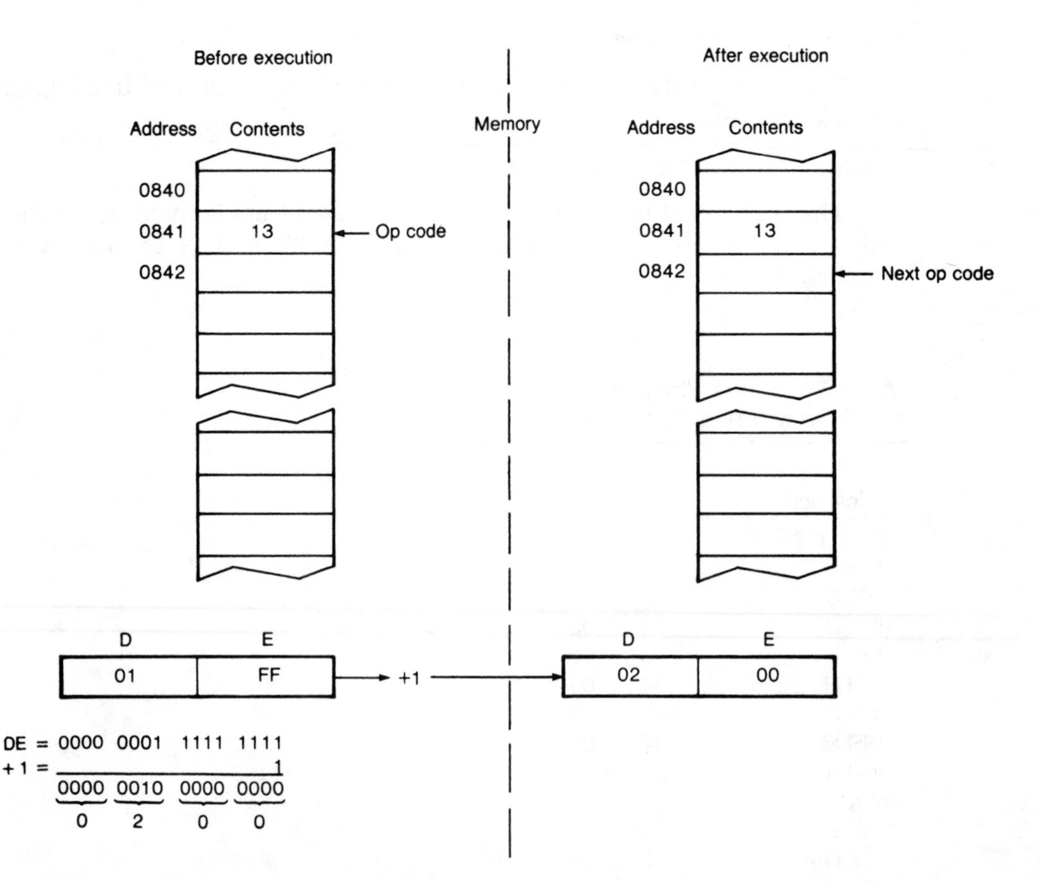

EXAMPLE 6-7 Memory and Register Contents before and after Execution of 8080A μP INX D Instruction

TABLE 6–10 8080A Microprocessor Decrement Instructions with Their Op Codes

	Op Code		
Instruction	Hex	Octal	Example
DCR r and DCR M			
DCR B	05	005	
DCR C	0D	015	
DCR D	15	025	
DCR E	1D	035	
DCR H	25	045	
DCR L	2D	055	
DCR M	35	065	6–8
DCR A	3D	075	
DCX rp			
DCX B	0B	013	
DCX D	1B	033	
DCX H	2B	053	
DCX SP	3B	073	

DCR M **Decrement Memory**

The contents of a memory location whose address is contained in the H and L registers are decremented by 1. All condition flags except CY are affected. Example 6–8 illustrates what happens in memory and the μP register when a DCR M instruction is executed.

DCX rp **Decrement Register Pair**

The contents of a register pair (rp) are decremented by 1. No flag bits are affected by this instruction. This instruction applies to four register pairs: BC, DE, HL, and SP.

6.5 LOGICAL INSTRUCTIONS

This section considers the instructions that perform logical operations (AND, OR, Exclusive OR, and complement) on data in registers and memory. Unless indicated otherwise, all instructions in this category affect the C, Z, S, P, and AC flag bits. Logical instructions with their op codes are listed in Table 6–11.

6.5.1 AND Instructions

The 8080A μP has three basic AND instructions. These instructions perform the logical AND operation between data in a register or memory and data in the accumulator. The result is automatically placed back in the accumulator. In addition to using the data in the accumulator, the first instruction listed below uses data from one of the μP registers; the second instruction uses data from memory; and the third instruction uses byte 2 of the instruction word.

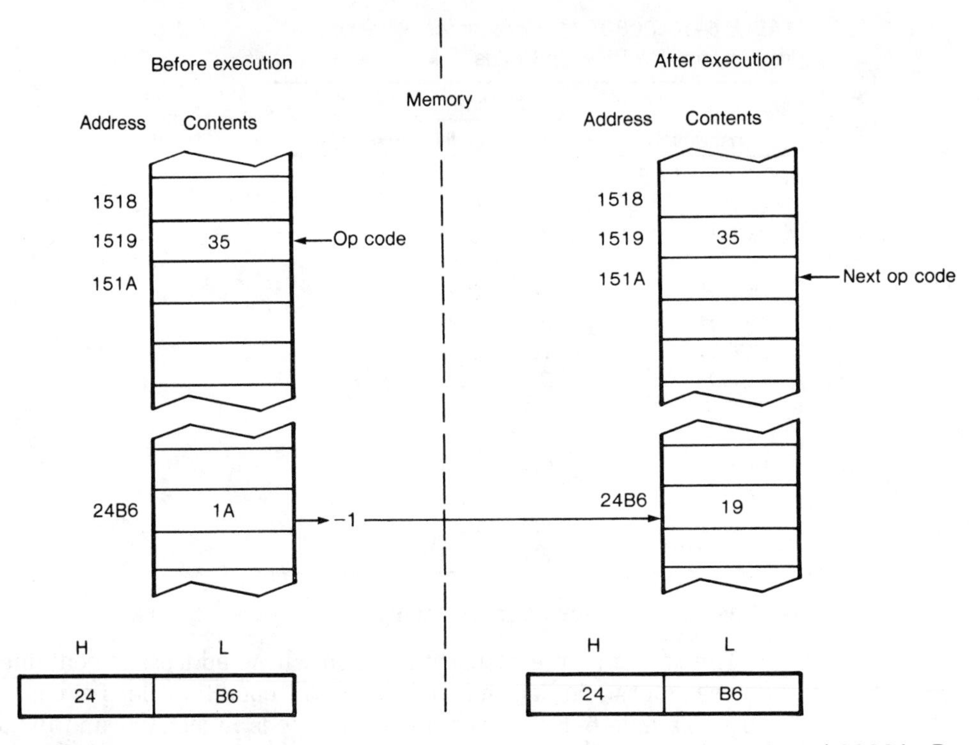

EXAMPLE 6–8 Memory and Register Contents before and after Execution of 8080A μP DCR M Instruction

ANA r AND Register

The contents of a μP register are logically ANDed with the contents of the accumulator. The result is placed in the accumulator. The carry flag is always cleared.

ANA M AND Memory

The contents of the memory location whose address is contained in the H and L registers are logically ANDed with the contents of the accumulator. The result is placed in the accumulator. The carry flag is always cleared. Example 6–9 shows what happens in memory and the μP register when an ANA M instruction is executed.

ANI data AND Immediate

This instruction is a two-byte instruction. The contents of the second byte of the instruction are ANDed with the contents of the accumulator. The result is placed in the accumulator. The carry flag and the auxiliary carry flag are always cleared. The d8 expression shown in Table 6–11 represents the data contained in the second byte of the instruction.

TABLE 6–11 8080A Microprocessor Logical Instructions with Their Op Codes

Instruction	Op Code Hex	Op Code Octal	Example
ANA r and ANA M			
ANA B	A0	240	
ANA C	A1	241	
ANA D	A2	242	
ANA E	A3	243	
ANA H	A4	244	
ANA L	A5	245	
ANA M	A6	246	6–9
ANA A	A7	247	
ANI data			
ANI d8	E6	346	
ORA r and ORA M			
ORA B	B0	260	
ORA C	B1	261	
ORA D	B2	262	
ORA E	B3	263	
ORA H	B4	264	
ORA L	B5	265	
ORA M	B6	266	
ORA A	B7	267	
ORI data			
ORI d8	F6	366	6–10
XRA r and XRA M			
XRA B	A8	250	
XRA C	A9	251	
XRA D	AA	252	
XRA E	AB	253	
XRA H	AC	254	6–11
XRA L	AD	255	
XRA M	AE	256	
XRA A	AF	257	
XRI data			
XRI d8	EE	356	
CMA	2F	057	
CMC	3F	077	
STC	37	067	

6.5.2 OR Instructions

The 8080A μP also has three OR instructions. Each OR instruction performs the logical OR operation between the contents of the accumulator and the contents of a μP register or memory. The result is automatically placed back in the accumulator. The OR instructions are described next.

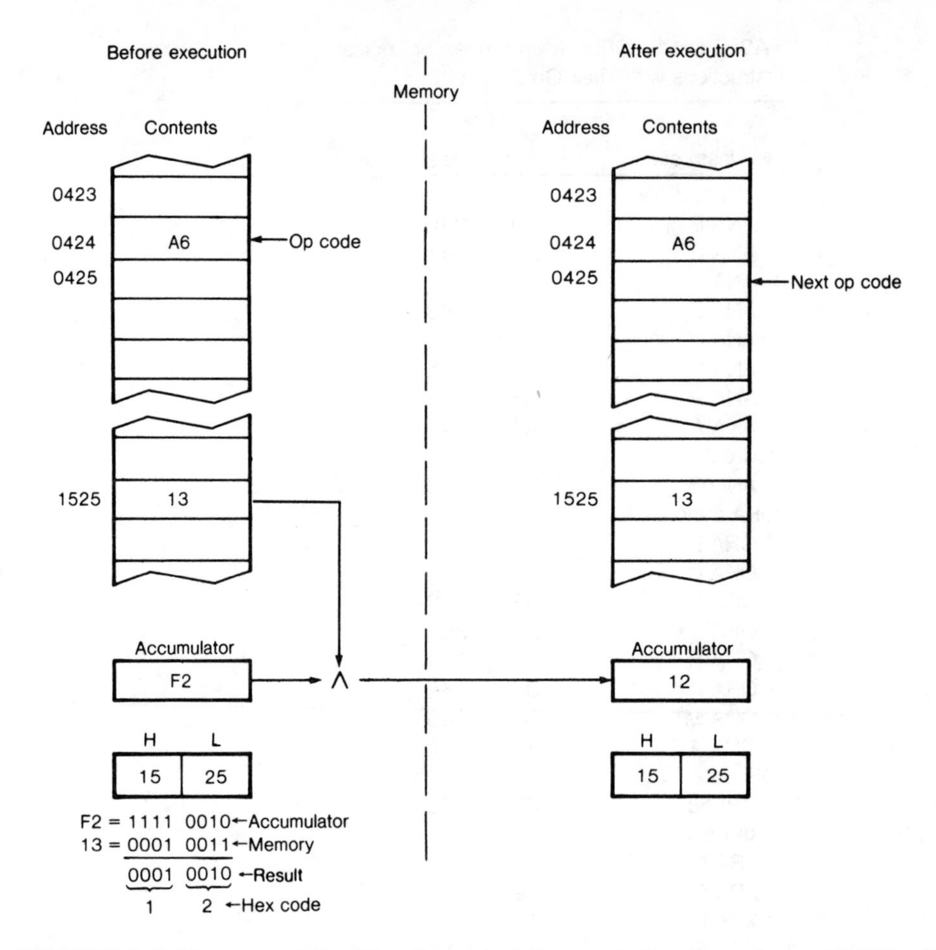

EXAMPLE 6–9 Memory and Register Contents before and after Execution of 8080A μP ANA M Instruction

ORA r OR Register

The contents of a μP register are ORed with the contents of the accumulator. The result is placed in the accumulator. The carry flag and the auxiliary carry flag are always cleared.

ORA M OR Memory

The contents of the memory location whose address is contained in the H and L registers are ORed with the contents of the accumulator. The result is placed in the accumulator. The carry flag and the auxiliary carry flag are always cleared.

ORI data OR Immediate

This instruction is a two-byte instruction. The contents of the second byte of the instruction are ORed with the contents of the accumulator. The result is placed in the accumulator. The carry flag and the auxiliary carry flag are always cleared. The d8 expression shown in Table 6–11 represents the data contained in the second byte of the instruction. Example 6–10 shows what happens in memory and the μP register when an ORI d8 instruction is executed.

6.5.3 Exclusive OR Instructions

The Exclusive OR instructions, like the AND and OR instructions, are divided into three groups. The first involves the accumulator and any μP register; the second involves the accumulator and data from a memory location; the third involves the accumulator and data from the second byte of the instruction word (the immediate addressing mode). Each instruction is described below.

XRA r **Exclusive OR Register**

The contents of a μP register are Exclusive ORed with the contents of the accumulator. The result is placed in the accumulator. The carry flag and the auxiliary flag are always cleared. *Note:* The accumulator can be Exclusive ORed with itself. This technique is used to clear the accumulator and the carry flag.

XRA M **Exclusive OR Memory**

The contents of the memory location whose address is contained in the H and L registers are Exclusive ORed with the contents of the accumulator. The result is placed in the accumulator. The carry flag and the auxiliary carry flag are always cleared. Example 6–11 illustrates what happens in memory and the μP registers when an XRA H instruction is executed.

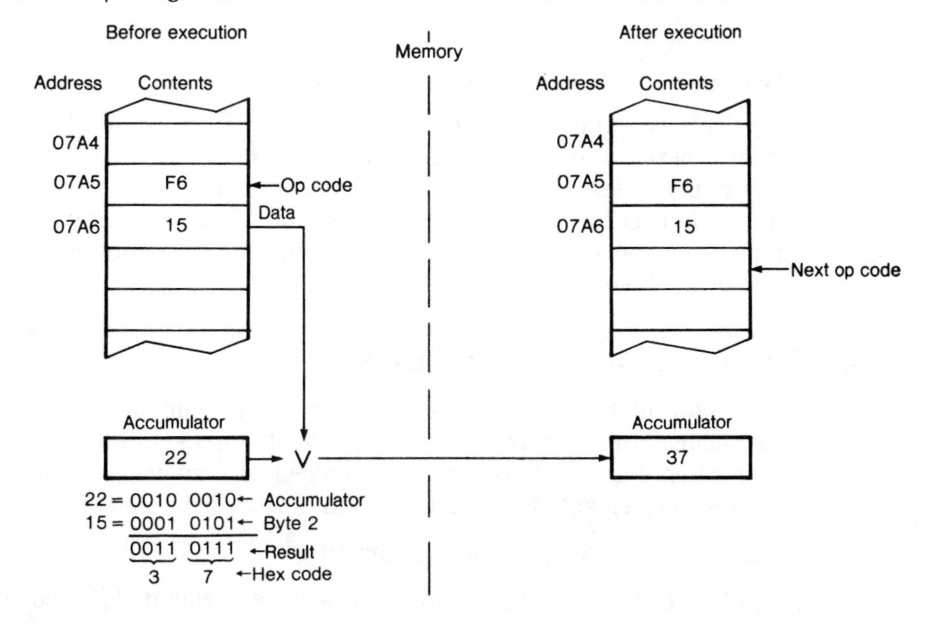

EXAMPLE 6–10 Memory and Register Contents before and after Execution of 8080A μP ORI Instruction

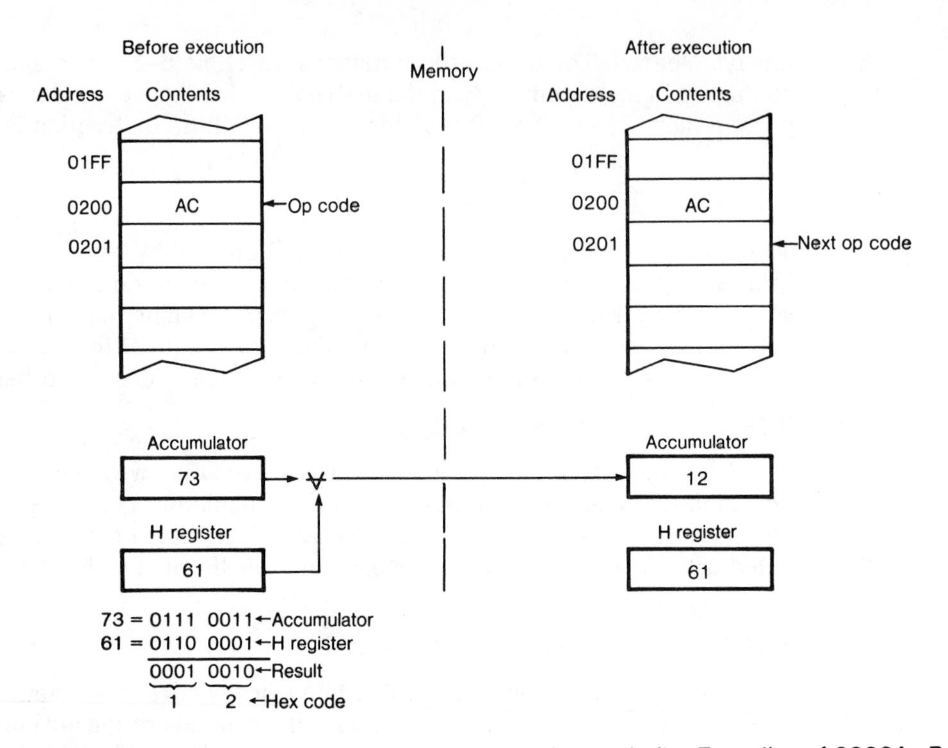

EXAMPLE 6–11 Memory and Register Contents before and after Execution of 8080A μP XRA H Instruction

XRI data **Exclusive OR Immediate**

This instruction is a two-byte instruction. The first byte is the op code; the second byte is data. The contents of the second byte of the instruction are Exclusive ORed with the contents of the accumulator. The result is placed in the accumulator. The carry flag and the auxiliary flag are always cleared. The d8 expression shown in Table 6–11 represents the data contained in the second byte of the instruction.

6.5.4 Complement and Set Instructions

The 8080A μP has two complement instructions. One instruction complements the accumulator, and the other complements the carry flag. There is also one instruction that sets the carry flag to a logic 1. The complement instruction is the 1's complement. These instructions are described below.

CMA **Complement Accumulator**

The contents of the accumulator are complemented (1's complement). No flags are affected.

CMC **Complement Carry**

The carry flag is complemented. No other flags are affected.

STC **Set Carry**

The carry flag is set to a logic 1. No other flags are affected.

6.6 COMPARE INSTRUCTIONS

In Chapter 5, we saw that a compare instruction is like a subtract instruction but that the result is not stored in the accumulator. A compare instruction does not include the carry flag in the subtraction, but the result does affect the carry flag. The 8080A μP has three compare instructions in its instruction set. Compare instructions with their op codes are listed in Table 6–12. The instructions are described next.

CMP r **Compare Register**

The contents of a μP register are subtracted from the contents of the accumulator. The result is not stored in the accumulator, and therefore the contents of the accumulator are unchanged. Condition flags are set as a result of the subtraction. The Z flag is set to a logic 1 if A = r, and the carry flag is set to a logic 1 if A < r.

CMP M **Compare Memory**

The contents of the memory location whose address is contained in the H and L registers are subtracted from the contents of the accumulator. The contents of the accumulator remain unchanged. The condition flags that are affected are the Z flag, which is set to a logic 1 if A = M, and the carry flag, which is set to a logic 1 if A < M. Example 6–12 shows what happens in memory and the μP registers when a CMP M instruction is executed.

TABLE 6–12 8080A Microprocessor Compare Instructions with Their Op Codes

Instruction	Op Code Hex	Op Code Octal	Example
CMP r and CMP M			
CMP B	B8	270	
CMP C	B9	271	
CMP D	BA	272	
CMP E	BB	273	
CMP H	BC	274	
CMP L	BD	275	
CMP M	BE	276	6–12
CMP A	BF	277	
CPI data			
CPI d8	FE	376	

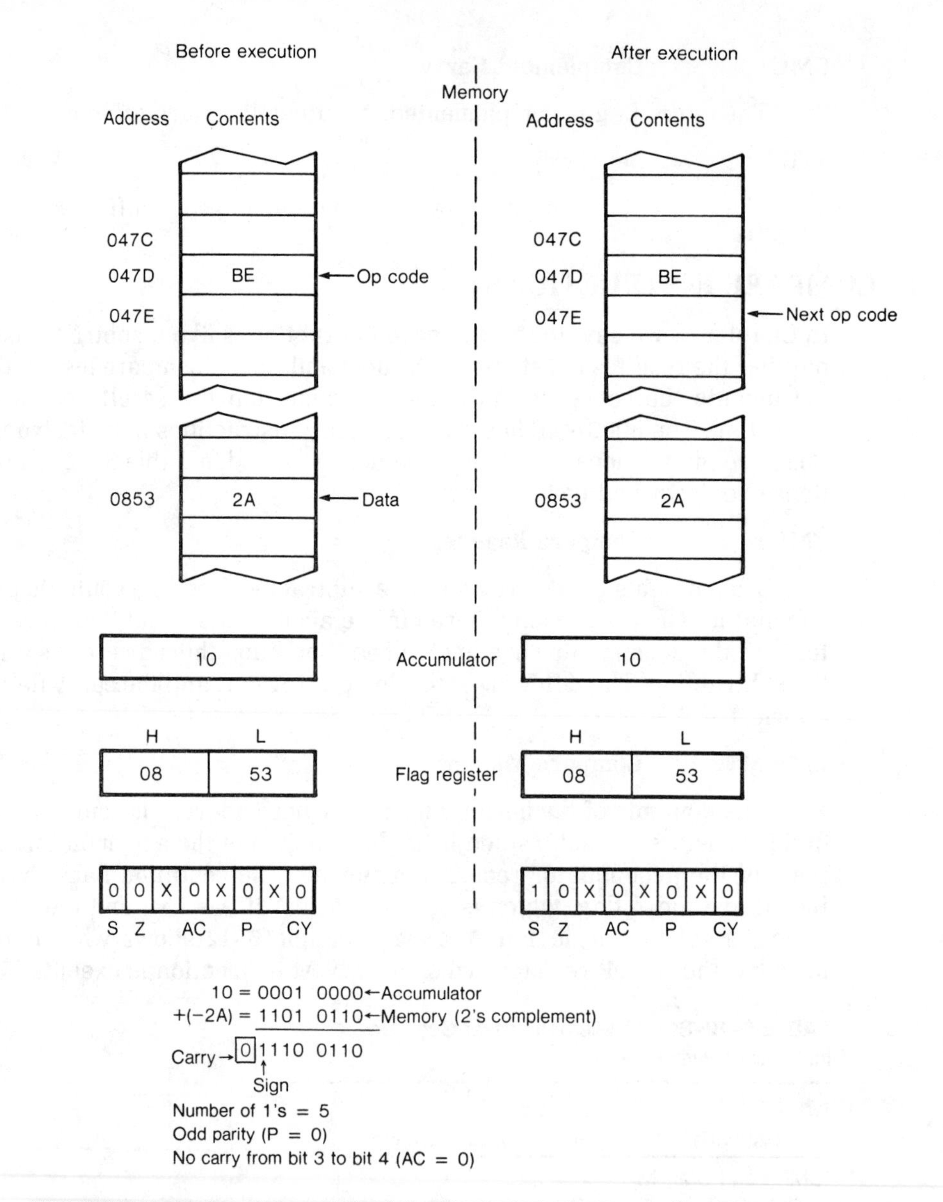

EXAMPLE 6–12 Memory and Register Contents before and after Execution of 8080A μP CMP M Instruction

CPI data Compare Immediate

Like most immediate addressing mode instructions, this instruction is a two-byte instruction. The contents of the second byte of the instruction are subtracted from the contents of the accumulator. The condition flags affected by the comparison are the Z flag, which is set to a logic 1 if A = byte 2, and the C flag, which is set to a logic 1 if A < byte 2. The d8 expression shown in Table 6–12 represents the 8 bits of data in the second byte of the instruction.

6.7 ROTATE INSTRUCTIONS

The 8080A μP has four rotate instructions: two to the right and two to the left. These instructions apply only to the accumulator. The carry flag is involved in all of the rotate instructions, but no other flag bits are affected. Rotate instructions with their op codes are listed in Table 6–13. The descriptions given below of the rotate instructions show their differences.

RLC **Rotate Left**

The contents of the accumulator are rotated left one bit. The high-order bit (bit 7) is rotated into the low-order bit (bit 0) and the carry flag, as shown in Figure 6–4.

RRC **Rotate Right**

The contents of the accumulator are rotated right one bit. The low-order bit (bit 0) is rotated into the high-order bit (bit 7) and the carry flag, as shown in Figure 6–5.

RAL **Rotate Left through Carry**

The contents of the accumulator are rotated left one bit through the carry flag. For this instruction, the expression "through the carry flag" means that

TABLE 6–13 8080A Microprocessor Rotate Instructions with Their Op Codes

Instruction	Op Code	
	Hex	Octal
RLC	07	007
RRC	0F	017
RAL	17	027
RAR	1F	037

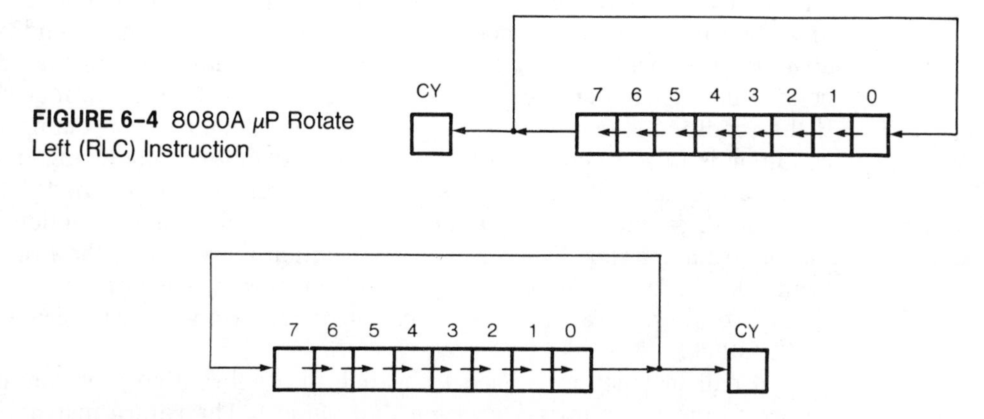

FIGURE 6–4 8080A μP Rotate Left (RLC) Instruction

FIGURE 6–5 8080A μP Rotate Right (RRC) Instruction

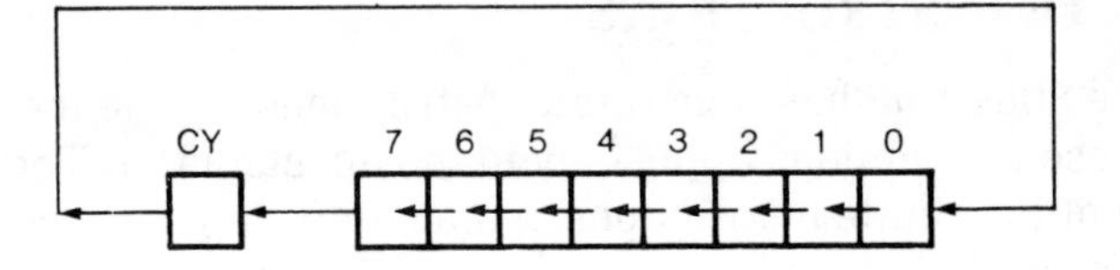

FIGURE 6–6 8080A μP Rotate Left through Carry (RAL) Instruction

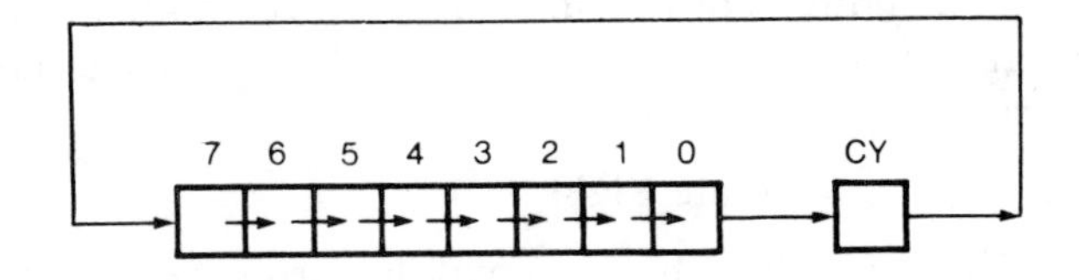

FIGURE 6–7 8080A μP Rotate Right through Carry (RAR) Instruction

bit 7 is rotated into the carry flag and the carry flag is rotated into bit 0. Figure 6–6 illustrates the RAL instruction.

RAR **Rotate Right through Carry**

The contents of the accumulator are rotated right one bit through the carry flag. For this instruction, the expression "through the carry flag" means that bit 0 is rotated into the carry flag and the carry flag is rotated into bit 7, as shown in Figure 6–7.

6.8 PROGRAM CONTROL INSTRUCTIONS

The 8080A μP has five categories of instructions that affect the program counter: *jump, call, return, restart,* and *transfer* instructions. There are two jump instructions, two call instructions, two return instructions, one restart instruction, and one transfer instruction. The jump, call, and return instructions are either *unconditional* or *conditional* instructions. When an unconditional instruction is executed, the program counter is automatically changed. When a conditional instruction is executed, the state of a flag bit must first be checked. If the condition is true (a yes answer), the program counter is changed. If the condition is false (a no answer), the program counter is not changed, and the next instruction in the program sequence is fetched and executed.

The difference between a jump instruction and a call instruction involves the program counter. When a jump instruction is executed, the present program counter is not stored on the stack. Therefore, we do not expect to return to the present program location. A call instruction saves the program counter on the stack.

A call instruction is used to branch to a subroutine program and then return to the place in the program that we left. The return instructions are used at the end of a subroutine program so that it is possible to return to the program that we left.

The restart instruction is an unconditional instruction, and the program counter is saved on the stack. This instruction allows the programmer to jump to one of 8 different memory locations. The transfer instruction moves the contents of the H and L registers to the program counter.

The condition flags are not affected by any instruction in this section. Now, let's examine each instruction.

JMP addr Jump

This instruction is a three-byte instruction. The first byte is the op code; the second and third bytes are a memory location. The program sequence jumps to the memory address specified by bytes 2 and 3. Byte 2 is moved into the low-order 8 bits of the program counter, and byte 3 is moved into the high-order 8 bits of the program counter. The unconditional jump instruction is shown in Table 6-14 with its op codes. The a16 expression indicates two bytes of address. Example 6-13 illustrates the execution of a JMP instruction. The program listing would be JMP 50E7.

Jcondition addr Conditional Jump

This instruction is a three-byte instruction. The first byte is the op code; the second and third bytes are a memory location. The op code tells the μP which flag bit to check. If the condition is true, the program jumps to the memory location whose address is specified by bytes 2 and 3. If the condition is false, the program continues sequentially.

Conditional instructions examine the logic state of the zero, carry, parity, or sign flag bits. There is no conditional branch instruction to check the auxiliary carry flag. A flip-flop can be either a logic 0 or a logic 1, and there is an instruction for each condition. Therefore, with four flag bits and two possible

TABLE 6-14 8080A Microprocessor Jump Instructions with Their Op Codes

Condition of Flag Bit	Instruction	Op Code Hex	Op Code Octal	Example
	Unconditional			
	JMP a16	C3	303	6-13
	Conditional			
Z = 0	JNZ a16	C2	302	6-14
Z = 1	JZ a16	CA	312	
CY = 0	JNC a16	D2	322	
CY = 1	JC a16	DA	332	
P = 0	JPO a16	E2	342	
P = 1	JPE a16	EA	352	
S = 0	JP a16	F2	362	
S = 1	JM a16	FA	372	

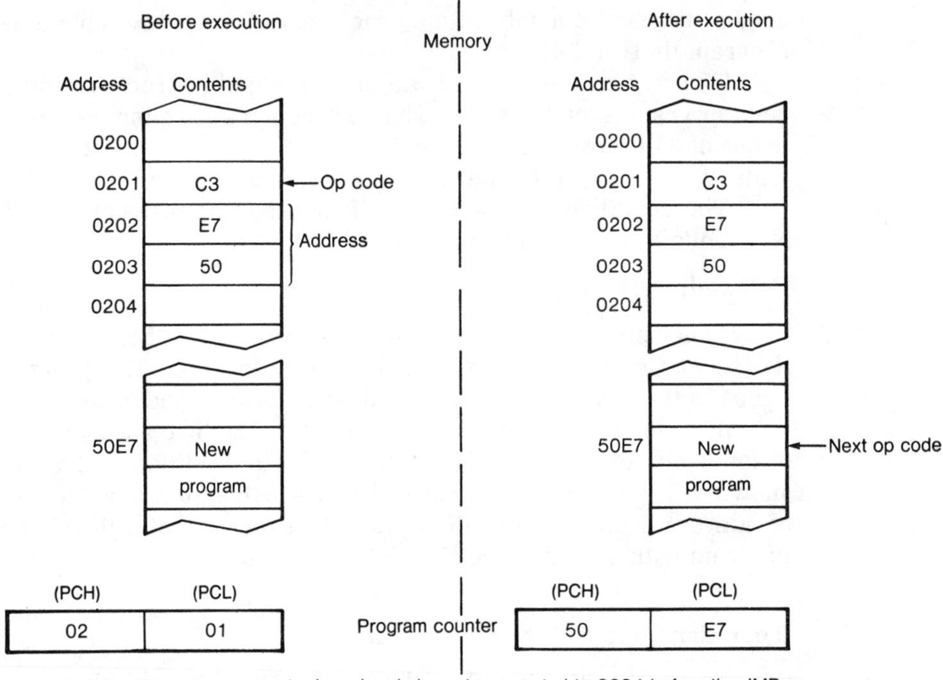

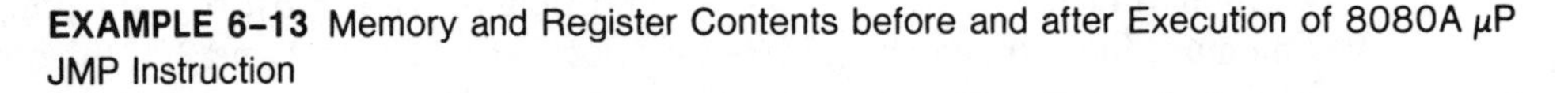

EXAMPLE 6–13 Memory and Register Contents before and after Execution of 8080A μP JMP Instruction

states for each, there is a total of 8 conditional jump instructions. They are listed in Table 6–14 with their op codes. The a16 expressions represent two bytes of address. Example 6–14 illustrates execution of a JNZ instruction. The program listing would be JNZ 104B.

CALL addr Call

This three-byte instruction is the unconditional call instruction. The first byte is the op code; the second and third bytes are the starting address of a subroutine program. After the call instruction is executed, the program counter will contain bytes 2 and 3 of the instruction. Before bytes 2 and 3 are moved into the program counter, however, a number of steps first take place in the μP. The present contents of the program counter are incremented so as to contain the next address—that is, the return address that will be stored on the stack. The stack pointer is decremented by 1, and the high contents of the program counter are stored at the address held by the stack pointer. The stack pointer is decremented again by 1, and the low address of the program counter is stored at the address held by the stack pointer. Byte 2 of the instruction is now moved into the low-order 8 bits of the program counter, and byte 3 is moved into the high-order 8 bits of the program counter. The unconditional call

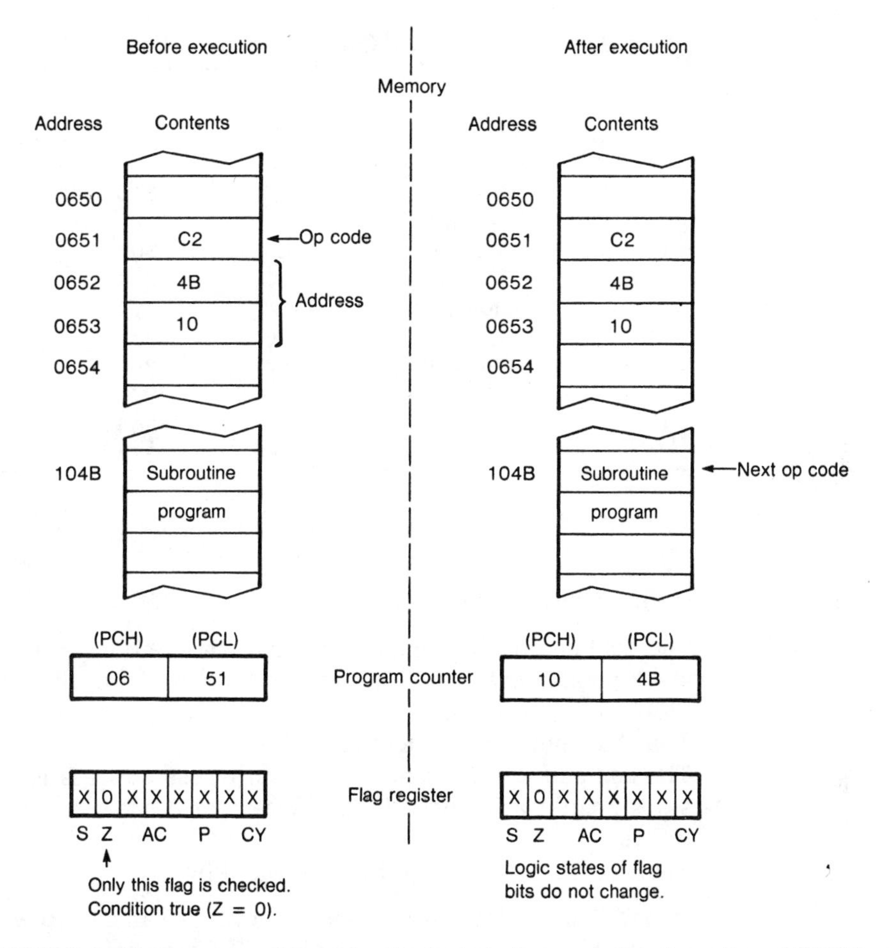

EXAMPLE 6–14 Memory and Register Contents before and after Execution of 8080A μP JNZ Instruction

instruction is shown in Table 6–15 with its op codes. Example 6–15 illustrates execution of a CALL instruction. The program listing would be CALL 062A.

Ccondition addr Conditional Call

This call instruction is conditional. Therefore, the μP first must check the condition of a flag bit. If the condition is true, a subroutine program is called; otherwise, the main program continues sequentially. The only flags that can be checked are the zero, carry, parity, and sign flag bits. The auxiliary carry flag cannot be checked. Since each flag bit can be either a logic 0 or a logic 1, there are 8 possible conditions. These conditions are described in Table 6–15. The a16 expressions represent two bytes for address.

RET Return

This one-byte instruction is unconditional. When this instruction is ex-

TABLE 6–15 8080A Microprocessor Call Instructions with Their Op Codes

Condition of Flag Bit	Instruction	Op Code Hex	Op Code Octal	Example
	Unconditional			
	CALL	CD	315	6–15
	Conditional			
Z = 0	CNZ a16	C4	304	
Z = 1	CZ a16	CC	314	
CY = 0	CNC a16	D4	324	
CY = 1	CC a16	DC	334	
P = 0	CPO a16	E4	344	
P = 1	CPE a16	EC	354	
S = 0	CP a16	F4	364	
S = 1	CM a16	FC	374	

ecuted, the following steps take place:

1. The contents of the memory location whose address is specified by the stack pointer are moved to the low-order 8 bits of the program counter (PCL).
2. The stack pointer is incremented by 1.
3. The contents of the memory location whose address is specified by the stack pointer are moved to the high-order 8 bits of the program counter (PCH).
4. The stack pointer is again incremented by 1.

The unconditional return instruction is shown in Table 6–16 with its op codes. Example 6–16 illustrates execution of an RET instruction.

TABLE 6–16 8080A Microprocessor Return Instructions with Their Op Codes

Condition of Flag Bit	Instruction	Op Code Hex	Op Code Octal	Example
	Unconditional			
	RET	C9	311	6–16
	Conditional			
Z = 0	RNZ	C0	300	
Z = 1	RZ	C8	310	
CY = 0	RNC	D0	320	6–17
CY = 1	RC	D8	330	
P = 0	RPO	E0	340	
P = 1	RPE	E8	350	
S = 0	RP	F0	360	
S = 1	RM	F8	370	

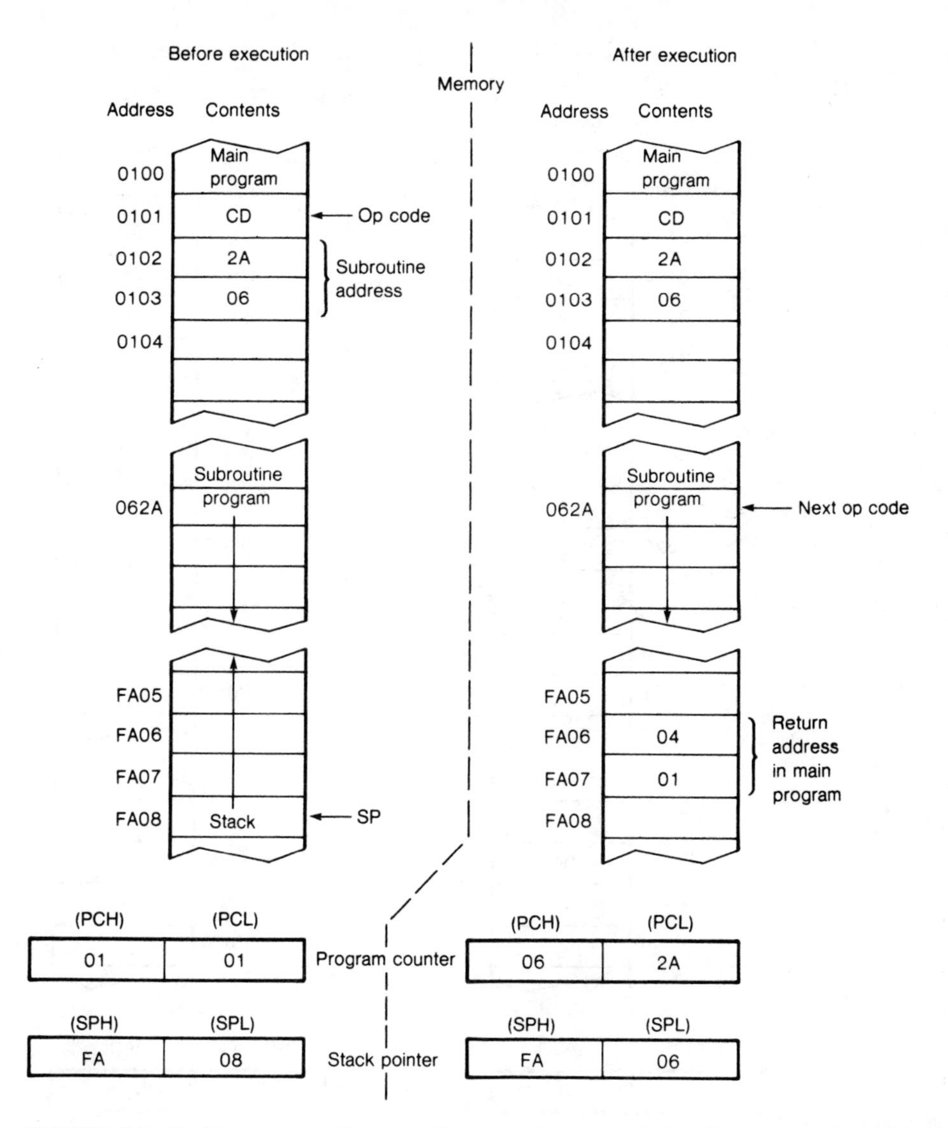

EXAMPLE 6–15 Memory and Register Contents before and after Execution of 8080A μP CALL Instruction

Rcondition Conditional Return

This one-byte instruction is conditional. The μP first checks a flag bit to see if the condition is true. If it is, then the actions specified in the return instruction (see the preceding list of steps) are performed; otherwise, the program being executed continues. Table 6–16 shows the 8 possible conditional return instructions along with their op codes. Example 6–17 illustrates execution of an RNC instruction (condition true).

RST n Restart

This restart instruction is a one-byte unconditional instruction. The pres-

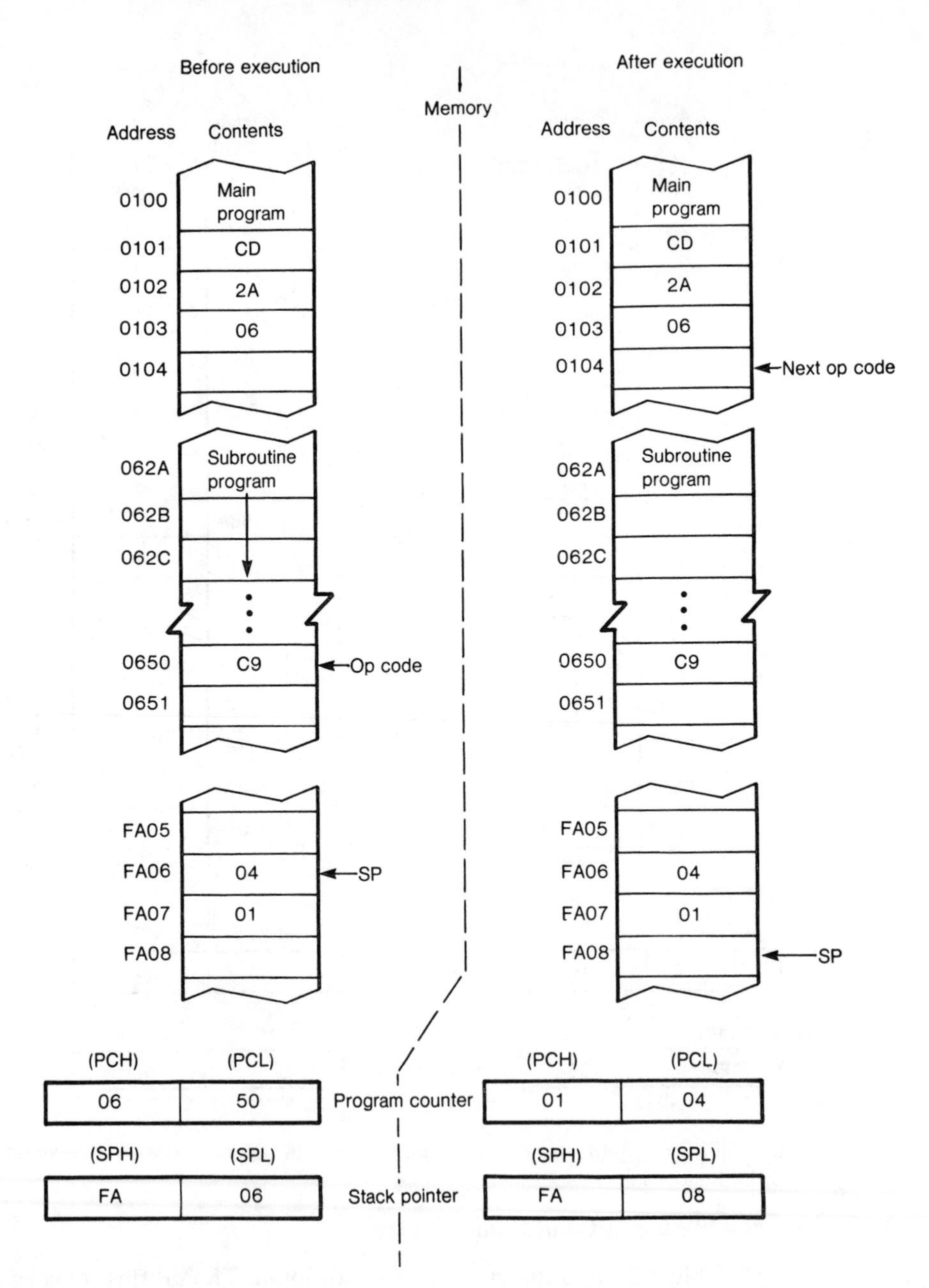

EXAMPLE 6–16 Memory and Register Contents before and after Execution of 8080A μP RET Instruction

ent contents of the program are saved on the stack so that the μP can return to its present program. The memory location to which the μP branches is determined by multiplying bits 3, 4, and 5 of the restart instruction by 8. These bits are labeled NNN in Figure 6–8A.

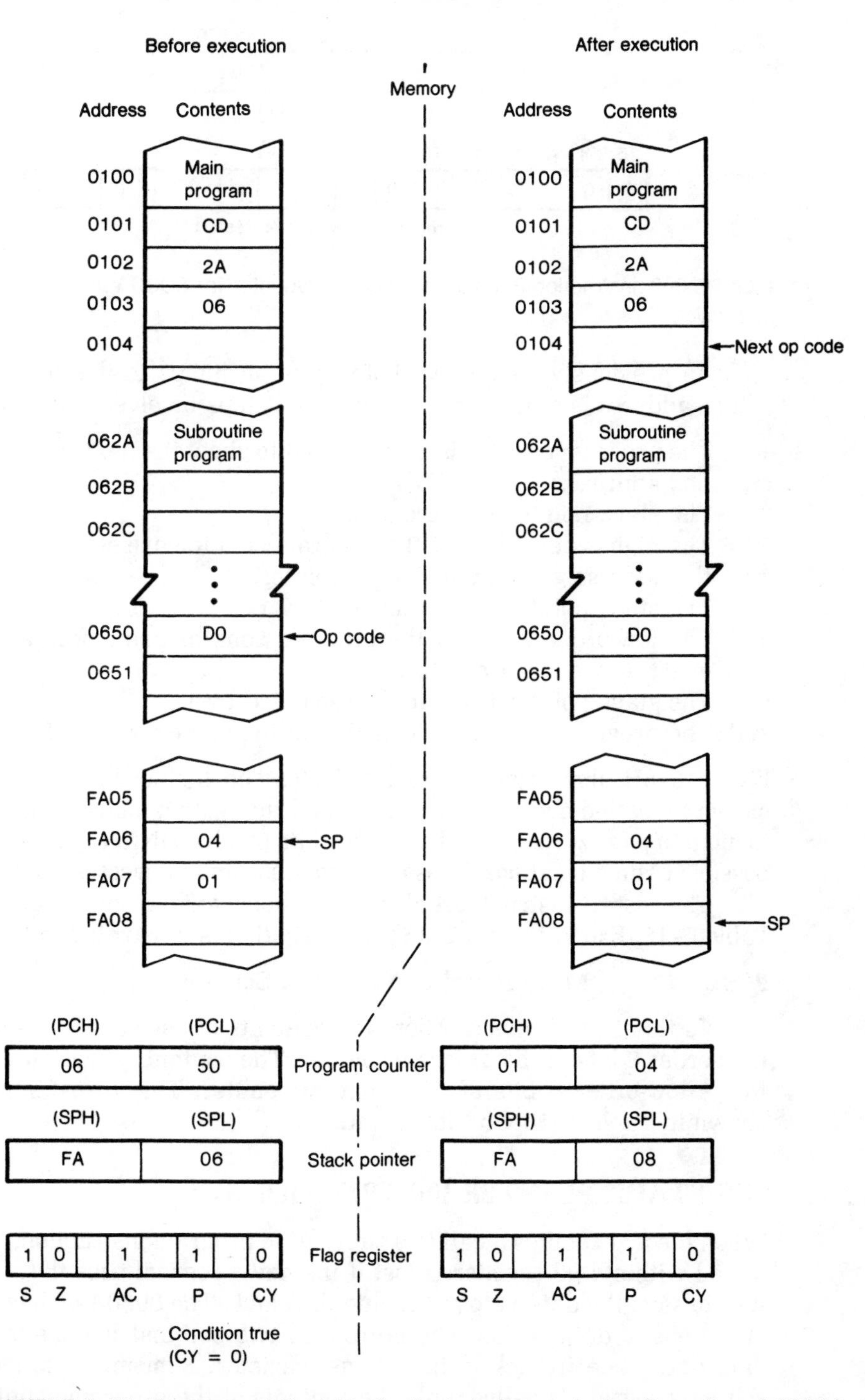

EXAMPLE 6-17 Memory and Register Contents before and after Execution of 8080A μP RNC Instruction (Condition True)

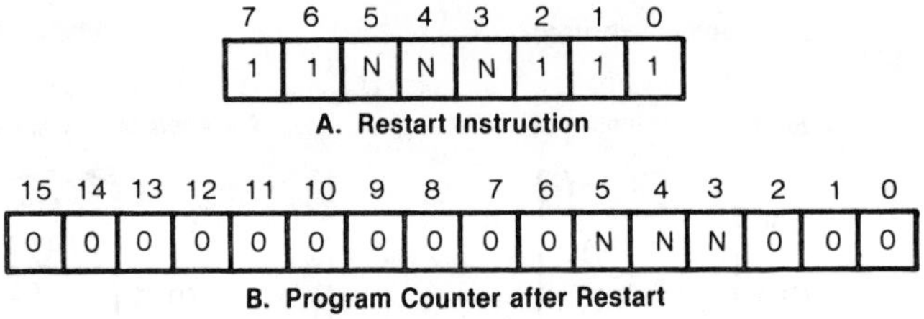

7	6	5	4	3	2	1	0
1	1	N	N	N	1	1	1

A. Restart Instruction

15	14	13	12	11	10	9	8	7	6	5	4	3	2	1	0
0	0	0	0	0	0	0	0	0	0	N	N	N	0	0	0

B. Program Counter after Restart

FIGURE 6–8 Instruction Format and Program Counter for 8080A μP Restart (RST) Instruction

As previously mentioned, before the μP jumps to the new location, the return address is stored on the stack. The steps involved are as follows:

1. The program counter is incremented to show the next sequential instruction address.
2. The stack pointer is decremented by 1.
3. The high-order 8 bits of the program counter are stored on the stack at the address given by the stack pointer.
4. The stack pointer is decremented by 1.
5. The low-order 8 bits of the program counter are stored at the address given by the stack pointer.
6. The stack pointer is again decremented by 1.
7. The program counter is loaded with the value 8 × NNN.

Figure 6–8B illustrates the result. *Note:* The high-order 8 bits of the new memory location are all 0s. Therefore, all the restart instructions cause the μP to jump to page zero. Since there are 3 bits involved (NNN), there are 8 ($2^3 = 8$) possible restart locations. These combinations and addresses are in Table 6–17.

The restart instructions along with their hex and octal codes are given in Table 6–18. Execution of an RST 3 instruction is illustrated in Example 6–18.

PCHL Move H and L to Program Counter

In this transfer instruction, the contents of register H are moved to the high-order 8 bits of the program counter. The contents of register L are moved to the low-order 8 bits of the program counter. This transfer instruction is shown in Table 6–18 with its op codes.

6.9 STACK/STACK POINTER INSTRUCTIONS

When the μP executes a call to a subroutine program instruction, the data contained within a μP register is lost if the new program uses that register. One way to save the data is to put it onto the stack. The 8080A μP has two push instructions to do just this. There are also two pop instructions to retrieve the data and place it back in its original register. Remember that when a subroutine program is called, only the contents of the program counter are automatically saved. All other registers are subject to the programmer's control. Stack/stack pointer instructions are listed with their op codes in Table 6–19; the instructions are described in the following.

TABLE 6–17 Effect of 8080A Microprocessor Restart Instruction on Program Counter

NNN	Decimal	8 × NNN in Decimal	8 × NNN in Hex	Program Counter after Restart, in Hex
000	0	0	00	0000
001	1	8	08	0008
010	2	16	10	0010
011	3	24	18	0018
100	4	32	20	0020
101	5	40	28	0028
110	6	48	30	0030
111	7	56	38	0038

TABLE 6–18 8080A Microprocessor Restart and Transfer Instructions with Their Op Codes

Instruction	Op Code Hex	Op Code Octal	Example
Restart			
RST 0	C7	307	
RST 1	CF	317	
RST 2	D7	327	
RST 3	DF	337	6–18
RST 4	E7	347	
RST 5	EF	357	
RST 6	F7	367	
RST 7	FF	377	
Transfer			
PCHL	E9	351	

PUSH rp Push a Register Pair

This instruction saves the contents of a register pair. The steps involved are the following:

1. The stack pointer is decremented by 1.
2. The contents of the high-order register of the register pair are moved to the memory location whose address is contained in the stack pointer.
3. The stack pointer is decremented by 1.
4. The contents of the low-order register of the register pair are moved to the memory location whose address is contained in the stack pointer.

Note: Only register pairs BC, DE, or HL may be saved.

PUSH PSW Push Processor Status Word

This instruction pushes the accumulator and the flag register onto the stack. The steps involved are as follows:

1. The stack pointer is decremented by 1.
2. The accumulator is stored at memory location given by stack pointer.
3. The stack pointer is again decremented by 1.
4. The contents of the flag register are stored at the memory location given by the stack pointer.

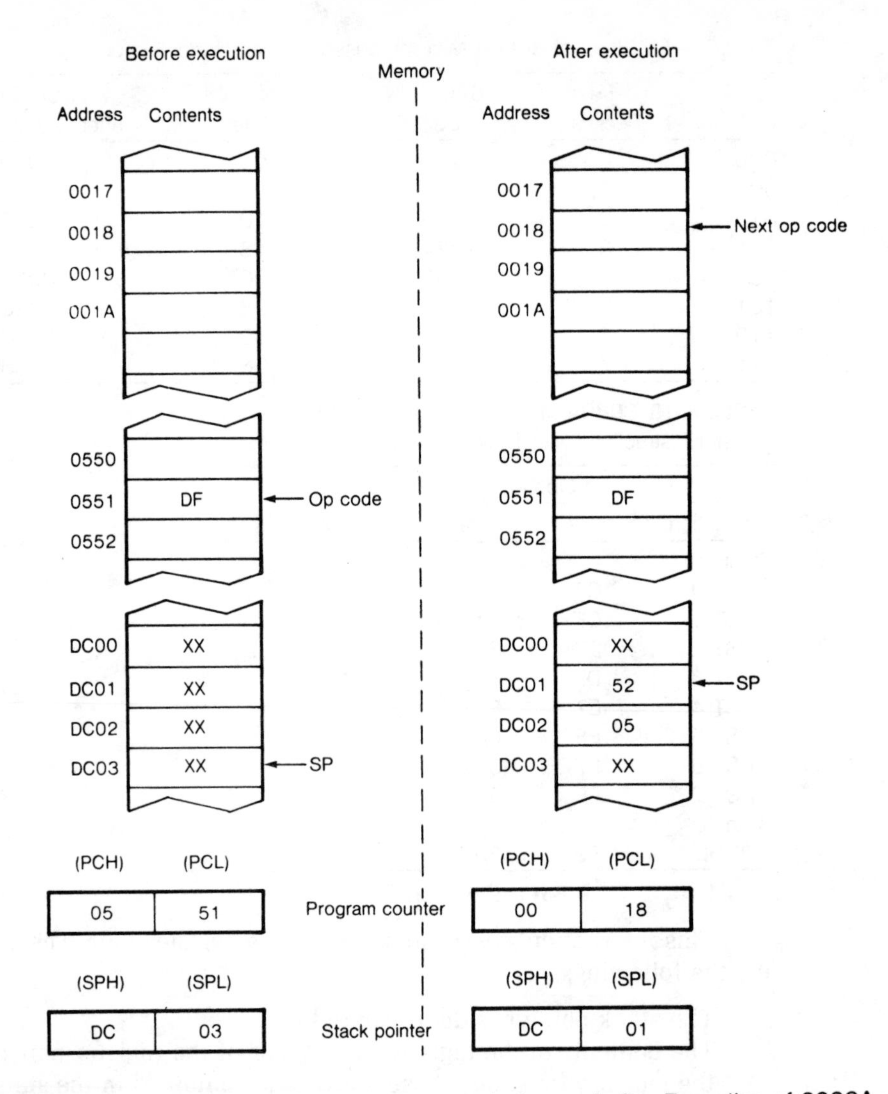

EXAMPLE 6–18 Memory and Register Contents before and after Execution of 8080A μP RST Instruction (NNN = 3)

Note: Although the flag register is 8 bits wide, the 8080A μP uses only 5 of these bits. In this instruction, those bits that are not specified are preloaded to a particular logic state. Bit D_1 is loaded to a logic 1, while bits D_3 and D_5 are loaded to a logic 0, as we saw in Figure 6–3. Example 6–19 illustrates execution of the PUSH PSW instruction.

POP rp **Pop a Register Pair**

This instruction restores the data that was stored on the stack to its original register pair. The steps involved are as follows:

TABLE 6–19 8080A Microprocessor Stack/Stack Pointer Instructions with Their Op Codes

Instruction	Op Code Hex	Op Code Octal	Example
PUSH rp			
PUSH B	C5	305	
PUSH D	D5	325	
PUSH H	E5	345	
PUSH PSW	F5	365	6–19
POP rp			
POP B	C1	301	
POP C	D1	321	
POP H	E1	341	
POP PSW	F1	361	
XTHL	E3	343	6–20
SPHL	F9	371	

1. The contents of the memory location whose address is specified by the stack pointer are moved to the low-order 8 bits of the register pair.
2. The stack pointer is incremented by 1.
3. The contents of the memory location whose address is now specified by the stack pointer are moved to the high-order 8 bits of the register pair.
4. The stack pointer is again incremented by 1.

Only register pairs BC, DE, or HL may be specified by this instruction.

POP PSW Pop Processor Status Word

This instruction restores the flag register and the accumulator. The steps involved are the following:

1. The contents of the memory location whose address is specified by the stack pointer are moved to the flag register.
2. The stack pointer is incremented by 1.
3. The contents of the memory location whose address is now specified by the stack pointer are moved to the accumulator.
4. The stack pointer is again incremented by 1.

XTHL Exchange Stack Top with H and L Registers

The contents of the L register are exchanged with the contents at the memory location specified by the stack pointer. The contents of the H register are exchanged with the contents specified by the stack pointer plus one. *Note:* The address stored by the stack pointer before and after execution of this instruction is the same. Example 6–20 illustrates execution of the XTHL instruction.

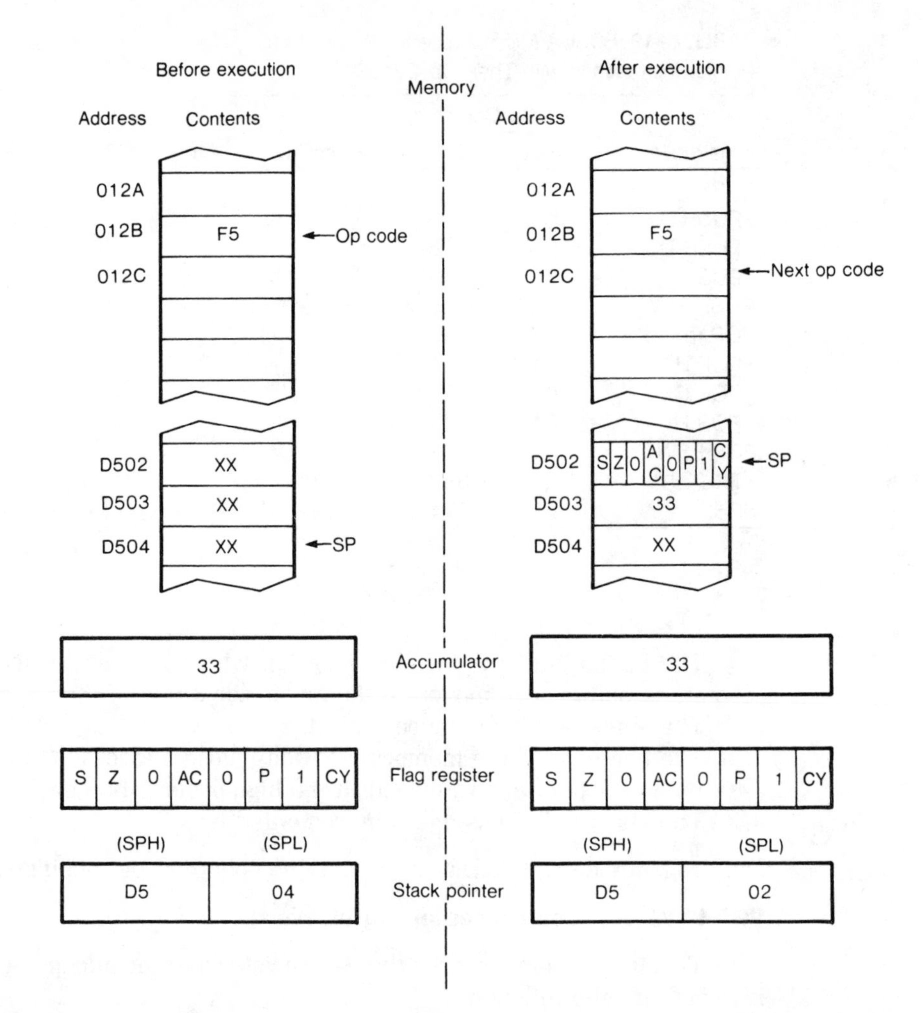

EXAMPLE 6–19 Memory and Register Contents before and after Execution of 8080A μP PUSH PSW Instruction

SPHL Move H and L to the Stack Pointer

The contents of registers H and L are moved to the stack pointer. Register L is moved to the low-order 8 bits of the stack pointer, while register H is moved to the high-order 8 bits of the stack pointer. *Note:* Registers H and L are moved to the stack pointer, not to the stack.

By loading data into registers H and L and then using this instruction to transfer the data to the stack pointer, the programmer initializes the stack pointer. This combination of loading and transferring data should always be used when power is first applied to the μP, so we know where the stack will be in memory.

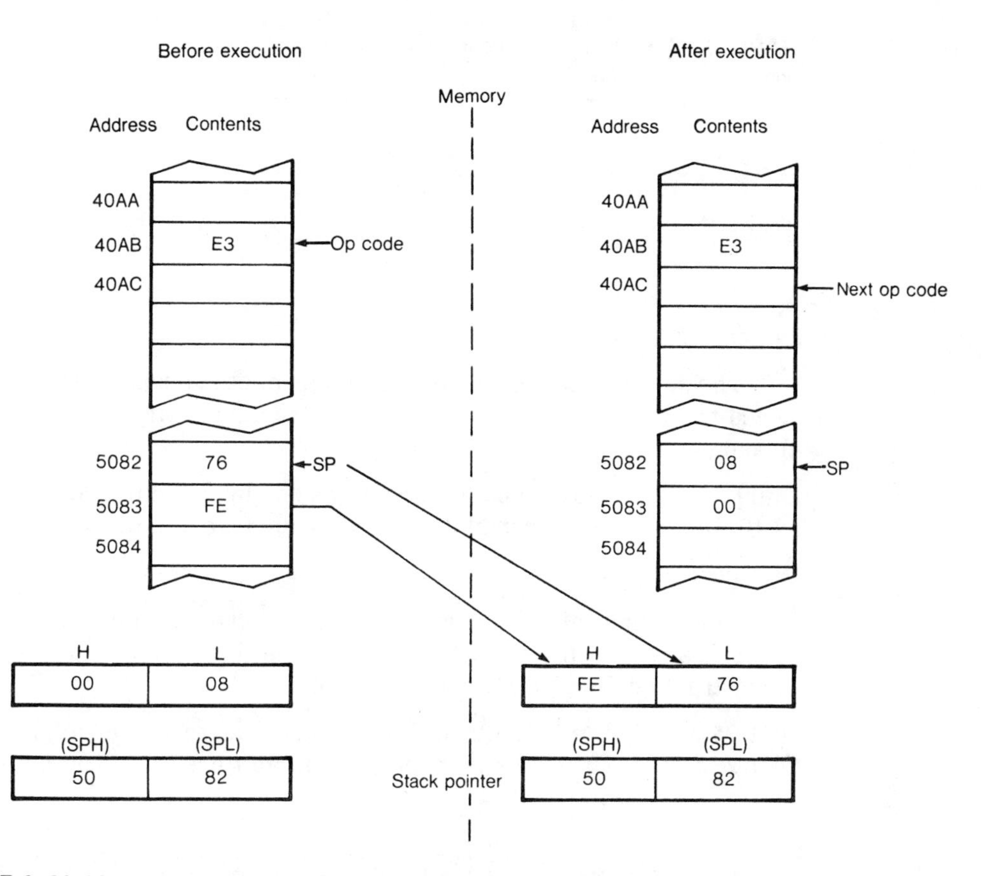

EXAMPLE 6-20 Memory and Register Contents before and after Execution of 8080A μP XTHL Instruction

6.10 INPUT/OUTPUT INSTRUCTIONS

This section describes the instructions that allow the 8080A μP to receive data from an external device or to send data to an external device. These instructions occupy two bytes of memory. The first byte is the op code telling the μP whether the instruction is an input instruction or an output instruction. The second byte is the port number (the number of the external device). Since there are 8 bits in a byte, there are 256 (2^8) possible ports that can be served by these instructions. Input/output instructions require hardware that is capable of decoding the port number. When these instructions are executed, the port number is placed on both the low address lines (A_0–A_7) and the high address lines (A_8–A_{15}). Data going between the external device and the μP moves across the data bus. Therefore, another requirement of the hardware is that it be capable of sending or receiving data when the device is selected. We will discuss the hardware aspects in later chapters. Input/output instructions with their op codes are listed in Table 6-20.

TABLE 6-20 8080A Microprocessor Input/Output Instructions with Their Op Codes

	Op Code	
Instruction	Hex	Octal
IN port	DB	333
OUT port	D3	323

IN port **Input**

The data placed on the 8-bit bidirectional data bus by the specified port is moved to the accumulator. When this instruction is written into a program it appears as follows:

IN 00 The accumulator receives one byte of data from port 00_{hex}.
IN 10 The accumulator receives one byte of data from port 10_{hex}.

OUT port **Output**

The contents of the accumulator are placed on the 8-bit bidirectional data bus for transmission to the specified port. The port number is given by byte 2 of the instruction. Two programming examples follow:

OUT 05 The contents of the accumulator are sent to output port 05_{hex}.
OUT 28 The contents of the accumulator are sent to output port 28_{hex}.

6.11 OTHER 8080A MICROPROCESSOR INSTRUCTIONS

In this section, we will discuss the remaining instructions for the 8080A μP. These instructions are (1) a decimal adjustment instruction, (2) two control the interrupt flags, (3) a halt instruction, and (4) a no operation instruction. These instructions with their op codes are listed in Table 6-21.

DAA **Decimal Adjust Accumulator**

This instruction is used after an addition instruction to adjust the result in

TABLE 6-21 Other 8080A Microprocessor Instructions with Their Op Codes

	Op Code	
Instruction	Hex	Octal
DAA	27	047
EI	FB	373
DI	F3	363
HLT	76	166
NOP	00	000

the accumulator into two binary-coded-decimal digits. The steps involved are as follows:

1. The least significant 4 bits of the accumulator are checked. If this result is greater than 9 or if the AC flag equals 1, then 6 is added to the least significant 4 bits of the accumulator.
2. The most significant 4 bits of the accumulator are checked. If this result is greater than 9 or if the CY flag equals 1, then 6 is added to the most significant 4 bits of the accumulator.

The DAA instruction affects all the flag bits.

EI **Enable Interrupt**

This instruction allows the μP to acknowledge an interrupt request following the execution of the next sequential instruction.

DI **Disable Interrupt**

The interrupt system is disabled immediately following the execution of the DI instruction. Therefore, following this instruction, the μP will not acknowledge any interrupt request until the DI signal is cleared.

HLT **Halt**

The program counter is incremented to the address of the next sequential instruction. The μP is stopped, and no activity occurs until an interrupt.

NOP **No Operation**

This instruction allows the μP only to increment the program counter to the next instruction. No other operation takes place.

6.12 SUMMARY

The 8080A's instruction set consists of 78 basic instructions. However, when they are combined with all the different addressing modes, the total is 244 different op codes. This total number of op codes is the entire instruction set of the 8080A μP. This instruction set should allow a programmer enough flexibility to write any program that is needed for either a dedicated control application or for a general-purpose μC application.

Appendix Table D–1 is a summary of the 8080A instruction set. This table offers a quick reference guide to check how an 8080A instruction works. It is particularly helpful when writing a program and may be used for reference during the next chapter.

PROBLEMS

The following problems apply only to the 8080A μP.

6–1 How many general-purpose registers are there inside the 8080A μP? 6

6–2 What are the register pairs in the 8080A? BC, DE, HL

6–3 Does the programmer have control over the register pair WZ? No

6–4 What information is held by the stack pointer?

6–5 What flag bits are there in the 8080A?
6–6 List the categories of data movement instructions.
6–7 Explain what happens when each of the following instructions is executed (data and address values given in hex): (a) MOV A, D; (b) MOV H, A; (c) MVI C, 57; (d) LDA 0100; (e) LXI H, 4128; (f) STAX B; (g) SHLD 0400; (h) LHLD FC0G; (i) STA 0000; (j) MVI B, 00; (k) LDA 04F5; and (l) STAX D.
6–8 Does the 8080A μP have an add instruction that includes the carry flag?
6–9 Do all the add instructions affect the carry flag?
6–10 When a DAD instruction is executed, where is the result placed?
6–11 Explain what happens when each of the following instructions is executed (the data and address are in hex): (a) ADD B, (b) ADD A, (c) ADI 05, (d) ADI 10, (e) DAD B, (f) ADC L, (g) ADC C, (h) ACI 07, (i) SUB D, (j) SUB L, (k) SUI 02, (l) SUI 08, (m) SBB H, (n) SBB E, (o) SBI 03, and (p) SBI 09.
6–12 Are the increment and decrement instructions part of the arithmetic category of instructions?
6–13 Explain the function of each of the following instructions: (a) INC A, (b) INC M, (c) INX B, (d) INX SP, (e) DCR C, (f) DCR L, (g) DCX D, and (h) DCX H.
6–14 List the 8080A's logical instructions.
6–15 Does the 8080A's complement instruction perform the 1's or 2's complement?
6–16 What steps are necessary to perform the 2's complement of data in the accumulator?
6–17 The result of all logical operations is placed in which register?
6–18 Explain what happens when each of the following instructions is executed: (a) ANA L, (b) ANA B, (c) ORA C, (d) ORA M, (e) ORI 0F, (f) XRA D, (g) XRA H, (h) CMA, (i) STC, and (j) CMC.
6–19 Does the compare instruction include the carry flag?
6–20 Can the accumulator be compared with each of the general-purpose registers?
6–21 Is the result of a compare instruction stored in the accumulator?
6–22 What flag bits are affected by a compare instruction?
6–23 Does the 8080A instruction set have a compare immediate instruction?
6–24 List the 8080A's rotate instructions.
6–25 Do all the rotate instructions affect the carry flag?
6–26 List the five categories of program control instructions.
6–27 Does the 8080A's instruction set have a conditional and an unconditional jump instruction?
6–28 Given the conditions Z = 0, CY = 0, P = 1, S = 1, determine whether the μP jumps to a new location when the following instructions are executed: (a) JNZ, (b) JZ, (c) JPO, (d) JC, and (e) JP.
6–29 What is the difference between a conditional jump and a conditional call instruction?
6–30 What is the last instruction of a subroutine?
6–31 What is the function of the PCHL instruction?
6–32 If the B register is to be saved on the stack, what instruction should be used?
6–33 Could the following be a solution to Problem 6–32?

```
MOV A, B
PUSH PSW
```

6–34 What do the following instructions accomplish?

```
LXI 02FF
SPHL
```

6–35 What instruction is needed to send the data in the accumulator out to port 6?
6–36 What instruction is used so that the μP ignores all interrupt request signals?

8080A/8085/Z80 Programs

7.0 INTRODUCTION

This chapter is a continuation of our discussion of 8080A μP software. Since any program written for the 8080A μP also works on an 8085 or Z80, the programs in this chapter can be used on any of these μPs. In this chapter, most of the 8080A instructions are assembled in short but commonly used programs—programs for binary addition and subtraction, BCD addition and subtraction, or movement of blocks of data from one part of memory to another; time delay programs; programs that use input and output instructions; programs that use the stack; and code conversion programs. These programs use mnemonics and an assembly language format. All data and addresses are given in hexadecimal code. Assembly language programs often use labels (a place in the program) to show the destination of a jump instruction. The format for these programs gives the labels in the first column, the instructions in the second column, and comments in the third column. Remember that there is no unique way to write a program, and thus some of the following programs could have been written with fewer instructions. In most cases, there is no particular reason why one register rather than another was chosen for a function. Remember from the previous chapter that some register pairs cannot do everything. Therefore, it may be necessary to use register pair BC or DE and not register pair HL.

7.1 ADDITION AND SUBTRACTION

Addition and subtraction programs are probably the most commonly used programs in a μC system. Sometimes, we need to add two 8-bit (one-byte) numbers; in other cases, we may need multiprecision addition or subtraction, as we do when we have a number that is two or more bytes in length. Sometimes, the addition has to be done in binary; other times, it must be done in BCD. Both types of programs are shown in this section.

As we saw in Chapter 6, the 8080A μP can do subtraction with and without the borrow bit (carry flag). The programs in this section show examples using both instructions. Subtraction programs use 2's complement arithmetic. The programmer does not have to worry about obtaining the 2's complement of a number because it is obtained automatically by the μP in the arithmetic and logic unit. If the result of a subtraction is negative, the answer is in 2's complement form. In binary subtraction, the most significant bit (MSB) can be used as the sign bit. If the MSB = 0, the number is positive. If the MSB = 1, the number is negative.

7.1.1 Single-Byte Binary Addition

Adding two 8-bit numbers requires loading the accumulator with one number and then adding to it a number from one of the six general-purpose μP registers or from a memory location. The result is automatically stored in the accumulator. If the result is to be saved, an MOV instruction must be used to move the data from the accumulator to a memory location.

In arithmetic terminology, the number placed in the accumulator is called the *augend*, and the number that is added to it is called the *addend*. The result is the *sum*. For example:

```
01010111  ←  augend
00011101  ←  addend
--------     ------
01110100  ←  sum
```

Example 7.1 shows how single-byte binary addition may be accomplished. For this example, consider that the data has already been stored in memory before the program begins.

EXAMPLE 7.1 Add the contents of memory location 0200 to the contents of memory location 0300. Place the result back in location 0300.

Solution

LXI H, 0300	Initialize register pair HL.
LDA 0200	Load accumulator directly with data (augend) at location 0200.
ADD M	Add accumulator + data (addend) at location 0300.
MOV M, A	Move result (sum) to location 0300.
HLT	End of program.

The program in Example 7.1 did not concern itself with saving the carry flag. In the event that there is a carry from the most significant bit and the carry is to be saved, then additional programming steps are needed, as shown in Example 7.2.

EXAMPLE 7.2 Continue the program of Example 7.1, but save the carry flag at memory location 0301.

Solution

LXI H, 0300	Initialize register pair HL.
LDA 0200	Load augend from location 0200.
ADD M	Add augend + addend.
MOV M, A	Move sum to location 0300.
MVI A, 00	Clear accumulator.
RAL	Rotate carry flag into accumulator.
INX H	Increment register pair HL.
MOV M, A	Move accumulator (carry flag) to location 0301.
HLT	End of program.

7.1.2 Double-Precision Addition

Double-precision addition means the addition of two 16-bit numbers. Since most 8-bit μPs can do only 8-bit addition, the addition of 16-bit numbers has to be done twice—thus, "double precision." The 8080A μP does have an instruction, DAD, that does double-precision addition between register pair HL and one of the other register pairs. The result is placed in the HL register pair. The following binary numbers show data that could be added by using this instruction:

most significant bytes	least significant bytes		
00110101	10011000	←	register pair HL
00000110	10000011	←	register pair DE
00111100	00011011	←	register pair HL

Example 7.3 shows how double-precision addition may be accomplished.

EXAMPLE 7.3 Add the data at locations 0200 and 0201 to the data at locations 0300 and 0301. Store the answer in locations 0300 and 0301. Do not save the carry flag. Assume that the data at locations 0200 and 0300 are the LS bytes and the data at locations 0201 and 0301 are the MS bytes.

Solution

LHLD 0200	Move data at locations 0200 and 0201 to L and H registers, respectively.
XCHG	Exchange H and L with D and E.
LHLD 0300	Move data at locations 0300 and 0301 to L and H registers, respectively.
DAD D	ADD H + D and L + E.
SHLD 0300	Store register L at location 0300 and register H at location 0301.
HLT	End of program.

7.1.3 Multiprecision Addition

Double-precision addition is actually multiprecision addition. The term *multi-* most often applies to addition programs where more than 16 bits have to be added, such as 24 bits (3 bytes) or 32 bits (4 bytes). Example 7.4 shows how 32-bit numbers can be added. It does not use the DAD instruction. Instead, as each 8 bits are added and stored, a counter (the D register) is decremented and a decision is made by the μP: Is the program complete or not? If the answer is yes, the program will jump to the halt instruction; if the answer is no, the program repeats until all 4 bytes are added.

EXAMPLE 7.4 Add the contents of locations 0200 to 0203 to the data in locations 0300 to 0303. Store the result in locations 0300 to 0303. Refer to Figure 7-1 to visualize what data is being added. In the figure, the augend values stored in page 02 are added to the addend values stored in page 03. The result is stored in page 03. The addend values are lost.

Solution

```
         XRA           Clear accumulator and carry flag.
         LXI B, 0200   Initialize register pair BC.
         LXI H, 0300   Initialize register pair HL.
         MVI D, 04     Initialize D register as a counter.
REPEAT:  LDAX B        Load augend, using register pair BC.
         ADC M         Add augend + addend.
         MOV M, A      Move sum to location given by HL.
         DCR D         Decrement counter.
         JZ HALT       If D = 0, then jump to HALT.
```

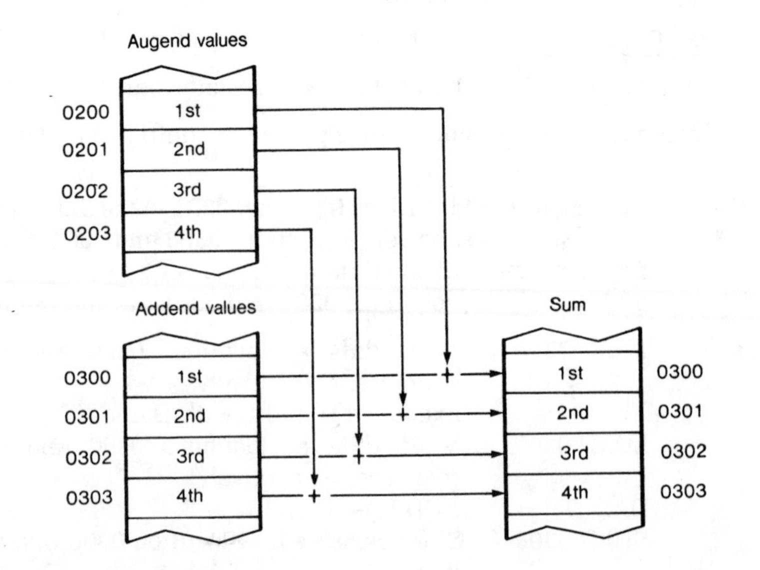

FIGURE 7-1 Multiprecision Addition

```
        INX B          Increment register pair BC.
        INX H          Increment register pair HL.
        JMP REPEAT     Jump back to REPEAT to complete program.
HALT:   HLT            End of program.
```

7.1.4 BCD Addition

The 8080A μP is capable of adding BCD numbers and producing a BCD result. This addition is done by using the decimal adjust instruction (DAA). Example 7.5 shows how Example 7.1 can be modified to do BCD addition. Remember that one byte contains two BCD numbers. In BCD addition, all numbers must be valid BCD numbers. Therefore, all the data in memory must already be in a BCD format before the addition process begins.

EXAMPLE 7.5 Repeat Example 7.1 for BCD addition.

Solution

```
LXI H, 0300    Initialize register pair HL.
LDA 0200       Load augend into accumulator.
ADD M          Add augend + addend.
DAA            Decimal adjust.
MOV M, A       Move sum to location 0300.
HLT            End of program.
```

7.1.5 BCD Double-Precision Addition

The decimal adjust instruction only adjusts a result in the accumulator. Therefore, when two 16-bit BCD numbers are to be added—that is, for a double-precision addition with BCD numbers—the addition must be done in the accumulator, not in the DE and HL register pairs, as was done in Example 7.3. Example 7.6 shows how BCD double-precision addition may be accomplished.

EXAMPLE 7.6 Add the contents of memory locations 0400 and 0401 to the contents of 0600 and 0601. Store the result in locations 0600 and 0601.

Solution

```
        LXI D, 0400    Initialize register pair DE.
        LXI H, 0600    Initialize register pair HL.
        MVI C, 02      Initialize C register as a counter.
        XRA A          Clear accumulator and carry flag.
DADD:   LDAX D         Load accumulator by using register pair DE.
        ADC M          Add accumulator + memory + carry.
        DAA            Decimal adjust.
        MOV M, A       Store accumulator.
        DCR C          Decrement counter.
```

```
        JZ HALT        If C = 0, then jump to HALT.
        INX D          Increment register pair DE.
        INX H          Increment register pair HL.
        JMP DADD       Jump back to DADD.
HALT:   HLT            End of program.
```

7.1.6 Single-Byte Binary Subtraction

In arithmetic terminology, the number in the accumulator is called the *minuend*, and the number being subtracted from it, which comes either from a μP register or from memory, is called the *subtrahend*. The answer is called the *difference*. For example:

```
01100101  ←  minuend
11000000  ←  subtrahend in 2's complement form
--------     ---------------------------------
00100101  ←  difference
```

Example 7.7 shows how single-byte binary subtraction may be accomplished.

EXAMPLE 7.7 Subtract the contents of memory location 0300 from the contents of location 0200. Place the result in location 0300. This problem is similar to the problem in Example 7.1 but involves subtraction.

Solution

```
LXI H, 0300    Initialize register pair HL.
LDA 0200       Load minuend into accumulator.
SUB M          Subtract minuend – subtrahend.
MOV M, A       Move difference to location 0300.
HLT            End of program.
```

7.1.7 Double-Precision Binary Subtraction

The DAD instruction is only for double-precision binary addition. Therefore, when a double-precision subtraction program is needed, the accumulator must be used. The procedure is as follows: First, subtract the least significant bytes, and store the result. Then subtract the most significant bytes, and store the result. This procedure could be continued to perform multiprecision subtraction of any number of bytes. In order for the μP to know if all the bytes have been subtracted, a counter must first be initialized with the number of times the subtraction process is to be done. In Example 7.8, register D is used as the counter.

EXAMPLE 7.8 Subtract the contents of locations 0600 and 0601 from the contents of locations 0500 and 0501, respectively. Store the result in memory locations 0600 and 0601.

Solution

```
       XRA          Clear accumulator and carry flag.
       LXI B, 0500  Initialize register pair BC.
       LXI H, 0600  Initialize register pair HL.
       MVI D, 02    Initialize D register as a counter.
SUBT:  LDAX B       Load minuend into accumulator.
       SBB M        Subtract minuend − subtrahend − CY.
       MOV M, A     Store difference.
       DCR D        Decrement counter.
       JZ HALT      If D = 0, then jump to HALT.
       INX B        Increment register pair BC.
       INX H        Increment register pair HL.
       JMP SUBT     Jump back to SUBT.
HALT:  HLT          End of program.
```

7.1.8 Decimal Subtraction

The DAA instruction permits the 8080A μP to do decimal addition. Therefore, decimal subtraction must be done by using complements. The procedure consists of first obtaining the 100's complement of the subtrahend and then adding the result to the minuend. As an example, consider the subtraction 68 − 15 = 53. The 100's complement of 15 is 85 (100 − 15 = 85). The 85 is added to the 68, yielding 153. The 1 indicates no borrow, and the result is 53, the correct answer. The lack of a carry from the most significant bit indicates that a borrow has been generated, and in the next subtraction of multibyte numbers, the 99's complement of the subtrahend must be obtained. The steps involved in doing a multidigit subtraction are as follows:

1. Set the carry bit to a logic 1 to indicate no borrow.
2. Load the accumulator with 99_{hex} to represent the decimal number 99.
3. Add 0 to the accumulator with the carry to produce either 99_{hex} or $9A_{hex}$ ($100_{decimal}$). The carry bit is also reset.
4. Subtract the subtrahend from the accumulator. The subtraction will generate either the 99's or the 100's complement.
5. Add the minuend to the accumulator.
6. Use the DAA instruction to ensure that the answer is a BCD number.
7. Store the result.
8. If the subtraction operation is not complete, go back to step 2. Otherwise, the program is finished.

Example 7.9 shows how double-precision decimal subtraction may be accomplished.

EXAMPLE 7.9 Write a double-precision decimal subtraction program using steps 1–8. Assume memory locations 0500 and 0501 contain the minuend and memory locations 0600 and 0601 hold the subtrahend. Store the result at locations 0500 and 0501.

Solution

```
       LXI D, 0500    Initialize register pair DE.
       LXI H, 0600    Initialize register pair HL.
       MVI C, 02      Initialize C register as a counter.
       STC            Set carry flag.
DSUB:  MVI A, 99      Load accumulator with 99.
       ACI 00         Add carry flag.
       SUB M          Form 99's or 100's complement.
       MOV B, A       Temporarily save result in B register.
       LDAX D         Load accumulator by using register pair DE.
       ADD B          Add B register without carry.
       DAA            Decimal adjust.
       STAX D         Store accumulator by using register pair DE.
       DCR C          Decrement counter.
       JZ HALT        If C = 0, then jump to HALT.
       INX D          Increment register pair DE.
       INX H          Increment register pair HL.
       JMP DSUB       Jump back to DSUB.
HALT:  HLT            End of program.
```

7.2 TIME DELAYS

Often the μP fetches and executes instructions in a few microseconds—far too fast, in many cases, for peripheral equipment to respond. For example, a signal can be sent from the μP to turn on a thermal printer. The printer may require from 50 to 100 ms to heat its print head before the first line can be printed. If the μP should send the printer a signal to turn on and then immediately begin sending data to the printer, the first line may not be printed at all or may be only partially printed. In this example, the μP should send the signal to turn on the printer and then wait a specified length of time before sending any data to be printed. Another example of having the μP wait occurs when the μP sends a line of data to a printer and then must wait while the printer prints the data before the μP can send the next line. The wait may be several hundred milliseconds. In both examples here, the μP must wait or idle for a certain length of time.

The 8080A μP can be made to wait by either a hardware condition or a software condition. The hardware condition results from application of an external signal to a pin on the μP chip. In this case, the μP fetches and executes no more instructions until the signal is removed. The hardware condition is studied in the next chapter. The software method causes the μP to execute a program over and over again for a specified length of time. Such a program is called a *time delay program*. Often, time delays are written as subroutine programs because they are needed in several places in a main program. Some applications that require μP time delay programs are waveform generation, no-bounce switches, polling peripheral devices at specified times, updating CRT displays, and waiting for slow memory devices.

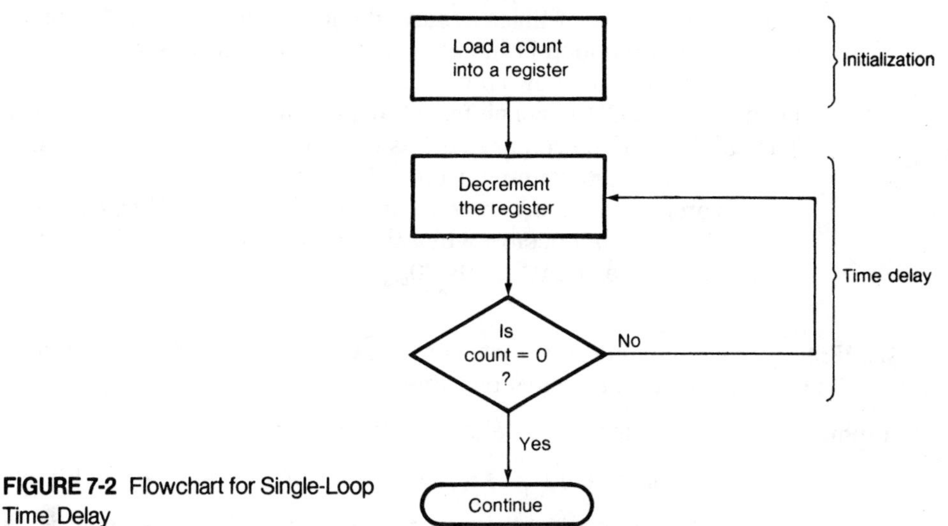

FIGURE 7-2 Flowchart for Single-Loop Time Delay

The principle behind all time delay programs is that a register is loaded with a particular binary pattern. The μP decrements the register and then checks the zero flag to see whether the register is zero. If it is not, the μP jumps back and decrements the register once again. Therefore, the μP is in a loop until the register is zero, at which time the μP executes the next instruction in the program. The binary pattern that is first loaded into the register determines the number of times the μP goes around the loop and thus the overall time delay. Figure 7-2 shows a flowchart for a single-loop time delay. Example 7.10 shows how a time delay may be programmed by using a single register.

EXAMPLE 7.10 Write a time delay subroutine program using the C register as a counter.

Solution

```
       MVI C, COUNT   Initialize C register as a counter (3.5 μs).
LOOP:  DCR C          Decrement counter (2.5 μs).
       RZ             If C = 0, return to main program (5.5 μs); if
                      C ≠ 0, continue (2.5 μs).
       JMP LOOP       Jump back to LOOP (5.0 μs).
```

In the program in Example 7.10, the times in parentheses are for the 8080A μP operating from a 2 MHz clock. Equation 7-1 shows how the overall time delay can be calculated:

$$\text{Time delay} = \underset{\text{MVI C}}{3.5\ \mu s} + (\underset{\text{DCR C}}{2.5\ \mu s} + \underset{\text{RZ}}{2.5\ \mu s} + \underset{\text{JMP}}{5.0\ \mu s})(\text{count} - 1) + \underset{\text{DCR C}}{2.5\ \mu s} + \underset{\text{RZ}}{5.5\ \mu s} \qquad \textbf{(7-1)}$$

Note: The number of times around the loop equals count − 1 because the last time through the loop is the return to the main program.

Example 7.10 shows a complete subroutine program. A call instruction is needed for the μP to branch from the main program to this subroutine program. The call instruction requires 8.5 μs to execute. This additional time should also be included in determining a total time delay.

Example 7.11 shows how to find the shortest and longest time delays. The shortest time delay occurs when the count equals 1_{hex}. The longest time delay occurs when the count equals 00_{hex}.

EXAMPLE 7.11 Use the time delay program of Example 7.10 to determine the shortest and longest time delays possible.

Solution The shortest time delay is calculated as follows:

$$\text{Time delay} = 3.5\ \mu s + (10.0\ \mu s)(0) + 8.0\ \mu s = 11.5\ \mu s$$

In the case of the longest time delay, the C register is decremented $256_{decimal}$ times before the C register is 0 again. The longest time delay is thus calculated as follows:

$$\text{Time delay} = 3.5\ \mu s + (10.0\ \mu s)(255) + 8.0\ \mu s = 2561.5\ \mu s$$

7.2.1 Time Delays Using a Register Pair

The 8080A μP has instructions to decrement not only a single register but also a register pair. Since a register pair is 16 bits wide, much longer time delays can be obtained by using them. Example 7.12 shows how a time delay may be programmed by using a register pair.

EXAMPLE 7.12 Use the register pair DE to write a general time delay program.

Solution

```
       LXI D, COUNT   Initialize register pair DE as a counter (5.0 μs).
LOOP:  DCX D          Decrement the counter (2.5 μs).
       MOV A, E       Move register E to accumulator (2.5 μs).
       ORA A, D       Inclusive OR (2.0 μs).
       JNZ LOOP       If result is not equal to 0, jump to LOOP (5.0 μs).
       RET            Return from subroutine.
```

This algorithm gives the following equation for the time delay:

$$\text{Time delay} = \underbrace{5.0\ \mu s}_{\text{LXI D}} + (\underbrace{2.5\ \mu s}_{\text{DCX D}} + \underbrace{2.5\ \mu s}_{\text{MOV A, E}} + \underbrace{2.0\ \mu s}_{\text{ORA A, D}} + \underbrace{5.0\ \mu s}_{\text{JNZ}})(\text{count}) + \underbrace{5.0\ \mu s}_{\text{RET}} \quad (7\text{-}2)$$

The additional time to execute the call instruction (8.5 μs) from the main program may be included in determining the total time delay.

Example 7.13 shows how to find the shortest and longest time delays. The shortest time delay occurs when the count equals 1. The longest time delay occurs when both the D and E registers are loaded with 00_{hex}.

EXAMPLE 7.13 Use the time delay program of Example 7.12 to determine the shortest and longest time delays possible by using a register pair.

Solution The shortest time delay is calculated as follows:

$$\text{Time delay} = 5.0\ \mu s + (12\ \mu s)(1) + 5\ \mu s = 22\ \mu s$$

In the case of the longest time delay, the register pair DE will be decremented $65{,}536_{decimal}$ times before it equals 0 again. Thus, the longest time delay is calculated as follows:

$$\text{Time delay} = 5.0\ \mu s + (12\ \mu s)(65{,}536) + 5\ \mu s \cong 786\ \text{ms}$$

7.2.2 Longer Time Delays

Longer time delays can be obtained by *nesting* time delay loops. In nesting, a delay loop is set up within a delay loop. In this procedure, both registers are initialized and the first delay loop is decremented until it reaches zero. Then a second delay counter is decremented once. If the second counter does not equal zero, the μP goes back to the first loop and repeats it. When the first loop reaches zero, the μP decrements the second counter again. This process is continued until both counters equal zero. The approximate time delay is the time delay of the first loop multiplied by the second counter. Figure 7-3 shows a flowchart for nesting two time delays. Example 7.14 shows how a nested time delay may be programmed.

EXAMPLE 7.14 Use the register pair DE and register B in a nested time delay program. Use register B as the second counter. Load all register bits with 0 for the longest possible delay.

Solution

```
        MVI B, 00     Initialize B register as a counter.
        LXI D, 0000   Initialize register pair DE as a counter.
LOOP:   DCX D         Decrement register pair DE.
        MOV A, E      Move register E to accumulator.
        ORA A, D      Inclusive OR.
        JNZ LOOP      If DE ≠ 0, then jump back to LOOP.
        DCR B         Decrement B register.
        JNZ LOOP      If B ≠ 0, then jump back to LOOP.
        RET           Return to main program.
```

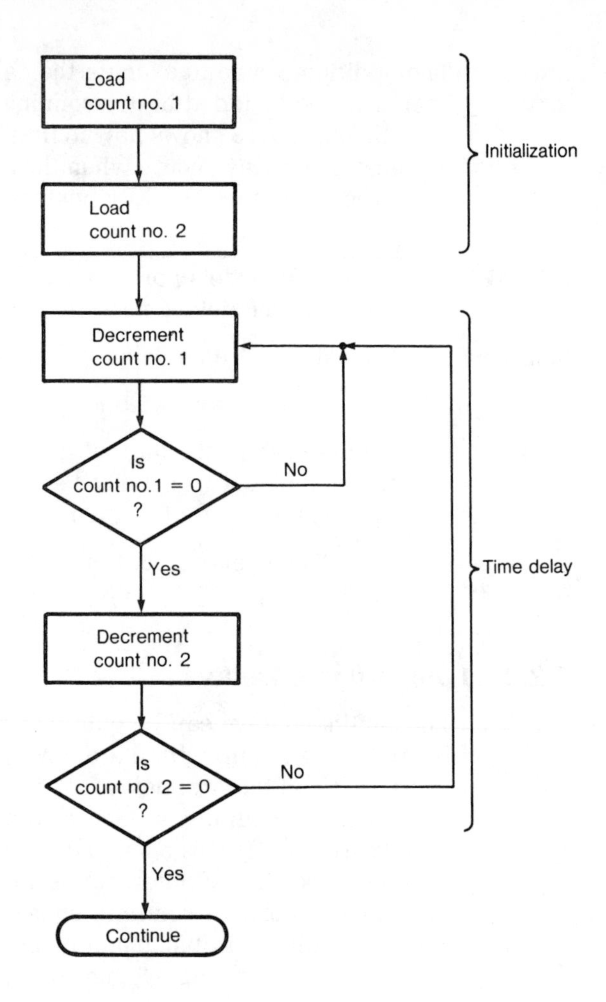

FIGURE 7-3 Flowchart for Nesting Two Time Delays

7.3 CLEARING A SECTION OF MEMORY

When power is first turned on, the binary data in read/write memory is random. In many programs, the programmer may wish to clear an entire section of memory before storing data in it. This procedure guarantees that only valid data or logic 0s are contained in the specified section of memory. Another application for clearing an entire section of memory is in quality control. For example, when read/write devices are purchased, the user may wish to insert the R/W device in a test socket, enter known data into the device, and read it back to see whether the memory chip holds the data. The user can check every bit in the device by this procedure. The program in Example 7.15 is written as a separate program, but it can easily be modified to be a subroutine.

EXAMPLE 7.15 Write a program to clear every byte in page 1 of memory. Remember, page 1 goes from memory location 0100 to location $01FF_{hex}$.

Solution

```
       LXI H, 0100  Load register pair HL with starting address.
       MVI C, 00    Load count 00hex.
LOOP:  MVI M, 00    Clear a memory location.
       INX H        Increment HL register pairs.
       DCR C        Decrement counter.
       JNZ LOOP     If C ≠ 0, then jump back to LOOP to complete
                    program.
HALT:  HLT          End of program.
```

The preceding program writes all 0s into every memory location in page 1. If after this task is done, it is necessary to read the data back and check it, additional programming steps are needed. Example 7.16 shows a program that loads page 1 with all 0s, reads each byte back, and compares it. It is not the shortest program that can be written to do this task, but it works.

EXAMPLE 7.16 Continue the program of Example 7.15 to read each byte in page 1 and check if it is 00_{hex}.

Solution

```
        LXI H, 0100   Initialize register pair HL.
        MVI C, 00     Load count 00hex.
WRITE:  MVI M, 00     Clear a memory location.
        DCR C         Decrement counter.
        JZ READ       If C = 0, then jump to READ program.
        INX H         Increment register pair HL.
        JMP WRITE     Jump to WRITE.
READ:   MOV A, M      Load accumulator.
        CPI 00        Accumulator − 00.
        JNZ ERROR     If Z = 0, jump to ERROR program (not shown).
        DCR C         Decrement counter.
        JZ HALT       If C = 0, jump to HALT.
        DCX H         Decrement register pair HL.
        JMP READ      Jump to READ.
HALT:   HLT           End of program.
```

In the read portion of the program in Example 7.16, the HL register pair and the counter, the C register, do not have to be reinitialized. The reason the C register does not have to be reloaded with 00 is that the C register has to be 00_{hex} for the μP to jump to the read program. The reason the HL register pair is not reinitialized is that, in the read portion of the program, the μP starts at location 01FF and decrements down to location 0100. Therefore, data is written into page 1 from 0100 to 01FF and read from memory from 01FF to 0100, thus saving two programming steps.

7.4 TRANSFERRING A BLOCK OF MEMORY

Programs are often needed to move blocks of data from one part of memory to another. For example, CRT displays always take data from one part of memory and display it on the screen. Therefore, if the data on the screen is to be changed, the specialized portion of memory used for the display (the buffer register) must be changed. Another application is in word processing. After working with data in one part of memory, we may wish to store that whole section of memory. Both applications require moving a number of bytes from one part of memory to another part. The program in Example 7.17 will transfer an entire page of memory.

EXAMPLE 7.17 Transfer the contents of page 1 to page 3 in memory. Use the L register as a counter.

Solution

Label	Instruction	Comment
	LXI B, 0100	Initialize register pair BC.
	LXI D, 0300	Initialize register pair DE.
	MVI L, 00	Initialize counter 00_{hex}.
REPEAT:	LDAX B	Load accumulator with data at location given by register pair BC.
	STAX D	Store accumulator at location given by register pair DE.
	DCR L	Decrement counter, L register.
	JZ HALT	If L = 0, then jump to HALT.
	INX B	Increment register pair BC.
	INX D	Increment register pair DE.
	JMP REPEAT	Jump back to REPEAT.
HALT:	HLT	End of program.

In the program in Example 7.17, whatever data was in page 3 is lost. In many applications, the loss of data is not a problem; in others, it is a problem. The next section shows how to exchange two blocks of memory.

7.5 EXCHANGING TWO BLOCKS OF MEMORY

In some word processing applications, it is necessary to move a block of data from storage memory to the CRT buffer register and move whatever is in the buffer register back to memory to be stored. These movements require exchanging two blocks of memory. The program in Example 7.18 modifies the program in Example 7.17 so that page 1 is exchanged with page 3.

EXAMPLE 7.18 Exchange the contents of page 1 with the contents of page 3. Use the L register as a counter.

Solution

```
         LXI B, 0100   Initialize register pair BC.
         LXI D, 0300   Initialize register pair DE.
         MVI L, 00     Initialize counter 00hex.
REPEAT:  LDAX B        Load accumulator with data given by register
                       pair BC.
         MOV H, A      Temporarily store accumulator in H register.
         LDAX D        Load accumulator with data given by register
                       pair DE.
         STAX B        Store accumulator at location given by register
                       pair BC.
         MOV A, H      Return data in H register to accumulator.
         STAX D        Store accumulator at location given by regis-
                       ter pair DE.
         DCR L         Decrement counter.
         JZ HALT       If L = 0, then jump to HALT.
         INX B         Increment register pair BC.
         INX D         Increment register pair DE.
         JMP REPEAT    Complete program by jumping to REPEAT.
HALT:    HLT           End of program.
```

In the program in Example 7.18, register pair BC holds the memory locations of page 1, while register pair DE holds the memory locations of page 3. During execution of this program, each byte from page 1 is brought into the accumulator, which then transfers it to the H register to be held temporarily. A byte from page 3 is then moved to the accumulator and then into page 1. The data that was temporarily in the H register is moved back to the accumulator and then back to page 3. The data has to be held in a register temporarily because the μP can do only one thing at a time and the accumulator can hold only one byte at a time. Temporary storage of data is an application for which the stack can be used. Example 7.18 is modified in the next section by use of the stack instead of the H register for temporary storage.

7.6 STACK POINTER PROGRAMS

In Chapter 5, the stack was defined as an area in memory that is used by the μP to store the contents of the program counter when a subroutine is called. Saving the present contents of the program counter before the μP jumps to a subroutine program guarantees that the μP will be able to return to the program from which it left. In Chapter 6, we saw that the program counter is automatically saved on the stack when the 8080A μP executes a call instruction. When the 8080A executes a return instruction, the address that was saved on the stack is returned to the program counter. However, saving the contents of the program counter is not the only purpose of the stack. It can be used at any time to store data temporarily.

7.6.1 Saving the Data of the Microprocessor Registers

The other μP registers, accumulator, flag register, and general-purpose registers (B, C, D, E, H, and L) are not saved automatically by the call instruction. Therefore, if a subroutine program uses any of these internal registers, the present data within them will be lost. The contents of the registers on the stack can be saved before the main portion of the subroutine program begins. A push instruction is needed to save the data; a pop instruction is needed to return it. Although the push and pop instructions are included in the overall subroutine program, the push instructions are executed before the main subroutine begins and the pop instructions are executed before the return instruction, as shown in Example 7.19.

EXAMPLE 7.19 Write the programming steps necessary to save and return all the data in the 8080A μP registers.

Solution

```
PUSH PSW    Save accumulator and flag register.
PUSH B      Save register pair BC.
PUSH D      Save register pair DE.
PUSH H      Save register pair HL.
   .            .
   .            .
            Subroutine program
   .            .
POP H       Return register pair HL.
POP D       Return register pair DE.
POP B       Return register pair BC.
POP PSW     Return accumulator and flag register.
RET         Return program counter.
```

Note: The pop instructions are in reverse order from the push instructions; otherwise, the data will not be returned to the proper registers.

7.6.2 Storing Data Temporarily

As previously mentioned, the stack can be used any time for temporary storage; it does not have to be used only when a subroutine program is called. The program in Example 7.20 is similar to that of Example 7.18 in which the contents of page 1 are exchanged with the contents of page 3. The program in Example 7.20 uses the stack instead of the H register for temporary storage. Using the stack for such an application is useful in the event that the H register contains data that should not be lost. The first instruction in the program initializes the stack pointer. It is included only to show that at the beginning of a main program, the stack must be initialized. Initialization is usually done right after power is turned on.

EXAMPLE 7.20 Exchange the contents of page 1 with page 3, using the stack for temporary storage. Use page 8 for the stack.

Solution

```
        LXI SP, 08FF    Initialize stack pointer.
        LXI B, 0100     Initialize register pair BC.
        LXI D, 0300     Initialize register pair DE.
        MVI L, 00       Initialize counter.
EXCH:   LDAX B          Load accumulator, using BC.
        PUSH PSW        Put accumulator and flag register onto stack.
        LDAX D          Load accumulator, using DE.
        STAX B          Store accumulator, using BC.
        POP PSW         Retrieve accumulator and flag register from
                        stack.
        STAX D          Store accumulator, using DE.
        DCR L           Decrement counter.
        JZ HALT         If L = 0, then jump to HALT.
        INX B           Increment register pair BC.
        INX D           Increment register pair DE.
        JMP EXCH        Jump back to EXCH.
HALT:   HLT             End of program.
```

7.7 INPUT/OUTPUT PROGRAMS

The input/output instructions allow the 8080A μP to communicate with peripheral equipment. In Chapter 2, we discussed examples of peripheral equipment. Input devices may be transducers, switches, relays, or keyboards, while peripheral output equipment may be valves, transistors, CRT displays, printers, or plotters. In Chapter 6, we saw what happens when the 8080A μP executes either an input or output instruction. In this section, we will use these instructions in a program.

7.7.1 Input Programs

Assume that an A/D converter is wired at address port 0. The program in Example 7.21 shows how a number of bytes can be taken in from this port and placed in memory.

EXAMPLE 7.21 Take in 10 bytes of data and store them in memory locations 0000 to 000A. The A/D converter is wired at port 0 (00_{hex}).

Solution

```
        LXI H, 0000     Initialize register pair HL.
        MVI C, 0A       Initialize counter 0A_hex = 10_decimal.
DATAIN: IN 00           Input data from port 0.
        MOV M, A        Store accumulator in memory.
        DCR C           Decrement counter.
```

```
        JZ HALT       If C = 0, then jump to HALT.
        INX H         Increment register pair HL.
        JMP DATAIN    Jump to DATAIN.
HALT:   HLT           End of program.
```

7.7.2 Output Programs

Consider that a printer is wired as output port 1 of an 8080A μC system. Therefore, every time the μP executes an output port 1 instruction, the data on the data bus is received by the printer and will be typed out. The output program in Example 7.22 shows not only how the output instruction works but also how code conversion works. Binary-coded-decimal numbers stored in memory are to be converted to ASCII code, and then the ASCII code will be sent to the printer. The reason for this conversion is that many printers are designed to receive only ASCII characters. The printer converts the ASCII character into an alphanumeric character and types the correct letter, number, punctuation mark, or other character.

EXAMPLE 7.22 Write a program that converts the BCD numbers shown in Table 7-1 into ASCII code and outputs the data to port 1 (01_{hex}).

Solution

```
         LXI D, 0150   Initialize register pair DE.
         MVI C, 05     Initialize C register as a counter; 5 bytes.
DATOUT:  LDAX D        Load accumulator, using register pair DE.
         ANI OF        Mask out the most significant 4 bits.
         ORI 30        Convert the least significant 4 bits to ASCII.
         OUT 01        Output the ASCII character to port 01.
         LDAX D        Reload accumulator, using register pair DE.
         ANI FO        Mask out the least significant 4 bits.
         RRC           Rotate right.
         RRC           Rotate right.
         RRC           Rotate right.
         RRC           Rotate right.
         ORI 30        Convert the most significant 4 bits to ASCII.
         OUT 01        Output the ASCII character to port 01.
         DCR C         Decrement counter.
         JZ HALT       If C = 0, then jump to HALT.
         INX D         Increment register pair DE.
         JMP DATOUT    Jump to DATOUT.
HALT:    HLT           End of program.
```

7.8 SUMMARY

Nearly all of the instructions for the 8080A μP were used in one or more of the programs in this chapter. But remember that, at the beginning of this chapter, we noted there is no unique way of writing a program. For example, in most

TABLE 7–1 Memory Locations and Decimal Equivalents of BCD Numbers Used in Example 7.22

Memory Location	BCD	Decimal
0150	0010 0100	24
0151	0111 1000	78
0152	0100 0101	45
0153	0110 0011	63
0154	0111 0000	70

programs in this chapter, another register could have been used as the counter register, or another register pair could have been used to hold the memory location. Also, all of the programs could have been written as subroutine programs. And, like the registers, the memory locations were chosen at random to show that the 8080A μP is capable of addressing any memory location.

In this chapter, we saw how the 8080A's instruction set can be used to write programs for binary and decimal addition and subtraction. Several programs in the examples also included single-byte and multiple-byte addition and subtraction.

When a μP is interfaced with slower peripheral equipment, time delay programs are often used. Thus, in this chapter, we examined several time delay programs for the 8080A μP. Also, we considered programs for clearing, transferring, and exchanging blocks of memory; such programs are often used in word processing applications.

As we saw in this chapter, the 8080A μP can be programmed to use the stack area of memory for storing data temporarily. In addition, the 8080A has instructions both for inputting and for outputting data to peripheral equipment; both instructions are required in most 8080A μC systems. Thus, as we have seen, the 8080A's instruction set covers a wide range of applications.

In this chapter and in the previous chapter, we have examined the software for the 8080A μP. In the next chapter, we consider the 8080A's hardware.

PROBLEMS

7–1 Write a program to add the contents of location 0040 to the contents at memory location 0075. Store the result in location 0075.

7–2 Modify Problem 7–1 to store the answer in location 0095.

7–3 Refer to Example 7.1. Was the carry flag included in the addition? Explain.

7–4 If the MVI A, 00 instruction had not been included in Example 7.2, what would have been stored at location 0301?

7–5 What does the expression *double-precision addition* mean?

7–6 Was the carry flag included in the addition in Example 7.3? Explain.

7–7 What modifications have to be made to Example 7.3 so that the carry flag can be saved at memory location 0302?

7–8 If the program of Example 7.4 were to be written as a subroutine, how would the JZ instruction have to be changed so that there would be a return to the main program?

7–9 If the program of Example 7.4 were used for 16-bit addition, what value would be put into the D register?

7-10 Write a program that adds the BCD values of location 0100 to the BCD values of location 0150. The result is to be placed in location 0200.

7-11 If the numbers being added in Problem 7-10 are not valid BCD numbers, will the DAA instruction correct them?

7-12 What change or changes have to be made in Example 7.6 so that the contents of memory locations 0400 through 0403 can be added to the contents of locations 0600 through 0603?

7-13 What modifications are needed in the program of Example 7.8 to make it a general multiprecision subtraction subroutine?

7-14 If the C register in Example 7.10 is initialized with 80_{hex}, what time delay will be generated by the program?

7-15 If register pair DE in Example 7.12 is initialized with 0400_{hex}, what time delay will be generated by the program?

7-16 What is the approximate time delay generated by the program of Example 7.14?

7-17 Does the following subroutine program clear every memory location in page 1?

```
      LXI H, 01FF
LOOP: MVI M, 00
      DCR L
      RZ
      JMP LOOP
```

7-18 Can the following subroutine program replace the program of Example 7.16?

```
       LXI H, 01FF
WRITE: MVI M, 00
       MVI A, M
       CPI 00
       JNZ ERROR
       DCR L
       RZ
       JMP WRITE
```

7-19 Can the following subroutine program replace the program of Example 7.17?

```
        LXI B, 01FF
        LXI D, 03FF
REPEAT: LDAX B
        STAX D
        DCR C
        DCR E
        RZ
        JMP REPEAT
```

7-20 Suppose a subroutine program saves the μP's registers in the following order:

```
PUSH H
PUSH D
PUSH B
PUSH PSW
```

What should be the last instructions of the subroutine program?

7-21 Refer to Example 7.21. What changes have to be made if (a) the input is 20 bytes of data, (b) data is to be stored at location 0400, and (c) the input port is wired as port 08?

8080A Microprocessor

8.0 INTRODUCTION

This chapter covers the hardware aspects of the 8080A μP, including pin descriptions, timing diagrams, and instruction cycle terminology. What happens when an instruction is fetched and executed, how to stop the μP from fetching and executing instructions, what happens when power is turned on, and what happens when an interrupt occurs are other hardware aspects that are discussed.

The 8080A is a complete central processing unit for a general-purpose μC system. However, it does require some circuitry in addition to memory and I/O devices. Figure 8-1 shows the 8080A μP along with its two basic support chips—the 8224, a clock generator and driver, and the 8228, a system controller and data bus driver.

The 8224 provides the required ϕ_1 and ϕ_2 nonoverlapping clock signals for the 8080A. These signals are not TTL compatible. However, the 8224 does provide a ϕ_2 TTL compatible clock signal for external timing purposes. This chip also provides other timing signals for the μP and for the 8228.

The 8228 provides two functions: (1) system control and (2) data bus buffering for the 8080A μP. As a system controller, it generates all the control signals required for the μP to interface with memory and I/O. At specific times, the 8080A places "status" information on the data bus. The 8228 latches this information and uses it to control the flow of data to and from the μP. The second function of the 8228 is data bus buffer. The 8080A's data lines require 3.3 V minimum for a logic 1. This voltage level is not TTL compatible (for a TTL, 2.0

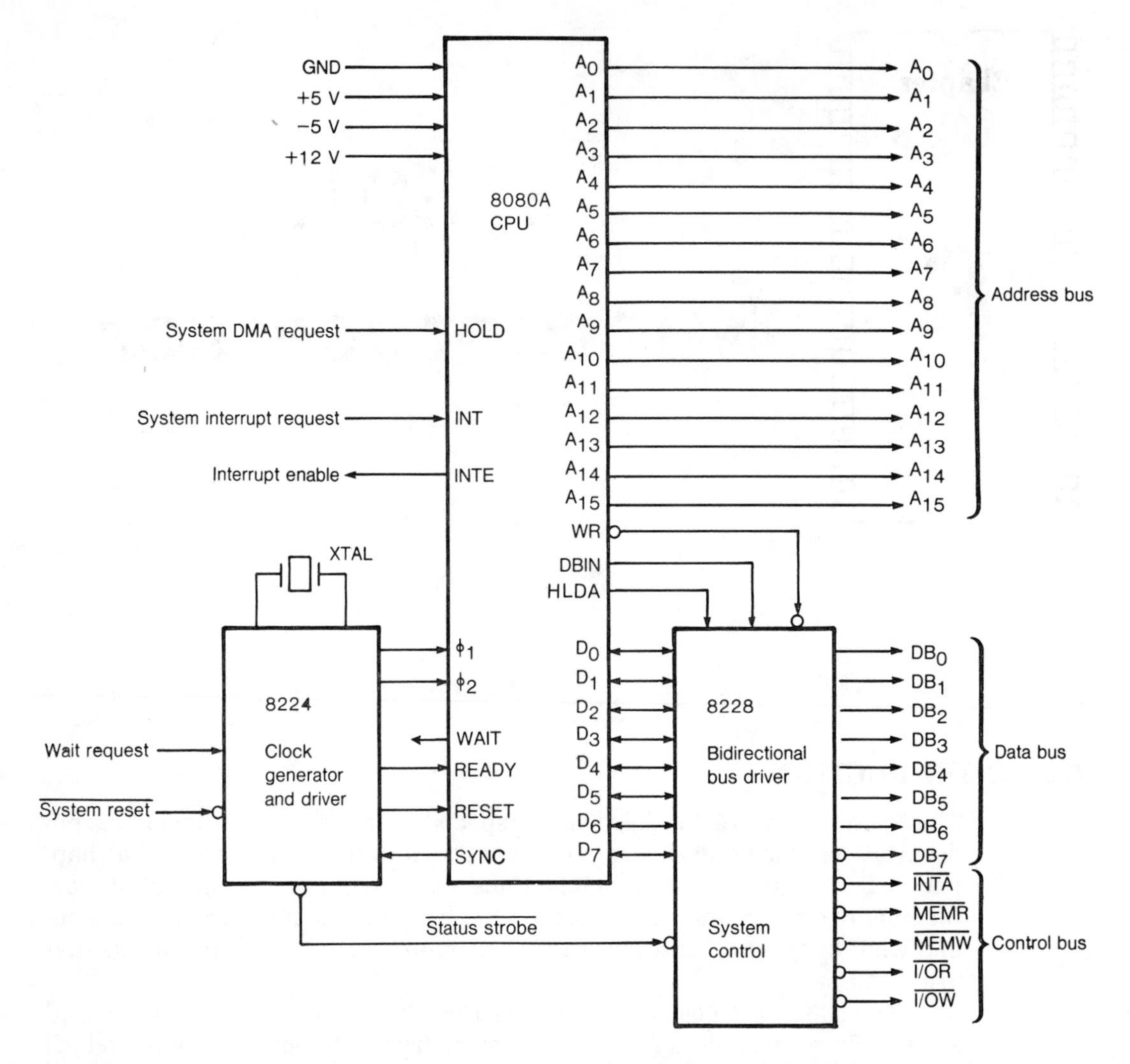

FIGURE 8–1 Schematic of 8080A CPU Group with 8080A, 8224, and 8228 (Redrawn from data sheet for 8224 clock generator and driver for 8080A CPU with permission. Intel Corporation, Santa Clara, CA)

V minimum = logic 1). Since most memory and I/O devices are at TTL logic levels, the 8080A data lines need either a 1 kΩ pull-up resistor or a data bus buffer. The 8228 is a better solution than a resistor because it guarantees all of the necessary logic levels and proper interfacing for the μP.

8.1 PIN DESCRIPTIONS

This section describes the functions of the 8080A's pins. Some descriptions use terms that are explained in more detail in later sections of this chapter. Figure 8–2 shows the pin designations for the 8080A μP.

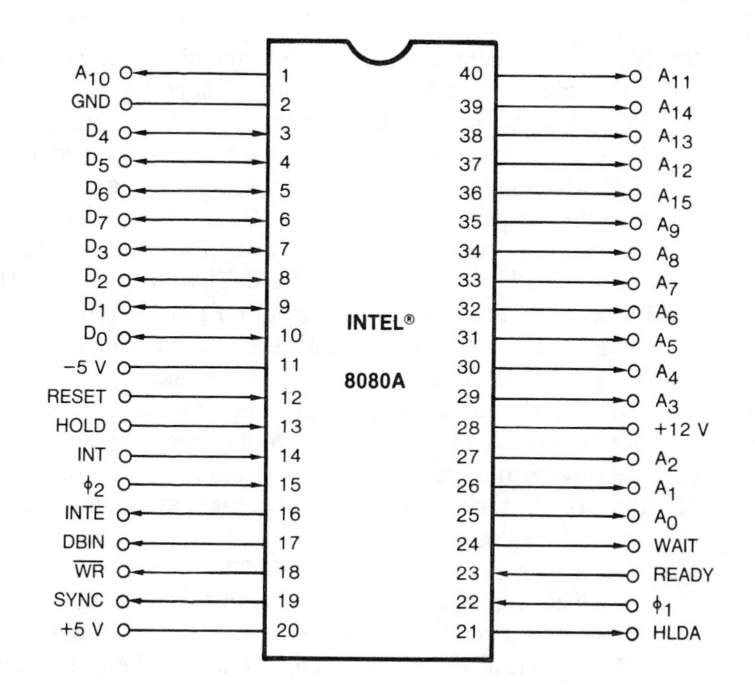

FIGURE 8-2 Pin Designations for the 8080A μP (Redrawn from data sheet for 8080A microprocessor with permission. Intel Corporation, Santa Clara, CA)

Address Bus (A_0–A_{15}): The 8080A's address bus provides either an address to memory (up to 64K bytes) or an I/O device number (up to 256 input devices and up to 256 output devices). A_0 is the least significant address bus line, and A_{15} is the most significant address bus line. All address lines are three state.

Data Bus (D_0–D_7): The data bus provides bidirectional communication among the μP, memory, and I/O devices for instructions and data transfers. At specific times, the data bus also contains status information, a topic covered in Section 8.5. D_0 is the least significant data bus line, and D_7 is the most significant data bus line. All data bus lines are three state.

Power: The 8080A has four pins that are connected to a power supply. They are as follows:

Pin 2	V_{SS}	Ground reference
Pin 28	V_{DD}	$+12$ V $\pm 10\%$
Pin 20	V_{CC}	$+5$ V $\pm 10\%$
Pin 11	V_{BB}	-5 V $\pm 10\%$

Clock Inputs: The ϕ_1 (pin 22) and ϕ_2 (pin 15) are the nonoverlapping clock signals from a clock generator circuit such as the 8224. Remember, these clock signals are not TTL compatible.

The 8080A receives control signals on four pins (RESET, HOLD, INT, and READY) and sends out timing and control signals on six pins (INTE, DBIN, $\overline{WR}$, SYNC, HLDA, and WAIT). These control signals work in the following ways:

RESET (Pin 12): When power is first turned on, the contents of the μP's internal registers come up at random. Therefore, it is necessary to apply a high reset pulse to pin 12. The duration of this signal must be at least three clock periods. The reset pulse forces the program counter to all 0s. Following the reset pulse back to its low state, the μP fetches the first instruction from memory location 0000_{hex}. *Note:* The reset pulse affects only the program counter—no other μP registers; it is left to the programmer to initialize all other registers. The INTE and HLDA flip-flops are also reset.

HOLD (Pin 13): A high control signal on pin 13 allows an external device to suspend the μP's operation of fetching another instruction from memory. This hold signal forces the μP's address and data buses to their three-state condition; the μP is said to be "floating." This condition allows the 8080A to have the feature of direct memory access (DMA). Thus, an external device and memory can communicate without intervention by the μP.

INT (Pin 14): A high pulse on pin 14 signals the μP that there is an external interrupt request.

READY (Pin 23): A low signal on pin 23 places the 8080A μP in a wait condition. This signal allows memory chips or external devices that operate at a slower speed than the μP to be used in the same system. As long as pin 23 is held low, the 8080A remains in a wait state and will not fetch or execute any more instructions.

INTE (Pin 16): When this line is high, the μP is able to acknowledge an interrupt signal. After an INT signal, this line goes low. This line can be used by an external device as an acknowledgement that the μP has received the interrupt. The logic state of this pin is under the programmer's control. INTE is the mnemonic for *interrupt enable*.

DBIN (Pin 17): When the 8080A μP is receiving data, it generates a high output pulse on pin 17. This signal from the μP can be used by memory chip(s) or external device(s) as an acknowledgement that the data has been received. DBIN is the mnemonic for *data bus input*.

$\overline{\text{WR}}$ (Pin 18): This pin is used by the 8080A to synchronize the transfer of data between the μP and memory or external devices. Although $\overline{\text{WR}}$ is the mnemonic for *write* (the μP is sending data), this line is used for both reading (the μP is receiving data) and writing. When this line goes low, the μP is writing data; when this line is high, the μP is reading data.

SYNC (Pin 19): At the beginning of each machine cycle, this line goes high and can be used as a signal that the μP's status information is available on the data bus.

HLDA (Pin 21): When the μP receives a hold signal, this line goes high as an acknowledgement that the μP has received the hold signal. HLDA is the mnemonic for *hold acknowledge*.

WAIT (Pin 24): This pin goes high when the μP is in a wait state. Thus, it is the μP's acknowledgement that it has received a ready signal.

8.2 8080A MICROPROCESSOR CYCLES

As we stated in Chapter 5, μPs are synchronous, sequential machines. The μP fetches an instruction from memory and then executes the instruction. In order to follow how and when these operations are carried out by the μP, we need timing diagrams. To understand these diagrams, we need to be familiar with three terms defined by the manufacturer of the 8080A: instruction cycle, machine cycle, and state.

An *instruction cycle* is the total time required to fetch and execute an instruction. Instruction cycles consist of one, two, three, four, or five machine cycles. A *machine cycle* is required every time the μP accesses memory or an I/O port. Each machine cycle consists of three, four, or five states. A *state* is the smallest unit of time in the processing activity. A state is defined as the time interval from the positive-going edge of the ϕ_1 clock pulse to the next positive edge of the ϕ_1 clock pulse.

The time interval of a state, as shown in Figure 8–3, includes a ϕ_1 clock signal as well as a ϕ_2 clock signal. The state time determines how fast the μP can operate and equals t_{cyc}. In most applications, the 8080A's clock frequency is 2 MHz; therefore, t_{cyc} = 500 ns.

To summarize the three types of cycles used for the 8080A μP: Each ϕ_1 clock signal period marks a state; three to five states constitute a machine cycle; and one to five machine cycles comprise an instruction cycle. Therefore, depending on the instruction that is being fetched and executed by the 8080A, an instruction cycle can require anywhere from four to eighteen states for completion.

There are three exceptions to the total number of states needed to complete an instruction cycle. They are (1) a wait state, (2) a hold state, or (3) a halt state. Each state is generated by events external to the μP. Therefore, the number of states needed to complete an instruction cycle cannot be determined for these conditions. These exceptions are covered in Sections 8.6, 8.8, and 8.9.

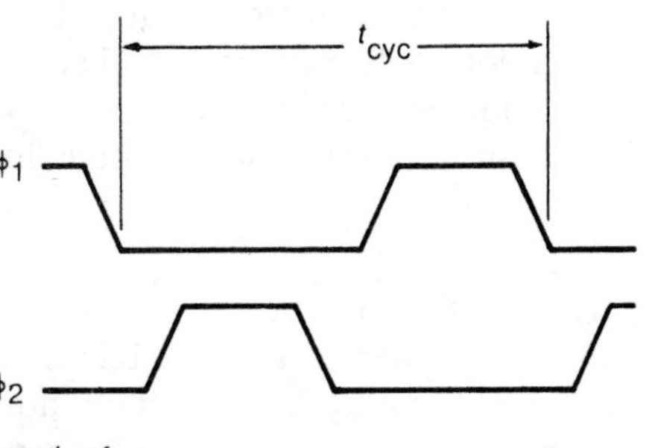

FIGURE 8–3 Time Interval of a State

8.3 MACHINE CYCLE IDENTIFICATION

The number of machine cycles required by the 8080A μP to fetch and execute an instruction equals the number of times the μP has to address memory or an I/O port. There is one exception: the DAD instruction. The 8080A μP has been designed so that it puts out only one address per machine cycle. For example, if an instruction requires the μP to address memory twice, then there are two machine cycles. If an instruction requires the μP to address memory five times, then there are five machine cycles.

Every instruction cycle addresses memory at least once because the instruction has to be fetched even if execution of the instruction requires no further references to memory. Therefore, the first machine cycle in every instruction cycle is a fetch. Beyond that, there are no rules. The number of cycles depends on the instruction that is fetched. The following examples demonstrate three different 8080A μP instructions and show why some instructions require more than one machine cycle.

EXAMPLE 8.1 The MOV r1, r2 instruction requires only one machine cycle (fetch) for completion. Only one cycle is needed since all the information necessary to execute the instruction is contained in the one-byte instruction. Remember from Chapter 6 that when this instruction is executed, the contents of register r2 are moved to register r1. When this instruction is decoded, the μP knows the type of instruction, the source register (r2), and the destination register (r1). Since registers r2 and r1 are inside the 8080A, the μP does not have to address memory again to execute the instruction. Therefore, the instruction cycle for MOV r1, r2 requires only one machine cycle.

Note: Although only one machine cycle is required for MOV r1, r2, five states are needed: one to fetch the instruction from memory and four additional states to increment the program counter, decode the instruction, and move the contents of register r2 to register r1. Therefore, for this instruction, the instruction cycle requires one machine cycle that consists of five states. Section 8.6 describes in more detail what happens in each state.

EXAMPLE 8.2 The MOV r, M instruction transfers the contents of a specific memory location to an internal register. Like the instruction of Example 8.1, this instruction is a one-byte instruction; however, an extra machine cycle is needed in order for the μP to address the desired memory location. Remember from Chapter 6 that the address where the data will be obtained is held in the H and L registers. This instruction requires the μP to address memory twice. Therefore, there are two machine cycles. The actual sequence is as follows.

For machine cycle 1, the μP fetches from memory the one-byte instruction and places it in the instruction register. The program counter is incremented by 1, to be used for the next instruction cycle. These steps take three states. An additional state is needed for decoding the instruction.

For machine cycle 2, the μP sends out on the address bus the contents of the H and L registers, which is the location where the data will be obtained. This machine cycle requires three states to retrieve the data and place it in the proper internal register.

Therefore, for a MOV r, M instruction, the entire instruction cycle requires two machine cycles with a total of seven states. The first machine cycle has four states, and the second machine cycle has three states.

EXAMPLE 8.3 SHLD addr is one of the longest instructions for the 8080A to complete. The entire instruction cycle requires five machine cycles and a total of sixteen states. The SHLD instruction is a three-byte instruction. The first byte is the μP op code, while the second and third bytes are an address. When this instruction is completed, the contents of the L register are moved to the memory location whose address is specified by bytes 2 and 3 of the instruction. The contents of the H register are moved to the next memory location. During the fetch and execution of this instruction, the following sequence of events occurs.

Machine cycle 1 is the fetch cycle and consists of four states. During the first three states, the μP fetches the instruction from memory, increments the program counter, and places the instruction in the instruction register. The fourth state is used for decoding the instruction.

Machine cycle 2 is called a memory read cycle and consists of three states. During this machine cycle, the μP reads the contents of the memory location indicated by the program counter. The contents are placed in the 8080A's Z register. The program counter is incremented again.

Machine cycle 3, like machine cycle 2, is a memory read cycle and consists of three states. The μP reads the memory location indicated by the program counter. The contents of memory are placed in the 8080A's W register. The program counter is incremented again. The new value in the program counter will not be used until the μP fetches the next instruction.

Machine cycle 4 is a memory write cycle and consists of three states. The contents of the W and Z registers are placed on the address bus. The data in the L register is stored at the memory location indicated by the W and Z registers. The contents of the W and Z registers are incremented by 1. *Note:* In this machine cycle, the W and Z registers are used in place of the program counter.

Machine cycle 5, like machine cycle 4, is a memory write cycle and consists of three states. The contents of the H register are stored at the memory location given by the new contents of the W and Z registers.

Therefore, a SHLD instruction takes five machine cycles and sixteen states.

Appendix Table D-2 lists the mnemonic, the binary pattern of the op code, the number of machine cycles, and the number of states for each 8080A instruction. The machine cycles are labeled M_1, M_2, M_3, M_4, and M_5. The states are labeled T_1, T_2, T_3, T_4, and T_5. Notes are given at the end of the table.

8.4 TYPES OF MACHINE CYCLES

Although no one instruction cycle consists of more than five machine cycles, the 8080A μP has ten different types of machine cycles that may occur. They are as follows:

1. Fetch (M_1)
2. Memory read
3. Memory write
4. Stack read
5. Stack write
6. Input
7. Output
8. Interrupt acknowledge
9. Halt
10. Interrupt acknowledge while halt

The machine cycles that actually occur in a particular instruction cycle depend upon the instruction. Remember that the *first machine cycle* in any instruction cycle is always a *fetch*. Thus, the M_1 expression has been added to the preceding list. We will now consider each type of machine cycle.

8.4.1 Fetch (M_1)

The fetch cycle consists of either four or five states. There are three exceptions: the wait, hold, and halt states. These exceptions are covered in later sections. For some 8080A μP instructions, the fetch cycle is the only machine cycle needed to fetch and execute the instruction. (An example was given in Section 8.3.) In multibyte instructions, during the fetch cycle, the op code is fetched from memory and transferred to the instruction register. During this cycle, the following steps may occur: A memory address is placed on the address bus; status information is made available by the external data bus (see Section 8.5); data is transferred between the μP registers; the program counter is incremented by 1; some simple arithmetic or logical operations are performed; and the instruction is decoded.

8.4.2 Memory Read

The memory read cycle consists of three states. During this cycle, data in a memory location indicated by the program counter or a register pair is transferred from memory to one of the 8080A's internal registers. These registers include the accumulator and the B, C, D, E, H, and L registers.

8.4.3 Memory Write

The memory write cycle consists of either three or four states. During this cycle, the contents of a μP register are transferred to the memory location pointed to by either a register pair or by the temporary WZ register pair. The register pair being used as a pointer to memory may also be incremented or decremented during this machine cycle.

8.4.4 Output

The output cycle consists of three states. During this cycle, the address code of the output port is made available on the 16-bit memory address bus, and the contents of the accumulator are sent out on the data bus. It is up to the peripheral equipment to decode the address and capture the data.

8.4.5 Input

The input cycle consists of three states. During this cycle, the input address code is made available on the address bus, and the data on the data bus is transferred to the accumulator. It is up to the peripheral equipment to decode the address and place the data on the data bus.

8.4.6 Stack Read

The stack read cycle consists of three states. During this cycle, the contents of the memory location indicated by the stack pointer are transferred to one of the 8080A internal registers. Such registers include the accumulator and the B, C, D, E, H, L, program counter, or flag registers.

8.4.7 Stack Write

The stack write cycle consists of three states. During this cycle, the contents of an internal register are transferred to the memory location indicated by the stack pointer. The registers that may be involved are the accumulator and the B, C, D, E, H, L, program counter, or flag registers.

8.4.8 Interrupt Acknowledge

The interrupt acknowledge cycle consists of five states. It resembles the fetch machine cycle, except that the program counter is not incremented. This cycle allows the program counter to be saved on the stack and will permit the 8080A μP to make an orderly return to the program after the interrupt request has been processed.

8.4.9 Halt

The halt cycle can contain any whole number of states greater than 3. The μP enters and remains in the halt state after it decodes the HLT instruction. There are three ways of getting the 8080A μP out of the halt state. They will be explained in Section 8.8.

8.4.10 Interrupt Acknowledge while Halt

The interrupt acknowledge while halt cycle consists of five states. One method of getting the μP out of the halt state is by having it recognize an interrupt request.

8.5 STATUS INFORMATION

As previously mentioned, the 8080A μP puts out status information on the data bus during state T_1 of every machine cycle. The eight status bits can be used for either (1) interfacing the 8080A μP with memory or peripheral devices or (2) identifying the type of machine cycle the μP is performing. The 8228 system controller shown in Figure 8–1 captures these status bits and uses them to generate the proper interfacing signals. However, the 8228 does not output all the status bits, so it cannot be used to identify which type of machine cycle is being executed. Identifying which machine cycle is being performed can be helpful in troubleshooting. Figure 8–4 shows how an 8212 IC is connected to the 8080A data bus to latch and output all the status bits. Table 8–1 lists the status bits with a description of each bit.

Table 8–2 lists the ten types of machine cycles and shows the corresponding status information for each cycle. Although the status bits are provided principally for controlling external circuitry, they can also be used for identifying the type of machine cycle in progress.

As an example of controlling external circuitry, consider Figure 8–5. The OUT line from the status latch enables the decoder. The output lines of the decoder chip enable eight output ports. Each port line goes to a separate piece of peripheral equipment. The 74LS138 chip is a 3-to-8 decoder. When this chip is enabled by the output line from the status latch, it decodes the binary pattern on address lines A_0, A_1, and A_2. Depending on the binary pattern, the corresponding output line of the decoder chip goes low. The output signal from the decoder is used to turn on the corresponding output port.

If the user wishes to use the status bits for machine cycle identification, LEDs may be connected to the output of each line of the status latch, as shown in Figure 8–6.

8.6 STATES

Each machine cycle has three to five states, labeled T_1, T_2, T_3, T_4, and T_5. The three exceptions are the wait, hold, and halt states. These states, which can last from three to an indefinite number of clock periods, are terminated only by

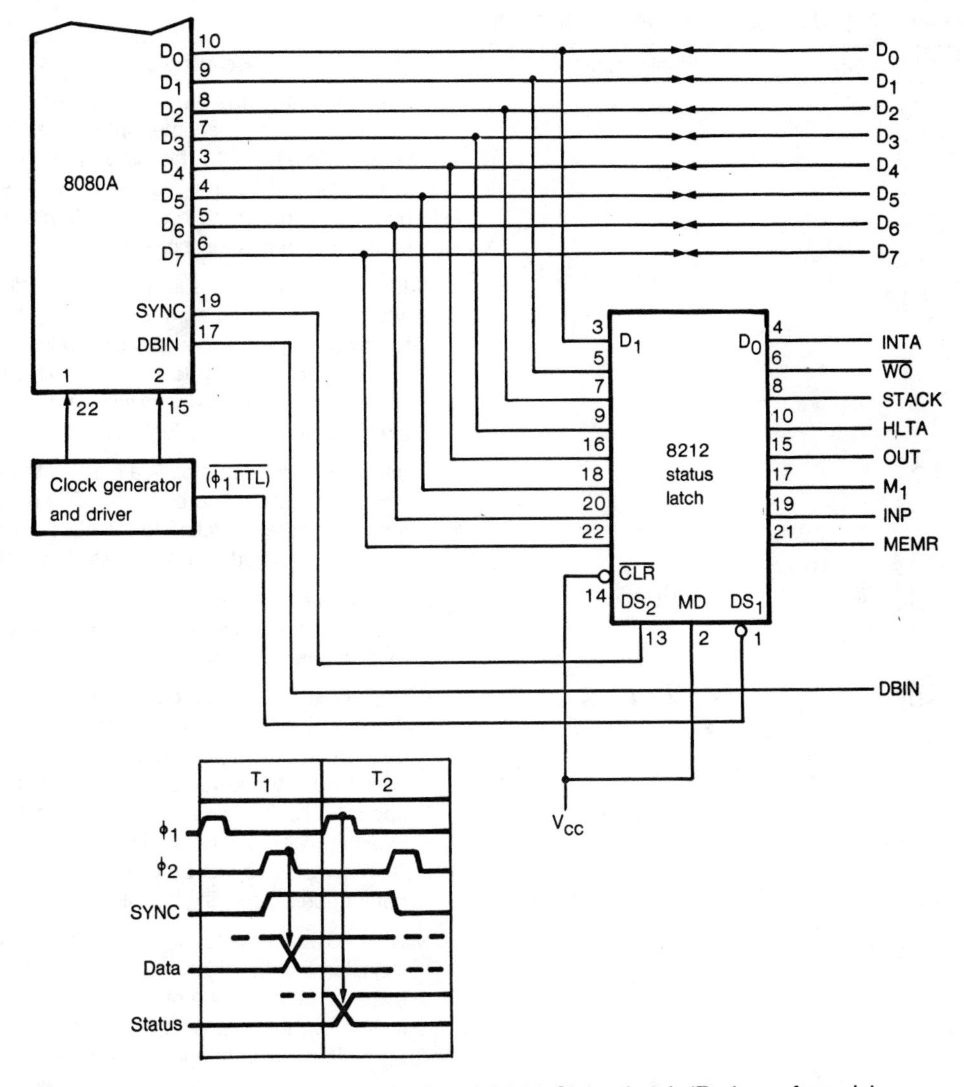

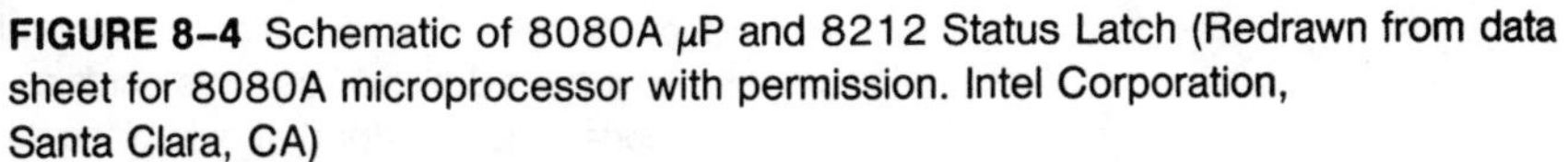

FIGURE 8–4 Schematic of 8080A μP and 8212 Status Latch (Redrawn from data sheet for 8080A microprocessor with permission. Intel Corporation, Santa Clara, CA)

external signals. The total number of states per instruction cycle is determined by the number of machine cycles times the number of states of each machine cycle. The simplest instruction in the 8080A μP instruction set has four states; the most complicated instruction has eighteen.

Every machine cycle has at least three states defined by the positive-going edge of the ϕ_1 clock pulse. Remember that each state contains two clock pulses, a ϕ_1 clock pulse and a ϕ_2 clock pulse. Events occur at the leading edge of a clock pulse or within 50 ns of the leading edge. The activities that occur during each state are discussed next.

TABLE 8–1 Identification and Description of Status Bits

Data Bus Bit	Identification	Description of Status Bit
D_0	INTA	Interrupt Acknowledge: When the μP acknowledges that it has received an interrupt request, this status bit goes to a logic 1. This signal, along with a logic 1 from the DBIN (pin 17 of the 8080A μP), should be used by peripheral equipment to place data onto the data bus for the restart (RST) instruction.
D_1	$\overline{WO}$	Write Output: If the μP is in a machine cycle in which data is being sent to a memory location or to an output port, this status bit is a logic 0. If the μP is in a machine cycle in which data is being received from a memory location or from an input port, this status bit is a logic 1.
D_2	STACK	Stack: When this status bit is a logic 1, the address bus holds a stack address. The μP is doing either a read or a write operation to the stack. The stack address originated in the μP's stack pointer (SP).
D_3	HLTA	Halt Acknowledge: When this status bit is a logic 1, it indicates an acknowledgement that the μP has received and decoded a halt (HLT) instruction.
D_4	OUT	Output: When this status bit is a logic 1, it indicates that the 16-bit address bus contains an address code of an output port. The address code is contained in the lower 8 bits and repeated in the upper 8 bits. The data bus will contain the data when the $\overline{WR}$ (pin 18 on the 8080A μP) is a logic 0. This status bit can be used as a signal to the output port's decoding circuitry.
D_5	M_1	Machine Cycle 1: When this status bit is a logic 1, it indicates that the 8080A μP is in the first machine cycle of an instruction cycle. In a multibyte instruction, this status bit is a logic 1 only when the op code is being fetched (first machine cycle).
D_6	INP	Input: When this status bit is a logic 1, it indicates that the 16-bit address bus contains an input port code. The input port should place its data onto the data bus when the DBIN (pin 17 on the 8080A μP) is a logic 1.
D_7	MEMR	Memory Read: When this status bit is a logic 1, it indicates that the μP is going to read data from memory.

8.6.1 State T_1

During state T_1, a memory address or I/O device number is placed on the address bus after the positive edge of the ϕ_2 clock pulse. A memory address can originate in the program counter, a register pair, the stack pointer, or the tem-

TABLE 8–2 Types of Machine Cycles and Corresponding Status Information

	MEMR	INP	M_1	OUT	HLTA	STACK	$\overline{WO}$	INTA	←Status information
Type of Machine Cycle	D_7	D_6	D_5	D_4	D_3	D_2	D_1	D_0	←Data bus bit
(1) Instruction fetch	1	0	1	0	0	0	1	0	
(2) Memory read	1	0	0	0	0	0	1	0	
(3) Memory write	0	0	0	0	0	0	0	0	
(4) Stack read	1	0	0	0	0	1	1	0	
(5) Stack write	0	0	0	0	0	1	0	0	
(6) Input	0	1	0	0	0	0	1	0	
(7) Output	0	0	0	1	0	0	0	0	
(8) Interrupt	0	0	1	0	0	0	1	1	
(9) Halt	1	0	0	0	1	0	1	0	
(10) Interrupt while halt	0	0	1	0	1	0	1	1	

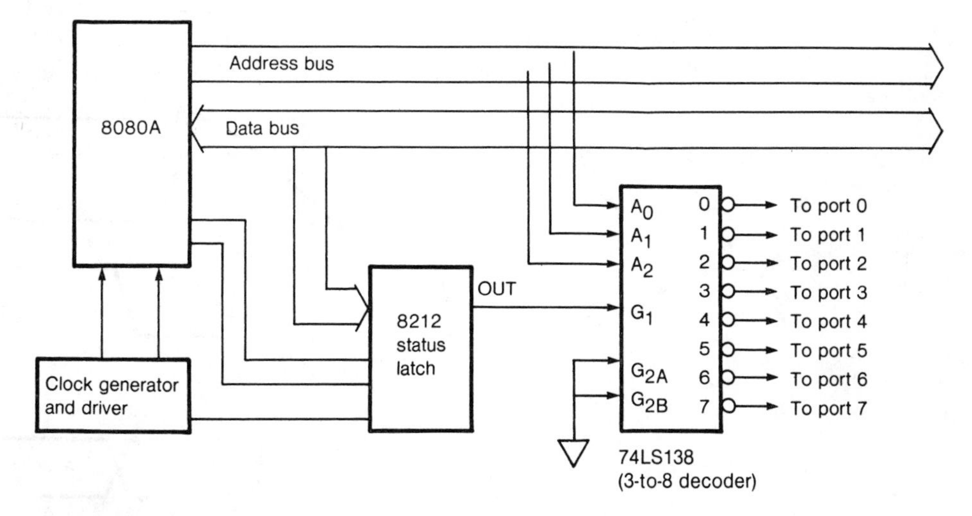

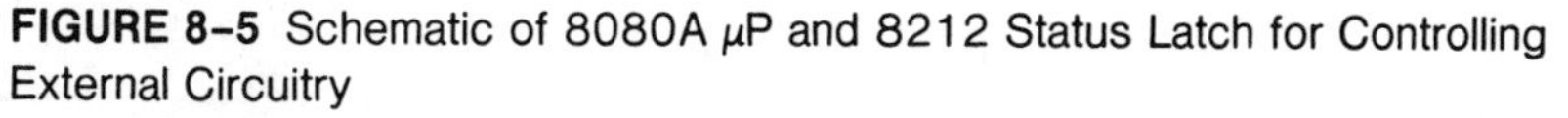
FIGURE 8–5 Schematic of 8080A μP and 8212 Status Latch for Controlling External Circuitry

porary register pair WZ. The eight status bits are placed on the external data bus after the positive edge of the ϕ_2 clock pulse. The SYNC output line goes to a logic 1 slightly after the positive edge of the ϕ_2 clock pulse. Figure 8–7 shows what happens during state T_1.

8.6.2 State T_2

During state T_2, the 8080A μP checks the logic states of the HOLD and READY input pins and also tests for a halt instruction. If a halt (HLT) instruction is decoded, the μP enters a wait state. If the μP does not decode a halt instruction, the μP checks the logic state on the READY pin. If the READY input is at a logic

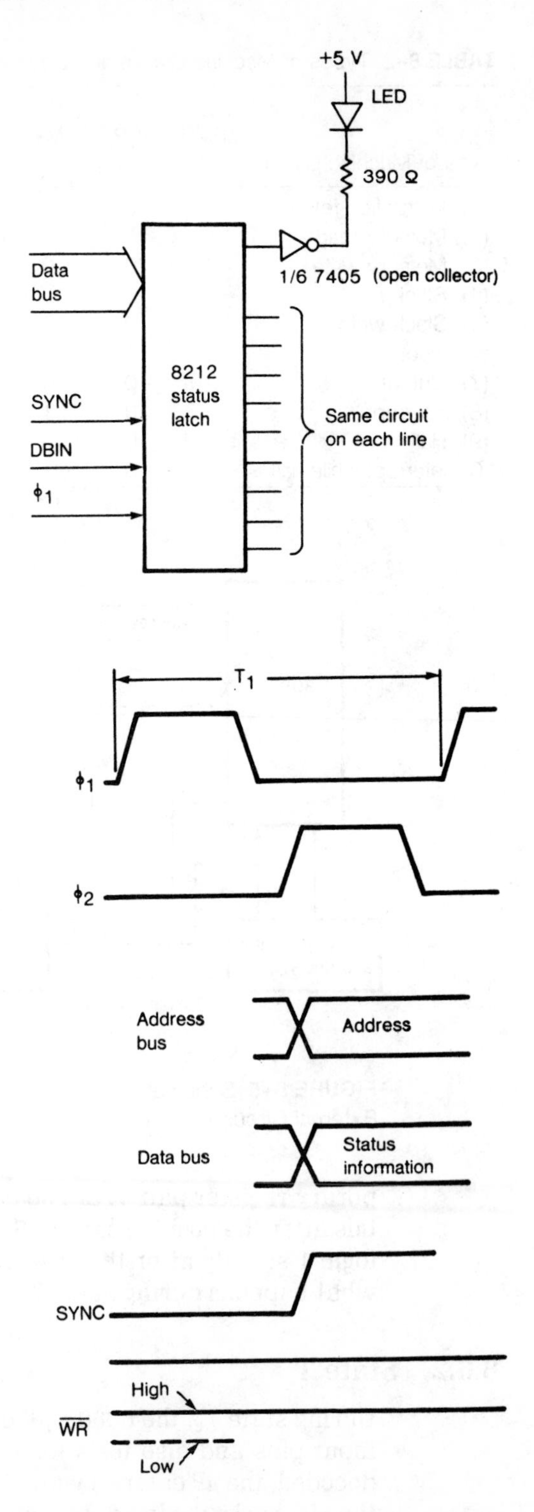

FIGURE 8-6 Inverter, Current-Limiting Resistor, and LED Connected to Each Output Line of 8212 Status Latch to Allow Identification of Each Machine Cycle

FIGURE 8-7 Timing Diagram for State T_1

1, the μP enters state T_3; if the READY input is at a logic 0, the 8080A μP goes into a wait state.

If the HOLD pin goes to a logic 1, the μP floats its address and data buses, thereby allowing an external device to control the μP bus lines. This feature allows the 8080A μP to provide for direct memory access (DMA) operations.

The SYNC output line goes to a logic 0 slightly after the positive edge of the ϕ_2 clock pulse. After the positive edge of the ϕ_2 clock pulse, the 8 bits of status information are replaced either by an instruction or by data. The data could be coming into the μP or going out of the μP. If the μP is receiving data, the data input signal, DBIN, goes to a logic 1 at the beginning of the ϕ_2 clock pulse. Figure 8–8 shows what happens during state T_2.

8.6.3 State T_W

State T_W is the optional wait state. The 8080A μP enters this state if the READY input line goes to a logic 0 or if a halt (HLT) instruction has been decoded. The 8080A μP acknowledges that it is in this wait state by placing a logic 1 on the wait pin at the positive edge of the ϕ_1 clock pulse. The wait period is of indefinite duration because an external signal must be applied to the μP's READY or INTERRUPT pin to end the period.

If a low on the READY line caused the μP to enter the wait state, then the μP remains in a wait state until an interrupt request is received or until the program counter is reset. The address on the address bus does not change during the wait state unless the μP receives a hold signal and a DMA operation is performed.

If the μP has decoded a write instruction, the $\overline{WR}$ line goes low at the beginning of the ϕ_1 clock pulse and remains low for the entire wait state and into the T_3 state. Figure 8–8 illustrates what occurs during the wait state.

8.6.4 State T_3

The events that take place during state T_3 are determined by the kind of machine cycle in progress. In a fetch machine cycle, the μP interprets the binary pattern on the data bus as an instruction and directs it to the instruction register. If the machine cycle is memory read or stack read, the binary pattern on the data bus is interpreted as data and forwarded to the appropriate μP register. If the machine cycle is memory write, the μP outputs data onto the data bus. During I/O operations, the μP either receives or sends data, depending on whether an input or output instruction is being executed.

The DBIN output pin on the 8080A goes low at the leading edge of the ϕ_2 clock pulse. The $\overline{WR}$ line remains high. *Note:* Machine cycles in which DBIN is available include fetch, memory read, stack read, and interrupt. The DBIN pin is initiated on the rising edge of the ϕ_2 clock pulse during state T_2 and ends at the rising edge of the ϕ_2 clock pulse during state T_3. If any wait states occur between T_2 and T_3, the DBIN signal will remain high for the entire wait condition.

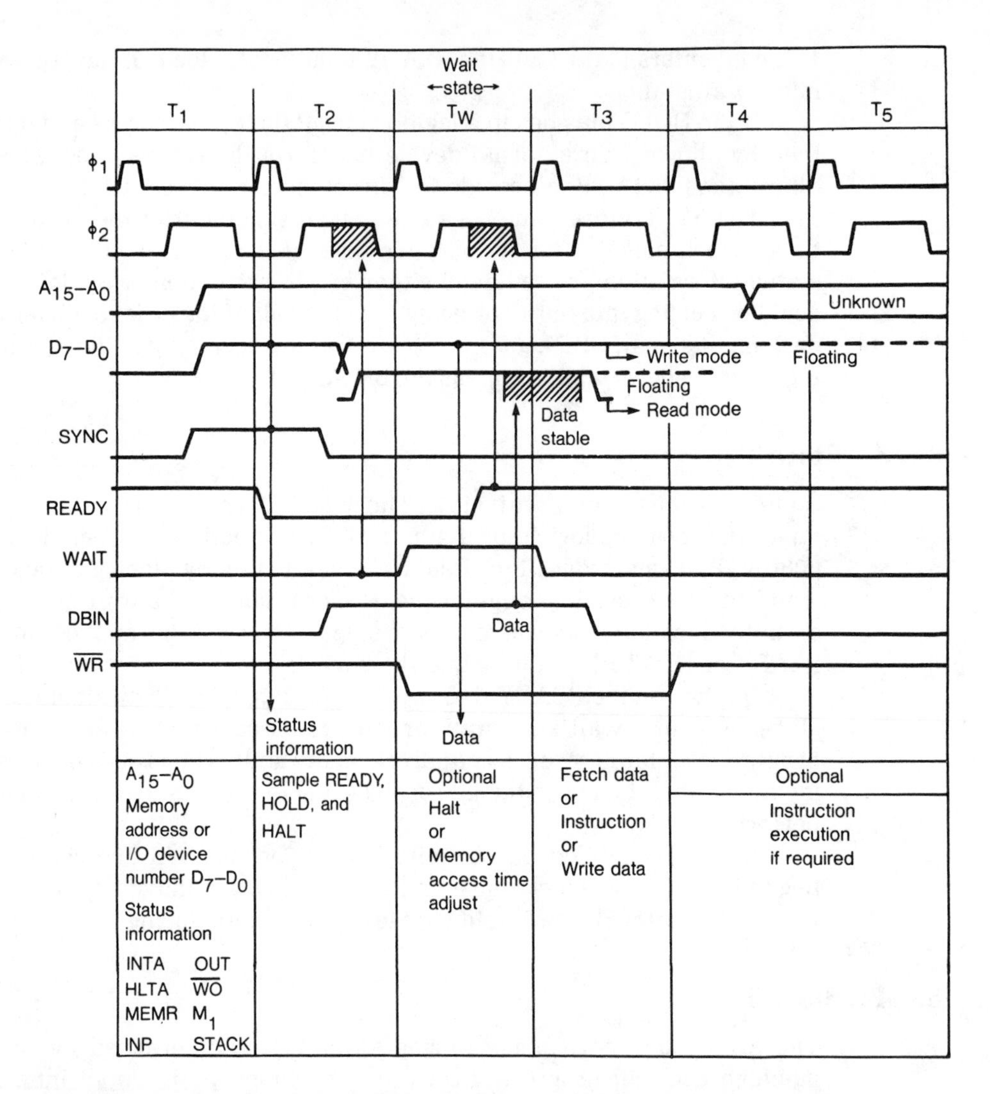

FIGURE 8–8 Timing Diagram for 8080A Machine Cycle Showing One Wait State (Redrawn from data sheet for 8080A microprocessor with permission. Intel Corporation, Santa Clara, CA)

If the μP is doing a write operation, the $\overline{WR}$ output pin goes low at the positive edge of the ϕ_1 clock pulse. The DBIN line is low. If there was a wait state and the $\overline{WR}$ output pin was low, it would remain low during this state. Both read and write conditions are shown in Figure 8–8.

8.6.5 States T_4 and T_5

States T_4 and T_5 are optional states used by the 8080A μP to complete the execution of some instructions. The μP may skip one or both of these states. They are used only for internal operations.

Figures 8–9 and 8–10 summarize the 8080A's activities during the states. Figure 8–9 shows what happens during states T_1, T_2, T_3, and T_4 when the 8080A μP reads data (an input instruction). Figure 8–10 illustrates what occurs during states T_1 through T_4 for a write operation (an output instruction).

8.7 STARTING OR RESETTING THE 8080A MICROPROCESSOR

The 8080A μP begins operating immediately when power is applied. However, the contents of its program counter, stack pointer, accumulator, and all other internal working registers come up at random. Therefore, after power is applied, it is necessary to have a reset condition.

When a high voltage level is applied to the 8080A's RESET pin for at least three clock cycles, the μP's internal program counter is automatically loaded with all 0s. After the reset signal goes low, the μP begins to fetch instructions, beginning at memory location 0000_{hex}. The programmer must remember that the reset signal has no effect on any registers other than the program counter. However, the HLDA and INTE flip-flops are cleared upon a reset signal. Therefore, if a particular binary pattern is needed in the accumulator, stack pointer, flag register, or any other register, then that register must be initialized by the program. In some systems, the designer may wish the μP to wait for an external signal before the program begins. For this type of application, the first two program steps should be EI, HLT. These steps will set the interrupt enable flip-flops and then halt the μP. The μP will remain in its wait state until it receives

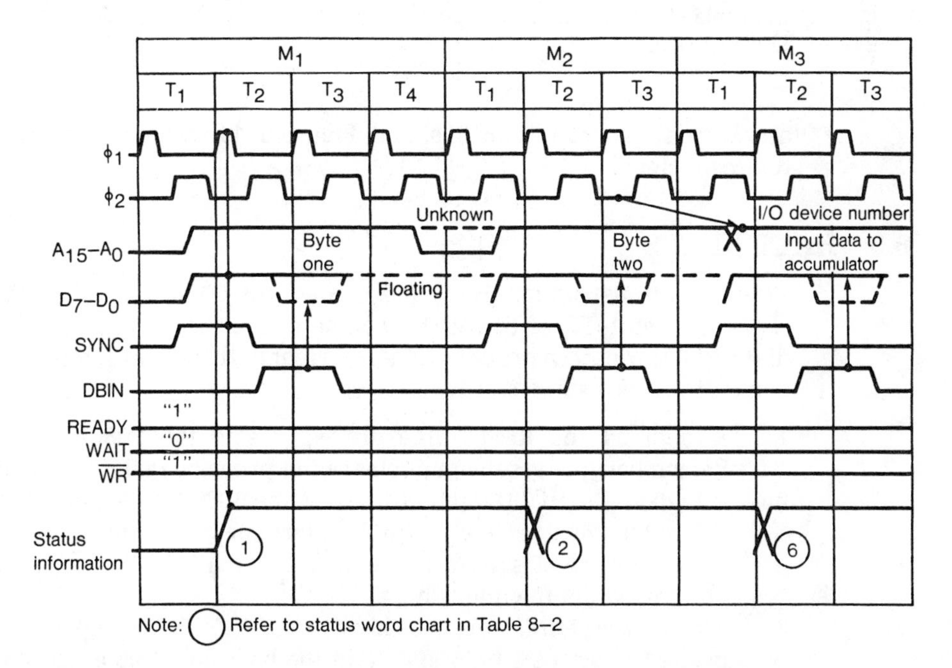

FIGURE 8–9 Timing Diagram for 8080A μP Input Instruction Cycle (Redrawn from data sheet for 8080A microprocessor with permission. Intel Corporation, Santa Clara, CA)

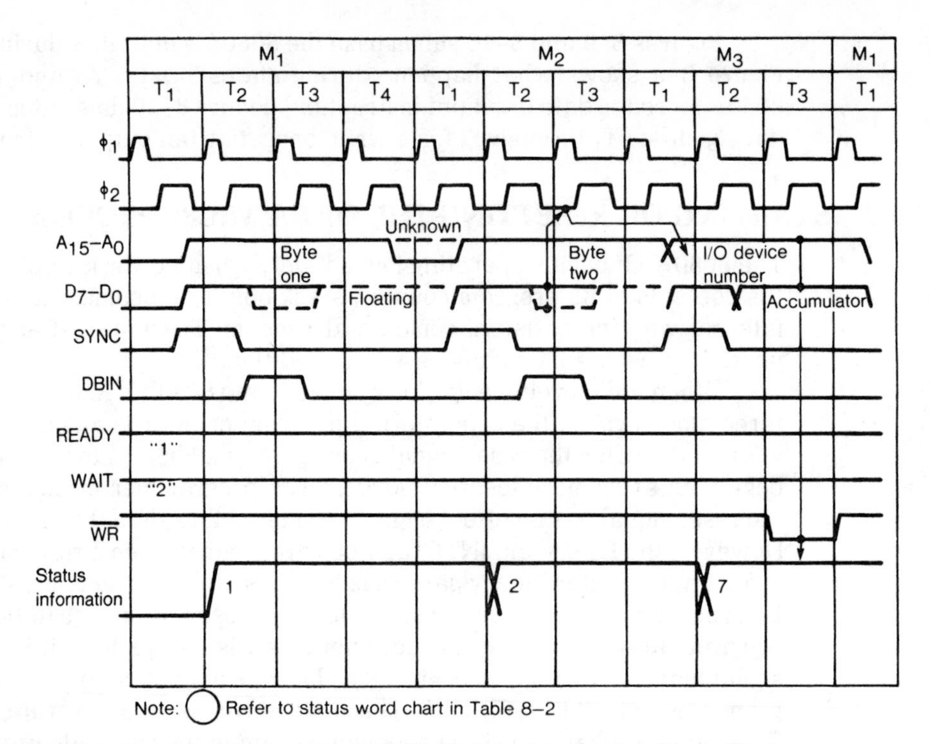

FIGURE 8–10 Timing Diagram for 8080A μP Output Instruction Cycle (Redrawn from data sheet for 8080A microprocessor with permission. Intel Corporation, Santa Clara, CA)

an external interrupt request signal. Figure 8–11 shows the timing diagram for the reset signal.

8.8 HALT STATE

When a halt instruction (HLT) is executed, the 8080A μP enters the halt state (T_{WH}) after state T_2 of the next machine cycle. Figure 8–12 shows the timing diagram for a halt instruction. There are only three ways in which the 8080A can exit the halt state:

1. A high on the RESET line always resets the 8080A μP to state T_1. Remember, the reset signal clears the program counter to logic 0.
2. A high on the HOLD input pin causes the 8080A μP to enter the hold state. When the line goes low, the μP reenters the halt state on the rising edge of the next ϕ_1 clock signal. Therefore, the μP leaves the halt state only temporarily while the line is high.
3. The interrupt (INT) line goes high, and the INTE flip-flop is enabled. These events cause the 8080A μP to exit the halt state and enter state T_1 on the rising edge of the next ϕ_1 clock pulse. *Note:* The interrupt enable (INTE)

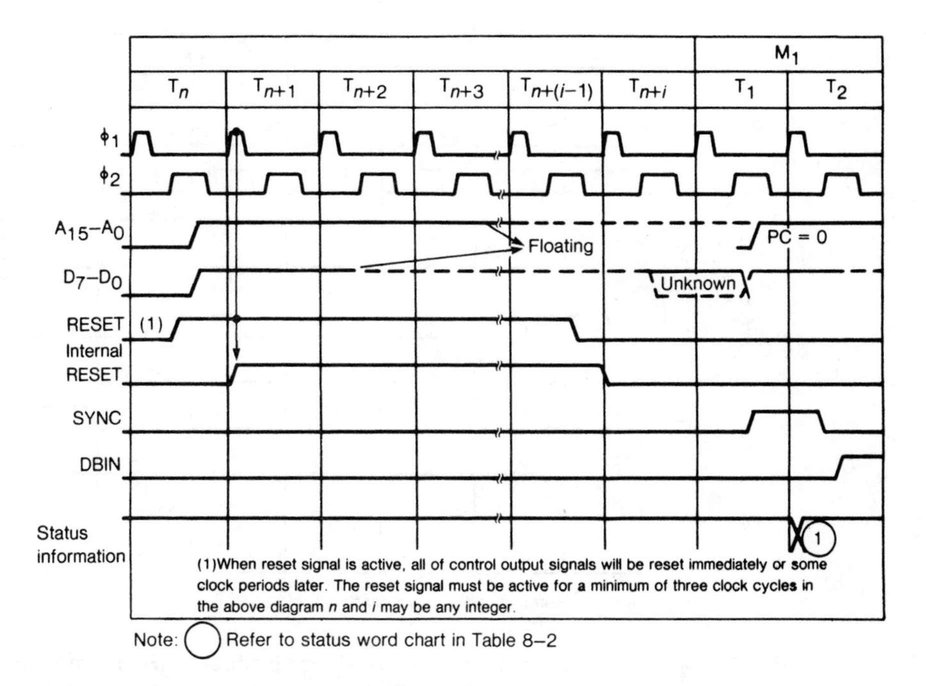

FIGURE 8–11 Timing Diagram for 8080A μP Reset Signal (Redrawn from data sheet for 8080A microprocessor with permission. Intel Corporation, Santa Clara, CA)

flag must be set when the halt state is entered; otherwise, the 8080A can only exit the halt state by a reset signal.

The flowchart of Figure 8–13 illustrates the halt sequence.

8.9 HOLD STATE

The 8080A μP contains circuitry that allows it to suspend its normal operations and relinquish control of the address and data buses. This circuitry is useful in applications such as direct memory access (DMA) operations or in computer systems that use two or more μPs connected to the same buses. An external device can cause the 8080A μP to suspend its normal operations by applying a high logic level to the HOLD pin. The μP responds by floating its buffers and placing a high logic level on its HLDA (hold acknowledge) pin. During the hold operation, the address and data buses are under the control of the external device that originated the request.

The hold input signal is synchronized internally. It must be stable prior to a hold setup time (t_{HS} = 140 ns minimum) that precedes the rising edge of a ϕ_2 clock pulse.

Figures 8–14 and 8–15 are timing diagrams for the hold operations. The hold request waveform is the signal from the external device. The hold waveform is the signal received internally by the μP and is synchronized with the

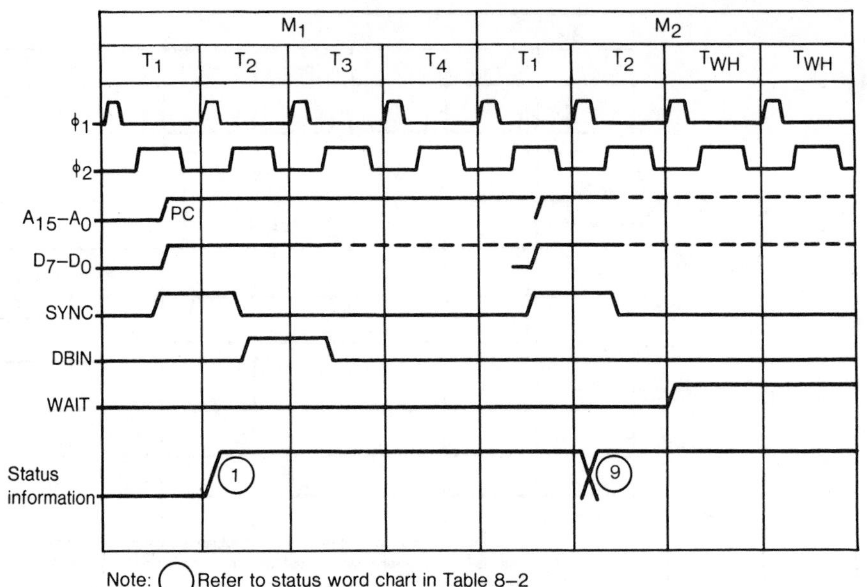

FIGURE 8–12 Timing Diagram for 8080A μP Halt Instruction (Redrawn from data sheet for 8080A microprocessor with permission. Intel Corporation, Santa Clara, CA)

clock pulse. Figure 8–14 shows that the ready line, the hold line, and the ϕ_2 clock pulse set the μP's internal hold flip-flop. This internal flip-flop and the next ϕ_1 clock pulse cause the HLDA line to go high.

The hold acknowledgement slightly precedes the μP's floating of the address and data lines. The μP acknowledges a hold at the beginning of T_3 if a read or an input machine cycle is in progress (see Figure 8–14). Otherwise, acknowledgement is deferred until the beginning of the state following T_3 (see Figure 8–15). In both cases, however, the hold acknowledge line goes high within a specified time delay (t_{DC} = 120 ns maximum) of the rising edge of the ϕ_1 clock pulse. Address and data lines are floated within a brief delay (less than 100 ns) after the rising edge of the next ϕ_2 clock pulse.

To all outward appearances, the μP has suspended its operations once the address and data buses are floated. Internally, however, the μP may continue certain functions. For example, if a machine cycle required five states and the hold request is acknowledged at state T_3, the μP will complete states T_4 and T_5 before ceasing its internal activities. This overlapping of internal μP functions with external operations improves efficiency and speed of the entire computer system.

For the 8080A μP to exit a hold state, the hold request must be removed—that is, the logic level on the hold line must go low. The hold acknowledge will go low following the next ϕ_1 clock pulse. The μP resumes with the machine cycle following the last machine cycle that was executed.

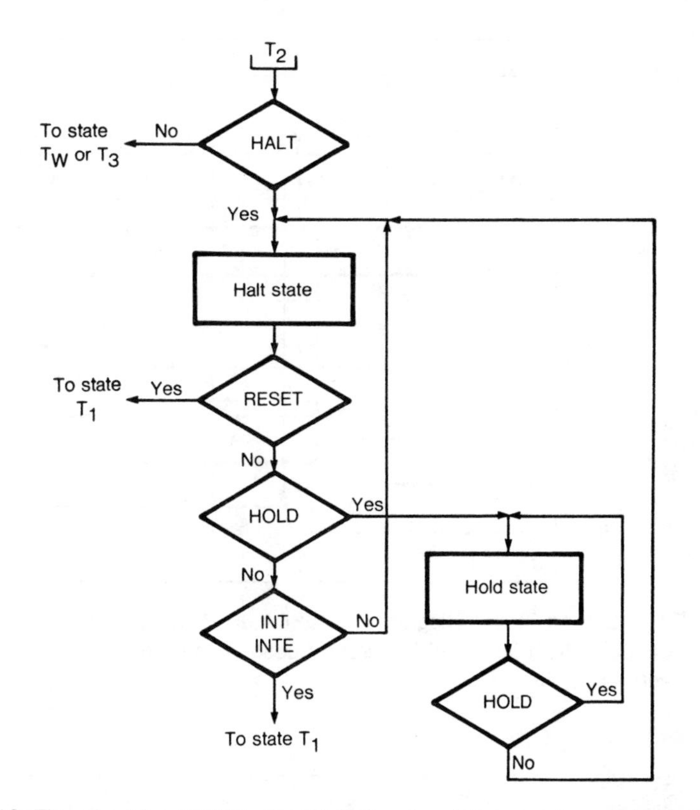

FIGURE 8-13 Flowchart for 8080A μP Halt Instruction (Redrawn from data sheet for 8080A microprocessor with permission. Intel Corporation, Santa Clara, CA)

8.10 INTERRUPT SEQUENCE

The 8080A μP has the ability to handle external interrupt requests. A peripheral device can initiate an interrupt simply by driving the μP's interrupt (INT) line high.

The interrupt (INT) input is asynchronous, which means that the interrupt request may originate at any time during the instruction cycle. The μP's internal logic reclocks the external request so that it will correspond with a clock pulse. For the 8080A to acknowledge an interrupt request signal, its internal interrupt enable (INTE) flip-flop must be in the logic 1 state. The timing diagram in Figure 8-16 shows an interrupt request (INT) arriving when the interrupt enable line (INTE) is high. These two signals act with the ϕ_2 clock pulse to set the internal interrupt latch. This event takes place during the last state of the instruction cycle in which the request occurs so that the instruction in progress is completed before the interrupt can be processed. The μP now begins to acknowledge the interrupt request.

The first machine cycle is called the interrupt machine cycle and resembles an ordinary fetch machine cycle in many respects. Figure 8-16

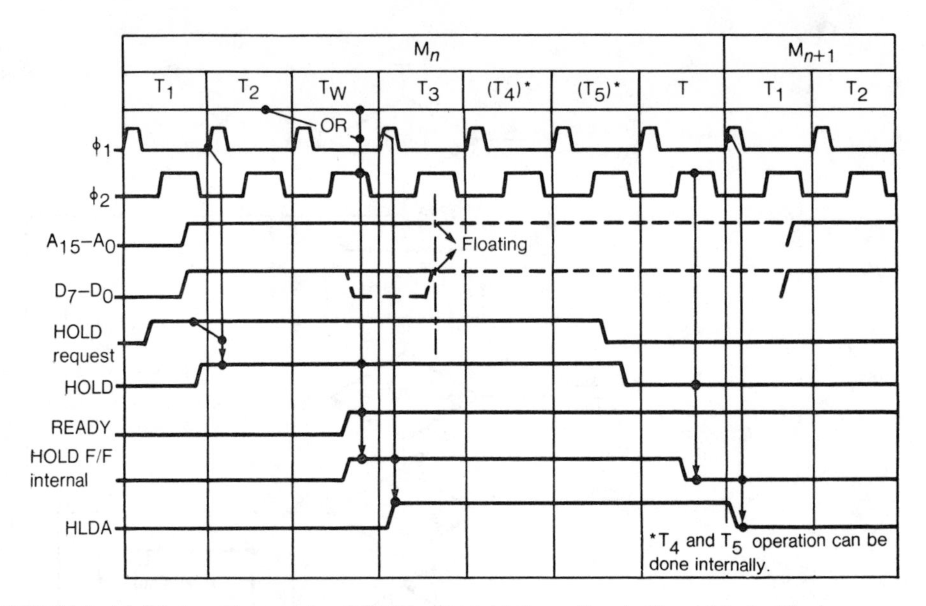

FIGURE 8–14 Timing Diagram for 8080A μP Hold Operation in Read Mode (Redrawn from data sheet for 8080A microprocessor with permission. Intel Corporation, Santa Clara, CA)

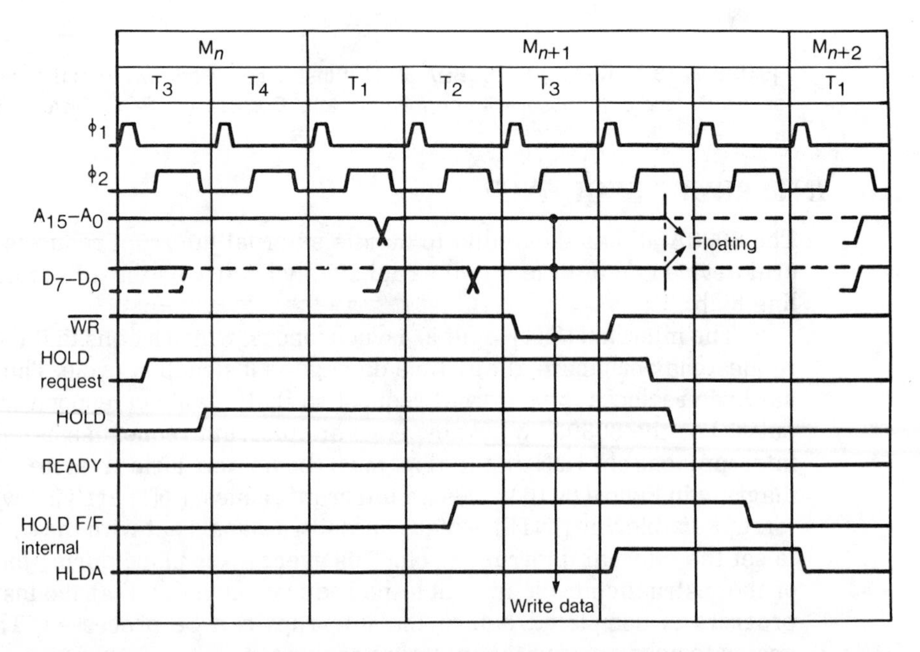

FIGURE 8–15 Timing Diagram for 8080A μP Hold Operation in Write Mode (Redrawn from data sheet for 8080A microprocessor with permission. Intel Corporation, Santa Clara, CA)

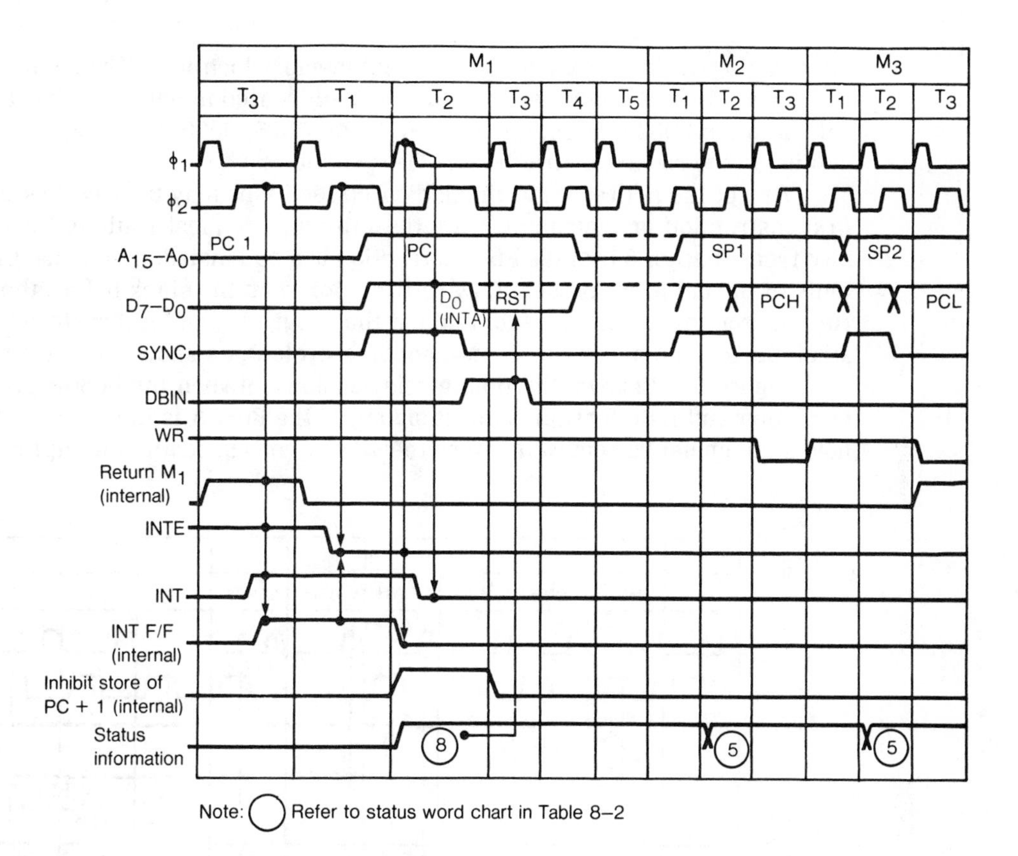

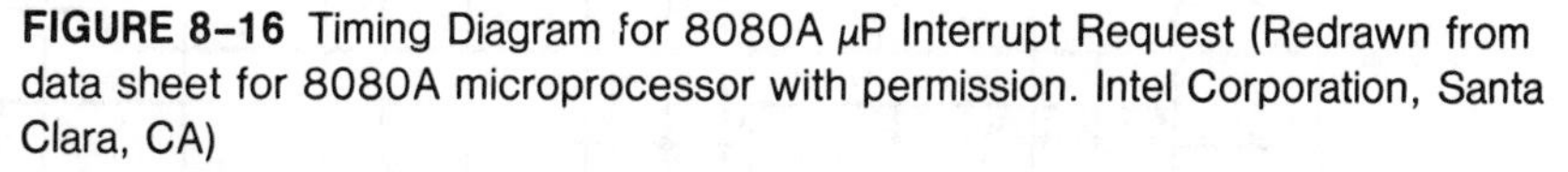

FIGURE 8–16 Timing Diagram for 8080A μP Interrupt Request (Redrawn from data sheet for 8080A microprocessor with permission. Intel Corporation, Santa Clara, CA)

shows the logic states of the individual status bits for a fetch and an interrupt acknowledge machine cycle. As in any fetch cycle, the contents of the program counter are latched onto the μP's address bus line during T_1, but the counter itself is not incremented during an interrupt machine cycle as it otherwise would be. The reason the counter is not incremented is that the present contents of the program counter will be stored on the stack so that the μP will be able to return to the main program after the interrupt request has been processed. The interrupt subroutine begins at the memory location established by the peripheral circuitry. It is the responsibility of the peripheral logic to "jam" an 8-bit interrupt instruction address onto the processor's data bus during state T_3. The "jamming" process requires that the data bus from memory be temporarily disconnected from the μP's data bus so that the peripheral logic can use the memory data bus without interference.

Remember from Chapter 6 that the 8080A's instruction set provides a special one-byte instruction that is used for calling interrupt subroutines, the restart instruction (RST). Three bits embedded in the 8-bit data word allow the interrupting device to call one of the eight memory locations. The hexadecimal addresses of these dedicated locations are all located in page 00. They are (all values in hex) 0000, 0008, 0010, 0018, 0020, 0028, 0030, and 0038. For more details on the restart instruction, review Section 6.8.

Any of the addresses of the dedicated locations may be used to store the first instruction or instructions for the interrupt request routine. Remember also from Chapter 6 that the RST instruction is a call instruction. Thus, the contents of the old program counter are first stored on the stack before the interrupt subroutine begins. The contents of the program counter are stored on the stack during machine cycle 2 and machine cycle 3, as shown in Figure 8–16.

Figure 8–17 shows the timing relationship between the 8080A μP's hold operation and its interrupt request signal. If the 8080A is in a hold state, the hold signal must be removed before the μP will recognize an interrupt request.

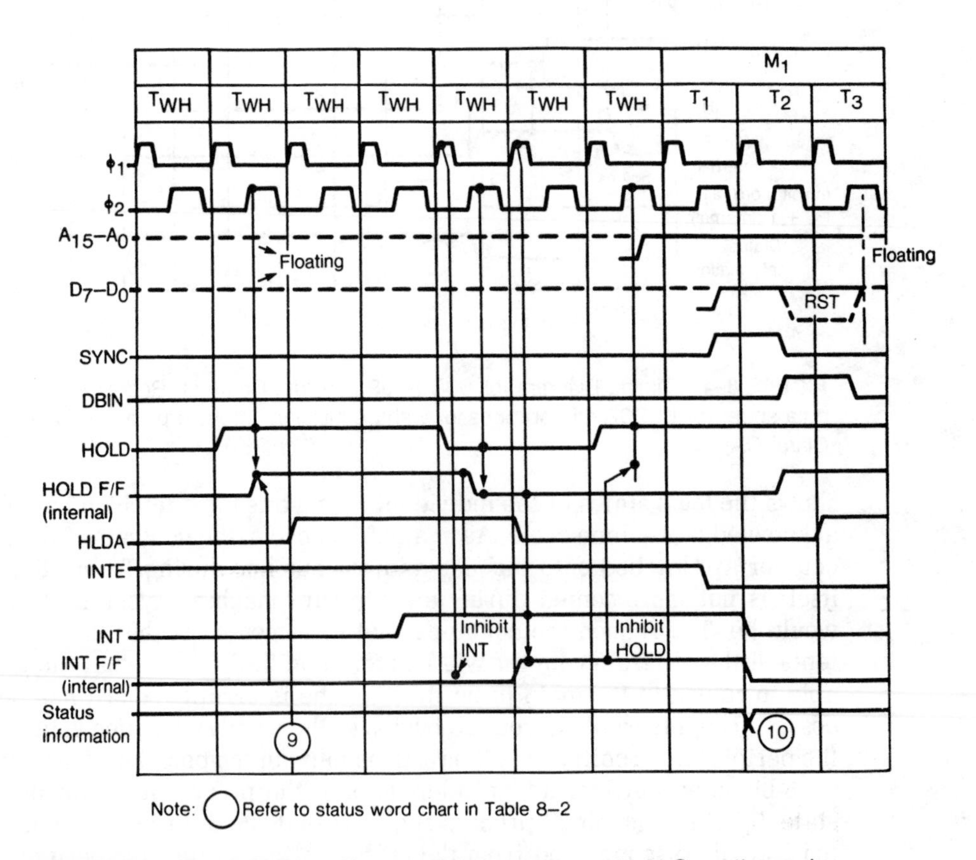

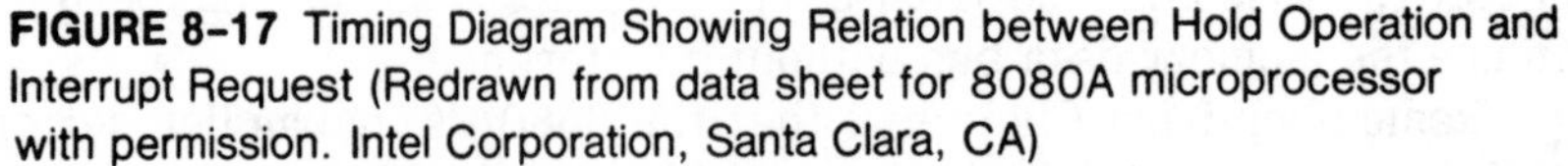

FIGURE 8–17 Timing Diagram Showing Relation between Hold Operation and Interrupt Request (Redrawn from data sheet for 8080A microprocessor with permission. Intel Corporation, Santa Clara, CA)

8.11 SUMMARY

Microprocessors have two aspects: software and hardware. Chapters 6 and 7 dealt with the 8080A's software; this chapter introduced its hardware and two support chips, the 8224 and 8228. Since the 8080A is a synchronous, sequential digital circuit, we must understand its clock signals and timing diagrams if we wish to be able to interconnect it with memory and I/O chips. This chapter covered the 8080A pin descriptions, timing cycles, machine cycles, reset condition, and the difference between its halt state and hold state. This chapter also covered the 8080A's interrupt sequence. A summary of the machine cycles of the 8080A is given in Appendix Table D-2.

PROBLEMS

All the following problems apply to the 8080A μP.

8-1 What are the two basic support chips that are needed by the 8080A μP?
8-2 What are the 8080A μP's power requirements?
8-3 Does the 8080A require two nonoverlapping clock signals?
8-4 When the RESET pin goes high, what data is forced into the program counter?
8-5 If the 8080A μP is doing a direct memory access operation, what pin must be high?
8-6 Does a high or low pulse on pin 14 signal an interrupt request?
8-7 What pin puts the 8080A μP in a wait state?
8-8 Which pin is the interrupt acknowledge pin?
8-9 When the $\overline{WR}$ pin is at a logic 1, is the μP receiving or sending data?
8-10 What pin is used as an acknowledgement that the μP is in a wait state?
8-11 What is the smallest unit of time in the 8080A's processing activity called?
8-12 Instruction cycles are made up of how many machine cycles?
8-13 Define state.
8-14 What is the cycle time used in many 8080A μP applications?
8-15 In all but one case, what determines the number of machine cycles?
8-16 Refer to Problem 8-15. What is the exception?
8-17 What is the first machine cycle in any instruction cycle?
8-18 How many types of machine cycles are there in the 8080A μP? What are they?
8-19 During what state does the μP put out status information?
8-20 How many bits are there in the status information?
8-21 What can the status information be used for?
8-22 Does the 8228 system controller output all of the status bits? If your answer is no, what chip is required?
8-23 The following binary patterns are status information. Give the type of machine cycle for each: (a) 10000010, (b) 00000100, (c) 01000010, and (d) 00100011.
8-24 How many states are there in a machine cycle?
8-25 What are the three exceptions to Problem 8-24?
8-26 What are the three ways to exit a halt state?
8-27 When an interrupt request signal is received by the 8080A μP, what must the peripheral circuitry accomplish?

6800 Microprocessor Instruction Set

9.0 INTRODUCTION

This chapter and Chapters 10 and 11 deal specifically with the 6800 μP. This chapter covers its instructions and addressing modes and provides examples that show the flexibility of the instruction set. Chapter 10 employs most of the instructions in a number of commonly used programs. Chapter 11 introduces the hardware aspects of the 6800 μP, such as pin designations, pin functions, and timing diagrams. Thus, Chapters 9 and 10 deal with the 6800 μP's software, while Chapter 11 deals with its hardware. Later chapters show how the 6800 can be connected to memory and peripheral devices.

The 6800 μP has 72 basic instructions. When these instructions are combined with the different addressing modes, the result is a total of 197 different op codes. These op codes comprise the entire instruction set for the 6800 μP. This instruction set gives a programmer enough flexibility to write any program for a dedicated control or a general-purpose μC application.

Chapter 5 introduced basic μP architecture and the options contained within the 6800 μP. Sections 9.1 and 9.2 of this chapter review the function of the 6800's registers and describe how its condition code register works. These sections can help us visualize what happens within the μP when an instruction is fetched and executed. Since most instructions affect a bit or bits within the condition code register, knowing how the bits are affected will help us understand what the μP will do after it checks one or more of these bits.

Figure 9-1 shows the pin assignments for the 6800 μP. The function of each pin is covered in detail in Chapter 11, so this figure may be used simply for reference in this and the next chapter.

Pin	Signal	Signal	Pin
1	V_{SS}	$\overline{Reset}$	40
2	$\overline{Halt}$	TSC	39
3	ϕ_1	NC	38
4	$\overline{IRQ}$	ϕ_2	37
5	VMA	DBE	36
6	$\overline{NMI}$	NC	35
7	BA	R/W	34
8	V_{CC}	D_0	33
9	A_0	D_1	32
10	A_1	D_2	31
11	A_2	D_3	30
12	A_3	D_4	29
13	A_4	D_5	28
14	A_5	D_6	27
15	A_6	D_7	26
16	A_7	A_{15}	25
17	A_8	A_{14}	24
18	A_9	A_{13}	23
19	A_{10}	A_{12}	22
20	A_{11}	V_{SS}	21

FIGURE 9–1 Pin Assignments for the 6800 μP (Redrawn from data sheet for MC6800 microprocessor with permission. Motorola Incorporated, Phoenix, AZ)

9.1 6800 INTERNAL ARCHITECTURE

Figure 9–2 is a functional block diagram that shows the internal architecture of a 6800 μP. The 6800 contains the basic blocks such as the arithmetic and logic unit, instruction register, decoding circuitry, timing and control section, address buffers, data buffers, and internal data bus. A major difference between the 6800 and most other μPs is that the 6800 has two accumulators—accumulator A and accumulator B. Both can store the results of arithmetic and logic operations. As we examine the 6800's instruction set, we will see that there are a few functions that can be done only by accumulator A. The 6800 μP has a 16-bit program counter and a 16-bit stack pointer. Since the stack pointer is 16 bits wide, the stack can be located anywhere in read/write memory. There is also a 16-bit index register. The index register is added to an instruction's operand address to calculate the final address where the μP will find the data. The 6800 μP also contains a condition code register, which we will examine in the next section.

9.2 CONDITION CODE REGISTER

The condition code register (CCR) for the 6800 μP is also called the *program status byte*. The 6800 μP uses 6 bits of the condition code register, as shown in Figure 9–3. Bits 6 and 7 are always set to a logic 1. The carry, overflow, and interrupt flag bits can be set or cleared directly by an instruction as well as by the result of an instruction. The zero, negative, and half-carry flag bits are set

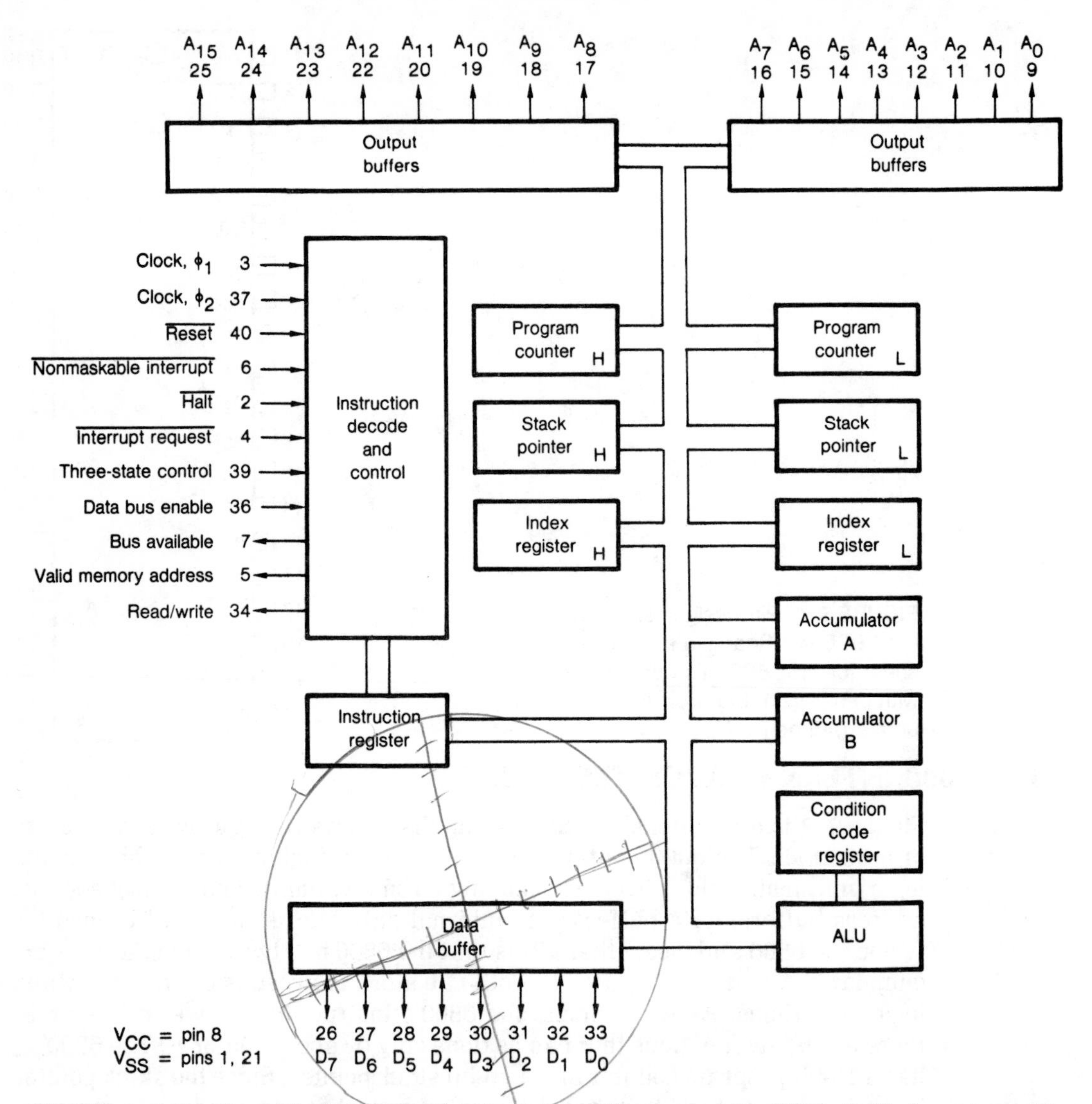

FIGURE 9–2 Functional Block Diagram Showing Internal Structure of the 6800 μP (Redrawn from data sheet for MC6800 microprocessor with permission. Motorola Incorporated, Phoenix, AZ)

or cleared only by the result of an instruction. Unless indicated otherwise, the results of instructions affect the flag bits in the following ways.

Carry Flag (C Flag): The carry flag bit is set to a logic 1 if there is a carry out of the most significant bit (bit 7) of the result; otherwise, C = 0.

Overflow Flag (V Flag): The overflow flag is set to a logic 1 if the result exceeds +127 or −128; otherwise, V = 0.

Zero Flag (Z Flag): The zero flag is set to a logic 1 when the result is 0 (that is, each bit of the register or memory location is 0); otherwise, Z = 0. Thus, if the result is 0, then Z = 1.

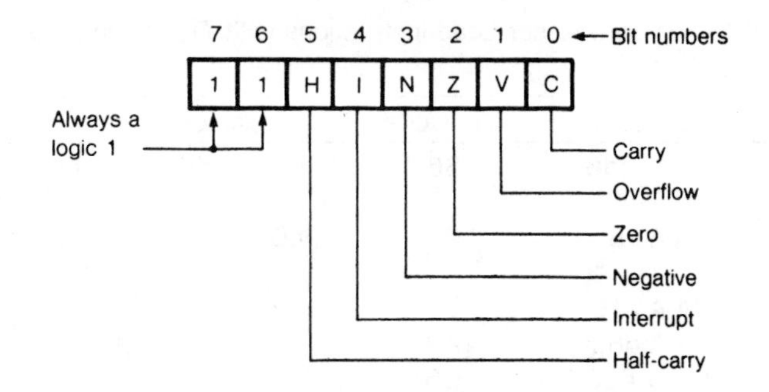

FIGURE 9–3 Condition Code Register for the 6800 μP

Negative Flag (N Flag): If the most significant bit of the result is a logic 1, then N = 1; otherwise, N = 0. The most significant bit of an 8-bit register or memory location is bit 7. The most significant bit of a 16-bit register is bit 15.

Interrupt Flag (I Flag): The interrupt flag bit enables or disables the interrupt line (pin 4). This flag can be set to a logic 1 either by an external interrupt request signal or by an instruction that will be discussed in Section 9.10. This flag is cleared by a return from interrupt instruction or by a clear interrupt instruction (both of these instructions are covered in later sections).

Half-Carry Flag (H Flag): The half-carry flag is set to a logic 1 if there is a carry from bit 3 to bit 4 of the result; otherwise, H = 0. This flag bit is only affected by three add instructions—ABA, ADD, and ADC.

9.3 DATA MOVEMENT INSTRUCTIONS

The 6800 has three groups of instructions that move data from one location to another. They are load instructions, store instructions, and transfer instructions. The load instructions move data from a memory location to a μP register. The store instructions move data from a μP register to a memory location. The transfer instructions move data from one μP register to another.

9.3.1 Load Instructions

The 6800 μP has three load instructions. In this section, we will consider two of these instructions; the third load instruction is used for the stack pointer and is covered in Section 9.9. The instructions that apply to the accumulator and the index register are as follows:

LDA	Load accumulator
LDX	Load index register

Table 9–1 is a listing of the 6800's load instructions. Since the 6800 has two accumulators (accumulator A and accumulator B), load instructions for both accumulators are listed in Table 9–1 along with their different addressing modes and op codes. The table also shows several examples of specific instructions.

TABLE 9-1 6800 Microprocessor Load Instructions with Addressing Modes, Op Codes, and Examples

Mode	Instruction	Op Code	Example	Explanation
Immediate	LDA A #d8	86	LDA A #07	Load accumulator A immediately with 07 hex
Direct	LDA A a8	96	LDA A 07	Load accumulator A with data at memory location 0007.
Extended	LDA A a16	B6		
Indexed	LDA A d8,X	A6		
Immediate	LDA B #d8	C6		
Direct	LDA B a8	D6		
Extended	LDA B a16	F6	LDA B 80CD	Load accumulator B with data at memory location 80CD.
Indexed	LDA B d8,X	E6	LDA B 58,X	Load accumulator B with data at memory location given by X register + 58_{hex}.
Immediate	LDX #d16	CE	LDX #1024	Load 1024 into X register, 10_{hex} into X_H and 24_{hex} into X_L.
Direct	LDX a8	DE		
Extended	LDX a16	FE		
Indexed	LDX d8,X	EE		

Load instructions affect the zero flag and the negative flag, as described in Section 9.2. The overflow is always cleared to a logic 0. A brief discussion of each load instruction follows.

LDA **Load Accumulator**

The LDA instruction moves the contents of a memory location into either accumulator A or accumulator B. The contents of the memory location are not changed because it is the source location.

LDX **Load Index Register**

The index register in the 6800 is 16 bits wide. Therefore, two bytes of data have to be loaded into the index register. The LDX instruction moves data from two consecutive memory locations to the index register. The first byte of data comes from the memory location specified by the instruction and is loaded into the index register's most significant bits, X_H (bits 8–15). The second byte of data comes from the memory location following that of the first byte and is stored in the index register's least significant bits, X_L (bits 0–7).

9.3.2 Store Instructions

The 6800 μP has three store instructions. Two of them are covered in this section; the store instruction that applies to the stack pointer is covered in Section 9.9. The instructions covered in this section are as follows:

TABLE 9–2 6800 Microprocessor Store Instructions with Addressing Modes, Op Codes, and Examples

Mode	Instruction	Op Code	Example	Explanation
Direct	STA A a8	97	STA A 3A	Store accumulator A at memory location 003A.
Extended	STA A a16	B7		
Indexed	STA A d8,X	A7	STA A 55,X	Store accumulator A at memory location given by X register + 55_{hex}.
Direct	STA B a8	D7		
Extended	STA B a16	F7	STA B 42DC	Store accumulator B at memory location 42DC.
Indexed	STA B d8,X	E7		
Direct	STX a8	DF		
Extended	STX a16	FF	STX AC45	Store X_H at location AC45; store X_L at location AC46.
Indexed	STX d8,X	EF		

STA Store accumulator
STX Store index register

Table 9–2 provides a listing of the 6800's store instructions with their addressing modes and op codes. Examples of specific instructions are also given in the table. The STA instruction includes store instructions for both accumulator A and accumulator B. Store instructions affect the zero flag and the negative flag, as described in Section 9.2. The overflow flag is always cleared to a logic 0. A brief description of each store instruction follows.

STA Store Accumulator

The STA instruction stores the contents of an accumulator in a memory location. In this instruction, the accumulator is the source and the memory location is the destination.

STX Store Index Register

The STX instruction stores the index register in two consecutive memory locations. The high-order byte, X_H (bits 8–15), is stored in the memory location specified by the instruction. The low-order byte, X_L (bits 0–7), is stored in the next memory location.

9.3.3 Transfer Instructions

There are six transfer instructions associated with the 6800 μP. Two of these instructions are used for the stack pointer and are covered in Section 9.9, along with the other stack instructions. The remaining four transfer instructions covered in this section are as follows:

TAB	Transfer accumulator A to accumulator B
TBA	Transfer accumulator B to accumulator A
TAP	Transfer accumulator A to condition code register
TPA	Transfer condition code register to accumulator A

Table 9-3 shows these instructions with their op codes. In literature from Motorola, the condition code register is used on block diagrams to indicate the flag register within the μP, but the condition code register is also referred to as the program status byte—hence, the letter P in the mnemonics TAP and TPA.

The four instructions are single bytes and use the inherent addressing mode. The instructions TAB and TBA affect the zero flag and the negative flag, as described in Section 9.2. The overflow flag is always cleared. A brief discussion of all four instructions follows.

TAB Transfer Accumulator A to Accumulator B

The TAB instruction transfers the contents of accumulator A to accumulator B. In this instruction, accumulator A is the source register and accumulator B is the destination register. Therefore, the contents of accumulator A are not changed, but the previous contents of accumulator B are lost.

TBA Transfer Accumulator B to Accumulator A

The TBA instruction transfers the contents of accumulator B to accumulator A. In this instruction, accumulator B is the source register and accumulator A is the destination register. Therefore, the contents of accumulator B are not changed, but the previous contents of accumulator A are lost.

TAP Transfer Accumulator A to Condition Code Register

The TAP instruction transfers the first 6 bits (bits 0–5) of accumulator A to the first 6 bits (bits 0–5) of the condition code register. When this transfer is executed, bits 6 and 7 of the condition code register are automatically set to a logic 1. This instruction either clears or sets the flag bits according to the data that is being transferred from accumulator A.

TPA Transfer Condition Code Register to Accumulator A

The TPA instruction transfers the contents of the condition code register to accumulator A. Unlike the TAP instruction, this instruction transfers 8 bits of data from the condition code register to accumulator A. The first 6 bits (bits 0–5) are the flag bits. Bit 6 and bit 7 are each a logic 1.

TABLE 9-3 6800 Microprocessor Transfer Instructions with Their Op Codes

Instruction	Op Code
TAB	16
TBA	17
TAP	06
TPA	07

9.4 ARITHMETIC INSTRUCTIONS

The 6800 μP has four groups of instructions that we will classify as arithmetic instructions. They are add instructions, subtract instructions, increment instructions, and decrement instructions.

The 6800 μP has three add instructions and three subtract instructions. Like the 8080A μP, the 6800 μP can add two 8-bit numbers with or without the carry flag. The two accumulators of the 6800 μP can be added or subtracted.

The increment and decrement instructions add 1 or subtract 1 from a register or memory location. There are three increment and three decrement instructions associated with the 6800 μP. Two of these instructions apply to the stack pointer and will be discussed in Section 9.9.

The 6800 μP can perform addition in either straight binary or in binary coded decimal. To perform a BCD arithmetic operation requires a special instruction following the add instruction. This special instruction, which allows two decimal numbers to be added and the result to be given as a decimal number, is called a *decimal adjust instruction* and is covered in Section 9.10.

9.4.1 Add Instructions

The 6800 μP has three add instructions:

ABA	Add accumulator A to accumulator B
ADD	Add without carry
ADC	Add with carry

Table 9-4 lists the 6800's add instructions with their addressing modes and op codes. Some specific examples of the ADD instruction and the ADC instruction are also listed in the table.

Each of the add instructions adds two 8-bit numbers in the arithmetic and logic unit (ALU) and stores the result in an accumulator. The flag bits that are affected are the carry, zero, negative, overflow, and half-carry, as described in Section 9.2. A brief description of the ABA, ADD, and ADC instructions follows.

ABA Add Accumulator B to Accumulator A

The ABA instruction adds the contents of accumulator B to the contents of accumulator A. The result is placed in accumulator A. The contents of accumulator B are not changed. This instruction does not include the carry flag in the addition. However, the carry flag may be affected by the result of the addition.

ADD Add without Carry

The ADD instruction adds the contents of an accumulator (either accumulator A or accumulator B) to the contents of a memory location. If accumulator A is used, the result goes into accumulator A. If accumulator B is used, the result goes into accumulator B. As its name implies, this instruction does not include the carry flag in the addition. The result of the addition, however, may affect the carry flag.

TABLE 9–4 6800 Microprocessor Add Instructions with Addressing Modes, Op Codes, and Examples

Mode	Instruction	Op Code	Example	Explanation
Implied	ABA	1B		
Immediate	ADD A #d8	8B	ADD A #50	Add accumulator A + 50_{hex} (result is placed in accumulator A).
Direct	ADD A a8	9B		
Extended	ADD A a16	BB		
Indexed	ADD A d8,X	AB		
Immediate	ADD B #d8	CB		
Direct	ADD B a8	DB		
Extended	ADD B a16	FB	ADD B 0375	Add accumulator B + data at location 0375 (result is placed in accumulator B).
Indexed	ADD B d8,X	EB	ADD B 48,X	Add accumulator B + data at location given by X register + 48_{hex} (result is placed in accumulator B).
Immediate	ADC A #d8	89	ADC A #32	Add accumulator A + C flag + 32_{hex} (result is placed in accumulator A).
Direct	ADC A a8	99	ADC A 10	Add accumulator A + C flag + data at location 0010 (result is placed in accumulator A).
Extended	ADC A a16	B9	ADC A D400	Add accumulator A + C flag + data at location D400 (result is placed in accumulator A).
Indexed	ADC A d8,X	A9		
Immediate	ADC B #d8	C9		
Direct	ADC B a8	D9		
Extended	ADC B a16	F9		
Indexed	ADC B d8,X	E9		

ADC **Add with Carry**

The ADC instruction adds the contents of an accumulator (accumulator A or accumulator B) and the contents of a memory location with the carry flag. If the addition uses accumulator A, the result is placed in accumulator A. If the addition uses accumulator B, the result is placed in accumulator B. This instruction is used when a program requires multiprecision addition. Such a program will be presented in the next chapter.

9.4.2 Subtract Instructions

There are three subtract instructions associated with the 6800 μP. They are as follows:

TABLE 9–5 6800 Microprocessor Subtract Instructions with Addressing Modes, Op Codes, and Examples

Mode	Instruction	Op Code	Example	Explanation
Implied	SBA	10		
Immediate	SUB A #d8	80		
Direct	SUB A a8	90		
Extended	SUB A a16	B0		
Indexed	SUB A d8,X	A0		
Immediate	SUB B #d8	C0	SUB B #0D	Subtract accumulator B − $0D_{hex}$ (result is placed in accumulator B).
Direct	SUB B a8	D0		
Extended	SUB B a16	F0	SUB B 2E30	Subtract accumulator B − data at location 2E30 (result is placed in accumulator B).
Indexed	SUB B d8,X	E0		
Immediate	SBC A #d8	82	SBC A #45	Subtract accumulator A − C flag − 45_{hex} (result is placed in accumulator A).
Direct	SBC A a8	92	SBC A 2D	Subtract accumulator A − C flag − data at location 002D (result is placed in accumulator A).
Extended	SBC A a16	B2		
Indexed	SBC A d8,X	A2		
Immediate	SBC B #d8	C2		
Direct	SBC B a8	D2		
Extended	SBC B a16	F2	SBC B 2C80	Subtract accumulator B − C flag − data at location 2C80 (result is placed in accumulator B).
Indexed	SBC B d8,X	E2		

SBA Subtract accumulator B from accumulator A
SUB Subtract
SBC Subtract with carry

Table 9–5 shows the 6800's subtract instructions with their addressing modes and op codes. Examples of the SUB and SBC instructions are also shown.

Each of the subtract instructions subtracts two 8-bit numbers in the arithmetic and logic unit (ALU). Subtraction is performed using 2's complement arithmetic. The flag bits that are affected are the carry, zero, negative, and overflow. The following discussion provides explanation of how the carry flag is affected for each instruction. The other flag bits are affected as described in Section 9.2.

SBA **Subtract Accumulator B from Accumulator A**

The SBA instruction subtracts the contents of accumulator B from accumulator A. The result is placed in accumulator A. This instruction does not involve the carry bit in the process of subtraction. However, the carry bit is affected by the result of the subtraction. The contents of accumulator B are not changed.

The carry bit is affected in the following way: C = 1 if the contents of accumulator B are greater than or equal to the contents of accumulator A; C = 0 if the contents of accumulator A are greater than the contents of accumulator B.

SUB **Subtract**

The SUB instruction subtracts the contents of a memory location from an accumulator (either accumulator A or accumulator B). If accumulator A is used, the result is placed in accumulator A. If accumulator B is used, the result is placed in accumulator B. The carry bit is not included in the subtraction operation, but the result may affect the carry bit in the following way: C = 1 if the contents of the memory location are greater than or equal to the contents of the accumulator; C = 0 if the contents of the accumulator are greater than the contents of the memory location.

SBC **Subtract with Carry**

The SBC instruction subtracts the contents of a memory location and the carry bit from an accumulator (either accumulator A or accumulator B). If the subtraction involves accumulator A, the result is placed in accumulator A. If the subtraction involves accumulator B, the result is placed in accumulator B. The result of the subtraction operation affects the carry bit in the following way: C = 1 if the contents of the memory location plus the carry bit are greater than or equal to the contents of the accumulator; C = 0 if the contents of the accumulator are greater than the contents of the memory location plus the carry bit.

9.4.3 Increment Instructions

The 6800 μP has three increment instructions. One instruction involves the stack pointer and is included with the stack pointer instructions in Section 9.9. The other two instructions are as follows:

INC Increment
INX Increment index register

Table 9-6 is a listing of the 6800 μP increment instructions INC and INX. Addressing modes, op codes, and examples are also provided in the table. The INC instruction applies to either accumulator or to a memory location. The contents of a memory location are incremented by a read/modify/write operation, as described in Section 5.3.2.

TABLE 9–6 6800 Microprocessor Increment Instructions with Addressing Modes, Op Codes, and Examples

Mode	Instruction	Op Code	Example	Explanation
Implied	INC A	4C		
Implied	INC B	5C	INC B	Add 1 to contents of accumulator B.
Extended	INC a16	7C	INC 507D	Add 1 to contents of memory location 507D.
Indexed	INC d8,X	6C		
Implied	INX	08		

These increment instructions produce a "roll-over" effect. That is, if a register is all 1s and it is incremented, the result is all 0s and the carry flag is not set. A brief discussion of each increment instruction follows.

INC **Increment**

The INC instruction adds 1 to the contents of either accumulator A or accumulator B or to the contents of a memory location. The INC instructions affect the N, Z, and V flags, as explained in Section 9.2.

INX **Increment Index Register**

The INX instruction adds 1 to the contents of the index register. The only flag bit affected is the zero flag: Z = 1 if all 16 bits of the index register are cleared to the logic 0 state; otherwise, Z = 0.

9.4.4 Decrement Instructions

The 6800 μP has three decrement instructions. One instruction involves the stack pointer and is covered in Section 9.9. The instructions covered in this section are the following:

DEC Decrement
DEX Decrement index register

Table 9–7 is a listing of the 6800's decrement instructions DEC and DEX. Addressing modes, op codes, and examples are also provided in the table. The DEC instruction applies to either accumulator or to a memory location. Like the increment instruction, the decrement instruction produces a roll-over effect. That is, a register that contains all 0s and is decremented produces a result of all 1s, but the carry flag is not affected. A brief description of the decrement instructions follows.

DEC **Decrement**

The DEC instruction subtracts 1 from the contents of either accumulator A or accumulator B or from the contents of a memory location. The flag bits that are affected are Z, N, and V. The N and Z flags are explained in Section 9.2. V = 1 if the operation produces a 2's complement overflow; otherwise,

TABLE 9–7 6800 Microprocessor Decrement Instructions with Addressing Modes, Op Codes, and Examples

Mode	Instruction	Op Code	Example	Explanation
Implied	DEC A	4A	DEC A	Subtract 1 from contents of accumulator A.
Implied	DEC B	5A		
Extended	DEC a16	7A		
Indexed	DEC d8,X	6A		
Implied	DEX	09		

V = 0. A 2's complement overflow occurs if the content of accumulator A, accumulator B, or the memory location is 80_{hex} before the instruction is executed.

DEX Decrement Index Register

The DEX instruction subtracts 1 from the contents of the index register. The Z flag is the only flag that is affected by this instruction (see Section 9.2).

9.5 LOGICAL INSTRUCTIONS

Like other μPs, the 6800 μP includes the basic logical instructions AND, OR, and Exclusive OR. This μP also has two other logical instructions: the 1's complement, COM, and a 2's complement, NEG. These instructions apply to both accumulators and to the contents of any memory location. Table 9–8 shows the 6800's logical instructions with their addressing modes and op codes. Specific examples are also shown for several instructions.

For the AND, OR, and Exclusive OR instructions, the flag bits affected are the N and Z flags, as described in Section 9.2. The V flag is always cleared to a logic 0. For the COM and NEG instructions, the flag bits will be discussed later. The five logical instructions are each described in the following discussion.

AND Logical AND

The AND instruction performs the logical AND operation between each bit of an accumulator and the corresponding bit of a memory location. If the instruction involves accumulator A, the result is placed in accumulator A. If the instruction involves accumulator B, the result is placed in accumulator B.

ORA Inclusive OR

The ORA instruction performs the logical OR operation between each bit of an accumulator and the corresponding bit of a memory location. The result is placed in accumulator A if the accumulator A instruction is used. The result is placed in accumulator B if the accumulator B instruction is used.

EOR Exclusive OR

The EOR instruction performs the Exclusive OR operation between each bit of an accumulator and the corresponding bit of a memory location. The result is placed in accumulator A if the A instruction is used. The result is placed in accumulator B if the B instruction is used.

TABLE 9–8 6800 Microprocessor Logical Instructions with Addressing Modes, Op Codes, and Examples

Mode	Instruction	Op Code	Example	Explanation
Immediate	AND A #d8	84	AND A #02	AND accumulator A with 02_{hex} (result is placed in accumulator A).
Direct	AND A a8	94		
Extended	AND A a16	B4		
Indexed	AND A d8,X	A4		
Immediate	AND B #d8	C4		
Direct	AND B a8	D4		
Extended	AND B a16	F4	AND B FFD0	AND accumulator B with data at location FFD0 (result is placed in accumulator B).
Indexed	AND B d8,X	E4	AND B 0F,X	AND accumulator B with data at location given by X register + $0F_{hex}$ (result is placed in accumulator B).
Immediate	ORA A #d8	8A		
Direct	ORA A a8	9A	ORA A 4B	OR accumulator A with data at location 004B (result is placed in accumulator A).
Extended	ORA A a16	BA	ORA A 3F80	OR accumulator A with data at location 3F80 (result is placed in accumulator A).
Indexed	ORA A d8,X	AA		
Immediate	ORA B #d8	CA	ORA B #47	OR accumulator B with 47_{hex} (result is placed in accumulator B).
Direct	ORA B a8	DA		
Extended	ORA B a16	FA		
Indexed	ORA B d8,X	EA		
Immediate	EOR A #d8	88	EOR A #FF	Accumulator A is ⊕ with FF_{hex} (result is placed in accumulator A).
Direct	EOR A a8	98		
Extended	EOR A a16	B8		
Indexed	EOR A d8,X	A8		
Immediate	EOR B #d8	C8		
Direct	EOR B a8	D8		
Extended	EOR B a16	F8	EOR B AA10	Accumulator B is ⊕ with data at location AA10 (result is placed in accumulator B).
Indexed	EOR B d8,X	E8		

TABLE 9–8 continued

Mode	Instruction	Op Code	Example	Explanation
Implied	COM A	43	COM A	Replace contents of accumulator A by their 1's complement.
Implied	COM B	53		
Extended	COM a16	73	COM C400	Replace contents of location C400 by their 1's complement.
Indexed	COM d8,X	63		
Implied	NEG A	40		
Implied	NEG B	50	NEG B	Replace contents of accumulator B by their 2's complement.
Extended	NEG a16	70		
Indexed	NEG d8,X	60		

COM Complement

The COM instruction takes the 1's complement of either accumulator A or accumulator B or of a memory location. Remember, the 1's complement of a binary number is formed when all 1s are changed to 0s and all 0s are changed to 1s. The flag bits affected are N, Z, V, and C. The N and Z flags are explained in Section 9.2. The V flag is always cleared to a logic 0, and the C flag is always set to a logic 1.

NEG Negative

The NEG instruction converts the contents of either accumulator A or accumulator B or of a memory location to their 2's complement. The flag bits affected are N, Z, V, and C. Refer to Section 9.2 for an explanation of the N and Z flags. V = 1 if the contents of the accumulator or of the memory location are 80_{hex} as a result of the execution of this instruction; otherwise, V = 0. C = 1 if the contents of an accumulator or of a memory location are 00_{hex} as a result of the execution of this instruction; otherwise, C = 0.

9.6 COMPARE AND TEST INSTRUCTIONS

Compare instructions are like subtract instructions, but the result is not put into the accumulator as it is with an ordinary subtract instruction. However, the flag bits are affected by a compare instruction. Compare instructions are used to compare the data in an accumulator with the contents of a memory location and to set or clear the appropriate flag bits. Since the data in the accumulator is not changed, this instruction is a rapid way of checking data between the accumulator and several different memory locations.

In addition to comparing data between an accumulator and a memory location, the 6800 μP instruction set also includes an instruction that allows the two accumulators to be compared. This μP also has an instruction to compare the contents of the index register with the contents of two memory locations.

The test instructions are a group of AND instructions. Again, the result is not stored in an accumulator, but the flag bits are affected. The 6800 μP has two test instructions: a bit test and a test for zero or minus. Table 9-9 is a listing of the 6800's compare and test instructions with their addressing modes and op codes. Specific examples are also listed. The instructions are briefly discussed next.

CBA Compare Accumulators

The CBA instruction subtracts the contents of accumulator B from the contents of accumulator A. The contents of neither accumulator are affected. This instruction is a single-byte instruction, and the flag bits affected are N, Z, V, and C, as explained in Section 9.2.

TABLE 9-9 6800 Microprocessor Compare and Test Instructions with Addressing Modes, Op Codes, and Examples

Mode	Instruction	Op Code	Example	Explanation
Implied	CBA	11		
Immediate	CMP A #d8	81	CMP A #08	Accumulator A − 08_{hex}.
Direct	CMP A a8	91	CMP A B4	Accumulator A − data at location 00B4.
Extended	CMP A a16	B1		
Indexed	CMP A d8,X	A1		
Immediate	CMP B #d8	C1		
Direct	CMP B a8	D1		
Extended	CMP B a16	F1	CMP B 40A7	Accumulator B − data at location 40A7.
Indexed	CMP B d8,X	E1		
Immediate	CPX #d16	8C	CPX #1045	X_H − 10_{hex} and X_L − 45_{hex}.
Direct	CPX a8	9C		
Extended	CPX a16	BC	CPX D800	X_H − data at location D800 and X_L − data at location D801.
Indexed	CPX d8,X	AC		
Immediate	BIT A #d8	85	BIT A #0F	AND accumulator A with $0F_{hex}$.
Direct	BIT A a8	95		
Extended	BIT A a16	B5	BIT A 48C0	AND accumulator A with data at location 48C0.
Indexed	BIT A d8,X	A5		
Immediate	BIT B #d8	C5		
Direct	BIT B a8	D5		
Extended	BIT B a16	F5		
Indexed	BIT B d8,X	E5		
Implied	TST A	4D	TST A	Determine logic state of Z and N flags according to contents of accumulator A.
Implied	TST B	5D		
Extended	TST a16	7D		
Indexed	TST d8,X	6D		

CMP **Compare**

The CMP instruction subtracts the contents of a memory location from either accumulator A or accumulator B. Neither the memory location nor the accumulator is changed. The flag bits affected are N, Z, V, and C, as described in Section 9.2.

CPX **Compare Index Register**

The CPX instruction subtracts the contents of two consecutive memory locations from the index register. Neither the contents of the index register nor the contents of the two memory locations are changed. The contents of the first memory location are subtracted from the index register's most significant byte, X_H (bits 15–8). The contents of the second memory location are subtracted from the index register's least significant byte, X_L (bits 7–0).

The flag bits affected are N, Z, and V. N = 1 if the most significant bit (bit 15) of the result is a logic 1; otherwise, N = 0. Z = 1 if all the bits of the result are a logic 0; otherwise, Z = 0. V = 1 if the subtraction from the most significant byte causes a 2's complement overflow; otherwise, V = 0.

BIT **Bit Test**

The BIT instruction performs the logical AND operation on each bit of an accumulator with the corresponding bit of a memory location. Neither the accumulator nor the contents of the memory location are affected. The N and Z flags are affected, as described in Section 9.2. The V flag is always cleared to a logic 0.

TST **Test (Zero or Minus)**

The TST instruction either clears or sets the Z and N flag bits according to the contents of accumulator A, accumulator B, or a memory location. Besides the Z and N flags, the C and V flag bits are always cleared.

9.7 SHIFT AND ROTATE INSTRUCTIONS

The 6800 μP has five shift and rotate instructions associated with it. They are as follows:

ASL	Arithmetic shift left
ASR	Arithmetic shift right
LSR	Logical shift right
ROL	Rotate left
ROR	Rotate right

Table 9–10 gives the 6800's shift and rotate instructions with their addressing modes and op codes. Some examples of these instructions are also given. Each instruction can be applied to accumulator A, accumulator B, or a memory location. A brief description of the shift and rotate instructions follows.

TABLE 9–10 6800 Microprocessor Shift and Rotate Instructions with Addressing Modes, Op Codes, and Examples

Mode	Instruction	Op Code	Example	Explanation
Implied	ASL A	48		
Implied	ASL B	58	ASL B	Shift contents of accumulator B left one bit.
Extended	ASL a16	78	ASL 60AD	Shift contents of location 60AD left one bit.
Indexed	ASL d8,X	68		
Implied	ASR A	47	ASR A	Shift contents of accumulator A right one bit.
Implied	ASR B	57		
Extended	ASR a16	77		
Indexed	ASR d8,X	67		
Implied	LSR A	44		
Implied	LSR B	54	LSR B	Shift contents of accumulator B right one bit.
Extended	LSR a16	74		
Indexed	LSR d8,X	64		
Implied	ROL A	49		
Implied	ROL B	59		
Extended	ROL a16	79	ROL 17D5	Rotate contents of location 17D5 left one bit.
Indexed	ROL d8,X	69		
Implied	ROR A	46		
Implied	ROR B	56		
Extended	ROR a16	76		
Indexed	ROR d8,X	66	ROR 5F,X	Rotate contents of location given by X register + $5F_{hex}$ right one bit.

ASL Arithmetic Shift Left

The ASL instruction shifts the contents of accumulator A, accumulator B, or a memory location one bit to the left. The most significant bit (bit 7) is transferred to the carry flag. A logic 0 is always loaded into the least significant bit (bit 0). Figure 9–4 illustrates the ASL instruction.

The flag bits affected are N, Z, V, and C. See Section 9.2 for explanations of the N and Z flags. V = 1 if, after the instruction is executed, either N = 1 and C = 0 *or* N = 0 and C = 1; otherwise, V = 0. C = 1 if, before the instruction is executed, the most significant bit (bit 7) is a logic 1; otherwise, C = 0.

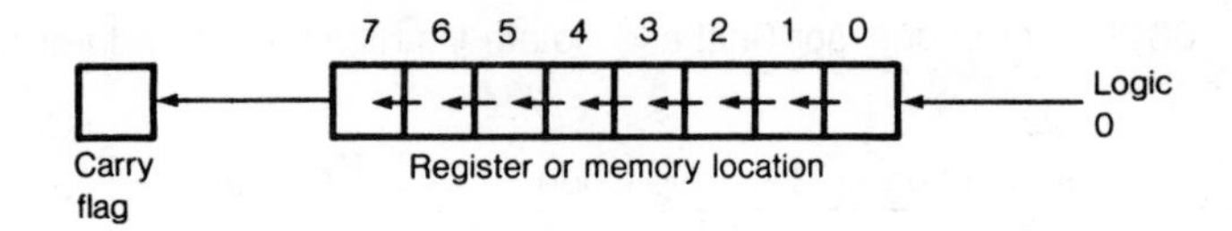

FIGURE 9-4 6800 μP Arithmetic Shift Left (ASL) Instruction

ASR Arithmetic Shift Right

The ASR instruction shifts the contents of accumulator A, accumulator B, or a memory location one bit to the right. Bit 0 is transferred to the carry flag. The contents of bit 7 are not changed. Figure 9-5 illustrates the ASR instruction.

The flag bits affected are N, Z, V, and C. See Section 9.2 for explanations of the N and Z flags. V = 1 if, after this instruction is executed, either N = 1 and C = 0 *or* N = 0 and C = 1; otherwise, V = 0. C = 1 if, before the instruction is executed, the least significant bit (bit 0) is a logic 1; otherwise, C = 0.

LSR Logical Shift Right

The LSR instruction shifts the contents of accumulator A, accumulator B, or a memory location one bit to the right. A logic 0 is loaded into bit 7, and bit 0 is shifted into the carry flag, as shown in Figure 9-6.

The flag bits affected are N, Z, V, and C. The Z flag follows the rules given in Section 9.2. The N flag is always cleared to a logic 0. V = 1 if, after this instruction is executed, either N = 1 and C = 0 *or* N = 0 and C = 1; otherwise, V = 0. C = 1 if, before this instruction is executed, the least significant bit (bit 0) is a logic 1; otherwise, C = 0.

ROL Rotate Left

The ROL instruction shifts the contents of accumulator A, accumulator B, or a memory location one bit to the left. Bit 7 is moved into the carry flag, and the carry flag is moved into bit 0, as shown in Figure 9-7.

The flag bits affected are N, Z, V, and C. See Section 9.2 for explanations of the N and Z flags. V = 1 if, after this instruction is executed, either N = 1 and C = 0 or N = 0 and C = 1; otherwise, V = 0. C = 1 if, before the instruction is executed, the most significant bit (bit 7) is a logic 1; otherwise, C = 0.

ROR Rotate Right

The ROR instruction shifts the contents of accumulator A, accumulator B, or a memory location one bit to the right. Bit 0 is moved into the carry flag, and the carry flag is moved into bit 7. Figure 9-8 illustrates the ROR instruction.

In addition to the carry flag, the N and Z flags are affected as described in Section 9.2. The V flag is also affected. V = 1 if, after the instruction is executed, either N = 1 and C = 0 *or* N = 0 and C = 1; otherwise, V = 0. C = 1 if, before the instruction is executed, the least significant bit (bit 0) is a logic 1; otherwise, C = 0.

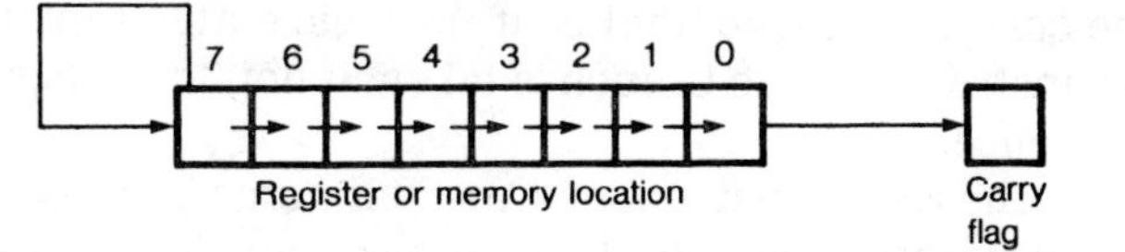

FIGURE 9–5 6800 μP Arithmetic Shift Right (ASR) Instruction

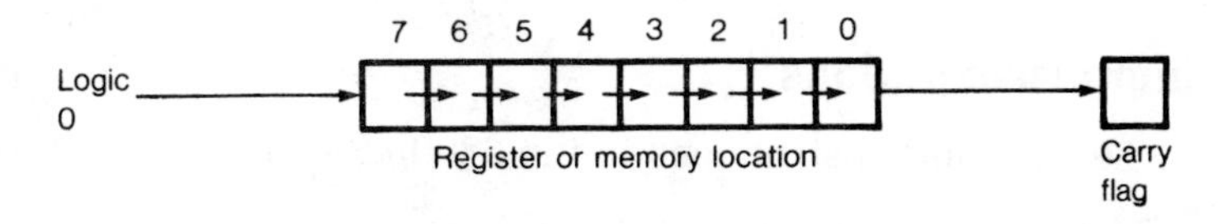

FIGURE 9–6 6800 μP Logical Shift Right (LSR) Instruction

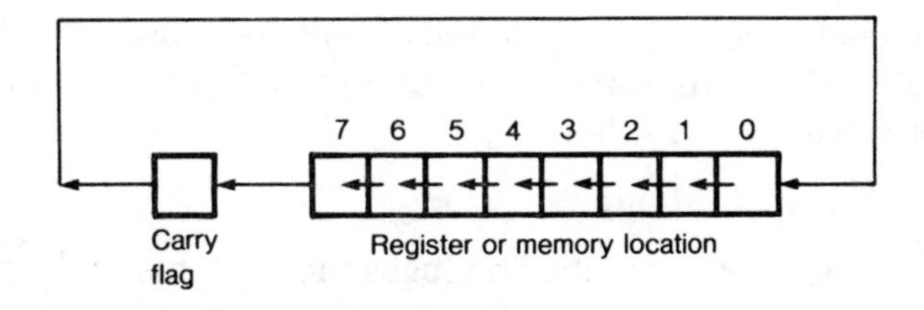

FIGURE 9–7 6800 μP Rotate Left (ROL) Instruction

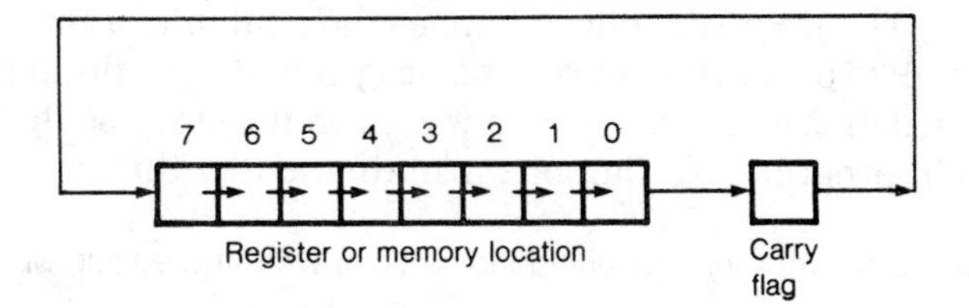

FIGURE 9–8 6800 μP Rotate Right (ROR) Instruction

9.8 PROGRAM CONTROL INSTRUCTIONS

The 6800 μP has three groups of instructions that change the contents of the program counter and thereby change the sequential flow of the program. These instructions are jump, branch, and return instructions. There are two jump instructions, sixteen branch instructions, and two return instructions.

The jump, return, and two of the branch instructions are *unconditional* instructions. That is, these instructions always change the contents of the program counter. The remaining fourteen branch instructions are *conditional* instructions. These instructions first check the logic state of a flag bit or bits: If the condition is true (that is, if the logic state of the flag bit or bits agrees with the instruction), the branch is taken; if not, the program continues in its normal sequence.

The return instructions, as their name implies, are used to return the flow of the program back to the main program. These instructions are used as the last instruction in a subroutine program or as the last instruction in an interrupt program. Let's examine each group of instructions and the instructions that fall within that group.

9.8.1 Jump Instructions

The two jump instructions in the 6800 μP instruction set are the following:

JMP Jump
JSR Jump to subroutine

Although both are unconditional instructions and both change the program counter, the JSR instruction saves a return address on the stack, while the JMP does not save a return address. Table 9–11 lists the 6800 μP jump instructions with their addressing modes and op codes. Examples of the instructions are also given in the table.

JMP Jump

The JMP instruction changes the contents of the program counter to allow the μP to execute a program in another part of memory. No flag bits are affected by this instruction.

JSR Jump to Subroutine

The JSR instruction changes the contents of the program counter to allow the μP to execute a subroutine program. Before the subroutine is executed, this instruction stores a return address on the stack so that the μP can return to the main program. No flag bits are affected by this instruction.

TABLE 9–11 6800 Microprocessor Jump Instructions with Addressing Modes, Op Codes, and Examples

Mode	Instruction	Op Code	Example	Explanation
Extended	JMP a16	7E	JMP 8A50	Program sequence jumps to memory location 8A50.
Indexed	JMP d8,X	6E	JMP 70,X	Program sequence jumps to memory location given by X register + 70_{hex}.
Extended	JSR a16	BD	JSR AD70	Program sequence jumps to memory location AD70. Return address saved.
Indexed	JSR d8,X	AD		

9.8.2 Branch Instructions

The 6800 μP has sixteen branch instructions. Two are unconditional and fourteen are conditional instructions. The unconditional branch instructions operate like the jump instructions in that they do not check any flag bits of the condition code register. The conditional branch instructions, however, check the logic state of one or more flag bits: If the condition is true, the branch is taken; otherwise, the program's normal sequence is executed.

All of the branch instructions require two bytes of program memory. The first byte is the op code, and the second byte is the offset. Offset values are expressed in 2's complement form, which allows the μP to branch forward and backward from + 127 to − 128, the maximum range that can be obtained from eight bits when using 2's complement form.

Note: When an instruction is being executed, the contents of the program counter already contain the address of the next instruction. Therefore, when the offset is added to the program counter, the program counter does not contain the address of the branch instruction; rather, it contains the address of the instruction following the offset.

The two unconditional branch instructions are as follows:

BRA Branch always
BSR Branch to subroutine

These instructions are similar to the JMP and JSR instructions, respectively. The BRA instruction is like the JMP instruction using an extended addressing mode. The difference between these two instructions is that the branch instruction is two bytes of program memory and the jump instruction is three bytes. The range of the branch instruction is limited from + 127 to − 128. The branch instruction always takes one more cycle to execute than the jump instruction, even though it has one less byte of program memory. Therefore, if range is not a problem, the trade-off between these two instructions is memory space for time.

The BSR and JSR instructions are also similar, except that the branch instruction has a limited range, whereas the jump instruction can be directed to any memory location. The BSR instruction requires one less byte of memory than the JSR instruction (two bytes versus three), and the BSR instruction requires one less cycle to execute. Table 9–12 shows the two unconditional branch instructions with their op codes.

TABLE 9–12 6800 Microprocessor Unconditional Branch Instructions with Their Op Codes

Instruction	Op Code
BRA	20
BSR	8D

BRA **Branch Always**

The BRA instruction adds the second byte of the instruction (the offset) to the contents of the program counter. This instruction does not store a return address on the stack. No flag bits are affected.

BSR **Branch to Subroutine**

The BSR instruction adds the second byte of the instruction (the offset) to the contents of the program counter. Before the addition is done, the μP stores the contents of the program counter on the stack so that when a return from subroutine instruction is executed, the μP will return to the main program. The steps involved in executing this instruction are as follows:

1. The low-order byte (bits 7–0) of the program counter is stored in memory at the address given by the stack pointer.
2. The stack pointer is decremented by 1.
3. The high-order byte (bits 15–8) of the program counter is stored in memory at the address given by the stack pointer.
4. The stack pointer is again decremented by 1.
5. The offset is added to the program counter.
6. The μP fetches the first op code from the subroutine program.

The 8080A and 6502 μPs have only eight conditional branch instructions. These μPs check the logic state (either 0 or 1) of four flag bits. The 6800 μP can check the logic state of these four flip-flops, and it also can check two or more flag bits at the same time. By doing so, the 6800 μP has fourteen conditional branch instructions, which are listed in Table 9–13.

9.8.3 Return Instructions

The two return instructions for the 6800 μP are as follows:

RTS	Return from subroutine
RTI	Return from interrupt

A subroutine program is executed by the μP when it decodes a JSR instruction or a BSR instruction. An interrupt program is executed by the μP as a result of a high-to-low transition on either the interrupt request pin ($\overline{\text{IRQ}}$ pin, pin 4) or the nonmaskable interrupt pin ($\overline{\text{NMI}}$ pin, pin 6). The difference between the RTS and RTI instructions is the amount of information returned to the μP from the stack. The RTS instruction restores only the program counter. The RTI instruction restores the contents of all the μP registers. Table 9–14 shows the two return instructions with their op codes.

RTS **Return from Subroutine**

The RTS instruction is the last instruction in a subroutine program. It restores the contents of the program counter so that the μP returns to the main program. The steps involved when this instruction is executed are as follows:

TABLE 9-13 6800 Microprocessor Conditional Branch Instructions with Their Op Codes

Condition(s)	Description	Instruction	Op Code
C = 0 and Z = 0	Branch if higher	BHI	22
C = 1 and/or Z = 1	Branch if lower or same	BLS	23
C = 0	Branch if carry clear	BCC	24
C = 1	Branch if carry set	BCS	25
Z = 0	Branch if not equal to zero	BNE	26
Z = 1	Branch if equal to zero	BEQ	27
V = 0	Branch if overflow clear	BVC	28
V = 1	Branch if overflow set	BVS	29
N = 0	Branch if plus	BPL	2A
N = 1	Branch if minus	BMI	2B
N = 0 and V = 0 or N = 1 and V = 1	Branch if greater than or equal to zero	BGE	2C
N = 0 and V = 1 or N = 1 and V = 0	Branch if less than zero	BLT	2D
Z = 0 and N = 0 and V = 0 or Z = 0 and N = 1 and V = 1	Branch if greater than zero	BGT	2E
Z = 1 or N = 1 and V = 0 or N = 0 and V = 1	Branch if less than or equal to zero	BLE	2F

TABLE 9-14 6800 Microprocessor Return Instructions with Their Op Codes

Instruction	Op Code
RTS	39
RTI	3B

1. The stack pointer is incremented by 1.
2. The contents of the memory location given by the stack pointer are loaded into the high-order byte (bits 15–8) of the program counter.
3. The stack pointer is again incremented by 1.
4. The contents of the memory location given by the stack pointer are loaded into the low-order byte (bits 7–0) of the program counter.
5. The next instruction is fetched from the main program.

RTI Return from Interrupt

Before the 6800 μP services an interrupt, it stores the contents of the following μP registers on the stack: the program counter, the index register, accumulator A, accumulator B, and the condition code register. Then the μP jumps to the interrupt program.

When the RTI instruction is executed, the contents of these μP registers are restored to the conditions they had before the interrupt. The memory locations holding the data are given by the stack pointer. The steps involved are as follows:

1. The stack pointer is incremented by 1.
2. The condition code register is returned.
3. The stack pointer is incremented by 1.
4. Accumulator A is returned.
5. The stack pointer is incremented by 1.
6. Accumulator B is returned.
7. The stack pointer is incremented by 1.
8. The high-order byte of the index register is returned.
9. The stack pointer is incremented by 1.
10. The low-order byte of the index register is returned.
11. The stack pointer is incremented by 1.
12. The high-order byte of the program counter is returned.
13. The stack pointer is incremented by 1.
14. The low-order byte of the program counter is returned.
15. The μP fetches the next instruction from memory, using the returned address of the program counter.

9.9 STACK/STACK POINTER INSTRUCTIONS

The stack pointer in the 6800 μP is 16 bits wide, which allows the programmer to have the stack located anywhere in read/write memory. There are six instructions that affect the stack pointer. They are load, store, increment, decrement, and two transfer instructions. There are also two instructions that move data between the μP and the stack. Table 9–15 shows the stack/stack pointer instructions, their addressing modes and op codes, and some examples. Now let's examine each instruction.

LDS Load Stack Pointer

The LDS instruction moves data from memory to the stack pointer. Since the stack pointer is 16 bits wide, two bytes of data must be transferred from memory to the stack pointer. These two bytes of data must be in consecutive memory locations. The first memory location contains the data that will be transferred to the stack pointer's most significant byte, S_H (bits 15–8). The second memory location contains the stack pointer's least significant byte, S_L (bits 7–0).

The flag bits affected are N, Z, and V. N = 1 if the most significant bit (bit 15) of the stack pointer is a logic 1; otherwise, N = 0. Z = 1 if all bits of the stack pointer are a logic 0; otherwise, Z = 0. The V flag is always cleared by this instruction, so V = 0.

TABLE 9–15 6800 Microprocessor Stack/Stack Pointer Instructions with Addressing Modes, Op Codes, and Examples

Mode	Instruction	Op Code	Example	Explanation
Immediate	LDS #d16	8E	LDS #12A7	Load S_H with 12_{hex} and S_L with $A7_{hex}$.
Direct	LDS a8	9E		
Extended	LDS a16	BE		
Indexed	LDS d8,X	AE		
Direct	STS a8	9F		
Extended	STS a16	BF	STS BF00	Store S_H at location BF00 and S_L at location BF01.
Indexed	STS d8,X	AF		
Implied	INS	31		
Implied	DES	34		
Implied	TSX	30		
Implied	TXS	35		
Implied	PSH A	36	PSH A	Put contents of accumulator A onto stack at address given by stack pointer.
Implied	PSH B	37		
Implied	PUL A	32	PUL A	Place contents of stack, at memory location given by incremented stack pointer, in accumulator A.
Implied	PUL B	33		

STS **Store Stack Pointer**

The STS instruction stores the stack pointer in two consecutive memory locations. The most significant byte of the stack pointer, S_H, is stored in the first memory location. The least significant byte of the stack pointer, S_L, is stored in the second memory location.

The flag bits affected are N, Z, and V. N = 1 if the most significant bit (bit 15) of the stack pointer is a logic 1; otherwise, N = 0. Z = 1 if all bits of the stack pointer are a logic 0; otherwise, Z = 0. The V flag is always cleared by this instruction, so V = 0.

INS **Increment Stack Pointer**

The INS instruction adds 1 to the stack pointer. Like other increment instructions, this instruction produces a roll-over effect. This instruction affects no flag bits.

DES **Decrement Stack Pointer**

The DES instruction subtracts 1 from the stack pointer. Like the increment instruction, this instruction produces a roll-over effect. It does not affect any flag bits.

TSX **Transfer from Stack Pointer to Index Register**

The TSX instruction transfers the contents of the stack pointer plus 1 to the index register. The contents of the stack pointer remain unchanged. This instruction allows the index register to hold the address of the last data byte put onto the stack. No flag bits are affected.

TXS **Transfer from Index Register to Stack Pointer**

The TXS instruction transfers the contents of the index register minus 1 to the stack pointer. The contents of the index register remain unchanged. This instruction causes the stack pointer to operate correctly when data is pulled from the stack because, before data is removed from the stack, the stack pointer is incremented by 1. No flag bits are affected by this instruction.

PSH **Push Data onto Stack**

The PSH instruction stores the contents of either accumulator A or accumulator B on the stack. The memory location at which the data is stored is given by the stack pointer. The stack pointer is then decremented by 1. The contents of the accumulator are not changed. This instruction affects no flag bits.

PUL **Pull Data from Stack**

The PUL instruction increments the stack pointer by 1 and then loads either accumulator A or accumulator B with the data at the memory location given by the stack pointer. This instruction affects no flag bits.

9.10 OTHER 6800 MICROPROCESSOR INSTRUCTIONS

In this section, we will look at condition code register instructions, two interrupt instructions, a decimal adjust instruction, a no operation instruction, and several clear instructions. These instructions, except for the clear instructions, and their op codes are listed in Table 9-16.

TABLE 9-16 Other 6800 Microprocessor Instructions

Description	Instruction	Op Code	Result
Clear overflow	CLV	0A	V = 0
Set overflow	SEV	0B	V = 1
Clear carry	CLC	0C	C = 0
Set carry	SEC	0D	C = 1
Clear interrupt mask	CLI	0E	I = 0
Set interrupt mask	SEI	0F	I = 1
Software interrupt	SWI	3F	
Wait for interrupt	WAI	3E	
Decimal adjust accumulator	DAA	19	
No operation	NOP	01	

9.10.1 Condition Code Register Instructions

In Section 9.3, we discussed two transfer instructions that involve the condition code register: the TAP and TPA instructions. These instructions transfer accumulator A to the condition code register and transfer the condition code register to accumulator A, respectively. Table 9–16 lists four instructions that either set or clear an individual bit of the condition code register. All of these instructions are one-byte instructions and affect no flag bits other than the one they clear or set, as shown in Table 9–16.

Table 9–16 also shows that the interrupt flag bit can either be cleared or set, which allows the μP either to acknowledge or not to acknowledge an interrupt signal on the interrupt request pin (pin 4). The SEI instruction is used, for example, when a portion of the program is of such high priority that the programmer does not wish the μP to recognize an interrupt signal. Then the SEI instruction is used at the beginning of the program. At the end of this priority program, the CLI instruction must be used; otherwise, the μP will still keep the interrupt flip-flop set and will not recognize an interrupt signal. The CLI instruction is also used, for example, after the μP has recognized an interrupt signal. Then the interrupt bit is automatically set and remains set until a return from interrupt (RTI) instruction is executed. However, even when an interrupt program is being executed, the user may wish the μP to be able to recognize another interrupt signal. For this type of application, one of the first instructions in the interrupt program that is being executed would be a CLI instruction.

9.10.2 Interrupt Instructions

The 6800 μP contains two interrupt instructions. They are listed in Table 9–16 with their op codes and are as follows:

SWI Software interrupt
WAI Wait for interrupt

These instructions allow the programmer to execute the interrupt program. The first instruction executes the interrupt program after the instruction is decoded. The second instruction places the μP in a wait state, and no instruction is executed until an interrupt signal is received by the μP on either the interrupt request pin (pin 4) or the nonmaskable interrupt pin (pin 6). Let's examine what happens when each instruction is decoded.

SWI Software Interrupt

The following steps are executed by the μP when the SWI instruction is decoded:

1. The program counter, the index register, accumulator A, accumulator B, and the condition code register are stored on the stack.
2. The interrupt mask bit is set (I = 1).

3. The program counter is loaded with the data contained at memory locations FFFA and FFFB. The contents of memory location FFFA are loaded into the high-order byte of the program counter, and the contents of memory location FFFB are loaded into the low-order byte of the program counter.
4. The μP fetches the first instruction from the interrupt program. The last instruction from this interrupt program must be an RTI instruction so that the μP can return to its place in the main program and all the μP's registers can return to their original states.

Only the interrupt flag bit is affected (I = 1). Note that the μP will recognize this instruction and execute the software interrupt program even if the interrupt flag bit is a logic 1.

WAI Wait for Interrupt

When the WAI instruction is decoded, the μP executes the following steps:

1. The program counter, the index register, accumulator A, accumulator B, and the condition code register are stored on the stack.
2. The μP is placed in a wait loop until an interrupt signal is acknowledged. The μP can recognize an interrupt signal only if the interrupt flag bit is a logic 0.

3a. If an $\overline{\text{IRQ}}$ signal is received, the I bit is set, and the program counter is loaded with the data contained at memory locations FFF8 and FFF9.

3b. If an $\overline{\text{NMI}}$ signal is received, the I bit is set, and the program counter is loaded with the data contained at memory locations FFFC and FFFD.

If the μP is to be returned to the main program, an RTI instruction must be executed. This instruction restores all the μP registers to their original states. The only flag bit that is affected by this instruction is the interrupt bit. The I flag is set to a logic 1 when an interrupt occurs.

9.10.3 Other Instructions

The 6800 μP instruction set also includes a decimal adjust instruction, a no operation instruction, and several clear instructions. These instructions are shown in Tables 9-16 and 9-17 with their op codes. A brief description of each instruction follows.

DAA Decimal Adjust Accumulator

The DAA instruction is used in BCD addition to adjust the binary answer. It is used following an ABA, ADD, or ADC instruction. The numbers that are being added must be BCD values and not hexadecimal values.

TABLE 9–17 6800 Microprocessor Clear Instructions with Addressing Modes, Op Codes, and Examples

Mode	Instruction	Op Code	Example	Explanation
Implied	CLR A	4F	CLR A	Clear accumulator A.
Implied	CLR B	5F		
Extended	CLR a16	7F		
Indexed	CLR d8,X	6F	CLR 18,X	Clear location given by X register + 18_{hex}.

NOP **No Operation**

The NOP instruction causes the μP to go to the next instruction in sequence. No flag bits are affected.

CLR **Clear**

The CLR instruction replaces the present contents of accumulator A, accumulator B, or a memory location with logic 0s. The N, V, and C flags are cleared. The Z flag is set.

9.11 SUMMARY

This chapter grouped similar types of instructions for the 6800 μP together, as was done in Chapter 5. However, when we are writing a program and want to check (1) how an instruction works, (2) its op code, (3) its addressing mode, (4) how long it takes to execute, or (5) what flag bits are affected, a reference table is the easiest way to find the answer. Therefore, the 6800's instructions are summarized in Appendix Tables D–3 through D–8.

This chapter began with the 6800 μP's pin assignments and internal architecture. Like many other μPs, the 6800 contains a program counter, stack pointer, index register, condition code register, and instruction register, along with the necessary buffers, latches, and control circuitry. Unlike most other μPs, however, the 6800 has two accumulators: accumulator A and accumulator B. Two accumulators give the programmer the flexibility of storing the results of an ALU operation in either accumulator. The condition code register (also called the program status register or the flag register) is the record-keeping register. There are six bits in the condition code register that are set or cleared as a result of an instruction—hence, the name record-keeping register.

In this chapter, we examined the 6800's instruction set, including the data movement, arithmetic, logical, compare and test, shift and rotate, program control, and stack/stack pointer instructions. Op codes and addressing modes were given for most of these instructions, and specific examples were provided to show the flexibility and comprehensiveness of the 6800's instruction set. The next chapter shows how these instructions are used to write programs.

PROBLEMS

All of the following problems apply to the 6800 μP.

9–1 How many basic instructions are there in the 6800 instruction set?

9–2 What is a major difference between the 6800 μP's internal architecture and the internal architecture of most other μPs?

9–3 How many 16-bit registers are there in the 6800 μP? Name them.

9–4 Name the flag bits in the 6800's condition code register.

9–5 If the result of a subtract instruction is zero, will the zero flag bit be cleared to a logic 0 or set to a logic 1?

9–6 Name the three groups of data movement instructions in the 6800 instruction set.

9–7 Explain what happens when each of the following instructions is executed (data and address values given in hex): (a) LDA A #04; (b) LDA A F800; (c) LDA B 50; (d) LDX #01FF; (e) STA A 0240; (f) STA B 07,X; (g) STX C000; (h) TBA; and (i) TPA.

9–8 What are three add instructions for the 6800 μP?

9–9 Explain the function of each of the following instructions: (a) ABA; (b) ADD A #03; (c) ADD B 0200; (d) ADC A 15; (e) SUB A #10; (f) SBC B 08,X; (g) INC A; (h) INC 0150; (i) DEC B; and (j) DEX.

9–10 What are the logical instructions in the 6800 μP's instruction set?

9–11 If data from memory location 0300 is ANDed with the contents of accumulator A, where is the result stored?

9–12 Can accumulator A be ANDed with accumulator B by one instruction?

9–13 Do all of the logical operations have indexed addressing mode capability?

9–14 What flag bits are affected by the 1's complement (NEG) instruction?

9–15 What flag bits are affected by the compare accumulator's instruction?

9–16 Explain what happens when each of the following instructions is executed (data and address values given in hex): (a) CMP A 57A2; (b) CMP B #14; and (c) CPX 20.

9–17 What flag bits are affected by (a) the BIT instruction and (b) the TST instruction?

9–18 Explain what the following instructions accomplish when executed: (a) BIT A #01; (b) TST A; (c) BIT A 4000; and (d) TST 4000.

9–19 List the five shift and rotate instructions that are in the 6800 μP instruction set.

9–20 What is the difference between the logical shift right instruction and the arithmetic shift right instruction?

9–21 Can any RAM memory location be rotated one bit to the right?

9–22 Can any ROM memory location be rotated one bit to the right?

9–23 Is the instruction ROL 0055 a read/modify/write instruction if location 0055 is in RAM?

9–24 Does the 6800 μP have an unconditional branch instruction? If your answer is yes, what is the instruction(s)?

9–25 How many branch instructions are there in the 6800 μP instruction set?

9–26 What is the difference between the JMP instruction and the JSR instruction?

9–27 Are both the JMP and the JSR instructions unconditional instructions?

9–28 Do jump instructions have offset values?

9–29 With the JMP instruction, can the μP jump to any location in memory?

9–30 Repeat Problem 9–29 for the JSR instruction.

9–31 What is the range that a branch instruction can take?

9–32 What is the (a) advantage and (b) disadvantage of the BSR instruction over the JSR instruction?

9–33 How many conditional branch instructions are there in the 6800's instruction set?

9–34 Given the following condition of the condition code register,

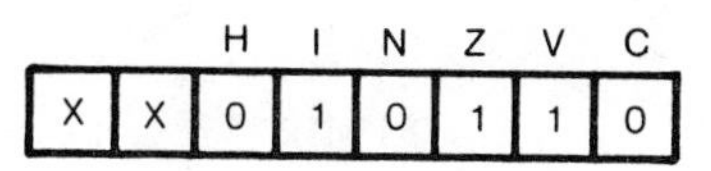

determine whether the branch be taken for the following instructions: (a) BHI, (b) BCC, (c) BNE, (d) BVS, (e) BLT, and (f) BLE.

9-35 What is the first step that the μP does after an RTS instruction is decoded?

9-36 What μP registers are returned from the stack when the 6800 μP executes an RTI instruction?

9-37 Name the instruction that affects the stack pointer.

9-38 List the different ways in which the data in the condition code register is saved on the stack.

6800 Programs

10.0 INTRODUCTION

In this chapter, we will use the 6800 μP's instructions to write some commonly used programs. These programs include binary and decimal addition, binary and decimal subtraction, adding a column of numbers, checking memory for a particular value, clearing memory, transferring blocks of data between sections of memory, using the stack, using time delays, converting binary to BCD, and multiplication. These programs can be used as a basis for longer and more complex programs. The programs are written by using the 6800 mnemonics and an assembly language format. All data and addresses are given in hexadecimal code. The first column is reserved for labels, the second column is for instructions, and the third column is for comments about the instructions. Keep in mind that the programs are general and are written to show different 6800 instructions. Also, remember that there is no unique way of writing a program, and many of these programs could have been written with fewer steps.

10.1 ADDITION AND SUBTRACTION

In nearly every long program, there is an addition or subtraction program. Sometimes, only two 8-bit numbers are involved—single-byte operation—and in other programs multiprecision addition or subtraction is needed. The 6800 can be programmed to do both binary and decimal addition or subtraction. Remember, subtraction is done by using 2's complement arithmetic. However, the programmer does not have to worry about obtaining the 2's complement of a number; that is done automatically by the μP in the arithmetic and logic unit whenever a subtraction instruction is decoded. If the result of a subtraction is negative, the answer is in 2's complement form.

10.1.1 Single-Byte Binary Addition

Adding two 8-bit numbers can be done in one of three ways in the 6800 μP: (1) Load accumulator A with one number and add to it a number from a memory location; (2) load accumulator B with one number and add to it another number from a memory location; or (3) add the contents of accumulator A to accumulator B. In any of the three cases, if we wish to save the result, then we must use a store instruction and move the data from an accumulator to a memory location.

Remember that augend, addend, and sum are the arithmetic terms commonly used in the process of addition. The number placed in the accumulator is the *augend*, and the number that is added to it is the *addend*. The result is the *sum*. When accumulator A and accumulator B are added, accumulator A holds the augend and accumulator B holds the addend; the sum goes into accumulator A.

The program in Example 10.1 shows single-byte addition. In the program, the data has already been stored at memory locations 0400 and 0500.

EXAMPLE 10.1 Add the contents of memory location 0400 to the contents of memory location 0500. Store the result at memory location 0600. Use accumulator A for the addition.

Solution

```
LDA A, 0400   Load accumulator A from location 0400.
ADD A, 0500   Add accumulator A + data from location 0500.
STA A, 0600   Store result at location 0600.
```

The program in Example 10.1 does not include the carry flag in the addition. However, the result does affect the carry flag, and it is possible that the carry flag was set. If there is a carry from the most significant bit, and if we wish to save it, then additional programming steps are needed, as shown in Example 10.2.

EXAMPLE 10.2 Repeat Example 10.1, but this time save the carry flag at memory location 0601. The carry flag should be in the least significant bit, and all other bits of location 0601 should be a logic 0.

Solution

```
LDA A, 0400   Load accumulator A from location 0400.
ADD A, 0500   Add accumulator A + data from location 0500.
STA A, 0600   Store result.
LDA A, #00    Clear accumulator A.
ROL A         Rotate carry flag into LSB of accumulator A.
STA A, 0601   Store accumulator A (carry flag).
```

Remember that the symbol # stands for the immediate addressing mode.

10.1.2 Double-Precision Addition

Double-precision addition means adding two 16-bit numbers. In the 6800 μP, this procedure requires adding the first two 8-bit numbers and storing the result, then adding the next two 8-bit numbers and storing the result. The following binary numbers show which bits are being added:

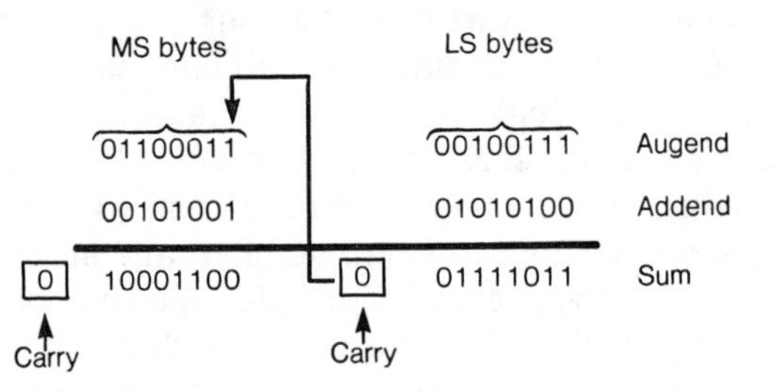

Double-precision addition requires use of the ADC instruction, because a carry from the least significant (LS) bytes must be brought forward to the most significant (MS) bytes. The program in Example 10.3 illustrates double-precision addition and the use of the ADC instruction.

EXAMPLE 10.3 Add the data at locations 0400 and 0401 to the data at locations 0500 and 0501. Store the result at locations 0600 and 0601. Use accumulator B for the addition.

Solution

```
LDA B, 0400   Load LS byte.
ADD B, 0500   Add accumulator B + data from memory.
STA B, 0600   Store result at location 0600.
LDA B, 0401   Load MS byte.
ADC B, 0501   Add accumulator B + carry + memory.
STA B, 0601   Store result at location 0601.
```

The program in Example 10.3 does not save the carry flag from the most significant bytes. Example 10.2 shows the programming steps that should be included to save the carry flag in another memory location such as 0602.

10.1.3 Multiprecision Addition

A multiprecision addition is one in which more than 8 bits are added. Therefore, double-precision addition is actually a multiprecision addition. The term *multi-* is most often applied to addition programs where more than 16 bits have to be added.

Example 10.4 shows how any number of bytes can be added. In writing a multiprecision addition program, we load one of the accumulators with a count equal to the number of times an 8-bit addition has to be performed, and we use the other accumulator for the actual addition. The program in Example 10.4 uses the index register as a pointer to memory for the augend values, addend values, and sum. The index register has to be temporarily stored in memory (page 0), because the index register is being used to hold different pointers to memory at different times, and we do not want to lose the old value. In this program, all the addend values will be lost, but this loss commonly occurs in multiprecision addition programs.

EXAMPLE 10.4 Write a multiprecision addition program that adds data in memory beginning at location 0400 to data in memory beginning at location 0500. Store the result in memory, beginning at location 0500. Use accumulator B to keep the count. Use memory locations 0020 and 0030 as temporary storage locations for the index register.

Solution

```
        LDX #0400     Initialize X index register.
        STX 20        Temporary storage 1 (location 0020).
        LDX #0500     Initialize X index register.
        STX 30        Temporary storage 2 (location 0030).
        CLC           Clear carry flag.
        LDA B, count  Load accumulator B with count.
MULTAD: LDX 20        Reload X register from temporary storage 1.
        LDA A 00,X    Load accumulator A, using X register.
        INX           Increment X register.
        STX 20        Restore X register at temporary storage 1.
        LDX 30        Load X register from temporary storage 2.
        ADC A 00,X    Add accumulator A + carry + memory.
        STA A 00,X    Store accumulator A, using X register.
        INX           Increment X register.
        STX 30        Restore X register at temporary storage 2.
        DEC B         Decrement count.
        BNE MULTAD    If count ≠ 0, go to MULTAD.
        RTS           Return from subroutine.
```

The program in Example 10.4 is written so that any count can be loaded into accumulator B. If we were doing a double-precision addition, the count would be 2. If we were adding 32 bits (4 bytes), the count would be 4. Thus, the count value equals the number of bytes being added.

10.1.4 BCD Addition

The 6800 μP is capable of adding binary-coded-decimal numbers and producing a BCD result. Like the 8080A μP, the 6800 μP has a decimal adjust (DAA) instruction. This instruction applies only to accumulator A. Therefore, the addition should be done in accumulator A. If the addition is done in accumulator B, the result has to be transferred to accumulator A, and then the decimal adjust instruction is executed. Remember, when we do BCD addition, all numbers must be valid BCD numbers, and one byte contains two BCD numbers.

Examples 10.5, 10.6, and 10.7 show how Examples 10.1, 10.3, and 10.4 can be modified to do BCD addition. In the programs, all numbers coming from memory are valid BCD numbers. If the data coming from memory were not in a BCD format, then we would first have to do a binary-to-BCD conversion.

EXAMPLE 10.5 Repeat Example 10.1 for BCD addition.

Solution

```
LDA A, 0400   Load accumulator A from location 0400.
ADD A, 0500   Add accumulator A + data from location 0500.
DAA           Decimal adjust.
STA A, 0600   Store result at location 0600.
```

EXAMPLE 10.6 Modify the double-precision binary addition program of Example 10.3 to perform BCD addition.

Solution Since Example 10.3 used accumulator B for addition, and since the DAA instruction applies only to accumulator A, then the addition should be done in accumulator A.

```
LDA A, 0400   Load LS byte.
ADD A, 0500   Add accumulator A + data from memory.
DAA           Decimal adjust LS byte.
STA A, 0600   Store result at location 0600.
LDA A, 0401   Load MS byte.
ADC A, 0501   Add accumulator A + carry + memory.
DAA           Decimal adjust MS byte.
STA A, 0601   Store result at location 0601.
```

Note: The decimal adjust instruction has to be included after every addition instruction.

EXAMPLE 10.7 What programming steps must be added to the multiprecision binary addition program of Example 10.4 to make it a multiprecision BCD program?

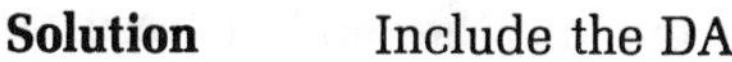

Solution Include the DAA instruction after the ADC A 00,X instruction, as shown below:

```
        .
        .
        .
ADC A 00,X
DAA             Decimal adjust.
STA A 00,X
        .
        .
        .
```

10.1.5 Single-Byte Binary Subtraction

As we saw in the previous chapter, the 6800 μP can do subtraction with and without the borrow bit (carry flag). The programs in Examples 10.8 and 10.9 use both instructions. As in addition, the 6800 μP can do three types of 8-bit subtraction. They are (1) subtract the contents of a memory location from accumulator A, (2) subtract the contents of a memory location from accumulator B, and (3) subtract accumulator B from accumulator A. The arithmetic terms commonly used in subtraction are *minuend*, the number in the accumulator; *subtrahend*, the number coming from the memory location; and *difference*, the answer. When accumulator B is subtracted from accumulator A, accumulator A holds the minuend and accumulator B holds the subtrahend. The difference is placed in accumulator A.

Remember that subtraction is done by 2's complement arithmetic. The arithmetic and logic unit automatically generates the 2's complement of the subtrahend. Example 10.8 illustrates binary subtraction.

EXAMPLE 10.8 Subtract the contents of memory location 0850 from the contents of memory location 0800. Place the result in memory location 0900. Use accumulator A for the subtraction.

Solution

```
LDA A 0800    Load accumulator A with minuend.
SUB A 0850    Subtract subtrahend.
STA A 0900    Store result.
```

10.1.6 Double-Precision Binary Subtraction

Double-precision binary subtraction involves subtracting one 16-bit number (two bytes) from another. Since the 6800 μP can only do one 8-bit subtraction at one time, the subtract instruction has to be used twice. In the first subtraction, one of the least significant bytes is subtracted from the other and the result is stored. Then one of the most significant bytes is subtracted from the other and the result is stored. This procedure is similar to the procedure in double-precision binary addition.

The program in Example 10.9 shows how a loop can be set up so that the least significant bytes can be subtracted and the results stored, and then the most significant bytes can be subtracted and the results stored. This program requires the use of the index X register and a counter.

EXAMPLE 10.9 Subtract the contents of memory locations 0020 and 0021 from the contents of memory locations 0010 and 0011. Store the result at memory locations 0050 and 0051. Use accumulator A for the subtraction, and use accumulator B as a counter.

Solution

```
      LDX #0000     Initialize X register with all 0s.
      LDA B #02     Initialize accumulator B with count = 2.
      CLC           Clear carry flag.
SUBT: LDA A 10,X    Load minuend from location 0010,X.
      SBC A 20,X    Subtract subtrahend (location 0020,X).
      STA A 50,X    Store difference at 0050,X.
      INX           Increment X register.
      DEC B         Decrement accumulator B.
      BNE SUBT      If B ≠ 0, branch to SUBT.
```

The program in Example 10.9 can be changed to a multiprecision binary subtraction by changing the count in accumulator B. The value of the count equals the number of bytes to be subtracted.

10.1.7 Decimal Subtraction

The DAA instruction permits the 6800 μP to do decimal addition. For decimal subtraction, complements must be used. In the procedure for decimal subtraction using the 6800 μP, we first obtain the 99's complement of the subtrahend, and then we add the result to the minuend plus the carry flag. In a one-byte subtraction, the carry flag is set once; in a multibyte subtraction, the carry flag is set before the first addition. The DAA instruction follows the addition so that the answer will be the correct decimal number.

The following steps show how a multibyte decimal subtraction can be done by using the 6800 μP:

1. Initialize the index register to 0.
2. Initialize a counter to the number of bytes to be subtracted.
3. Load the accumulator with 99_{hex} (this value represents the decimal number 99).
4. Subtract the subtrahend from the accumulator (this step generates the 99's complement).

5. Temporarily store the 99's complement in memory.
6. If the 99's complement of each byte of the subtrahend has been obtained, go on. Otherwise, go back to step 3.
7. Reinitialize the index register.
8. Reinitialize the counter.
9. Set the carry flag to a logic 1.
10. Load the first byte of the minuend.
11. Add the minuend plus the carry flag plus the first byte of the 99's complement of the subtrahend.
12. Decimal adjust the answer.
13. Store the result.
14. If each byte of the minuend, the carry flag, and the 99's complement of the subtrahend has been added, the program is complete. Otherwise, go back to step 10.

Steps 1–14 show that each byte of the subtrahend is complemented, before any addition is done, so the 6800 μP programmer may use the index register. However, temporary storage of the 99's complement values is required.

Example 10.10 shows a multibyte decimal subtraction program using steps 1–14. As each byte of the subtrahend is complemented, it is stored in the memory location from which it came. Thus, the original subtrahend bytes are lost. If we wish to keep the original subtrahend values, we must choose another area of memory for temporary storage of the complemented values.

EXAMPLE 10.10 Write a multibyte decimal subtraction subroutine program, using accumulator A for the subtraction and addition operations and using accumulator B as a counter. The subtrahend values begin at memory location 0010, and the minuend values begin at memory location 0020. Use the subtrahend area of memory for temporary storage and for the final answer.

Solution

```
        LDX #0000      Initialize index register with all 0s.
        LDA B # count  Use accumulator B as a counter.
COMP:   LDA A #99      Initialize accumulator A for 99's complement.
        SUB A 10,X     Find 99's complement of subtrahend.
        STA A 10,X     Store 99's complement temporarily.
        INX            Increment index register.
        DEC B          Decrement accumulator B.
        BNE COMP       If B ≠ 0, branch to COMP.
        LDX #0000      Reinitialize index register.
        LDA B # count  Reinitialize counter.
        SEC            Set carry flag.
SUBT:   LDA A 20,X     Load minuend.
        ADC A 10,X     Add accumulator A + carry + 99's comple-
                       ment.
        DAA            Decimal adjust.
        STA A 10,X     Store result at location 0010,X.
        INX            Increment index register.
```

```
        DEC B          Decrement counter.
        BNE SUBT       If B ≠ 0, branch to SUBT.
        RTS            Return from subroutine.
```

In the program in Example 10.10, the count value is set to the number of bytes that have to be subtracted. For example, for a double-precision decimal subtraction (two bytes), the count value equals 2.

10.2 TIME DELAYS

A program can be written so that the μP serves as a timer for control applications, for sending or receiving data, for generating waveforms, for polling peripheral devices at specified times, or for any other application in which the μP operates too fast for peripheral equipment to respond to it. Such programs are called time delays, timing loops, or delay generation.

All time delay programs have the μP repeat a set of instructions. Since each instruction requires a certain amount of time for execution, a time delay can be generated. If the μP executes the same set of instructions, a time delay loop is created, as shown in the flowchart in Figure 10–1. A counter is decremented each time the μP goes through the loop. The μP gets out of the loop when the counter equals 0. The flowchart in Figure 10–1 is for a time delay program that uses only accumulator A. Example 10.11 illustrates the program for the flowchart.

EXAMPLE 10.11 Write a time delay program for the flowchart of Figure 10–1. Use accumulator A.

Solution

```
        LDA A, count   Initialize accumulator A with count (2 μs).
DELAY:  DEC A          Decrement accumulator A (2 μs).
        BNE DELAY      If A ≠ 0, branch to DELAY (4 μs).
```

The times in parentheses in the program of Example 10.11 are for a 6800 μP operating from a 1 MHz clock. Equation 10–1 shows how the overall time delay can be calculated:

$$\text{Time delay} = \underset{\text{LDA}}{2\ \mu s} + (\underset{\text{DEC A}}{2\ \mu s} + \underset{\text{BNE}}{4\ \mu s}) \times \text{count} \tag{10-1}$$

Example 10.12 shows how to calculate the shortest and longest time delays for the program illustrated in Example 10.11.

EXAMPLE 10.12 Determine the shortest and longest time delays possible for the time delay program of Example 10.11.

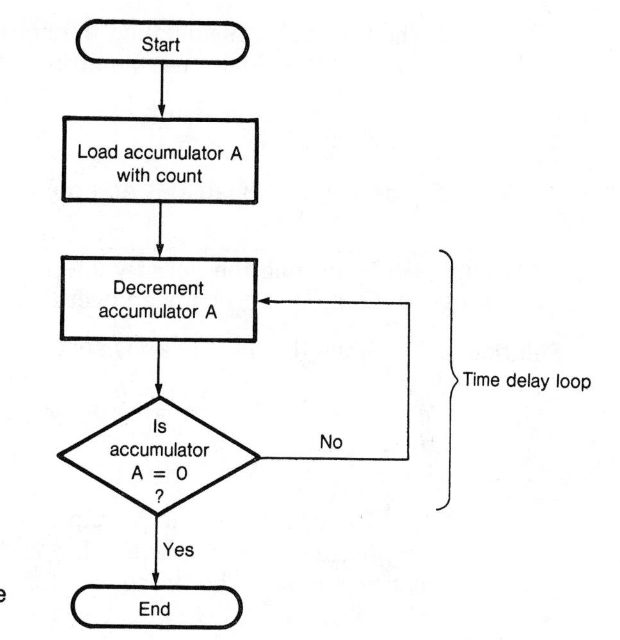

FIGURE 10-1 Flowchart for Time Delay Program

Solution The shortest time delay occurs when count = 01_{hex}. The shortest time delay is as follows:

$$\text{Time delay} = 2\ \mu s + (6\ \mu s)(1) = 8\ \mu s$$

The longest time delay occurs when accumulator A is loaded with 00_{hex}. The accumulator must be decremented $256_{decimal}$ times before accumulator A is 00 again. The longest time delay is as follows:

$$\text{Time delay} = 2\ \mu s + (6\ \mu s)(256) = 1538\ \mu s$$

The range of times in Example 10.12 is from 8 μs to 1538 μs. Therefore, we see that, by varying the count value, we can vary the overall time delay of the program. Section 10.2.1 shows how to determine the count, and Section 10.2.2 shows how to trim the program for a specified time.

10.2.1 Calculating the Count Value

Rearranging Equation 10-1 to solve for the count value yields the following equation:

$$\text{Count} = \frac{\text{Time delay} - \text{LDA A}}{\text{DEC A} + \text{BNE}} \qquad (10\text{-}2)$$

If the time delay is specified in microseconds and the 6800 μP is being driven from a 1 MHz clock, then Equation 10–2 can be written as follows:

$$\text{Count} = \frac{\text{Time delay} - 2}{6} \quad \textbf{(10–3)}$$

Example 10.13 illustrates an application of Equation 10–3.

EXAMPLE 10.13 Determine the count value that has to be loaded into accumulator A of Example 10.11 for an overall time delay of 764 μs.

Solution Since the time delay is specified in microseconds, we use Equation 10–3:

$$\text{Count} = \frac{764 - 2}{6} = 127_{\text{decimal}} = 7F_{\text{hex}}$$

The count value in Example 10.13 is a whole number. If it had not been, the program of Example 10.11 would have had to be modified to give the correct time delay. The procedure for making these modifications is called *trimming*, a procedure we turn to next.

10.2.2 Trimming Time Delays

If the count value of Equation 10–3 produces a whole number and a fraction, then the timing delay program must be trimmed. Trimming means adding additional program instructions (usually NOPs) to generate the correct overall time delay. Trimming is illustrated in Example 10.14.

EXAMPLE 10.14 Write a program to generate a time delay of 1.0 ms (1000 μs).

Solution Begin by using Equation 10–3:

$$\text{Count} = \frac{1000 - 2}{6} = 166.333_{\text{decimal}}$$

The count value equals the whole part of the number, 166_{decimal} ($A6_{\text{hex}}$). If only the whole part of the number were considered, the time delay would be only 998 μs. This value is considered the untrimmed time delay value:

$$\text{Time delay (untrimmed)} = 2\ \mu\text{s} + (6\ \mu\text{s}) \times 166 = 998\ \mu\text{s}$$

Execution of an NOP instruction takes 2 μs. Therefore, adding one NOP instruction at the end of the program generates the correct overall time delay. The program is as follows:

```
        LDA A,A6    Initialize accumulator A with count.
DELAY:  DEC         Decrement counter.
```

```
BNE DELAY     If accumulator A ≠ 0, branch to DELAY.
NOP           Additional 2 μs delay.
```

Therefore, the trimmed time delay is as follows:

$$\text{Time delay (trimmed)} = 2\ \mu s + (6\ \mu s) \times 166 + 2\ \mu s = 1000\ \mu s = 1\ ms$$

10.2.3 Nesting Time Delays

Longer time delays can be generated by a time delay loop inside a time delay loop. This technique is called *nesting time delay loops*. Figure 10-2 shows a flowchart for nesting time delay loops. In this flowchart, accumulator A is used for the inside loop counter, and accumulator B is used for the outside loop counter. Depending on the initial counts put into accumulator A and accumulator B, the overall time delay can be determined as shown in Example 10.15.

EXAMPLE 10.15 Write a time delay program by using the flowchart of Figure 10-2.

Solution

```
        LDA A, count no. 1   Initialize accumulator A with count no. 1
                             (2 μs).
        LDA B, count no. 2   Initialize accumulator B with count no. 2
                             (2 μs).
DELAY:  DEC A                Decrement accumulator A (2 μs).
        BNE DELAY            If A ≠ 0, branch to DELAY (4 μs).
        DEC B                Decrement accumulator B (2 μs).
        BNE DELAY            If B ≠ 0, branch to DELAY (4 μs).
```

The total time delay for the program in Example 10.15 is given by the following equation:

$$\text{Total time delay} = \text{Initialization} + (\text{loop A} \times \text{count no. 2}) + \text{loop B} \quad \textbf{(10-4)}$$

where:

$$\text{Initialization} = \underset{\text{LDA A}}{2\ \mu s} + \underset{\text{LDA B}}{2\ \mu s} = 4\ \mu s$$

$$\text{Loop A} \times \text{count no. 2} = \underbrace{(\underset{\text{DEC A}}{2\ \mu s} + \underset{\text{BNE}}{4\ \mu s}) \times \text{count no. 1}}_{\text{Loop A}} \times \text{count no. 2}$$

$$\text{Loop B} = (\underset{\text{DEC B}}{2\ \mu s} + \underset{\text{BNE}}{4\ \mu s}) \times \text{count no. 2}$$

Example 10.16 illustrates an application of Equation 10-4.

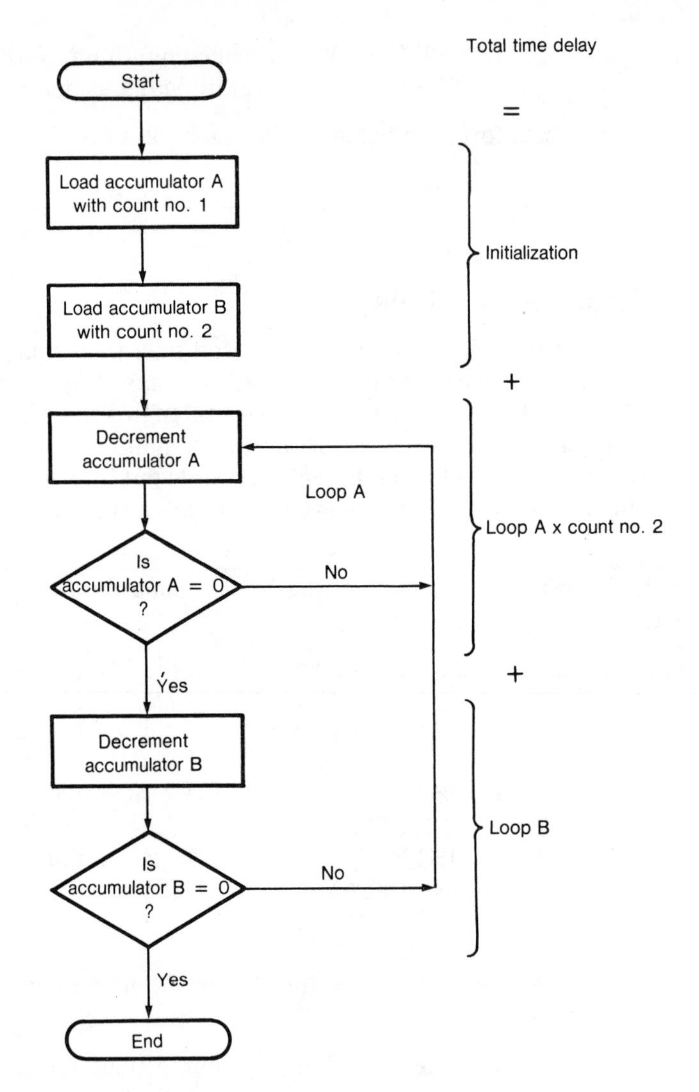

FIGURE 10–2 Flowchart for Nesting Timing Delay Loops

EXAMPLE 10.16 What is the shortest and the longest time delay that can be generated from the program in Example 10.15?

Solution The shortest time delay occurs when both counts equal 1. Applying Equation 10–4 yields the result:

$$\text{Total time delay} = 4\ \mu\text{s} + (6\ \mu\text{s}) \times 1 \times 1 + (6\ \mu\text{s}) \times 1 = 16\ \mu\text{s}$$

The longest time delay is generated when both accumulators are loaded with 00_{hex}. Applying Equation 10–4 yields the result:

$$\text{Total time delay} = 4\ \mu\text{s} + (6\ \mu\text{s}) \times 256 \times 256 + (6\ \mu\text{s}) \times 256 \cong 0.395\ \text{s}$$

Therefore, nesting two time delay loops yields a range from 16 μs to approximately 0.4 s.

Since the 6800 μP has a decrement memory location instruction, we can use memory locations for additional nested time delays, thereby generating any time delay that we need. Remember, when the μP is executing a time delay program, it cannot execute any other program. Thus, time delay programs can be a considerable waste of μP time. To avoid wasting μP time, manufacturers make timing chips. The count is loaded into the timing chips, and they automatically decrement. When they equal zero, a signal can be sent to the μP on the interrupt request line so that the μP knows the count is finished. Timing chips free the μP to execute other programs.

10.3 CHECKING FOR KNOWN DATA

The compare instruction is useful when it is necessary to check memory for a specified or known value. The known value is loaded into an accumulator, and each byte of memory is compared with the accumulator value. A branch instruction follows the compare instruction so that the μP can make a decision. For example, if we want to find all the values less than or equal to 5 in a section of memory, we use the BLS instruction after the compare instruction. In program execution, every time the number from memory is less than or equal to 5, the μP will branch to another program. This new program could output the data to a CRT display or to a printer. This type of program is used when we want to check memory for a particular number, letter, or name, as shown in Example 10.17.

EXAMPLE 10.17 Write a program that checks page 4 for all values less than or equal to 5. Use accumulator A for the comparison, and use accumulator B as a counter.

Solution

```
       LDX #0400     Initialize X with starting address.
       LDA B, #00    Initialize accumulator B as a counter.
       LDA A, 05     Load accumulator A with desired value.
COMP:  CMP A 00,X    Compare accumulator A and memory.
       BLS PRINT     Branch if memory ≤ accumulator A (branch to
                     new program).
       INX           Increment X register.
       DEC B         Decrement count.
       BNE COMP      If B ≠ 0, branch to COMP.
```

10.4 CHECKING THE STACK

In Chapter 5, we saw that the stack is an area in memory that is used by the μP to store the contents of the program counter when a subroutine is called. Saving the present contents of the program counter before the μP jumps or branches to a subroutine program guarantees that the μP will be able to return to the program it left. Although the stack is used automatically by the μP whenever a subroutine program is called, the stack can be used at any time by the programmer. In fact, it is an ideal location for the temporary storage of data.

10.4.1 Saving the Data of the Microprocessor Registers

When the 6800 μP executes either a jump or a branch subroutine program, only the contents of the program counter are saved. In most applications, we want to save the contents of both accumulators and the contents of the condition code register. To do so, we have to use push (PSH) and pull (PUL) instructions. Data is put onto the stack by push instructions, and it is retrieved by pull instructions. Push instructions have to be executed before the main part of the subroutine program begins. Pull instructions have to be executed at the end of the subroutine program but before the return instruction. Example 10.18 shows the use of push and pull instructions.

EXAMPLE 10.18 Write the programming steps necessary to save and return all of the data in the 6800 μP registers.

Solution

```
PSH A     Save accumulator A.
PSH B     Save accumulator B.
TPA       Transfer CCR to accumulator A.
PSH A     Save accumulator A (condition code register).
  .         .
  .         .
  .         .
          Main subroutine program.
  .         .
  .         .
  .         .
PUL A     Retrieve accumulator A (condition code register).
TAP       Transfer accumulator A to CCR.
PUL B     Retrieve accumulator B.
PUL A     Retrieve accumulator A.
RTS       Retrieve original program counter.
```

Note: The 6800 μP does not have a push or pull instruction for the condition code register. This register can be saved on the stack, though, by transferring it to the accumulator and then using the PSH A instruction. The condition code register is retrieved from the stack by first executing a PUL A instruction and then a TAP instruction. Remember that the data has to be retrieved in the reverse order in which it was saved.

10.4.2 Temporary Storage

The stack does not have to be reserved for subroutine programs. It can also be used at any time for temporary storage of data. Often, the stack is used to hold incoming or outgoing data temporarily. The program in Example 10.19 shows how data can be brought into the μP and put onto the stack.

Remember that the 6800 μP does not have input or output instructions. It uses memory-mapped I/O, for which a peripheral chip is wired to the system bus and appears as a memory location to the μP. For example, if a peripheral device is wired as memory location 4000, then when the μP executes a load the accumulator instruction from memory location 4000, any data that is located at this address is put into the accumulator. Peripheral devices are covered in detail in Chapters 17, 18, and 19.

EXAMPLE 10.19 Write a program that brings in 10 bytes of data from an input device and stores each byte in the stack. The input device is wired as memory location 4000. Use accumulator A for bringing in the data, and use accumulator B as a counter. Use page 1 for the stack.

Solution

	LDS #01FF	Initialize starting location of stack pointer.
	LDA B #0A	Initialize accumulator B ($0A_{hex} = 10_{dec}$).
INPUT:	LDA A 4000	Load accumulator A from location 4000.
	PSH A	Save data on stack.
	DEC B	Decrement counter.
	BNE INPUT	If B ≠ 0, branch to INPUT.

The program in Example 10.20 shows how the data that has been stored on the stack by the program in Example 10.19 can be added. The program uses the TSX instruction to transfer the contents of the stack pointer plus 1 (the location of the first byte of data in the stack) to the index register. Then, by using the indexed addressing mode, we can remove a byte of data from the stack and add it to the contents of the accumulator. At the end of the program, we can store the total sum in memory.

EXAMPLE 10.20 Write a single-byte addition program to add the data that was stored on the stack in Example 10.19. Use accumulator A for the addition, and use accumulator B as a counter. Store the result in memory location 0500.

Solution

	TSX	Transfer stack + 1 to index register.
	LDA B #0A	Initialize accumulator B ($0A_{hex} = 10_{decimal}$).
	CLR A	Clear accumulator A and carry flag.
REPEAT:	ADC A 00,X	Add accumulator A + data in stack + carry flag.
	DEC B	Decrement counter.
	BNE REPEAT	If B ≠ 0, branch to REPEAT.
	STA 0500	Store sum at location 0500.

10.5 MULTIPLICATION

The 6800 μP does not have a multiplication instruction. Therefore, if we wish to multiply two numbers, we have to write a program to do so. The following description shows how two 8-bit positive numbers can be multiplied. When two 8-bit numbers are multiplied, the result is a 16-bit answer. Because the 6800 μP does not have any 16-bit registers, we need to use some memory locations as working registers. The memory locations in page 0 are usually used so that we can utilize the direct addressing mode.

The arithmetic terms used in multiplication are as follows:

```
  42  ←Multiplicand
  35  ←Multiplier
 ----
 210 }
126  }  Partial product
 ----
1470  ←Product
```

The values shown above are decimal numbers.

Before the multiplication program begins, the multiplicand and the multiplier have to be stored in memory. Remember that the product is eventually going to consist of 16 bits. The low-order 8 bits are referred to as the least significant (LS) byte of the product and the high-order 8 bits are referred to as the most significant (MS) byte.

The steps involved in multiplication are as follows:

1. Check the least significant bit of the multiplier. If it is 0, rotate both bytes of the product one bit to the right. If it is 1, add the multiplicand to the most significant byte of the product, and then rotate both bytes of the product one bit to the right.
2. If all bits of the multiplier have been checked, the program is finished. Otherwise, repeat step 1.
3. Store the result.

Table 10–1 shows how 42 is multiplied by 35, using the binary number system and the steps just described. Note in the multiplication that the shift operation is done by rotate right instructions. Since the multiplier is represented by 8 bits, step 1 has to be done 8 times. A counter keeps track of the number of times step 1 has been done. The count is shown in column 1 in Table 10–1. Column 2 shows the logic state of the multiplier for each test, starting with the least significant bit. Column 3 describes what is happening. Column 4 shows the addition that is done in the accumulator. Column 5 shows the contents of a working register, which holds the contents of the LS byte of the partial product. After the last rotation, the accumulator contains the most significant byte of the product, and the working register holds the least significant byte. Example 10.21 illustrates a program for 8-bit multiplication.

TABLE 10–1 Steps Involved in Binary Multiplication of Two 8-Bit Numbers (42 × 35 = 1470)

Count	Multiplier Logic State	Comments	Accumulator	Working Register
Start			00000000	
1	1	Add multiplicand	00101010	
		Shift right	00010101	0
2	1	Add multiplicand	00111111	0
		Shift right	00011111	10
3	0	Shift right	00001111	110
4	0	Shift right	00000111	1110
5	0	Shift right	00000011	11110
6	1	Add multiplicand	00101101	11110
		Shift right	00010110	111110
7	0	Shift right	00001011	0111110
8	0	Shift right	00000101 (MS byte of product)	10111110 (LS byte of product)

Note: 42 = 00101010 is the multiplicand; 35 = 00100011 is the multiplier.

EXAMPLE 10.21 Write an 8-bit multiplication program using the steps outlined above and the memory locations in page 0, shown in Table 10–2, as working registers.

Solution

```
        LDA A #08     Load accumulator A with number of bits to be
                      multiplied.
        STA A 20      Store count in location 0020.
        CLR A         Clear accumulator A and carry flag.
        LDA B 21      Load accumulator B with multiplicand.
MULT:   LSR 22        Shift multiplier right (bit 0 into carry).
        BCC ROTATE    If carry = 0, branch to ROTATE.
        ABA           Add multiplicand to accumulator A.
ROTATE: ROR A         Rotate accumulator A.
        ROR 24        Rotate location 0024.
        DEC 20        Decrement count.
        BNE MULT      If location 0020 ≠ 0, branch to MULT.
        STA A 23      Store MS byte in location 0023.
```

Note: Motorola's *Application Manual* (pages 2–12 to 2–21 of the *Manual*) describes how the 6800 μP can be programmed to multiply two 16-bit numbers. This multiplication generates a 32-bit product.

TABLE 10–2 Memory Locations to Be Used in Example 10.21

Memory Location	Purpose
0020	Count
0021	Multiplicand
0022	Multiplier
0023	MS byte of product
0024	LS byte of product

10.6 SUMMARY

In this chapter, we saw many of the 6800 μP instructions used in a number of different programming applications. As in previous chapters, the memory locations were chosen at random. Also, the programs could have been inserted into a main program or written as a subroutine. If programs are written as a subroutine, remember that the last instruction has to be an RTS instruction. If they are written as an interrupt subroutine program, the last instruction has to be an RTI instruction.

Section 10.1 showed how binary and decimal addition and subtraction can be accomplished using the 6800 μP. When two 8-bit numbers are being added or subtracted, the operation is a single-byte operation. A multiprecision program is needed when the numbers to be added or subtracted are longer than 8 bits. If two 16-bit numbers (2 bytes) are being operated upon, the multiprecision program is known as a double-precision program.

Section 10.2 showed the μP can be programmed for time delays. In the event that a time delay loop does not generate the exact delay, a time delay program can be trimmed, as described in Section 10.2.2.

A program that searches through memory for a particular value was illustrated in Section 10.3. The stack can be a very efficient area in memory for storing data temporarily. Several examples of how to use the stack instructions were given in Section 10.4.

Like most μPs, the 6800 has to be programmed to do multiplication. Section 10.5 showed a program for multiplying two 8-bit positive numbers. This multiplication program produces a 16-bit answer. Therefore, the product requires two memory locations to store the answer.

PROBLEMS

These problems are for the 6800 μP.

10–1 Write a program that adds the contents of location 0150 to the contents of location 0160. Store the result at memory location 0160. Use accumulator B.

10–2 Continue the program of Problem 10–1 so that the carry flag is saved at memory location 0161.

10-3 Does the following program add a column of five numbers at locations 0400 to 0404 and store the result at location 0030? The result does not produce a carry,

```
        CLC
        LDA B #05
        LDX #0400
        LDA A #00
COLADD: ADC A 00,X
        INX
        DEC B
        BNE COLADD
        STA A, 0030
```

10-4 What would be the count value in Example 10.4 for a 24-bit addition program?

10-5 Can a decimal adjust be made for accumulator B?

10-6 Repeat Problem 10-1 for BCD addition.

10-7 Repeat Problem 10-1 for binary subtraction.

10-8 What instruction or instructions have to be modified so that the program in Example 10.9 subtracts the contents of locations 0020 to 0023 from the contents of locations 0010 to 0013?

10-9 If accumulator A in Example 10.11 is initialized with 48_{hex}, what time delay will be generated?

10-10 With what value must accumulator A in Example 10.11 be initialized for a time delay of 842 μs?

10-11 What time delay would be generated in Example 10.14 if the NOP instruction were accidentally inserted between the DEC instruction and the BNE instruction?

10-12 Refer to Example 10.15. If count no. 1 = 00_{hex} and count no. 2 = 80_{hex}, what time delay is generated by the program?

10-13 What data will be lost if the programming steps of Example 10.18 are written as follows?

```
.
.
.
TPA
PHA
PHB
PHA
.
.
.
```

10-14 Modify Example 10.19 for 20 bytes of data.

10-15 Continue Example 10.19 so that, after 10 bytes of data have been stored on the stack, the μP will add the column of numbers in BCD. Use accumulator A for the addition, use accumulator B for a counter, and store the result at location 0750. Use the PUL A instruction.

6800 Microprocessor

11.0 INTRODUCTION

This chapter deals with the 6800 μP's pin descriptions, timing diagrams, events that occur when an instruction is fetched and executed, events that occur when power is applied, and procedure for handling interrupts.

The 6800 μP is a central processing unit around which an entire μC system can be built. It is fabricated using NMOS technology and is housed in a 40-pin dual-in-line package. Like the 8080A, the 6800 requires an external circuit to generate the two-phase nonoverlapping clock pulses. Figure 11-1 shows the 6800 μP along with a 6870A clock generator circuit. The 6800 μP needs an external clock driver, such as the MC6870A, to generate the ϕ_1 and ϕ_2 nonoverlapping clock pulses. The 6870A provides not only the clock signals for the μP, but also a ϕ_2 clock pulse that is TTL compatible and other control signals.

11.1 PIN DESCRIPTIONS

The following paragraphs briefly describe the functions of the 6800's pins. Figure 11-2 shows the pin designations for this μP.

Address Bus (A_0–A_{15}): There are 16 address bus pins that allow the 6800 μP to address 64K bytes. Each pin is capable of driving one standard TTL load and 130 pF. All the lines have three-state drivers that allow this μP to perform direct memory access (DMA) operations.

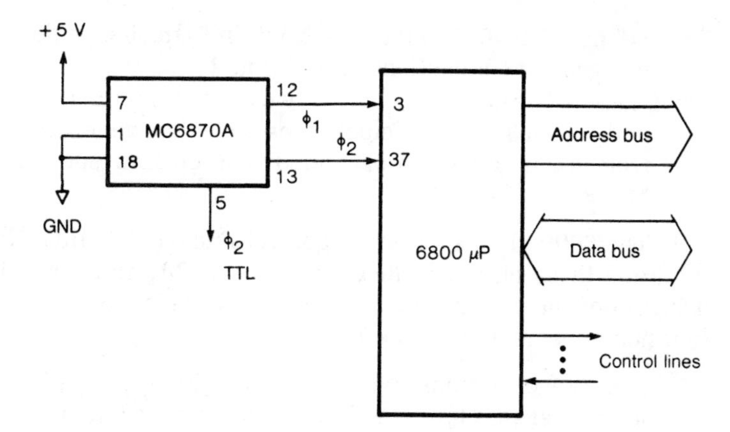

FIGURE 11–1 6800 μP with 6870 Clock Generator Circuit

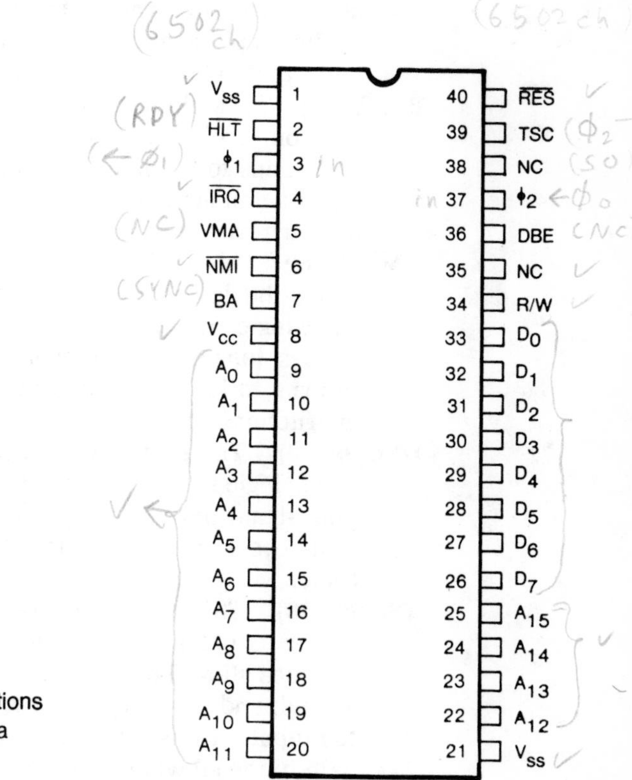

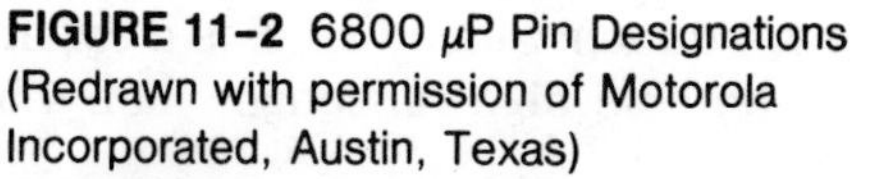
FIGURE 11–2 6800 μP Pin Designations (Redrawn with permission of Motorola Incorporated, Austin, Texas)

Data Bus (D_0–D_7): There are eight bidirectional data bus pins that allow the μP to communicate with memory and peripheral chips. When the μP is sending data, the output buffers are capable of driving one standard TTL load and 130 pF. Each pin has three-state capability.

Power Pins: The 6800 μP is a +5 V (pin 8) device. It does, however, require two ground connections (pins 1 and 21).

Clock Pins: The 6800 μP requires two nonoverlapping clock signals—ϕ_1 (pin 3) and ϕ_2 (pin 37). These clock signals must be generated externally to the μP from a clock generator and driver circuit, such as the MC6870A or MC6871.

The 6800 μP has six input control lines ($\overline{\text{HLT}}$, $\overline{\text{IRQ}}$, $\overline{\text{NMI}}$, DBE, TSC, and $\overline{\text{RES}}$) and three output control lines (VMA, BA, and R/W). The bar over a pin designation means that this line's active state is low. A brief description of the function of each control pin follows.

$\overline{\text{HLT}}$ (Pin 2): In normal operation, the logic level on pin 2 is high. When the logic level goes low, the μP finishes the instruction it is executing and then halts (no more instructions are fetched and executed). This permits an external signal to control the execution of the program. This feature is often used during program debugging. When the $\overline{\text{HLT}}$ line goes low, the bus available pin goes high, the valid memory address line goes low, and all other three-state lines go to their three-state condition.

$\overline{\text{IRQ}}$ (Pin 4): The abbreviation IRQ stands for *interrupt request.* When the logic level on this line goes low, the μP finishes the instruction it is executing and jumps to the interrupt service routine, provided that the μP's interrupt flag bit is not set. The μP returns to the program it left after decoding a return from interrupt instruction.

$\overline{\text{NMI}}$ (Pin 6): This pin is the nonmaskable interrupt request pin. This interrupt cannot be disabled by the programmer or by the μP. When pin 6 receives a low logic level, the μP finishes executing its present instruction and then always jumps to its nonmaskable interrupt service program. The μP returns to its normal operation after decoding a return from interrupt instruction.

DBE (Pin 36): The abbreviation DBE stands for *data bus enable.* When there is a high logic level input on this line, the μP's data bus buffers are enabled. This signal permits the μP to send data out onto the data bus during a write cycle. In most applications, the DBE signal comes from the ϕ_2 clock cycle.

TSC (Pin 39): TSC stands for *three-state control.* A high logic level on this line causes the μP's address lines and the R/W line to go into their high impedance state. The VMA and BA lines go low. The ϕ_1 and ϕ_2 clock inputs go high and low, respectively. *Caution:* Since the μP is a dynamic device, the input on this line cannot be held high for longer than 4.5 μs, or the data in the μP will be lost.

$\overline{\text{RES}}$ (Pin 40): This pin is the reset pin. It is used to initialize the program counter after power is first turned on. If the reset pin is held low for at least 8 clock cycles and is brought back high, the μP retrieves data at location FFFE and then the data at FFFF. The data stored at these two successive memory locations should be the starting address of the main program.

VMA (Pin 5): The abbreviation VMA stands for *valid memory address*. When this line goes high, it is a signal to all other devices that there is a valid address on the address bus lines.

BA (Pin 7): The abbreviation BA stands for *bus available*. When the μP is controlling the system, the logic level on this pin is low. When this line goes to a high logic level, the μP address and data bus are in the high impedance state. This line goes high under two conditions: (1) when the μP receives a $\overline{\text{HLT}}$ signal or (2) if the μP decodes a wait for interrupt instruction.

R/W (Pin 34): The read/write line indicates whether the μP is receiving data or sending data. When this line is high, the μP is reading (receiving) data from memory or an I/O device. When this line is low, the μP is writing (sending) data to memory or an I/O device.

11.2 ϕ_1 AND ϕ_2 CLOCK SIGNALS

Figure 11–3 shows typical ϕ_1 and ϕ_2 clock signals for the 6800 μP. The electrical characteristics are given in Table 11–1. The frequency range for the 6800 is from 100 kHz to 1 MHz. This frequency range causes a range of cycle times from 1.0 μs to 10 μs. The minimum pulse width high times are specified as $PW_{\phi H}$. The high input clock voltage level is given by V_{IHC} and the low input clock voltage level is given by V_{ILC}. The overshoot voltage is V_{OS} (see Figure 11–3). The value t_{ut} is the total up time. It is used by a designer to guarantee that the required access times for memory and peripheral chips are met. Time t_d is the delay or separation time measured at a maximum overlap voltage, V_{OV} (see Figure 11–3). This separation time ensures that the nonoverlapping requirement is met.

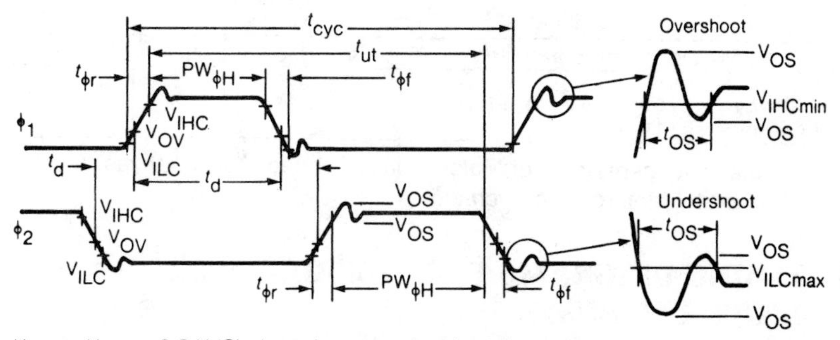

FIGURE 11–3 Clock Timing Waveform (Redrawn with permission of Motorola Incorporated, Austin, Texas)

TABLE 11–1 Electrical and Timing Characteristics for ϕ_1 and ϕ_2 Clock Pulses

DC ELECTRICAL CHARACTERISTICS (V_{CC} = 5.0 Vdc, ±5%, V_{SS} = 0, T_A = T_L to T_H unless otherwise noted)

Characteristic		Symbol	Min	Typ	Max	Unit
Input High Voltage	Logic	V_{IH}	$V_{SS}+2.0$	–	V_{CC}	V
	ϕ1, ϕ2	V_{IHC}	$V_{CC}-0.6$	–	$V_{CC}+0.3$	
Input Low Voltage	Logic	V_{IL}	$V_{SS}-0.3$	-	$V_{SS}+0.8$	V
	ϕ1, ϕ2	V_{ILC}	$V_{SS}-0.3$	–	$V_{SS}+0.4$	
Input Leakage Current (V_{in} = 0 to 5.25 V, V_{CC} = Max)	Logic	I_{in}	–	1.0	2.5	μA
(V_{in} = 0 to 5.25 V, V_{CC} = 0 V to 5.25 V)	ϕ1, ϕ2		–	–	100	
Three-State Input Leakage Current (V_{in} = 0.4 to 2.4 V, V_{CC} = Max)	D0-D7	I_{IZ}	–	2.0	10	μA
	A0-A15, R/$\overline{W}$		–	–	100	
Output High Voltage (I_{Load} = −205 μA, V_{CC} = Min)	D0-D7	V_{OH}	$V_{SS}+2.4$	–	–	V
(I_{Load} = −145 μA, V_{CC} = Min)	A0-A15, R/$\overline{W}$, VMA		$V_{SS}+2.4$	–	–	
(I_{Load} = −100 μA, V_{CC} = Min)	BA		$V_{SS}+2.4$	–	–	
Output Low Voltage (I_{Load} = 1.6 mA, V_{CC} = Min)		V_{OL}	–	–	$V_{SS}+0.4$	V
Internal Power Dissipation (Measured at $T_A = T_L$)		P_{INT}	–	0.5	1.0	W
Capacitance (V_{in} = 0, T_A = 25°C, f = 1.0 MHz)	ϕ1	C_{in}	–	25	35	pF
	ϕ2		–	45	70	
	D0-D7		–	10	12.5	
	Logic Inputs		–	6.5	10	
	A0-A15, R/$\overline{W}$, VMA	C_{out}	–	–	12	pF

CLOCK TIMING (V_{CC} = 5.0 V, ±5%, V_{SS} = 0, T_A = T_L to T_H unless otherwise noted)

Characteristic		Symbol	Min	Typ	Max	Unit
Frequency of Operation	MC6800	f	0.1	–	1.0	MHz
	MC68A00		0.1	–	1.5	
	MC68B00		0.1	–	2.0	
Cycle Time	MC6800	t_{cyc}	1.000	–	10	μs
	MC68A00		0.666	–	10	
	MC68B00		0.500	–	10	
Clock Pulse Width (Measured at $V_{CC}-0.6$ V)	ϕ1, ϕ2 – MC6800	$PW_{\phi H}$	400	–	9500	ns
	ϕ1, ϕ2 – MC68A00		230	–	9500	
	ϕ1, ϕ2 – MC68B00		180	–	9500	
Total ϕ1 and ϕ2 Up Time	MC6800	t_{ut}	900	–	–	ns
	MC68A00		600	–	–	
	MC68B00		440	–	–	
Rise and Fall Time (Measured between $V_{SS}+0.4$ and $V_{CC}-0.6$)		t_r, t_f	–	–	100	ns
Delay Time or Clock Separation (Measured at $V_{OV} = V_{SS}+0.6$ V@$t_r = t_f \leq 100$ ns)		t_d	0	–	9100	ns
(Measured at $V_{OV} = V_{SS}+1.0$ V@$t_r = t_f \leq 35$ ns)			0	–	9100	

Source: Reprinted with permission of Motorola Incorporated, Austin, Texas.

11.3 TIMING DIAGRAMS FOR THE ADDRESS AND DATA BUSES

Figures 11–4 and 11–5 show the timing diagrams for a read and write operation, respectively. Table 11–2 gives the names and specifications for all the times. A cycle starts when the ϕ_1 clock signal rises to 0.3 V. The address, R/W signal, and VMA signal are stable after t_{AD}, address delay time. The read access time is t_{acc}, followed by the data setup time, t_{DSR}. The data coming into the μP is latched at the end of the ϕ_2 clock signal. To guarantee that the μP latches the data, the data on the data bus is held there for an additional hold time, t_H.

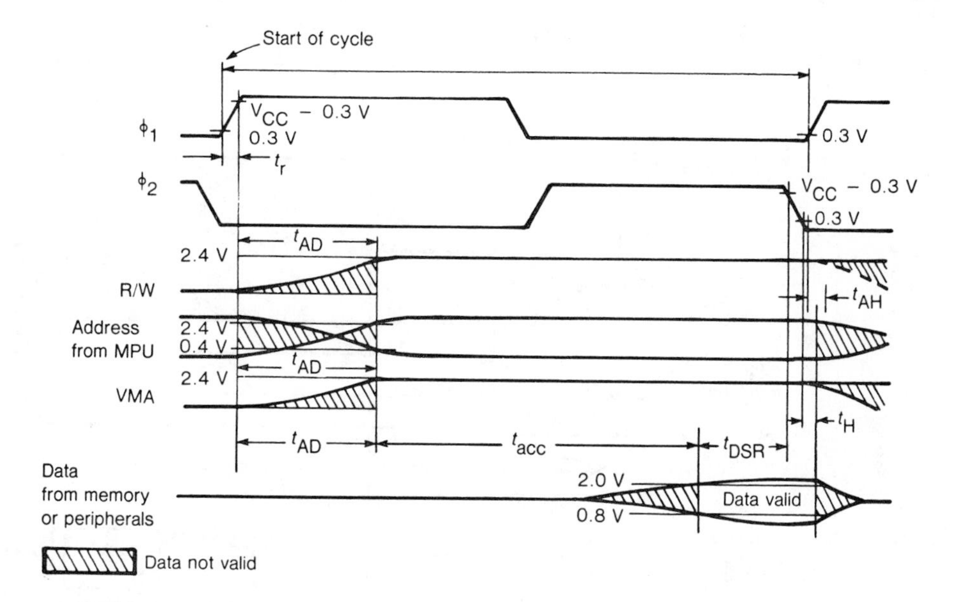

FIGURE 11–4 Timing Diagram for Reading Data from Memory or Peripherals (Redrawn with permission of Motorola Incorporated, Austin, Texas)

TABLE 11–2 Read and Write Timing Characteristics

Characteristic	Symbol	MC6800			MC68A00			MC68B00			Unit
		Min	Typ	Max	Min	Typ	Max	Min	Typ	Max	
Address Delay											
C = 90 pF	t_{AD}	–	–	270	–	–	180	–	–	150	ns
C = 30 pF		–	–	250	–	–	165	–	–	135	
Peripheral Read Access Time $t_{acc} = t_{ut} - (t_{AD} + t_{DSR})$	t_{acc}	605	–	—	400	–	—	290	–	—	ns
Data Setup Time (Read)	t_{DSR}	100	–	–	60	–	–	40	–	–	ns
Input Data Hold Time	t_H	10	–	–	10	–	–	10	–	–	ns
Output Data Hold Time	t_H	10	25	–	10	25	–	10	25	–	ns
Address Hold Time (Address, R/$\overline{W}$, VMA)	t_{AH}	30	50	–	30	50	–	30	50	–	ns
Enable High Time for DBE Input	t_{EH}	450	–	–	280	–	–	220	–	–	ns
Data Delay Time (Write)	t_{DDW}	–	–	225	–	–	200	–	–	160	ns
Processor Controls											
Processor Control Setup Time	t_{PCS}	200	–	–	140	–	–	110	–	–	ns
Processor Control Rise and Fall Time	t_{PCr}, t_{PCf}	–	–	100	–	–	100	–	–	100	
Bus Available Delay	t_{BA}	–	–	250	–	–	165	–	–	135	
Three-State Enable	t_{TSE}	–	–	40	–	–	40	–	–	40	
Three-State Delay	t_{TSD}	–	–	270	–	–	270	–	–	220	
Data Bus Enable Down Time During ϕ1 Up Time	t_{DBE}	150	–	–	120	–	–	75	–	–	
Data Bus Enable Rise and Fall Times	t_{DBEr}, t_{DBEf}	–	–	25	–	–	25	–	–	25	

Source: Reprinted with permission of Motorola Incorporated, Austin, Texas.

When the 6800 μP writes data, the address bus, R/W, and VMA signals are stabilized by the end of the address delay time, t_{AD}. The data bus enable (DBE) pin must be brought high. After a data delay write time, t_{DDW}, the data on the data bus is valid. In most systems, the DBE is connected to the ϕ_2

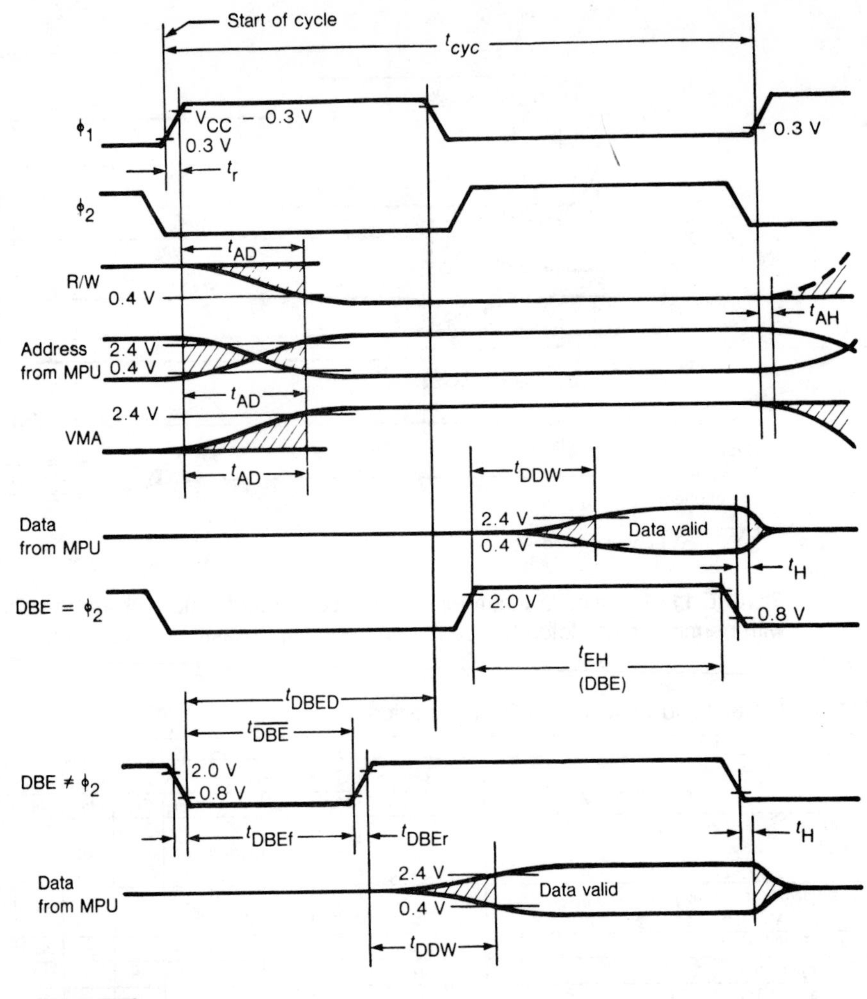

FIGURE 11–5 Timing Diagram for Writing Data to Memory or Peripherals (Redrawn with permission of Motorola Incorporated, Austin, Texas)

clock signal. Figure 11–5 shows the timing diagrams when DBE = ϕ_2 and when DBE ≠ ϕ_2.

11.4 CYCLE-BY-CYCLE OPERATION

The 6800 μP has 72 different types of instructions and seven addressing modes. This section gives a cycle-by-cycle description of what happens on the address and data buses when an instruction is fetched and executed by the μP. The section is subdivided according to addressing modes. In the following examples, a clock cycle is t_{cyc}, the time for a complete ϕ_1 and ϕ_2 clock pulse. The memory locations have been chosen at random.

11.4.1 Immediate Addressing Mode

The immediate addressing mode is an addressing technique in which the first byte of the instruction is the op code and the second byte is the data (operand). Exceptions to this are the CPX, LDS, and LDX instructions, which have the operand in the second and third bytes of the instruction.

Figure 11–6 shows a timing diagram for the immediate addressing mode. Data buses for a two-byte and a three-byte instruction are illustrated. Referring to Figure 11–6, we see that, during the first half of cycle 1, the program counter's (PC) current address is put on the address bus, the R/W line goes high designating a read operation, and VMA goes high designating that the current address is a valid memory address. The program counter is incremented on the falling edge of ϕ_1. During the second half of cycle 1, the op code is put on the data bus from memory and loaded into the μP. The new value in the program counter (PC) goes out on the address bus and the operand, which is usually data, is loaded into the μP at the end of cycle 2. The PC has been incremented again. The op code of the next instruction is fetched on the next cycle if the immediate addressing mode instruction was two bytes long. For the CPX, LDS, and LDX instructions, cycle 3 is needed for the μP to receive the third byte of the instruction. A summary of instructions and cycle-by-cycle operation for the immediate addressing mode is given in Table 11–3. Examples 11.1 and 11.2 illustrate determinations of the number of clock cycles needed for certain program listings.

EXAMPLE 11.1 Show the clock cycles needed to load accumulator A immediately with data 00.

Program Listing	Memory Listing		
C400 LDA A #00	C400	86	Op code
	C401	00	Data

Solution

Clock Cycle	Address Bus	Data Bus	Internal Operation
1	C400	86	Fetch op code; increment PC to C401.
2	C401	00	Decode op code 86; increment PC to C402; latch data 00 into μP.
3	C402	Next op code	

The LDA A immediate instruction takes two clock cycles because on the third clock cycle, the next op code is being fetched by the μP. The data at the end of clock cycle 2 is latched into the μP.

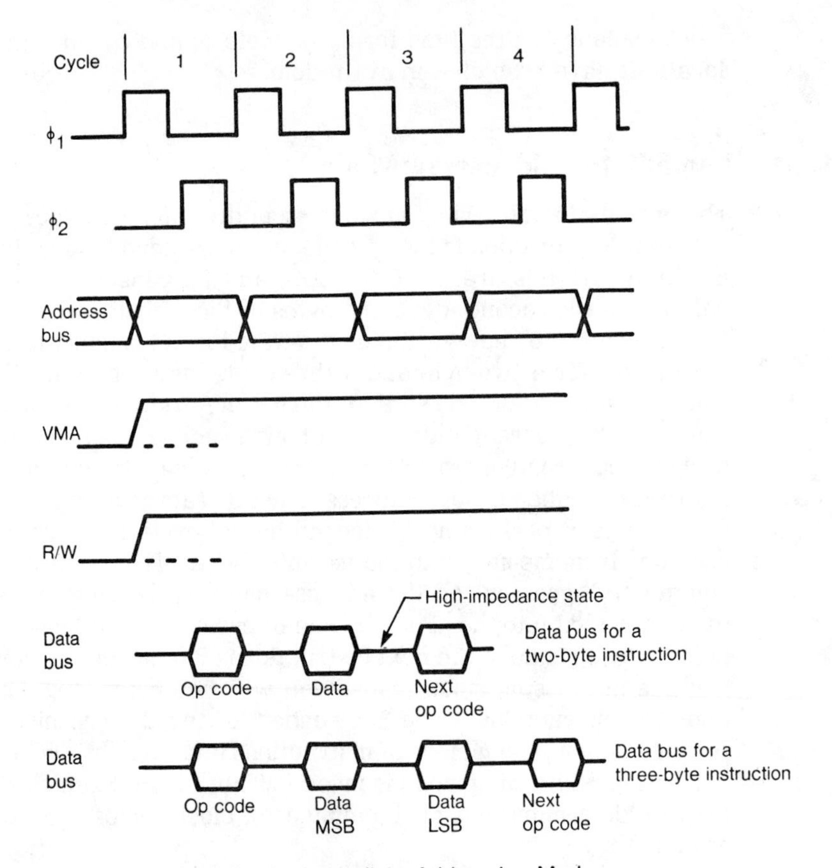

FIGURE 11-6 Timing Diagram for Immediate Addressing Mode

TABLE 11-3 Summary of Immediate Addressing Mode Instructions

Instructions	Cycles	Cycle #	VMA Line	Address Bus	R/$\overline{W}$ Line	Data Bus
ADC EOR ADD LDA AND ORA BIT SBC CMP SUB	2	1	1	Op Code Address	1	Op Code
		2	1	Op Code Address + 1	1	Operand Data
CPX LDS LDX	3	1	1	Op Code Address	1	Op Code
		2	1	Op Code Address + 1	1	Operand Data (High Order Byte)
		3	1	Op Code Address + 2	1	Operand Data (Low Order Byte)

Source: Reprinted with permission of Motorola Incorporated, Austin, Texas.

EXAMPLE 11.2 Show the number of clock cycles needed to load the X index register immediately with data 0010. Remember, the X register is a 16-bit register.

Program Listing	Memory Listing		
F850 LDX #0010	F850	CE	Op code
	F851	00	Data (high byte)
	F852	10	Data (low byte)

Solution

Clock Cycle	Address Bus	Data Bus	Internal Operation
1	F850	CE	Fetch op code; increment PC to F851.
2	F851	00	Decode op code (CE); increment PC to F852; latch data 00 into X register.
3	F852	10	Increment PC to F853; latch data into X register.
4	F853	Next op code	Fetch next op code; increment PC to F854.

11.4.2 Direct Addressing Mode

The direct addressing mode for the 6800 μP is a two-byte instruction. The first byte is the op code and the second byte is the low byte of the operand address. The high byte is understood by the μP to be in page zero. This addressing mode allows the user to address directly the lowest 256 bytes in memory (locations 0 through 255). This allows faster execution times by storing or retrieving data in these locations. In most configurations, these locations should be a random access memory. The 6800 μP has 16 instructions that can use the direct addressing mode. Although all of them are two bytes long, their execution times may require 3, 4, or 5 clock cycles, depending on the instruction. A summary of instructions and cycle-by-cycle operation for the direct addressing mode is given in Table 11-4. Example 11.3 illustrates the clock cycles needed in a program listing.

TABLE 11-4 Summary of Direct Addressing Mode Instructions

Instructions	Cycles	Cycle #	VMA Line	Address Bus	R/$\overline{W}$ Line	Data Bus
ADC EOR ADD LDA AND ORA BIT SBC CMP SUB	3	1	1	Op Code Address	1	Op Code
		2	1	Op Code Address + 1	1	Address of Operand
		3	1	Address of Operand	1	Operand Data
CPX LDS LDX	4	1	1	Op Code Address	1	Op Code
		2	1	Op Code Address + 1	1	Address of Operand
		3	1	Address of Operand	1	Operand Data (High Order Byte)
		4	1	Operand Address + 1	1	Operand Data (Low Order Byte)
STA	4	1	1	Op Code Address	1	Op Code
		2	1	Op Code Address + 1	1	Destination Address
		3	0	Destination Address	1	Irrelevant Data
		4	1	Destination Address	0	Data from Accumulator
STS STX	5	1	1	Op Code Address	1	Op Code
		2	1	Op Code Address + 1	1	Address of Operand
		3	0	Address of Operand	1	Irrelevant Data
		4	1	Address of Operand	0	Register Data (High Order Byte)
		5	1	Address of Operand + 1	0	Register Data (Low Order Byte)

Source: Reprinted with permission of Motorola Incorporated, Austin, Texas.

EXAMPLE 11.3 Show the clock cycles needed for loading accumulator B with data from page 00.

Program Listing	Memory Listing	Data at Location 0070
0400 LDA B 70	0400 D6 Op code	85
	0401 70 ABL	

Solution

Clock Cycle	Address Bus	Data Bus	Internal Operation
1	0400	D6	Fetch op code; increment PC to 0401.
2	0401	70	Decode op code D6; increment PC to 0402.
3	0070	85	Latch data (85) into μP.
4	0402	Next op code	Fetch next op code; increment PC to 0403.

Figure 11-7 shows the timing diagram for a load the accumulator instruction using the direct addressing mode. The address in the program counter is put on the address bus and the LDA op code is loaded into the μP during cycle 1. The program counter is incremented. During cycle 2, 8 bits of address are loaded into the μP's address bus low (ABL) register. The upper 8 bits are forced to all zeros. In cycle 3, the new address is put on the address bus and the operand is loaded in the μP. Example 11.4 illustrates the clock cycles needed for a store instruction.

EXAMPLE 11.4 Show the number of clock cycles needed to complete the following store instruction:

Program Listing	Memory Listing	Accumulator B
5740 STA B 20	5740 D7 Op code	F1
	5741 20 ABL	

Solution

Clock Cycle	Address Bus	Data Bus	Internal Operation
1	5740	D7	Fetch op code; increment PC to 5741.
2	5741	20	Decode op code D7; increment PC to 5742; latch ABL (20).
3	0020	Data (irrelevant)	Bring R/W line low.
4	0020	F1	Data F1 from accumulator B is sent to location 0020.
5	5742	Next op code	Fetch next op code; increment PC to 5743.

This store instruction requires four clock cycles. On the fifth clock cycle, the 6800 μP fetches the next op code.

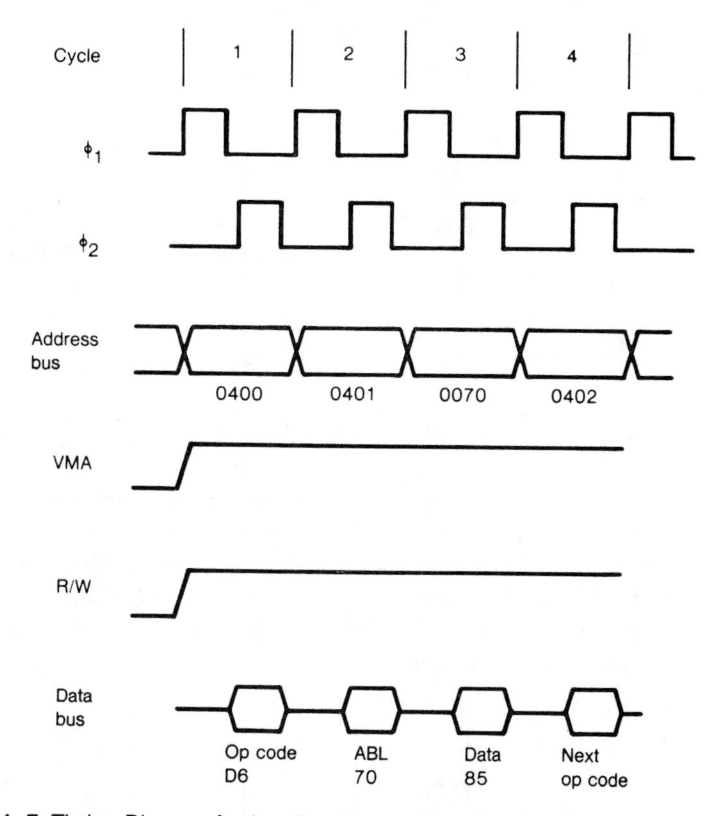

FIGURE 11-7 Timing Diagram for Loading Accumulator B with Data from Page 00

A STA instruction is handled in the same manner as an LDA instruction, except that there is an additional cycle for the STA instruction, due to the μP's architecture. This additional cycle is required to move the accumulator internally, and it occurs during clock cycle 3 in the preceding example. During this cycle, the data bus is in an indeterminate state and the VMA line is low. The actual storing of data occurs on cycle 4. The next instruction follows on the next clock cycle. Figure 11-8 shows the timing diagram for an STA instruction. Example 11.5 shows what happens on each clock cycle when the μP executes an STX instruction.

EXAMPLE 11.5 Show the number of clock cycles needed to store the following data in the X register at an address in page 00:

Program Listing	Memory Listing	X Register
C200 STX 80	C200 DF Op code	471E
	C201 80 ADL	

Solution

Clock Cycle	Address Bus	Data Bus	Internal Operation
1	C200	DF	Fetch op code; increment PC to C201.
2	C201	80	Decode op code DF; increment PC to C202; latch ADL.
3	0080	Data (irrelevant)	VMA line is low; bring R/W line low for next cycle.
4	0080	47	Send high byte of X register to location 0080; increment address to 0081.
5	0081	1E	Send low byte of X register to location 0081.
6	C202	Next op code	Fetch next op code; increment PC to C203.

This instruction requires one more clock cycle than the instruction in Example 11.4 because two bytes of data have to be stored in memory. If we continue Example 11.5, the contents of the program counter (C202) that has been held since clock cycle 2 are placed on the address bus on the next clock cycle. Figure 11-9 shows a timing diagram for the instruction in this example.

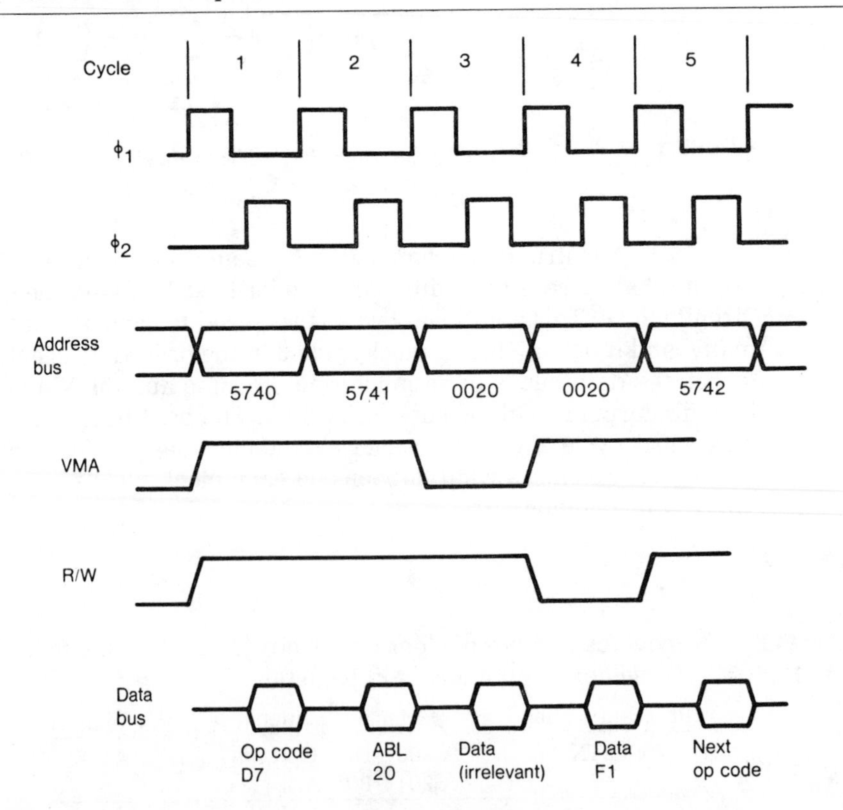

FIGURE 11-8 Timing Diagram for Storing Data in Page 00

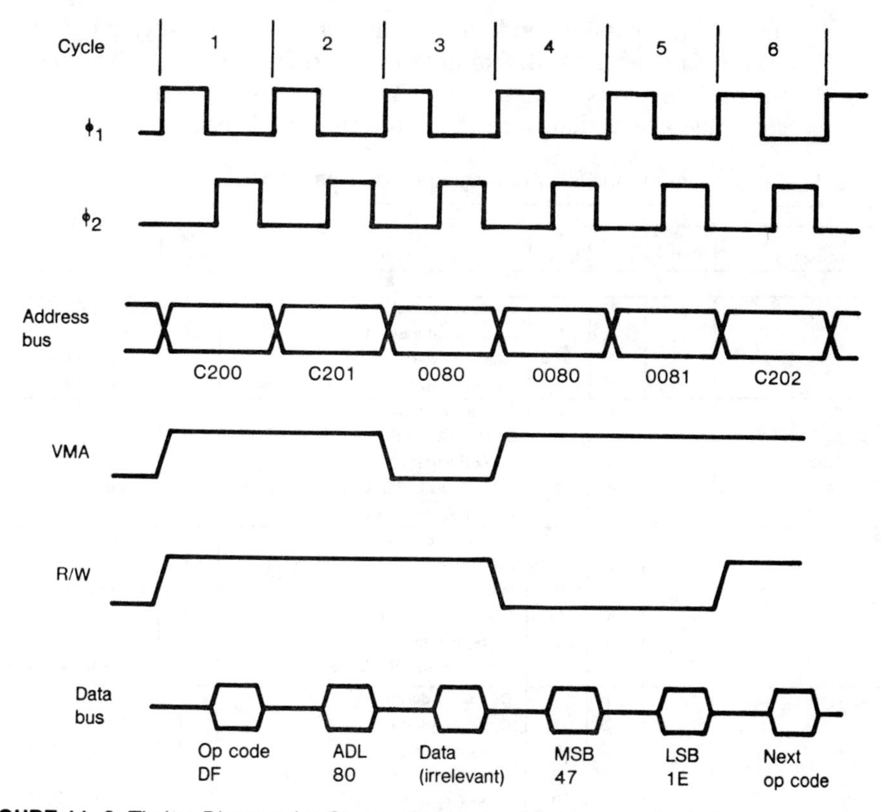

FIGURE 11–9 Timing Diagram for Storing Contents of Index Register in Page 00

11.4.3 Indexed Addressing Mode

An indexed addressing mode instruction is a two-byte instruction. The first byte is the op code, while the second byte is an offset value. The address contained in the second byte of the instruction is added to the lowest 8 bits of the index register. This result is then used to address memory. The modified address is held in a temporary address register, so there is no change to the index register or the program counter.

In the first two cycles of an LDA indexed address instruction, the op code is loaded into the μP, followed by the index offset. In the third cycle, the low-order byte of the index register is added to the offset; the carry propagates during cycle 4. The VMA goes low during these two cycles, while the μP is preparing the indexed address. The new address than goes on the address bus during cycle 5.

The STA indexed instruction is handled in the same manner as the LDA instruction; however, an additional cycle is required for the STA indexed instruction, due to the μP's architecture. VMA is held low, then, for three bytes for the STA instruction instead of two for the LDA instruction. The 6800 μP's indexed addressing mode instructions and cycle-by-cycle operations are summarized in Table 11–5. Example 11.6 and Figure 11–10 show the steps involved for an STA indexed instruction. The contents of the index register and the offset value are added to produce the final address.

TABLE 11–5 Summary of Indexed Addressing Mode Instructions

Instructions	Cycles	Cycle #	VMA Line	Address Bus	R/$\overline{W}$ Line	Data Bus
JMP	4	1	1	Op Code Address	1	Op Code
		2	1	Op Code Address + 1	1	Offset
		3	0	Index Register	1	Irrelevant Data
		4	0	Index Register Plus Offset (w/o Carry)	1	Irrelevant Data
ADC EOR ADD LDA AND ORA BIT SBC CMP SUB	5	1	1	Op Code Address	1	Op Code
		2	1	Op Code Address + 1	1	Offset
		3	0	Index Register	1	Irrelevant Data
		4	0	Index Register Plus Offset (w/o Carry)	1	Irrelevant Data
		5	1	Index Register Plus Offset	1	Operand Data
CPX LDS LDX	6	1	1	Op Code Address	1	Op Code
		2	1	Op Code Address + 1	1	Offset
		3	0	Index Register	1	Irrelevant Data
		4	0	Index Register Plus Offset (w/o Carry)	1	Irrelevant Data
		5	1	Index Register Plus Offset	1	Operand Data (High Order Byte)
		6	1	Index Register Plus Offset + 1	1	Operand Data (Low Order Byte)
STA	6	1	1	Op Code Address	1	Op Code
		2	1	Op Code Address + 1	1	Offset
		3	0	Index Register	1	Irrelevant Data
		4	0	Index Register Plus Offset (w/o Carry)	1	Irrelevant Data
		5	0	Index Register Plus Offset	1	Irrelevant Data
		6	1	Index Register Plus Offset	0	Operand Data
ASL LSR ASR NEG CLR ROL COM ROR DEC TST INC	7	1	1	Op Code Address	1	Op Code
		2	1	Op Code Address + 1	1	Offset
		3	0	Index Register	1	Irrelevant Data
		4	0	Index Register Plus Offset (w/o Carry)	1	Irrelevant Data
		5	1	Index Register Plus Offset	1	Current Operand Data
		6	0	Index Register Plus Offset	1	Irrelevant Data
		7	1/0 (Note 2)	Index Register Plus Offset	0	New Operand Data
STS STX	7	1	1	Op Code Address	1	Op Code
		2	1	Op Code Address + 1	1	Offset
		3	0	Index Register	1	Irrelevant Data
		4	0	Index Register Plus Offset (w/o Carry)	1	Irrelevant Data
		5	0	Index Register Plus Offset	1	Irrelevant Data
		6	1	Index Register Plus Offset	0	Operand Data (High Order Byte)
		7	1	Index Register Plus Offset + 1	0	Operand Data (Low Order Byte)
JSR	8	1	1	Op Code Address	1	Op Code
		2	1	Op Code Address + 1	1	Offset
		3	0	Index Register	1	Irrelevant Data
		4	1	Stack Pointer	0	Return Address (Low Order Byte)
		5	1	Stack Pointer – 1	0	Return Address (High Order Byte)
		6	0	Stack Pointer – 2	1	Irrelevant Data
		7	0	Index Register	1	Irrelevant Data
		8	0	Index Register Plus Offset (w/o Carry)	1	Irrelevant Data

Source: Reprinted with permission of Motorola Incorporated, Austin, Texas.

EXAMPLE 11.6 Show the number of clock cycles needed to store accumulator A using the indexed addressing mode.

Program Listing	Memory Listing			X Register	Accumulator A
D900 STA A 10,X	D900	EF	Op code	3050	E4
	D901	10	Offset		

Solution

Clock Cycle	Address Bus	Data Bus	Internal Operation
1	D900	EF	Fetch op code; increment PC to D901.
2	D901	10	Decode op code EF.
3	3050	Data (irrelevant)	Add 50 + 10 = 60 (no internal carry).
4	3060	Data (irrelevant)	Add 30 + internal carry = 30.
5	3060	Data (irrelevant)	Bring R/W line low for next clock cycle.
6	3060	E4	Send out data E4 to location 3060.

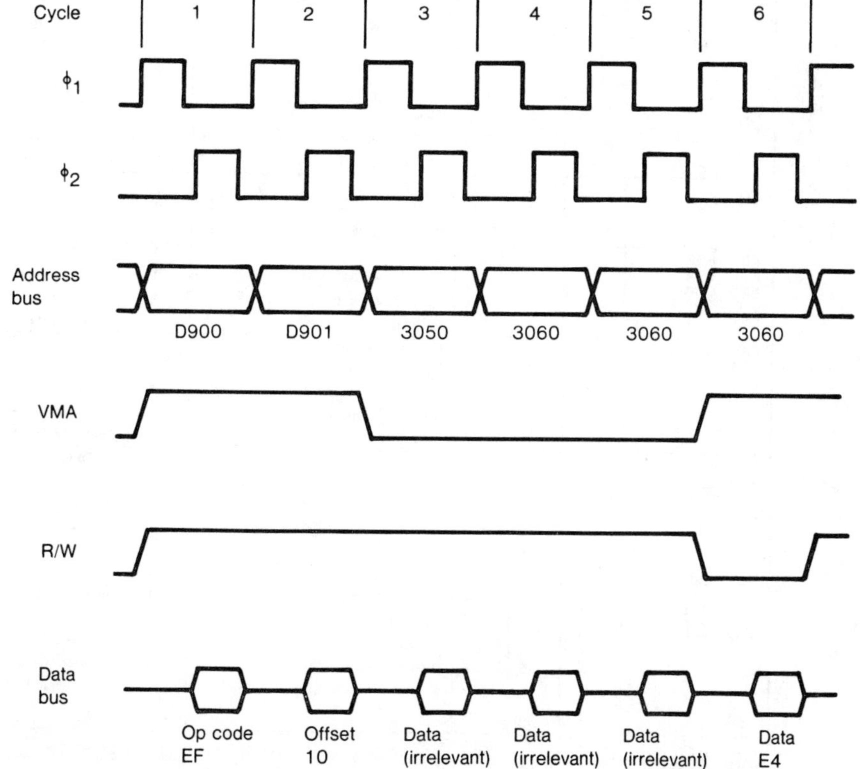

FIGURE 11-10 Timing Diagram for STA Indexed Instruction

11.4.4 Extended Addressing Mode

All extended addressing mode instructions are three-byte instructions. The first byte is the op code, the second byte is the eight high-order address bits. The third byte of the instruction contains the low-order eight bits of the address. Table 11–6 gives a summary of the instructions for the extended addressing mode. Notice in Table 11–6 and in Examples 11.7 and 11.8 that the VMA line is low for some instructions. This is again due to the internal architecture of the μP. When the VMA line is low, it signifies that the data bus is in an indeterminate state and the data is considered to be irrelevant. Examples 11.7 and 11.8 show what happens on each clock cycle for loading and storing data in the accumulator using the extended addressing mode.

TABLE 11–6 Summary of Extended Addressing Mode Instructions

Instructions	Cycles	Cycle #	VMA Line	Address Bus	R/$\overline{W}$ Line	Data Bus
STS STX	6	1	1	Op Code Address	1	Op Code
		2	1	Op Code Address + 1	1	Address of Operand (High Order Byte)
		3	1	Op Code Address + 2	1	Address of Operand (Low Order Byte)
		4	0	Address of Operand	1	Irrelevant Data
		5	1	Address of Operand	0	Operand Data (High Order Byte)
		6	1	Address of Operand + 1	0	Operand Data (Low Order Byte)
JSR	9	1	1	Op Code Address	1	Op Code
		2	1	Op Code Address + 1	1	Address of Subroutine (High Order Byte)
		3	1	Op Code Address + 2	1	Address of Subroutine (Low Order Byte)
		4	1	Subroutine Starting Address	1	Op Code of Next Instruction
		5	1	Stack Pointer	0	Return Address (Low Order Byte)
		6	1	Stack Pointer 1	0	Return Address (High Order Byte)
		7	0	Stack Pointer 2	1	Irrelevant Data
		8	0	Op Code Address + 2	1	Irrelevant Data
		9	1	Op Code Address + 2	1	Address of Subroutine (Low Order Byte)
JMP	3	1	1	Op Code Address	1	Op Code
		2	1	Op Code Address + 1	1	Jump Address (High Order Byte)
		3	1	Op Code Address + 2	1	Jump Address (Low Order Byte)
ADC EOR ADD LDA AND ORA BIT SBC CMP SUB	4	1	1	Op Code Address	1	Op Code
		2	1	Op Code Address + 1	1	Address of Operand (High Order Byte)
		3	1	Op Code Address + 2	1	Address of Operand (Low Order Byte)
		4	1	Address of Operand	1	Operand Data
CPX LDS LDX	5	1	1	Op Code Address	1	Op Code
		2	1	Op Code Address + 1	1	Address of Operand (High Order Byte)
		3	1	Op Code Address + 2	1	Address of Operand (Low Order Byte)
		4	1	Address of Operand	1	Operand Data (High Order Byte)
		5	1	Address of Operand + 1	1	Operand Data (Low Order Byte)
STA A STA B	5	1	1	Op Code Address	1	Op Code
		2	1	Op Code Address + 1	1	Destination Address (High Order Byte)
		3	1	Op Code Address + 2	1	Destination Address (Low Order Byte)
		4	0	Operand Destination Address	1	Irrelevant Data
		5	1	Operand Destination Address	0	Data from Accumulator
ASL LSR ASR NEG CLR ROL COM ROR DEC TST INC	6	1	1	Op Code Address	1	Op Code
		2	1	Op Code Address + 1	1	Address of Operand (High Order Byte)
		3	1	Op Code Address + 2	1	Address of Operand (Low Order Byte)
		4	1	Address of Operand	1	Current Operand Data
		5	0	Address of Operand	1	Irrelevant Data
		6	1/0	Address of Operand	0	New Operand Data

Source: Reprinted with permission of Motorola Incorporated, Austin, Texas.

EXAMPLE 11.7 Show the number of clock cycles that are needed for loading accumulator A using the extended addressing mode.

Program Listing	Memory Listing	Data in Memory
0350 LDA A 4712	0350 B6 Op code	4712 1D
	0351 47 ADH	
	0352 12 ADL	

Solution

Clock Cycle	Address Bus	Data Bus	Internal Operation
1	0350	B6	Fetch op code; increment PC to 0351.
2	0351	47	Decode op code B6; increment PC to 0352.
3	0352	12	Hold ADH (47); increment PC to 0353.
4	4712	1D	Latch incoming data.
5	0353	Next op code	Fetch next op code; increment PC to 0354.

Figure 11-11 shows the timing diagram for a load the accumulator instruction using the extended addressing mode. The contents (1D) of memory location 4712 are being transferred to accumulator A.

EXAMPLE 11.8 Show the number of clock cycles needed to store accumulator A in the following program:

Program Listing	Memory Listing	Accumulator A
8450 STA A 27FA	8450 B7 Op code	11
	8451 27 ADH	
	8452 FA ADL	

Solution

Clock Cycle	Address Bus	Data Bus	Internal Operation
1	8450	B7	Fetch op code; increment PC to 8451.
2	8451	27	Decode op code B7; increment PC to 8452.
3	8452	FA	Hold ADH (27); increment PC to 8453.
4	27FA	Data (irrelevant)	VMA line is low; bring R/W line low for next clock cycle.
5	27FA	11	Send out data (11) from accumulator A to location 27FA.
6	8453	Next op code	Fetch next op code; increment PC to 8454.

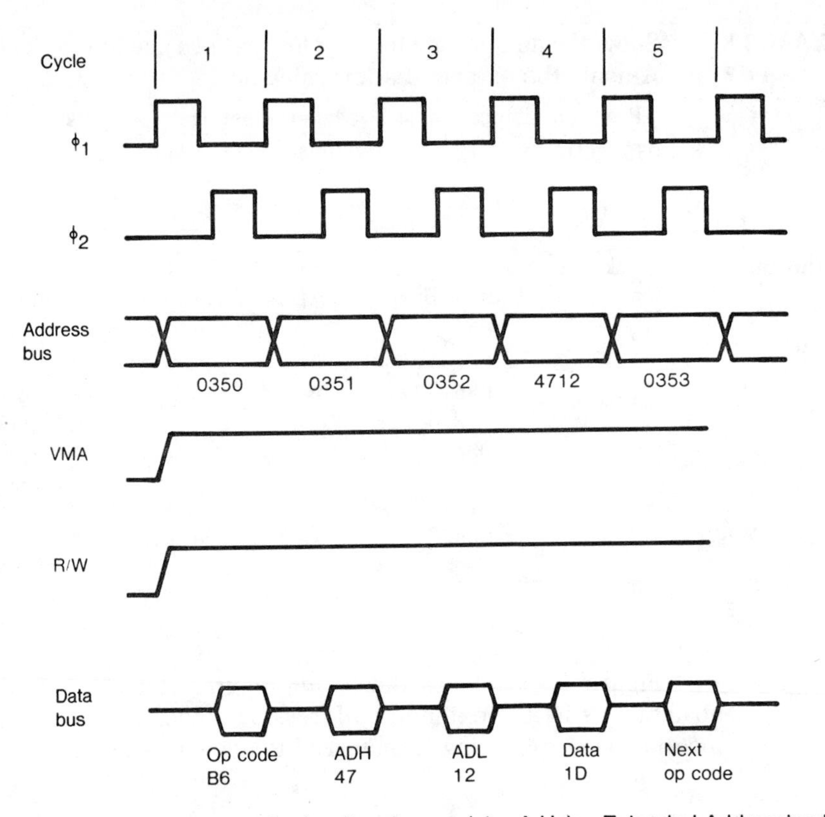

FIGURE 11–11 Timing Diagram for Loading Accumulator A Using Extended Addressing Mode

Figure 11–12 shows the timing diagram for a store the accumulator instruction using the extended addressing mode. The contents (11) of accumulator A are stored at memory location 27FA.

11.4.5 Inherent Addressing Mode

For the 6800 μP, the inherent addressing mode is divided into two addressing modes—implied and accumulator. Both types are one-byte instructions.

Implied Addressing Mode

There are two types of implied addressing mode instructions; those that require an operand address and those that do not. An example of an instruction that does not is the TBA instruction. This instruction causes the μP to move the contents of accumulator B to accumulator A. The binary patterns on the address and data buses are valid only on the first cycle of the instruction. For those instructions that do require an address, the address is held by an internal μP register such as the stack pointer. Thus, no additional data is required

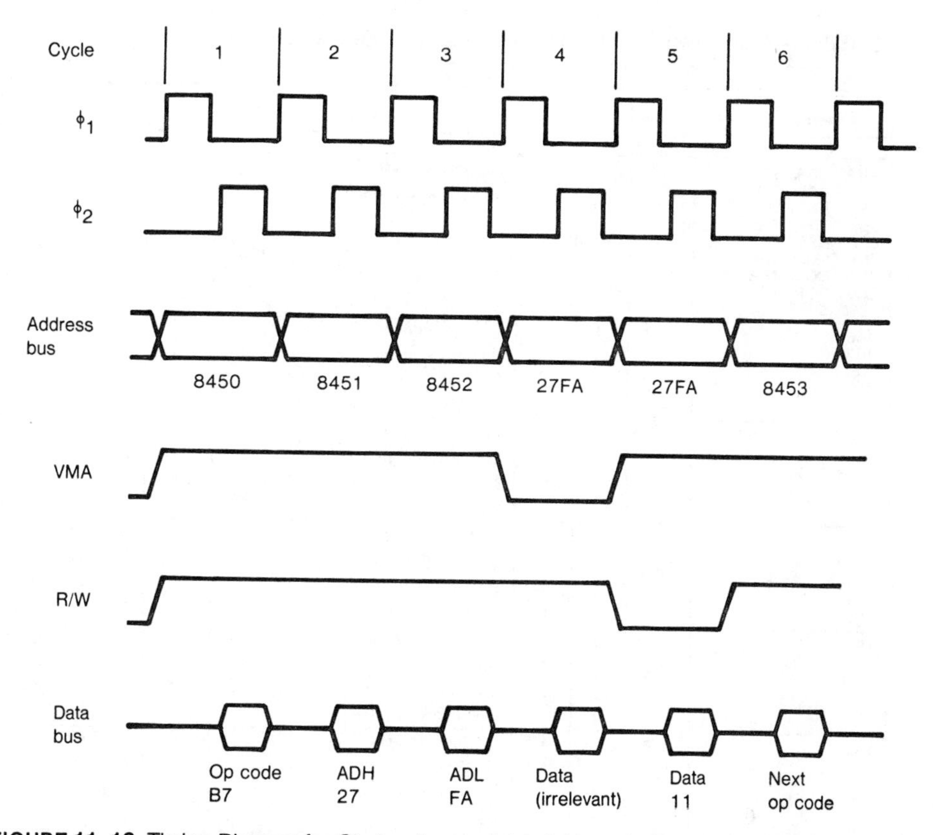

FIGURE 11–12 Timing Diagram for Storing Accumulator A Using Extended Addressing Mode

from memory to develop an address. An example of this type of instruction is PSH.

Accumulator Addressing Mode

In accumulator only addressing, either accumulator A or accumulator B is specified. An example is ASL A (arithmetic shift left on the A accumulator).

These are one-byte, two-cycle instructions and the address and data buses are active only during the first cycle of the instruction when the operator is being loaded from memory. During the second cycle, the machine performs the operation and VMA is high.

Table 11–7 gives a summary of the instructions and a cycle-by-cycle timing description for the 6800 μP's inherent addressing mode. Example 11.9 shows the cycle-by-cycle operation for a one-byte accumulator addressing mode instruction. Example 11.10 shows what happens for a two-byte accumulator addressing mode instruction.

TABLE 11-7 Summary of Inherent Addressing Mode Instructions

Instructions	Cycles	Cycle #	VMA Line	Address Bus	R/$\overline{W}$ Line	Data Bus
ABA DAA SEC ASL DEC SEI ASR INC SEV CBA LSR TAB CLC NEG TAP CLI NOP TBA CLR ROL TPA CLV ROR TST COM SBA	2	1	1	Op Code Address	1	Op Code
		2	1	Op Code Address + 1	1	Op Code of Next Instruction
DES DEX INS INX	4	1	1	Op Code Address	1	Op Code
		2	1	Op Code Address + 1	1	Op Code of Next Instruction
		3	0	Previous Register Contents	1	Irrelevant Data
		4	0	New Register Contents	1	Irrelevant Data
PSH	4	1	1	Op Code Address	1	Op Code
		2	1	Op Code Address + 1	1	Op Code of Next Instruction
		3	1	Stack Pointer	0	Accumulator Data
		4	0	Stack Pointer – 1	1	Accumulator Data
PUL	4	1	1	Op Code Address	1	Op Code
		2	1	Op Code Address + 1	1	Op Code of Next Instruction
		3	0	Stack Pointer	1	Irrelevant Data
		4	1	Stack Pointer + 1	1	Operand Data from Stack
TSX	4	1	1	Op Code Address	1	Op Code
		2	1	Op Code Address + 1	1	Op Code of Next Instruction
		3	0	Stack Pointer	1	Irrelevant Data
		4	0	New Index Register	1	Irrelevant Data
TXS	4	1	1	Op Code Address	1	Op Code
		2	1	Op Code Address + 1	1	Op Code of Next Instruction
		3	0	Index Register	1	Irrelevant Data
		4	0	New Stack Pointer	1	Irrelevant Data
RTS	5	1	1	Op Code Address	1	Op Code
		2	1	Op Code Address + 1	1	Irrelevant Data
		3	0	Stack Pointer	1	Irrelevant Data
		4	1	Stack Pointer + 1	1	Address of Next Instruction (High Order Byte)
		5	1	Stack Pointer + 2	1	Address of Next Instruction (Low Order Byte)

EXAMPLE 11.9 Show the clock cycles needed for transferring the contents of accumulator B to accumulator A.

Program Listing	Memory Listing
0200 TBA	0200 17

Solution

Clock Cycle	Address Bus	Data Bus	Internal Operation
1	0200	17	Fetch op code; increment PC to 0201.
2	0201	Next op code	Decode op code (17); increment PC to 0202.
3	0202	Next byte from memory	Transfer the contents of accumulator B to accumulator A; increment PC to 0203.

TABLE 11-7 continued

Instructions	Cycles	Cycle #	VMA Line	Address Bus	R/$\overline{W}$ Line	Data Bus
WAI	9	1	1	Op Code Address	1	Op Code
		2	1	Op Code Address + 1	1	Op Code of Next Instruction
		3	1	Stack Pointer	0	Return Address (Low Order Byte)
		4	1	Stack Pointer – 1	0	Return Address (High Order Byte)
		5	1	Stack Pointer – 2	0	Index Register (Low Order Byte)
		6	1	Stack Pointer – 3	0	Index Register (High Order Byte)
		7	1	Stack Pointer – 4	0	Contents of Accumulator A
		8	1	Stack Pointer – 5	0	Contents of Accumulator B
		9	1	Stack Pointer – 6	1	Contents of Cond. Code Register
RTI	10	1	1	Op Code Address	1	Op Code
		2	1	Op Code Address + 1	1	Irrelevant Data
		3	0	Stack Pointer	1	Irrelevant Data
		4	1	Stack Pointer + 1	1	Contents of Cond. Code Register from Stack
		5	1	Stack Pointer + 2	1	Contents of Accumulator B from Stack
		6	1	Stack Pointer + 3	1	Contents of Accumulator A from Stack
		7	1	Stack Pointer + 4	1	Index Register from Stack (High Order Byte)
		8	1	Stack Pointer + 5	1	Index Register from Stack (Low Order Byte)
		9	1	Stack Pointer + 6	1	Next Instruction Address from Stack (High Order Byte)
		10	1	Stack Pointer + 7	1	Next Instruction Address from Stack (Low Order Byte)
SWI	12	1	1	Op Code Address	1	Op Code
		2	1	Op Code Address + 1	1	Irrelevant Data
		3	1	Stack Pointer	0	Return Address (Low Order Byte)
		4	1	Stack Pointer – 1	0	Return Address (High Order Byte)
		5	1	Stack Pointer – 2	0	Index Register (Low Order Byte)
		6	1	Stack Pointer – 3	0	Index Register (High Order Byte)
		7	1	Stack Pointer – 4	0	Contents of Accumulator A
		8	1	Stack Pointer – 5	0	Contents of Accumulator B
		9	1	Stack Pointer – 6	0	Contents of Cond. Code Register
		10	0	Stack Pointer – 7	1	Irrelevant Data
		11	1	Vector Address FFFA (Hex)	1	Address of Subroutine (High Order Byte)
		12	1	Vector Address FFFB (Hex)	1	Address of Subroutine (Low Order Byte)

Source: Reprinted with permission of Motorola Incorporated, Austin, Texas.

Although this instruction is listed as requiring only two clock cycles, the actual transfer takes place during the third clock cycle. This internal operation does not interfere with other operations, so the instruction is considered to need only two clock cycles.

EXAMPLE 11.10 Show the clock cycles needed for the following push instruction:

Program Listing	Memory Listing	Accumulator	Stack Pointer
B460 PSH A	B460 36 Op code	70	02FF

Solution

Clock Cycle	Address Bus	Data Bus	Internal Operation
1	B460	36	Fetch op code; increment PC to B461.
2	B461	Next op code (to be ignored)	Decode op code 36; ignore incoming op code; hold PC at B461.
3	02FF	70	Data (70) is sent from accumulator A to stack.
4	02FF	70	Stack pointer is decremented at this time; VMA = 0; R/W = 1.

Although the contents (70) of accumulator A are actually stored on the stack by the end of the third clock cycle, the 6800 μP takes an additional clock cycle (clock cycle 4) to decrement the stack pointer. This leaves the stack pointer holding the next available address where data can be stored. Figure 11–13 shows the timing diagrams for a push instruction.

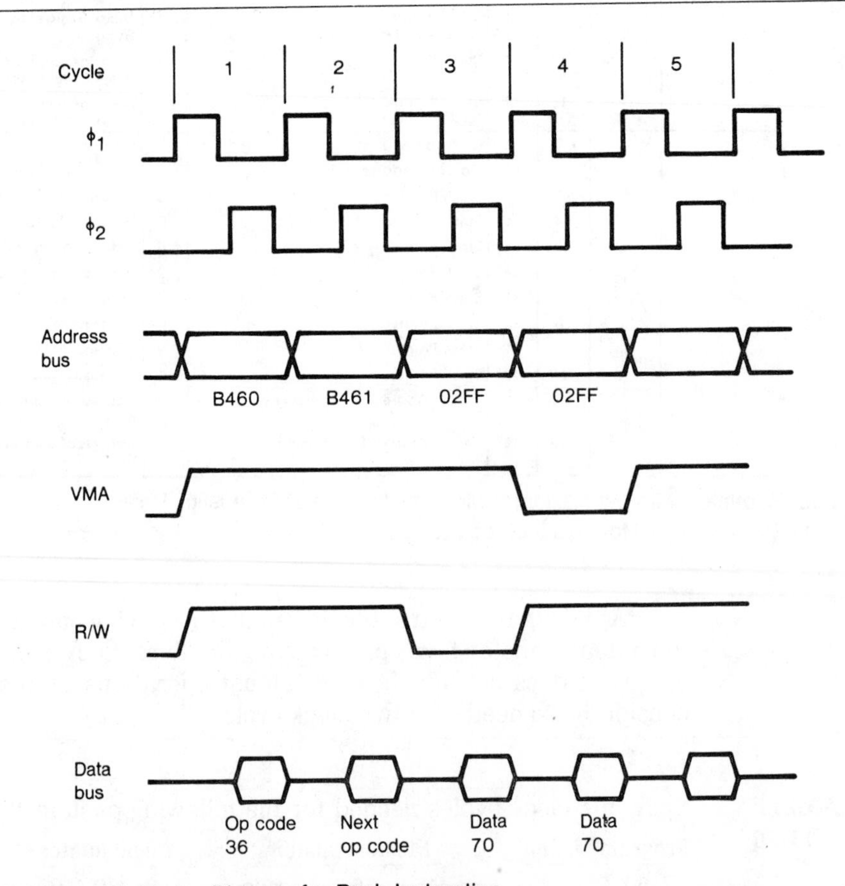

FIGURE 11–13 Timing Diagram for Push Instruction

11.4.6 Relative Addressing Mode

This addressing mode is the addressing mode for the branch instruction. Remember from Chapter 10 that branch instructions are two-byte instructions. The first byte is the op code and the second byte is the offset.

When a branch instruction is executed, the sequence of events is as follows:

1. The op code is fetched from the memory and stored in the instruction register during cycle 1.
2. The offset is loaded into the μP during cycle 2.
3. The offset is added to the low-order bits of the program counter in cycle 3 and the carry is propagated during cycle 4.
4. During cycles 3 and 4, the VMA line goes low while the μP is operating on the offset.
5. The next instruction is loaded during cycle 5.

Table 11–8 is a cycle-by-cycle description of what happens during a relative addressing mode. Figure 11–14 shows the timing diagram for a branch instruction using the relative addressing mode. The following four examples show what happens during each clock cycle for different situations that could occur when the μP is executing a branch instruction.

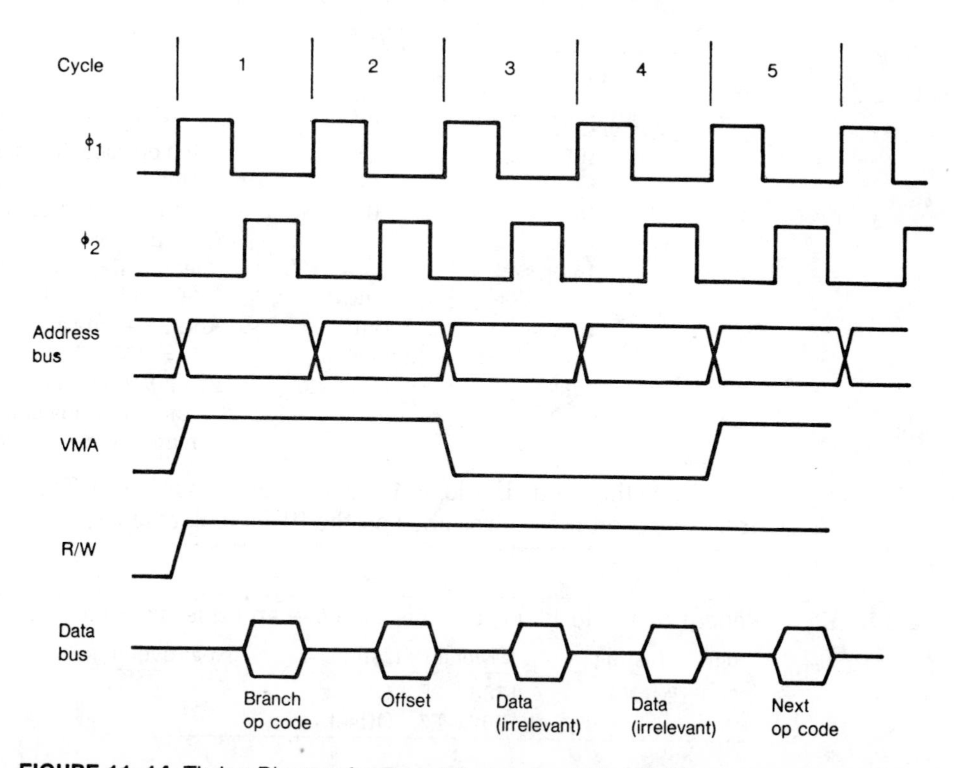

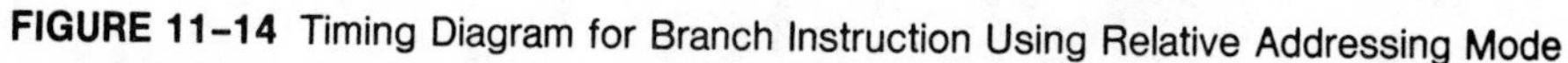
FIGURE 11–14 Timing Diagram for Branch Instruction Using Relative Addressing Mode

TABLE 11-8 Summary of Relative Addressing Mode Instructions

Instructions	Cycles	Cycle #	VMA Line	Address Bus	R/$\overline{W}$ Line	Data Bus
BCC BHI BNE BCS BLE BPL BEQ BLS BRA BGE BLT BVC BGT BMI BVS	4	1	1	Op Code Address	1	Op Code
		2	1	Op Code Address + 1	1	Branch Offset
		3	0	Op Code Address + 2	1	Irrelevant Data
		4	0	Branch Address	1	Irrelevant Data
BSR	8	1	1	Op Code Address	1	Op Code
		2	1	Op Code Address + 1	1	Branch Offset
		3	0	Return Address of Main Program	1	Irrelevant Data
		4	1	Stack Pointer	0	Return Address (Low Order Byte)
		5	1	Stack Pointer − 1	0	Return Address (High Order Byte)
		6	0	Stack Pointer − 2	1	Irrelevant Data
		7	0	Return Address of Main Program	1	Irrelevant Data
		8	0	Subroutine Address	1	Irrelevant Data

Source: Reprinted with permission of Motorola Incorporated, Austin, Texas.

EXAMPLE 11.11 Show the clock cycles needed to execute the following branch on minus instruction. The offset value is positive (04 = +4) and there is no page crossing.

Program Listing	Memory Listing	Negative Flag
1586 BMI 04	1586 2B Op code 1587 04 Offset	1

Solution

Clock Cycle	Address Bus	Data Bus	Internal Operation
1	1586	2B	Fetch op code; increment PC to 1587.
2	1587	04	Decode op code 2B; increment PC to 1588.
3	1588	Data (irrelevant)	Check N flag; add 88 + 04 = 8C (no internal carry).
4	158C	Data (irrelevant)	Add 15 + internal carry (15 + 0 = 15).
5	158C	Next op code	Bring VMA line back high; fetch new op code; increment the new PC to 158D.

Since the N flag is a logic 1, then the branch is taken. The branch address is put on the address bus on the fifth clock cycle.

EXAMPLE 11.12 Repeat Example 11.11, but this time use an offset value of $-9 = F7_{hex}$.

Program Listing	Memory Listing	Negative Flag
1586 BMI F7	1586 2B Op code 1587 F7 Offset	1

Solution

Clock Cycle	Address Bus	Data Bus	Internal Operation
1	1586	2B	Fetch op code; increment PC to 1587.
2	1587	F7	Decode op code 2B; increment PC to 1588.
3	1588	Data (irrelevant)	Bring VMA line low; check N flag; add 88 + F7 = 7F with no internal borrow.
4	157F	Data (irrelevant)	Subtract 15 − 0 = 15.
5	157F	Next op code	Bring VMA line back high; fetch new op code; increment the new PC to 1580.

EXAMPLE 11.13 Repeat Example 11.11 with a positive offset of 7C. This offset value causes a page crossing.

Program Listing	Memory Listing	Negative Flag
1586 BMI 7C	1586 2B Op code 1587 7C Offset	1

Solution

Clock Cycle	Address Bus	Data Bus	Internal Operation
1	1586	2B	Fetch op code; increment PC to 1587.
2	1587	7C	Decode op code 2B; increment PC to 1588.
3	1588	Data (irrelevant)	Bring VMA line low; check N flag; add 88 + 7C = 04 with an internal carry.
4	1504	Data (irrelevant)	Add 15 + 1 = 16.
5	1604	Next op code	Bring VMA line back high; fetch new op code; increment new PC to 1605.

EXAMPLE 11.14 Show the clock cycles needed for the following negative branch. The offset value EC causes a page crossing in the negative direction.

Program Listing	Memory Listing	Negative Flag
1536 BMI EC	1536 2B Op code 1537 EC Offset	1

Solution

Clock Cycle	Address Bus	Data Bus	Internal Operation
1	1536	2B	Fetch op code; increment PC to 1537.
2	1537	EC	Decode op code 2B; increment PC to 1538.
3	1538	Data (irrelevant)	Bring VMA line low; check N flag; add 38 + EC = 24 with an internal borrow.
4	1524	Data (irrelevant)	Subtract 15 − 1 = 14.
5	1424	Next op code	Bring VMA line back high; fetch new op code; increment PC to 1425.

11.5 INTERRUPTS

The 6800 μP has four different types of interrupts: reset ($\overline{RST}$), nonmaskable ($\overline{NMI}$), software (SWI), and interrupt request ($\overline{IRQ}$). Three of these interrupts ($\overline{RST}$, $\overline{NMI}$, and $\overline{IRQ}$) are hardware interrupts because they are activated by signals external to the μP. The fourth interrupt (SWI) is a software interrupt because it is initiated when the μP decodes the SWI instruction. Regardless of which type of interrupt occurs, the μP fetches the starting address of the interrupt service program from memory. The starting address (not the program) must be stored in the following locations:

Reset ($\overline{RST}$)	FFFE FFFF
Nonmaskable interrupt ($\overline{NMI}$)	FFFC FFFD
Software interrupt (SWI)	FFFA FFFB
Interrupt request ($\overline{IRQ}$)	FFF8 FFF9

These eight addresses are called *vectors* or *vector addresses* because they contain information that points the μP to an interrupt service routine. Let's consider the timing diagrams for each type of interrupt.

11.5.1 Reset

A reset signal is used to initialize the μP after power is turned on or to reinitialize the μP at any time. If the reset line goes low for at least eight clock cycles and then goes high, the μP resets itself. The following conditions occur after eight clock cycles:

1. The interrupt mask bit is set. This is the I bit of the condition code register.
2. The address bus contains FFFE.
3. The R/W line is high (read condition).
4. The VMA line goes low.
5. The data bus lines are in their high impedance state.
6. The BA line goes low.

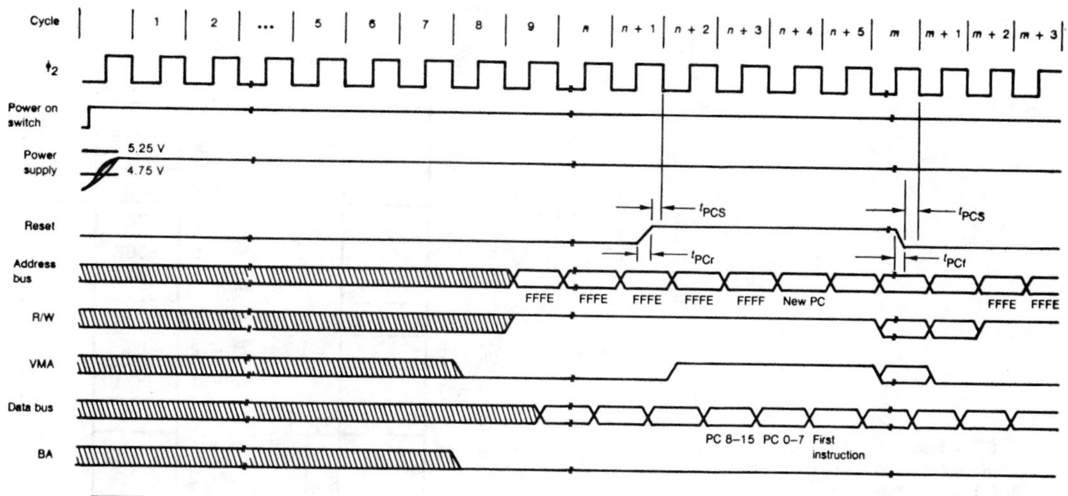

FIGURE 11–15 Timing Diagram for Reset Condition (Redrawn with permission of Motorola Incorporated, Austin,Texas)

Note: Although the address bus line contains an address (FFFE), neither memory chips nor peripheral devices respond to it because the VMA line is low. The VMA line goes high after the reset line goes high. Figure 11–15 shows the timing diagram for the reset condition.

11.5.2 $\overline{\text{NMI}}$, SWI, and $\overline{\text{IRQ}}$

The 6800 μP handles the $\overline{\text{NMI}}$, SWI, and $\overline{\text{IRQ}}$ interrupts similarly, except that each has its own vector address. For the nonmaskable interrupt ($\overline{\text{NMI}}$) and the interrupt request ($\overline{\text{IRQ}}$), the μP completes the instruction in progress before beginning the interrupt sequence. For the software interrupt (SWI), after this instruction is decoded, the μP begins the interrupt sequence. Before the vector address is fetched, the μP stores on the stack the contents of the program counter, the index register, accumulator A, accumulator B, and the condition code register. Figure 11–16 shows this data being stored on the stack. Figure 11–17 shows the timing diagram for the $\overline{\text{NMI}}$ and $\overline{\text{IRQ}}$ interrupts.

Remember from Chapter 5 that the difference between an interrupt request and a nonmaskable interrupt is that the μP can be stopped from recognizing an interrupt request signal but it cannot be stopped from recognizing a nonmaskable interrupt request signal. If the I bit in the condition code register is set, the μP will not recognize an interrupt request. The I bit is set in one of the following ways:

1. By a reset condition,
2. With an SEI (set interrupt flag) instruction,
3. By recognizing an interrupt request signal,
4. By recognizing a nonmaskable interrupt signal,
5. By executing an SWI (software interrupt).

The CLI (clear interrupt flag) instruction resets the I bit to a logic 0.

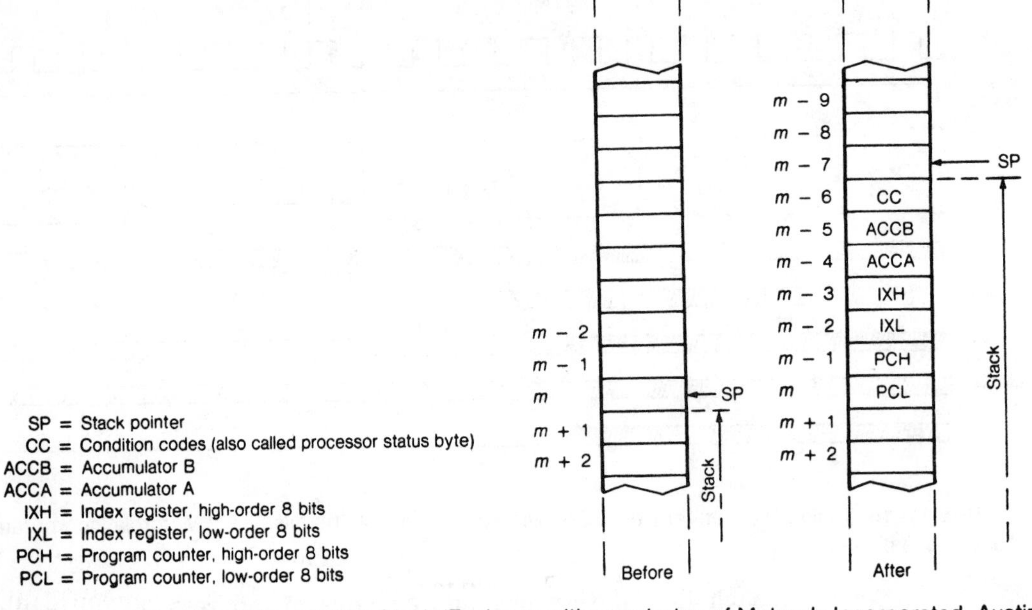

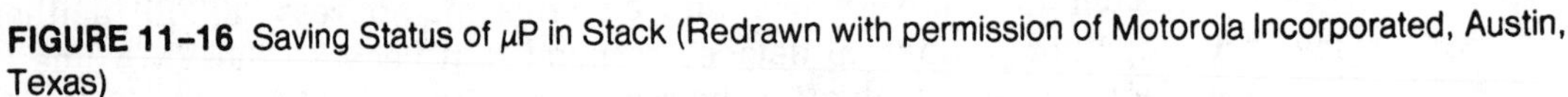

FIGURE 11–16 Saving Status of μP in Stack (Redrawn with permission of Motorola Incorporated, Austin, Texas)

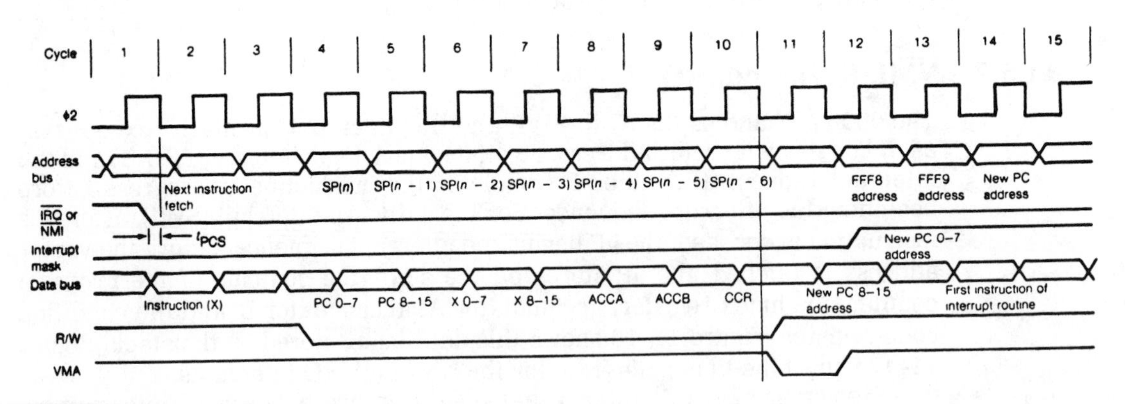

FIGURE 11–17 Timing Diagram for $\overline{NMI}$ and $\overline{IRQ}$ Interrupts (Redrawn with permission of Motorola Incorporated, Austin, Texas)

11.6 WAIT FOR INTERRUPT

In Chapter 9, we saw that the 6800 μP has a WAI (wait for interrupt) instruction. This instruction suspends all μP operation so that the μP does not fetch and execute any more instructions. After a WAI instruction has been executed, the μP stores the contents of the program counter, the index register, accumulator A, accumulator B, and the condition code register on the stack. The

μP's address, data, and R/W lines go to their high impedance state. The VMA line goes low and the BA line goes high. These conditions remain until the μP receives an $\overline{\text{IRQ}}$ or an $\overline{\text{NMI}}$ signal. Remember, however, that if the I bit is set, the μP can never recognize an $\overline{\text{IRQ}}$ signal. If the I bit is set, the μP can only recognize a nonmaskable interrupt or reset signal. The μP recognizes a reset condition at any time. A reset overrides any operation. The timing diagram for the WAI instruction is shown in Figure 11–18.

11.7 HALT AND SINGLE INSTRUCTION EXECUTION

The $\overline{\text{HLT}}$ line allows an external signal to stop the μP from fetching and executing any more instructions. Controlling the μP in this way is primarily used for two purposes: (1) DMA (direct memory access) operation and (2) single instruction execution.

In normal operation, the $\overline{\text{HLT}}$ line is high and the μP fetches and executes the program instructions. When the $\overline{\text{HLT}}$ line goes low, the μP stops all activity. As a response, the μP brings the bus available (BA) line high. This is a signal from the μP that the address bus, data bus, and R/W lines have gone to their high impedance states. The μP is said to be "floating" because it no longer controls the buses. So that no memory chip or peripheral device is falsely activated, the VMA line goes low. When the μP is in this condition, data can be quickly transferred between memory and peripheral equipment because the data does not have to go through the μP. This condition is called *direct memory access* (DMA). In order to do DMA operations, a special peripheral device called a DMA controller is needed.

The second purpose of using the $\overline{\text{HLT}}$ line is to allow debugging of a program by execution of one instruction at a time. When the $\overline{\text{HLT}}$ line goes low, the μP completes the instruction it is executing and then stops all activity. The $\overline{\text{HLT}}$

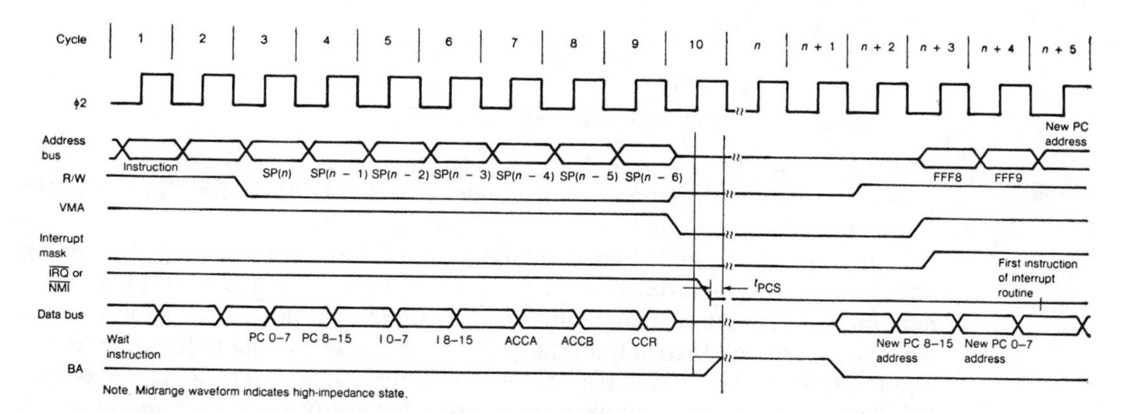

FIGURE 11–18 Timing Diagram for Wait Instruction (Redrawn with permission of Motorola Incorporated, Austin, Texas)

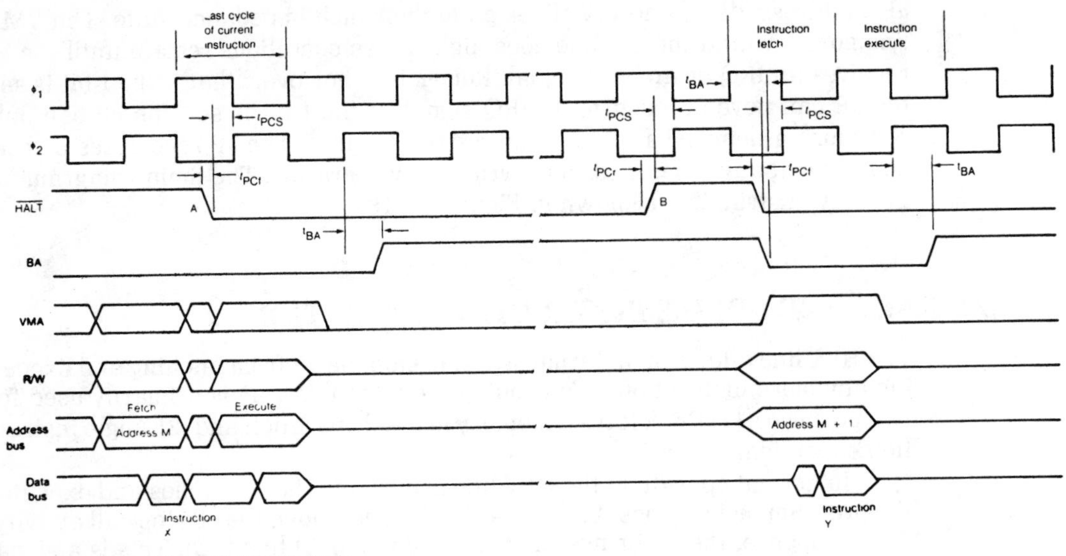

FIGURE 11–19 HALT and Single Instruction Execution for System Debugging (Redrawn with permission of Motorola Incorporated, Austin, Texas)

line must go low before the trailing edge of the ϕ_1 clock pulse of the last cycle of an instruction. Point A of Figure 11–19 shows this condition. The minimum time in Figure 11–19 is shown as t_{PCS}.

If either a nonmaskable interrupt or interrupt request signal occurs while the μP is halted, the signal is latched into the μP. However, the μP will not respond to the interrupt until the $\overline{HLT}$ line goes back high. If a reset signal occurs while the μP is halted, the following conditions occur:

1. VMA line remains low.
2. BA line goes low.
3. Data bus remains in its high impedance state.
4. R/W line goes high.
5. Address bus contains the address FFFE.

As long as the $\overline{HLT}$ line remains low, conditions 1–5 hold. When the $\overline{HLT}$ line goes high, the μP addresses the reset vector location (FFFE and FFFF) and the reset program is executed.

In order to do single-step execution, the $\overline{HLT}$ line must be brought high for one μP cycle and then returned low, as shown by point B in Figure 11–19. This condition allows the μP to execute one instruction and then halt. Each time we want to execute an instruction, the $\overline{HLT}$ line must be brought high and then low again. The right half of Figure 11–19 shows the timing diagram for a one-byte, two-cycle instruction, such as an inherent addressing mode instruction.

11.8 SUMMARY

This chapter covered the hardware aspects of the 6800 μP from its pin descriptions to how it handles an interrupt request, including its clock signals, timing diagrams, cycle-by-cycle operations, and interrupts. Remember that the number of clock cycles required to execute an instruction depends on the type of instruction and the addressing mode. Therefore, choice of the right addressing mode allows the μP and μC system to operate most efficiently by storing the program in the fewest number of bytes or by executing an instruction with the fewest number of clock cycles. As an example, Section 11.4 showed examples and timing diagrams for different 6800 instructions and addressing modes. Several examples compared the 6800's extended addressing mode with its direct addressing mode.

Section 11.5 covered the 6800's hardware and software interrupts. The hardware interrupts are reset ($\overline{RST}$), nonmaskable interrupt request ($\overline{NMI}$), and interrupt request ($\overline{IRQ}$). There is one software interrupt request instruction (SWI). Each interrupt request has its own pair of vector addresses.

The 6800 μP has a WAI instruction. This instruction permits the μP to stop fetching and executing any more instructions until an interrupt request signal is received.

In Section 11.7, we saw how an external signal can be used to halt the μP from fetching and executing any more instructions. This method of halting the μP can be used to debug programs when it is used as a single step feature.

PROBLEMS

11-1 Does the 6800 μP require an external circuit to generate the two-phase nonoverlapping clock pulses?

11-2 What are the power requirements for the 6800 μP?

11-3 Name the input and output control lines.

11-4 When the $\overline{HLT}$ pin goes low, does the μP finish executing the present instruction before halting?

11-5 What do the following abbreviations stand for? (a) $\overline{IRQ}$, (b) $\overline{NMI}$, (c) DBE, (d) TSC, (e) $\overline{RES}$, (f) VMA, and (g) BA.

11-6 What does the line over the control symbols represent?

11-7 For a 1 MHz system, what is the minimum pulse width time?

11-8 When is the data coming into the μP latched?

11-9 How many clock cycles are needed for an LDX immediate addressing mode instruction?

11-10 When, during the clock cycle, is the program counter incremented to the next memory location?

11-11 Does the direct addressing mode for the 6800 μP apply only to page zero?

11-12 What is the advantage of using the direct addressing mode?

11-13 How many bytes is the indexed addressing mode instruction?

11-14 During what clock cycle(s) in an indexed addressing mode are the index register and the offset value added?

11-15 When the 6800 μP's VMA line is low, what does it signify?

11-16 Does the VMA line go low in all extended addressing mode instructions?
11-17 Are all inherent addressing mode instructions one-byte instructions?
11-18 What are the two groups of inherent addressing mode instructions?
11-19 How many clock cycles are required by a PSH B instruction? What is accomplished on the last clock cycle?
11-20 Does the relative addressing mode apply only to the branch instructions?
11-21 Examples 11.11 to 11.14 show that, when a branch is taken, the 6800 μP requires four clock cycles. Does the 6800 μP also require four clock cycles if the branch is not taken? If yes, during what clock cycle(s) is the VMA line low?
11-22 List the four different types of interrupts for the 6800 μP.
11-23 What are the interrupt vectors for each type of interrupt?
11-24 Why does the μP set the interrupt flag bit during a reset operation?
11-25 Name two reasons for using the $\overline{\text{HLT}}$ line.
11-26 What does the term *floating* mean?

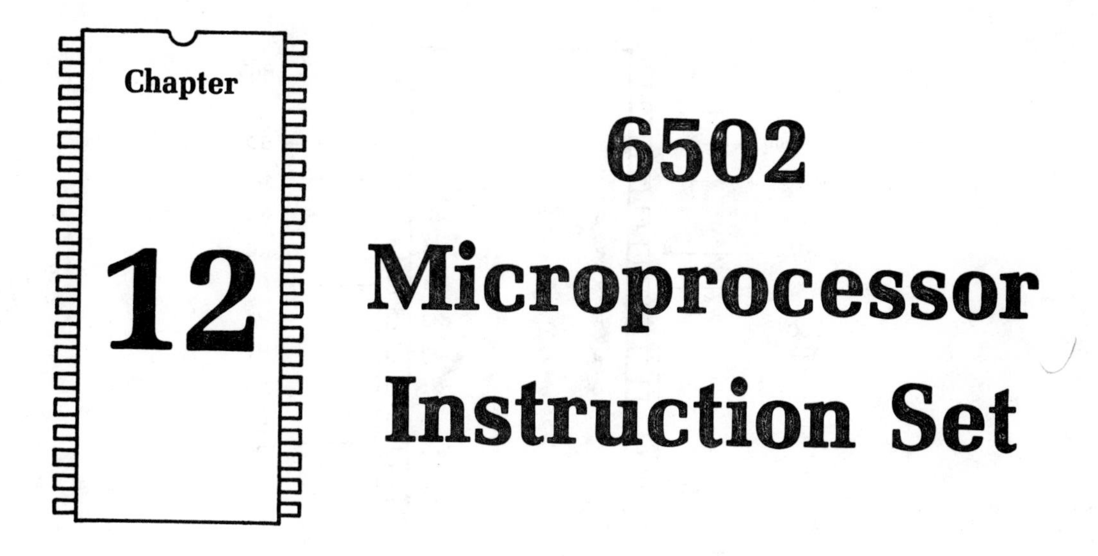

6502 Microprocessor Instruction Set

12.0 INTRODUCTION

This chapter and the next deal with the 6502 μP's software, instruction set, and programs. Chapter 14 covers pin designations, timing, reset operation, and other hardware aspects of the 6502 μP.

The 6502 μP has 56 basic instructions and 13 addressing modes. When the instructions are combined with their different addressing modes, there is a total of 151 different op codes, comprising the entire instruction set for the 6502 μP. This μP, like others, can be used either for dedicated control applications or in a general-purpose μC such as the Apple system.

This chapter covers the internal architecture (programmer's model), the processor status register, and the 6502's instruction set. Figure 12–1 gives the pin designations for the 6502 μP. The 6502 μP is housed in a 40-pin dual-in-line package. The pins are labeled so that the figure can be used for reference in this or the next chapter. A complete description of all the pins is given in Chapter 14.

12.1 6502 INTERNAL ARCHITECTURE

The basic programmer's model of the 6502 μP was shown in Chapter 5. The diagram of Figure 12–2 is more complete than the diagram shown in Chapter 5 in that it shows the address and data buffers and latches. As in other μPs, an instruction enters the 6502 μP on the data bus and is routed into the instruction

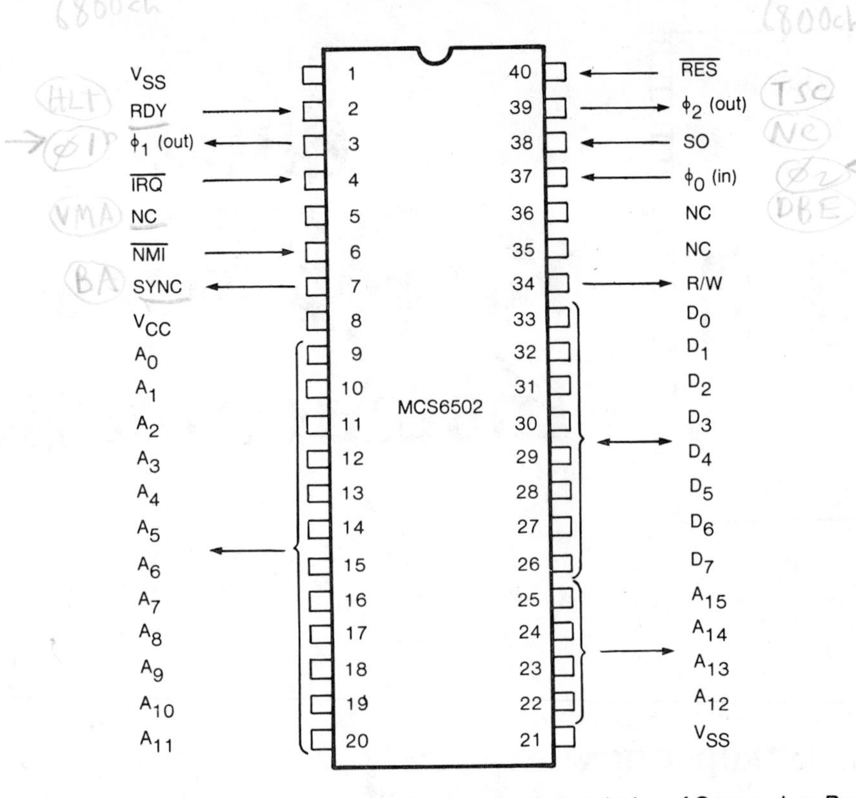

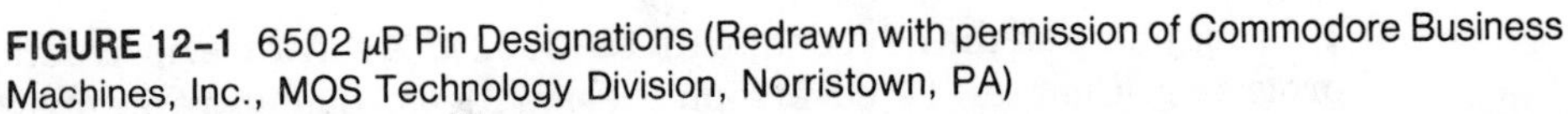
FIGURE 12–1 6502 μP Pin Designations (Redrawn with permission of Commodore Business Machines, Inc., MOS Technology Division, Norristown, PA)

register, where it is held while being decoded. The decoding circuitry, along with the μP timing signals generate all of the control signals for the μP and thus for the rest of the system.

Additional control lines that affect an instruction's execution come from the interrupt logic circuitry and processor status register. The processor status register indicates the results of arithmetic and logical operations and the status of other μP operations. This register is covered in the next section.

If the clock frequency is 1 MHz, then data comes into the μP from memory or an I/O device in the last 100 ns of the ϕ_2 clock cycle. The μP does not attempt to operate on the data in this short time interval. Instead, data is trapped in the input data latch register and is used in the next clock cycle. At that time, the data is transferred onto one of the internal data buses and from there into an internal register. Internal data transfers take place during the ϕ_1 clock cycle.

The stack pointer of the 6502 μP always points to stack locations in page 01_{hex}. Only the low-order 8 bits of the stack pointer can be programmed. Hardware designers must remember that the stack has to be located in page 01 so that the memory chips will be connected correctly.

The 6502 μP has two 8-bit index registers, X and Y. The contents of these registers can be used to calculate an address from which data can be obtained or where data can be stored.

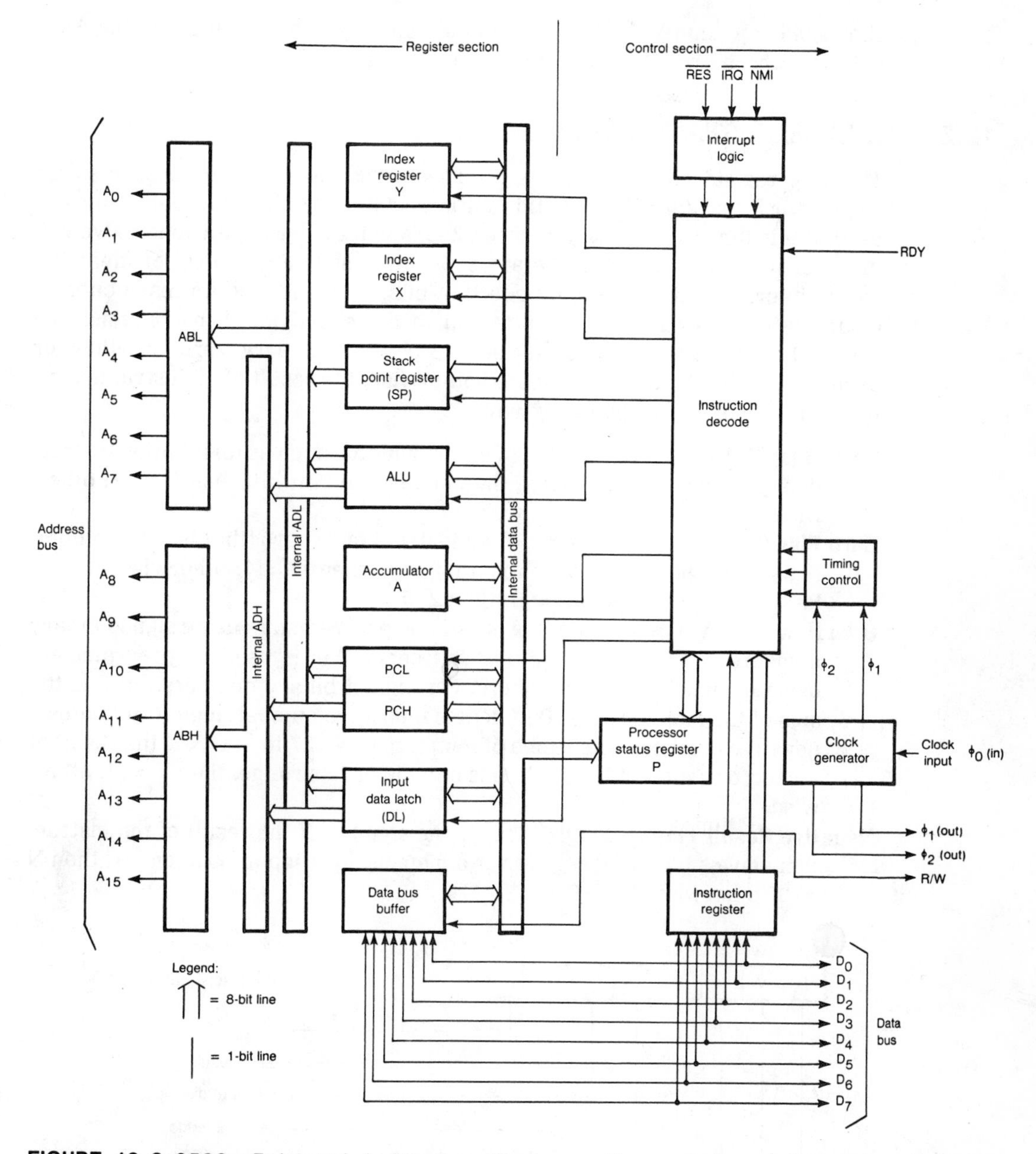

FIGURE 12–2 6502 μP Internal Architecture (Redrawn with permission of Commodore Business Machines, Inc., MOS Technology Division, Norristown, PA)

The address buffers (ABH, ABL) consist of a set of latches and TTL compatible drivers. Remember that the address lines of the 6502 μP are not three state.

The program counter (PCH, PCL), the arithmetic and logic unit (ALU), and the accumulator operate similarly to those of other μPs. Although Figure 12–2 shows only one internal data bus and only one multiline bus input to the ALU, note that there are other internal buses for control signals.

12.2 PROCESSOR STATUS REGISTER

The flag register in the 6502 is often referred to as the *processor status register* or *P register*. Although this status register is 8 bits wide, only 7 bits are used at this time. As shown in Figure 12–3, one bit is for expansion. As we will discover in Section 12.10, there are separate instructions to set or clear the carry, interrupt, and decimal mode flag bits. There is also an instruction to clear the overflow flag bit. In addition to these individual instructions, the *result* of many instructions either sets or clears the carry, zero, overflow, or negative result bits. Unless indicated otherwise, the result of an instruction affects these bits in the following ways:

Carry Flag (C Flag): If the result of an instruction, such as an addition instruction, produces a carry from the most significant bit, then C = 1; otherwise, C = 0.

Zero Flag (Z Flag): If the result of an instruction is zero (that is, each bit of a register or memory location is a logic 0), then Z = 1; otherwise, Z = 0. Remember, if the result = 0, then Z = 1.

Overflow Flag (V Flag): This flag is used by programmers using signed binary numbers in the same way that the carry flag is used by programmers using unsigned binary numbers. For signed binary numbers, bit 7 is the sign of the number (logic 0 indicates a positive number, logic 1 indicates a negative number). The range of numbers is + 127 to − 128. If the result of an add or subtract instruction is outside of this range, then V = 1; otherwise, V = 0.

Negative Result Flag (N Flag): This is the sign bit. If the result of the instruction causes bit 7 of a register or a memory location to be a logic 1, then N = 1; otherwise, N = 0.

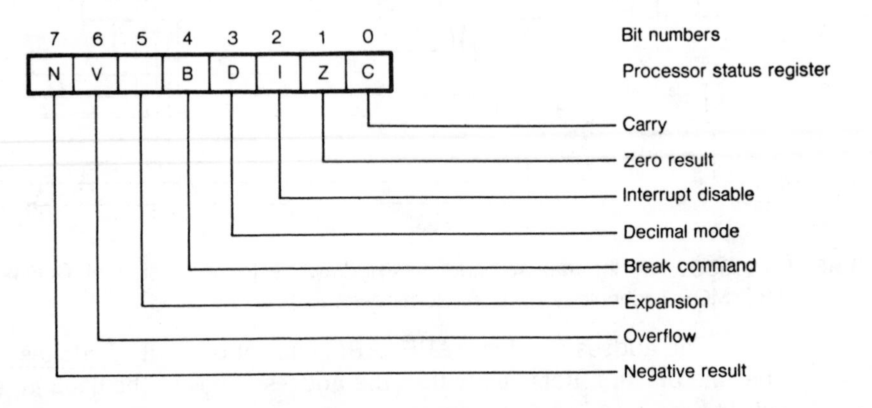

FIGURE 12–3 6502 μP Processor Status Register (Redrawn with permission of Commodore Business Machines, Inc., MOS Technology Division, Norristown, PA)

The three remaining flag bits are used by the μP in the following ways:

Interrupt Flag (I Flag): This flip-flop is used by the programmer and the μP to control the interrupt request pin. This bit enables or disables the interrupt request pin (pin 4). If this bit is a logic 0, then the μP will acknowledge an interrupt request signal. If it is a logic 1, an interrupt request signal will not be acknowledged by the μP. (Interrupt request and nonmaskable interrupt signals are covered in Section 14.7.)

If the I flag is a logic 0, it can be set to a logic 1 by (1) the use of a set an interrupt instruction (see Section 12.10), (2) an interrupt request signal, (3) a nonmaskable interrupt request signal, or (4) a reset signal.

If the I flag is a logic 1, it can be cleared to a logic 0 by (1) the use of a clear interrupt instruction (see Section 12.10) or (2) the decoding by the μP of a return from interrupt instruction (see Section 12.8).

Decimal Mode Flag (D Flag): This flip-flop controls the adder circuit operation of the ALU. If D = 0, then all additions and subtractions are done in straight binary. If D = 1, then all additions and subtractions are done as decimal numbers. Unlike the 8080A or 6800, in the 6502 μP once this flag is set, the arithmetic mode does not change until the programmer changes it. The 8080A and 6800 decimal adjust instructions are only for addition, whereas the 6502 μP is capable of performing both decimal addition and subtraction by setting the D flag.

Break Command Flag (B Flag): This flag can be set or cleared only by the μP. The logic state of this flip-flop indicates whether the μP jumped to an interrupt service subroutine program because of an external interrupt request signal or because the μP decoded a break instruction. A logic 0 in this bit means an external signal on the $\overline{\text{IRQ}}$ pin caused the jump to the subroutine program. A logic 1 in this bit means that a break instruction has been decoded by the μP.

12.3 DATA MOVEMENT INSTRUCTIONS

There are three groups of data movement instructions for the 6502 μP. They are the *load* instructions, *store* instructions, and *transfer* instructions. When data is moved from memory to a μP register, the instruction used is a load instruction. When data is moved from a μP register to memory, the instruction used is a store instruction. Transfer instructions refer to movement between μP registers. The three μP registers that are involved in data movement instructions are the accumulator, the X register, and the Y register. When a μP is executing a load instruction, the μP is said to be "reading" data from memory or I/O. When the μP is executing a store instruction, it is said to be "writing" data to memory or I/O.

Each load and store instruction for the 6502 μP has a number of addressing modes associated with it. For example, load the accumulator instruction has eight addressing modes associated with it, while load the X and Y register instructions each have five addressing modes. Store the accumulator instruction has seven addressing modes associated with it, while store the X and Y register instructions each have three addressing modes.

The transfer instruction allows the contents of the accumulator to be moved to either the X or Y register or vice versa. *Note:* In the 6502 μP, data cannot be transferred directly between the X and Y registers. For example, if we want to transfer data from the X register to the Y register, we must first transfer it to the accumulator and then transfer it from the accumulator to the Y register.

There are two other transfer instructions. They allow the contents of the X register to be moved to the stack pointer or vice versa. These instructions will be covered in Section 12.9 dealing with the stack operation. Table 12–1 is a listing of the data movement instructions for the 6502 μP with the addressing modes that these instructions use and their op codes. Several example instructions are also listed.

12.3.1 Load Instructions

The 6502 μP has three load instructions:

LDA Load accumulator
LDX Load X register
LDY Load Y register

These instructions are either two or three bytes long, depending on the addressing mode used. Each of these instructions affects the zero flag and the negative flag as described in Section 12.2. A brief discussion of each load instruction follows.

LDA Load Accumulator

The LDA instruction moves the contents of a memory location to the accumulator.

LDX Load X Register

The LDX instruction moves the contents of a memory location to the X register.

LDY Load Y Register

The LDY instruction moves the contents of a memory location to the Y register.

12.3.2 Store Instructions

The 6502 μP has three store instructions:

STA Store accumulator
STX Store X register
STY Store Y register

TABLE 12–1 6502 Microprocessor Data Movement Instructions with Addressing Modes, Op Codes, and Examples

Addressing Mode	Assembly Language Form	Op Code	Example	Explanation
Immediate	LDA #Oper	A9	LDA #40	Load accumulator immediately with 40_{hex}.
Zero page	LDA Oper	A5	LDA 40	Load accumulator with data at memory location 0040.
Zero page,X	LDA Oper,X	B5	LDA 40,X	Load accumulator with data at memory location 0040 + X register.
Absolute	LDA Oper	AD	LDA 1040	Load accumulator with data at memory location 1040.
Absolute,X	LDA Oper,X	BD	LDA 1040,X	Load accumulator with data at memory location 1040 + X register.
Absolute,Y	LDA Oper,Y	B9	LDA 1040,Y	Load accumulator with data at memory location 1040 + Y register.
(Indirect,X)	LDA (Oper,X)	A1		
(Indirect),Y	LDA (Oper),Y	B1		
Immediate	LDX #Oper	A2	LDX #75	Load X register immediately with 75_{hex}.
Zero page	LDX Oper	A6		
Zero page,Y	LDX Oper,Y	B6	LDX 30,Y	Load X register with data at memory location 0030 + Y register.
Absolute	LDX Oper	AE		
Absolute,Y	LDX Oper,Y	BE	LDX 182A,Y	Load X register data at memory location 182A + Y register.
Immediate	LDY #Oper	AØ		
Zero page	LDY Oper	A4	LDY 80	Load Y register with data at memory location 0080.
Zero page,X	LDY Oper,X	B4		
Absolute	LDY Oper	AC	LDY 45B0	Load Y register with data at memory location 45B0.
Absolute,X	LDY Oper,X	BC	LDY 0100,X	Load Y register with data at memory location 0100 + X register.
Zero page	STA Oper	85	STA 00	Store contents of accumulator in memory location 0000.
Zero page,X	STA Oper,X	95	STA 50,X	Store contents of accumulator in memory location 0050 + X register.
Absolute	STA Oper	8D	STA 0485	Store contents of accumulator in memory location 0485.
Absolute,X	STA Oper,X	9D	STA 0070,X	Store contents of accumulator in memory location 0070 + X register.
Absolute,Y	STA Oper,Y	99	STA 2075,Y	Store contents of accumulator in memory location 2075 + Y register.

TABLE 12–1 continued

Addressing Mode	Assembly Language Form	Op Code	Example	Explanation
(Indirect,X)	STA (Oper,X)	81		
(Indirect),Y	STA (Oper),Y	91		
Zero page	STX Oper	86		
Zero page,Y	STX Oper,Y	96		
Absolute	STX Oper	8E	STX A4B1	Store contents of X register in memory location A4B1.
Zero page	STY Oper	84	STY 6A	Store contents of Y register in memory location 006A.
Zero page,X	STY Oper,X	94		
Absolute	STY Oper	8C		
Implied	TAX	AA		
Implied	TXA	8A		
Implied	TAY	A8		
Implied	TYA	98		

These instructions, like the load instructions, are either two or three bytes long, depending on the addressing mode. These instructions move the data from a μP register to a memory location. None of the store instructions affects any of the μP flag bits. We will discuss each of the store instructions in turn.

STA **Store Accumulator**

The contents of the accumulator are moved to a memory location.

STX **Store X Register**

The contents of the X register are moved to a memory location.

STY **Store Y Register**

The contents of the Y register are moved to a memory location.

12.3.3 Transfer Instructions

There are four instructions that allow the accumulator and the index registers, X and Y, to transfer data:

TAX Transfer accumulator to X register
TXA Transfer X register to accumulator
TAY Transfer accumulator to Y register
TYA Transfer Y register to accumulator

All of these instructions are single-byte instructions. These instructions affect only the zero flag and the negative flag, as described in Section 12.2. These instructions do not exchange the contents of the registers. Rather, one register is the source register and another register is the destination register. A brief discussion of the transfer instructions follow.

TAX **Transfer Accumulator to X Register**

The TAX instruction transfers the contents of the accumulator to the index register X. For this instruction, the accumulator is the source and the X register is the destination. The contents of the accumulator are unchanged.

TXA **Transfer X Register to Accumulator**

The TXA instruction transfers the contents of the index register X to the accumulator. For this instruction, the X register is the source and the accumulator is the destination. The contents of the X register are unchanged.

TAY **Transfer Accumulator to Y Register**

The TAY instruction transfers the contents of the accumulator to the index register Y. The accumulator is the source register and the Y register is the destination register. The contents of the accumulator remain unchanged.

TYA **Transfer Y Register to Accumulator**

The TYA instruction transfers the contents of the index register Y to the accumulator. The Y register is the source register and the accumulator is the destination register. The contents of the Y register remain unchanged.

12.4 ARITHMETIC INSTRUCTIONS

The 6502 has four groups of instructions that we will classify as arithmetic instructions. They are the *add* instruction, *subtract* instruction, *increment* instructions, and *decrement* instructions. Unlike the 8080A and 6800, the 6502 μP has only one add instruction and one subtract instruction. Both instructions include the carry bit. For the add instruction, the carry flag must first be cleared to a logic 0. For the subtract instruction, the carry flag must first be set to a logic 1. The 6502, like the 6800, includes in its instruction set instructions either to clear or to set the carry flag. These instructions are covered in Section 12.10.

The add and subtract instructions of the 6502 μP have eight addressing modes associated with each instruction. There are also three increment and three decrement instructions (not including their addressing modes). Table 12-2 shows the arithmetic instructions for the 6502 μP with their addressing modes and op codes. Some examples are also shown.

12.4.1 Add Instruction

The 6502 μP has only one add instruction.

ADC **Add Memory, Accumulator, and Carry**

The ADC instruction adds the contents of a memory location and the carry bit to the accumulator. The result is automatically placed in the accumulator. The flag bits that are affected are the carry flag, the zero flag, the negative flag, and the overflow flag, as described in Section 12.2.

TABLE 12–2 6502 Microprocessor Arithmetic Instructions with Addressing Modes, Op Codes, and Examples

Addressing Mode	Assembly Language Form	Op Code	Example	Explanation
Immediate	ADC #Oper	69	ADC #05	Add accumulator, carry flag, and hex number 05.
Zero page	ADC Oper	65		
Zero page,X	ADC Oper,X	75	ADC 8A,X	Add accumulator, carry flag, and contents of memory location 008A + X register.
Absolute	ADC Oper	6D	ADC 4250	Add accumulator, carry flag, and contents of memory location 4250.
Absolute,X	ADC Oper,X	7D	ADC 010D,X	Add accumulator, carry flag, and contents of memory location 010D + X register.
Absolute,Y	ADC Oper,Y	79		
(Indirect,X)	ADC (Oper,X)	61		
(Indirect),Y	ADC (Oper),Y	71		
Immediate	SBC #Oper	E9	SBC #18	Subtract accumulator, carry flag, and value 18_{hex}.
Zero page	SBC Oper	E5		
Zero page,X	SBC Oper,X	F5		
Absolute	SBC Oper	ED	SBC 0200	Subtract contents of memory location 0200 and carry flag from accumulator.
Absolute,X	SBC Oper,X	FD	SBC 0465,X	Subtract contents of memory location 0465 + X register and carry flag from accumulator.
Absolute,Y	SBC Oper,Y	F9	SBC 0200,Y	Subtract contents of memory location 0200 + Y register and carry flag from accumulator.
(Indirect,X)	SBC (Oper,X)	E1		
(Indirect),Y	SBC (Oper),Y	F1		
Zero page	INC Oper	E6	INC 05	Add 1 to contents of memory location 0005.
Zero page,X	INC Oper,X	F6		
Absolute	INC Oper	EE	INC 03FA	Add 1 to contents of memory location 03FA
Absolute,X	INC Oper,X	FE		
Implied	INX	E8		
Implied	INY	C8		
Zero page	DEC Oper	C6	DEC BC	Subtract 1 from contents of memory location 00BC.
Zero page,X	DEC Oper,X	D6		
Absolute	DEC Oper	CE		
Absolute,X	DEC Oper,X	DE	DEC 0402,X	Subtract 1 from contents of memory location 0402 + Y register.
Implied	DEX	CA		
Implied	DEY	88		

12.4.2 Subtract Instruction

The 6502 μP has only one subtract instruction.

SBC Subtract Memory, Accumulator, and Borrow Bit

The SBC instruction subtracts the value of memory and the borrow bit ($\overline{C}$) from the accumulator. The result is placed in the accumulator. Subtraction is done using 2's complement arithmetic. The borrow bit is defined as the complement of the carry flag. Since the subtract instruction includes the carry flag, it must be set (a logic 1) before a subtraction operation. This instruction affects the carry, zero, negative, and overflow flags as described in Section 12.2.

12.4.3 Increment Instructions

The 6502 μP has three increment instructions:

INC	Increment memory
INX	Increment X index register
INY	Increment Y index register

An increment instruction adds 1 to the contents of the specified memory location or register. The 6502 μP instruction set does not include an instruction to increment the accumulator. Therefore, there are three ways to add 1 to the accumulator: (1) use an add instruction; (2) transfer the accumulator to either the X or Y register, do the increment, and then transfer the result back to the accumulator; or (3) move the contents of the accumulator to a memory location, do the increment, and move the result back to the accumulator.

Remember from Section 5.3.2 that all increment instructions are considered to be roll-over instructions, and the actual operation is done in the arithmetic and logic unit (ALU). To increment a memory location requires a read/modify/write operation, as described in Section 5.3.2.

The only flag bits that are affected by these increment instructions are the zero flag and the negative flag, as described in Section 12.2. We will discuss each of the increment instructions next.

INC Increment Memory

The INC instruction adds 1 to the contents of the specified memory location. The increment memory instruction does not affect the accumulator or the X or Y registers.

INX Increment X Index Register

The INX instruction adds 1 to the contents of the X index register.

INY Increment Y Index Register

The INY instruction adds 1 to the contents of the Y index register.

12.4.4 Decrement Instructions

The 6502 μP has three decrement instructions:

DEC	Decrement memory
DEX	Decrement X index register
DEY	Decrement Y index register

A decrement instruction subtracts 1 from a specified memory location or register.

The decrement instructions, like the increment instructions, apply only to the μP's X and Y registers. There is no instruction in the 6502 μP that allows the user to decrement the accumulator with a single instruction. Therefore, we must decrement the accumulator in a way similar to the way we increment the accumulator. The decrement instructions are done in the ALU, and there is a roll-over effect if a register or memory location is all 0s and is decremented. A memory location is decremented by a read/modify/write operation.

Unlike the subtraction instruction, the decrement instruction does not require the carry flag to be set. This instruction affects only the zero and negative flags, as described in Section 12.2. A brief discussion of the decrement instructions follows.

DEC Decrement Memory

The DEC instruction subtracts 1 from the contents of a specified memory location.

DEX Decrement X Index Register

The DEX instruction subtracts 1 from the current value of the X index register.

DEY Decrement Y Index Register

The DEY instruction subtracts 1 from the contents of the Y index register.

12.5 LOGICAL OPERATIONS

This group of instructions performs the Boolean logic operations of AND, OR, and Exclusive OR. These instructions work by transferring the contents of the memory location and the accumulator to the arithmetic and logic unit (ALU), where the logic operation is performed on the corresponding bits. That is, the logic operation is performed between bit 1 of the memory location and bit 1 of the accumulator, and so on. The result is automatically placed in the accumulator. These instructions affect the zero flag and the negative flag, as described in Section 12.2. Table 12-3 lists the logical instructions for the 6502 μP with their addressing modes and op codes. Specific examples are also listed.

TABLE 12-3 6502 Microprocessor Logical Instructions with Addressing Modes, Op Codes, and Examples

Addressing Mode	Assembly Language Form	Op Code	Example	Explanation
Immediate	AND #Oper	29	AND #0F	AND accumulator with hex number 0F.
Zero page	AND Oper	25		
Zero page,X	AND Oper,X	35		
Absolute	AND Oper	2D	AND 0410	AND accumulator with contents of memory location 0410.
Absolute,X	AND Oper,X	3D		
Absolute,Y	AND Oper,Y	39		
(Indirect,X)	AND (Oper,X)	21		
(Indirect),Y	AND (Oper),Y	31		
Immediate	ORA #Oper	Ø9		
Zero page	ORA Oper	Ø5	ORA 16	OR accumulator with contents of memory location 0016.
Zero page,X	ORA Oper,X	15		
Absolute	ORA Oper	ØD		
Absolute,X	ORA Oper,X	1D	ORA 0100,X	OR accumulator with contents of memory location 0100 + X register.
Absolute,Y	ORA Oper,Y	19		
(Indirect,X)	ORA (Oper,X)	Ø1		
(Indirect),Y	ORA (Oper),Y	11		
Immediate	EOR #Oper	49	EOR #FF	Exclusive OR accumulator with FF_{hex}.
Zero page	EOR Oper	45		
Zero page,X	EOR Oper,X	55		
Absolute	EOR Oper	4D		
Absolute,X	EOR Oper,X	5D		
Absolute,Y	EOR Oper,Y	59		
(Indirect,X)	EOR (Oper,X)	41		
(Indirect),Y	EOR (Oper,Y	51		

12.5.1 AND Instruction

The 6502 μP has only one AND instruction.

AND **AND Memory with Accumulator**

The AND instruction performs the logical AND operation between the contents of memory and the corresponding bit of the accumulator. The result is placed in the accumulator. The zero and negative flags are affected.

12.5.2 OR Instruction

There is only one OR instruction for the 6502 μP.

ORA **OR Memory with Accumulator**

The ORA instruction performs the logical OR operation between the contents of a memory location and the corresponding bit of the accumulator. The result is placed in the accumulator. The zero and negative flags are affected.

12.5.3 Exclusive OR Instruction

The 6502 μP has one Exclusive OR instruction.

EOR **Exclusive OR Memory with Accumulator**

The EOR instruction performs the logical Exclusive OR operation between the contents of a memory location and the corresponding bit of the accumulator. The result is placed in the accumulator. Only the zero and negative flags are affected.

Note: The Exclusive OR instruction for the 8080A μP is an operation between the accumulator and a μP register (including the accumulator). As mentioned in Chapter 5, the Exclusive OR instruction is often used to clear the accumulator and the carry flag when a program is written that uses the 8080A μP. In the 6502 μP, the Exclusive OR instruction operates only between data in memory and the accumulator. Therefore, when we use the 6502, we cannot Exclusive OR the accumulator with itself, and we cannot Exclusive OR the accumulator with any other μP register (the X register or the Y register).

12.6 COMPARE AND TEST INSTRUCTIONS

In this section, we will look at three compare instructions and a bit test instruction for the 6502 μP. The compare instructions are as follows:

CMP	Compare memory with accumulator
CPX	Compare memory with X register
CPY	Compare memory with Y register

The bit test instruction is as follows:

BIT	Bit test

Like the compare instructions for previous μPs, the 6502 compare instructions are designed to compare two values (by subtracting them) but not to store the result. The bit test instruction is used to test individual bits of a memory location with the accumulator (by ANDing them), but not to store the result.

All compare instructions and the bit test instruction affect flag bits. The compare instructions affect the carry flag, zero flag, and negative flags, as described in Section 12.2. The flag bits affected by the bit test instruction are covered when that instruction is discussed. Table 12–4 is a listing of the compare and test instructions for the 6502 μP with their addressing modes and op codes. Several example instructions are also listed.

Let's study the comparison and bit test instructions for the 6502 μP.

TABLE 12-4 6502 Microprocessor Compare and Test Instructions with Addressing Modes, Op Codes, and Examples

Addressing Mode	Assembly Language Form	Op Code	Example	Explanation
Immediate	CMP #Oper	C9		
Zero page	CMP Oper	C5		
Zero page,X	CMP Oper,X	D5	CMP 60,X	Compare accumulator with data at memory location 0060 + Y register.
Absolute	CMP Oper	CD		
Absolute,X	CMP Oper,X	DD		
Absolute,Y	CMP Oper,Y	D9		
(Indirect,X)	CMP (Oper,X)	C1		
(Indirect),Y	CMP (Oper),Y	D1		
Immediate	CPX #Oper	EØ		
Zero page	CPX Oper	E4	CPX 4D	Compare X register with data at memory location 004D.
Absolute	CPX Oper	EC		
Immediate	CPY #Oper	CØ		
Zero page	CPY Oper	C4		
Absolute	CPY Oper	CC	CPY 4DF0	Compare Y register with data at memory location 4DF0.
Zero page	BIT Oper	24	BIT 6A	Test accumulator with data at memory location 006A; bits 6 and 7 at memory location 006A loaded into V and N flag bits, respectively.
Absolute	BIT Oper	2C	BIT 8000	Test accumulation with data at memory location 8000; bits 6 and 7 at memory location 8000 loaded into V and N flag bits, respectively.

CMP Compare Memory with Accumulator

The CMP instruction subtracts the contents of memory from the contents of the accumulator. The result is not stored. The carry flag does not have to be set by the programmer.

CPX Compare Memory with X Register

The CPX instruction subtracts the contents of memory from the contents of the X register. The result of the comparison is not stored. The carry flag does not have to be set first.

CPY Compare Memory with Y Register

The CPY instruction subtracts the contents of memory from the contents of the Y register. Like other compare instructions, the result of this instruction is not stored and the carry flag does not have to be set.

BIT **Bit Test**

The BIT instruction performs an AND operation between data in memory and the accumulator. The result is not placed in the accumulator. This instruction affects the zero flag, the negative flag, and the overflow flag as follows:

1. Z = 1 if the result of the AND operation between the accumulator and the data from memory is zero; Z = 0 if the result is not zero.
2. N = 1 if the value of bit 7 of the memory location is a logic 1; N = 0 if the value of bit 7 of the memory location equals a logic 0.
3. V = 1 if bit 6 of the data from the memory location is a logic 1; V = 0 if bit 6 of the data from the memory location is a logic 0.

This instruction can be used for two applications. The first allows the examination of individual bits without disturbing the value in the accumulator. If the bits in the accumulator and the data from memory agree, the zero flag is set (a logic 1); otherwise, it is reset. Therefore, if we were using the bit instruction in this way, we would follow it by a branch instruction.

The second use of the bit instruction is based on the fact that it transfers bit 6 and bit 7 of the data from memory into the V and N flags, respectively. This transfer occurs automatically regardless of the value in the accumulator. Therefore, by checking the V and N flags, we know what the contents of bit 6 and bit 7 of the memory location are. The advantage to this feature is that the 6502 μP is often used with the 6821 input/output device. This device has its interrupt status bits reflected into bit 6 and bit 7 of a register. By using the bit instruction on an I/O device, bit 6 and bit 7 are automatically sent to the V and N flags, respectively. Both of these flag bits can be checked by branch instructions. This technique is used in Chapter 19 for a software polling routine.

12.7 SHIFT AND ROTATE INSTRUCTIONS

The 6502 μP has both shift and rotate instructions. The shift instructions are as follows:

ASL Arithmetic shift left
LSR Logical shift right

The rotate instructions are as follows:

ROL Rotate left
ROR Rotate right

Both the shift and rotate instructions can be applied to the accumulator and a memory location. They do not apply to the X or Y register. Therefore, to shift or rotate either of those registers, the programmer must transfer their contents to either the accumulator or a memory location, perform the operation, and then transfer the data back to the register. Table 12–5 shows the shift and rotate instructions for the 6502 μP with their addressing modes and op codes. Examples of some specific instructions are also shown. Now, let's look briefly at each instruction.

TABLE 12-5 6502 Microprocessor Shift and Rotate Instructions with Addressing Modes, Op Codes, and Examples

Addressing Mode	Assembly Language Form	Op Code	Example	Explanation
Accumulator	ASL A	ØA	ASL A	Shift left contents of accumulator.
Zero page	ASL Oper	Ø6		
Zero page,X	ASL Oper,X	16		
Absolute	ASL Oper	ØE	ASL 1A40	Shift left contents of memory location 1A40.
Absolute,X	ASL Oper,X	1E		
Accumulator	LSR A	4A		
Zero page	LSR Oper	46	LSR A5	Shift right contents of memory location 00A5.
Zero page,X	LSR Oper,X	56	LSR 74,X	Shift right contents of memory location 0074 + X register.
Absolute	LSR Oper	4E		
Absolute,X	LSR Oper,X	5E		
Accumulator	ROL A	2A		
Zero page	ROL Oper	26	ROL D4	Rotate left contents of memory location 00D4.
Zero page,X	ROL Oper,X	36		
Absolute	ROL Oper	2E		
Absolute,X	ROL Oper,X	3E	ROL E300,X	Rotate left contents of memory location E300 + X register.
Accumulator	ROR A	6A		
Zero page	ROR Oper	66		
Zero page,X	ROR Oper,X	76		
Absolute	ROR Oper	6E		
Absolute,X	ROR Oper,X	7E		

ASL Arithmetic Shift Left

The ASL instruction shifts either the contents of the accumulator or the contents of a memory location one bit to the left. Bit 0 is always cleared to a logic 0, and bit 7 is transferred to the carry flag, as shown in Figure 12-4. This instruction affects the zero flag and the negative flag as well as the carry flag.

LSR Logical Shift Right

The LSR instruction shifts the contents of the accumulator or the contents of a specified memory location one bit to the right. Bit 7 is always cleared to a logic 0, and bit 0 is transferred to the carry flag, as shown in Figure 12-5. This instruction also affects the zero flag and the negative flag.

ROL Rotate Left

The ROL instruction shifts either the contents of the accumulator or the contents of a specified memory location left one bit. In this instruction, the carry flag is transferred to bit 0, and bit 7 is transferred to the carry flag, as shown in Figure 12-6. This instruction also affects the zero flag and the negative flag.

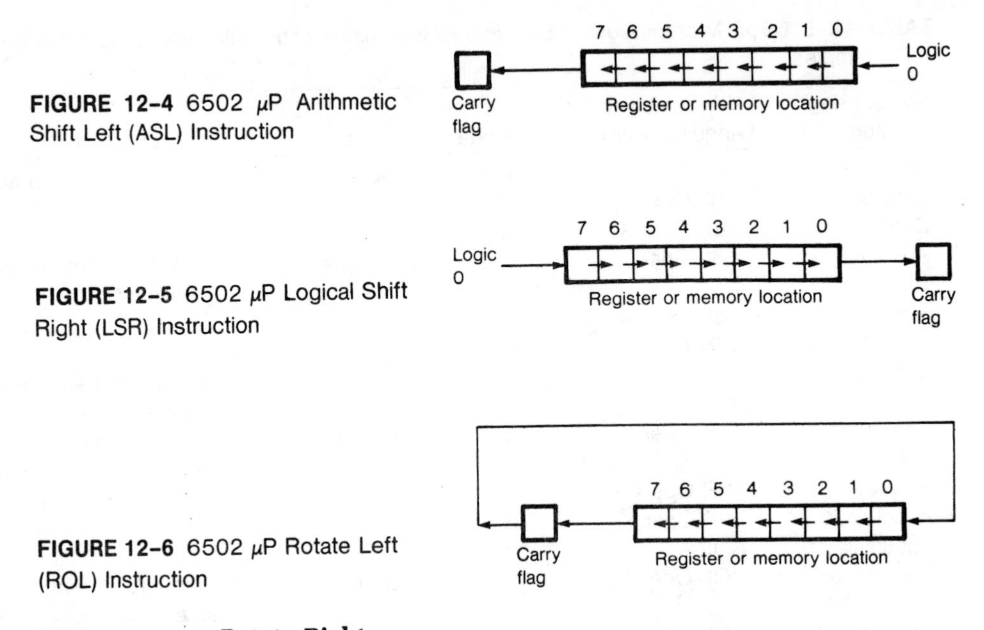

FIGURE 12-4 6502 μP Arithmetic Shift Left (ASL) Instruction

FIGURE 12-5 6502 μP Logical Shift Right (LSR) Instruction

FIGURE 12-6 6502 μP Rotate Left (ROL) Instruction

ROR Rotate Right

The ROR instruction shifts the contents of either the accumulator or a specified memory location right one bit. Bit 0 is transferred to the carry flag, and the carry flag is transferred to bit 7, as shown in Figure 12-7. Like the previous shift and rotate instructions, this instruction also affects the zero flag and the negative flag.

12.8 PROGRAM CONTROL INSTRUCTIONS

The 6502 μP has three groups of instructions that affect the program counter: *jump, branch,* and *return* instructions. The jump and return instructions are unconditional instructions. That is, when the op code for these instructions is decoded by the μP, the program counter will always be changed. The branch instructions, however, are conditional instructions. A flag bit must first be checked. If the condition is true, then the branch will be taken; if not, the program continues sequentially. There are four flag bits that can be checked in the 6502 μP. They are the carry flag, the zero flag, the negative flag, and the overflow flag. Since each flag bit can be either a logic 0 or a logic 1, there are eight possible branch instructions. Table 12-6 lists the program control instructions for the 6502 μP with their addressing modes and op codes. Examples of several instructions are also listed. For the eight branch instructions, the offset value is in hexadecimal.

There are two jump instructions: JMP and JSR. The difference between them is that the JSR instruction saves a return address on the stack while the JMP instruction does not. The JSR instruction is used to jump to a subroutine, and a return address is needed to get back to the main program. The JMP in-

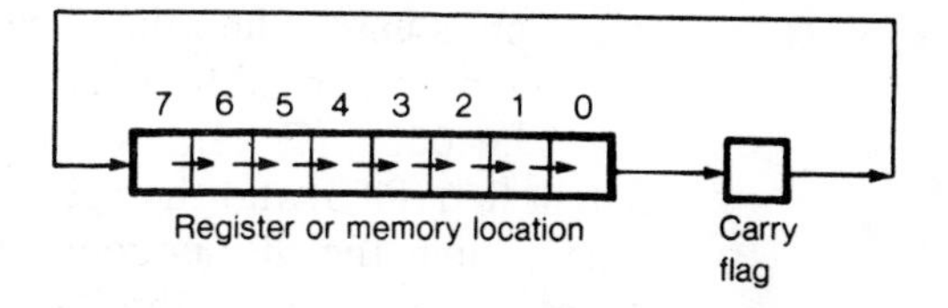

FIGURE 12–7 6502 μP Rotate Right (ROR) Instruction

TABLE 12–6 6502 Microprocessor Program Control Instructions with Addressing Modes, Op Codes, and Examples

Condition	Description	Addressing Mode	Instruction	Op Code	Example	Explanation
		Absolute	JMP Oper	4C	JMP FA40	Jump to memory location FA40.
		Indirect	JMP (Oper)	6C		
		Absolute	JSR Oper	20	JSR B475	Jump to subroutine at memory location B475.
C = 0	Branch on carry clear	Relative	BCC	90	BCC 08	Test carry flag and add 08 to PC if C flag is a logic 0.
C = 1	Branch on carry set	Relative	BCS	B0	BCS 1A	Test carry flag and add 1A to PC if C flag is a logic 1.
Z = 0	Branch on result not zero	Relative	BNE	D0	BNE 4C	Test zero flag and add 4C to PC if Z flag is a logic 0.
Z = 1	Branch on result zero	Relative	BEQ	F0	BEQ FD	Test zero flag and add FD to PC if Z flag is a logic 1.
N = 0	Branch on result plus	Relative	BPL	10	BPL 0D	Test negative flag and add 0D to PC if N flag is a logic 0.
N = 1	Branch on result minus	Relative	BMI	30	BMI 74	Test negative flag and add 74 to PC if N flag is a logic 1.
V = 0	Branch on overflow clear	Relative	BVC	50	BVC 10	Test overflow flag and add 10 to PC if V flag is a logic 0.
V = 1	Branch on overflow set	Relative	BVS	70	BVS C5	Test overflow flag and add C5 to PC if V flag is a logic 1.
		Implied	RTS	60		
		Implied	RTI	40		

struction is used when the programmer wishes to jump to a new memory location and a return address is not needed.

The 6502 μP has two return instructions: the return from subroutine instruction (RTS) and the return from interrupt instruction (RTI). Both instructions return the μP sequence to its original program; however, the RTI instruction also returns the flag register to its original condition.

12.8.1 Jump Instructions

Both the JMP and JSR instructions are three-byte instructions. The first byte is the op code while the second and third bytes are the address of the first instruction of the new program. When these jump instructions are decoded, the second byte is transferred to the low-order 8 bits of the program counter and the third byte of the instruction is transferred to the high-order 8 bits of the program counter. These instructions do not affect any flag bits. A brief discussion of the jump instructions follows.

JMP Jump to New Location

The JMP instruction changes the program sequence to access either an old or a new program by placing byte 2 and 3 of the instruction in the program counter. This instruction does not check any condition flags, so it is an unconditional jump instruction. When this instruction is decoded, byte 2 is placed in the low-order 8 bits of the program counter, and byte 3 is placed in the high-order 8 bits of the program counter.

JSR Jump to New Location Saving Return Address

The JSR instruction, like the JMP instruction, changes the program counter by placing bytes 2 and 3 in the program counter. The difference between the JMP instruction and the JSR instruction is that the JSR instruction is used to call a subroutine program and saves the next address of the main program on the stack. This procedure allows the programmer to use a return instruction and be guaranteed a return to the instruction following the JSR instruction. The JSR instruction has only one type of addressing mode and affects no flag bits.

The return address that is placed on the stack is placed there before bytes 2 and 3 are placed into the program counter. As for the JMP instruction, byte 2 is placed into the low-order 8 bits of the program counter, and byte 3 is placed into the high-order 8 bits of the program counter.

12.8.2 Branch Instructions

These instructions are conditional instructions. That is, a flag bit must be checked first. When these instructions are executed, the μP decodes the op code, tests the appropriate flag bit, and changes the program counter if the condition is true (if the logic state of the flag bit agrees with the instruction). If the condition is not true, the program continues in its normal sequence, and the next instruction following the branch instruction is executed.

The branch instructions are two-byte instructions. The first byte is the op code, and the second byte is the offset. If a condition is true, the offset is added to the present contents of the program counter. Remember from Section 5.6 that the offset is in 2's complement form.

12.8.3 Return Instructions

The 6502 μP has two return instructions:

RTS Return from subroutine
RTI Return from interrupt

The RTS instruction is used as the last instruction in a subroutine program. This instruction allows the μP to find its way back to the main program and allows the μP to execute the rest of the program. Remember that a subroutine program is initiated by the μP decoding a JSR instruction.

The RTI instruction is the last instruction in an interrupt program and allows the μP to find its way back to the main program. However, an interrupt program is not initiated by the μP decoding an instruction but, rather, by a high-to-low transition either on the interrupt request pin ($\overline{IRQ}$) or on the non-maskable pin ($\overline{NMI}$). A brief discussion of each return instruction follows.

RTS Return from Subroutine

The RTS instruction transfers two bytes of information from the stack to the μP's program counter. When this instruction is decoded and executed, the steps involved are as follows:

1. The stack pointer is incremented by 1.
2. The contents of the memory location given by the stack pointer are transferred to the low-order 8 bits of the program counter.
3. The stack pointer is again incremented by 1.
4. The contents of the new memory location given by the stack pointer are transferred to the high-order 8 bits of the program counter.
5. The program counter is incremented by 1.
6. The program counter is now sent to the address bus, and the next op code is fetched by the μP.

The RTS instruction is a single-byte instruction and does not affect any flag bits. The only register involved is the program counter.

RTI Return from Interrupt

The RTI instruction transfers three bytes of information from the stack to the μP. The first byte is the processor status register, while the second and third bytes are sent to the program counter. When this instruction is decoded and executed, the steps involved are as follows:

1. The stack pointer is incremented by 1.
2. The contents of the memory location given by the stack pointer are transferred to the processor status register.

3. The stack pointer is again incremented by 1.
4. The contents of the memory location given by the stack pointer are transferred to the low-order 8 bits of the program counter (PCL).
5. The stack pointer is again incremented by 1.
6. The contents of the memory location given by the stack pointer are transferred to the high-order 8 bits of the program counter (PCH).

Like the RTS instruction, the RTI instruction is a single-byte instruction and does not affect any μP registers other than the processor status register and the program counter. Remember that this instruction returns the processor status register to the condition that it was in before the interrupt occurred.

12.9 STACK/STACK POINTER INSTRUCTIONS

The instructions covered in this section are used by the programmer to put data onto the stack, to remove data from the stack, or to transfer data between the low-order 8 bits of the stack pointer and the X register. Table 12–7 shows the stack/stack pointer instructions for the 6502 μP with their addressing modes and op codes. A brief discussion of each instruction follows.

PHA **Push Accumulator on Stack**

The PHA instruction transfers the contents of the accumulator to the memory location given by the stack pointer. The stack pointer is automatically decremented by 1. This instruction is a single-byte instruction and affects no flag bits.

PLA **Pull Accumulator from Stack**

The PLA instruction is a two-step operation. First, this instruction increments the current value of the stack pointer by 1. Second, the contents of the memory location given by the stack pointer are transferred to the accumulator.

PHP **Push Processor Status Register on Stack**

The PHP instruction transfers the current contents of the processor status register to the stack. The memory location is given by the stack pointer. The stack pointer is decremented by 1.

TABLE 12–7 6502 Microprocessor Stack/Stack Pointer Instructions with Addressing Modes and Op Codes

Addressing Mode	Assembly Language Form	Op Code
Implied	PHA	48
Implied	PLA	68
Implied	PHP	08
Implied	PLP	28
Implied	TXS	9A
Implied	TSX	BA

PLP **Pull Processor Status Register from Stack**

The PLP instruction increments the stack pointer by 1 and then transfers the contents of the memory location given by the stack pointer to the processor status register.

TXS **Transfer Index Register to Stack Pointer**

The TXS instruction transfers the value of the X register to the low-order 8 bits of the stack pointer. The high-order 8 bits for the 6502 μP are always 01_{hex}. This instruction is used in the beginning of a program to initialize the stack pointer. The programmer loads the X register and then transfers it to the stack pointer.

TSX **Transfer Stack Pointer to X Register**

The TSX instruction transfers the low-order 8 bits of the stack pointer to the X register. This instruction affects the zero and negative flags.

12.10 OTHER 6502 MICROPROCESSOR INSTRUCTIONS

In this section, we will examine the remaining 6502 μP instructions. They are as follows:

1. Those that clear (a logic 0) or set (a logic 1) some of the processor status bits,
2. A no operation instruction,
3. A break instruction.

Table 12–8 is a listing of clear, set, and other instructions for the 6502 μP with their addressing modes and op codes.

12.10.1 Clear and Set Instructions

We have seen how, for other instructions, some flag bits are automatically cleared to a logic 0 or set to a logic 1 by the operation. For example, the result of an addition can affect the carry flag, the zero flag, the overflow flag, and the

TABLE 12–8 6502 Microprocessor Clear and Set, No Operation, and Break Instructions with Addressing Modes and Op Codes

Addressing Mode	Assembly Language Form	Op Code
Implied	CLC	18
Implied	SEC	38
Implied	CLI	58
Implied	SEI	78
Implied	CLV	B8
Implied	CLD	D8
Implied	SED	F8
Implied	NOP	EA
Implied	BRK	00

negative flag. At times, however, the programmer needs to clear or set a particular flag bit either to control the μP's actions or to execute a program properly. There are four bits of the processor register that can be either cleared or set by the programmer. They are the carry flag, the decimal mode flag, the interrupt flag, and the overflow flag. Each of these instructions is a single byte and uses the implied addressing mode. Let's turn now to a brief discussion of each instruction.

CLC **Clear Carry Flag**

The CLC instruction clears the carry flag to a logic 0. It often precedes an add program, as we will see in Section 13.1.1.

SEC **Set Carry Flag**

The SEC instruction sets the carry flag to a logic 1. It normally precedes a subtract program, as we will see in Section 13.1.6.

CLI **Clear Interrupt Flag**

The CLI instruction clears the interrupt flag to a logic 0. This allows the μP to acknowledge interrupt signals that occur on the interrupt request pin (pin 4).

SEI **Set Interrupt Flag**

The SEI instruction sets the interrupt flag to a logic 1. It is used by the programmer to disable the interrupt line so that the μP will not acknowledge any interrupt signals that occur on the interrupt request pin.

CLV **Clear Overflow Flag**

The CLV instruction clears the overflow flag to a logic 0. There is no instruction to set the overflow flag. However, there is a pin (pin 38) that is used to receive a signal that allows an external device to set the overflow flag.

CLD **Clear Decimal Load Flag**

The CLD instruction clears the decimal flag to a logic 0. This causes all addition and subtraction operations following the CLD instruction to be carried out as binary operations.

SED **Set Decimal Mode Flag**

The SED instruction sets the decimal mode flag to a logic 1. This setting causes all addition and subtraction operations following the SED instruction to be carried out as decimal operations. If a programmer wishes to execute an entire program using decimal numbers, then this flag would have to be set only once at the beginning of the program.

12.10.2 Other Instructions

In this section, we will examine two other 6502 μP instructions: no operation and break.

NOP **No Operation**

The NOP instruction affects no register or carry bits, and only the program counter is incremented by 1. It is a single-byte instruction and uses the implied addressing mode.

BRK **Force Break**

The BRK instruction causes the μP to go through an interrupt sequence under program control. Thus, the program counter is automatically stored on the stack along with the processor status register. This instruction is used during program debugging. By allowing the programmer to enter the code for the break instruction, the program will execute up to the break instruction, at which point it will automatically jump to the interrupt vector location. In order to know whether the vector was fetched in response to an interrupt signal or in response to a break instruction, the B flag of the processor status register is checked. It will contain a logic 1 if the interrupt was caused by a break instruction; otherwise, it will contain a logic 0. Like the other instructions in this section, the break instruction is a single-byte instruction and uses the implied addressing mode.

12.11 INDIRECT ADDRESSING MODE

Indirect addressing is an advanced addressing mode that is not used by all μPs. It is a valuable tool for many applications, in particular, those of data processing. For this mode, the address specified by the instruction is only used as a pointer to memory to pick up the final (effective) address. For example, in Figure 12-8, IAL and IAH are the indirect address low and high bytes, respectively. When the instruction is executed, IAH, IAL point to a memory location where the final address may be obtained. Since an address requires two bytes of memory, the μP has been designed to retrieve both bytes, ADL and ADH. An example showing that this addressing mode is valuable is as follows: Consider a program that refers to a particular memory location 50 times. If the location is changed, it must be changed every place in the program—which means 50 modifications. If the indirect addressing mode is used, only ADL and ADH have to be changed—one change as opposed to 50 changes. The 6502 μP has an indirect addressing mode similar to that shown in Figure 12-8 for its JMP instructions. It also has two other modes of indirect addressing: (1) indexed indirect and (2) indirect indexed.

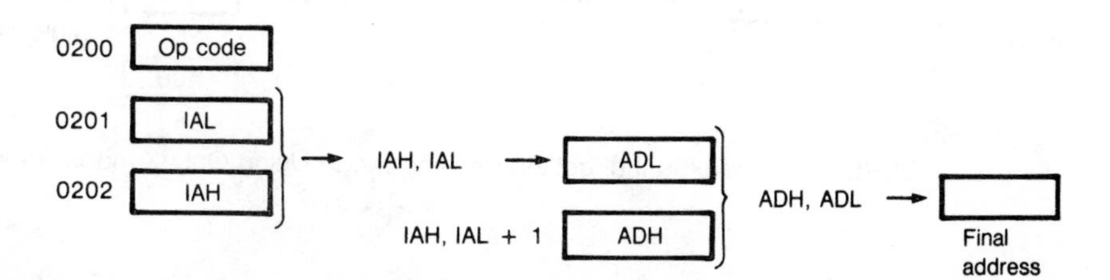

FIGURE 12-8 Indirect Addressing Mode for 6502 μP

12.11.1 Indexed Indirect Addressing Mode

The 6502's instructions that have this addressing mode capability are as follows:

ADC	LDA
AND	ORA
CMP	SBC
EOR	STA

The indexed indirect addressing mode differs from the indirect mode previously described in that IAH = 00. Therefore, the final address will always be found in page 0. Another difference is that the X index register is added to IAL. The indirect address is [00, IAL + X register]. Figure 12–9 shows how this addressing mode works. The technique of using the index register allows easy polling of I/O devices, or any other string operation, because the X register can be incremented or decremented. This addressing mode uses only the X register for indexing. When IAL is added to the X register, there is no carry because the indirect address must always be found on page 0.

12.11.2 Indirect Indexed Addressing Mode

The 6502 instructions that have this addressing mode capability are as follows:

ADC	LDA
AND	ORA
CMP	SBC
EOR	STA

This addressing mode is a two-byte instruction. The first byte is the op code, and the second byte is the indirect address pointer to a location on page 0. From page 0, a base address (BAH, BAL) is retrieved. Now, the Y index register is added to the base address to produce the final address. The Y register is actually added only to BAL. If there is a carry, it is added to BAH. Figure 12–10 shows how this addressing mode operates.

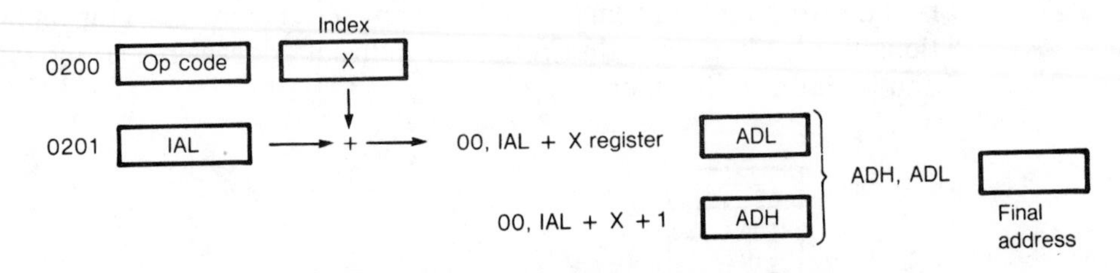

FIGURE 12–9 Indexed Indirect Addressing Mode Using Only X Index Register

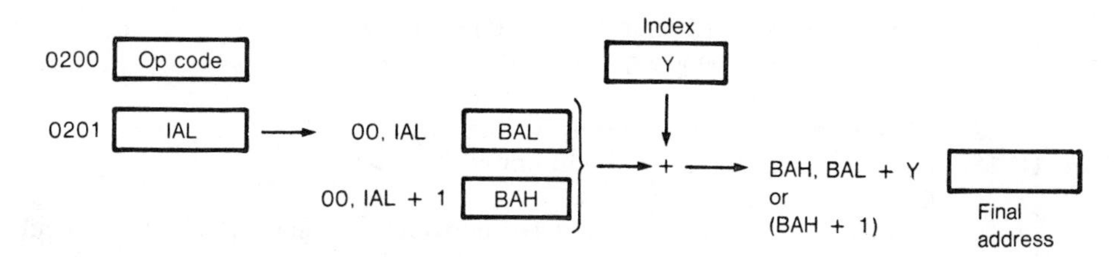

FIGURE 12–10 Indirect Indexed Addressing Mode Using Only Y Index Register

12.12 SUMMARY

This chapter followed the format that was established in Chapter 5 for grouping similar instructions. However, when we are writing a program and need a quick reference guide for checking (1) an op code, (2) an addressing mode, (3) execution times, or (4) the flag bits affected, an alphabetical listing, such as the one shown in Appendix Table D–9, is often the easiest way to find the answer.

In this chapter, we began our study of the 6502 μP's instruction set by examining its internal architecture. The block diagram shown in Figure 12–2 is helpful in visualizing what happens when the μP is fetching and executing an instruction. We also saw that the 6502's processor status register contains four flag bits: the carry, zero, sign, and overflow bits. Similarly, the P register contains three bits for telling the μP the status of different conditions. These bits are the interrupt, decimal mode, and break command bits.

In succeeding sections of the chapter, we discussed the 6502's instructions, grouped into eight categories: data movement, arithmetic, logical, compare and test, shift and rotate, program control, stack/stack pointer, and other 6502 instructions. The 6502 does not have separate input/output instructions. Therefore, all I/O operations are done through memory-mapped I/O similar to what is done in the 6800 μP.

We concluded the chapter by examining, in detail, the indirect addressing capabilities of the 6502 μP.

PROBLEMS

These problems apply to the 6502 μP.

12–1 How many basic instructions are there in the 6502's instruction set? 56
12–2 When does the μP trap the incoming data from the data bus? (The clock frequency is 1 MHz.)
12–3 Where is the stack located in the 6502 μP?
12–4 How many index registers are there?
12–5 Are the address bus lines TTL or three state?
12–6 Name the processor status bits.
12–7 Is the I flag under the programmer's control?
12–8 Is the 6502 μP capable of doing both decimal addition and decimal subtraction? Yes

12-9 Does the 6502 μP have an exchange instruction?
12-10 What are the three groups of data movement instructions?
12-11 What flag bits are affected by a load instruction?
12-12 What flag bits are affected by a store instruction?
12-13 Can the X register be stored at any RAM location?
12-14 List the transfer instructions.
12-15 Can the X register be transferred directly to the Y register? If not, how could the transfer take place?
12-16 What type of addressing mode is used for the transfer instructions?
12-17 Explain what happens when each of the following instructions is executed (data and address are given in hex): (a) LDA #FF; (b) LDA 0020; (c) LDA 4500,X; (d) LDX #00; (e) LDY 0100; (f) STA 80; (g) STA 0600,Y; and (h) STY 0F37.
12-18 List the four groups of arithmetic instructions.
12-19 Does the 6502 μP have an add instruction that does not include the carry flag?
12-20 What flag bits are affected by the ADC instruction?
12-21 Are the results of all the add instructions placed automatically in the accumulator?
12-22 Can any RAM memory location be incremented?
12-23 Can any ROM memory location be incremented?
12-24 Can the accumulator be decremented with a single instruction?
12-25 What are the four addressing modes for the increment and decrement instructions?
12-26 Explain what happens when each of the following instructions is executed (data and address are given in hex): (a) ADC #03; (b) ADC 0760; (c) ADC 0760,X; (d) SBC #04; (e) SBC 0310; (f) INX; (g) INC 0080; and (h) DEY.
12-27 What are the logical operations for the 6502 μP?
12-28 Does the 6502 μP have an instruction that Exclusive ORs the accumulator with the X register?
12-29 Explain what happens for each of the following instructions (data and addresses are given in hex): (a) AND #F0; (b) AND 5700; (c) ORA #C0; (d) ORA 14; and (e) EOR #80.
12-30 What is the difference between the compare instruction and the subtract instruction?
12-31 List the shift and rotate instructions.
12-32 Is the carry flag affected by all the shift and rotate instructions?
12-33 Which μP registers can be shifted right?
12-34 If the accumulator is shifted nine times to the left, what data will it contain?
12-35 If the accumulator is rotated nine times to the left, what data will it contain?
12-36 What are the instructions that affect the program counter?
12-37 How many branch instructions are there for the 6502 μP?
12-38 What are the flag bits that can be checked by branch instructions?
12-39 What is the difference between the RTS and the RTI instructions?
12-40 Are both the JMP and the JSR three-byte instructions?
12-41 Are the branch instructions two or three bytes long?
12-42 Are all the branch instructions conditional instructions?
12-43 Given the following logic states of the flag register:

N	V		B	D	I	Z	C
1	0	X	0	1	0	1	0

Determine whether the μP will branch to a new location for the following instructions: (a) BCC, (b) BNE, (c) BVC, and (d) BMI.

12-44 How many bytes is the RTS instruction? Are the flag bits affected by this instruction?

12-45 List the stack/stack pointer instructions.

12-46 Can the X and Y registers be saved by using one μP instruction?

12-47 When the TXS instruction is executed, is the X register transferred to the stack or to the stack pointer?

12-48 Can the high byte of the stack pointer be changed?

12-49 What is the purpose of the SEI instruction?

12-50 Does the 6502 μP use a decimal adjust instruction? Explain.

6502 Programs

13.0 INTRODUCTION

This chapter is a continuation of our study of the 6502 μP's software. In it, most of the instructions from the previous chapter will be used to write programs such as binary and decimal addition and subtraction, adding a column of numbers, determining the largest value in a column of numbers, time delay programs, exchanging sections of memory, multiplication programs, and a binary-to-BCD conversion program. These programs are similar to those presented for the 8080A and 6800 μPs. They can be used as building blocks to write longer and more complex programs. The programs are written by using the 6502 mnemonics and in an assembly language format. All data and addresses are in hexadecimal code. The first column is reserved for labels, the second column is for instructions, and the third column is for comments about the instructions. As was true of the other programming chapters, the programs in this chapter are general and are written to show different 6502 instructions. Remember that the symbol # stands for the immediate addressing mode.

13.1 ADDITION AND SUBTRACTION

There are some differences between how the 6502 μP and either the 8080A or the 6800 μP does addition and subtraction. The 6502 μP has only one add and one subtract instruction (not including the addressing modes). The carry flag is included in both the add and subtract instructions for the 6502. When addition is being done, the carry flag first has to be cleared. When subtraction is being done, the carry flag first has to be set. The programs for decimal addition and subtraction are a lot shorter than those for the other μPs. The reason is the 6502's decimal mode flag bit. When this bit is set, the μP automatically does decimal arithmetic, and, therefore, no decimal adjust instruction is needed. When the decimal mode flag has cleared, the 6502 μP does binary arithmetic.

13.1.1 Single-Byte Binary Addition

Adding two 8-bit binary numbers requires five steps:

1. Clear the decimal mode flag.
2. Clear the carry flag.
3. Load the accumulator with one number.
4. Add the accumulator to the contents of a memory location.
5. Store the result.

The number placed in the accumulator is called the *augend*, the number that is added to it is called the *addend*, and the result is the *sum*. In the following examples, assume that the data has already been stored at the particular memory location. Example 13.1 is a general 8-bit addition program; Example 13.2 shows how a constant value can be added to the accumulator.

EXAMPLE 13.1 Add the contents of memory location 0200 to the contents of memory location 0250. Store the result at memory location 0300.

Solution

```
CLD        Clear decimal flag (binary addition).
CLC        Clear carry flag.
LDA 0200   Load accumulator with data at location 0200.
ADC 0250   Add accumulator + data at 0250 + carry.
STA 0300   Store sum at 0300.
```

The program in Example 13.1 uses the 6502's absolute addressing mode for the load, add, and store instructions. In some programs, we may want to add a particular value to the contents of the accumulator. For this type of program, we should use the immediate addressing mode, as Example 13.2 shows.

EXAMPLE 13.2 Add the contents of memory location 0200 to the value 60_{hex}. Store the result at memory location 0300.

Solution

```
CLD        Clear decimal flag (binary addition).
CLC        Clear carry flag.
LDA 0200   Load accumulator with data at location 0200.
ADC #60    Add accumulator + 60hex + carry.
STA 0300   Store sum at 0300.
```

13.1.2 Double-Precision Addition

When two 16-bit numbers are added, the addition is called *double precision*. Like the 6800 μP, the 6502 has to add 8-bit numbers and store the result. Then, it adds the next two 8-bit numbers and stores the result. The carry flag is not cleared between the first and second additions. The following binary numbers show which bits are added:

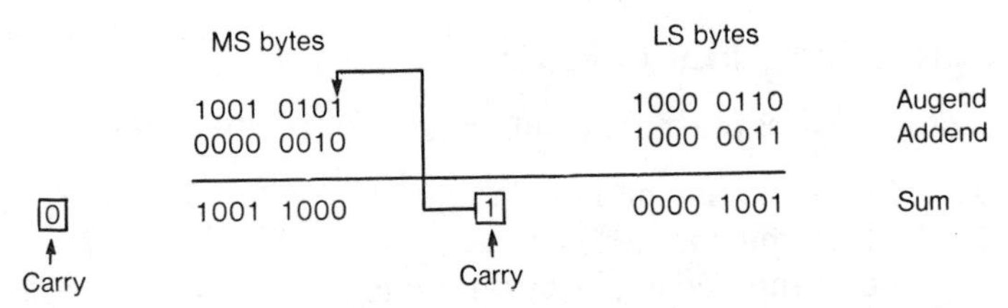

Example 13.3 shows the programming steps for a double-precision addition. The Y register is used as a counter. It is initialized to the value 2 because the add instruction has to be done twice. The X register is initialized for indexing because the augend and addend values are stored in consecutive memory locations.

EXAMPLE 13.3 Add the data at locations 0400 and 0401 to the data at locations 0500 and 0501. Store the result at locations 0600 and 0601.

Solution

```
      CLD           Clear decimal flag (binary addition).
      CLC           Clear carry flag.
      LDY #02       Load Y register for count = 2.
      LDX #00       Load X register for indexing.
ADD:  LDA 0400,X    Load accumulator with data at location 0400
                    + X register.
      ADC 0500,X    Add to accumulator data at location 0500 + X
                    register.
      STA 0600,X    Store answer at location 0600 + X register.
      INX           Increment X register.
      DEY           Decrement Y register.
      BNE ADD       If Y ≠ 0, branch to ADD.
```

The program in Example 13.3 uses the indexed addressing mode for the load, add, and store instructions. With the INX instruction, the 6502 μP can easily handle data that is stored in consecutive memory locations.

13.1.3 Multiprecision Addition

The double-precision addition program of the previous section can be expanded to a general multiprecision addition program by loading the Y register with a count equal to the number of bytes that have to be added. The index register of the 6502 μP works differently from the index register of the 6800 μP. For this reason, a multiprecision addition program using the 6502 μP requires fewer steps than a similar program using the 6800 μP. If we compare Example 13.4 with Example 10.4, we will find that the index register does not have to be stored temporarily during the program. The 6502 μP is considered to have true indexing because its index register can be added to a complete 16-bit address.

EXAMPLE 13.4 Write a multiprecision addition program that adds data in memory beginning at location 0400 to data in memory beginning at location 0500. Store the result in memory beginning at location 0600.

Solution

```
      CLD            Clear decimal mode (binary addition).
      CLC            Clear carry flag.
      LDY #count     Load Y register with count = number of bytes.
      LDX #00        Initialize X index register.
ADD:  LDA 0400,X     Load accumulator with augend.
      ADC 0500,X     Add accumulator + addend + carry.
      STA 0600,X     Store sum.
      INX            Increment X index register.
      DEY            Decrement count.
      BNE ADD        If Y register ≠ 0, branch to ADD.
```

The program in Example 13.4 is just a modification of the double-precision program of Example 13.3. If we were adding 32-bit numbers (4 bytes), the Y register would be loaded with a count equal to 4. Therefore, the count value equals the number of bytes to be added.

13.1.4 BCD Addition

The 6502 μP is capable of doing binary-coded-decimal addition. Unlike the 8080A and 6800 μPs, the 6502 does not need a decimal adjust instruction. Any 6502 binary addition program can be changed to a BCD addition program by changing the CLD instruction to an SED instruction. When doing BCD addition, remember that all numbers must be valid BCD numbers and that one byte contains two BCD numbers. In the program in Example 13.5, consider the data stored in memory to be valid BCD numbers.

EXAMPLE 13.5 Modify the multiprecision binary addition program of Example 13.4 to perform BCD addition.

Solution Change CLD to SED. All other programming steps remain the same.

```
      SED            Set decimal flag (decimal addition).
      CLC            Clear carry flag.
      LDY #count     Load Y register with count = number of bytes.
      LDX #00        Initialize X index register.
```

```
ADD: LDA 0400,X     Load accumulator with augend.
     ADC 0500,X     Add accumulator + addend + carry.
     STA 0600,X     Store sum.
     INX            Increment X index register.
     DEY            Decrement count.
     BNE ADD        If Y register ≠ 0, branch to ADD.
```

The program in Example 13.5 is a general-purpose decimal addition program. Single-byte as well as double-precision decimal addition may be done using this program. In single-byte decimal addition, the count value would equal 1. In double-precision decimal addition, the count value would equal 2.

13.1.5 Adding a Column of Numbers

When numbers in a column are to be added, they are usually stored in consecutive memory locations. This allows us to use the indexed addressing mode. The program in Example 13.6 shows how to add a column of 10 numbers and store the result in two consecutive memory locations. Each value in the column is added to the least significant byte of the answer (memory location 0300), and the carry flag is added to the most significant byte of the answer (memory location 0301).

EXAMPLE 13.6 Write a decimal addition program that adds 10 bytes of data stored in memory beginning at location 0200. Store the result at memory locations 0300 and 0301. Use the Y register as a counter, and use the X register for indexing.

Solution

```
        SED          Set decimal flag.
        CLC          Clear carry flag.
        LDY #0A      Load Y register with 0A_hex = 10_decimal.
        LDX #00      Load X register immediately.
        TXA          Clear accumulator.
        STA 0300     Clear location 0300.
        STA 0301     Clear location 0301.
REPEAT: LDA 0300     Load accumulator with data at location 0300.
        ADC 0200,X   Add data at location (0200 + X register).
        STA 0300     Store result.
        LDA #00      Clear accumulator; carry flag is not cleared.
        ADC 0301     Add carry flag to data at location 0301.
        STA 0301     Store result.
        INX          Increment X register.
        DEY          Decrement Y register.
        BNE REPEAT   If Y ≠ 0, branch to REPEAT.
```

The program in Example 13.6 could be changed to a binary addition program simply by changing the SED instruction to a CLD instruction.

13.1.6 Single-Byte Subtraction

The 6502 μP can do either binary or decimal subtraction, depending on the logic state of the decimal mode flag. If the decimal mode flag is cleared, binary subtraction is done. If the decimal mode flag is set, BCD subtraction is done. In either type of subtraction, the carry flag must be set. The steps for doing single-byte subtraction are as follows:

1. Clear or set the decimal mode flag.
2. Set the carry flag.
3. Load the accumulator with one number.
4. Subtract the contents of memory from the accumulator.
5. Store the result.

The arithmetic terminology for subtraction is as follows: The number in the accumulator is the *minuend*, the number coming from memory is the *subtrahend*, and the result is the *difference*.

Like the other μPs, the 6502 μP uses 2's complement arithmetic to do subtraction. The 2's complement of the subtrahend is obtained automatically, and, therefore, the programmer does not have to worry about it. If the answer is negative, it will be stored in 2's complement form. Examples 13.7 and 13.8 show the programming steps required for a general-purpose binary and decimal subtraction program, respectively.

EXAMPLE 13.7 Write a binary subtraction program that subtracts the contents of memory location 0150 from the contents of memory location 0100. Store the result in memory location 0200.

Solution

```
CLD          Clear decimal flag (binary subtraction).
SEC          Set carry flag.
LDA 0100     Load accumulator with data at 0100.
SBC 0150     Subtract data at 0150.
STA 0200     Store answer at 0200.
```

EXAMPLE 13.8 What modification has to be made to the program in Example 13.7 so it will perform an 8-bit decimal subtraction?

Solution Change the CLD instruction to an SED instruction. All other instructions remain the same.

Like decimal addition, decimal subtraction requires the data in memory to be valid BCD numbers.

13.1.7 Multiprecision Subtraction

The 6502 μP can perform multiprecision binary or decimal subtraction as easily as it can perform multiprecision addition. The multiprecision binary subtraction program is similar to the multiprecision binary addition program, except for two changes: (1) The CLC instruction is changed to an SEC instruction, and (2) the ADC instruction is changed to an SBC instruction.

A multiprecision decimal subtraction program using the 6502 μP does not require finding the complements of the subtrahend, as was required when using the 8080A or 6800 μP. Besides the two changes just mentioned, all that is needed is to change the CLD instruction to an SED instruction. Examples 13.9 and 13.10 show a multiprecision binary and decimal subtraction program, respectively.

EXAMPLE 13.9 Write a multiprecision binary subtraction program that subtracts the data beginning at memory location 0150 from the data beginning at memory location 0100. Store the result in memory beginning at location 0200. Use the Y register as a counter and the X register for indexing.

Solution

```
       CLD          Clear decimal flag (binary subtraction).
       SEC          Set carry flag.
       LDY #count   Load Y register with count.
       LDX #00      Initialize X index register.
SUBT:  LDA 0100,X   Load accumulator with data at 0100 + X
                    register.
       SBC 0150,X   Subtract data at location 0150 + X register.
       STA 0200,X   Store result at 0200 + X register.
       INX          Increment X index register.
       DEY          Decrement Y register.
       BNE SUBT     If Y ≠ 0, branch to SUBT.
```

EXAMPLE 13.10 Modify the program of Example 13.9 for decimal subtraction.

Solution

```
SED          Set decimal mode flag (decimal subtraction).
 .           All other instructions remain the same.
 .
 .
```

In either Example 13.9 or 13.10, the count value equals the number of bytes to be subtracted. If a double-precision subtraction were being performed, then the count value would equal 2.

13.2 DETERMINING THE LARGEST VALUE

In Chapter 5 and again in Chapter 9, we saw that the compare instruction is a subtract instruction. However, the carry flag is not included in the subtraction and the result is not stored in the accumulator. The compare instruction is useful when we want to check the contents of the accumulator with data from memory and determine which number is larger or smaller, or if the numbers are equal. Depending on what we want to do, the compare instruction is followed by a branch instruction. The program in Example 13.11 checks for the largest value among ten numbers. The numbers are considered to be in consecutive memory locations beginning at location 0200. The program is written as a subroutine to show where the RTS instruction goes.

EXAMPLE 13.11 Write the programming steps needed to find the largest value among ten numbers beginning at memory location 0200. Store the largest value at memory location 0300. Use the Y register as a counter and the X register for indexing.

Solution

	LDX #00	Load X register immediately with 00_{hex}.
	LDY #0A	Load Y register with $0A_{hex} = 10_{decimal}$.
	LDA 0200	Load accumulator with first number.
P_2:	CMP 0201,X	Compare accumulator with data at location 0201 + X register.
	BPL P_1	If plus, branch to P_1.
	LDA 0201,X	Load accumulator with larger value if $M \geq A$.
P_1:	INX	Increment X register.
	DEY	Decrement Y register.
	BNE P_2	If $Y \neq 0$, branch to P_2.
	STA 0300	Store largest value at location 0300.
	RTS	Return from subroutine.

13.3 TIME DELAYS

A commonly used program is a time delay program, which we have covered for the 8080A and 6800 μPs. Its primary function is to force the μP to wait for slow peripheral equipment to operate. All time delay programs are based on the same procedure, loading a register or memory location with a particular count and then decrementing that count until it equals 0. Since each instruction requires a certain amount of time for execution, a time delay is generated. The time delay loop is created by having the μP execute the same set of instructions over and over again until the count equals 0. Figure 13–1 shows a flowchart for a time delay program. In the chapters on the 8080A and 6800 μPs, we used registers internal to the μP to store the count. In the examples that follow, memory locations are used as temporary working registers to store the count.

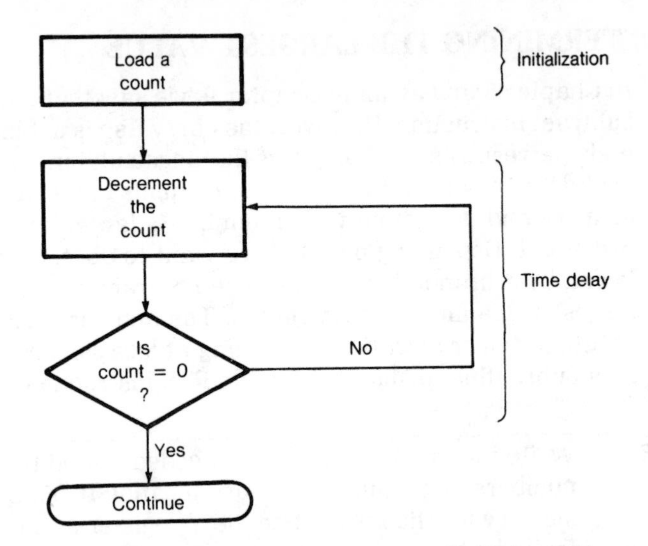

FIGURE 13–1 Flowchart for Loading and Decrementing a Register or Memory Location

The X or Y registers could have been used, but these programs show how the DEC instruction can be used. The examples in this section show how programs having 1, 2, and 3 time delay loops can be written.

EXAMPLE 13.12 For the flowchart of Figure 13–1, write a time delay program. Use memory location 0020 as a working register.

Solution

```
        LDA #count   Load the accumulator with initial value (2 μs).
        STA 0020     Store the accumulator at location 0020 (4 μs).
DELAY:  DEC 0020     Decrement location 0020 (6 μs).
        BNE DELAY    If location 0020 ≠ 0, then branch to DELAY
                     (2 μs/3 μs/4 μs).
```

The times in parentheses are for the 6502 μP operating from a 1 MHz clock. The BNE instruction has three times associated with it: (1) If the branch is not taken, then the time is 2 μs; (2) if the branch is taken and the location is on the same page, then the time is 3 μs; and (3) if the branch is taken and the location is on another page, then the time is 4 μs.

The following equation shows how the overall time delay can be calculated:

$$\text{Time delay} = \underset{\text{LDA}}{2\ \mu s} + \underset{\text{STA}}{4\ \mu s} + (\underset{\text{DEC}}{6\ \mu s} + \underset{\text{BNE}}{3\ \mu s \text{ or } 4\ \mu s}) \times (\text{count} - 1) + (\underset{\text{DEC}}{6\ \mu s} + \underset{\text{BNE}}{2\ \mu s}) \qquad \textbf{(13–1)}$$

In the program of Example 13.12, the count value would be in hexadecimal code, but in Equation 13–1, the count value must be in decimal.

EXAMPLE 13.13 What is the time delay in the previous example if memory location 0020 is loaded with 00_{hex}?

Solution The hexadecimal code 00 causes the longest time delay because memory location 0020 would have to be decremented 256 times before it is 0 again. Therefore, inserting 256 as the count value in Equation 13–1 yields the following:

$$\text{Time delay} = 6\ \mu s + [(9\ \mu s) \times 255] + 8\ \mu s = 2309\ \mu s \cong 2.3\ \text{ms}$$

Longer time delays can be generated by programming one time delay loop inside another. This technique is called *nesting time delays*. Figure 13–2 shows a flowchart for nesting two time delay loops using memory locations 0020 and 0021 as working registers.

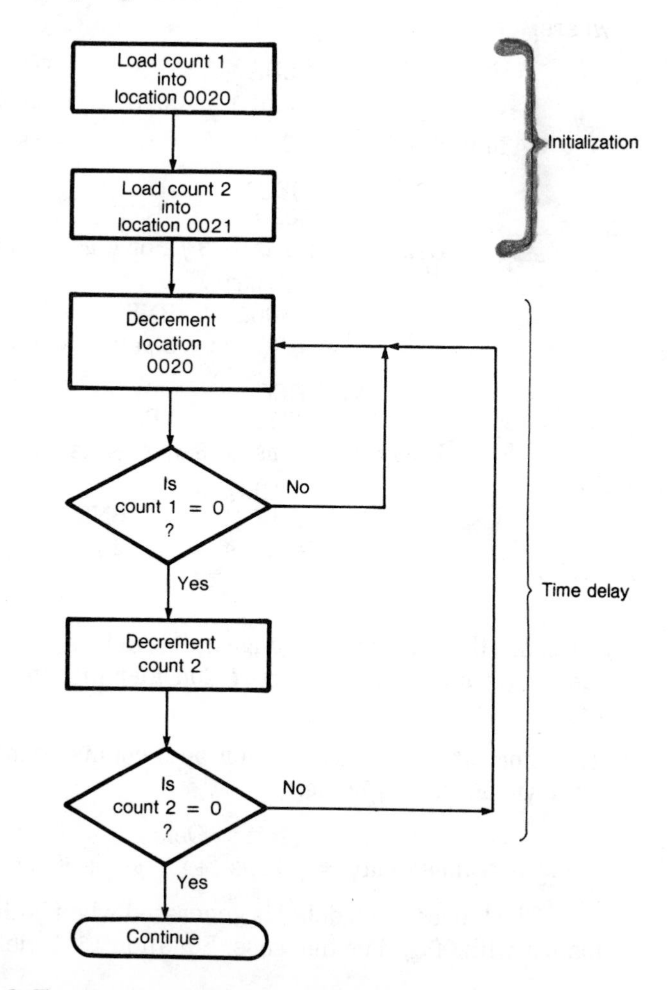

FIGURE 13–2 Flowchart for Two Nested Time Delays

EXAMPLE 13.14 Write a time delay program using Figure 13-2. Consider count 1 = 00_{hex} to give a consistent time delay.

Solution

```
        LDA #count 1   Load accumulator with count 1.
        STA 0020       Store accumulator in location 0020.
        LDA #count 2   Load accumulator with count 2.
        STA 0021       Store accumulator in location 0021.
DELAY:  DEC 0020       Decrement location 0020.
        BNE DELAY      If location 0020 ≠ 0, branch to DELAY.
        DEC 0021       Decrement location 0021.
        BNE DELAY      If location 0021 ≠ 0, branch to DELAY.
```

The total time delay for this program is given by the following equation:

$$\text{Total time delay} = \text{Initialization} + \text{delay 1} + \text{delay 2} \qquad \textbf{(13-2)}$$

where:

$$\text{Initialization} = \underset{\substack{\text{LDA}\\ \text{count 1}}}{2\ \mu s} + \underset{\substack{\text{STA}\\ \text{0020}}}{4\ \mu s} + \underset{\substack{\text{LDA}\\ \text{count 2}}}{2\ \mu s} + \underset{\substack{\text{STA}\\ \text{0021}}}{4\ \mu s}$$

$$\text{Delay 1} = [(\underset{\substack{\text{DEC}\\ \text{0020}}}{6\ \mu s} + \underset{\text{BNE}}{3\ \mu s \text{ or } 4\ \mu s}) \times (\text{count 1} - 1) + (\underset{\substack{\text{DEC}\\ \text{0020}}}{6\ \mu s} + \underset{\text{BNE}}{2\ \mu s})] \times \text{count 2}$$

$$\text{Delay 2} = (\underset{\substack{\text{DEC}\\ \text{0021}}}{6\ \mu s} + \underset{\text{BNE}}{3\ \mu s \text{ or } 4\ \mu s}) \times (\text{count 2} - 1) + \underset{\substack{\text{DEC}\\ \text{0021}}}{6\ \mu s} + \underset{\text{BNE}}{2\ \mu s}$$

EXAMPLE 13.15 What are the shortest and longest time delays that can be generated from the program of Example 13.14? Consider that the branch is on the same page.

Solution The shortest time delay is when both counts equal 1. Applying Equation 13-2 yields the following:

$$\text{Total time delay} = \underset{\text{Init.}}{12\ \mu s} + \underset{\text{Delay 1}}{8\ \mu s} + \underset{\text{Delay 2}}{8\ \mu s} = 28\ \mu s$$

The longest time delay is generated when both memory locations are loaded with 00_{hex}. For this case, Equation 13-2 yields the following:

Initialization	=	12 μs
Delay 1 = [(9 μs)(255) + 8 μs] × 256	=	589,568 μs
Delay 2 = (9 μs)(255) + 8 μs	=	2,303 μs
Total time delay	=	591,883 μs
	≅	0.6 s

Example 13.5 shows that nesting two time delay loops can yield delays ranging from about 28 μs to approximately 0.6 s.

Equation 13–2 can be approximated by Equation 13–3:

$$\text{Total time delay} \cong 9\ \mu\text{s} \times \text{count } 1 \times \text{count } 2 \quad \textbf{(13–3)}$$

EXAMPLE 13.16 Use Equation 13–3 and repeat Example 13.15.

Solution Loading both memory locations with 1 yields the shortest time delay, and Equation 13–3 yields the result:

$$\text{Total time delay} \cong 9\ \mu\text{s} \times 1 \times 1 = 9\ \mu\text{s}$$

When both memory locations are loaded with 00_{hex}, the longest time delay is generated. Applying Equation 13–3 yields the result:

$$\text{Total time delay} \cong 9\ \mu\text{s} \times 256 \times 256 = 589{,}824\ \mu\text{s} \cong 0.6\ \text{s}$$

Longer time delay loops can be generated by nesting more loops. Figure 13–3 shows a flowchart for nesting three time delay loops. It uses memory locations 0020, 0021, and 0022 as temporary working registers.

EXAMPLE 13.17 The following program is written from the flowchart of Figure 13–3. Calculate the approximate time delay using Equation 13–3.

```
        LDA #00      Load accumulator with 00hex.
        STA 0020     Store accumulator in location 0020.
        STA 0021     Store accumulator in location 0021.
        LDA #10      Load accumulator with 10hex.
        STA 0022     Store accumulator in location 0022.
DELAY:  DEC 0020     Decrement location 0020.
        BNE DELAY    Branch to DELAY.
        DEC 0021     Decrement location 0021.
        BNE DELAY    Branch to DELAY.
        DEC 0022     Decrement location 0022.
        BNE DELAY    Branch to DELAY.
```

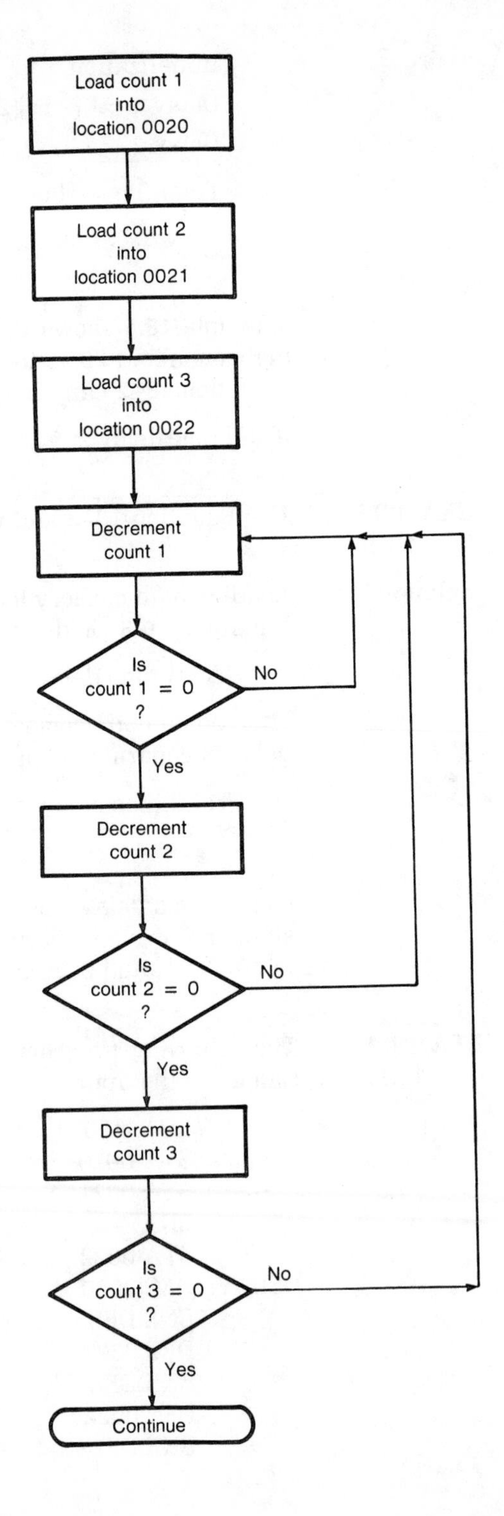

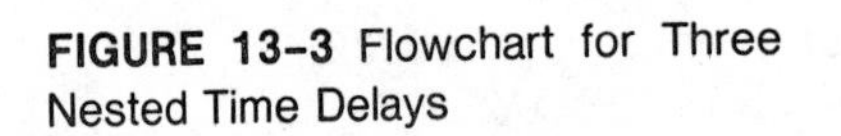
FIGURE 13–3 Flowchart for Three Nested Time Delays

Solution Equation 13–3 can be expanded to three nested time delays by the following expression:

$$\text{Total time delay} \cong 9\ \mu s \times \text{count 1} \times \text{count 2} \times \text{count 3} \qquad \textbf{(13-4)}$$

From the program, counts 1 and 2 equal 00_{hex} ($256_{decimal}$), and count 3 equals 10_{hex} ($16_{decimal}$). Therefore, the total time delay is as follows:

$$\text{Total time delay} \cong 9\ \mu s \times 256 \times 256 \times 16 \cong 9.4\ s$$

This program causes a total time delay of approximately 9.4 s. Thus, execution of this program uses 9.4 s of computer time.

In many applications, we cannot use the amount of time shown in Example 13.17 on a timing loop program. Another solution would be to use a timing chip. The count is loaded into this chip, and the count is automatically decremented. When the count equals 0, the timing chip can be programmed to send an interrupt request signal to the μP so the μP knows that the timing loop is over. Thus, these timing chips free the μP to execute other programs. Use of these chips is a hardware solution to generating a time delay. The programs that we used in this section are a software solution to generating a timing delay.

13.4 MOVING A SECTION OF MEMORY

Programs that are written for word processing machines contain a program that is capable of moving a section of memory. The operator can thus edit or assemble the text in any desired way. Even dedicated control applications may require a section of memory to be moved from one part of memory to another. For example, data may have to be collected and stored in one section of memory so that it can be sent to a printer or a CRT display. In either case, the 6502 μP can easily handle moving a section of memory by using the indexed addressing mode. Example 13.18 shows how 20 bytes of data can be moved from page 4 to page 8. Example 13.19 shows how the entire page 4 can be moved to page 8.

EXAMPLE 13.18 Transfer the first 20 bytes of data from page 4 to page 8. Use the X register for indexing and the Y register as a counter. Write the program as a subroutine program.

Solution

```
       LDX #00       Initialize X index register.
       LDY #14       Count 14hex = 20decimal.
MOVE:  LDA 0400,X    Load accumulator with data on page 04.
       STA 0800,X    Store data on page 08.
       INX           Increment X register.
       DEY           Decrement count register.
       BNE MOVE      If Y ≠ 0, branch to MOVE.
       RTS           Return from subroutine.
```

The program in Example 13.19 shows how the X register can be used for both indexing and counting. When the entire page of data has been transferred, the X register will again be equal to 0. The μP can then execute the RTS instruction.

EXAMPLE 13.19 Transfer all the data on page 4 to page 8. Write the program as a subroutine program, and use the X register for both indexing and counting.

Solution

```
       LDX #00       Initialize X index register.
MOVE:  LDA 0400,X    Load accumulator with data on page 04.
       STA 0800,X    Store the data on page 08.
       INX           Increment X register.
       BNE MOVE      If X ≠ 0, branch to MOVE.
       RTS           Return from subroutine.
```

The technique of using the X register for two purposes (indexing and counting) eliminates two instructions, LDY and DEY. We could have used this technique in Example 13.18, but the X register would be loaded with 14_{hex} and the INX instruction has to be changed to DEX. Also, the LDY and DEY instructions have to be deleted.

The programs in this section took data in page 4 and transferred it to page 8. Any data that was in page 8 would have been lost. In some word processing applications, we want to exchange the data in two sections of memory. This type of program is shown in the next section.

13.5 PROGRAMS USING THE STACK

The stack is an area in memory that is used automatically by the μP to save the contents of the program counter when a subroutine is called. However, the programmer can use the stack at any time for temporary storage of data that is in the accumulator. A single PHA instruction pushes the data onto the stack and a PLA instruction pulls the data from the stack. These one-byte instructions are all that is required because the stack pointer automatically keeps the address.

13.5.1 Saving the Microprocessor Registers

Like the 8080A and 6800 μPs, when the 6502 μP executes a jump to subroutine program, only the contents of the program counter are automatically saved on the stack. Usually we also want to save the contents of the accumulator, the X register, the Y register, and the flag register. Although the 6502 has instructions to save only the accumulator and the flag register, it does have instructions to transfer the X register to the accumulator and an instruction to transfer the Y register to the accumulator. By using the transfer instructions, we can save the contents of the X register and the Y register. Example 13.20 shows how the contents of all the registers can be saved.

EXAMPLE 13.20 Write the programming steps necessary to save and return the contents of all of the 6502 μP registers.

Solution

```
PHP     Save μP status register.
PHA     Save the accumulator.
TXA     Transfer X register to accumulator.
PHA     Save accumulator (X register).
TYA     Transfer Y register to accumulator.
PHA     Save accumulator (Y register).
 .        .
 .        .
 .        .
        Main subroutine program.
 .        .
 .        .
 .        .
PLA     Retrieve accumulator (Y register).
TAY     Transfer accumulator to Y register.
PLA     Retrieve accumulator (X register).
TAX     Transfer accumulator to X register.
PLA     Retrieve accumulator.
PLP     Retrieve μP status register.
RTS     Retrieve program counter.
```

In the program in Example 13.20, the push instructions have to be executed before the main subroutine program, and the pull instructions have to be executed before the RTS instruction. The data has to be retrieved in reverse order from which it was saved; otherwise, data will not be returned to the proper register.

13.5.2 Temporary Storage

As previously mentioned, the stack can be used to store data temporarily. The following programs show how to exchange sections of memory using the stack as temporary storage. In each example, consider that the stack pointer has been initialized by the main program. Example 13.21 shows how to exchange a portion of a page; Example 13.22 shows how to exchange an entire page.

EXAMPLE 13.21 Write a program that exchanges the first 20 bytes of data in page 4 with the first 20 bytes of data in page 8. Use the X register for indexing and the Y register for counting.

Solution

```
      LDX #00       Initialize X index register.
      LDY #14       Load count 14hex = 20decimal.
EXCH: LDA 0400,X    Load accumulator with data in page 04.
      PHA           Save data on stack.
      LDA 0800,X    Load accumulator with data in page 08.
      STA 0400,X    Store data in page 04.
      PLA           Pull data from stack.
      STA 0800,X    Store data in page 08
      INX           Increment index register.
      DEY           Decrement count.
      BNE EXCH      If Y ≠ 0, branch to EXCH.
      RTS           Return from subroutine.
```

EXAMPLE 13.22 Write a program that exchanges all of the bytes of page 4 with all of the bytes of page 8. Use the X register for both indexing and counting.

Solution

```
      LDX #00       Initialize X index register.
EXCH: LDA 0400,X    Load accumulator with data in page 04.
      PHA           Push data onto stack to save it.
      LDA 0800,X    Load accumulator with data in page 08.
      STA 0400,X    Store data in page 04.
      PLA           Pull data from stack.
      STA 0800,X    Store data in page 08.
      INX           Increment index register.
      BNE EXCH      If X ≠ 0, branch to EXCH.
      RTS           Return from subroutine.
```

13.6 MULTIPLICATION

Like the 8080A and 6800 μPs, the 6502 μP does not have a multiplication instruction. Therefore, we have to write a program to multiply two numbers. The program in Example 13.23 uses the same procedure that was described in Section 10.5 for the 6800 μP. Section 10.5 should be reviewed before proceeding with the next example.

EXAMPLE 13.23 Write an 8-bit multiplication program using the steps described in Section 10.5. Use the following memory locations in page 0 as working registers, and use the Y register as a counter:

Memory Location	Purpose
0000	Multiplier
0001	Multiplicand
0005	LS byte of product
0006	MS byte of product

Solution

```
          CLC           Clear carry flag.
          LDA #00       Clear accumulator.
          LDY #08       Count = 8.
MULT:     LSR 0000      Shift multiplier one bit into C flag.
          BCC ROTATE    If C = 0, branch to ROTATE.
          CLC           Clear carry flag.
          ADC 0001      Add multiplicand to accumulator.
ROTATE:   ROR           Rotate accumulator.
          ROR 0005      Rotate LS byte of the answer.
          DEY           Decrement Y register.
          BNE MULT      If Y ≠ 0, branch to MULT.
          STA 0006      Store accumulator (MS byte of the answer).
          RTS           Return from subroutine.
```

Since most multiplication programs are written as subroutines, the RTS instruction has been included at the end of the preceding program.

13.7 BINARY-TO-BCD CONVERSION

A procedure for converting binary numbers to BCD numbers is the add three algorithm. This procedure is described in detail in Motorola's "Application Note AN-757." The technique requires having enough memory locations to contain the final BCD number. Remember, each byte of memory contains two BCD numbers. The steps in the conversion are as follows:

1. Check each BCD register for a value of 5 or greater.
2. If a BCD value is greater than 5, then add 3. If the value is less than 5, do not add 3.
3. Shift the binary and BCD registers left one bit. The carry out of the previous register is the carry into the next register.
4. Continue steps 1–3 until the registers have been shifted N times, where N = the number of bits in the initial binary number. $N = 8$ for an 8-bit binary number, $N = 16$ for a 16-bit binary number, and so on.

Figure 13–4 shows a flowchart of the binary-to-BCD conversion. Table 13–1 shows the steps involved in converting an 8-bit binary number to its BCD equivalent. The initial 8-bit binary word contains all 1s. After the eighth shift, the BCD registers contain 255. Since three BCD numbers have to be stored in two memory locations, the actual value stored in memory would be 0255. Example 13.24 shows how to use the above four steps in a program.

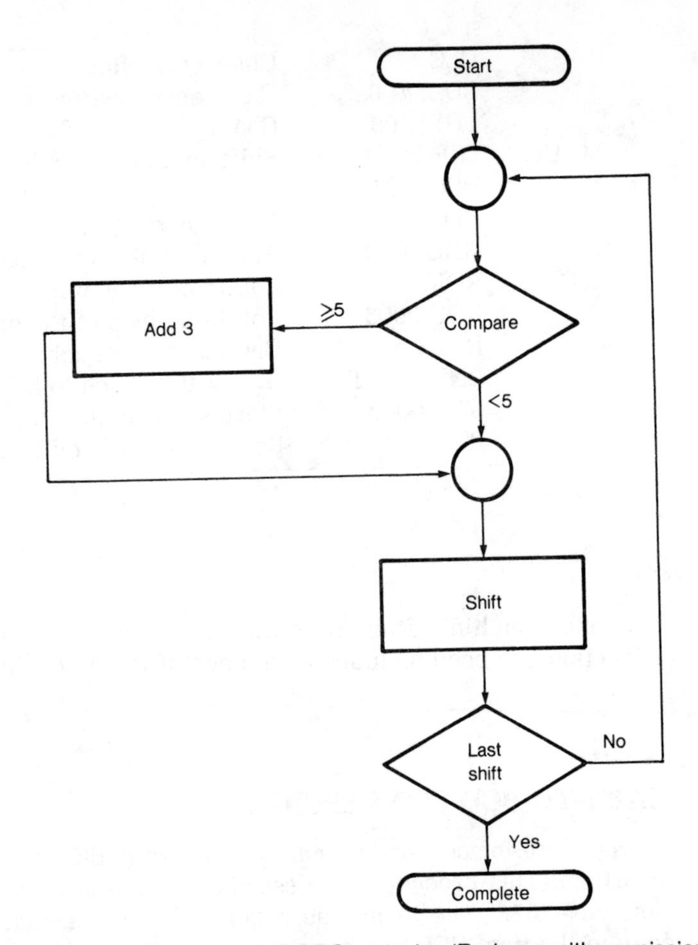

FIGURE 13–4 Flowchart for Binary-to-BCD Conversion (Redrawn with permission of Motorola Incorporated, Phoenix, AZ)

TABLE 13–1 Binary-to-BCD Conversion

Hundreds	Tens	Units	8-Bit Binary	
			11111111	
		1	1111111	Shift
		11	111111	Shift
		111	11111	Shift
		1010	11111	Add 3 to units
	1	0101	1111	Shift
	1	1000	1111	Add 3 to units
	11	0001	111	Shift
	110	0011	11	Shift
	1001	0011	11	Add 3 to tens
1	0010	0111	1	Shift
1	0010	1010	1	Add 3 to units
10	0101	0101		Shift
2	5	5		Total shifts: 8

EXAMPLE 13.24 Write a binary-to-BCD conversion program using steps 1–4 and the following memory locations in page 0 as working registers:

Memory Location	Purpose
001C	Count register
001F	Binary number
0020	Tens and units answer
0021	Thousands and hundreds answer
0022	Temporary storage location

Locations 0020, 0021, and 0022 contain an initial value = 00_{hex}.

Solution

```
BEGIN: LDA 0020     Load accumulator from location 0020.
       AND #0F      Mask out high four bits.
       CMP #05      Are low four bits ≥ 5?
       BMI TEMP     If accumulator < 5, branch to TEMP.
       CLC          Clear carry flag.
       ADC #03      Add 3 to accumulator.
TEMP:  STA 0022     Store accumulator temporarily.
       LDA 0020     Reload accumulator from location 0020.
       AND #F0      Mask out low four bits.
       CMP #50      Are high four bits ≥ 50?
       BMI SHIFT    If accumulator < 50, branch to SHIFT.
       CLC          Clear carry flag.
       ADC #30      Add +30 to accumulator.
SHIFT: ORA 0022     Logical OR accumulator with data at 0022.
       STA 0020     Store result at 0020.
       ASL 001F     Shift binary number.
       ROL 0020     Rotate tens and units location.
       ROL 0021     Rotate thousands and hundreds location.
       DEC 001C     Decrement counter.
       BNE BEGIN    If count ≠ 0, branch to BEGIN.
       RTS          Return from subroutine.
```

Motorola's "Application Note AN-757" shows how to convert a 16-bit number into BCD.

13.8 SUMMARY

This chapter showed how to use many of the 6502 μP instructions in different programming applications. As was mentioned in other programming chapters, there is no unique way of writing a program; therefore, all of the programs could have been written using other instructions or other memory locations (the memory locations for the programs were chosen at random). Furthermore, some of the programs were written as subroutines to show how the RTS instruction is used, but all of the programs could have been written as subroutines.

We began this chapter by examining single-byte and multibyte addition and subtraction programs. We saw how easy it is to do decimal addition and subtraction with the 6502 μP. Next, we saw how to program the 6502 to determine the largest value in a column of numbers. This program along with others showed the advantage of the 6502's indexing mode capabilities.

Like the 6800, the 6502 μP can increment or decrement a memory location. Therefore, long time delay programs are easily written and executed, as we saw in this chapter.

Next, we examined how blocks of data can be moved between memory locations without using the stack. Then, we saw how they can be moved using the stack. Stack operations usually result in a more efficient program. Both methods, however, use the indexed addressing mode. We also examined how the 6502 can be programmed to multiply two 8-bit positive numbers, a procedure similar to that given for the 6800 μP.

To output numerical data to a printer, plotter, or CRT display, a binary-to-BCD conversion program is usually required. A typical conversion program was presented in the final section of this chapter.

PROBLEMS

13–1 Add the contents of memory location 0420 to the contents of memory location 0430. Store the result at memory location 0450. Use binary addition.

13–2 What programming changes have to be made in Problem 13–1 if decimal addition is to be used?

13–3 What is the largest 8-bit binary number that can be an answer without generating a carry? Repeat for a BCD number.

13–4 Refer to Example 13.3. Could the X register be initialized as a counter and the Y register used for indexing?

13–5 Refer to Example 13.3. Assume that the LS bytes of data are in locations 0401 and 0501 and that the MS bytes of data are in locations 0400 and 0500. Write a double-precision addition program that uses the X register both as the counter and as the index register.

13–6 What value should be put into the Y register in Example 13.4 for a 24-bit addition?

13–7 Write an 8-bit binary addition program that adds a column of 20 numbers stored in memory beginning at location 0600. The result is to be stored at location 0320. Consider that the answer will not produce a carry.

13–8 Write a binary subtraction program that subtracts the contents of memory location 0200 from the contents of memory location 0400. Store the result in memory location 0050.

13–9 Refer to Example 13.9. If the program is to be used for a 32-bit subtraction, what value must be loaded into the Y register?

13–10 What modifications must be made in Example 13.11 so that the program checks for the smallest number?

13–11 Refer to Example 13.12. If the accumulator is loaded with a value of 80, what time delay is generated by the program? The entire program is written on the same page.

13–12 Refer to Example 13.14. Count 1 = 00_{hex} and count 2 = 80_{hex}. What time delay is generated by the program?

13–13 For a 0.1 s time delay, calculate the approximate value of count 2 in the program of Example 13.14. Let count 1 = 00_{hex}.

13–14 Refer to Example 13.17. What value should be stored at memory location 0022 for a time delay of approximately 4 s?

13–15 What modifications have to be made in Example 13.19 if the Y register is used for indexing and counting?

13–16 Could the X register be used for both indexing and counting in Example 13.18? If your answer is yes, write the program.

13–17 Refer to Example 13.20. What changes should be made in the program if the subroutine is called because of an interrupt request signal?

13–18 What change(s) has to be made in Example 13.21 if 40 bytes of data have to be moved instead of 20 bytes of data?

13–19 What change(s) has to be made in Example 13.22 if all the data on page 4 is to be moved to page $C5_{hex}$ instead of page 8?

6502 Microprocessor

14.0 INTRODUCTION

The 6502 μP is an NMOS central processing unit around which a complete μC can be designed. It is housed in a 40-pin dual-in-line package, as shown in Figure 14–1. Although the package has 40 pins, not all are used. The pins (5, 35, and 36) that are labeled NC have no internal connection. The 6502 has 16 address bus lines, but unlike the 8080A and 6800 μPs, these lines are not three state. They are TTL, which means that the 6502 μP cannot be used for direct memory access (DMA) without using three-state address buffers. At first glance, this may appear to be a disadvantage, but since most DMA applications require buffers anyway, it is not a major disadvantage. The data bus lines are three state. Like the other μPs covered in this text, the 6502 μP is an 8-bit μP because 8 bits of data are operated on at a time. Data is transferred between the μP and memory or I/O devices across the eight data bus lines.

Unlike the 8080A and 6800 μPs, the 6502 μP contains an on-the-chip oscillator and clock drivers that generate the two-phase nonoverlapping clock signals. The oscillator circuit requires an input signal that can come from an *RC* combination or, if more clock stability is required, a crystal should be used. The input clock signal is applied to pin 37, and the μP's internal circuitry produces ϕ_1 at pin 3 and ϕ_2 at pin 39.

In this chapter, we will examine the 6502's pin descriptions, timing diagrams, a cycle-by-cycle description of what happens when an instruction is fetched and executed, what happens when power is applied, and how interrupts are handled.

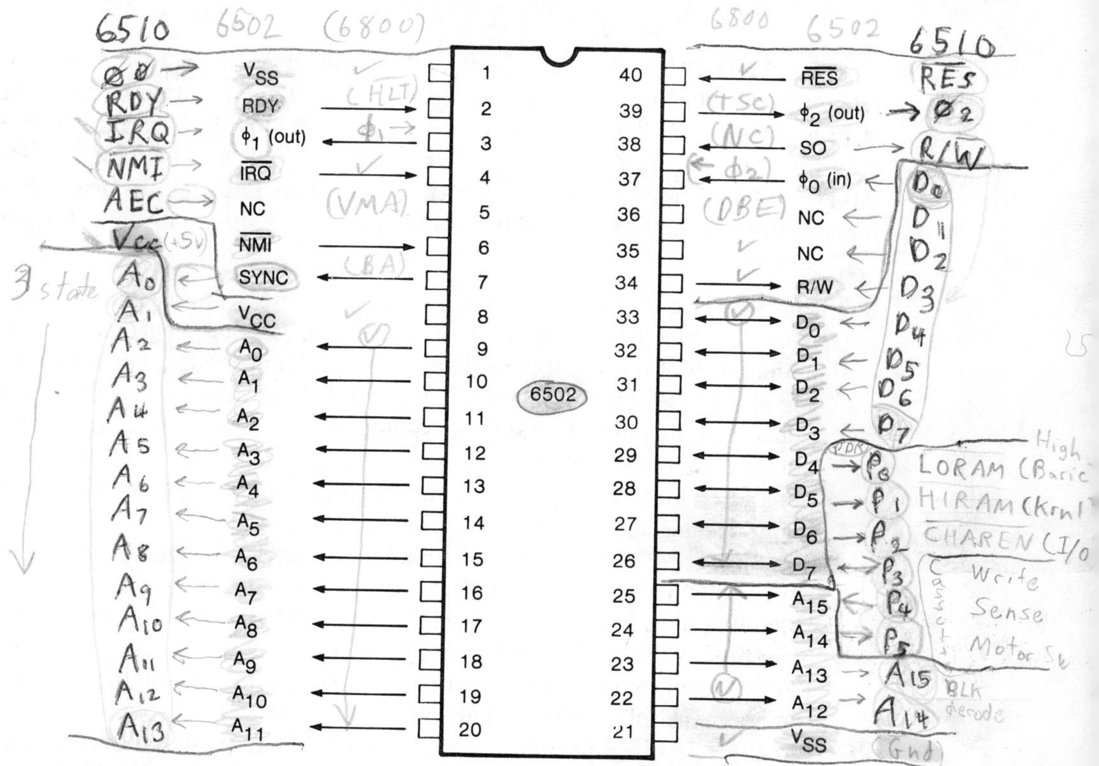

FIGURE 14–1 6502 μP Pin Designations (Redrawn with permission of Commodore Business Machines, Inc., MOS Technology Division, Norristown, PA)

14.1 PIN DESCRIPTIONS

Figure 14–1 shows the pin designations for the 6502 μP. The function of each pin is given next.

Address Bus (A_0–A_{15}): There are sixteen address bus pins that allow the 6502 μP to address 64K locations. Each pin is capable of driving one standard TTL load and 130 pF. These lines do not have three-state capability, only TTL capability.

Data Bus (D_0–D_7): There are eight bidirectional data bus pins that allow the μP to communicate with either memory or peripheral devices. The output buffers are capable of driving one standard TTL load and 130 pF when the μP is sending data. Each pin has three-state capability.

Power Pins: The 6502 μP is a +5 V (pin 8) device. It requires two ground connections (pins 1 and 21).

Clock Pins: The 6502 μP generates the two-phase nonoverlapping clock signals, ϕ_1 and ϕ_2, internally. These signals are available to the user: ϕ_1 at pin 3 and ϕ_2 at pin 39. The ϕ_2 signal is used most often because this clock pulse is used by memory chips and peripheral devices to synchronize the flow of data. To generate the ϕ_1 and ϕ_2 clock pulses, the μP must receive an input master clock signal at pin 37, ϕ_0. Section 14.2 shows several ways of generating the master clock signal.

The 6502 μP has five input control lines ($\overline{IRQ}$, $\overline{NMI}$, $\overline{RES}$, RDY, and SO) and two output control lines (SYNC and R/W). The 6502 μP has two pins to receive interrupt requests. They are the interrupt request pin (pin 4) and the nonmaskable interrupt request pin (pin 6). The reset pin (pin 40) also can be used to interrupt the μP from its normal operating sequence. Let's look at brief descriptions of the function of each of these pins as well as the other control pins.

$\overline{IRQ}$ (Pin 4): The $\overline{IRQ}$ pin is the maskable interrupt request pin. Remember from Chapter 5 that the term *maskable* means the programmer can, by using instructions, enable or disable the μP from recognizing an interrupt request signal. Like the 6800 μP, the 6502 μP's interrupt request signal is a low logic level on the $\overline{IRQ}$ pin. When the μP recognizes an interrupt request, it automatically loads into the program counter the data at locations FFFE and FFFF. These two memory locations must contain the starting address of the interrupt subroutine.

$\overline{NMI}$ (Pin 6): The $\overline{NMI}$ pin is the nonmaskable interrupt request pin. An interrupt request signal on this pin cannot be disabled by the programmer. When the logic level goes from high to low, the μP completes its present instruction and then loads the program counter with data at FFFA and FFFB. These two memory locations must contain the starting address of the nonmaskable interrupt subroutine.

$\overline{RES}$ (Pin 40): The $\overline{RES}$ pin is the μP's reset pin. When power is first turned on, the μP's internal registers come up at random. To initialize the program counter to a known memory location, this line is held low and then brought high, after which the program counter is automatically loaded with data retrieved from location FFFC. This data must be part of the first address (low byte) of the main program. The μP then automatically retrieves data from memory location FFFD. This data must be the remaining part of the first address (high byte) of the main program. The μP is now ready to jump to the main program and start executing it.

RDY (Pin 2): The ready pin is used to delay execution of an instruction. If this line is pulled low, the μP enters a wait state. This feature allows the μP to be used with slower memories or I/O devices. The ready function does not stop the μP during a write operation. If the RDY line should go from high to low during a write operation, the μP executes the write instruction and stops in the next read operation.

SO (Pin 38): The SO pin can be used to set the overflow flag. If there is a high-to-low transition on the SO pin, the μP's overflow flag bit is set to a logic 1. In most applications, this pin should not be used. It has been designed for future I/O devices.

SYNC (Pin 7): SYNC is an abbreviation for *synchronization*. The SYNC line goes high every time the μP fetches an op code. It remains high for one cycle, and it goes low if the μP is fetching an operand. This line is often used during troubleshooting.

R/W (Pin 34): The R/W line controls the direction of data. If this line is high, the μP is reading (receiving) data from memory or an I/O device. If this line goes low, the μP is writing (sending) data to memory or an I/O device.

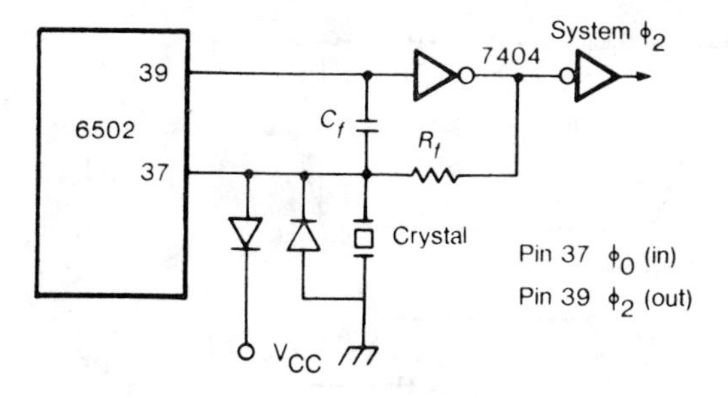

A. Parallel Mode Crystal-controlled Oscillator

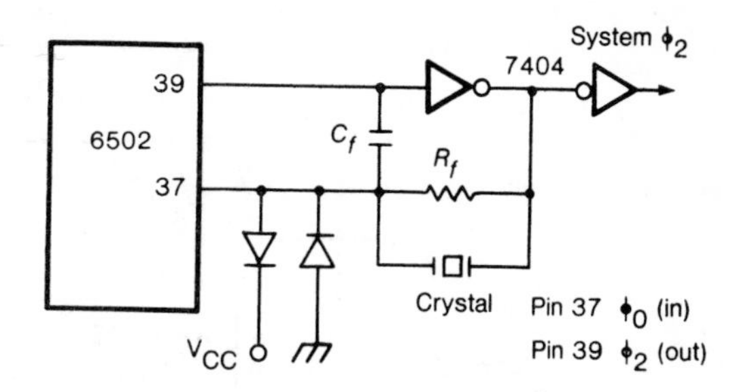

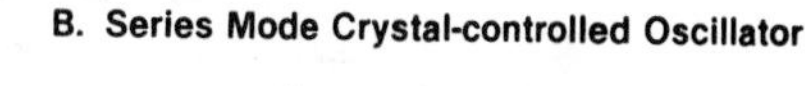
B. Series Mode Crystal-controlled Oscillator

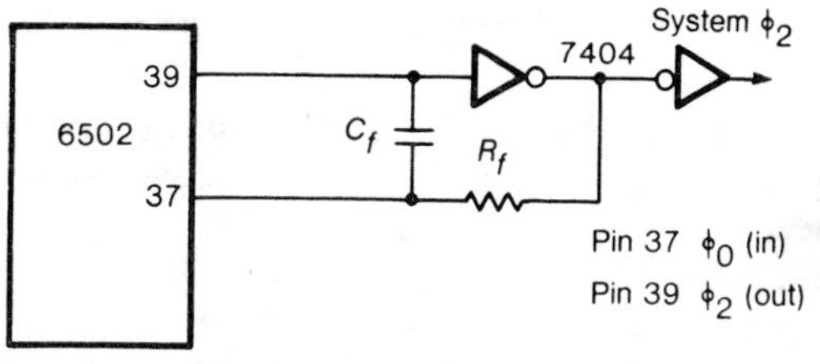

C. RC Network

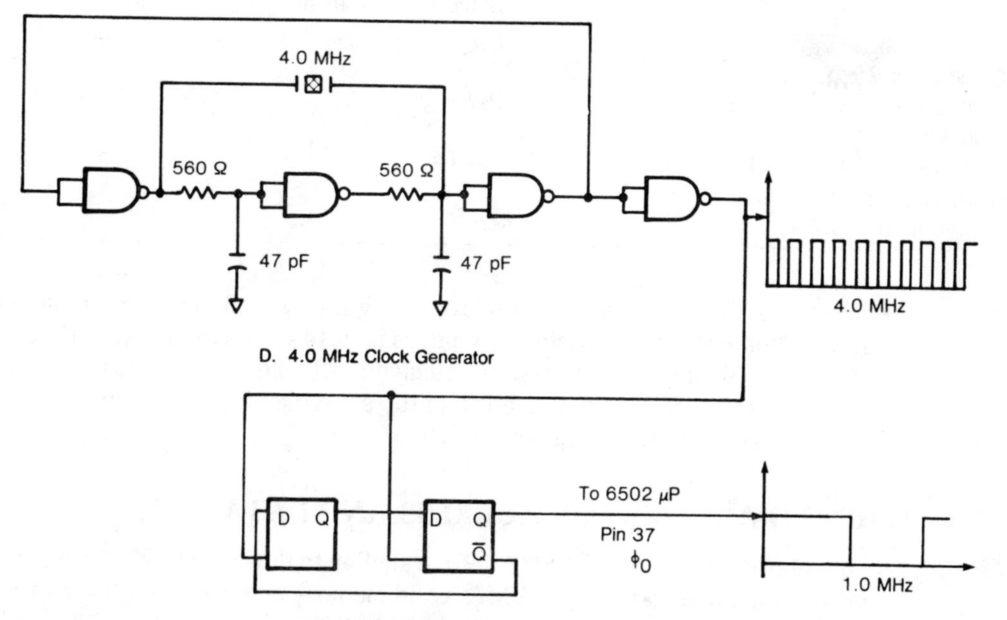

E. Two D Flip-Flops as Divide-by-4 Network and Signal Applied to μP

FIGURE 14–2 Circuits for Generating ϕ_0 Clock Signal for 6502 μP (Redrawn with permission of Commodore Business Machines, Inc., MOS Technology Division, Norristown, PA)

14.2 CLOCK SIGNALS

The 6502 μP receives an input clock signal, ϕ_0, on pin 37 and internally generates the two-phase nonoverlapping clock signals ϕ_1 and ϕ_2. The frequency range for the 6502 is from 100 kHz to 1 MHz. This range of frequency causes

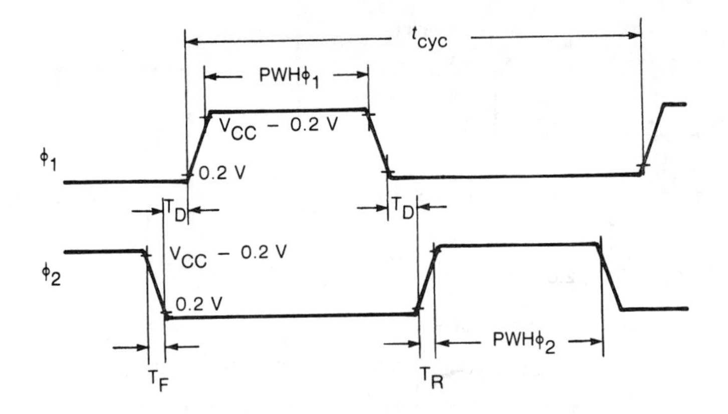

FIGURE 14-3 6502 μP ϕ_1 and ϕ_2 Clock Signals (Redrawn with permission of Commodore Business Machines, Inc., MOS Technology Division, Norristown, PA)

TABLE 14-1 Timing Characteristics of Clock Pulses for 1 MHz Operation

Characteristic		Symbol	Minimum	Typical	Maximum	Unit
Cycle time		t_{cyc}	1.0 μs	—	—	μs
Clock pulse width	ϕ_1	PWHϕ_1	430	—	—	ns
(measured at V_{CC} − 0.2 V)	ϕ_2	PWHϕ_2	430			
Rise and fall times (measured from 0.2 V to V_{CC} − 0.2 V)		T_F, T_R	—	—	25	ns
Delay time between clocks (measured at 0.2 V)		T_D	0	—	—	ns

cycle times ranging from 1.0 μs to 10 μs. Figure 14-2 shows some typical circuits for generating the ϕ_0 clock signal. Figure 14-3 shows the ϕ_1 and ϕ_2 clock pulses; their timing characteristics are given in Table 14-1. Since the 6502 has on board clock generation, there is usually a saving of time, money, and space for the microcomputer designer.

14.3 TIMING DIAGRAMS FOR ADDRESS AND DATA BUSES

The timing diagrams for the 6502 μP are similar to those for the 6800 μP, except that the 6502 does not have a VMA (valid memory address) signal. The reason that the 6502 does not need this signal is that the address lines are TTL and not three state. All addresses are valid 300 ns maximum after the rising edge of the ϕ_1 clock signal.

Figures 14-4 and 14-5 show the timing diagrams for a read and a write operation, respectively. Table 14-2 gives the names and specifications for all the times. The clock cycle begins when the ϕ_1 clock signal rises to 0.2 V. Data coming into the μP is latched at the end of the ϕ_2 clock signal.

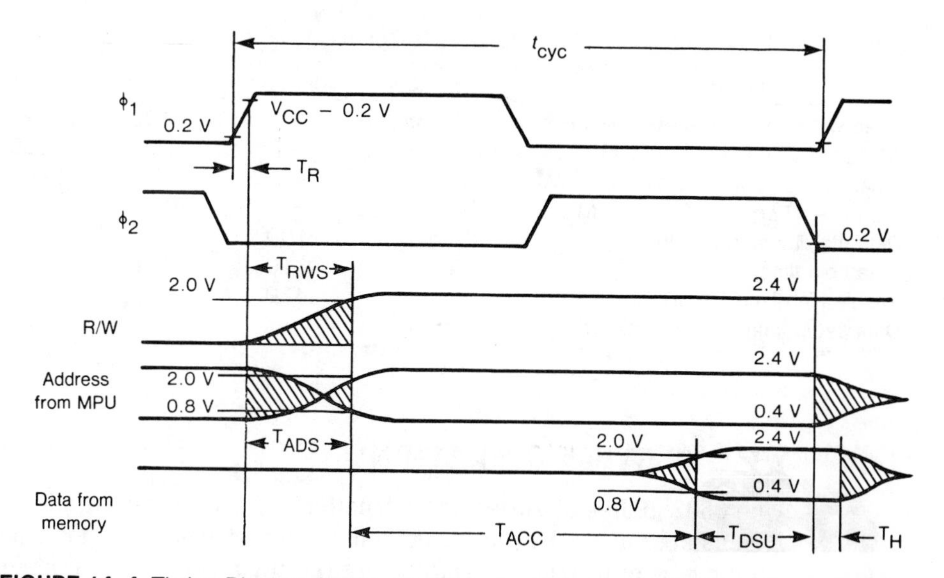

FIGURE 14–4 Timing Diagram for Reading Data from Memory or Peripherals (Redrawn with permission of Commodore Business Machines, Inc., MOS Technology Division, Norristown, PA)

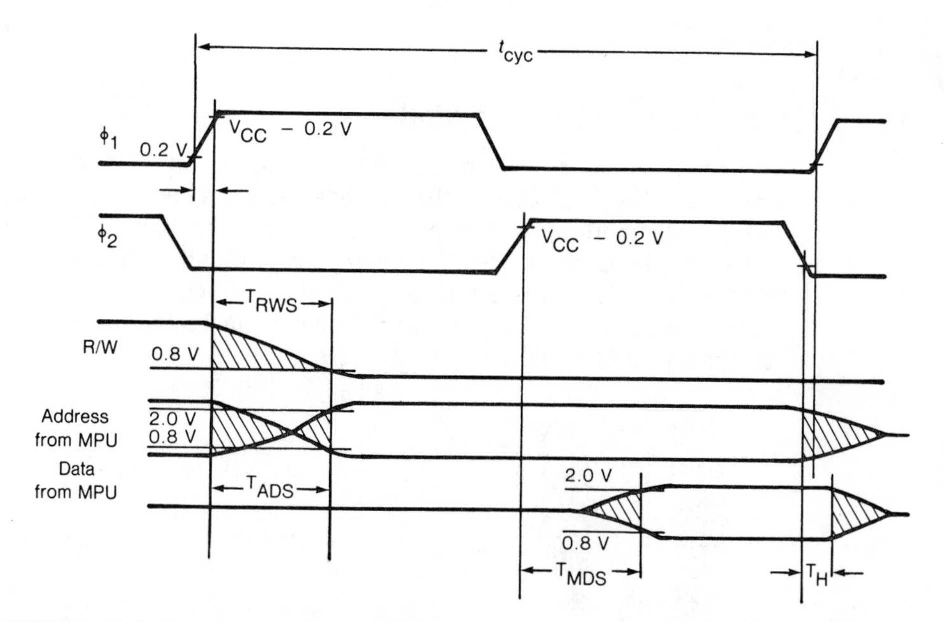

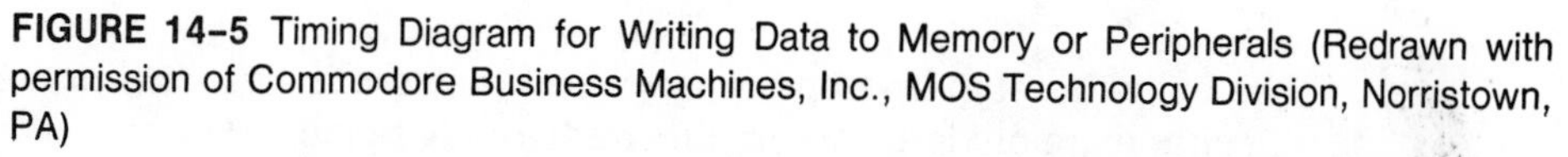
FIGURE 14–5 Timing Diagram for Writing Data to Memory or Peripherals (Redrawn with permission of Commodore Business Machines, Inc., MOS Technology Division, Norristown, PA)

TABLE 14–2 Read/Write Timing Table for 1 MHz Operation

Characteristic	Symbol	Minimum	Typical	Maximum	Unit
Read/write setup time from MCS650X	T_{RWS}	—	100	300	ns
Address setup time from MCS650X	T_{ADS}	—	200	300	ns
Memory read access time T_R $t_{cyc} - (T_{ADS} - T_{DSU} - tr)$	T_{ACC}	—	—	500	ns
Data stability time period	T_{DSU}	100	—	—	ns
Data hold time	T_H	10	30	—	ns
Enable high time for DBE input	T_{EH}	430	—	—	ns
Data setup time from MCS650X	T_{MDS}	—	150	200	ns

14.4 CYCLE-BY-CYCLE OPERATION

The 6502 μP has 56 different instructions and 13 different addressing modes. The number of clock cycles needed to fetch and execute an instruction depends on the type of instruction and the addressing mode. This section gives a cycle-by-cycle description of what happens on the address bus, data bus, and in the μP's internal operation for different instructions. The section is subdivided according to addressing modes. In the examples, one clock cycle is the time for a complete ϕ_1 and ϕ_2 clock pulse. The memory locations have been chosen at random.

14.4.1 Immediate Addressing Mode

All immediate addressing mode instructions for the 6502 μP are two-byte instructions. The first byte is the op code, and the second byte is the operand (data). The manufacturer's sheet specifies that this type of addressing mode requires only two clock cycles. The instruction actually is not completed until the third clock cycle. There is overlap on the third clock cycle when the instruction is being completed and a new instruction is being fetched. The instructions that use the immediate addressing mode are:

ADC	LDA
AND	LDX
CMP	LDY
CPX	ORA
CPY	SBC
EOR	

The following step-by-step breakdowns illustrate the general procedure, and a specific example is given for this addressing mode.

General operation of clock cycles for the immediate addressing mode is as follows:

Clock Cycle	Address Bus	Data Bus	Internal Operation
1	PC	Op code	Finish previous instruction; increment PC (PC + 1).
2	PC + 1	Data	Decode op code; latch incoming data; increment PC (PC + 2).
3	PC + 2	Next op code	Fetch next op code; execute immediate addressing mode instruction; increment PC (PC + 3).

A specific example using the immediate addressing mode for the X register is shown in Example 14.1.

EXAMPLE 14.1 Show the clock cycles needed for loading the X register immediately with data 00.

Program Listing	Memory Listing
0200 LDX #00	0200 A2 op code
	0201 00 data

Solution

Clock Cycle	Address Bus	Data Bus	Internal Operation
1	0200	A2	Finish previous instruction; increment PC to 0201.
2	0201	00	Decode op code A2; increment PC to 0202; latch 00 into μP.
3	0202	Next op code	Move 00 from input latch to X register; increment PC to 0203.

Figure 14-6 shows the timing diagram for Example 14.1.

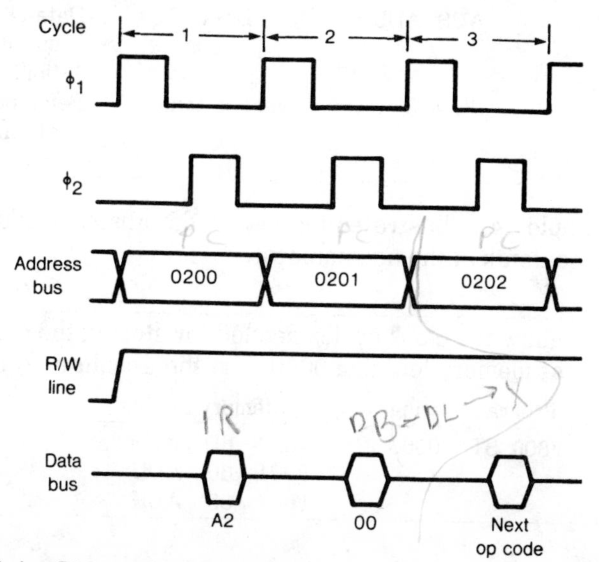

FIGURE 14-6 Timing Diagram for Example 14.1

14.4.2 Absolute Addressing Mode

The absolute addressing mode is a three-byte instruction. The first byte is the op code, the second byte is the line address, and the third byte is the page address. Most of the instructions that use this addressing mode require four clock cycles. However, one instruction requires only three clock cycles, while read/modify/write instructions and the jump to subroutine instruction require six clock cycles each. The completion of some instructions may not occur until the next clock cycle, when the μP is fetching another op code. Instructions that use the absolute addressing mode are as follows:

ADC	CPY	LDA	SBC
AND	DEC	LDX	STA
ASL	EOR	LDY	STX
BIT	INC	LSR	STY
CMP	JMP	ORA	
CPX	JSR	ROL	

The general cycle-by-cycle procedure for four and six clock cycles is given next, followed by specific examples.

General operation of clock cycles for the absolute addressing mode is as follows:

Clock Cycle	Address Bus	Data Bus	Internal Operation
1	PC	Op code	Finish previous instruction; increment PC (PC + 1).
2	PC + 1	ADL	Decode op code; latch low byte of address; increment PC (PC + 2).
3	PC + 2	ADH	Hold ADL; latch high byte of address; increment PC (PC + 3).
4	ADH, ADL	Data	Data is either latched into or sent out of μP, depending on instruction.
5	PC + 3	Next op code	Fetch next op code; finish executing absolute addressing mode instruction; increment PC (PC + 4).

Example 14.2 illustrates the use of the absolute addressing mode for storing the contents of the accumulator.

EXAMPLE 14.2 Show the clock cycles needed for storing the contents of the accumulator at memory location 0060. Use the absolute addressing mode.

Program Listing	Memory Listing			Accumulator
F800 STA 0060	F800	8D	op code	75
	F801	60	ADL	
	F802	00	ADH	

Solution

Clock Cycle	Address Bus	Data Bus	Internal Operation
1	F800	8D	Finish previous instruction; increment PC to F801.
2	F801	60	Decode op code 8D; increment PC to F802.
3	F802	00	Hold 60; increment PC to F803.
4	0060	75	Data 75 is sent to location 0060.
5	F803	Next op code	Increment PC to F804.

The timing diagram for Example 14.2 is shown in Figure 14–7. During clock cycle 4, the R/W line goes low, indicating that the μP is writing (sending) data to memory.

General operation of clock cycles for the read/modify/write operation (absolute addressing mode) is as follows:

Clock Cycle	Address Bus	Data Bus	Internal Operation
1	PC	Op code	Finish previous instruction; increment PC (PC + 1).
2	PC + 1	ADL	Decode op code; latch low byte of address; increment PC (PC + 2).
3	PC + 2	ADH	Hold ADL; latch high byte of address; increment PC (PC + 3).

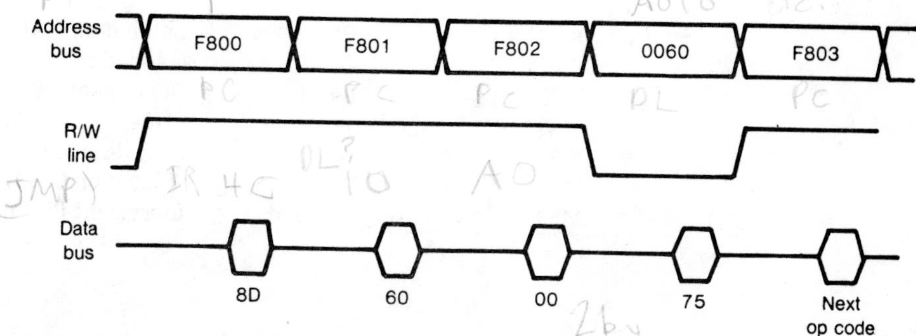

FIGURE 14–7 Timing Diagram for Example 14.2

4	ADH, ADL	Data	Read operation (incoming data is latched).
5	ADH, ADL	Data (to be ignored)	Modify operation (data is shifted or rotated in ALU); R/W line goes low.
6	ADH, ADL	Modified data	Write operation (modified data is returned to memory); set or clear flags.
7	PC + 3	Next op code	Increment PC (PC + 4).

The preceding timing steps are for the absolute addressing mode. If we are modifying data in a memory location in zero page, we can use the zero page addressing mode. In this situation, cycle 3 is deleted, making the overall operation shorter by one clock cycle. If we do use the zero page, addressing mode ADH = 00. Comparison of Example 14.3 with Example 14.5 will show the difference.

EXAMPLE 14.3 Show the clock cycles needed for decrement memory, location 0020. Use the absolute addressing mode.

Program Listing	Memory Listing	Contents of Location 0020
0850 DEC 0020	0850 CE op code	04
	0851 20 ADL	
	0852 00 ADH	

Solution

Clock Cycle	Address Bus	Data Bus	Internal Operation
1	0850	CE	Finish previous instruction; increment PC to 0851.
2	0851	20	Decode op code CE; increment PC to 0852.
3	0852	00	Hold ADL (20); increment PC to 0853.
4	0020	04	Latch data (04) coming from location 0020.
5	0020	04 (to be ignored)	Decrement data 04 in ALU (04 − 1 = 03).
6	0020	03	New data (03) is sent back to location 0020.
7	0853	Next op code	Increment PC to 0854.

Figure 14–8 is the timing diagram for Example 14.3. It shows what happens for a read/modify/write instruction. Notice that the R/W line does not go low until clock cycle 6.

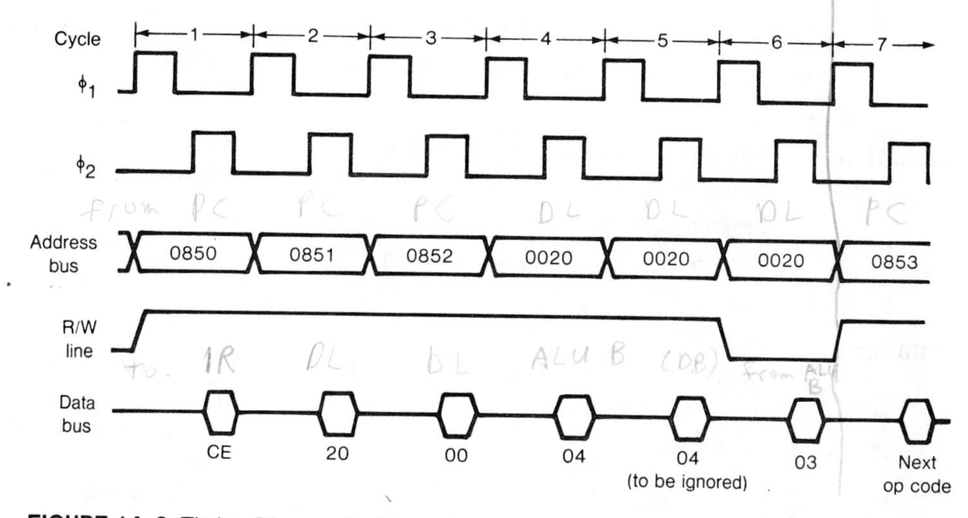

FIGURE 14–8 Timing Diagram for Example 14.3

14.4.3 Zero Page Addressing Mode

The zero page addressing mode is a two-byte instruction. The first byte is the op code, and the second byte is the line address in page zero. Manufacturers' data sheets specify that this instruction requires three clock pulses, but actually it may not be completed until the fourth clock pulse. On some instructions, there is an overlap on the fourth pulse between the completion of the instruction and the fetching of the next op code. Instructions that have the zero page addressing mode are as follows:

ADC	CPX	LDA	ROL
AND	CPY	LDX	SBC
ASL	DEC	LDY	STA
BIT	EOR	LSR	STX
CMP	INC	ORA	STY

The cycle-by-cycle description is given next, followed by specific examples.

General operation of clock cycles for the zero page addressing mode is as follows:

Clock Cycle	Address Bus	Data Bus	Internal Operation
1	PC	Op code	Finish previous instruction; increment PC (PC + 1).
2	PC + 1	ADL	Decode op code; latch low byte of address; increment PC (PC + 2).
3	00, ADL	Data	Data is either latched into or sent out of μP, depending on instruction.
4	PC + 2	Next op code	Finish executing zero page addressing mode instruction; increment PC (PC + 3).

Examples 14.4 and 14.5 show the differences between storing data and a read/modify/write instruction using the zero page addressing mode.

EXAMPLE 14.4 Show the clock cycles needed for storing the contents of the accumulator in memory location 0060. Use the zero page addressing mode.

Program Listing	Memory Listing			Accumulator
F800 STA 60	F800	85	op code	75
	F801	60	ADL	

Solution

Clock Cycle	Address Bus	Data Bus	Internal Operation
1	F800	85	Finish previous operation; increment PC to F801.
2	F801	60	Decode op code 85; increment PC to F802.
3	0060	75	Data (75) is sent to location 0060.
4	F802	Next op code	Increment PC to F803.

The zero page addressing mode requires one less byte of memory to store the program and one less clock cycle than the absolute addressing mode of Example 14.2. The timing diagram for Example 14.4 is shown in Figure 14–9.

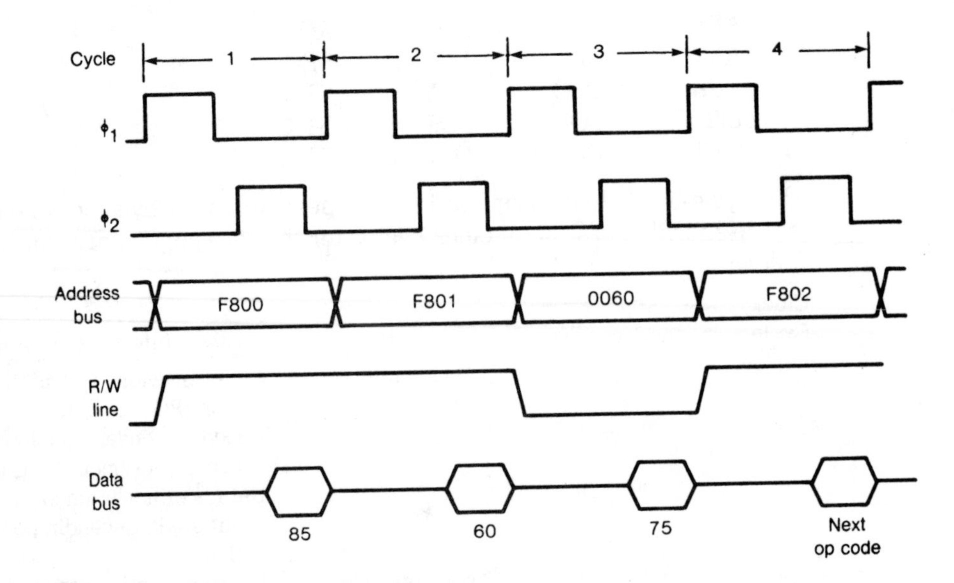

FIGURE 14–9 Timing Diagram for Example 14.4

EXAMPLE 14.5 Repeat Example 14.3, but this time use the zero page addressing mode.

Program Listing	Memory Listing			Contents of Location 0020
0850 DEC 20	0850	C6	op code	04
	0851	20	ADL	

Solution

Clock Cycle	Address Bus	Data Bus	Internal Operation
1	0850	C6	Finish previous instruction; increment PC to 0851.
2	0851	20	Decode op code (C6); increment PC to 0852.
3	0020	04	Latch data (04) coming from location 0020.
4	0020	04 (to be ignored)	Decrement data 04 in ALU (04 − 1 = 03).
5	0020	03	New data (03) is sent back to location 0020.
6	0852	Next op code	Increment PC to 0853.

The zero page addressing mode of Example 14.5 has executed the instruction in one less cycle than the absolute addressing mode of Example 14.3. The timing diagram for Example 14.5 is shown in Figure 14–10.

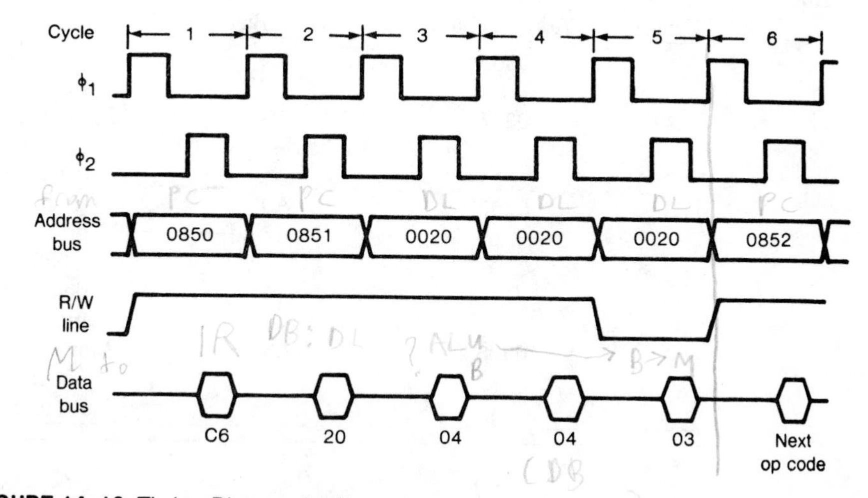

FIGURE 14–10 Timing Diagram for Example 14.5

14.4.4 Accumulator Addressing Mode

All accumulator addressing mode instructions are one-byte, two-cycle instructions. This addressing mode applies only to the rotate and shift accumulator instructions. They are as follows:

ASL	ROL
LSR	ROR

The following procedure shows what happens on each clock cycle for any accumulator addressing mode instructions. Example 14.6 shows a specific example, LSR A.

General operation of clock cycles for the accumulator addressing mode is as follows:

Clock Cycle	Address Bus	Data Bus	Internal Operation
1	PC	Op code	Finish previous instruction; increment PC.
2	PC + 1	Next op code (to be ignored)	Decode op code; hold PC; ignore incoming op code.
3	PC + 1	Next op code	Execute the instruction; decode new op code; increment PC.

EXAMPLE 14.6 Show the clock cycles needed for shifting the accumulator right one bit.

Program Listing	Memory Listing			Accumulator
0306 LSR A	0306	4A	op code	00000010
0307 LDY #05	0307	A0	next op code	
	0308	05	data	

Solution

Clock Cycle	Address Bus	Data Bus	Internal Operation
1	0306	4A	Finish previous instruction; increment PC to 0307.
2	0307	A0 (to be discarded)	Decode op code 4A; hold PC at 0307; ignore incoming op code A0.
3	0307	A0 (repeated)	Shift the accumulator one bit to the right ($00000001 = 01_{hex}$); decode op code A0; increment PC to 0308.
4	0308	05	Move result (01_{hex}) back to accumulator; increment PC to 0309.

Figure 14–11 gives the timing diagram for Example 14.6.

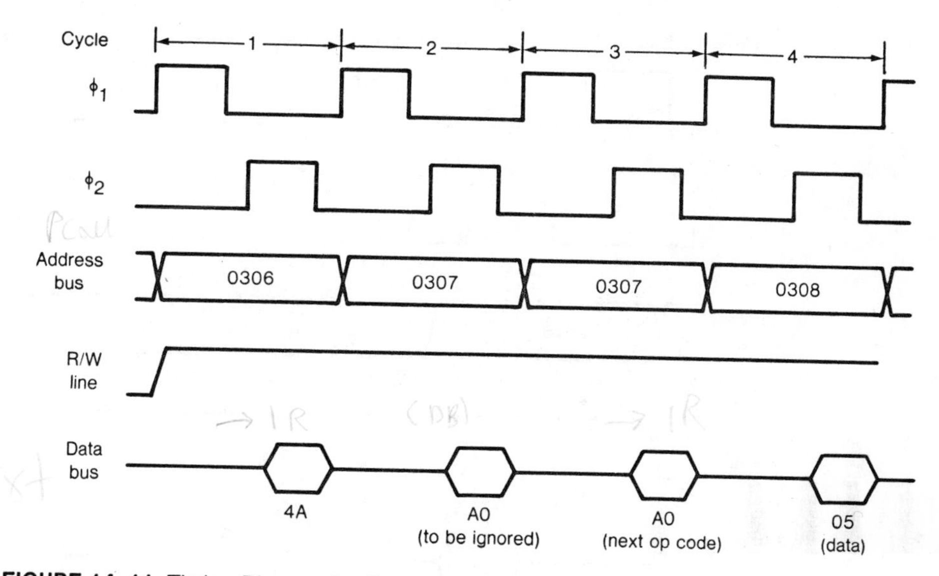

FIGURE 14–11 Timing Diagram for Example 14.6

14.4.5 Implied Addressing Mode

All the instructions that use this addressing mode are one-byte instructions. However, the number of clock cycles ranges from 2 to 7. The following instructions use this addressing mode:

BRK (7)	DEX (2)	PHA (3)	RTS (6)	TAY (2)
CLC (2)	DEY (2)	PHP (3)	SEC (2)	TSX (2)
CLD (2)	INX (2)	PLA (4)	SED (2)	TXA (2)
CLI (2)	INY (2)	PLP (4)	SEI (2)	TXS (2)
CLV (2)	NOP (2)	RTI (6)	TAX (2)	TYA (2)

The number in parentheses is the number of clock cycles required to complete each instruction. The step-by-step procedure and an example are shown next.

General operation of clock cycles for the implied addressing mode is as follows:

Clock Cycle	Address Bus	Data Bus	Internal Operation
1	PC	Op code	Finish previous instruction; increment PC (PC + 1).
2	PC + 1	Next byte from memory	Decode op code; ignore incoming byte.
3	PC + 1	Next op code	Fetch next op code; execute implied addressing mode instruction; increment PC (PC + 2).

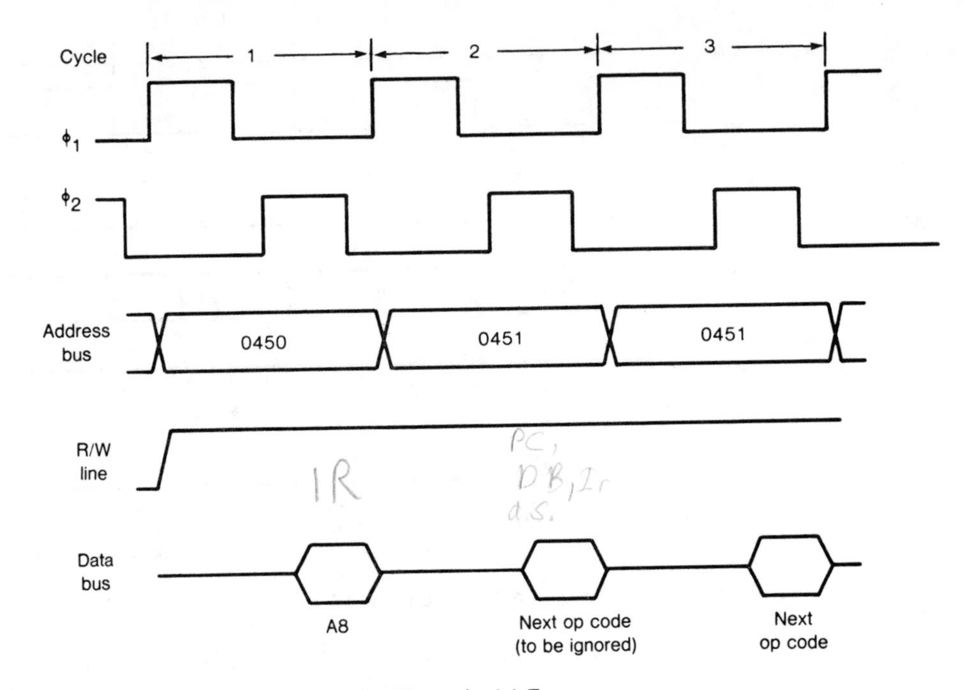

FIGURE 14–12 Timing Diagram for Example 14.7

EXAMPLE 14.7 Show the clock cycles needed for transferring the contents of the accumulator to the Y register.

Program Listing	Memory Listing
0450 TAY	0450 A8 op code

Solution

Clock Cycle	Address Bus	Data Bus	Internal Operation
1	0450	A8	Finish previous instruction; increment PC to 0451.
2	0451	Next op code (to be ignored)	Decode op code A8; ignore incoming new op code.
3	0451	Next op code	Transfer contents of accumulator to Y register; increment PC to 0452.

Figure 14–12 shows the timing diagram for Example 14.7.

14.4.6 Relative Addressing Mode

Like the 6800 μP, all of the branch instructions for the 6502 use the relative addressing mode. Unlike the 6800, however, the number of cycles needed for the 6502 to complete an instruction depends on whether the branch is taken or not, and, if it is taken, on whether or not a page boundary is crossed. The following 6502 instructions use the relative addressing mode:

BCC	BNE	BVC
BEQ	BPL	BVS
BMI	BCS	

Both general and specific examples are shown next.

Clock cycles for the relative addressing mode (no page crossing) are as follows:

Clock Cycle	Address Bus	Data Bus	Internal Operation
1	PC	Op code	Finish executing previous instruction; increment program counter (PC + 1).
2	PC + 1	Offset	Decode op code; increment program counter (PC + 2).
3	PC + 2	Next op code from memory	Check flags; add offset to present value program counter (PC + 2 + offset); increment program counter (PC + 3); op code ignored.
4	PC + 2 + offset	New op code	Transfer results to PCL; increment new program counter.

The above timing steps are for the μP taking the branch but with no page crossing. The branch could be either forward or backward, but the value in the PCH does not change. (This means the same page.) If the branch is not taken (the μP checks the appropriate flag and the answer is false), step 4 is deleted and the μP does not ignore the op code in step 3. In either case, the op code is directed to the instruction register and the program continues.

Examples 14.8, 14.9, and 14.10 show the difference between the clock cycles required for a branch instruction when the branch is not taken and when the branch is taken, regardless of a positive or negative offset.

EXAMPLE 14.8 Show the clock cycles needed for a branch on carry clear instruction, but because the carry flag is a logic 1, the branch is not taken.

Program Listing	Memory Listing			Carry Flag
0420 BCC 05	0420	90	op code	1
	0421	05	offset	

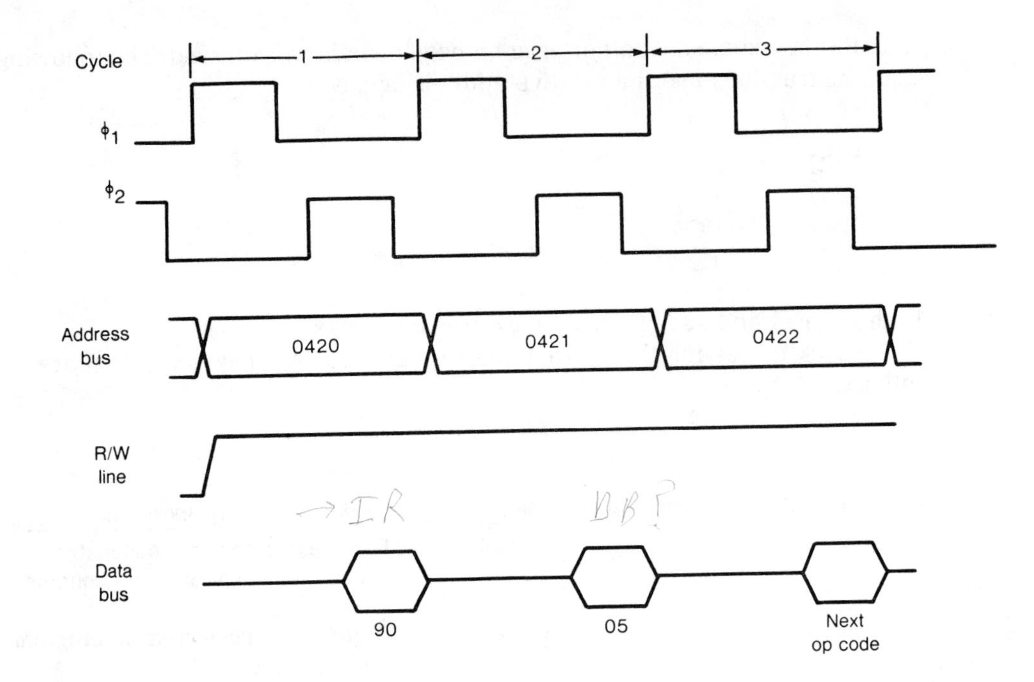

FIGURE 14–13 Timing Diagram for Example 14.8

Solution

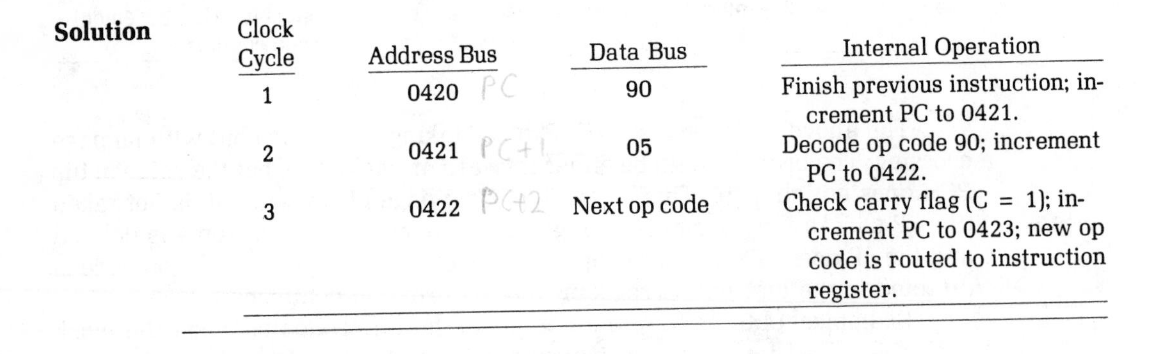

Clock Cycle	Address Bus	Data Bus	Internal Operation
1	0420	90	Finish previous instruction; increment PC to 0421.
2	0421	05	Decode op code 90; increment PC to 0422.
3	0422	Next op code	Check carry flag (C = 1); increment PC to 0423; new op code is routed to instruction register.

The timing diagram for Example 14.8 is shown in Figure 14–13.

EXAMPLE 14.9 Show the clock cycles needed for a branch on carry clear instruction with a positive offset.

Program Listing	Memory Listing			Carry Flag
0420 BCC 05	0420	90	op code	0
	0421	05	offset	

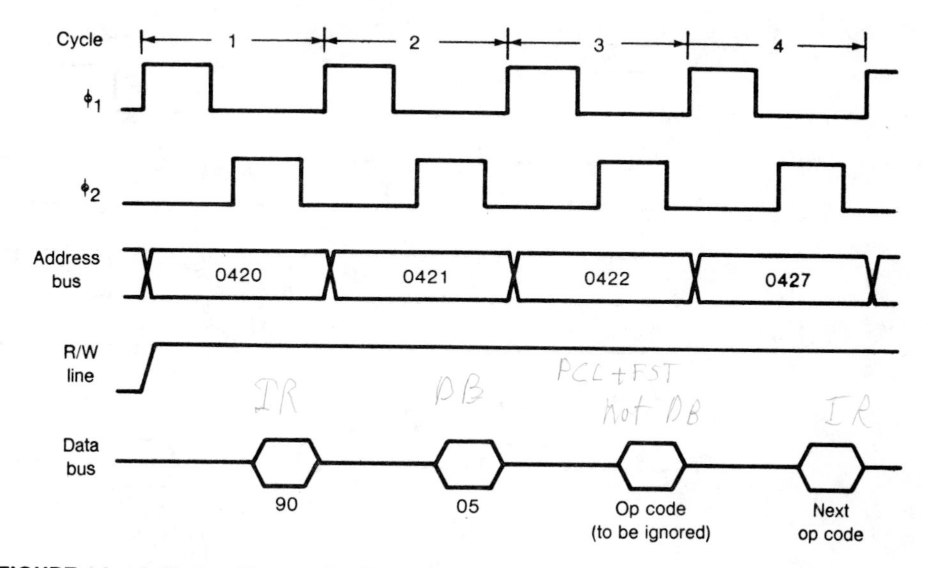

FIGURE 14–14 Timing Diagram for Example 14.9

Solution

Clock Cycle	Address Bus	Data Bus	Internal Operation
1	0420	90	Finish previous instruction; increment PC to 0421.
2	0421	05	Decode op code 90; increment PC to 0422.
3	0422	Op code (to be ignored)	Check carry flag (C = 0); add 0422 + 05 = 0427.
4	0427	Next op code	Increment PC to 0428.

In Example 14.9, when the offset value is added to the program counter, there is no page crossing. Therefore, three clock cycles are needed to fetch and execute the instruction. Figure 14–14 gives the timing diagram.

EXAMPLE 14.10 Repeat Example 14.9, but now there is a negative offset value $FB_{hex} = -5_{decimal}$.

Program Listing	Memory Listing	Carry Flag
0420 BCC F3	0420 90 op code	0
	0421 FB offset	

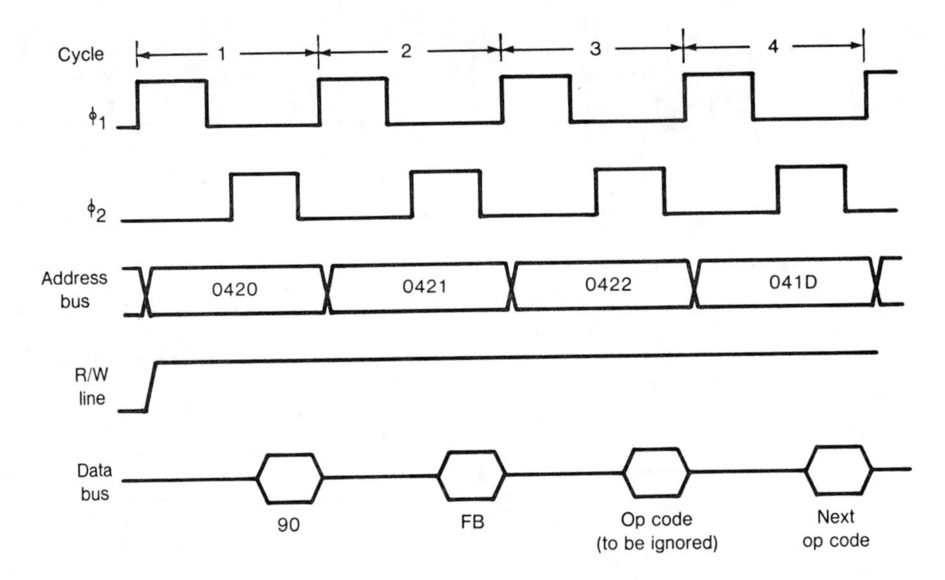

FIGURE 14–15 Timing Diagram for Example 14.10

Solution

Clock Cycle	Address Bus	Data Bus	Internal Operation
1	0420	90	Finish previous instruction; increment PC to 0421.
2	0421	FB	Decode op code 90; increment PC to 0422.
3	0422	Op code (to be ignored)	Check carry flag (C = 0); add 0422 + FB = 041D.
4	041D	Next op code	Transfer 1D to PCL; increment PC to 041E.

As in Example 14.9, the branch is taken in Example 14.10, and the offset is added to the program counter, but there is no page crossing. Once again, PCH does not change. Figure 14–15 shows the timing diagram.

Clock cycles for the relative addressing mode (with page crossing) are as follows:

Clock Cycle	Address Bus	Data Bus	Internal Operation
1	PCH, PCL	Op code	Finish previous instruction; increment program counter.
2	PCH, PCL + 1	Offset	Decode op code, increment program counter.

3	PCH, PCL + 2	Next op code from memory (to be ignored)	Check flags; add offset to present low byte of program counter; discard incoming op code.
4	PCH, PCL + 2 + offset	Data or op code from memory (to be ignored)	Store previous result in PCL; add or subtract 1 from PCH.
5	PCH ± 1, PCL + 2 + offset	Next op code	Increment new value in program counter.

Examples 14.11 and 14.12 show that it takes five clock cycles for a branch instruction to execute when a page boundary is crossed, regardless of a positive or negative page crossing.

EXAMPLE 14.11 Show the clock cycles needed for a branch on carry clear instruction with a page crossing.

Program Listing	Memory Listing	Carry Flag
04D0 BCC 70	04D0 90 op code	0
	04D1 70 offset	

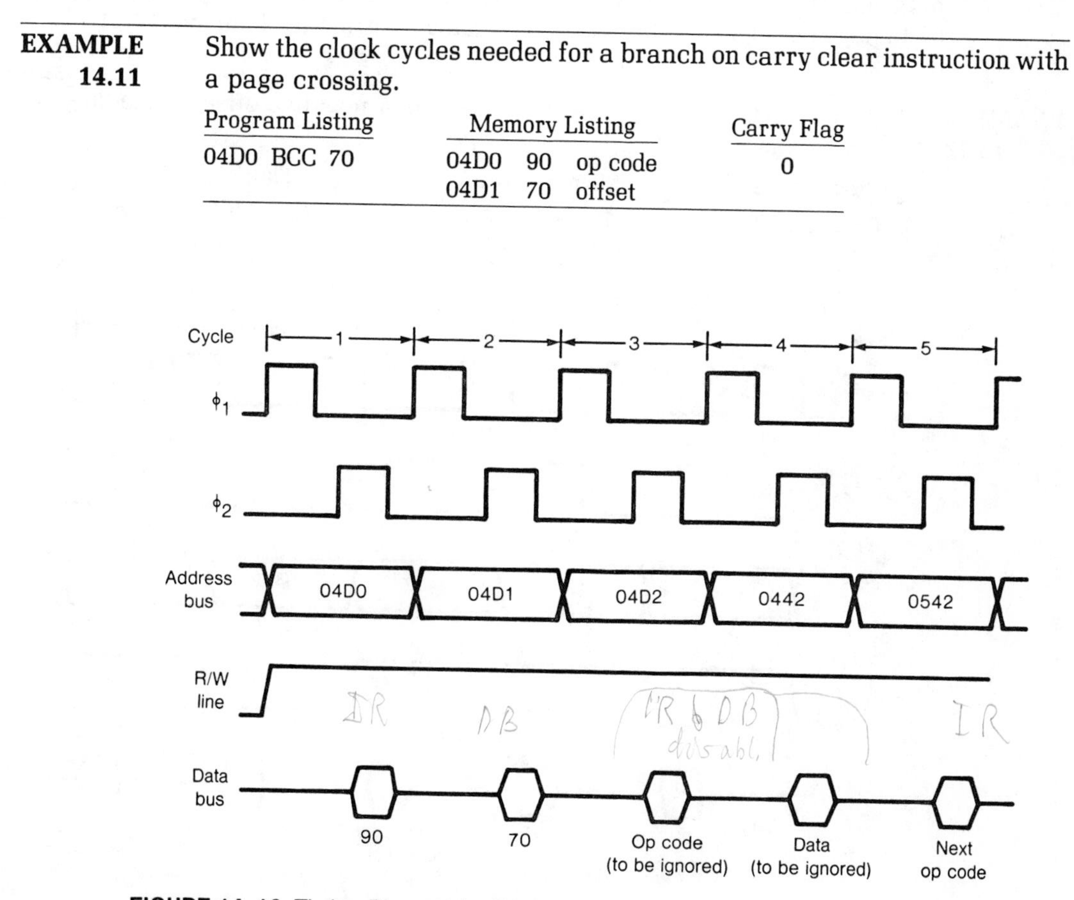

FIGURE 14–16 Timing Diagram for Example 14.11

Solution

Clock Cycle	Address Bus	Data Bus	Internal Operation
1	04D0	90	Finish previous instruction; increment PC to 04D1.
2	04D1	70	Decode op code 90; increment PC to 04D2.
3	04D2	Op code (to be ignored)	Check carry flag (C = 0); add D2 + 70 = 42; there is an internal carry of +1.
4	0442	Data (to be ignored)	Store 42 in PCL; add 04 + 1 = 05.
5	0542	Next op code	Increment PC to 0543.

The offset value in Example 14.11 is positive because the most significant bit is a logic 0 (70 = 01110000). However, when the offset value is added to the program counter, there is a page crossing in the positive direction from page 04 to page 05. Figure 14–16 gives the timing diagram for Example 14.11.

EXAMPLE 14.12 Repeat Example 14.11, but now there is a negative offset value $80_{hex} = -128_{decimal}$.

Program Listing	Memory Listing	Carry Flag
0420 BCC 80	0420 90 op code	0
	0421 80 offset	

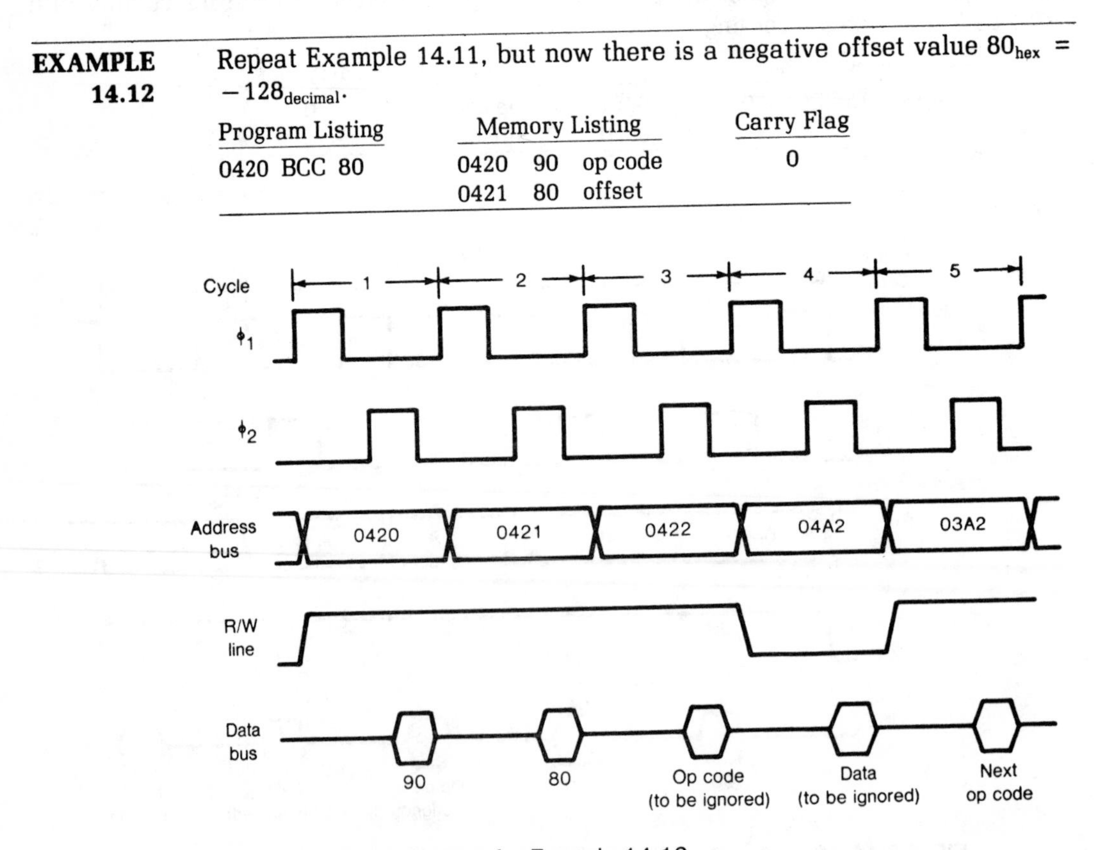

FIGURE 14–17 Timing Diagram for Example 14.12

Solution

Clock Cycle	Address Bus	Data Bus	Internal Operation
1	0420	90	Finish previous operation; increment PC to 0421.
2	0421	80	Decode op code 90; increment PC to 0422.
3	0422	Op code (to be ignored)	Check carry flag (C = 0); add 22 + 80 = A2; there is an internal borrow of 1.
4	04A2	Data (to be ignored)	Transfer A2 to PCL; subtract 1 from PCH (04 − 1 = 03).
5	03A2	Next op code	Increment PC to 03A3.

In Example 14.12, when the offset value is added to the program counter, the result causes a negative branch with a page crossing from page 04 to page 03. The timing diagram in Figure 14–17 shows what happens on the bus lines for each clock cycle of the example.

14.4.7 Indexed Addressing Mode

The number of clock cycles needed to complete this addressing mode depends on whether it is being used with the absolute addressing mode or with the zero page addressing mode. An absolute indexed addressing mode requires six clock cycles, while the zero page indexed addressing mode requires five clock cycles.

The following instructions use both the absolute and zero page indexed addressing modes:

ADC	EOR	ORA
AND	INC	ROL
ASL	LDA	ROR
CMP	LDY	SBC
DEC	LSR	STA

The STY instruction also has indexed addressing mode capability, but only when the zero page mode is used. The general step-by-step procedure and specific examples for both types of indexed addressing modes are shown next.

General operation of clock cycles for the absolute indexed addressing mode is as follows:

Clock Cycle	Address Bus	Data Bus	Internal Operation
1	PC	Op code	Finish previous instruction; increment PC (PC + 1).
2	PC + 1	BAL	Decode op code; increment PC (PC + 2).

3	PC + 2	BAH	Add BAL + index register; increment PC (PC + 3).
4	BAH, BAL + index register	Data (to be ignored)	Add BAH + 1.
5	BAH + 1, BAL + index register	Data	Latch data into or send data out of μP, depending on instruction.
6	PC + 3	Next op code	Finish instruction; increment PC (PC + 4).

The preceding timing steps are for an absolute indexed addressing mode instruction with a page crossing. This is shown by BAH + 1 in clock cycle 5. If there is no page crossing, clock cycle 5 is deleted, and the data in clock cycle 4 is valid. The next two examples show the number of clock cycles with and without page crossing.

EXAMPLE 14.13 Show the clock cycles needed for storing the contents of the accumulator using the absolute indexed addressing mode.

Program Listing	Memory Listing	Accumulator	X Register
F800 STA 0740,X	F800 9D op code	25	06
	F801 40 BAL		
	F802 07 BAH		

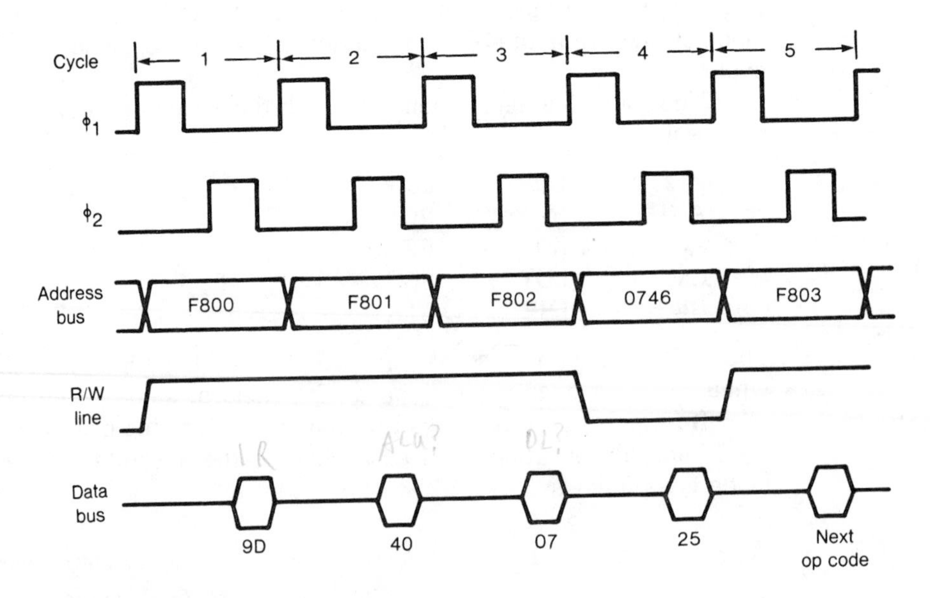

FIGURE 14–18 Timing Diagram for Example 14.13

Solution

Clock Cycle	Address Bus	Data Bus	Internal Operation
1	F800	9D	Finish previous instruction; increment PC to F801.
2	F801	40	Decode op code 9D; increment PC to F802.
3	F802	07	Add 40 + 06 = 46; increment PC to F803.
4	0746	25	Send data 25 to location 0746.
5	F803	Next op code	Increment PC to F804.

Example 14.13 did not involve a page crossing because the high byte of the base address (BAH) did not have to be incremented. Figure 14–18 shows the timing diagram for Example 14.13.

EXAMPLE 14.14 Repeat Example 14.13, but this time there is a page crossing.

Program Listing	Memory Listing	Accumulator	X Register
F800 STA 0740,X	F800 9D op code	30	C5
	F801 40 BAL		
	F802 07 BAH		

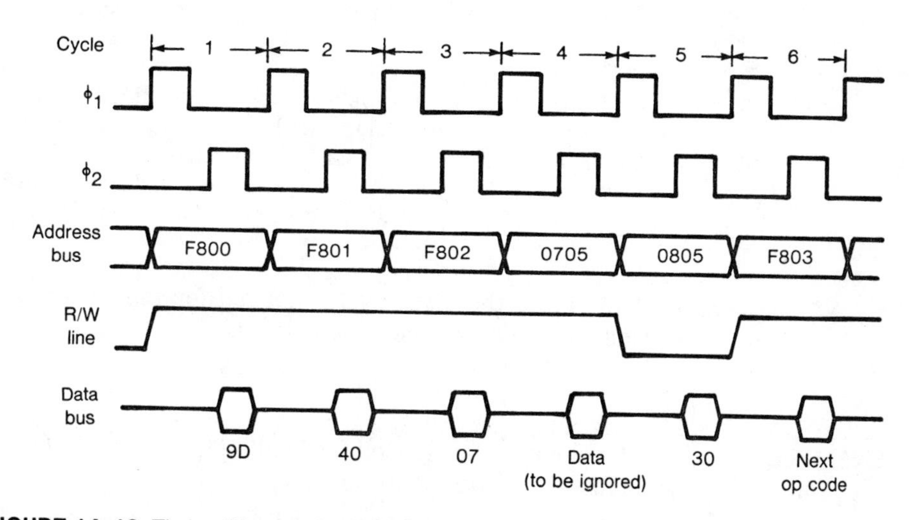

FIGURE 14–19 Timing Diagram for Example 14.14

Solution

Clock Cycle	Address Bus	Data Bus	Internal Operation
1	F800	9D	Finish previous instruction; increment PC to F801.
2	F801	40	Decode op code 9D; increment PC to F802.
3	F802	07	Add 40 + C5 = 05 with internal carry; increment PC to F803.
4	0705	Data (to be ignored)	Hold 05; add 07 + 1 = 08.
5	0805	30	Data 30 from accumulator is sent to location 0805.
6	F803	Next op code	Increment PC to F804.

Example 14.14 required one more clock cycle than Example 14.13 because BAH had to be incremented. Compare the timing diagram in Figure 14–18 with the diagram in Figure 14–19, which is the timing diagram for Example 14.14.

General operation of clock cycles for the zero page indexed addressing mode is as follows:

Clock Cycle	Address Bus	Data Bus	Internal Operation
1	PCH, PCL	Op code	Finish executing previous instruction; increment PC.
2	PCH, PCL + 1	BAL	Decode op code; increment PC.
3	00, BAL	Data (to be ignored)	Add BAL + index register; discard data; increment PC.
4	00, BAL + index register	Data	Latch data into or send data out of μP, depending on instruction.
5	PCH, PCL + 2	Next op code	Finish instruction; increment PC.

Example 14.15 shows the clock cycles needed for the zero page indexed addressing mode when loading the accumulator.

EXAMPLE 14.15 Show the clock cycles needed for loading the accumulator using the zero page indexed addressing mode.

Program Listing	Memory Listing	X Register	Location 0025
0300 LDA 20,X	0300 B5 op code	05	FD
	0301 20 BAL		

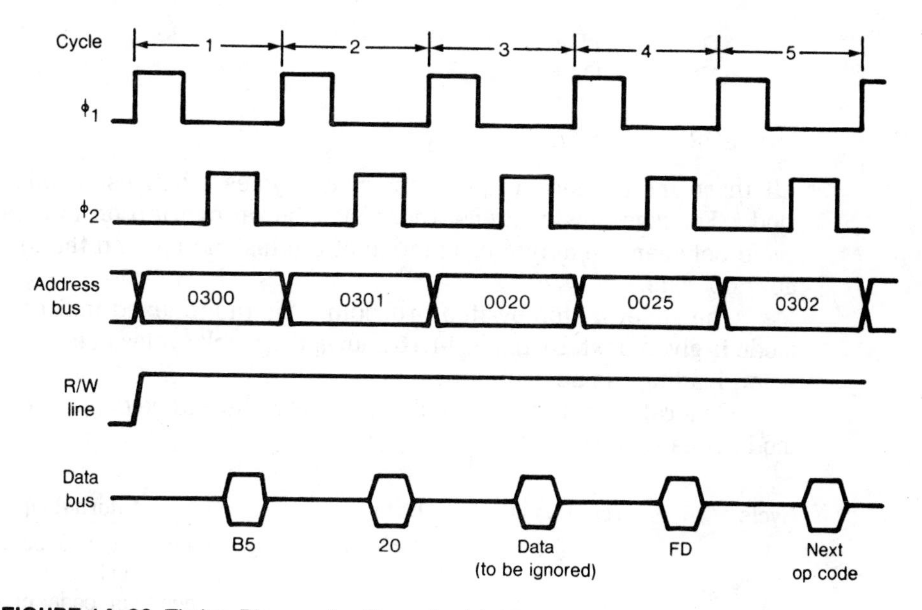

FIGURE 14–20 Timing Diagram for Example 14.15

Solution

Clock Cycle	Address Bus	Data Bus	Internal Operation
1	0300	B5	Finish previous instruction; increment PC to 0301.
2	0301	20	Decode op code B5; increment PC to 0302.
3	0020	Data (to be ignored)	Add 20 + 05 = 25.
4	0025	FD	Latch data (FD) into μP.
5	0302	Next op code	Transfer FD from latch to accumulator; increment PC to 0303.

Example 14.15 shows that since the data is coming from page zero, the program can be stored in two bytes in memory and requires one less clock cycle than the program of Example 14.14. Figure 14–20 shows the timing diagram for Example 14.15.

14.4.8 Indexed Indirect Addressing Mode

Instructions that use this type of addressing mode are two-byte instructions. The first byte is the op code and the second byte is a base address to which the X register will be added. Instructions which use this addressing mode are as follows:

ADC	LDA
AND	ORA
CMP	SBC
EOR	STA

All these instructions require six clock cycles when using this addressing mode. For some instructions, there may be an overlap on the seventh clock cycle between the actual completion of the instruction and the fetching of the next op code.

The general step-by-step procedure for the indexed indirect addressing mode is given next. Example 14.16 shows the clock cycles needed for this mode when loading the accumulator.

General operation of clock cycles for the indexed indirect addressing mode is as follows:

Clock Cycle	Address Bus	Data Bus	Internal Operation
1	PC	Op code	Finish previous operation; increment PC.
2	PC + 1	BAL	Decode op code; increment PC.
3	00, BAL	Data (to be discarded)	Add BAL + X register.
4	00, BAL + X register	ADL	Add 1 to BAL + X register.
5	00, BAL + X register + 1	ADH	Hold ADL.
6	ADH, ADL	Data	Latch data into or send data out of μP, depending on instruction.
7	PC + 2	Next op code	Finish operation; increment PC.

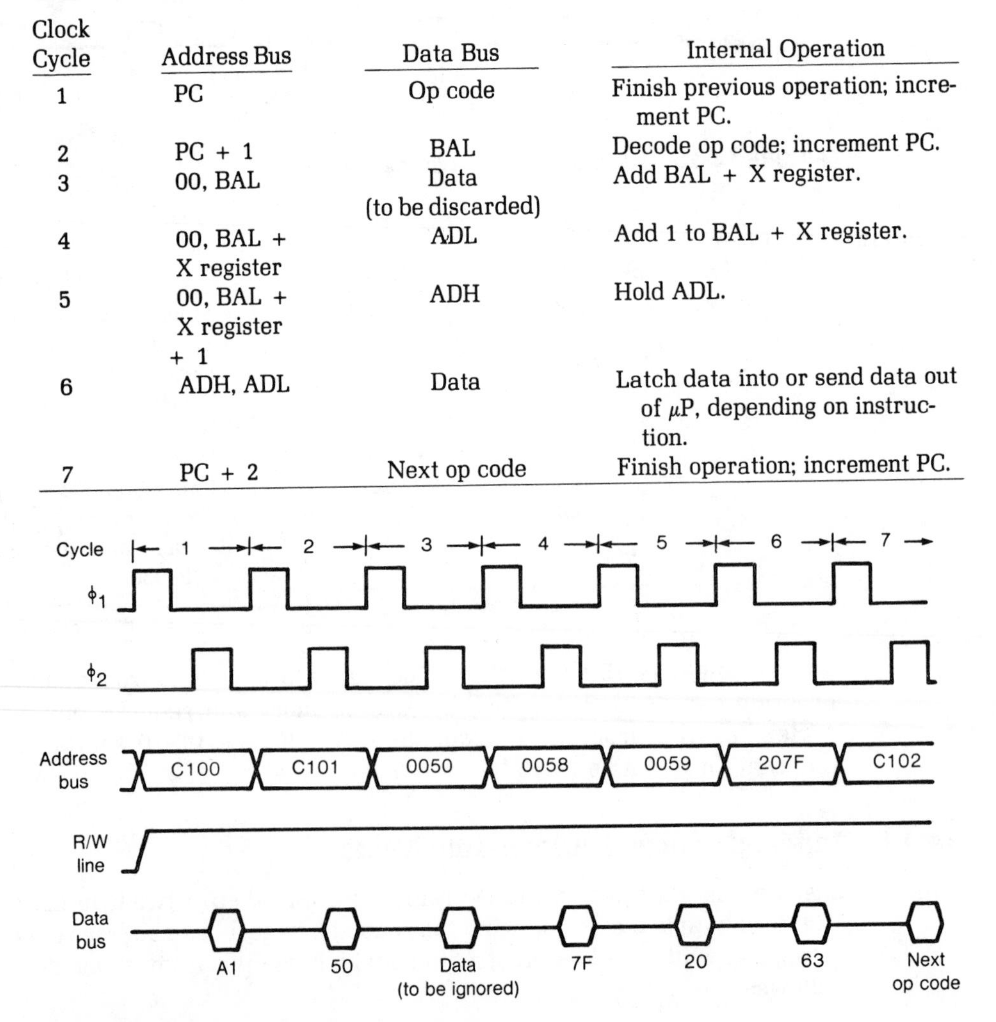

FIGURE 14–21 Timing Diagram for Example 14.16

EXAMPLE 14.16 Show the clock cycles needed for loading the accumulator using the indexed indirect addressing mode.

Program Listing	Memory Listing			Accumulator	X Register	Other Locations	
C100 LDA (50,X)	C100	A1	op code	14	08	0058	7F
	C101	50	BAL			0059	20
						207F	63

Solution

Clock Cycle	Address Bus	Data Bus	Internal Operation
1	C100	A1	Finish previous instruction; increment PC to C101.
2	C101	50	Decode op code A1; increment PC to C102.
3	0050	Data (to be ignored)	Add 50 + 08 = 58.
4	0058	7F	Add 1 to 58 = 59.
5	0059	20	Hold 7F.
6	207F	63	Latch data (63) into μP.
7	C102	Next op code	Transfer data 63 from input latch to accumulator; increment PC to C103.

The timing diagram for Example 14.16 is shown in Figure 14–21.

14.4.9 Indirect Indexed Addressing Mode

Instructions that use this type of addressing mode are two-byte instructions. The first byte is the op code and the second byte is the indirect address (IAL) in page zero. The following instructions use this type of addressing mode:

ADC	LDA
AND	ORA
CMP	SBC
EOR	STA

All the instructions that use this addressing mode, except the STA instructions, require five clock cycles. The STA instruction requires six clock cycles. The general step-by-step procedure that follows shows what happens on each clock cycle. Examples 14.17 and 14.18 give the clock cycles needed for this mode in loading the accumulator.

General operation of clock cycles for the indirect indexed addressing mode is as follows:

Clock Cycle	Address Bus	Data Bus	Internal Operation
1	PC	Op code	Finish previous instruction; increment PC.
2	PC + 1	IAL	Decode op code.
3	00, IAL	BAL	Add 1 to IAL.
4	00, IAL + 1	BAH	Add BAL + Y register.
5	BAH, BAL + Y register	Data (to be ignored)	Add 1 to BAH.
6	BAH + 1, BAL + Y register	Data	Latch data into or send data out of μP, depending on instruction.
7	PC + 2	Next op code	Finish operation; increment PC.

The number of clock cycles shown above is needed if there is a page crossing. This is indicated by BAH + 1. If there is no page crossing, clock cycle 6 is deleted and the data at clock cycle 5 is valid. The next two examples illustrate loading the accumulator using the indirect indexed addressing mode with and without a page crossing.

EXAMPLE 14.17 Show the clock cycles needed for loading the accumulator using the indirect indexed addressing mode.

Program Listing	Memory Listing	Y Register	Other Locations
A500 LDA (60),Y	A500 B1 op code	12	0060 10
	A501 60 IAL		0061 40
			4022 D3

Solution

Clock Cycle	Address Bus	Data Bus	Internal Operation
1	A500	B1	Finish previous instruction; increment PC to A501.
2	A501	60	Decode op code (B1); increment PC to A502.
3	0060	10	Add 1 + 60 = 61.
4	0061	40	Add 12 + 10 = 22.
5	4022	D3	Latch data D3 into μP.
6	A502	Next op code	Transfer data D3 from input latch to accumulator; increment PC to A503.

In Example 14.17, there is no page crossing, because when the Y register is added to IAL (12 + 10 = 22), there is no internal carry. Figure 14–22 shows what happens during each clock cycle in Example 14.17.

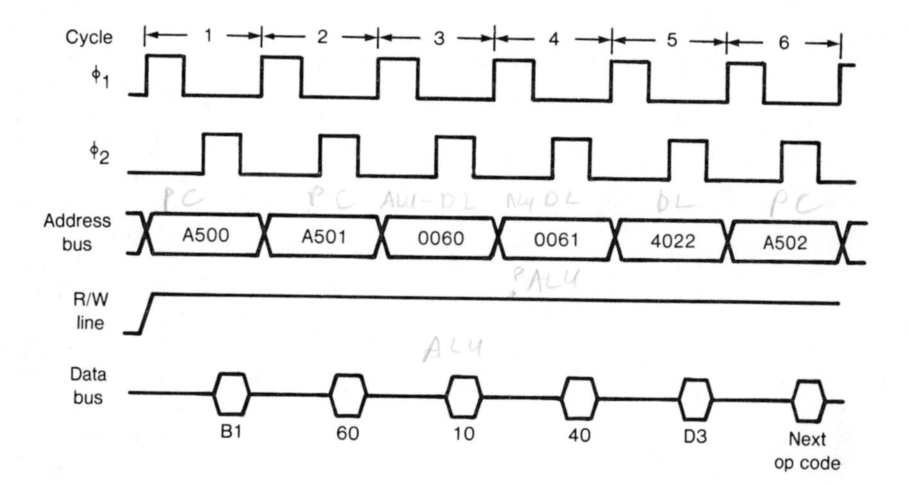

FIGURE 14–22 Timing Diagram for Example 14.17

EXAMPLE 14.18

Repeat Example 14.17, but now there will be a page crossing.

Program Listing	Memory Listing	Y Register	Other Locations
A500 LDA (60),Y	A500 B1 op code	F2	0060 10
	A501 60 IAL		0061 40
			4102 C4

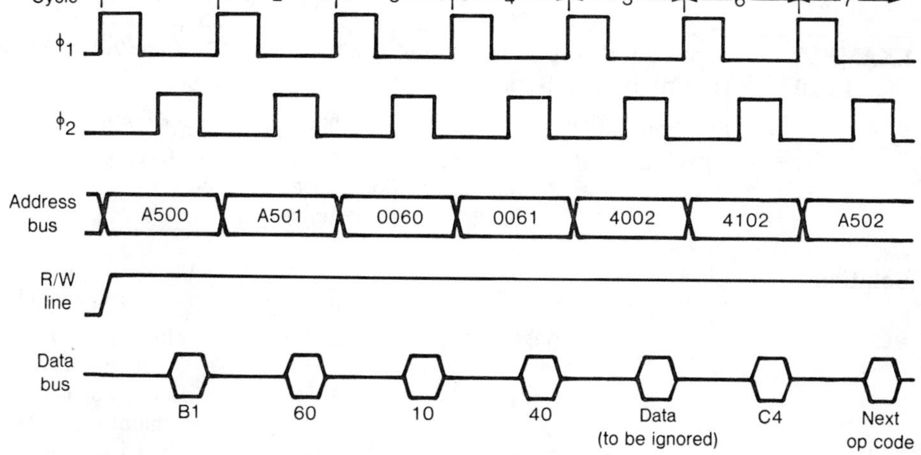

FIGURE 14–23 Timing Diagram for Example 14.18

Solution

Clock Cycle	Address Bus	Data Bus	Internal Operation
1	A500	B1	Finish previous instruction; increment PC to A501.
2	A501	60	Decode op code (B1); increment PC to A502.
3	0060	10	Add 1 + 60 = 61.
4	0061	40	Add F2 + 10 = 02 plus an internal carry.
5	4002	Data (to be ignored)	Add 1 + 40 = 41.
6	4102	C4	Latch data C4 into μP.
7	A502	Next op code	Transfer data C4 from input latch to accumulator; increment PC to A503.

Although Example 14.18 did not require any more memory locations to store the program than did Example 14.17, it did require an additional clock cycle because of the page crossing from page 40 to page 41. Compare the timing diagram of Figure 14–22 with that of Figure 14–23, which is the timing diagram for Example 14.18.

14.5 JUMP TO SUBROUTINE

The jump to subroutine instruction is a three-byte instruction. It loads the starting address of the subroutine into the program counter, but first it stores a return address on the stack. For the 6502 μP, the last byte of the JSR instruction is the information stored on the stack. For Example 14.19, the stack pointer is initialized to 01FF. This instruction does not affect any flag bits.

EXAMPLE 14.19 Show what happens for each clock cycle for the following jump to subroutine instruction.

Program Listing	Memory Listing			Stack Pointer	Other Locations	
0370 JSR 4510	0370	20	op code	01FF	01FD	XX
	0371	10	line address		01FE	XX
	0372	45	page address		01FF	XX

Solution

Clock Cycle	Address Bus	Data Bus	Internal Operation
1	0370	20	Finish previous instruction; increment PC to 0371.
2	0371	10	Decode op code (20); increment PC to 0372.
3	01FF	Data (ignored)	Hold 10.
4	01FF	03	Store 03 on stack; decrement SP to 01FE.

5	01FE	72	Store 72 on stack; decrement SP to 01FD.
6	0372	45	Fetch page address.
7	4510	Next op code	First op code of subroutine program.

The return address is stored on the stack, as follows:

01FD XX
01FE 72
01FF 03

Remember, for the 6502 μP, the stack is always located in page 01. The stack can be initialized to 01FF by the following programming steps:

```
LDX #FF
TXS
```

14.6 RETURN FROM SUBROUTINE

The return from subroutine instruction (RTS) is a one-byte instruction that retrieves an address from the stack. The RTS instruction does not affect any flag bits. Example 14.20 examines what happens during each cycle.

EXAMPLE 14.20 The last instruction of a subroutine program is an RTS instruction. Show how the μP returns to the main program of Example 14.19 at location 0373.

Program Listing	Memory Listing	Stack Pointer	Other Locations
453A RTS	453A 60 op code	01FD	01FD XX
			01FE 72
			01FF 03

Solution

Clock Cycle	Address Bus	Data Bus	Internal Operation
1	453A	60	Finish previous instruction; increment PC to 453B.
2	453B	Data (ignored)	Decode op code (60).
3	01FD	Data (ignored)	Increment stack pointer to 01FE.
4	01FE	72	Increment stack pointer to 01FF.
5	01FF	03	Hold 72.
6	0372	Data (ignored)	Increment PC to 0373.
7	0373	Next op code of main program	Increment PC to 0374.

Although the RTS instruction is only a one-byte instruction, it requires six clock cycles to complete.

14.7 INTERRUPTS

The 6502 μP has three different types of hardware interrupts: reset ($\overline{RES}$), nonmaskable ($\overline{NMI}$), and interrupt request ($\overline{IRQ}$). These interrupts are hardware interrupts because they are activated by something external to the μP. The 6502 μP has a software interrupt instruction, the break command instruction (BRK). When an interrupt signal is received, the μP first fetches from memory the starting address of the interrupt service program. The starting addresses (not the program) must be stored in the following locations:

Nonmaskable interrupt ($\overline{NMI}$)	FFFA–FFFB
Reset ($\overline{RST}$)	FFFC–FFFD
Interrupt request ($\overline{IRQ}$) and break command (BRK)	FFFE–FFFF

These six addresses are called *vectors* or *vector addresses* because they contain information that points the μP to an interrupt service routine. Figure 14–24 shows the memory map for the 6502 μP interrupt vectors. These interrupt vectors are located in the six highest memory locations.

Let's consider the timing diagrams for each type of interrupt.

14.7.1 Reset

A reset signal ($\overline{RES}$) is needed to initialize the μP after power is turned on, or a reset can be used at any time to reinitialize the μP. In either case, the reset line (pin 40) must be held low for two clock cycles and then brought high before the μP's reset sequence can start. In the case when power is first applied, the reset line must be held low for two clock cycles after V_{CC} reaches 4.75 V. When the reset line goes back high, the R/W line goes high, and the μP uses the next six clock cycles to reset itself. After these six clock cycles, the following functions occur:

1. The interrupt mask bit is set. This is the I bit of the condition code register.
2. The program counter is loaded with the data at locations FFFC and FFFD.

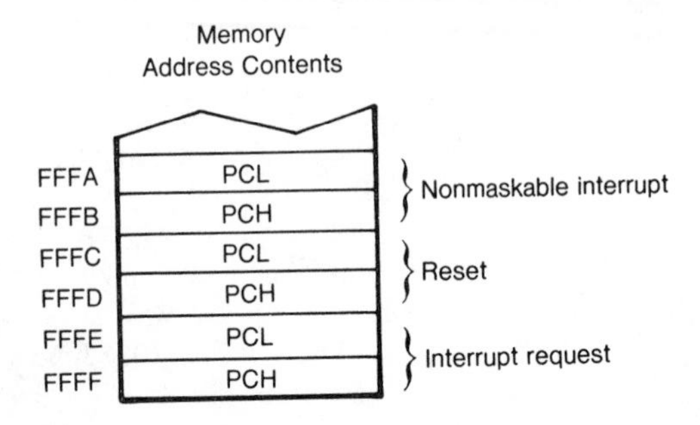

FIGURE 14–24 Memory Map for 6502 μP Interrupt Vectors

While the reset line is low, the μP is inhibited from receiving or sending any data. Figure 14–25 shows the timing diagram for the reset sequence.

14.7.2 Interrupt Request

An interrupt request signal is a low level (logic 0) on the $\overline{IRQ}$ line (pin 4). The $\overline{IRQ}$ pin is sampled during the ϕ_2 clock pulse. The μP will complete the current instruction before recognizing the interrupt request. Before the μP services an interrupt request, it checks the interrupt mask bit (I bit) in the condition code register. If the I bit is a logic 0, the μP begins its interrupt service sequence, which is as follows:

1. Store the present contents of the program counter in the stack.
2. Store the condition code register in the stack.
3. Set the I flag. This inhibits the μP from recognizing any further interrupts.
4. Load the program counter with the data at locations FFFE and FFFF.

For the μP to recognize an interrupt request, the ready line (pin 2) must be high.

The interrupt request pin on the 6502 μP is the open drain for a wire-OR operation. A 3kΩ resistor must be connected between V_{CC} and pin 4.

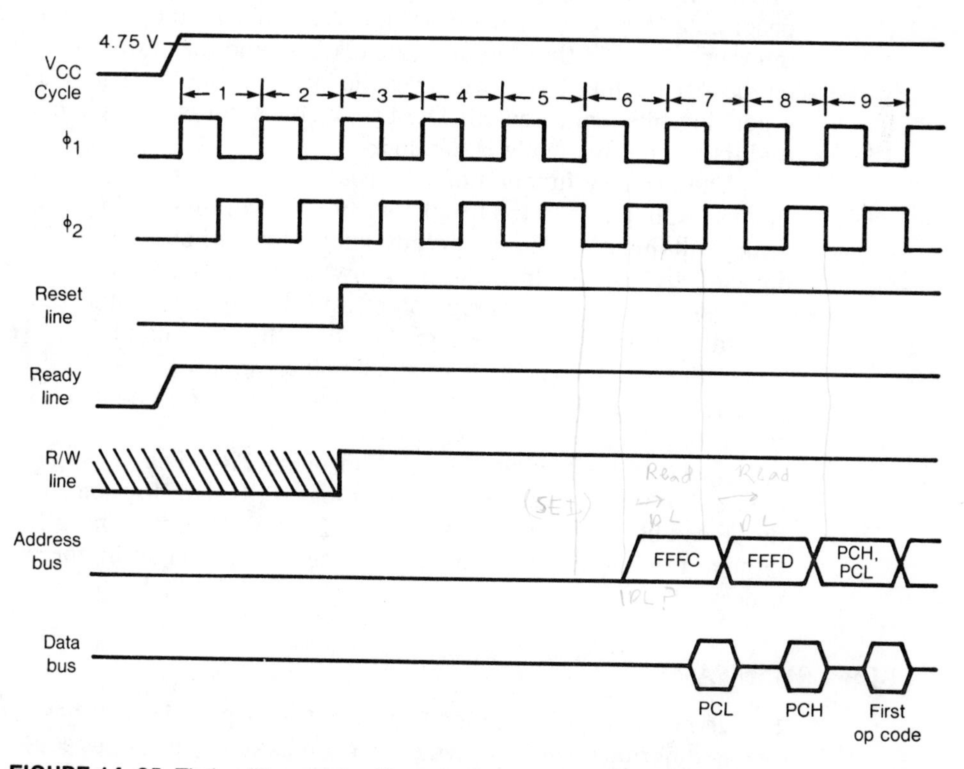

FIGURE 14–25 Timing Diagram for Start-up Sequence of 6502 μP

14.7.3 Nonmaskable Interrupt

A nonmaskable interrupt signal is a high-to-low transition on the $\overline{NMI}$ pin (pin 6). This pin is sampled during the ϕ_2 clock pulse. The present instruction is completed, and the μP begins executing the nonmaskable sequence beginning at the next appropriate ϕ_1 clock pulse. When the μP begins a nonmaskable interrupt sequence, it does not check the I bit. Therefore, the programmer cannot inhibit the μP from recognizing this signal. The steps performed by the μP after recognizing this type of interrupt are as follows:

1. Store the present contents of the program counter on the stack.
2. Store the condition code register on the stack.
3. Set the I bit. This inhibits the μP from recognizing any further interrupt request (not nonmaskable interrupt requests or a reset signal).
4. Load the program counter with the data at locations FFFA and FFFB.

A 3 kΩ resistor must be connected between V_{CC} and pin 6 for proper wire-OR operation for the nonmaskable line.

14.7.4 Break Command

The break command (BRK) allows the μP to jump to the interrupt subroutine program under program control. The break command is treated by the μP as an interrupt signal in that the program counter and the status register are stored on the stack before the μP retrieves the interrupt vector. The B flag is set but no other flag bits are affected. The break command is a single-byte instruction, and its addressing mode is implied.

The primary function of the break command is in debugging a program. The user can patch in the break instruction over an existing code, and the program will jump to the interrupt subroutine when the BRK instruction is decoded by the μP. In order to know whether the vector was retrieved in response to the break instruction or an interrupt request signal, the B flag in the status register that has been stored on the stack can be checked. The location of the status register is at stack pointer plus 1 (SP + 1). If the B flag is a logic 1, a BRK instruction has been decoded. If the B flag is a logic 0, an interrupt request signal has been received.

The BRK instruction is 00_{hex}. Therefore, PROMs may be patched by burning all the fusible links in a byte to a logic 0. If the BRK command is decoded, the μP can be directed to another PROM or EPROM chip. This allows a designer to have the additional memory chip used for patching in corrected codes or programs.

14.8 SUMMARY

In this chapter, we examined the 6502 μP's pin descriptions, clock signals, timing diagrams, cycle-by-cycle operations, and interrupt request signals. As in the 6800 μP, the number of clock cycles needed to execute a 6502 instruction depends on the type of instruction and the addressing mode. As we saw, the 6502 has its clock generator circuit within the μP, which is a major difference between this device and either the 8080A or the 6800. When the 6502 is used, the number of external components needed to build a μC system is reduced. Therefore, it is an easier and simpler design for many applications.

The 6502 μP performs many internal operations when it is fetching new information or data from memory. This overlapping of jobs is called pipelining. Pipelining allows a μP to execute programs faster, because several functions are being done at the same time. We saw many of these overlapping operations in this chapter when we studied the 6502's cycle-by-cycle operations and timing diagrams for different instructions and addressing modes.

Like all μPs, the 6502 has the ability to jump to and return from a subroutine. In this chapter, we examined what information is stored on and retrieved from the stack when the 6502 μP executes a JSR or RTS instruction.

Finally, we saw that the 6502 has three interrupt request pins: reset ($\overline{RST}$), nonmaskable interrupt request ($\overline{NMI}$), and interrupt request ($\overline{IRQ}$). Each interrupt has a pair of vector addresses. The six vector addresses are located in the six most significant memory locations, FFFA to FFFF. The break command instruction uses the same vector address as the interrupt request.

PROBLEMS

14-1 What is the difference between the 6502's address bus lines and the 6800's address bus lines?

14-2 What is the advantage of having a μP with an on-the-chip oscillator?

14-3 Is the 6502 a +5 V device?

14-4 To which pin on the 6502 μP must the master clock signal be applied?

14-5 In addition to the reset pin, which two pins are interrupt request pins?

14-6 What are the interrupt request vectors for the 6502 μP?

14-7 What is the function of the $\overline{RES}$ pin?

14-8 What is the function of the RDY pin?

14-9 If the clock frequency is 1 MHz, how long does it take the address bus lines to stabilize with a valid address?

14-10 How many basic instructions are there in the 6502's instruction set?

14-11 For an immediate addressing mode instruction, in which clock cycle is the instruction completed?

14-12 Do all absolute addressing mode instructions require the same number of clock cycles? If your answer is no, give an example.

14-13 For the STA 0010 instruction, how many clock cycles are saved if the zero page addressing mode is used instead of the absolute addressing mode?

14-14 List the accumulator's addressing mode instructions.

14-15 What is the difference between the number of clock cycles required by the 6800 μP and the number required by the 6502 μP for a branch instruction?

14-16 During what clock cycle of a branch instruction is the flag bit checked?

14-17 If the branch is taken, during what clock cycle is the offset value added?

14-18 Show the hex digits that would appear on the address bus and data bus for the following instruction:

C540 LDA 0200,X

The X register contains 07, and the memory location contains FF.

14–19 Refer to Example 14.16. Suppose the program listing changes to the following:

F765 LDA (50,X)

Does the data on the data bus change? If your answer is yes, list the changes.

14–20 Both the indexed indirect and relative addressing modes apply to instructions that require only two bytes. The second byte of the indexed indirect is called the base address low byte (BAL). The second byte of the branch instruction is called the offset. Does the 6502 μP treat the BAL and offset values in the same way? If your answer is no, what is the difference?

14–21 For the following instruction, what data is stored in the stack?

0208 JSR 1465

14–22 Does the RTS instruction always require six clock cycles even if the μP is to return to a location on page zero?

14–23 List the vector addresses for (a) the reset operation and (b) the nonmaskable interrupt operation.

14–24 Does a reset signal always reinitialize the μP's program counter?

14–25 Does the μP complete the present instruction before recognizing an interrupt request?

14–26 Before the μP recognizes a nonmaskable interrupt request must the I flag be checked?

Semiconductor Memories

15.0 INTRODUCTION

In Chapter 2, we examined the three major parts of a μC system: the μP, memory, and input/output ports. In Chapters 6–14, we dealt with the hardware and software aspects of three different μPs: the 8080A, 6800, and 6502. We saw that all μPs fetch and execute instructions that are stored in memory. In this chapter, we will look at the memory devices that are most often used in μC systems. Chapter 16 will cover specific memory chips and show how to connect them to the μP.

Memories store information. The information may be instructions, alphanumeric data, punctuation marks, special characters, and so forth. There are many different ways and devices for storing information, so let's first consider the different memory categories.

15.1 MEMORY CLASSIFICATIONS

Memories may be classified in a number of different ways. Some are (1) material used—semiconductor versus magnetic; (2) retention of information when power is turned off—volatile versus nonvolatile; (3) access to data—serial versus random. Let's look at each classification.

15.1.1 Semiconductor versus Magnetic

Memory IC chips are manufactured using either bipolar or MOS technology. These devices are called *semiconductor memories*. They use either the principle of a flip-flop to store a logic 1 and a logic 0 or a charge on a capacitor for a logic 1 and no charge for a logic 0.

Another method of storing logic 1s and logic 0s uses magnetic materials. Before 1970, the most popular type of memory unit was the ferrite core. These doughnut-shaped rings were magnetized in one direction for a logic 1 and in the other direction for a logic 0. Although ferrite cores are seldom used now, they enabled computers to store large amounts of data in a relatively small area. Their disadvantages were high cost, large power consumption, low speed, and low density. Although the ferrite core is seldom used today, the principle of storing binary information on magnetic material is still used with μC systems in the form of tape cassettes, floppy disks, and bubble memories. The emphasis in this text, however, is on semiconductor memories because they are used in every system, both dedicated control and general-purpose μC systems.

15.1.2 Volatile versus Nonvolatile

A *volatile memory* is one that loses its information when power is turned off or if there is a power failure. In other words, power must be kept on to retain the information in memory. Sometimes the word *temporary* is used in place of volatile.

A *nonvolatile memory* is one that retains its information when power is turned off or if there is a power failure. This type of memory is also known as *permanent* memory. Magnetic memories are nonvolatile. Semiconductor memories may be either volatile or nonvolatile.

15.1.3 Serial versus Random

This classification deals with the way information can be written to or retrieved from memory. Each instruction or piece of data is stored at a memory address. On magnetic tape, all information is stored in sequence. Therefore, if we want to go to a new address, the tape must be moved forward or backward to that address. For example, if the tape is at address 0100_{hex} and we wish to go to 0200_{hex} (256 addresses away), the tape must be moved forward from address 0100 to address 0200 before the data can be accessed. All the data between these two addresses must pass by the tape head before the new address is reached. Thus, all the data is in series. This type of memory is also called *sequential access memory*.

Even with high-speed tape drives, sequential access memories are slow. Tapes do have their advantages, however, in that they can store large amounts of data in a small area, and they are inexpensive.

Random access memories are the fastest because any memory location can be addressed directly. Therefore, reading or writing data is very fast because we do not have to pass sequentially through many locations. Semiconductor memories used in μC systems use the principle of random access.

Let's consider a comparison to the example just given for access to a magnetic tape memory. If the μP is to access location 0100_{hex}, the following steps occur:

1. The μP puts 0100 onto the address bus.
2. The address is decoded by external decoders, the memory chip(s), or both.
3. Information is either sent to or received from the μP across the data bus.

If the μP wishes to access location 0200_{hex}, steps 1–3 are repeated, except that address 0200 is put onto the address bus. Therefore, information at every location can be obtained in the same amount of time.

The term *random access memory* is used in two ways: (1) for the way a μP can address a memory location or (2) for a type of semiconductor memory. We have just used the first definition to compare sequential access with random access. Let's now consider the second definition.

As previously mentioned, a semiconductor memory can be either volatile or nonvolatile. A volatile semiconductor memory is also known as a *random access memory* (RAM) device. A nonvolatile semiconductor memory is known as a *read-only memory* (ROM) device. Every address in each type of memory chip (both RAM and ROM) can be accessed by the μP in the same amount of time. Hence, every memory location in either a RAM or ROM chip is accessed at random rather than in sequence.

15.2 SEMICONDUCTOR MEMORY TECHNOLOGY

Semiconductor memories can be subdivided according to the technology used in their manufacturing process, either bipolar technology or metal-oxide semiconductor (MOS) technology. In bipolar technology, manufacturers have most often used transistor-transistor logic (TTL), Schottky TTL, and emitter-coupled logic (ECL). In MOS technology, memory devices have been manufactured using P channel MOS (PMOS), N channel MOS (NMOS), and complementary MOS (CMOS). These technologies allow manufacturers to improve or trade off speed, density, and power consumption. Trade-offs have been made in all digital logic circuits, including the μP chip itself. For example, the fastest memories are bipolar, particularly those using ECL technology. The trade-off is that as speed increases, so does power consumption.

Semiconductor manufacturers have shifted from making PMOS memory devices to making NMOS memory devices because the latter allow increased speed and packaging density. CMOS devices consume the least power but are slightly more expensive.

Manufacturers have increased the speed of NMOS devices so that their access times approach—and in some cases overlap—the TTL bipolar memories and they consume less power than TTL devices. NMOS memories are the backbone of μC memory systems. If speed is the primary consideration, then a designer usually chooses ECL memories. To improve speed, manufacturers are now using a high-speed NMOS device, called a HMOS. Most memory devices (both RAMs and ROMs) in μC systems use NMOS technology. To allow the μP memory and peripheral devices to be interconnected easily, all the voltage levels are TTL compatible. We will now consider the different types of RAMs and ROMs that are available.

15.3 RANDOM ACCESS MEMORIES (RAMS)

As previously mentioned, the term *random access memory* refers to a volatile memory. A RAM device allows the μP to read data from or write data to the device. Therefore, RAMs are also referred to as read/write (R/W) memories. The term *read/write memory* is often more descriptive than the term *random access memory* because we can visualize the μP receiving (reading) and sending (writing) data to memory. The term *random access memory* is more descriptive when we study a timing diagram because every address can be accessed in the same amount of time. There are two types of RAMs—static and dynamic. We now look at each type in more detail.

A *static* RAM is a memory device that stores information in a flip-flop. As long as power is applied, the information is held. Remember, however, that if the power is lost, the information is lost.

A *dynamic* RAM is a memory device that stores data on a capacitor. With time, the capacitor loses its charge, and therefore even when power is applied the charge on the capacitor must be refreshed periodically to maintain the data. Most dynamic RAMs require a refresh signal every 2 ms, and some can go as long as 4 ms between refresh signals. In order to provide this refresh signal, some additional circuitry is required. Let's consider some of the advantages and disadvantages of each type of RAM.

The obvious advantage of the static RAM is that it is easier to use because it requires no additional circuitry. Static RAMs are also faster than dynamic RAMs and consume less power than dynamic RAMs. Static RAMs are available in bit-wide, byte-wide (8 bits) or half-byte-wide (4 bits) formats. This flexibility allows memory systems to be built quite rapidly. For example, a popular static RAM is the 2114. It is organized as 1024 words $\times$ 4 bits. Therefore, two of these chips give the user 1K $\times$ 8 bits of memory in two ICs.

Although dynamic RAMs require periodic refreshing, they have a lower cost per bit and are available in denser packages than the static RAMs. A denser package means that there are more bits per package. Dynamic RAMs only come one bit wide. Some of the commonly used dynamic RAMs are 4K $\times$ 1, 16K $\times$ 1, 32K $\times$ 1, and 64K $\times$ 1. Soon there will be on the market a 128K $\times$ 1 and a 256K $\times$ 1 dynamic RAM. As technology improves, the speed of dynamic RAMs is decreasing and more of the external circuitry is either put into the memory chip or contained in a single IC. Earlier dynamic RAMs required three power supplies, + 12 V and $\pm$5 V, but the newer dynamic RAMs, including the 64K dynamic RAM, require only a single supply, + 5 V.

15.4 STATIC NMOS RAM DEVICES

In many systems, the static NMOS RAM is the backbone of the memory system. Table 15-1 gives data for some of the static NMOS RAMs manufactured by Intel and Motorola.

All input and output lines of NMOS RAMs are TTL compatible. All output data lines are also three state, except in the 2125A and the 2125H devices. Their output lines are open collectors, not three state.

The automatic power down column in Table 15-1 indicates those static RAMs that draw less current from the power supply when the device is not selected. For example, the 2148, when it is selected, draws a maximum current of 140 mA. But when the device is not selected, it draws only a maximum of 30 mA. This feature is different from the low-power version. For example, the 2114, with a maximum current of 100 mA, is also available in a low-power version, the 21L14, which has a maximum current of only 70 mA. These devices do not have an automatic power down, which means that their maximum current could be drawn whether the device is selected or not. Low-power versions

TABLE 15-1 Static NMOS RAMs

Number	Organization	Access Time (ns max.)	Number of Pins	Low-Power Version Available	Automatic Power Down Capability
Motorola and Intel					
2114	1024 x 4	200–450	18	Yes	No
2115A[1]	1024 x 1	45–70	16	Yes	No
2115H[2]	1024 x 1	20–35	16	No	No
2125A	1024 x 1	45–70	16	Yes	No
2125H	1024 x 1	20–35	16	No	No
2147	4096 x 1	55–100	18	No	Yes
2147H	4096 x 1	35–55	18	No	Yes
2148	1024 x 4	70–85	18	No	Yes
2148H	1024 x 4	45–55	18	No	Yes
2149H	1024 x 4	45–55	18	No	No
Motorola					
MCM2167	16,384 x 1	55–100	20	No	Yes
MCM4016	2,048 x 8	20–200	24	No	Yes
MCM6641	4,096 x 1	200–450	18	Yes	No
MCM6810	128 x 8	250–450	24	No	No
Intel					
2101A	256 x 6	250–450	22	No	No
2102A	1024 x 1	250–450	16	Yes	Yes
2111A	256 x 4	250–450	18	No	No
2112A	256 x 4	250–450	16	No	No
2141	1024 x 4	120–450	18	Yes	Yes
2142	1024 x 1	200–450	20	No	No

[1] A indicates an improved version with lower access times. In many cases, only the A version is now being manufactured.

[2] H stands for high speed.

usually cost more and, therefore, the additional cost has to be taken into consideration when a system is being designed. The trade-off is the cost and, possibly, the size of the power supply versus the cost of the memory chips.

15.5 STATIC NMOS RAM CELL

The two types of MOS static RAMs that are primarily used in μC systems are the NMOS and CMOS devices. An NMOS device is faster and costs less than a CMOS device. However, CMOS devices have the advantage of low power, and they are used in many portable μP-controlled instruments. The design of the basic memory cell is similar for both devices.

Figure 15–1 shows a basic NMOS memory cell. It is a static cell because it requires no additional clock signals to refresh the data. Q_1 and Q_2 are used as high-resistance loads. Q_3 and Q_4 form a flip-flop. Q_5 and Q_6 act as switches to allow the memory cell to be read from and written to. The circuit in Figure 15–1 shows only one address line, X. X and Y address lines will be discussed in Section 15.5.3.

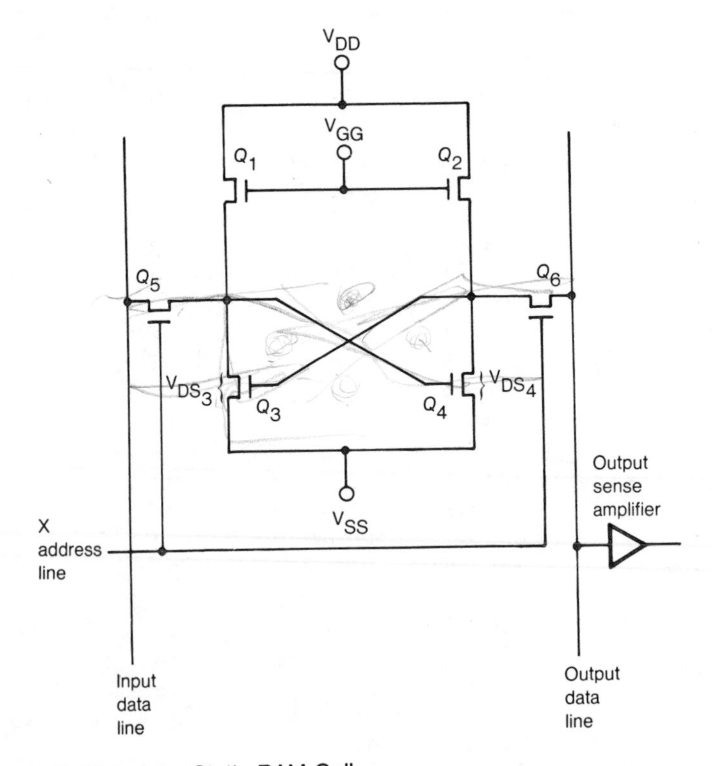

FIGURE 15–1 Six-Transistor Static RAM Cell

15.5.1 Circuit Operation

Voltage V_{DS_3} is the drain-to-source voltage of Q_3. It is also the gate-to-source voltage of Q_4 because of the cross-coupling nature of the flip-flop. Voltage V_{DS_4} is the drain-to-source voltage of Q_4 and is also the gate-to-source voltage of Q_3. If Q_3 is on—that is, if the drain-to-source of Q_3 is conducting current—then V_{DS_3} is very small. This low voltage causes Q_4 to be off. When Q_4 is off, its drain-to-source voltage is large, so that V_{DS_4} is approximately V_{DD}. The large voltage of V_{DS_4} keeps Q_3 on.

15.5.2 Switching Action

To change the state of the flip-flop, a positive signal is applied on the X address line and on the input line. This positive input signal increases V_{DS_3}. As V_{DS_3} increases, Q_4 begins to conduct, which in turn reduces V_{DS_4}. As V_{DS_4} decreases, the current to Q_3 decreases, thus increasing V_{DS_3} further. This process keeps repeating until Q_3 is cut off and Q_4 is conducting. Thus, the state of the flip-flop has changed, so that Q_3 is off and Q_4 is on.

If we want to change the state of the flip-flop back to Q_3 on and Q_4 off, the steps are as follows: (1) Bring the X address line high, and (2) bring the input data line low. The gate-to-source voltage of Q_4 will then be low, which cuts off Q_4. When Q_4 is off, Q_3 will conduct and will remain on. Although the circuit on Figure 15-1 shows the output data line to be the complement of the input data line, RAM cells have an additional inverter so that the input and output polarities are the same. A block diagram for this static memory cell is shown in Figure 15-2.

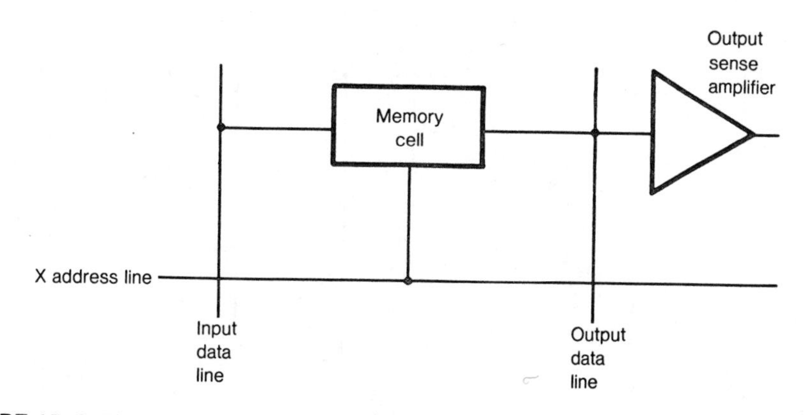

FIGURE 15-2 Block Diagram for Static Memory Cell

15.5.3 Memory Array

Figure 15-3 shows a 2 × 2 memory array using four of the memory cells of Figure 15-1. This circuit uses both X and Y address lines. The X address line chooses a particular row and the Y address line chooses a particular column of cells. A particular memory cell is chosen only when there is a logic 1 on both a row line and a column line. For example, if we want to address memory cell 1,1 then a logic 1 has to be placed on the X_1 line and on the Y_1 line. A logic 1 placed on the X_1 line addresses all of the memory cells of the first row. A logic 1 placed on the Y_1 line addresses all the memory cells of the first column. Remember, only one row line at a time can be a logic 1 and only one column line at a time can be a logic 1. When the Y_1 line is a logic 1, Q_A and Q_B conduct and all the data lines of the first column are connected to the drain of Q_{in}. The logic 1 on the Y_1 line also causes all of the output data lines of the first column of memory cells to be connected to the drain of Q_{out}.

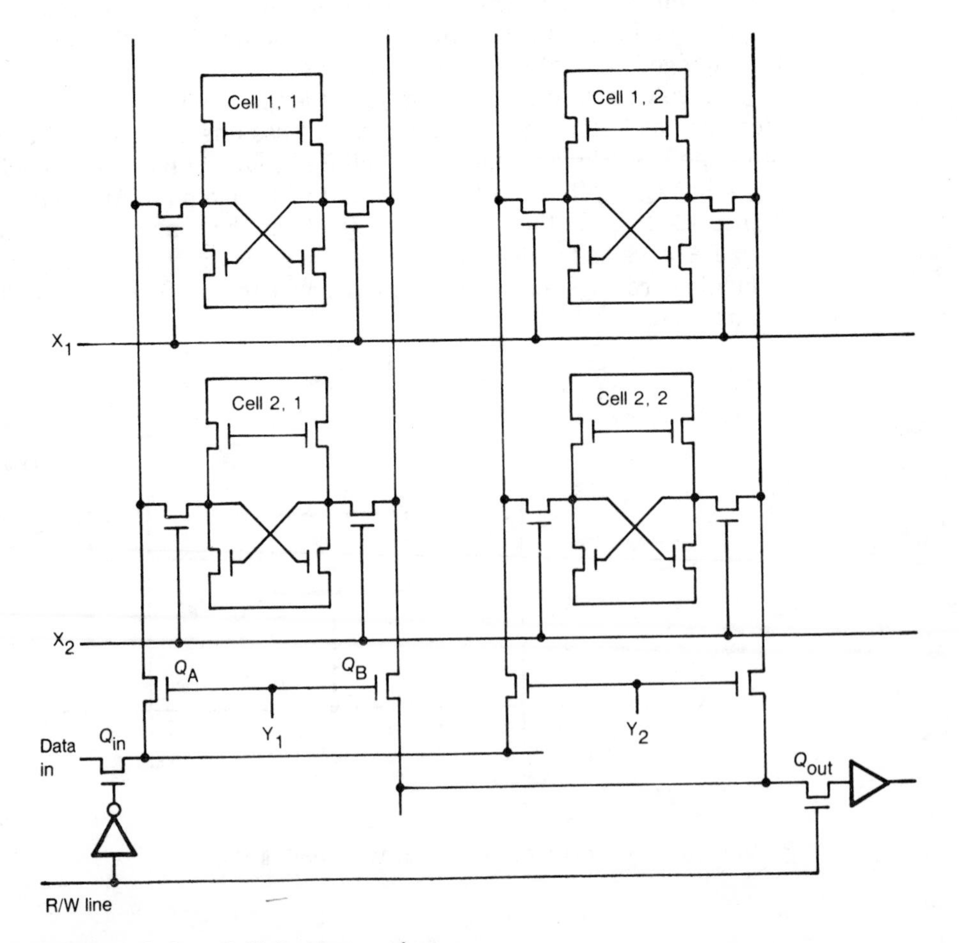

FIGURE 15-3 2 × 2 Static Memory Array

The read/write (R/W) line is used by the μP either to read data from a memory cell or to write data to a memory cell. If the R/W line is high, the μP is reading data from a memory cell. When this line is high, it causes Q_{in} to be off and Q_{out} to be on. In the circuit shown in Figure 15–3, the output data line contains the complemented logic state of the addressed memory cell. This complement can be corrected by another inverter at the output.

If the R/W line is low, the μP is writing data to a memory cell. When this line is low, it causes Q_{in} to be on and Q_{out} to be off. Now the logic level on the data input line is directed to the addressed cell.

The circuit of Figure 15–3 shows how each individual memory cell can be addressed by the μP. This is how a one-bit-wide static RAM device could be arranged. In static RAM devices that are organized as half-byte-wide (4 bits) or full-byte-wide (8 bits) devices, as shown in Figure 15–4, the Y address lines select four memory cells or eight memory cells at a time. Obviously, these devices have four or eight input and output lines, respectively. In Figure 15–4, each block contains four memory cells. When a particular row and column are selected, the four cells associated with that block are connected to the data lines. The logic level on the R/W line (not shown) determines whether data is being received or sent.

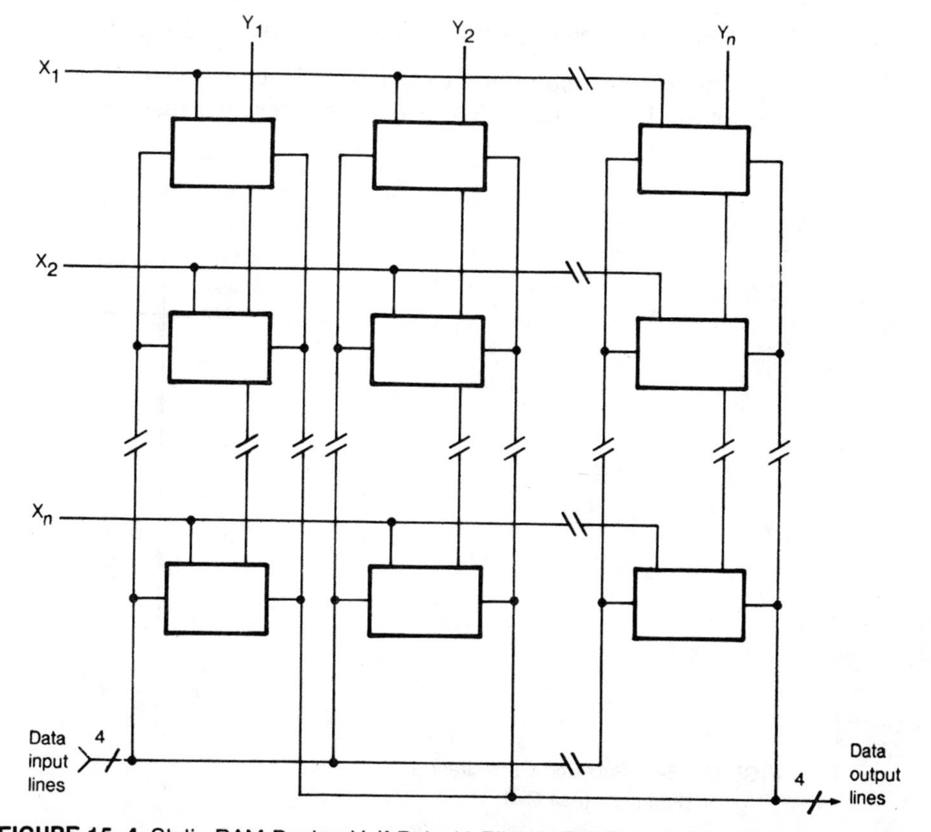

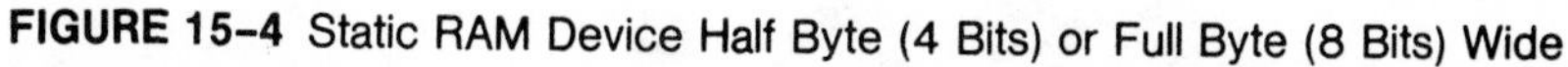

FIGURE 15–4 Static RAM Device Half Byte (4 Bits) or Full Byte (8 Bits) Wide

15.6 DYNAMIC RAMS

Dynamic RAMs store data as a charge on a capacitor instead of in a flip-flop, as in a static RAM. The capacitor is referred to as a *parasitic capacitor* because it is not a separate element but, rather, is the gate capacitance of a MOS transistor. Figure 15–5 is a diagram of a three-transistor RAM cell showing the parasitic capacitance (C_S) from gate to source (Q_2). In order to emphasize the presence of the parasitic capacitance, it is drawn as a separate element on circuit diagrams, as shown in Figure 15–5. As with any capacitor, this capacitor eventually loses its charge and therefore must be periodically refreshed. Most devices require every cell to be refreshed within 2 ms. Some dynamic RAMs, such as Texas Instruments' TMS 4164, can go as long as 4 ms without being refreshed. As previously mentioned, dynamic RAMs require additional circuitry to provide the refreshing, and this is a disadvantage. Much of the additional circuitry has been incorporated into either the RAM chip itself, or into the μP (not the 8080A, 6800, or 6502), or into a single IC controller chip. Therefore, dynamic RAMs are becoming easier to use. Remember, the advantages of dynamic RAMs over static RAMs are as follows:

1. More bits per device (denser packaging),
2. Less cost per bit,
3. Less power consumed per bit, both active and standby.

The reason manufacturers can fabricate dynamic RAMs with more bits per IC is that these RAMs require fewer transistors per cell than do

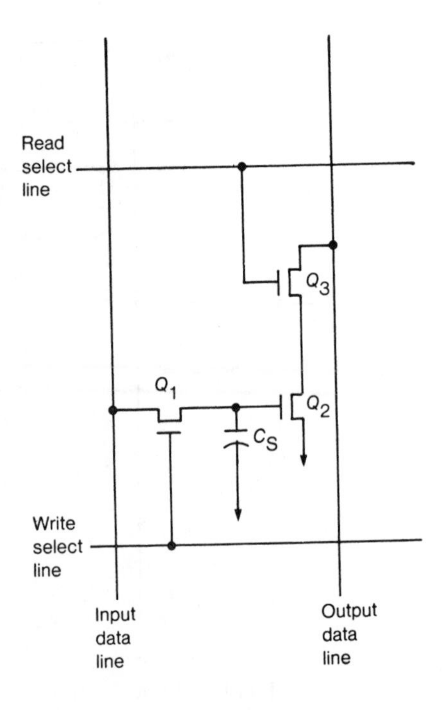

FIGURE 15–5 Parasitic Capacitance (C_S) for Dynamic RAM Cell

static RAMs; therefore, they are less expensive to make and consume less power per bit.

15.6.1 Cell Design

Dynamic cell designs, like other devices, have changed over the past few years. Earlier dynamic RAMs used three transistors per memory cell, although some manufacturers did experiment with four transistors per cell in a configuration similar to a static RAM cell. To increase package density, all of the newest dynamic RAMs now use a single transistor per cell. These devices include the 16,384 × 1, 32,768 × 1, and 65,536 × 1 memory chips. The break between the three-transistor and single-transistor devices occurred in the 4096 × 1 device. Some 4K devices use three transistors, while others are designed with a single transistor. Three-transistor cells tend to be more temperature stable and need less internal sense circuitry. Single-transistor cells allow more bits to be packaged in the same area.

15.6.2 Three-Transistor Dynamic Memory Cell

The circuit in Figure 15–6 shows a three-transistor dynamic memory cell. It requires two select lines (read and write) and two data lines (input and output). This is the basic storage cell used in the 1103 dynamic RAM. The device was first introduced in 1970 and was instrumental in the increased use of semiconductor memory rather than core memories.

Write Operation

Data is written into the three-transistor cell by the following steps (refer to Figure 15–6):

1. Data is put onto the input data line.
2. The write select line is brought to a logic 1, turning Q_1 on.
3. C_S charges or discharges to the logic level on the data line.
4. After sufficient time (~115 ns) to allow C_S to charge or discharge, the write select line can go low to turn off Q_1.

Note: The 115 ns in step 4 is not the total cycle time but rather is the minimum time the data has to be stable. The total access time has to be greater than 580 ns.

Read Operation

Data is read from the three-transistor cell by the following steps (refer to Figure 15–6):

1. The precharge transistor, Q_P, is turned on by a signal ϕ_P. This is called a precharge signal.
2. The reference capacitor, C_R, is charged to a logic 1 when Q_P is turned on.
3. The precharge signal is removed, causing Q_P to turn off and C_R to remain charged.

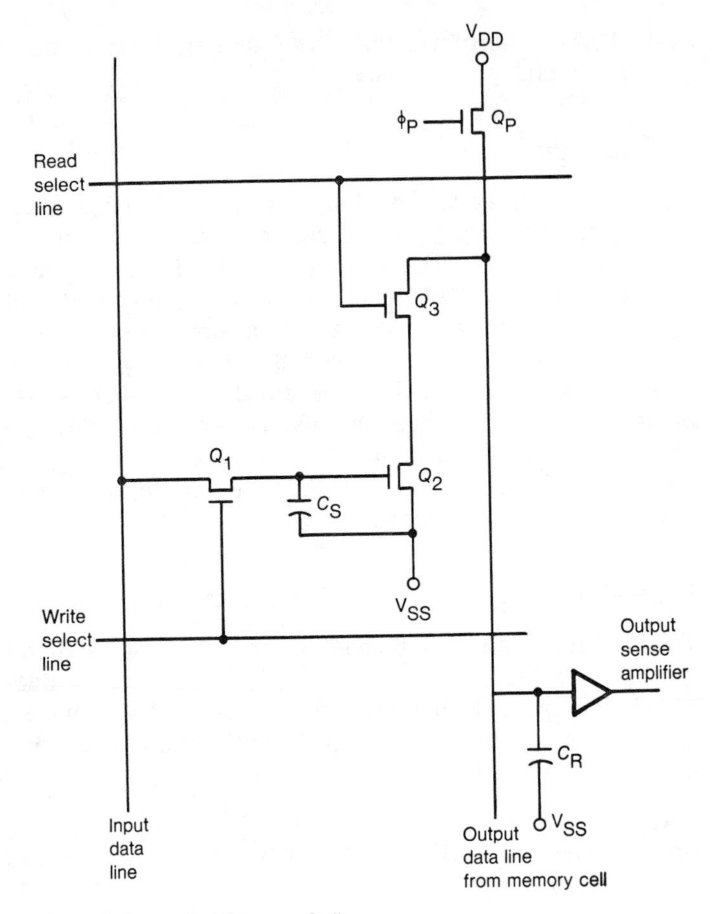

FIGURE 15–6 1103 Dynamic Memory Cell

4. The read select line goes to a logic 1, which turns Q_3 on.
5. Capacitor C_R remains charged or discharges, depending on the logic level on C_S: If C_S is at a logic 0, then Q_2 remains off and C_R cannot discharge. If C_S is at a logic 1, then Q_2 is turned on and C_R can discharge through Q_2 and Q_3.
6. The sense amplifier reads the logic state of C_R, which is the complement of C_S. The data output line of the 1103 is complemented.

Refresh Operation

The charge on C_S is refreshed by a modified read and write operation. Each cell in a row is refreshed at the same time, as shown in Figure 15–7. The steps for refreshing are as follows:

1. The precharge transistor, Q_P, is turned on and capacitor C_R is initially charged. Then Q_P is turned off.
2. The read select line is brought to a logic 1 and Q_3 is turned on. Capacitor C_R can remain charged or can discharge in the same manner as in the read operation, step 5. The read select line is turned off.

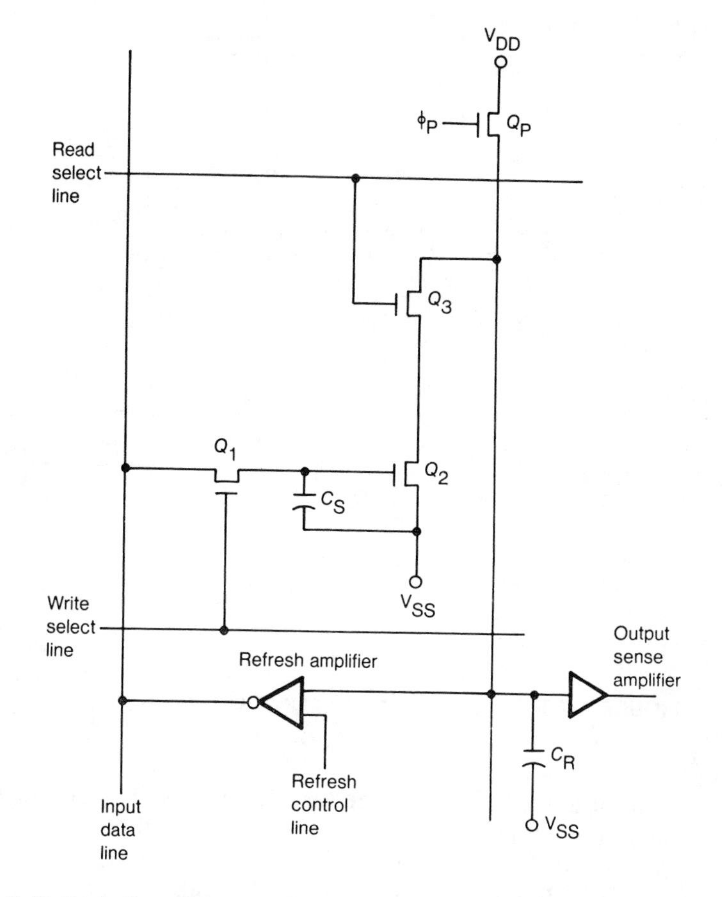

FIGURE 15–7 Refresh Operation

3. The control line on the refresh amplifier is activated.
4. The logic level on C_R is the input to the refresh amplifier.
5. The refresh amplifier inverts the signal and puts it onto the input data line.
6. The write select line is activated and the storage capacitor, C_S, is refreshed.

Steps 1–6 would take place even if C_S initially had no charge on it. This procedure would guarantee that C_S remained uncharged and that no stray charge "leaked" onto it. The refresh amplifier is a sense amplifier with an inverter.

15.6.3 Single-Transistor Dynamic Memory Cell

In order to fabricate more dynamic memory cells on a substrate, manufacturers have turned to the single-transistor memory cell, which is shown in Figure 15–8. Transistor Q_1 acts as a switch so that data can be read from or

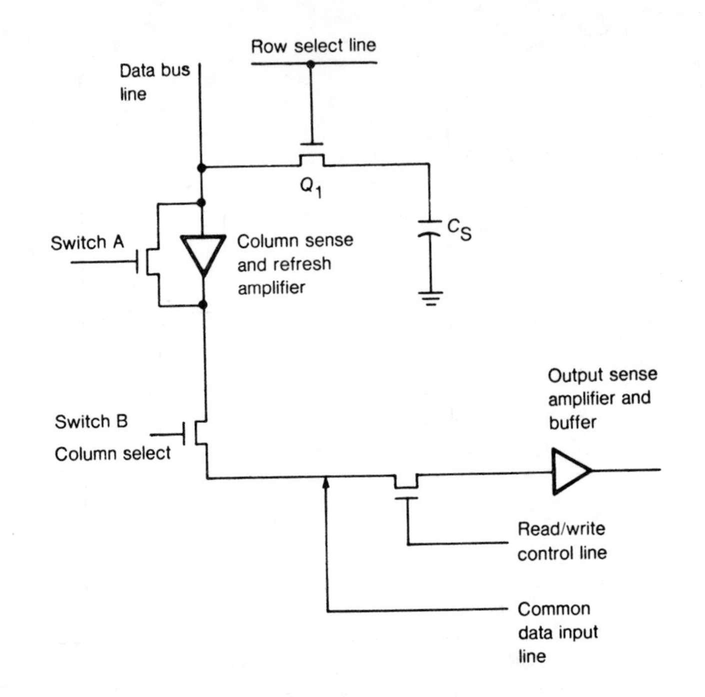

FIGURE 15–8 Single-Transistor Memory Cell

written to the storage capacitor, C_S. The row select line is used for both reading and writing. The data line is used for both reading data and writing data. The cell shown in Figure 15–8 requires additional internal circuitry to direct the input signal to C_S and to sense the voltage on C_S.

Write Operation

The following steps are used to write data into the single-transistor cell:

1. The row select line is brought to a logic 1, turning Q_1 on.
2. Switches A and B are turned on.
3. The logic level on the data line either charges or discharges the storage capacitor, C_S.
4. Switches A and B and the row select line are returned to a logic 0, turning off switches A and B and Q_1, allowing C_S to hold the data.

Read Operation

The steps involved in reading data from the single-transistor cell are as follows:

1. The row select line is brought to a logic 1, to turn on Q_1 and to put the charge held by C_S on the data line.
2. Switches A and B are put into the read and data output positions, respectively.
3. The sense amplifier senses the signal placed on the data line by C_S,

amplifies the signal so that the output is at a "clean" logic 1 or logic 0 state, sends the amplified signal to the memory's output amplifier and buffers, and returns the amplified signal to the data line so as to recharge or discharge C_S to its initial logic state.

4. Switches A and B are returned to their off state and Q_1 is turned off.

Refresh Operation

The refresh operation is similar to the read operation. The steps are as follows:

1. The row select line is brought to a logic 1 and the charge on C_S is placed on the data line.
2. Switch A is placed in the read position; switch B is left in the off position.
3. The sense amplifier works in the same way as in the read operation, step 3.

There are several ways of doing the refresh operation. In some cases, the output buffers are left open in their high impedance state; in other cases they are not, and the data appears on the output lines. There is one sense amplifier per column and each memory cell in a row is refreshed at the same time. Therefore, if a dynamic memory has 128 rows, then refreshing requires 128 refresh cycles. There are some exceptions to this rule because some memory chips allow two rows to be refreshed at the same time. In this case, only 64 refresh cycles would be required.

15.6.4 Need for Sense/Rewrite Amplifier

Unlike the three-transistor dynamic memory cell, the single-transistor cell is a destructive memory cell. This means that the charge on C_S is partially lost during a read operation. For this reason, the data must be rewritten into the cell on every read operation. Let's examine why.

Figure 15–9 illustrates why the sense/rewrite amplifier is needed. Every memory cell in a column is connected to the same data line; this adds capacitance to the line. In fact, the line capacitance, C_L, in Figure 15–9, may be 10 to 20 times the capacitance of a single storage cell. When the transistor Q_1 is turned on, there is a voltage division between C_L and C_S and a loss of charge on C_S. Voltage V_i is reduced. Therefore, the sense/rewrite amplifier does not receive all of the voltage that was on C_S and any loss of charge must be replaced.

The voltage received by the sense/rewrite amplifier is given by the voltage division law for capacitors:

$$V_{S/R} = \left(\frac{C_S}{C_S + C_L}\right) V_i \qquad (15\text{–}1)$$

where

$V_{S/R}$ = Input voltage to sense/rewrite amplifier
C_S = Value of storage capacitance
C_L = Value of data line capacitance
V_i = Initial voltage on C_S

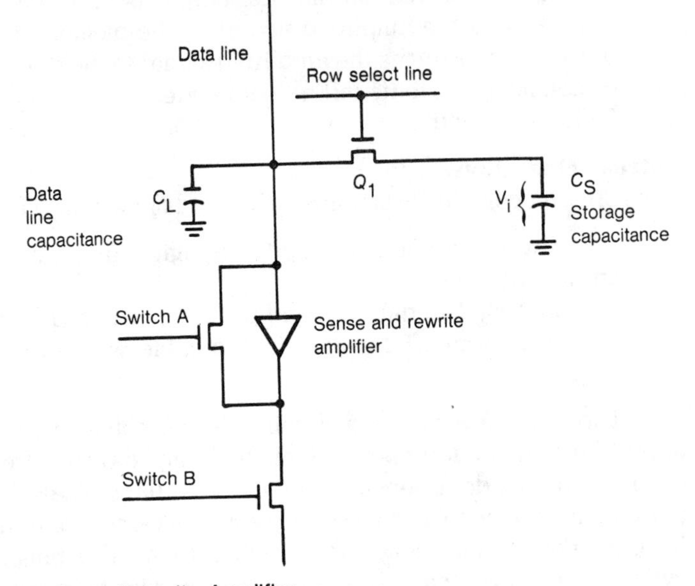

FIGURE 15–9 Sense/Rewrite Amplifier

EXAMPLE 15.1 Some typical values of voltage and capacitance are $C_S = 0.05$ pF, $C_L = 1.0$ pF, and $V_i = 10$ V. Calculate the input voltage to the sense/rewrite amplifier.

Solution Applying Equation 15–1 yields

$$V_{S/R} = \frac{0.05 \text{ pF}}{0.05 \text{ pF} + 1.0 \text{ pF}} \times 10 \text{ V}$$

$$\cong \frac{1}{20} \times 10 \text{ V}$$

$$= 500 \text{ mV}$$

The voltage $V_i = 10$ V indicates that the capacitor C_S is initially charged to a logic 1. A logic 0 would be stored as 0 V. In this example, the amplifier must be capable of detecting 500 mV as a logic 1. (Most dynamic memory devices use amplifiers that are capable of detecting at least 200 mV as a logic 1.) The amplifier amplifies the 500 mV back to 10 V and reapplies it to the data line, thereby recharging C_S.

15.6.5 Charge on C_S

The equation for capacitance in terms of charge, Q, and voltage, V, is as follows:

$$C = \frac{Q}{V} \tag{15–2}$$

When the storage cell's capacitance is initially charged to a voltage V_i, then the charge stored on the plates of C_S is given by Equation 15-3:

$$Q_i = C_S \times V_i \qquad (15\text{-}3)$$

When the cell is being read, V_i changes to $V_{S/R}$, a final voltage, and the charge on C_S at this time is given by Equation 15-4:

$$Q_f = C_S \times V_{S/R} \qquad (15\text{-}4)$$

Q_f and $V_{S/R}$ represent the charge and voltage, respectively, on C_S before it is recharged by the sense/rewrite amplifier during a read operation.

EXAMPLE 15.2 Using the values in Example 15.1, calculate Q_i and Q_f.

Solution From Example 15.1, $C_S = 0.05$ pF, $V_i = 10$ V and $V_f = 500$ mV. Therefore:

$$Q_i = 0.05 \text{ pF} \times 10 \text{ V} = 500 \times 10^{-15} \text{ coulombs}$$

and

$$Q_f = 0.05 \text{ pF} \times 500 \text{ mV} = 25 \times 10^{-15} \text{ coulombs}$$

Example 15.1 has C_S storing a logic 1 represented by $V_i = 10$ V. If C_S had stored a logic 0, then V_i would be 0 V and Q_i and Q_f would be 0. This is actually the ideal case, because some charge could "leak" onto C_S and therefore Q_i would not be 0. Even if C_S were an ideal capacitor and Q_i were 0, Q_f would not be 0 because of the presence of noise on the data line. For these reasons, sense/rewrite operation is needed to ensure that a logic 0 remains stored in the memory cell.

15.7 NONVOLATILE MEMORIES

As previously mentioned, semiconductor RAMs (either static or dynamic) are volatile memories—the programs and data are lost when the power is turned off. There are many applications, however, when it is necessary to save information in a nonvolatile memory after power is turned off. A semiconductor device is needed so that it can be mounted on a PC board. The nonvolatile memory should also have fast access time and enough bits to store a program of reasonable size (at least 1K words). Obviously, we do not want to go back to large and bulky core memories, and disk or magnetic tape systems are impractical and too expensive for many applications such as consumer products—microwave ovens, dishwashers, games, and so on. Even in systems in which general-purpose programs are entered through a keyboard or from disks or tapes, there is a program stored in the computer that allows the user to enter a program and operate the system.

Hence, there is a need to provide nonvolatile memory storage for μCs.

Although magnetic disks and tapes are nonvolatile storage, here we will consider only nonvolatile semiconductor memories. There are six types of nonvolatile semiconductor memories that are often used with μPs:

1. ROM, maskable read-only memory;
2. PROM, programmable read-only memory;
3. EPROM, erasable (using ultraviolet light) and reprogrammable read-only memory, sometimes referred to as UV PROM;
4. EEROM, electrically erasable read-only memory, also abbreviated as E^2ROM, and sometimes referred to as EAROM (electrically alterable read-only memory);
5. Battery back-up for RAM devices;
6. MBM, magnetic bubble memory.

No one μC system uses all of the memory methods. The first five are used most often. Magnetic bubble memories are being used more often now, but they are still few and far between. Let's concentrate on the first four devices.

15.7.1 ROM

A read-only memory, ROM, chip is permanently programmed at the factory by the semiconductor manufacturer. This IC device is sometimes referred to as a maskable ROM to distinguish its programming method from that of other ROM chips. In the last (or last two) manufacturing step, the binary pattern is entered by a technique called *masking*. Usually manufacturers will make ROMs only in lots of hundreds, thousands, or tens of thousands. Obviously, ROMs are used in high-volume products such as microwave ovens, games, and so forth. The program sent to the ROM manufacturer must be correct. Otherwise, the factory will produce hundreds or thousands of worthless devices. There is a method of working around errors that exist in a maskable ROM chip. The technique is called *patching*. However, this method requires another chip, and the system has to have been designed to take the additional chip. Most consumer products are not designed with this additional flexibility. Therefore, in most cases, ROMs that have an error are worthless devices. Although the cost of an error in a ROM chip is high, the cost of the ROM chip on a per-bit basis is the lowest of all the permanent memory chips.

15.7.2 PROM

ROM chips are not suitable for many μC applications. Instead, μC users usually need a nonvolatile storage device that satisfies one or more of the following criteria:

1. A piece of equipment that is not designed for high-volume production;
2. A nonvolatile memory chip with the same pin configuration as ROM, to use until ROM chips are delivered;
3. A nonvolatile memory chip that can be programmed in the field or laboratory for last-minute design modifications.

Semiconductor manufacturers have responded to these demands with the programmable read-only memory, PROM. These devices can be programmed only once. They are designed with fusible links that can be "blown" or not, depending on the binary pattern of the program. New PROMs, with all the fuses intact, are called clean PROMs.

In order to "burn" or blow the fusible links to enter the program into a PROM, the user needs a PROM programmer (a piece of equipment, not a person). Commercially available PROM programmers are easy to use because they are complete packages containing socket(s), power supply, additional working memory (buffer memory), serial or parallel keyboard interface, hex keyboard, seven-segment display readout of address and data, and, most important of all, the correct voltage levels and proper timing pulses.

Like ROMs, there is no margin for error in the use of PROMs. Once a fusible link has been blown, it cannot be changed. Therefore, once a PROM is programmed, it cannot be reprogrammed, and it is essential to be sure the program is correct before a PROM is programmed. An error is not as costly, however, as it is with a ROM device. An error wastes only one PROM, not hundreds or thousands of them. The cost per bit of a PROM is more than the cost per bit of a ROM, but in many cases it is well worth the extra money.

15.7.3 EPROM

Both the ROM and PROM chips can only be programmed once. During design development stages, and in some low-volume production of μC applications, designers need a memory device in which the program can be erased and the device can then be reprogrammed. Two devices are presently being marketed that are reprogrammable nonvolatile memories: the erasable programmable read-only memory, EPROM, and the electrically erasable programmable read-only memory, EEPROM or E^2PROM. This section introduces the EPROM and Section 15.7.4 covers the EEPROM.

The reprogrammable memory device most often used today is the EPROM or UV PROM. Like the PROM, EPROMs are usually programmed using a PROM programmer. The EPROMS are erased by placing them under an ultraviolet lamp (hence UV PROM) for a specified amount of time. Typically, erasure times are from 15 minutes to one hour.

The major advantage of EPROMs is that they can be erased and reprogrammed. Other advantages are that these devices operate from a single + 5 V power supply. This is not the programming voltage, but the operating voltage in the μC system. Many manufacturers have a ROM chip that is pin compatible with the EPROM. Therefore, when a design is finalized and it is going to be used in a large volume item, a ROM chip can be ordered and inserted into the same printed circuit board without any modifications.

Disadvantages of the EPROM are the following:

1. They have to be removed from the circuit to be erased.
2. They require a long time for erasure.
3. They have a limited life cycle (100 to 1000 erasures and reprogrammings).
4. The entire device is erased (block erasure), not just an individual byte.

There are some development systems that place the erasure unit on the PC board so that the EPROM does not have to be removed for erasure. There are not many of these systems, however, because the entire system has to be stopped while the EPROM is erased. Therefore, most development is done by using a zero insertion socket in the PC board and inserting and removing the EPROM when necessary. When a programming bug(s) is to be corrected, the EPROM is removed and placed under the ultraviolet lamp, and a blank EPROM is programmed using a PROM programmer (usually requiring 1 to 2 minutes) and inserted into the PC board socket. The new program can be tested while the old EPROM is being erased. Therefore, a separate erasure unit, PROM programmer, and extra EPROMs are the quickest and most convenient method of using EPROMS.

15.7.4 EEPROM

The electrically erasable programmable read-only memory, EEPROM or E^2PROM, is a nonvolatile reprogrammable memory chip. This device is sometimes referred to as an electrically alterable read-only memory, EAROM. The EAROM is actually an older version, and the way each cell is made is different from the way the cells are made in the EEPROM. Most manufacturers refer only to EEPROMS.

Like the PROM and EPROM, the EEPROM is purchased blank and is programmed by the user. Remember that PROMs cannot be erased, but EPROMS can be erased by using an ultraviolet lamp. EEPROMs are erased and programmed using an electrical pulse. This feature allows both erasing and programming to be done right on the PC board without removing the EEPROM.

Some EEPROMs have only block erasure (all bits are cleared), while others allow the user to erase one byte at a time. Byte erasure is a convenient feature because usually the user only needs to change one byte or at most a few bytes at a time when debugging a program. Devices that can be debugged on a per-byte basis are usually slower than block erasure devices.

Although the operating voltage for these devices is + 5 V, the erasing and programming voltage is usually + 17 V to + 20 V. To leave the EEPROM in the circuit and have the μP do the erasing and programming, additional support logic is required as well as the + 17 V to + 20 V.

Although binary patterns can be written into EEPROMs by the μP using the additional circuitry, EEPROMs are not intended to be used as read/write memories, but rather they are intended to be used as read mostly memory (RMM). Manufacturers' specifications list the data retention time as between 10 and 20 years. The more often these devices are erased and reprogrammed, the shorter their lifespan becomes. Most users probably do not have to worry about this problem, however, because many EEPROMs can be programmed tens of thousands of times without any deterioration.

15.8 NONVOLATILE MEMORY DEVICES IN SYSTEM DEVELOPMENT

Before a program is finalized and ready to be placed in a μC system, it has gone through a number of programming and reprogramming steps to get all of the bugs out of it. If the final program is to be stored in a PROM or ROM chip, it has usually gone through several stages using the different nonvolatile memory chips. Most μP programs are designed by the use of a RAM-to-ROM procedure. This is a multistep procedure resulting in a finalized program. First, the program is entered into RAM, where it is run, tested, and debugged. This step may take weeks or even months. After the programmer is satisfied that the program and the system are operating correctly, the program can be transferred to an EEPROM. Since this chip is a nonvolatile memory, the system may be turned off and on at different times to see if it responds as it should. If any additional errors are found or if other program modifications have to be made, they can be made on the EEPROM almost as easily as on the RAM chips. The next step after the EEPROM would be an EPROM. Using a PROM programmer, the designer could insert the chip into the final PC board. Last-minute modifications can still be made by removing the EPROM, erasing it, and reprogramming it. When all of the bugs are removed and the system is operating correctly, the program is ready to be burned into a PROM chip for low-volume applications or into a ROM chip for high-volume applications.

Users of ROM chips have to plan for the semiconductor manufacturer's turn-around time. That is, the time between when the manufacturer receives a program and when the user receives the ROM chips has to be included in the schedule for design development. In most cases, 4 to 6 weeks should be allowed for delivery. While the user is waiting for the ROM chips, many manufacturers will begin shipping products containing PROM chips.

15.9 MEMORY SPEED

Most 8-bit μPs operate on frequencies between 1 MHz and 2 MHz. This means the μP's clock cycle time is from 500 ns to 1 μs. So that the μP does not wait for data coming from memory, the memory chip should be fast enough to respond to the μP. This means we have to consider the memory chip's access time and cycle time.

Access time is the time interval between the instant at which the memory chip receives a valid address and the instant at which the output data is valid. For writing data into a memory chip, access time is the time between the instant at which the memory chip receives a valid address and the instant at which the storage is completed. In fully static ROMs, PROMs, EPROMs, and RAMs, the access time and the cycle time are equal. In dynamic RAMs and in some dynamic ROMs, cycle time and access time are not the same.

Cycle time is the time required to complete an entire memory cycle. It includes the access time, regeneration time, and any additional time until the memory chip can receive the next address. Many dynamic RAMs have destructive readouts—that is, when the data is read out, it is also destroyed. Therefore, the chip must regenerate or refresh the storage cell. Refreshing takes additional time, and this added time is why the cycle time is not equal to the access time.

Some ROM chips are fully static, while others are edge enabled. In the fully static ROM, access time and cycle time are the same. In the edge-enabled ROM, additional time is needed to precharge the support circuitry. The advantage of these devices is that they consume less power when the chip is not selected. The disadvantage, however, is that the chip enable line must go to the high state and then back to the low state every time a new address is selected.

15.10 ALLOWING ENOUGH TIME FOR DATA TO BE RECEIVED

First-time users of a μP may think that only the access time or cycle time of the memory chip must be considered to have the μP receive valid data from memory. Let's look at an example in which the access time and the cycle time each is equal to 450 ns, a typical access time for a static RAM. In Figure 15–10,

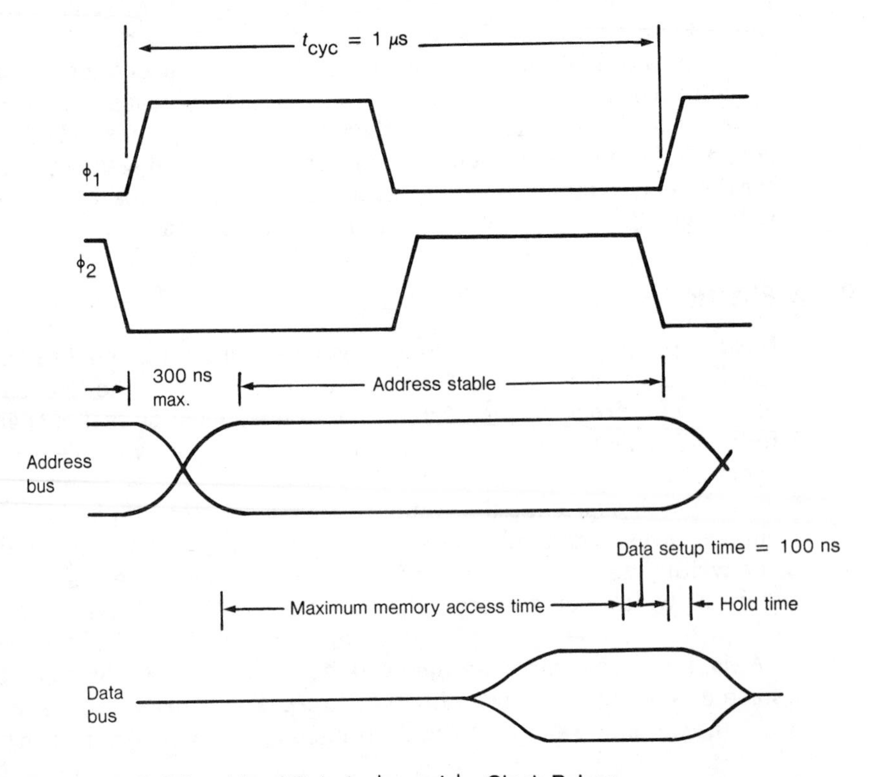

FIGURE 15–10 Relationship of Data to ϕ_1 and ϕ_2 Clock Pulses

typical ϕ_1 and ϕ_2 clock cycles are shown for either the 6800 μP or the 6502 μP operating at 1 MHz. The cycle time is 1 μs. The μP manufacturer guarantees that 300 ns after the ϕ_1 clock signal goes high the address on the address bus is valid. Therefore, for the worst possible case, 300 ns could be wasted while the μP places a valid address on the address bus. Let's consider negligible time for the memory chip to receive this valid address. If the memory chip's access time is 450 ns, then a total of 750 ns (300 ns + 450 ns) is the time used before the data is valid on the data bus. This leaves 250 ns for the μP to receive the data, which is plenty of time. See Figure 15–10.

If the μP's clock frequency is changed to 2 MHz (this corresponds to the μP's cycle time of 500 ns), let's see what could happen. The manufacturer states that the address from the μP is valid 150 ns after the ϕ_1 clock signal goes high. Although this time has been reduced from 300 ns to 150 ns, the memory chip's access time has not been reduced; it is still 450 ns. Therefore, the total time is 600 ns (150 ns + 450 ns). This means that the μP has entered the next cycle before the memory has been able to respond. If the μP has not been placed in a wait state, it will never receive valid data and the system will never work. We see, then, that running the μP at a faster frequency without considering the access and cycle times of the memory chips will lead to disaster.

15.11 SUMMARY

All computers require memory to store programs and data. In this chapter, we examined the different classifications of memories: (1) semiconductor versus magnetic, (2) volatile versus nonvolatile, and (3) serial versus random.

Two of the most commonly used semiconductor memories in μC systems are RAMs and ROMs. RAM devices are either static or dynamic. Static devices are easier to use and are faster. However, dynamic RAMs can be manufactured with greater density. The disadvantage most often cited for dynamic RAMs is the need for periodic refreshing of the individual bits. Section 15.6 shows different cell designs that are used for dynamic RAMs. Nonvolatile memories that are found in μC systems are ROMs, PROMs, and EPROMs, and EEPROMs.

Regardless of the type of memory chip used, access time or cycle time must be considered when a system is designed. This is to ensure that the μP receives or sends data to the right memory location. Section 15.10 discusses the factors that must be considered when memory chips are added to a μC system. The next chapter focuses on how these memory chips are interconnected to form a workable memory system.

PROBLEMS

15–1 What is the primary function of memories?
15–2 List the different classifications of memories.
15–3 What are the principle semiconductor technologies used for memory devices?
15–4 Define (a) volatile memory and (b) nonvolatile memory.

15–5 Is a volatile memory device a temporary or a permanent memory?

15–6 In most applications, are serial access memory devices faster or slower than random access memories?

15–7 What are the two ways the term *random access* is used?

15–8 Is the data in a ROM chip accessed as a random memory?

15–9 What is the fastest type of semiconductor technology?

15–10 What is the advantage of CMOS memory devices?

15–11 What are the two types of random access memories?

15–12 What is the principle storage element for (a) static memories and (b) dynamic memories?

15–13 List the advantages of static RAMs over dynamic RAMs.

15–14 Refer to Figure 15–1 and consider that Q_3 is on and Q_4 is off. What steps are required to switch the state of the memory cell?

15–15 Refer to Figure 15–3 and consider that memory cell 2,2 is to store a logic 0. What steps are required?

15–16 What is the name of the capacitor in a dynamic memory cell?

15–17 What are the advantages of dynamic RAMs?

15–18 Does the capacitor in a dynamic cell have to have a refresh signal to maintain a logic 0? Explain your answer.

15–19 List six types of nonvolatile memories.

15–20 What are some applications for maskable ROM chips?

15–21 Are PROM devices reusable?

15–22 What is the difference between erasing an EPROM chip and erasing an EEPROM chip?

15–23 Do EPROMs have block erasure or byte erasure?

15–24 Define access time.

Memory Chips and Organization

16.0 INTRODUCTION

Chapter 15 dealt with the different types of memories that are available. In this chapter, we will look at some of the more commonly used memory chips and see how they are connected to the μP. Although a designer may choose a specific μP, such as an 8080A, a 6800, or a 6502, the choice of a memory is more general because memory chips from one manufacturer usually can be used with any μP. Some semiconductor manufacturers specialize in making only memory chips.

One of the first decisions that must be made concerns the number of bytes of temporary and permanent memory that are to be included. Then, a decision on the type of temporary memory—static or dynamic—and on the type of permanent memory—ROM, PROM, EPROM, or EEPROM—must be made. In this chapter, we will see how to connect static RAMs, dynamic RAMs, and EPROMs into a system. These three devices cover a wide range of applications.

16.1 2114 STATIC RAM

The 2114 static RAM and its low-power version, the 21L14, are read/write memory devices that are often used. Both devices are housed in an 18-pin dual-in-line package and both have the same pin designations. The pin designations are shown in Figure 16-1. The device requires only + 5 V. It contains 4096 static memory cells organized as 1024 words × 4 bits. Therefore, two packages are required for 1K of memory in an 8-bit μC system. All lines are TTL compatible, which simplifies the interconnections. Besides the low-power version, this device can also be purchased with different maximum access times (200 ns, 250 ns, 300 ns, and 450 ns). Sections 16.1.1 and 16.1.2 show how to wire this memory chip to a μP.

Figure 16–1 shows that this device has 10 address lines, labeled A_0 to A_9. These lines allow the μP to address any one of 1024 words ($2^{10} = 1024$). The I/O lines are connected to the data bus so that the μP can read and write data. The write enable ($\overline{W}$) line is connected to the μC system's read/write line. As will be shown in Section 16.3, the system read/write line is derived from the μP's R/W line.

16.1.1 1K of Memory Using the 2114

Figure 16–2 shows how two 2114 packages can be arranged for 1K × 8 bits of memory. The address lines are connected either directly to the μP or through address buffers to the μP. In either case, the address lines are labeled to correspond to the μP terminology. Line A_0 eventually goes back to pin A_0 on the μP, line A_1 to pin A_1 on the μP, and so forth.

The connections to the data bus are not quite as straightforward as they are for the address bus. One package is chosen to hold the least significant four bits of data and the other package to hold the most significant four bits. In Figure 16–2, the package on the right contains the least significant four bits and is wired to data bus lines D_0 to D_3. The package on the left is wired to data bus lines D_4 to D_7 and contains the most significant four bits. Each 2114 package contains four data input/output lines, labeled I/O_1 to I/O_4. When the memory chip is being wired to the data bus, the I/O_1 pin must be connected to the data bus line with the lowest number in the group of four. Pin I/O_4 must be connected to the data bus line with the highest number in the group of four. Figure 16–2 shows to which data bus line each I/O pin must be connected.

The $\overline{W}$ pin is the read/write enable pin. When the logic level on this line is high, the μP is reading (receiving) data from the memory chips. When the $\overline{W}$

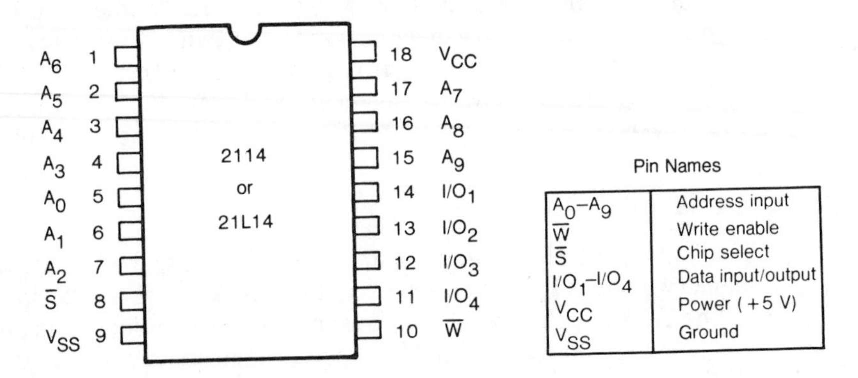

FIGURE 16–1 Pin Designations for 2114 or 21L14 Static RAM

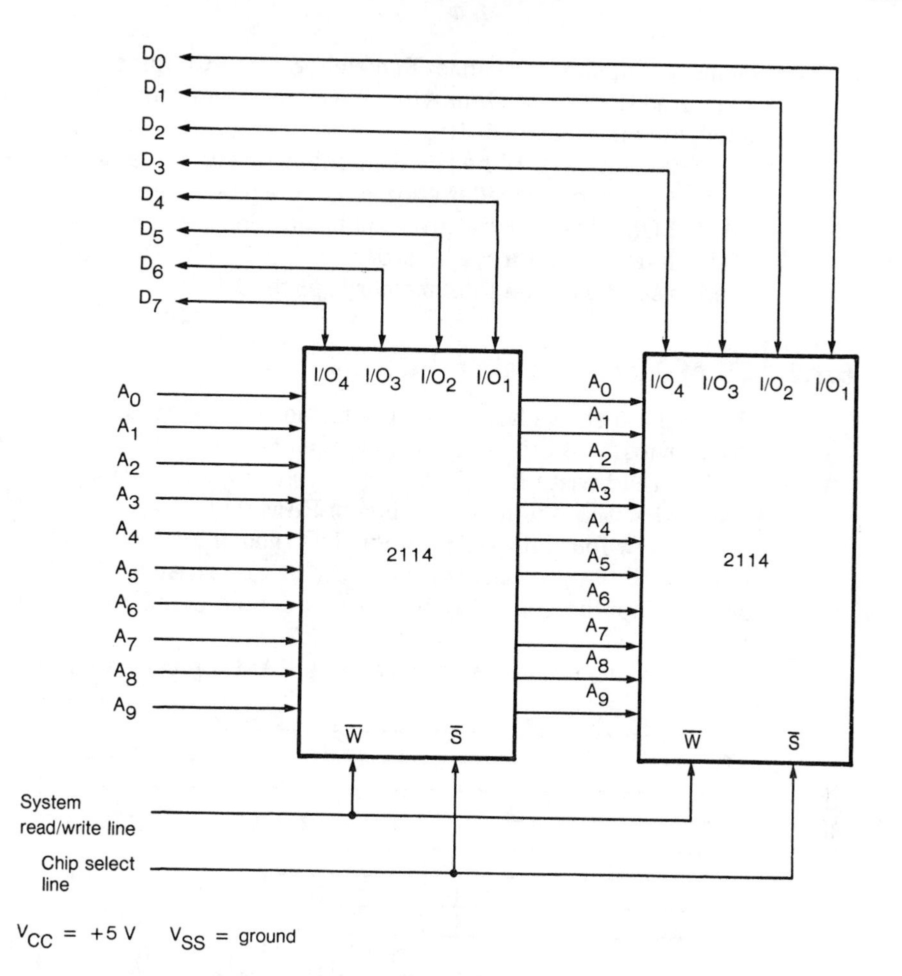

FIGURE 16–2 Two 2114 Packages for 1K of Memory

line goes low, the μP is writing (sending) data to memory. This line must be held high until the address information is stable so as to prevent the μP from erroneously writing data to a memory location. Section 16.3 shows the necessary circuitry needed between the μP and the $\overline{W}$ pin to prevent false data from reaching the memory chips.

The chip select pin ($\overline{S}$) enables or disables the I/O pin circuitry. When the chip select line goes high, the I/O pins are in their high impedance state. When this line goes low, the I/O circuitry is enabled either as input latches or as output buffers. Which condition exists depends on the logic level on the read/write line. If the R/W line is low, the input latches are enabled and the memory chips will trap the data on the data bus at the falling edge of the ϕ_2 clock cycle. When the $\overline{S}$ line is low and the R/W line is high, the memory chip's output buffers are enabled. The memory chips will put the data on the data bus at the end of the memory chips' access time. Remember, from Chapter 15, that access time is measured from the instant when the memory chip receives a stable address, as illustrated in Figure 15–10.

The chip select line is wired either directly to a μP address line, such as A_{14} or A_{15}, or to a decoder chip. Since the 64K of memory are divided between RAM, ROM, I/O, and future expansion, decoder chips are used much more often than a μP address line. Section 16.4 shows how decoder chips can be used to subdivide the total memory space.

16.1.2 2K of Memory Using the 2114

Figure 16–3 shows how four 2114 memory chips can be interconnected to yield 2048 bytes × 8 bits of RAM memory. The ten address lines (A_0–A_9) and the system read/write line (R/W) are wired to each memory chip. The chips are grouped so that the high four bits of RAM 0 and RAM 1 are next to each other and the low four bits are together. The reason for this is so that the printed circuit board can be laid out with few or no crossovers on the data bus lines. Microcomputer boards normally are double sided and many are multilayer boards.

The two packages that make up RAM 0 must be wired so they have the

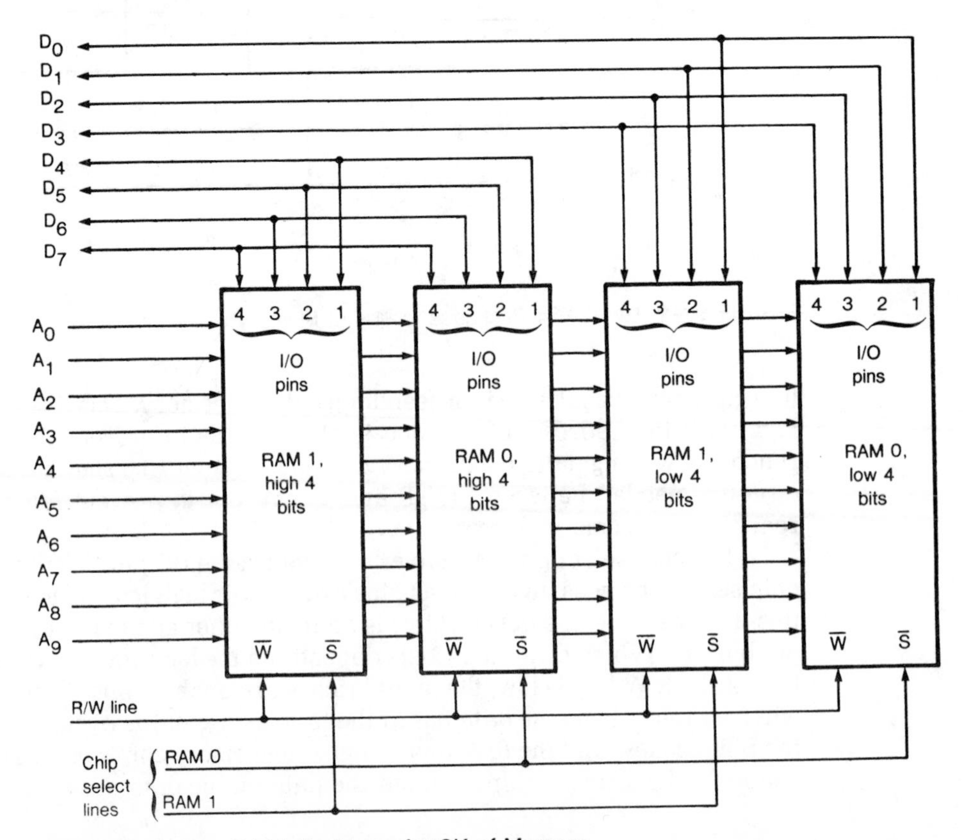

FIGURE 16–3 Four 2114 Packages for 2K of Memory

same chip select line. The $\overline{S}$ pins of RAM 1 must also be connected together. Therefore, there is a chip select line for every two packages. These lines go back to other μP address lines or to decoder chips, as discussed in Section 16.4.

Although the 2114 can be used to expand memory even further, there are some hardware problems that should be considered, and another memory chip might be a better choice. Let's consider what goes into the decision.

16.2 MEMORY EXPANSION

When a μC system requires 4K, 8K, 16K, 32K, or more bytes of temporary memory, the 2114 may not be the best choice. The loading effect on each data bus line should be considered. Look at Figure 16-3 again, and note that each data bus line is connected to two 2114 packages. This means that the loading effect on each line is 2. Another way of stating this is to say that when the 2114 memory chip is used, the loading on each line equals the following expression:

$$\frac{\text{Number of bytes}}{\text{K}} \quad (16\text{-}1)$$

Applying Equation 16-1 to Figure 16-3 yields the next equation:

$$\frac{2\text{K}}{\text{K}} = 2$$

Figure 16-4 shows how 4K of memory can be connected to the μP. Each data bus line is connected to four packages, producing a loading effect of 4. Although most μC systems need data bus buffers, the loading effect on each line should still be taken into consideration so that no limitations are exceeded. Let's now look at how the loading effect, not the package count, can be reduced.

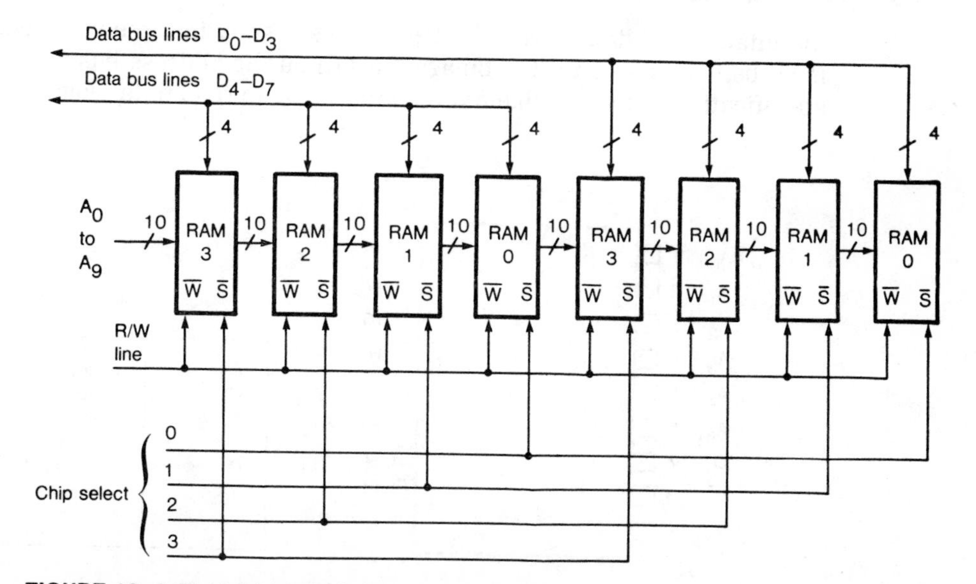

FIGURE 16-4 Eight 2114 Packages for 4K of Memory

16.2.1 2147 Static RAM

The 2147 is a 4096-bit static random access memory organized as 4096 words × 1 bit. This device has automatic power down, which means that when the device is not selected there is a considerable saving of power. The pin designations for the 2147 are shown in Figure 16–5. The 2147 is housed in an 18-pin dual-in-line package. Twelve pins are used for the address lines A_0–A_{11}. The μC system's read/write line is connected to the write enable pin, $\overline{W}$. The chip selected pin is labeled $\overline{E}$, which stands for chip enable. Power, + 5 V, is applied to the V_{CC} pin and ground to the V_{SS} pin. The 2147 has an input data pin, D, and an output data pin, Q. Thus, the 2147 can be used in systems that have separate input and output data bus lines. The majority of μC systems, however, have only eight common data bus lines. Therefore, each data bus line is used for inputting and outputting data. The 2147 allows the D and Q pins to be wired together for such systems.

16.2.2 4K of Memory Using the 2147

Since the 2147 is a 4K × 1-bit memory device, a system requires eight 2147 packages to produce a 4K × 8-bit static random access memory, as shown in Figure 16–6. This memory system requires the same number of packages as the system in Figure 16–4, but the loading effect on each data bus line is different. In the system of Figure 16–4, there are four packages connected to each data bus line. In the memory system of Figure 16–6, however, there is only one package connected to each data bus line, thus reducing the loading effect by a factor of 4.

16.3 SYSTEM READ/WRITE LINE

Manufacturers' data sheets for RAM chips specify that the write enable line must be held high until the binary pattern on the address bus is stable. This specification is not a problem if the μP is going to read data from memory, but

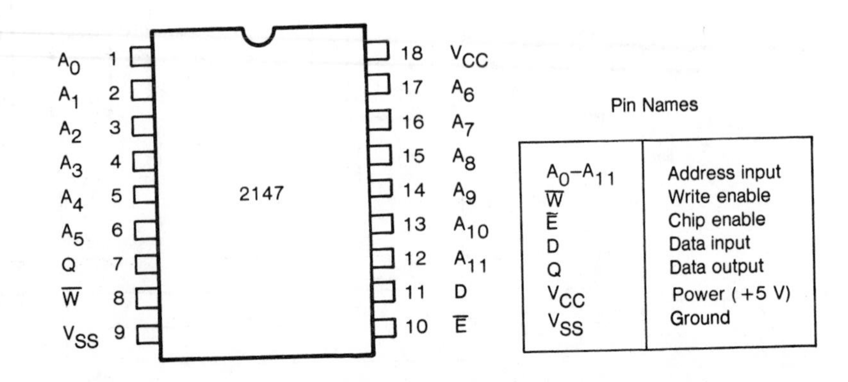

FIGURE 16–5 Pin Designations for 2147 Static RAM

when the μP is going to write data, this specification must be taken into account. The write enable line cannot go low until the address bus is stable.

In an 8080A μC system, the write enable line is held high by the 8228 controller chip. In a 6800 system, the μP's valid memory address (VMA) line is used in conjunction with an address line wired to the memory chip select pin or with the μP's R/W line wired to the write enable pin on the memory package.

The 6502 μP does not use a controller chip nor does it have a VMA line. Therefore, a digital circuit must be designed to keep the read/write line high until the address bus is stable. Figure 16–7A shows such a circuit; its timing diagrams are shown in Figures 16–7B and 16–7C. In the case of a write operation, the system read/write line will not go low until the ϕ_2 clock pulse goes high. Figure 14–5 showed that the ϕ_2 clock pulse goes high well after the address bus is stable. The circuit of Figure 16–7 can be used as is, either for the 6502 μP or the 6800 μP. If we want to use this circuit and the 6800's VMA line, then we must replace the ϕ_2 line from the μP with the VMA line.

16.4 DECODING THE MEMORY SPACE

At some point in the design of a μC system, a decision has to be made about how much temporary memory, permanent memory, and I/O are to be included. Next a decision has to be made about where in the total memory system everything will be placed. Let's consider that a system is to have 4K of RAM, 2K of EPROM, and 16 bytes of I/O. RAM is to be located from page 00 to page 0F. ROM is to be located at the highest memory locations from page F8 to FF. The 16 bytes of I/O are to be wired at memory locations 4000 to 400F. Figure 16–8 is a memory map that shows where everything is to be placed in the total memory space.

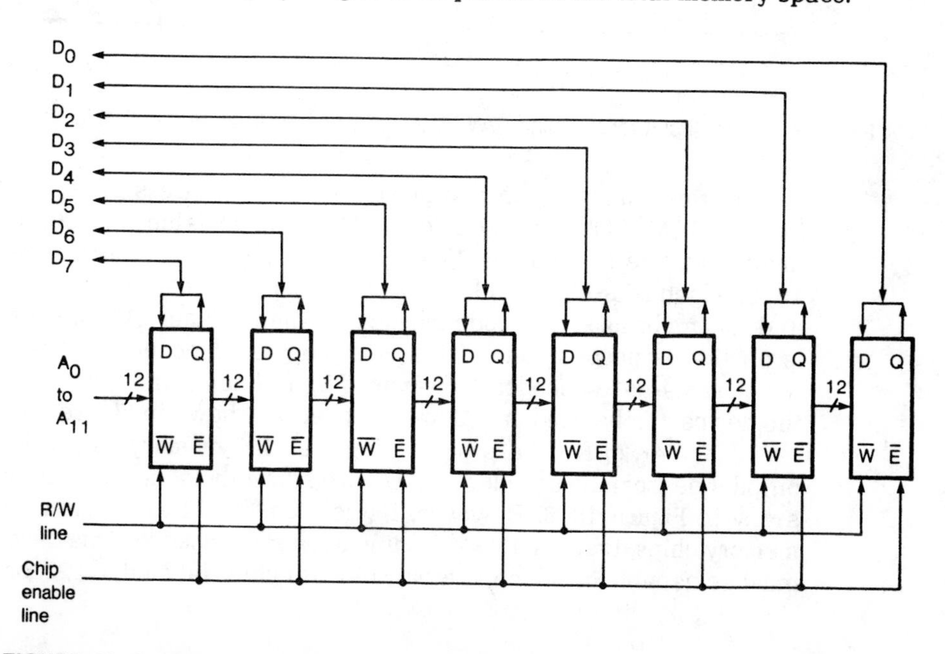

FIGURE 16–6 Eight 2147 Packages for 4K of Memory

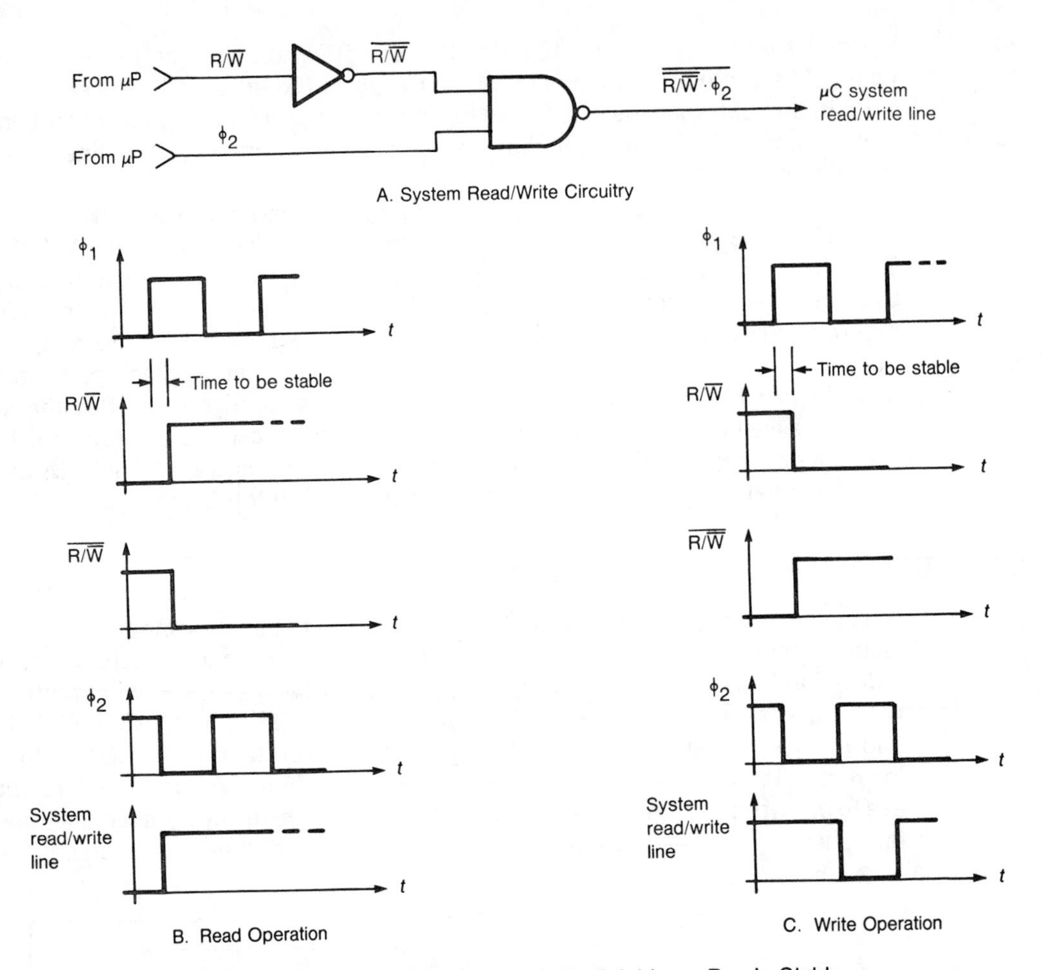

FIGURE 16–7 Digital Circuit for Keeping R/W Line High Until Address Bus Is Stable

In this example, the two most significant address lines can be used to identify RAM, ROM, and I/O. For RAM, the logic values are 00; for ROM, the logic levels are 11; and for I/O, they are 01. These values are shown in Figure 16–9, which is a diagram of the 74LS42 decoder. Therefore, address lines A_{14} and A_{15} can be used to decode the memory map of Figure 16–8. A 2-to-4 decoder is all that is needed. One of the most popular decoder chips is the 74LS42, which is a 4-to-10 decoder. However, if input lines C and D are grounded, then the device can be used as a 2-to-4 decoder, as shown in Figure 16–9.

If the 4K of RAM are built using the 2147 memory chips, then the RAM output line from the decoder chip is wired directly to the chip enable line of the array in Figure 16–6. However, if the 4K of RAM are built using the 2114 memory chips, then another decoding network is needed. This decoding circuit must be capable of selecting a pair of RAM chips labeled 0, 1, 2, or 3 in Figure

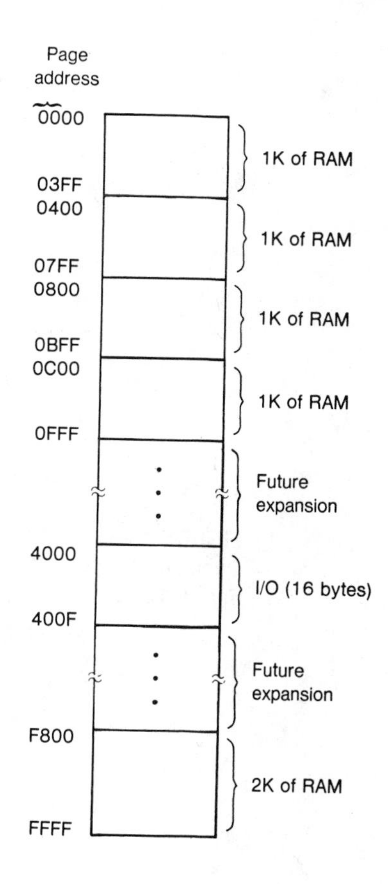

FIGURE 16–8 Typical Memory Map

16–4. Another 74LS42 can also be used for this decoding application, as shown in Figure 16–10. The figure also shows which address bus lines must be decoded and where the RAM output line of the memory map decoder is connected. The line (C) from the memory map decoder is used to enable or disable the chip decoder. When the memory map line is high, the four chip select lines are high, regardless of the logic levels on address lines A_{10} and A_{11}. When the RAM memory map line is low, then the logic levels on lines A_{10} and A_{11} determine which chip select line goes low. This allows the μP to communicate with one pair of memory chips.

In some larger μC systems, address lines A_{12}, A_{13}, A_{14}, and A_{15} all have to be decoded. Four address lines produce 16 possible outputs ($2^4 = 16$). Although a 4-to-16 decoder chip, such as the 74154, is available, there are some reasons for not using it:

1. It is housed in a 24-pin package. This means that this may be the only chip of its size on the PC board, and it may require special handling and insertion.

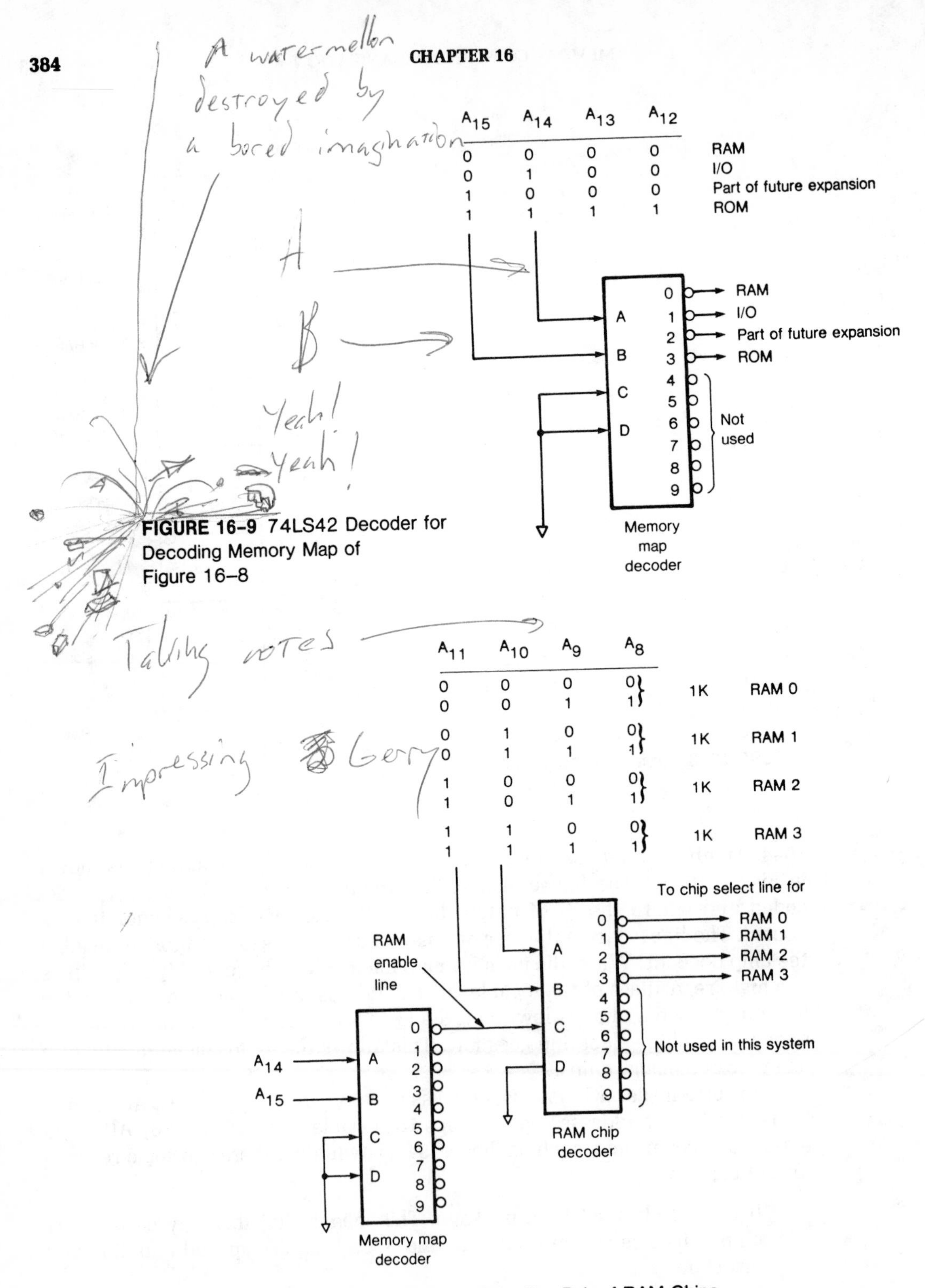

FIGURE 16–9 74LS42 Decoder for Decoding Memory Map of Figure 16–8

FIGURE 16–10 74LS42 Decoder for Selecting Pair of RAM Chips

2. It is usually the only 4-to-16 decoder being used. Thus, the user must order, handle, store, and check an extra part. (Also, it won't be possible to buy it in large quantities to obtain maximum discount.)
3. The 74154 is available only as a standard TTL or low-power chip, not in a low-power Schottky, LS, version. A standard TTL input has twice the input loading effect as does an LS version. Therefore, a standard TTL input loads the bus lines more than an LS input.

To overcome these problems, system designers try to use an LS package in as many places as possible. As previously mentioned, the 74LS42 IC is a popular and commonly used decoder chip. Figures 16–9 and 16–10 showed how it could be wired in two applications. Two 74LS42 ICs and an inverter can be interconnected to produce a 4-to-16 decoder, as shown in Figure 16–11. Certainly there are disadvantages with this circuit; one is that two decoder packages are needed, which means that additional drill holes and another package to which V_{CC} and ground must be connected are needed. The inverter gate usually comes from another package that contains an extra inverter, a NAND or NOR gate. The NAND and NOR gates have to be wired for inversion, as shown in Figure 16–11. These are some of the considerations that must be thought of by the system designer.

Although Figure 16–11 shows address lines A_{12}, A_{13}, A_{14}, and A_{15} connected to the circuit, any four address lines can be used. Note, in Figure 16–11, that outputs 8 and 9 of both decoders are not used. (The numbers 0 to 15 on the outside of the packages are the 16 output lines.)

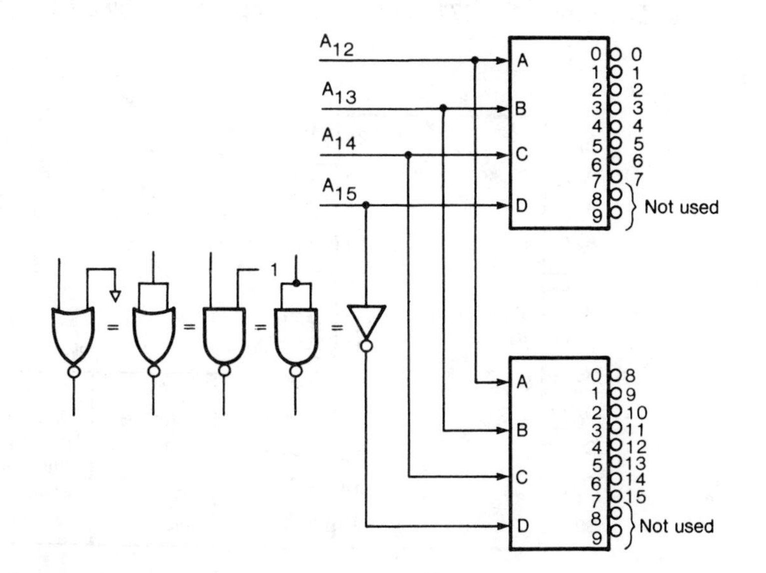

FIGURE 16–11 4-to-16 Decoder

16.5 2716 EPROM

The 2716 IC is an ultraviolet erasable programmable read-only memory (UV EPROM). It is a 16,384-bit device organized as 2048 bytes × 8 bits. A transparent lid on the top of the package allows the entire device to be erased by ultraviolet light. An erase operation causes every bit to go to the logic 1 state. When the device is programmed, only the bits that contain logic 0 change state.

Figure 16–12 shows the pin designations for the 2716. This device is housed in a 24-pin dual-in-line package. There are 11 address pins, A_0 to A_{10}, that enable the device to address 2048 bytes ($2^{11} = 2048$). The eight DQ pins, DQ_0 to DQ_7, are pins connected to the data bus. They are also used to input data during programming. One of the reasons that this device is so popular is that it requires only +5 V for the read operation. This voltage is not the programming voltage, which is +25 V.

16.5.1 Programming the 2716

The 2716 is set up in the programming mode under the following conditions:

$$V_{CC}\text{ (pin 24)} = +5\text{ V}$$
$$\overline{G}\text{ (pin 20)} = V_{IH}$$
$$V_{PP}\text{ (pin 21)} = +25\text{ V}$$

The data is entered in 8-bit words through the DQ pins. Remember, only 0s will be programmed when 0s and 1s are entered. After the address and data lines are set up, a program pulse is applied to the $\overline{E}$/Prog pin (pin 18). The recommended program pulse is a low-to-high pulse, V_{IL} to V_{IH}, with a pulse width of 2 ms. Therefore, the 2716 cannot be programmed by a DC signal.

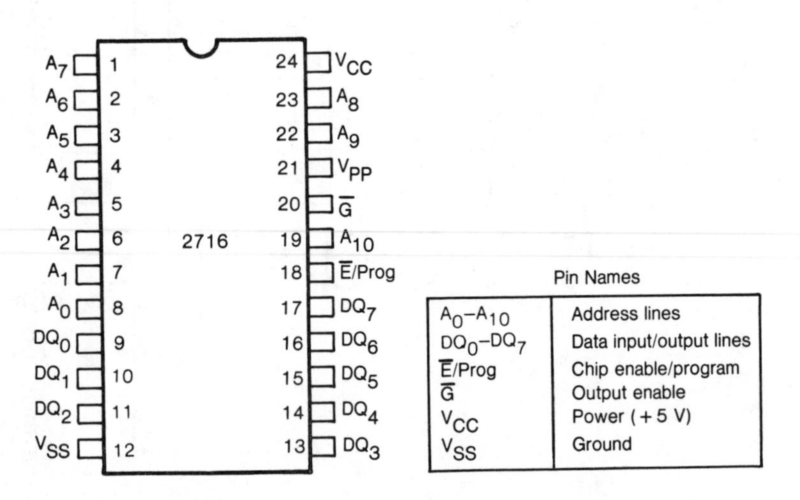

FIGURE 16–12 Pin Designations for 2716 EPROM

16.5.2 Read Operation

After the address is stable and at the end of the access time, data is valid at the DQ pins. The 2716 has a stand-by mode to reduce power dissipation when the device is not selected. The 2716 is in the stand-by mode when the $\overline{E}$/Prog pin is high, V_{IH}. In this mode, the output pins are in their high impedance state.

16.5.3 Erase Operation

The 2716 is erased by exposure to ultraviolet light. The recommended wavelength is 2537 angstroms. Like all EPROMs, when this device is erased, all the bits are erased. This procedure is called *block erasure*. An erased bit is a logic 1 for the 2716.

16.5.4 Wiring the 2716 into the System

The 2716 is actually easier to wire into a μC system than the 2114 or the 2147 static RAMs. The reason is that the 2716 EPROM is not split between two or more chips and, therefore, the eight data pins are connected directly to the data bus.

Figure 16–13 shows how the 2716 can be connected to a system. The eleven address lines, A_0–A_{10}, are wired directly back to the μP. In many systems, address buffers are connected between the μP and memory to reduce loading effects on the μP's lines. Their input pins are connected to the μP, and the corresponding output pin is connected to a memory line.

The eight data bus lines, DQ_0–DQ_7, are connected to the μP's corresponding data bus lines. Like the address lines, data lines often require buffering.

After the 2716 is programmed and inserted into a system, the V_{PP} cannot be left floating; it must be tied to V_{CC}. When the $\overline{G}$ pin is high, the output lines are disabled. This means that the output data lines remain in their high impedance state regardless of the logic state of the $\overline{E}$/Prog pin. Therefore, for normal operation, the $\overline{G}$ pin is tied to ground.

The chip is selected or deselected by the $\overline{E}$/Prog pin, pin 18. As shown in Figure 16–13, this pin is connected to the memory map decoder. When address lines A_{14} and A_{15} go to a logic 1 state, output line 3 of the decoder goes low. This low logic level is the signal to the 2716 that the μP is selecting it and wishes to receive data from it. An EPROM does not need a read/write line because data can only be read from it.

16.6 4517 DYNAMIC RAM

The 4517 is a 16,384-bit dynamic RAM. It is organized as 16,384 words × 1 bit. Therefore, by interconnecting eight of these devices, 16K of memory can be added to a μC system. This memory chip requires only + 5 V to operate. Each memory cell is designed using a single transistor, and each cell has to be

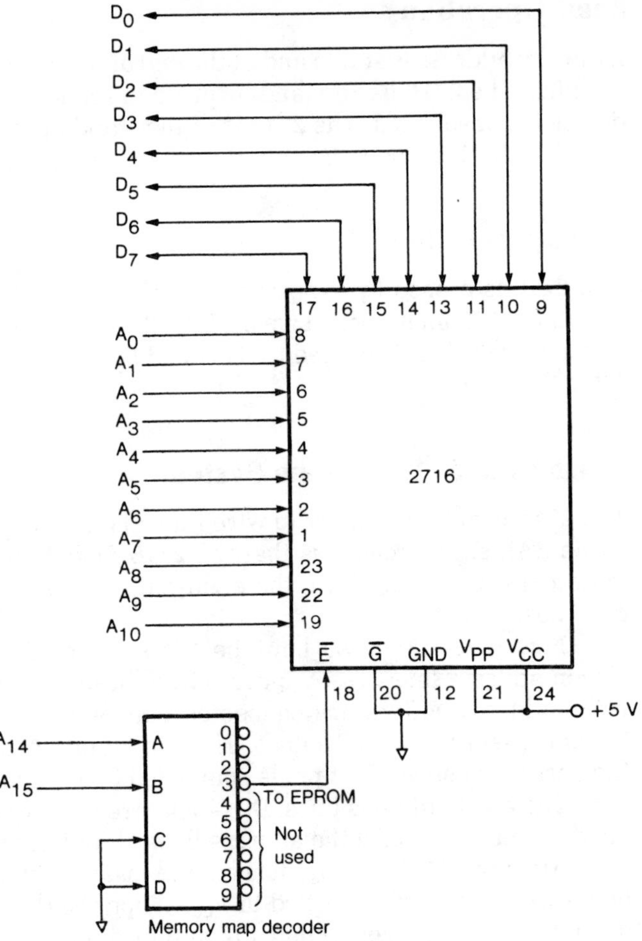

FIGURE 16–13 2716 EPROM Wired into μC System

refreshed within 2 ms. The device is housed in a 16-pin dual-in-line package, as shown in Figure 16–14. The figure also gives the pin assignments and names.

Note that there are only seven address pins, which would usually indicate that there can be only 128 ($2^7 = 128$) memory locations within the device. Manufacturers have designed dynamic memories, however, so that each address pin is used twice. This accounts for the 16,384 ($2^{14} = 16{,}384$) words within the memory chip. First, a row address is sent to the memory chip through the seven address pins, and then a column address is sent to the memory chip through the same address pins. This requires a multiplexer IC to be connected between the μP and the dynamic RAMs. Therefore, when dynamic RAMs are added to a μC system, we must consider two items that did not exist with static RAMs: (1) a multiplexer IC and (2) refresh cycles.

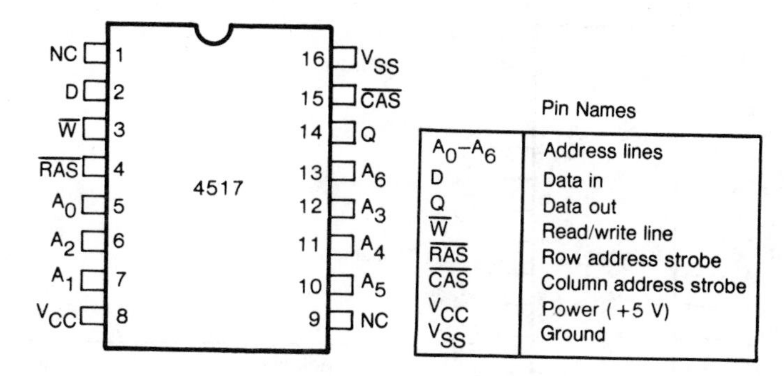

FIGURE 16–14 Pin Designations for 4517 Dynamic RAM

16.6.1 Address Line Multiplexer

The 3242A is a memory address multiplexer and refresh counter for 16K dynamic RAMs. It is the type of interface chip needed between the μP and the memory chips. Figure 16–15 shows the pin designations for the 3242A. The binary pattern on the μP's address lines A_0 to A_6 is sent to the memory chips as the row address. The binary pattern on the μP's address lines A_7 to A_{13} is sent to the memory chips as the column address. As Figure 16–16A shows, it is the function of the 3242A to latch the addresses coming from the μP and then send out the row address followed by the column address. In order for the multiplexer to know which position of the address to send, it uses its refresh enable and row enable lines, as shown in the truth table of Figure 16–16B. The refresh enable and row enable lines are controlled by a dynamic memory controller chip, such as the MC3480 IC.

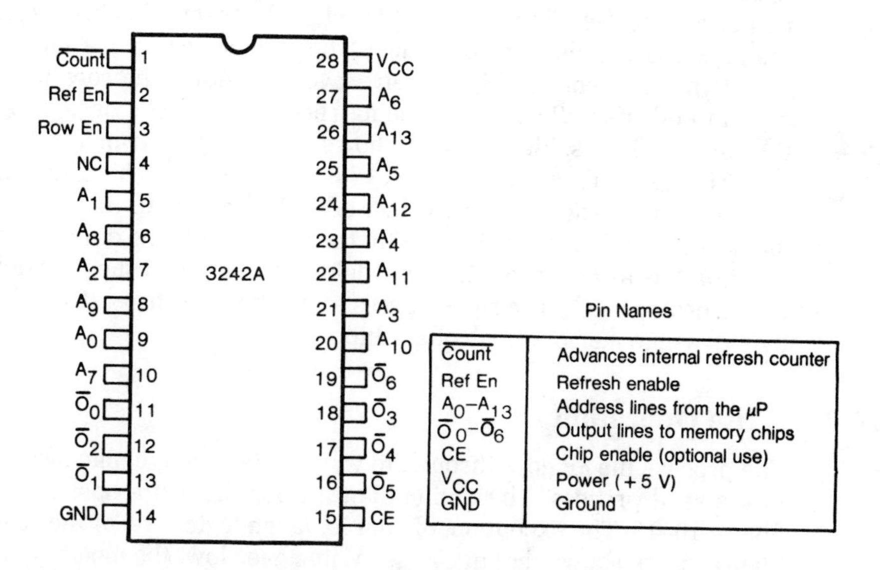

FIGURE 16–15 Pin Designations for 3242A Multiplexer

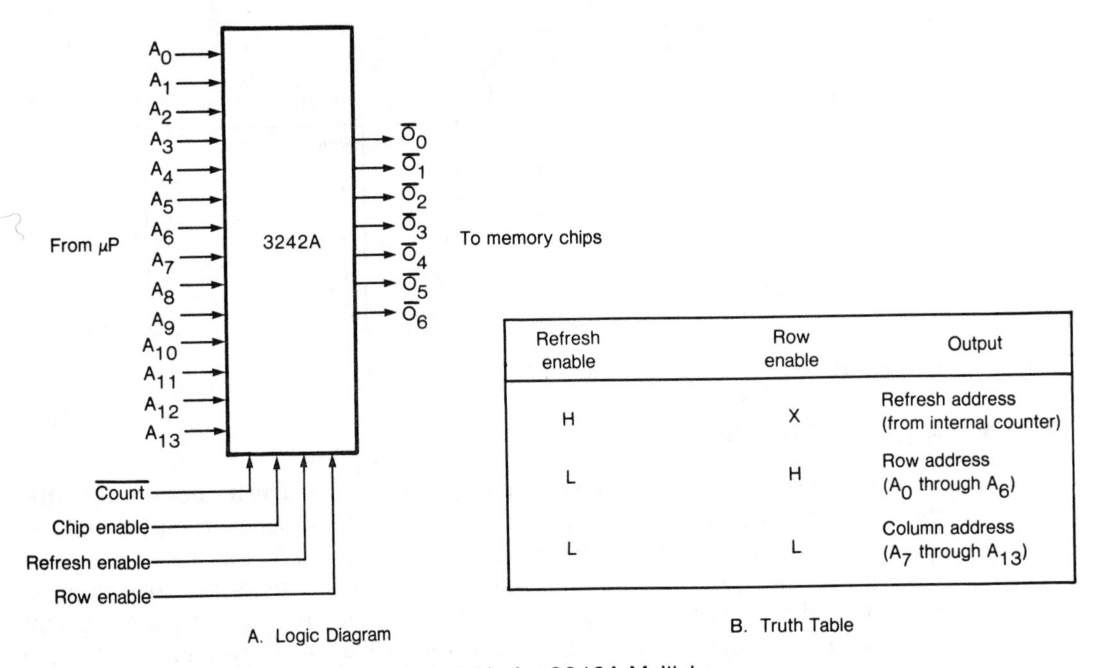

Refresh enable	Row enable	Output
H	X	Refresh address (from internal counter)
L	H	Row address (A_0 through A_6)
L	L	Column address (A_7 through A_{13})

FIGURE 16–16 Logic Diagram and Truth Table for 3242A Multiplexer

16.6.2 Read Operation

Remember that the terms *read* and *write* always refer to the μP reading (receiving) or writing (sending) data, not to what the memory chips are doing. When the μP is reading data from memory, the memory chips are sending the data.

Dynamic memory chips receive two addresses, the row address and the column address. Which one is being received depends on the logic levels of $\overline{RAS}$ and $\overline{CAS}$ lines. Figure 16–17 shows the timing diagram for the read operation. The figure shows that when $\overline{RAS}$ is low and $\overline{CAS}$ is high, the memory chips are receiving a row address. When both $\overline{RAS}$ and $\overline{CAS}$ lines are low, the column address is being received. With the $\overline{W}$ line high, the data becomes valid on the data bus after a specified time delay (the length of the time delay depends on the device used). The row address and column address strobe lines are sent by a dynamic memory controller chip.

16.6.3 Write Operation

The process the μP goes through to write data to a dynamic memory is similar to the read process. The timing diagram for the write operation is shown in Figure 16–18. The exception, of course, is the logic level of the read/write line. Figure 16–18 shows that after the $\overline{W}$ line goes low, the memory chip is able to receive valid data.

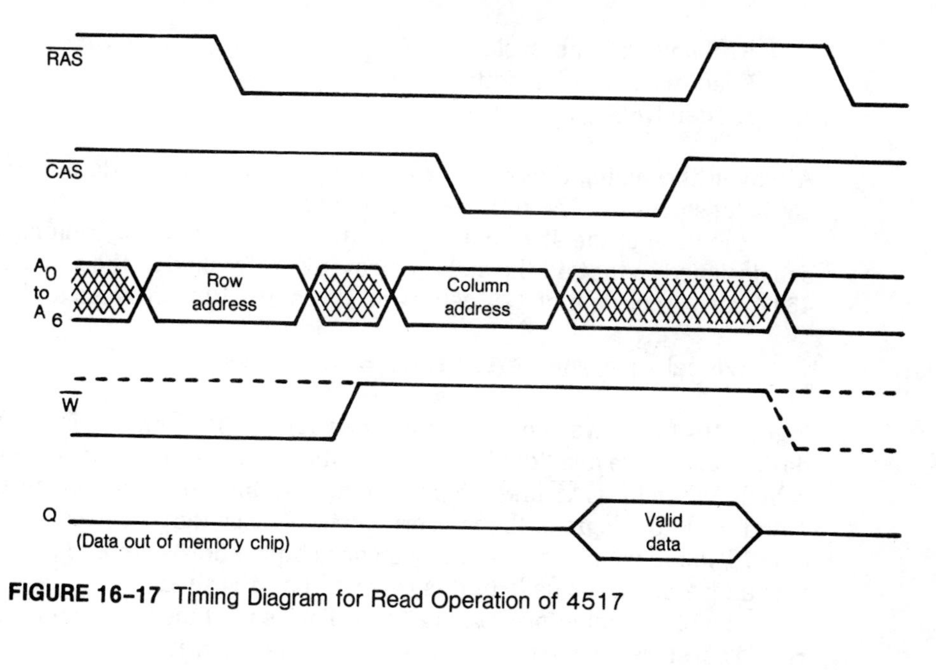

FIGURE 16–17 Timing Diagram for Read Operation of 4517

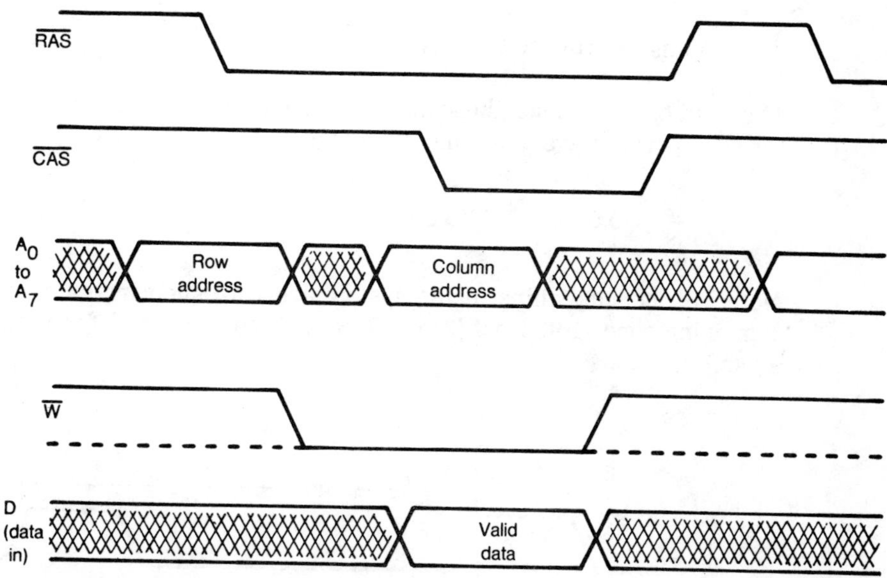

FIGURE 16–18 Timing Diagram for Write Operation of 4517

16.6.4 Dynamic Refresh

In order to keep the capacitor of a dynamic memory cell charged to its logic state, a refresh signal is required. The 4517 dynamic memory can be refreshed in three ways:

1. $\overline{RAS}$-only refresh cycle,
2. Read–write/read–modify cycle,
3. Hidden $\overline{RAS}$-only refresh cycle.

Although the timing diagram for each method is given in data sheets for the 4517, let's consider the first method in detail.

Each cell of the 4517 has to be refreshed within 2 ms. Dynamic memories are designed so that all the cells in a row are refreshed at the same time. In the 4517, a row consists of 128 cells, and there are 128 rows. As a check:

$$128 \text{ cells per row} \times 128 \text{ rows} = 16{,}384 \text{ cells}$$

Figure 16–19 shows the timing diagram for the $\overline{RAS}$-only refresh cycle. The data-in and write are "don't care" conditions and are not shown. The $\overline{CAS}$ line is high. When the $\overline{CAS}$ line is high and the $\overline{RAS}$ line goes from a logic 0 to a logic 1 and back to a logic 0, the memory device senses that a refresh cycle is to be done. The binary pattern on the memory chip's address pins, A_0–A_6, defines a row address. All the cells in this row will be refreshed.

A typical cycle time, t_{RC}, is 250 ns. This is the time required to refresh one row. Therefore, to refresh 128 rows takes the following time:

$$250 \text{ ns per row} \times 128 \text{ rows} = 32\ \mu\text{s}$$

Thus, out of every 2 ms, these memory devices require 32 μs to be refreshed. In terms of percent, we have the following:

$$\frac{32\ \mu\text{s}}{2\text{ ms}} = 0.016 \text{ or } 1.6\%$$

Note: All memory chips in the system are refreshed in the same 32 μs. The remaining time, 1.968 ms (2 ms − 32 μs), can be used for normal program execution.

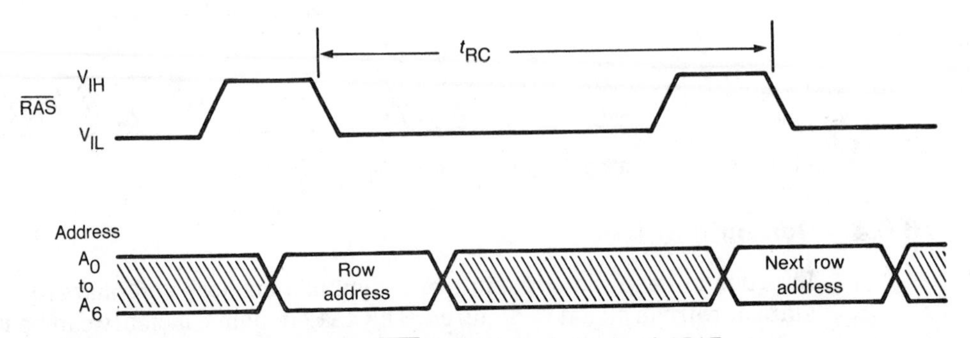

FIGURE 16–19 Timing Diagram for $\overline{RAS}$-Only Refresh Cycle of 4517

16.7 SUMMARY

This chapter showed how memory chips can be interconnected to form the memory portion of a μC. The popular 2114 static RAM is organized as 1024 words × 4 bits, so two of these devices yield 1K of memory. In Section 16.2, the 2147 static RAM, organized as 4096 words × 1 bit, was discussed. We found that comparisons can be made among the different types of static memory chips that are available.

The 2716 EPROM is one of the most widely used UV PROMs. This device gives the user 2048 words × 8 bits of permanent memory. Once programmed, it is easily connected to a system and operates from + 5 V.

The 4517 is a 16,384-bit dynamic RAM. Like all other dynamic RAMs, it needs additional support circuitry, such as a multiplexer and a dynamic memory controller. In Section 16.6, we looked at some of the problems encountered when dynamic memories are used.

PROBLEMS

16-1 What is the word size of a 2114 static RAM?

16-2 How many 2114 memory chips are required in a 3K × 8 system?

16-3 How many address pins are there on the (a) 2114 and (b) 2147 memory chips?

16-4 When the $\overline{W}$ pin on the 2114 chip goes low, is the memory chip receiving or sending data?

16-5 Why must the $\overline{W}$ pin be high until the address information is stable?

16-6 What is the function of the $\overline{S}$ pin on the 2114?

16-7 When does the memory chip put data on the data bus?

16-8 In a 3K × 8 memory system using the 2114, how many chip select lines are there?

16-9 For the memory system of Problem 16-8, what is the loading factor on each data bus line?

16-10 What does the expression *automatic power down* mean? Which memory chip has this feature?

16-11 Which pin is the chip select pin on the 2147?

16-12 Are both the 2114 and the 2147 + 5 V devices?

16-13 What is an advantage and a disadvantage of the 2147 memory chip over the 2114 memory chip?

16-14 Why does the circuit of Figure 16-7 also prevent any unwanted glitches from occurring on the system read/write line?

16-15 Refer to Figure 16-9. What section of the total memory space does output line 3 decode?

16-16 Consider that a system is to have 5K of RAM using the 2114 chip. What changes have to be made in the circuit of Figure 16-10 so the circuit will be able to decode the next 1K of RAM?

16-17 Consider that another 2716 EPROM has to be connected to the memory space outlined in Figure 16-8. What locations should the device occupy to avoid adding another decoder chip? (*Hint:* See Figure 16-9 and Problem 16-15.)

16-18 When a 2716 EPROM is erased, what is the logic state of each bit?

16-19 What is the function of a multiplexer IC in a dynamic RAM system?

16-20 What do the abbreviations $\overline{RAS}$ and $\overline{CAS}$ represent?

Interface Devices

17.0 INTRODUCTION

In Chapter 1, we looked at the μC system's three main building blocks: the μP, memory, and interface devices (also called interface chips). Interface devices allow the μP to communicate with peripheral equipment such as keyboards, printers, plotters, CRT displays, storage devices, solid state switches, relays, transducers, or even other computers. Semiconductor manufacturers have designed into a single IC package the circuitry the μP needs to interface with commonly used peripheral equipment. They have also designed some general-purpose interface devices that can be used for a wide variety of applications. These ICs use LSI technology, and they can replace 50 to 100 SSI packages. The interface devices are also programmable; that is, they are under the programmer's control. Although many interface chips have been designed for a specific function, the manufacturer has designed into the chip the usual methods of doing the same job, such as the rate at which data is transmitted or received. The programmer chooses the method by having the μP send a specific binary pattern to the interface device. By changing the binary pattern, the programmer chooses another method.

General-purpose interface devices are also programmable and allow the user great flexibility in design. In addition, the programmer may change the way the device does a job at any time. For example, the programmer may wish to receive data from peripheral equipment at one rate for part of a program and change the rate for another part of the program.

Although interface devices are designed for general or specific applications, they have many points in common. In this chapter, we will study these common points, while in the following chapters we will examine some of the commonly used interface chips.

The list that follows contains the interface IC devices frequently used with Intel and Motorola μPs:

Intel products:

8212	8-Bit Input/Output Port
8214	Priority Interrupt Control Unit
8251A	Programmable Communication Interface
8253	Programmable Interface Timer
8255A	Programmable Peripheral Interface
8257	Programmable DMA Controller
8259	Programmable Interrupt Controller
8271	Programmable Floppy Disk Controller
8273	Programmable Protocol Controller
8275	Programmable CRT Controller
8278	Programmable Keyboard Interface
8279	Programmable Keyboard Display Interface
8294	Data Encryption Unit

Motorola products (can also be used with the 6502 μP):

MC6821	Peripheral Interface Adapter (PIA)
MC6828	Priority Interrupt Controller (PIC)
MC6840	Programmable Timer Module (PIM)
MC6843	Floppy Disk Controller (FDC)
MC6844	Direct Memory Access Controller (DMAC)
MC6845	CRT Controller (CRTC)
MC6846	ROM–I/O–Timer
MC6847	Video Display Generator (VDG)
MC6850	Asynchronous Communication Interface Adapter (ACIA)
MC6852	Synchronous Serial Data Adapter (SSDA)
MC6854	Advanced Data Link Controller
MC6860	0–600 bps Digital Modem
MC6862	2400 bps Digital Modulator
MC68488	General-Purpose Interface Adapter

The list shows the principal manufacturer of these devices. However, many of these devices are also built by other IC manufacturers. Although the Intel and Motorola interface devices are normally used with their own μPs, they can be used with other 8-bit μPs.

17.1 PIN ASSIGNMENTS

The interface devices in the list just given are housed in either a 24-, a 28-, or a 40-pin dual-in-line package. Most devices can be purchased in either a plastic package or in a ceramic package for better heat dissipation.

An interface device is the link between the μP and peripheral equipment, so the device may be visualized as having a μP side and a peripheral side, as shown in the logic diagram of Figure 17–1.

On the μP side are the pins that are connected to the address bus, data bus, and control bus. On the peripheral side are the input and output (I/O) lines. The I/O lines are either for general-purpose applications or for a specific purpose, depending on the device.

Many interface devices have all the μP pins arranged on one side and the I/O lines on the other side of the device. This allows for easy PC board layout.

Figure 17–2 shows the pin assignments for Motorola's 6821 peripheral interface adapter, which is a general-purpose interface device. The MC6821 device has all of the μP connections on one side of the chip and all but two (CA_1 and CA_2) of the peripheral lines on the other. Pins 1 and 20 are the power supply pins. Pins 2–19 and pins 39 and 40 are for the peripheral equipment. Pins 21–38 are to be connected to the μP bus lines. Figure 17–2 shows that this device can easily be wired to the μP's bus lines and connected to peripheral equipment. More detailed discussion of the MC6821 is found in Chapter 19.

17.2 CONNECTIONS TO THE MICROPROCESSOR

An interface device has pins that are to be connected to the μP's address bus, data bus, and control bus. Let's look at the pins in each group.

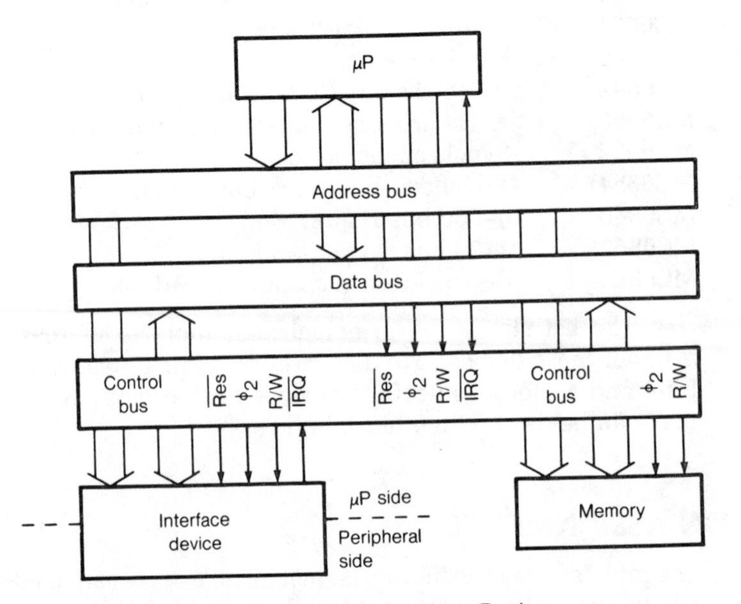

FIGURE 17–1 Typical μP System, Including Interface Device

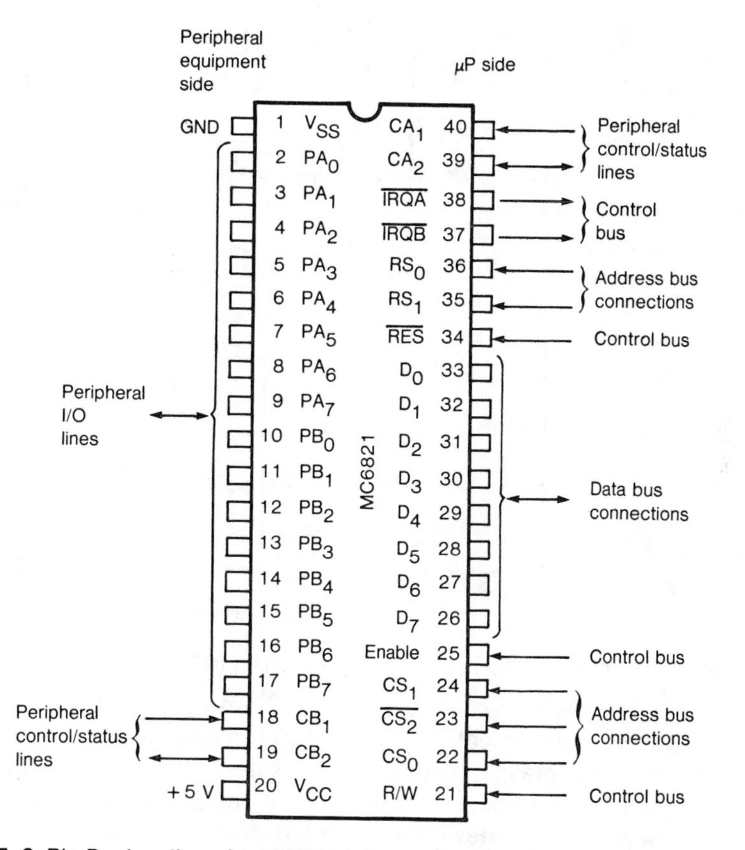

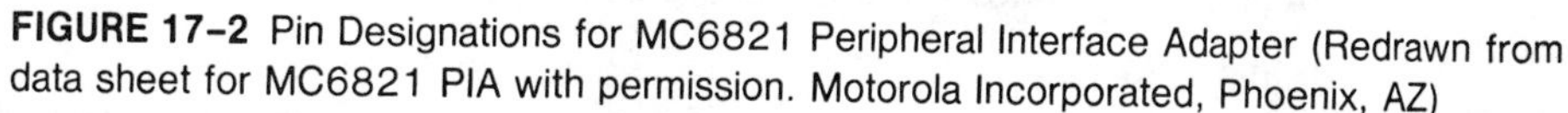

FIGURE 17–2 Pin Designations for MC6821 Peripheral Interface Adapter (Redrawn from data sheet for MC6821 PIA with permission. Motorola Incorporated, Phoenix, AZ)

17.2.1 Address Bus Connections

Chip Select

Interface devices have one or more chip select (CS) lines. In small systems, these lines are, or may be, connected directly to the μP's address lines, as shown in Figure 17–3A. In larger systems, interface devices (as well as memory) are connected to decoder chips, as shown in Figure 17–3B. Remember, from Chapter 16, that decoder chips allow more or all of the total memory space to be used.

In devices with only one chip select line, the active state of the line is usually low. That is, when either the μP's address line or the output of the decoder, wired to the chip select line, goes low, the interface device is enabled and can communicate with the μP. Devices with two or more chip select lines must have the correct logic state applied to all chip select lines to enable the device. All chip select lines must be used; they cannot be left floating. Devices with multiple chip select lines usually will have at least one of the lines with an

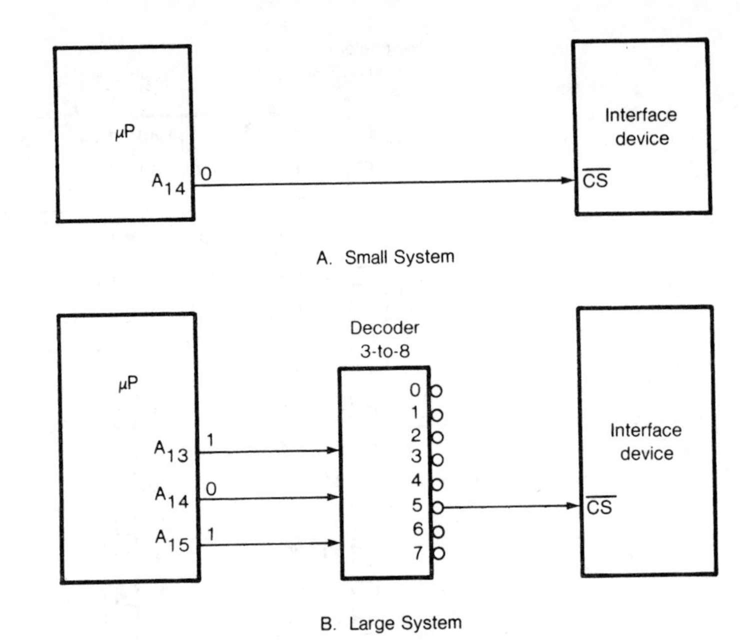

FIGURE 17–3 Connections for Chip Select (CS) Lines

active low state. Since the output lines of decoder chips are active low states, they can be directly connected to the chip select line. Figure 17–4 illustrates four possible connections to chip select lines. An interface device's chip select pins can be connected directly to the μP, as in Figure 17–4A, or indirectly through a decoder chip, as in Figure 17–4B.

Register Select

Besides the chip select pins, interface devices have one or more additional pins connected to the address bus. This line (or lines) is the register select line. It is used by the μP to communicate with a particular register within the interface device.

Register select lines are usually connected to the lowest-numbered address lines of the μP. For example, if the interface device has only one register select pin, it should be connected to the μP's A_0 address line. If there are two register select pins, they should be connected to the μP's A_0 and A_1 address lines.

Unlike the chip select lines, which may be connected to a decoder chip, register select pins are always connected directly to the address lines, as shown in Figure 17–5.

Some manufacturers, such as Intel, do not call this pin (or pins) "register select." Instead, they use the name of the actual register that is being addressed. Since the name of the register may be different for different interface devices, the name of the pin is not always the same. In either case, there should be no problem because it is important to be familiar with manufacturers' data sheets for any device and to learn the function of each pin and each internal register before using the device.

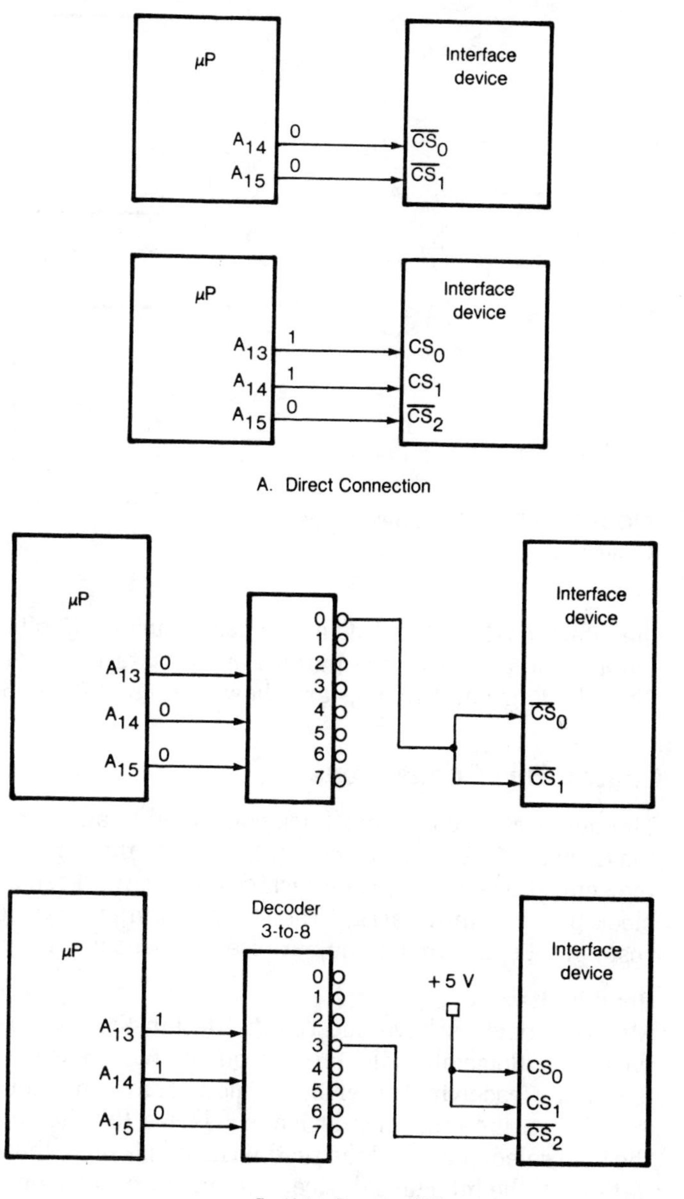

FIGURE 17–4 Four Possible Connections to Chip Select Lines

17.2.2 Data Bus Connections

Interface devices have eight bidirectional data lines that connect directly to the μP's data bus lines. Figure 17–6 shows that pin D_0 of the interface device is connected to D_0 in the μP, D_1 is connected to D_1, and so forth. These lines allow

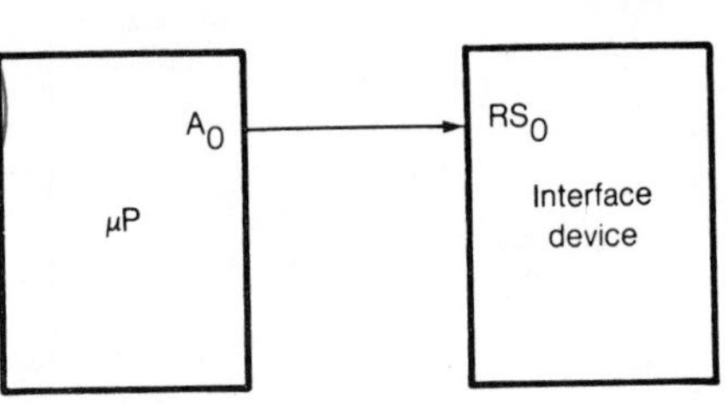

A. Single Register Select Line

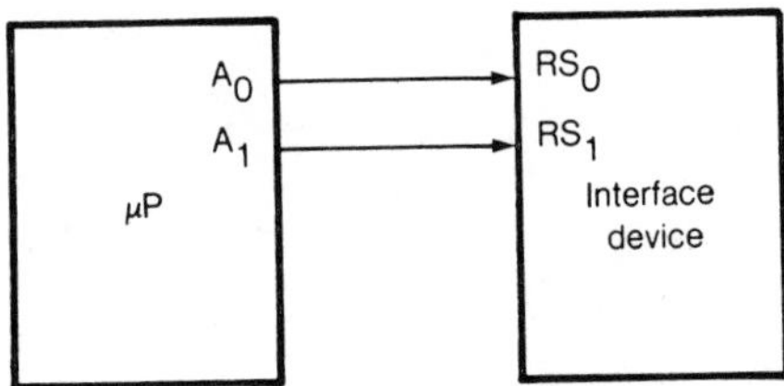

B. Two Register Select Lines

FIGURE 17–5 Register Select Line Connections

the interface device to send and receive one byte (8 bits) of data at a time from the μP. The actual wiring pattern of the data bus is shown in Figure 17–6A. Simplified circuit drawings are shown in Figures 17–6B and 17–6C.

17.2.3 Control Bus Connections

The number of control bus lines connected to an interface device depends on the device. Most chips, however, have from three to six pins that are wired to the control bus lines. Most interface chips have a read/write pin (or pins), a ϕ_2 clock pin, and an interrupt request pin. Many interface devices also have a reset pin. Let's examine the purposes of these control pins.

Read/Write

Motorola devices have one read/write pin that is wired to the system read/write line. Remember, the terms *read* and *write* always refer to whether the μP is reading (receiving) or writing (sending) data, and not to the interface device.

When the interface device is selected (by the correct binary pattern on the chip select pins) and the read/write line is high, the μP is reading (receiving) data from the interface device. The binary pattern on the register select lines determines which register within the interface device is sending data to the μP.

If the interface device is selected and the read/write is low, then the μP is writing (sending) data to the interface chip. The binary pattern on the register select lines determines which register within the interface device is receiving the data.

Intel products have two control pins for the read/write operation, one pin for the read operation and one pin for the write operation. Again, the terms *read* and *write* refer to what the μP is doing and not to what the interface

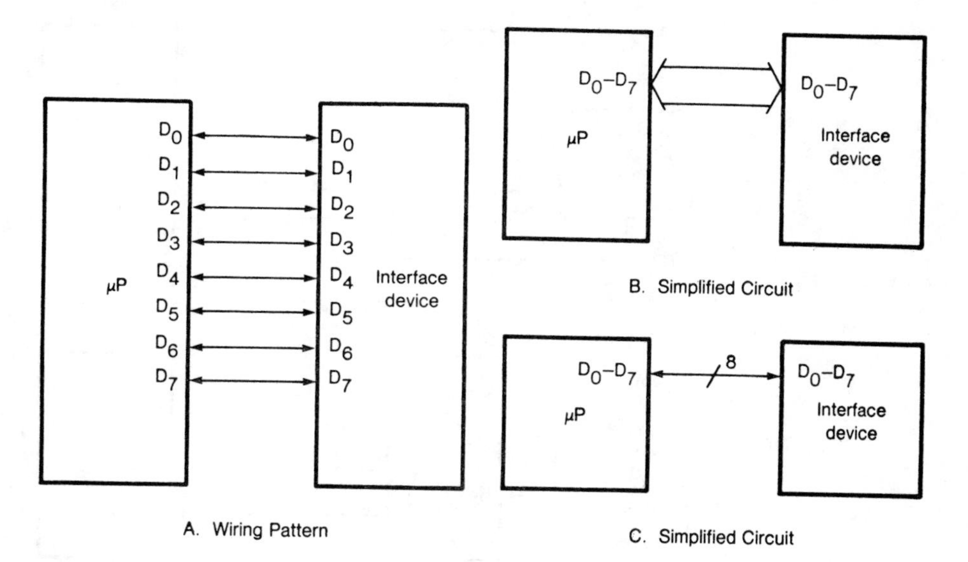

FIGURE 17–6 Data Bus Connections

device is doing. The pins are labeled $\overline{RD}$ and $\overline{WR}$. The bar indicates that these inputs are active low states. When the chip is selected and the $\overline{RD}$ pin is brought low, the μP is reading data from one of the registers within the interface chip. When the chip is selected and the $\overline{WR}$ pin is at a low logic level, the μP is writing data to one of the interface device's registers.

ϕ_2 Clock

The ϕ_2 clock input pin is used to receive the ϕ_2 clock signal so that all data transferred to and from the interface device is synchronized with the μP. This clock signal is used by many interface devices to generate their own internal timing signals.

On data sheets for Intel products, this pin is labeled clock (CLK) input. On Motorola data sheets, the term *enable* is used. When the 6800 μP is used, the ϕ_2 (TTL) line must be ANDed with the μP's VMA (valid memory address) line. The output of the AND gate is then connected to the interface device's enable pin. Figure 17–7A shows the clock line for the 6800. Figure 17–7B shows that a 6502 μP's ϕ_2 clock line can be connected directly to the enable pin—that is, this μP does not have a VMA pin.

On some Motorola data sheets, the term *clock* may be used, but it is intended for a clock signal other than the ϕ_2 clock signal. Thus, it is important to check the data sheet for each interface device carefully before using it.

Interrupt Request

Interface devices usually have one or more interrupt request pins. An interrupt request is a signal from an interface device to the μP. The signal indicates that the interface device needs servicing from the μP. Since the 8080A, 6800, and 6502 μPs have only one interrupt request pin (not counting the nonmask-

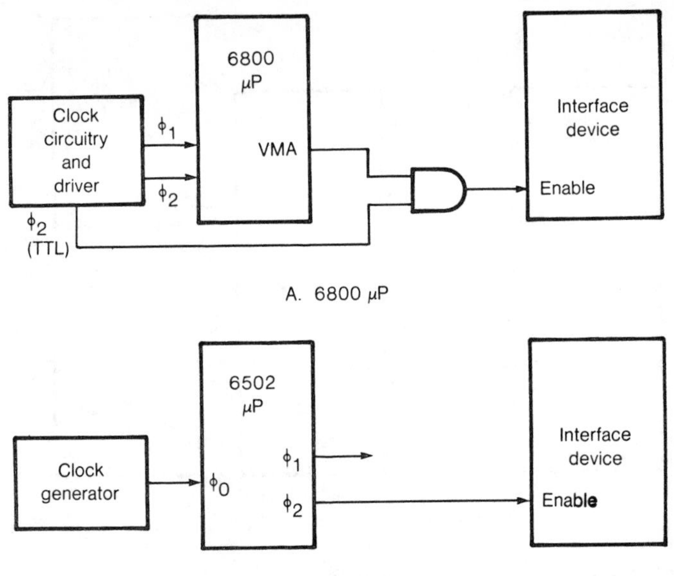

FIGURE 17–7 ϕ_2 Clock Lines for 6800 μP and 6502 μP

able interrupt pin of the 6800 and 6502), then all interrupt request lines from interface devices must be wired together, as shown in Figure 17–8. In order to be able to tie a number of interface interrupt request pins together, manufacturers have used open drain circuitry on this pin. Therefore, a pull-up resistor is needed on the interrupt request line, and that is the function of the 3.0-kilohm resistor in Figure 17–8.

If a number of interrupt request lines are tied together, then the μP has to have a way of determining which interrupt needs servicing. This is done by a program called an interrupt polling routine. The μP checks the status of the interrupt request line of each interface device. The order in which they are checked is determined by the writer of the polling routine program. Obviously, this technique takes time, especially if a number of interrupt request lines are tied together.

Another technique for determining which I/O device is signaling the μP is a hardware approach. All interrupt request lines are wired to an interrupt controller chip. The function of this chip is to determine the order in which interrupt request lines need servicing and also to send one signal to the μP. The μP checks the controller chip to find out which interface device needs servicing.

Reset

Some interface devices have a reset pin that is connected to the system's master reset line. The 6800 and 6502 μP systems have active low reset lines, while an 8080A system has an active high reset line. That is, when the reset

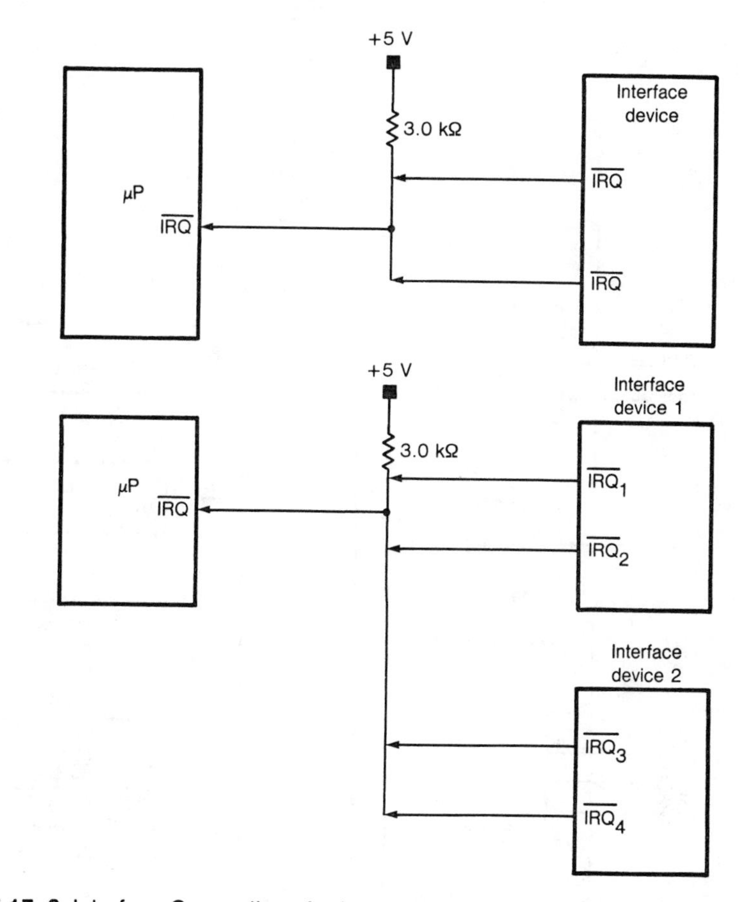

FIGURE 17–8 Interface Connections for Interrupt Request Pins

line goes to its active state, all devices wired to it set their internal registers to a predetermined logic state. In most cases, that state is a logic 0.

Some interface devices do not have a reset pin. The internal registers of these devices go to a predetermined logic state (usually logic 0) by circuitry within the device that senses the voltage level of the power supply line (the V_{CC} line). The term *predetermined logic state* means that the logic state is determined by the manufacturer, not by the user.

17.3 INTERNAL BLOCK DIAGRAMS

The internal block diagram for each peripheral device is different because of the different functions the devices perform. However, there are many common points, and Figure 17–9 shows some block diagrams and terms that are applicable to many interface devices.

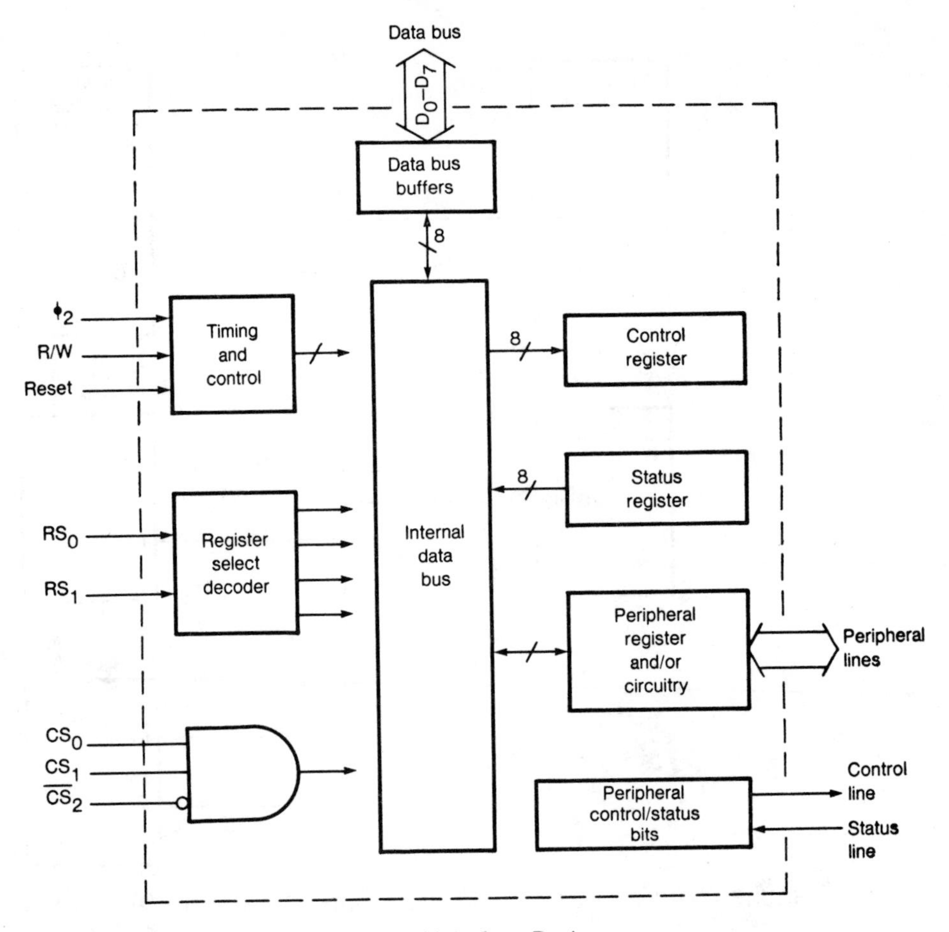

FIGURE 17–9 General Block Diagram of Interface Device

17.3.1 Address Decoding

Chip Select

Like memory chips, interface devices have internal circuitry that enables them. In other words, this circuitry "tells" the device whether or not the μP wishes to communicate with it. For the three chip select lines shown in Figure 17–9, the circuit is a three-input AND gate. The output of this gate activates the timing and control section.

Register Select

Besides the chip select circuitry, the interface device must have circuitry to decode the particular register that is going to communicate with the μP. As with any decoder, the number of output lines equals 2^n, where n equals the number of input lines. Figure 17–9 shows two register select input lines and four ($2^2 = 4$) output lines. Therefore, the μP is able to communicate with four internal registers of the interface device. In general, the number of register select lines determines the number of registers that can communicate with the μP. As we study some interface devices, however, we will see that manufacturers sometimes use other techniques.

Manufacturers may show the chip and register select circuitry as a single block or in a block with the device's timing and control circuitry.

17.3.2 Timing and Control

The function of this block is to receive the ϕ_2 clock signal, the read/write signal (or signals), and the reset signal (if the device has a reset pin), and to generate the internal timing and control pulses to allow data to flow from one internal interface register to another, from an interface register to the μP or from the μP to an interface register.

The direction of data to and from the μP is determined by the logic state of the read/write line. This logic state, in conjunction with circuitry of the timing and control section, determines what happens in the data bus buffer section.

17.3.3 Data Bus Buffers

The data bus buffers allow the transfer of data between the μP and the interface device. The circuitry in this block has output drivers that are three-state devices. When the interface chip is not selected, the drivers are in their high impedance (off) state. When the μP has selected the interface chip and is going to read data from it, the output drivers are turned on and are TTL compatible. Remember, when the μP is reading data, the interface device is sending it.

When the μP is writing (sending) data to the interface chip, the output drivers are turned off and the data is received through this block and either transferred to the appropriate register or captured in an input data latch network (not shown in Figure 17–9).

17.3.4 Internal Bus Structure

Interface devices move data between registers 8 bits (one byte) at a time. Therefore, each device has an 8-bit internal data bus. In addition, interface devices also have internal control lines.

Control lines originate at the control and timing block and go to the appropriate registers. Other signal lines are sometimes needed between registers so that the logic state of a bit (or bits) can be monitored.

The internal structure of interface devices is not considered to have an address bus. An address is decoded, as previously mentioned, and a control signal is sent to the appropriate register telling it to be ready to send or receive data.

17.3.5 Control Register

Large-scale-integration (LSI) interface devices are programmable devices. That is, a binary pattern sent to these devices determines how they will operate. For example, a binary pattern to an interface adapter chip determines which line (or lines) is input and which is output. An asynchronous interface chip uses a binary pattern to know at what rate to transmit and receive data. A timer interface chip uses a binary pattern to determine the time interval between the pulses that it generates. Some interface chips can perform different functions or the same function at different speeds, or can disable or enable the interrupt request line, or can perform several other operations. Therefore, by changing the binary pattern, the user can make use of a number of options for the best overall design.

Most interface devices have what is known as a *control register*. The binary pattern loaded into this register programs how the interface chip will do a job, and in some cases the binary pattern programs the choice of job. The binary pattern that the μP sends to this register is often referred to as the *control word*. The control register in some interface devices is a register to which the μP can only write data. For these devices, the μP cannot read data from the control register. Other interface devices allow the μP to read and write data to and from the control register. Each bit of the control register has a specific function in determining how the interface device will operate.

17.3.6 Status Register

As data or control signals are transferred between the μP and an internal register, between registers, or between the interface device and peripheral equipment, the interface chip must keep a "record" of these transfers so that the μP can periodically check the record and know that everything is operating correctly. This record-keeping register is most often referred to as the *status register*. As with other registers, this is an 8-bit register. Each bit is a record of a different function. Status registers are read-only registers; that is, the μP can read data from the register but cannot write data to it. Once the μP has read the data, it can check the logic state of each bit and make a decision about what to do next.

Some interface devices do not need an 8-bit control register and an 8-bit status register. In these chips, there may be one control/status register. Part of the register is used for control and the remaining part for status. When the μP sends an 8-bit binary pattern to this type of dual function register, the data will enter only those bits that are the control bits. All other bits are ignored. When the μP reads this type of register to find out the logic state of the status bit(s), the control bits are often sent too. However, the program can be written to ignore the control bits and concentrate only on the status bits.

17.3.7 Peripheral Registers or Circuitry

The registers, or circuitry, that are connected to the peripheral lines are usually labeled for the specific function that they perform. For example, in the CRT (cathode ray tube) controller chip, the circuitry that controls the video is labeled the video output. In an asynchronous interface chip, the register that is used to send data to peripheral equipment is labeled the transmit shift register, while the register that receives the data is labeled the receive shift register. General-purpose interface adapter chips refer to the register that is connected to the I/O lines as either a peripheral register or as a port.

17.3.8 Peripheral Status/Control Logic

In addition to the peripheral lines, many interface devices are designed to send or receive control signals from peripheral equipment and act on these signals. Depending on the interface device, these signals may be used by the device without disturbing the μP. In other cases, the μP must be notified of what is happening, and for those cases an interrupt request signal is sent to the μP.

The circuitry in the control block works with the status and control registers. Some differences are: There are usually only one or two bits associated with this block and the μP does not have access to it. The μP has access only to the status and control registers. Therefore, if the logic state of the peripheral control block is to be interpreted by the μP, it is interpreted through the status register. Likewise, if an interface device has a peripheral control logic circuit, then its logic state is usually set by the μP through the control register. This procedure allows two or more bits of the control register to determine the logic state for a single control line.

17.4 SUMMARY

Microprocessor manufacturers have designed a number of general-purpose and specific-purpose interface devices. Although they have been built to do many different jobs, there are many similarities among interface devices. In this chapter, we examined the common points from pin designations to internal architecture.

As the link between the μP and peripheral equipment, the interface device can be visualized as having a μP side and a peripheral side. On the μP side, the pins are connected to the address, data, and control buses. On the peripheral side, the interface device's I/O lines are connected to the external equipment.

Some of the common points of the internal architecture are shown in Section 17.3. They are: address bus decoding circuitry; timing and control circuitry; data bus buffers; control, status, and peripheral registers; and peripheral status/control logic. The next two chapters focus on two popular interface chips, how they are connected to the buses, and how they are programmed to send or receive data between the μP and peripheral equipment.

PROBLEMS

17-1 What is the purpose of an interface device?

17-2 Why are interface devices programmable?

17-3 Are interface devices connected to the μP's address, data, and control buses?

17-4 What pins on the interface device are used by the μP to indicate that the μP wants to communicate with it?

17-5 Can unused chip select lines be left "floating"?

17-6 What is the purpose of the register select lines?

17-7 To what bus lines should the register select lines be connected?

17-8 Are register select lines connected to decoder chips or directly to the μP?

17-9 How are the interface chip's data lines connected to the μP?

17-10 What are the most common control bus connections?

17-11 What is the purpose of the ϕ_2 pin on the interface device?

17-12 On the interface device, is the interrupt request line an input or output control line?

17-13 What is the name of the program used to identify the interrupt that needs servicing?

17-14 What is the function of a reset pin?

17-15 List the internal blocks that are common to many interface devices.

17-16 For most peripheral devices, if there are two register select lines, with how many internal registers can the μP communicate?

17-17 When a device is not selected, what state are the data lines in?

17-18 Which register receives the binary pattern that programs the device? What is the binary pattern called?

17-19 Which register keeps a "record" of what is happening in the interface device?

Chapter 18

Programmable Peripheral Interface 8255A

18.0 INTRODUCTION

Intel's 8255A is a general-purpose input/output device. It is referred to as a programmable peripheral interface (PPI) device. Although it has been designed for use in Intel μC systems, it can be used with other μPs. It is housed in a standard 40-pin dual-in-line package, as shown in Figure 18-1. Of the 40 pins, 24 are for input/output lines. The 8255A is used as the interface device between peripheral equipment—such as paper tape, printers, keyboards, A-to-D and D-to-A converters, CRT controllers, and floppy disk controllers—and the μP. As its name implies, the 8255A can be programmed so that in most applications no external logic is necessary for the peripheral equipment to interact with the rest of the μC system.

18.1 8255A PIN DESCRIPTIONS

I/O Pins: The 8255A's 24 I/O pins are grouped as three ports—port A, PA_0–PA_7; port B, PB_0–PB_7; and port C, PC_0–PC_7.

V_{CC}, GND: These are the power supply pins. They are connected to the μC's power supply lines. V_{CC} = +5 V.

Reset: This pin is connected to the μC's reset lines. When the logic level of the reset pin goes high, all the 8255A's internal registers go to a logic 0. In addition, the I/O line and the 8255A's data bus lines go to a high impedance state.

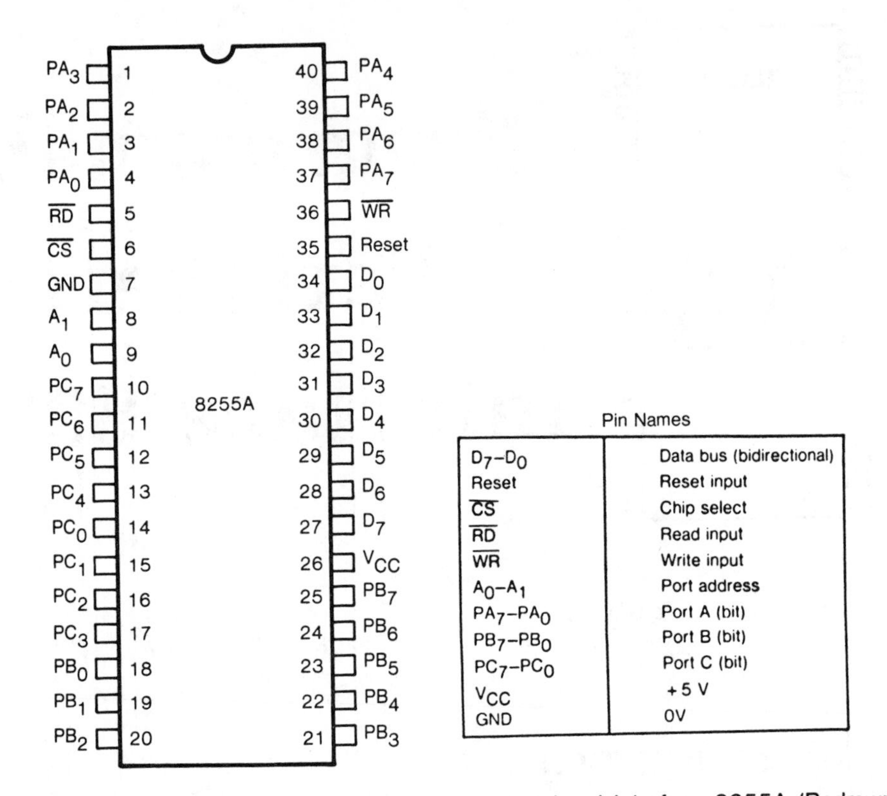

Pin Names

D_7–D_0	Data bus (bidirectional)
Reset	Reset input
$\overline{CS}$	Chip select
$\overline{RD}$	Read input
$\overline{WR}$	Write input
A_0–A_1	Port address
PA_7–PA_0	Port A (bit)
PB_7–PB_0	Port B (bit)
PC_7–PC_0	Port C (bit)
V_{CC}	+5 V
GND	0V

FIGURE 18–1 Pin Assignments for Programmable Peripheral Interface 8255A (Redrawn from data sheet for 8255A PPI with permission. Intel Corporation, Santa Clara, CA)

Data Bus (D_0–D_7): The 8255A's data bus is a bidirectional three-state bus. The eight lines of this data bus are connected to the corresponding eight lines of the μP's data bus. When the device is not selected by the μP, the 8255A's data bus goes to its high impedance state. All data, control words, and status information between the μP and the 8255A are transmitted across this bus.

Chip Select ($\overline{CS}$): This pin is the master chip select for the 8255A. If a logic 0 is applied to this pin, the device is selected; that is, the μP and the 8255A can communicate across the data bus. If the logic level on the chip select pin is high, the device is deselected and the data bus buffer goes to its high impedance state.

Port/Register Select (A_0–A_1): If the 8255A is selected using the $\overline{CS}$ pin, then pins A_0 and A_1 select which of the three ports or the control register is to be connected to the μP. These pins are normally connected to the μP's address lines A_0 and A_1, respectively, as shown in Figure 18–2. Table 18-1 shows how the chip select pin and address pins A_0 and A_1 are used to select a particular port or control register.

Read ($\overline{RD}$): When the voltage level on this pin goes low (logic 0), the μP is receiving data from the 8255A.

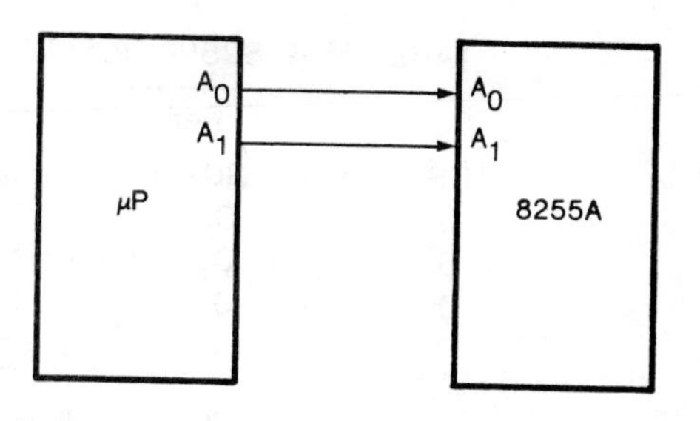

FIGURE 18–2 Connections for 8255A Port/Register Select Pins

TABLE 18–1 8255A Port/Register Selection

$\overline{CS}$	A_1	A_0	Selected Port/Register
0	0	0	Port A
0	0	1	Port B
0	1	0	Port C
0	1	1	Control register
1	X[1]	X[1]	Device not selected

[1]X = logic 0 or logic 1.

Write ($\overline{WR}$): When the voltage level on this pin goes low (logic 0), the μP is sending data or control words to the 8255A. Table 18–2 shows how the logic levels on the read and write pins, along with logic levels on the $\overline{CS}$, A_0, and A_1 pins, work to connect the μP to an 8255A device. The direction of data flow is also shown in the table.

18.2 PORTS A, B, AND C

The 8255A contains three 8-bit ports (A, B, and C).

Port A: Port A can be programmed as either an input port or an output port or as a bidirectional port. When this port is programmed as a bidirectional port, it acts as an extension of the data bus.

Port B: Port B can be programmed as either an input or an output port. It cannot be programmed as a bidirectional port.

Port C: Port C can be programmed as an 8-bit port for either input or output. This port can also be divided into two 4-bit ports, port C upper (PC_4–PC_7) and port C lower (PC_0–PC_3). The upper half can be programmed as an output port and the lower half can be programmed as an input port, or vice versa. In addition, port C can be used in conjunction with ports A and B to indicate output control signals or input status signals.

Thus, we see that ports A, B, and C all can be programmed but not necessarily in the same way. Since ports A, B, and C can be programmed in different ways, the 8255A can be used in a wide variety of applications. The way ports A, B, and C are used depends on the 8255A's mode of operation.

TABLE 18–2 8255A Read/Write Operation

Read Operation					
$\overline{CS}$	A_1	A_0	$\overline{RD}$	$\overline{WR}$	Direction of Data
0	0	0	0	1	Port A to μP
0	0	1	0	1	Port B to μP
0	1	0	0	1	Port C to μP
0	1	1	0	1	Illegal condition[1]
Write Operation					
$\overline{CS}$	A_1	A_0	$\overline{RD}$	$\overline{WR}$	Direction of Data
0	0	0	1	0	μP to port A
0	0	1	1	0	μP to port B
0	1	0	1	0	μP to port C
0	1	1	1	0	μP to control register
Three-State Condition					
$\overline{CS}$	A_1	A_0	$\overline{RD}$	$\overline{WR}$	Data Buffers
1	X[2]	X[2]	X[2]	X[2]	High-impedance state
0	X[2]	X[2]	1	1	High-impedance state

[1] μP cannot read data from the control register.
[2] X = logic 0 or logic 1.

18.3 MODE SELECTION

The 8255A has three modes of operation that can be selected by the computer program. They are as follows:

Mode 0, basic input/output
Mode 1, strobed input/output
Mode 2, bidirectional bus

Port A can be programmed in any one of the three modes. Port B can only be programmed in mode 0 or mode 1. Port A and port B do not have to be programmed in the same mode at the same time. When port A is programmed in one mode and port B in another, this is called *mode combination* and is covered in Section 18.7.

The mode of port C cannot be programmed independently. Port C is divided into two portions (the upper part, PC_4–PC_7, and the lower part, PC_0–PC_3). Port C upper assumes the same mode as port A. Port C lower assumes the same mode as port B. Therefore, the 8255A has three ports, but they are programmed as two groups, control group A and control group B:

Control group A, port A and port C upper
Control group B, port B and port C lower

Figure 18–3 shows which internal blocks of the 8255A are in group A and which are in group B. Each of the control blocks (group A and group B) accepts signals from the read/write control logic block, accepts control words from the

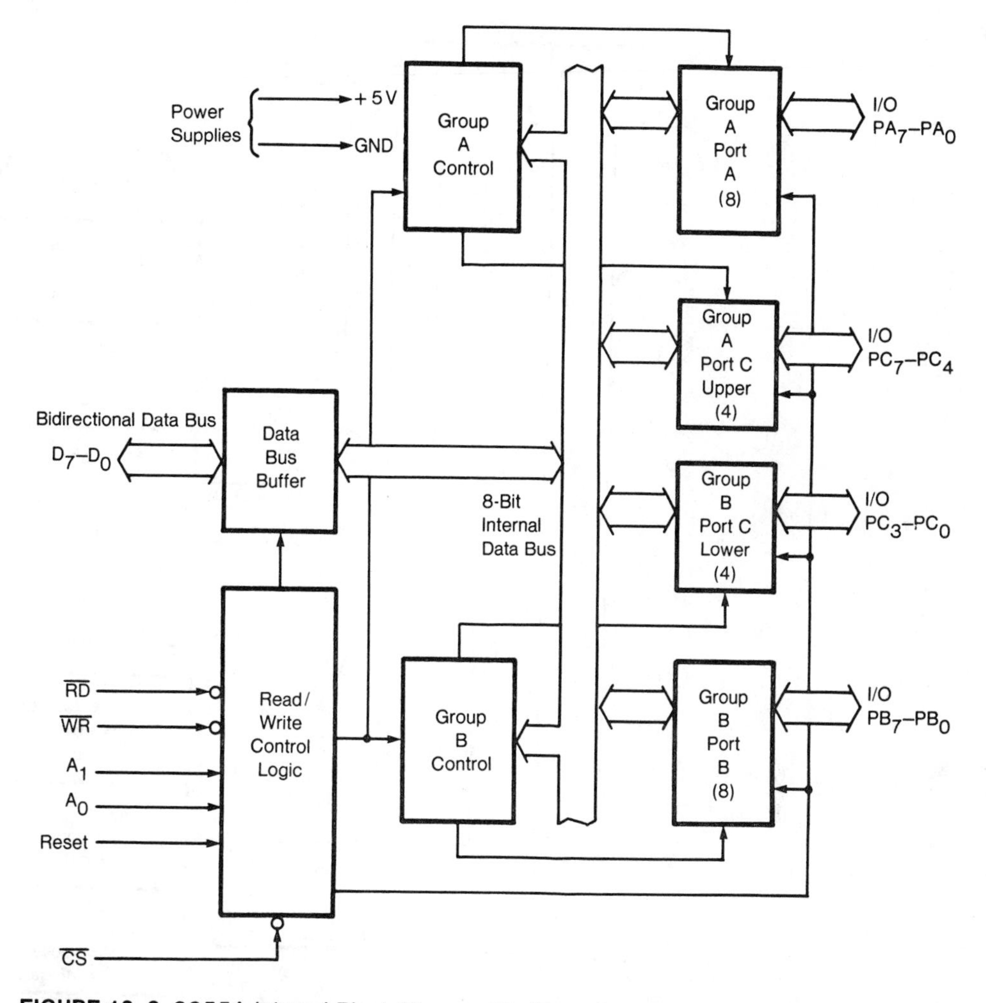

FIGURE 18–3 8255A Internal Block Diagram (Redrawn from data sheet for 8255A PPI with permission. Intel Corporation, Santa Clara, CA)

μP, and then sends the proper signals to its associated ports. The control word sent to the 8255A from the μP tells the 8255A which mode each group will be in and which ports will be input or output.

When the 8255A is used, a control word is first sent to the device from the μP. This 8-bit control word is decoded in the group A and group B control blocks. The control word contains the mode of operation for both group A and group B and denotes which ports will be input or output ports. The format for the control word is shown in Figure 18–4, where the control word is the binary pattern in the control register. In order for one of the modes to be selected, bit 7 of the control word must be a logic 1. If bit 7 of the control word is a logic 0, then the programmer is using another feature of the 8255A called single-bit set/reset. This feature will be covered in Section 18.9.

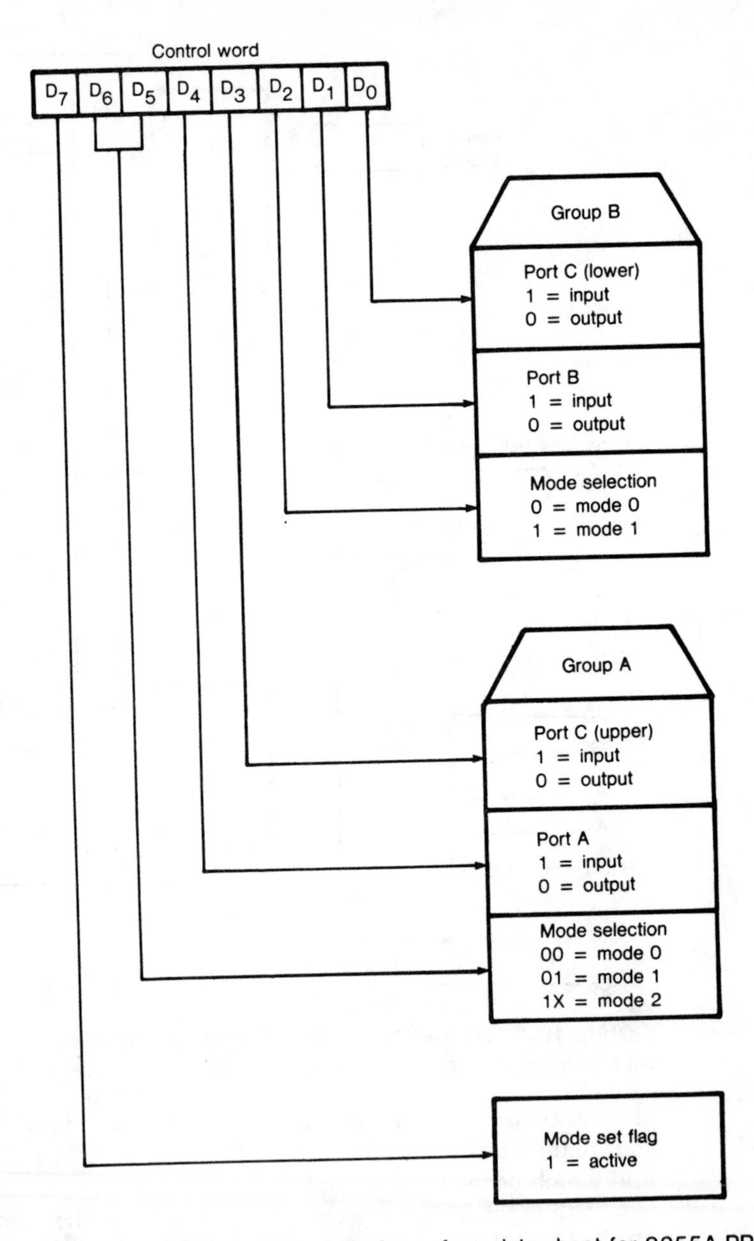

FIGURE 18–4 Format for Control Word (Redrawn from data sheet for 8255A PPI with permission. Intel Corporation, Santa Clara, CA)

Figure 18–4 shows that bits 0, 1, and 2 of the control word define the mode of operation for group B, determine whether port B is an input or an output port, and determine whether the lower part of port C is an input or an output port. Figure 18–4 also shows that bits 3, 4, 5, and 6 of the control word define the mode of operation for group A, determine whether port A is input or output, and determine whether the upper half of port C is input or output.

18.4 MODE 0 (BASIC INPUT/OUTPUT)

In this section, we will examine what is referred to as the basic or simple input/output configuration for the 8255A. It is called this because both group A and group B are programmed for mode 0 operation. This mode allows the μP to write or read data from any specified port. In this mode of operation, there is no "handshaking" between peripheral equipment and the interface device. The 8255A device operates in the following manner when it is programmed in mode 0 operation:

1. Port A can be programmed as either an input or an output port.
2. Port B can also be programmed as either an input or an output port.
3. Port C is divided into two 4-bit ports and each portion can be programmed as either an input or an output port.
4. When any port is programmed as an output port, data is latched; that is, the data is held by the port until new data is sent to that port by the μP.
5. Input ports do not latch data in this mode.
6. In the control word format of Figure 18–4, bits D_2, D_5, D_6, and D_7 must be programmed as $D_2 = 0$, $D_5 = 0$, $D_6 = 0$, and $D_7 = 1$.
7. The remaining four bits (D_0, D_1, D_3, and D_4) determine how port A, port B, and both parts of port C are to operate. These four bits produce 16 different input/output configurations in mode 0. These 16 possible configurations are listed in Table 18–3.

TABLE 18–3 Mode 0 Operation

A		B		GROUP A			GROUP B	
D_4	D_3	D_1	D_0	PORT A	PORT C (UPPER)	#	PORT B	PORT C (LOWER)
0	0	0	0	OUTPUT	OUTPUT	0	OUTPUT	OUTPUT
0	0	0	1	OUTPUT	OUTPUT	1	OUTPUT	INPUT
0	0	1	0	OUTPUT	OUTPUT	2	INPUT	OUTPUT
0	0	1	1	OUTPUT	OUTPUT	3	INPUT	INPUT
0	1	0	0	OUTPUT	INPUT	4	OUTPUT	OUTPUT
0	1	0	1	OUTPUT	INPUT	5	OUTPUT	INPUT
0	1	1	0	OUTPUT	INPUT	6	INPUT	OUTPUT
0	1	1	1	OUTPUT	INPUT	7	INPUT	INPUT
1	0	0	0	INPUT	OUTPUT	8	OUTPUT	OUTPUT
1	0	0	1	INPUT	OUTPUT	9	OUTPUT	INPUT
1	0	1	0	INPUT	OUTPUT	10	INPUT	OUTPUT
1	0	1	1	INPUT	OUTPUT	11	INPUT	INPUT
1	1	0	0	INPUT	INPUT	12	OUTPUT	OUTPUT
1	1	0	1	INPUT	INPUT	13	OUTPUT	INPUT
1	1	1	0	INPUT	INPUT	14	INPUT	OUTPUT
1	1	1	1	INPUT	INPUT	15	INPUT	INPUT

Source: Reprinted with permission of Intel Corporation, Santa Clara, CA.

18.5 MODE 1 (STROBED INPUT/OUTPUT)

In this section, we will see how both group A and group B can be programmed for mode 1 operation. In this mode, port A and port B use lines on port C to generate or accept handshaking signals. Let's list what can be expected in this mode:

1. Port A can be programmed as either an input or an output port.
2. Port B can be programmed as either an input or an output port.
3. Port C is divided into three sections. Three port C lines generate or accept signals for port A. Another three port C lines generate or accept signals for port B. The remaining two port C lines can be programmed as two input lines or two output lines, but not one of each.
4. When both port A and port B are programmed for mode 1 operation, the following control bits are fixed—$D_2 = 1, D_5 = 1, D_6 = 0$, and $D_7 = 1$. Control word bit D_0 can be either a logic 0 or a logic 1 because this bit is used by neither port nor is it used to indicate an I/O condition.
5. When port A is programmed as an input port, PC_3, PC_4, and PC_5 are used in conjunction with port A. For this condition, port lines PC_6 and PC_7 are the I/O lines.
6. When port A is programmed as an output port, PC_3, PC_6, and PC_7 are used with port A for the handshaking signals. For this condition, port lines PC_4 and PC_5 are port C's I/O lines.
7. Port C lines PC_0, PC_1, and PC_2 are used with port B, regardless of whether port B is programmed as an input port or an output port.

18.5.1 Input Control Signals

In this section, we will examine how both port A and port B are programmed as input ports in mode 1 operation. The following descriptions apply to those lines of port C that indicate status and control for this type of operation. To see which port C lines apply to port A and port B, refer to Figure 18–5A for port A operation and Figure 18–5B for port B operation.

In mode 1 operation, peripheral equipment supplies data to the input port and a control signal called *strobe input*. In response, the 8255A can send a signal back to the peripheral equipment and an interrupt signal to the μP. Let's examine how the lines function.

$\overline{\text{STB}}$ (Strobe Input): A low (logic 0) on this line loads the data from peripheral equipment into the input port where it is latched.

IBF (Input Buffer Full): After the data has been loaded and latched into the input port, a flip-flop within the 8255A is set (logic 1). The output of this flip-flop is the IBF line. This line is used as an acknowledgment to the peripheral equipment that the 8255A has received the data. This is a handshake signal. Note that the IBF line is set when the $\overline{\text{STB}}$ input is low. The timing diagram is shown in Figure 18–6. The IBF line is reset (logic 0) by the rising edge of the $\overline{\text{RD}}$ input, as shown in Figure 18–6.

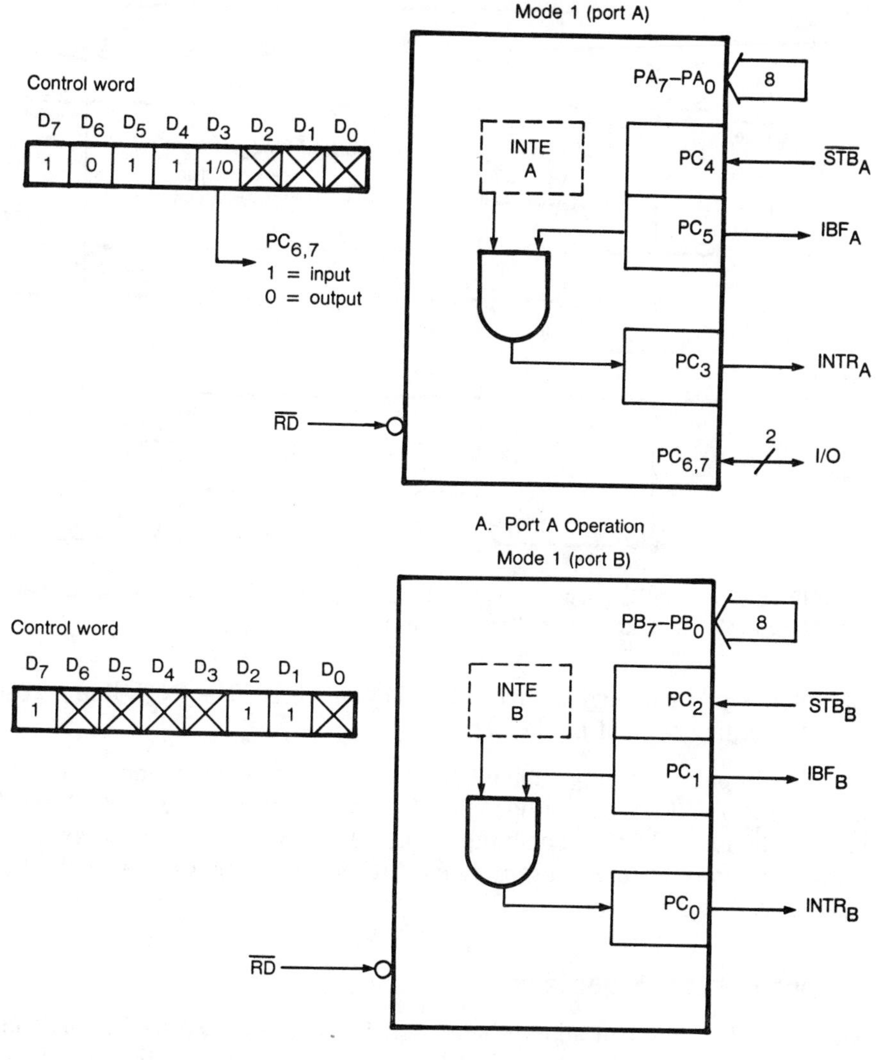

FIGURE 18–5 Port A and Port B Mode 1 Input Operation (Redrawn from data sheet for 8255A PPI with permission. Intel Corporation, Santa Clara, CA)

INTR (Interrupt Request): A high (logic 1) on this line can be used as an interrupt signal to the μP. This signal tells the μP that a piece of peripheral equipment has sent data to the 8255A and the 8255A is requesting service. For the INTR line to go high, the following conditions must be met—(1) $\overline{\text{STB}}$ must be in a logic 1 state, (2) IBF must be in a logic 1 state, and (3) INTE must be in a logic 1 state. INTE is a flip-flop inside the 8255A that can be programmed as either a logic 0 or as a logic 1. How this flip-

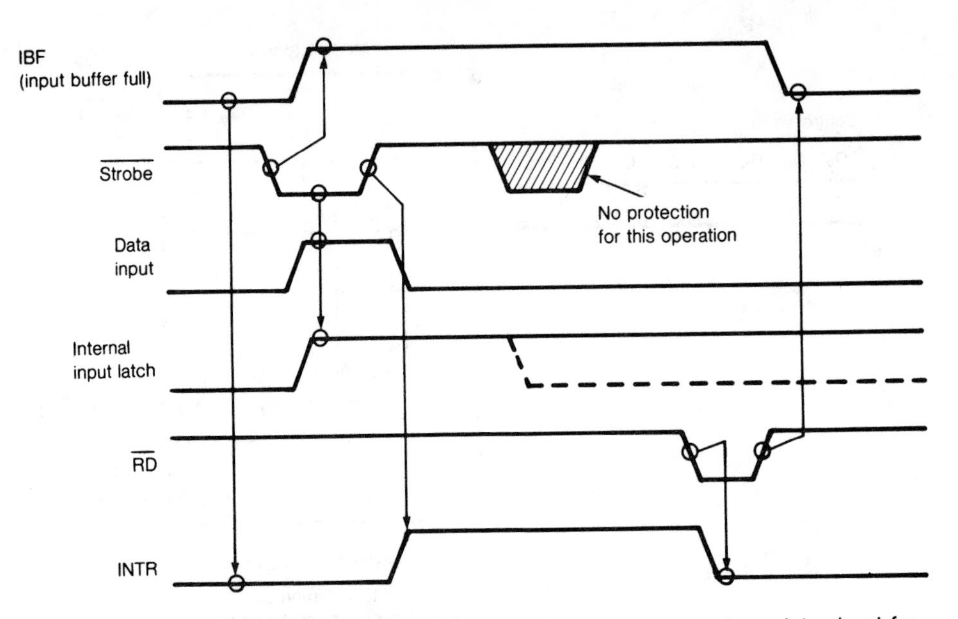

FIGURE 18–6 Timing Diagram for Mode 1 Input Operation (Redrawn from data sheet for 8255A PPI with permission. Intel Corporation, Santa Clara, CA)

flop is programmed is covered in Section 18.10. The INTR line is reset by the falling edge of the $\overline{\text{RD}}$ signal.

When port A is programmed as an input port in mode 1 operation, port C lines 6 and 7 automatically become I/O lines. If bit 3 of the control word is a logic 1, then both lines become input lines. If bit 3 is programmed as a logic 0, then both lines become output lines. Figure 18–5 shows the mode 1 input operation.

18.5.2 Output Control Signals

Mode 1 output control signals are used when the μP wants to send data to peripheral equipment and receive an acknowledgment that the data has been received. To do this, the μP sends the data to an output port of the 8255A. Then the 8255A sends a signal to the peripheral equipment telling the equipment that data is ready. When the peripheral equipment has taken the data, it sends back to the 8255A an acknowledgment signal. After receiving the acknowledgment signal, the 8255A can send an interrupt signal to the μP. The μP uses this interrupt signal as an acknowledgment that data has been sent and received by the peripheral equipment. Let's go over each output control line in more detail.

In this discussion of control lines, both port A and port B are programmed as output ports in mode 1 operation. Figure 18–7A shows the control lines that work with port A, and Figure 18–7B shows the control lines that work with port B. The following descriptions of the port control lines apply for both port A and port B when they are operating in mode 1.

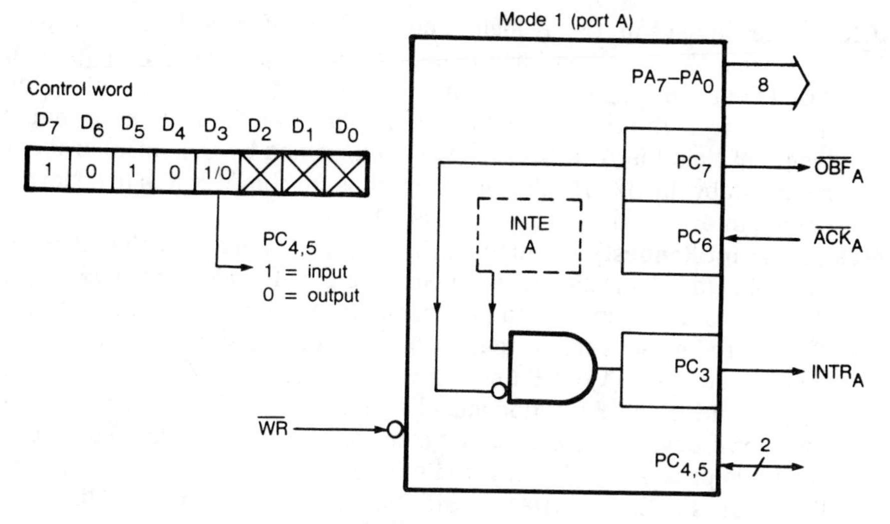

A. Port A Operation

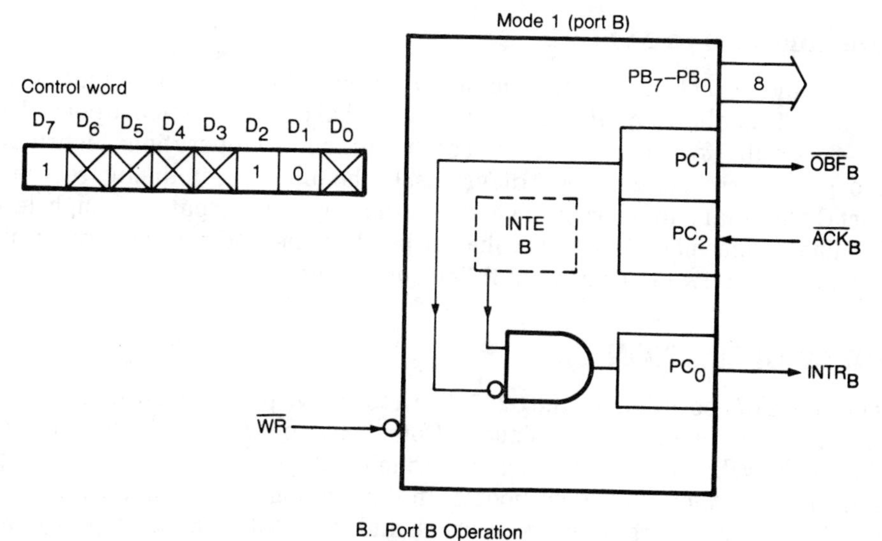

B. Port B Operation

FIGURE 18–7 Port A and Port B Mode 1 Output Operation (Redrawn from data sheet for 8255A PPI with permission. Intel Corporation, Santa Clara, CA)

$\overline{\text{OBF}}$ (Output Buffer Full): After the μP has sent (written) data to the 8255A, a flip-flop within the 8255A is cleared to a logic 0. The output of this flip-flop is the $\overline{\text{OBF}}$ line. Figure 18–8 shows the timing diagram. *Note:* From Figure 18–8, we see that the $\overline{\text{OBF}}$ line goes to the 0 state after the rising edge of the $\overline{\text{WR}}$ signal. This timing guarantees that the correct data has been written into the 8255A from the μP. The $\overline{\text{OBF}}$ line returns to its high state after the acknowledge, $\overline{\text{ACK}}$, signal.

$\overline{\text{ACK}}$ (Acknowledge Input): A logic 0 on this line informs the 8255A that the data from the port has been accepted by the peripheral equipment. In essence, it is a response from the peripheral equipment indicating that it has received the data sent by the μP. This is a handshake signal. The length of time the $\overline{\text{ACK}}$ line is low is determined by the peripheral equipment, not by the 8255A. The minimum time for the $\overline{\text{ACK}}$ line to be low, so it can be interpreted by the 8255A, is 300 ns.

INTR (Interrupt Request): A high on this line can be used by the μP as an interrupt signal. This signal can be used to give the μP an acknowledgment that the data transmitted to the peripheral equipment has been received. The interrupt request line goes to the logic 1 state when the following conditions are met—(1) $\overline{\text{OBF}}$ line must be a logic 1, (2) $\overline{\text{ACK}}$ line must be a logic 1, and (3) INTE flip-flop must be a logic 1. The INTE flip-flop is within the 8255A device and can be programmed to either a logic 0 or a logic 1. How it is programmed is covered in Section 18.10. The interrupt request line returns to the logic 0 state with the falling edge of the $\overline{\text{WR}}$ line. Figure 18–8 shows the timing diagram.

18.5.3 Combinations in Mode 1

Port A and port B can be individually programmed as input or output ports in mode 1. This allows a wide variety of handshake control applications. Table 18–4 lists the four possible combinations in mode 1 operation. Figure 18–9 shows the corresponding logic diagrams. In the table and in the figure, the two port C lines that can be programmed as either input or output are simply left as I/O lines. Remember that the value in bit 3 of the control word determines whether these two lines are input lines or output lines.

18.6 MODE 2 OPERATION

This mode of operation for the 8255A device allows port A to become a bidirectional bus with handshaking signals. *Note:* Only port A can be programmed in this mode. When port A is being used in mode 2, port B would have to be programmed in either mode 0 or mode 1. In this section, we will not consider port B. We will concentrate on how port A and the control lines of port C work together in this mode. The following list gives the functions that occur in mode 2 operation:

1. Port A becomes a bidirectional bus. Therefore, it can be used as an extension of the data bus to peripheral equipment.
2. Five lines of port C are used for handshaking signals. They are PC_3, PC_4, PC_5, PC_6, and PC_7.
3. The remaining three lines of port C can be programmed one of two ways. PC_0, PC_1, and PC_2 can be programmed as three input lines or three output lines if port B is programmed in mode 0 operation. Or, PC_0, PC_1, and PC_2 become handshake lines for port B if port B is programmed in mode 1 operation.

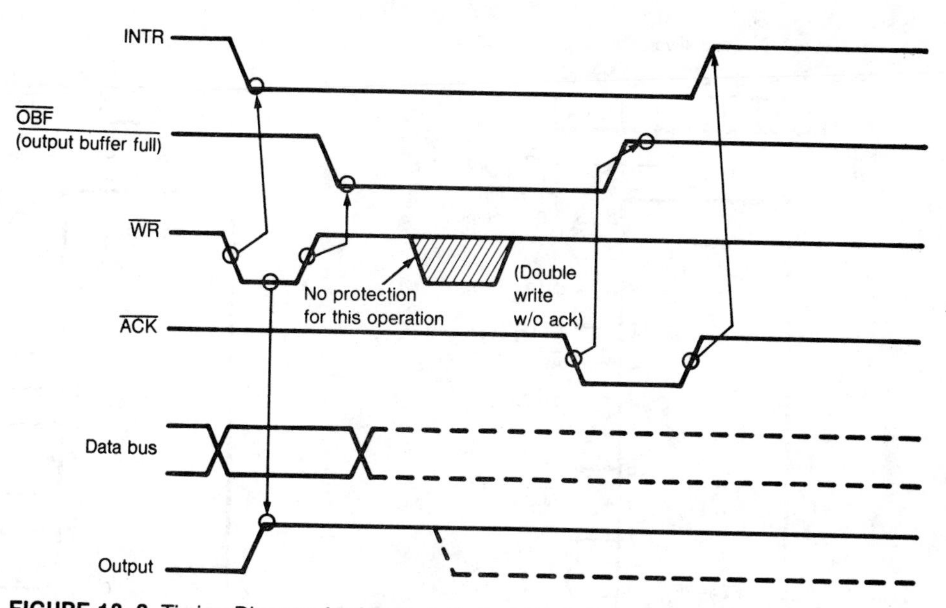

FIGURE 18–8 Timing Diagram for Mode 1 Output Operation (Redrawn from data sheet for 8255A PPI with permission. Intel Corporation, Santa Clara, CA)

TABLE 18–4 Mode 1 Combinations

Port A	Port B	Port C								See Figure
		PC_7	PC_6	PC_5	PC_4	PC_3	PC_2	PC_1	PC_0	
Output	Output	$\overline{OBF}_A$	$\overline{ACK}_A$	I/O	I/O	$INTR_A$	$\overline{ACK}_B$	$\overline{OBF}_B$	$INTR_B$	18–9A
Output	Input	$\overline{OBF}_A$	$\overline{ACK}_A$	I/O	I/O	$INTR_A$	$\overline{STB}_B$	IBF_B	$INTR_B$	18–9B
Input	Output	I/O	I/O	IBF_A	$\overline{STB}_A$	$INTR_A$	$\overline{ACK}_B$	$\overline{OBF}_B$	$INTR_B$	18–9C
Input	Input	I/O	I/O	IBF_A	$\overline{STB}_A$	$INTR_A$	$\overline{STB}_B$	IBF_B	$INTR_B$	18–9D

4. In terms of the control word format of Figure 18–4, only D_6 and D_7 are needed to specify mode 2 operation ($D_6 = 1$ and $D_7 = 1$). Control bits D_3, D_4, and D_5 may be either a logic 0 or a logic 1.
5. Input and output data at port A are latched.

This section covers only mode 2 operation. Combinations of different modes are left to Section 18.7. Let's consider what happens during input and output operations in mode 2.

18.6.1 Input Operations

The μP receives data from peripheral equipment through the 8255A in mode 2 operation in the same manner as it did in mode 1 operation. Figure 18–10 shows a logic diagram, and Figure 18–11 shows a timing diagram. Remember, mode 2 operation only applies to port A. The control lines of port C operate in the following manner.

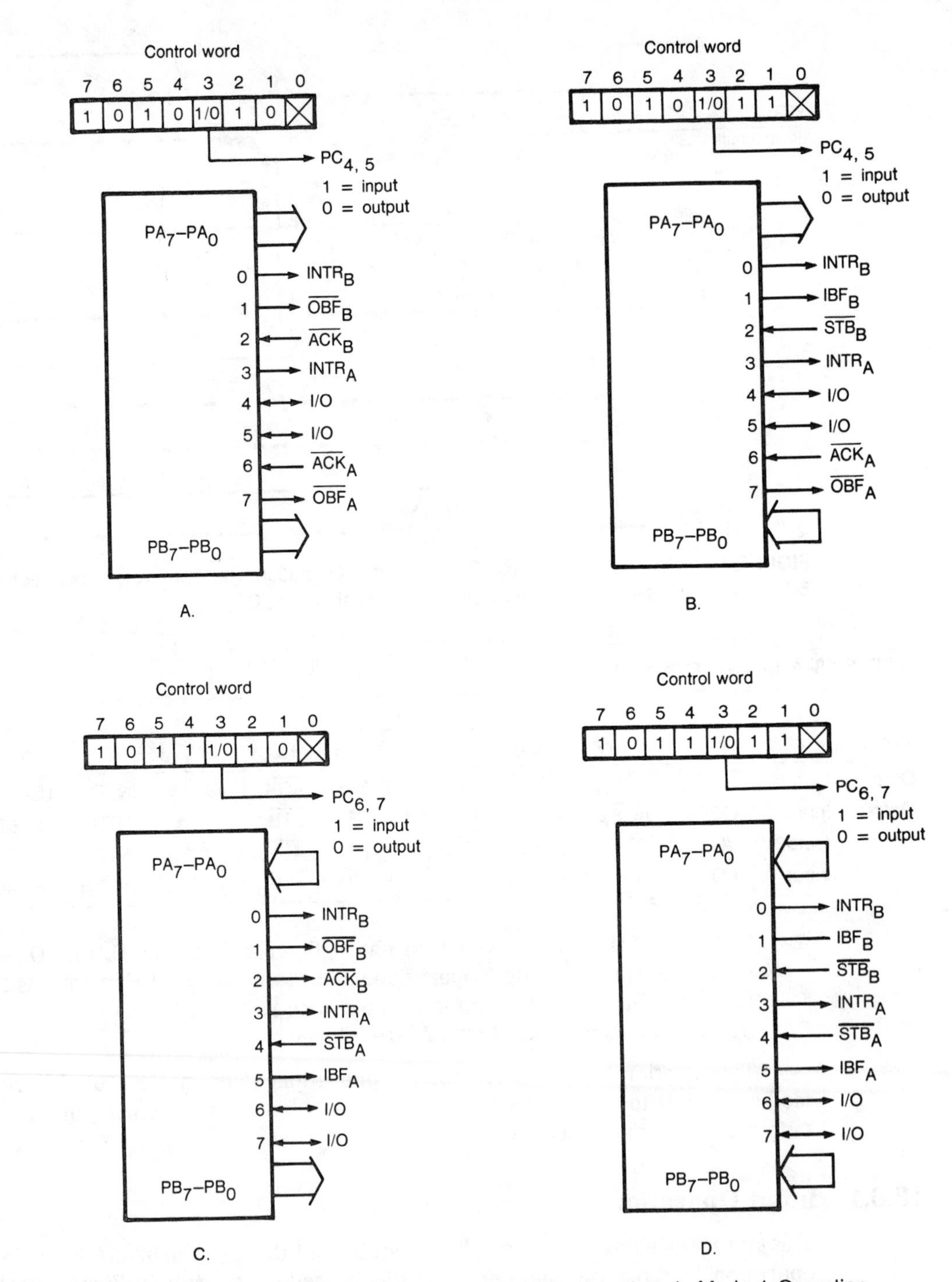

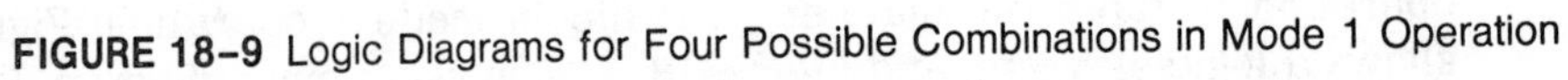
FIGURE 18–9 Logic Diagrams for Four Possible Combinations in Mode 1 Operation

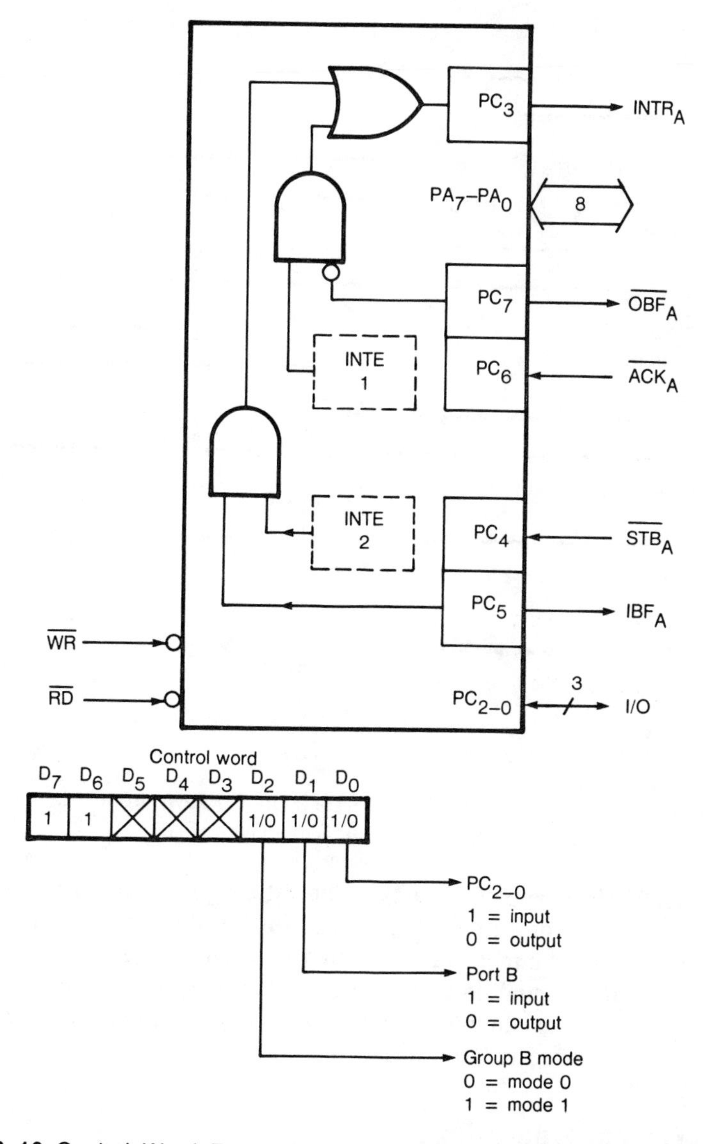

FIGURE 18–10 Control Word Format and Port C Control Lines for Mode 2 Operation (Redrawn from data sheet for 8255A PPI with permission. Intel Corporation, Santa Clara, CA)

$\overline{\text{STB}}$ (Strobe Input): A low on this input from peripheral equipment loads data into the input latch.

IBF (Input Buffer Full): After the data has been latched in the input port, a flip-flop within the 8255A is set. The output of this flip-flop is the IBF line. Therefore, this line goes high to indicate that the data has been loaded into the input port.

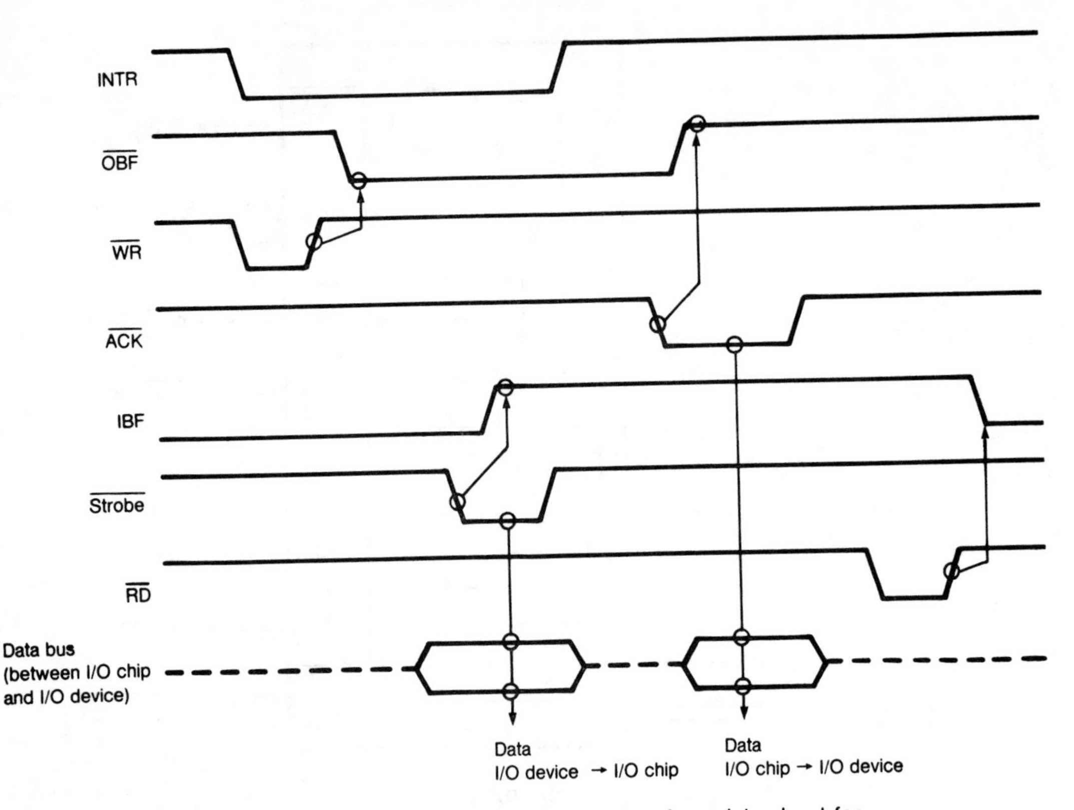

FIGURE 18–11 Timing Diagram for Mode 2 Operation (Redrawn from data sheet for 8255A PPI with permission. Intel Corporation, Santa Clara, CA)

INTR (Interrupt Request): The interrupt request line can be used for either input or output operations. For input operations, the following conditions must be met—(1) $\overline{\text{STB}}$ must be a logic 1, (2) IBF must be a logic 1, and (3) INTE must be a logic 1. INTE is a flip-flop within the 8255A device. It can be programmed as either a logic 0 or a logic 1. How it is programmed is covered in Section 18.10.

18.6.2 Output Operations

Output operation in mode 2 works in the same way as programming port A as an output port and using mode 1 operation. This situation allows the μP to send data to peripheral equipment through the 8255A device. The following descriptions show how the lines of port C operate in this mode.

$\overline{\text{OBF}}$ (Output Buffer Full): After the μP has written data out to port A, a flip-flop within the 8255A goes to a logic 0 state. The output of this flip-flop is the $\overline{\text{OBF}}$ line. This line is used as a signal to the peripheral equipment that data is ready at port A.

$\overline{\text{ACK}}$ (Acknowledge): After the peripheral equipment receives the $\overline{\text{OBF}}$ signal, it sends an acknowledge signal to the 8255A device. When the acknowledge line goes low, it enables the three-state output buffer of port

TABLE 18–5 Possible Combinations of Modes for 8255A

Mode 0, Port A	Mode 1, Port B	Mode 1, Port A	Mode 0, Port B	Mode 2, Port A	Mode 0, Port B	Mode 2, Port A	Mode 1, Port B
Input	Input	Input	Input	Bidirectional	Input	Bidirectional	Input
Input	Output	Input	Output	Bidirectional	Output	Bidirectional	Output
Output	Input	Output	Input				
Output	Output	Output	Output				

TABLE 18–6 Port C Status Word Format

		Port C							
Port A	Port B	PC_7	PC_6	PC_5	PC_4	PC_3	PC_2	PC_1	PC_0
Output	Output	$\overline{OBF}_A$	$INTE_A$	I/O	I/O	$INTR_A$	$INTE_B$	$\overline{OBF}_B$	$INTR_B$
Output	Input	$\overline{OBF}_A$	$INTE_A$	I/O	I/O	$INTR_A$	$INTE_B$	IBF_B	$INTR_B$
Input	Output	I/O	I/O	IBF_A	$INTE_A$	$INTR_A$	$INTE_B$	$\overline{OBF}_B$	$INTR_B$
Input	Input	I/O	I/O	IBF_A	$INTE_A$	$INTR_A$	$INTE_B$	IBF_B	$INTR_B$

A to send the data. If the acknowledge signal is not received by the 8255A, the output buffer of port A will remain in its high impedance state.

INTR (Interrupt Request): As previously mentioned, the INTR line can be used as an interrupt signal to the μP for either input operations or output operations. When it is used for output operations, the following conditions must be met—(1) $\overline{OBF}$ must be high, (2) $\overline{ACK}$ line must be high, (3) $\overline{WR}$ line must be high, and (4) INTE must be high. The INTE is a flip-flop within the 8255A. It can be cleared or set by the programmer.

18.7 MODE COMBINATION

As mentioned in Section 18.3, different modes of operation can be combined when the 8255A device is used. In Section 18.4, we saw how the device operates when both port A and port B are programmed for mode 0 operation. In Section 18.5, we saw how the 8255A works when both port A and port B are programmed for mode 1 operation. Table 18–5 is a listing of other possible combinations of modes for the 8255A.

18.8 READING PORT C STATUS

In mode 0, port C transfers data to or from the peripheral device. When the 8255A is programmed to function in modes 1 or 2, port C generates or accepts handshaking signals. Reading the contents of port C allows the programmer to test or verify the "status" of each peripheral device and change the program flow accordingly.

There is no special instruction to read the status information from port C. A normal read operation of port C is all that is necessary. Port C status word format is given in Table 18–6. Note that when port C is read for status information, the interrupt enable flip-flops are read, not the strobe input or acknowledge line signals. Therefore, Table 18–6 should be used to interpret port C status information, not Table 18–4.

18.9 SINGLE-BIT SET/RESET OF PORT C

Any of the 8 bits of port C can be programmed to a logic 1 state (set) or to a logic 0 state (reset) by a feature called single-bit set/reset. This feature allows the programmer to load a particular bit pattern into port C even when that port is being used for status and control lines, such as in mode 1 and mode 2 operations. The individual bits of port C are set or reset just as if they were data output ports. The difference is, however, that when port C is programmed as an output port (mode 0 operation), a byte of data is sent to port C from the μP. When the single-bit feature is used, only one bit of port C can be programmed at a time. For example, if the programmer wishes to set or reset four bits of port C, then four control words are needed to accomplish the task. *Note:* It is a control word that is sent to the 8255A device from the μP and stored in the control word register. Data is not sent directly to port C. The control word format for the bit set/reset feature of port C is shown in Figure 18–12. When bit 7 of

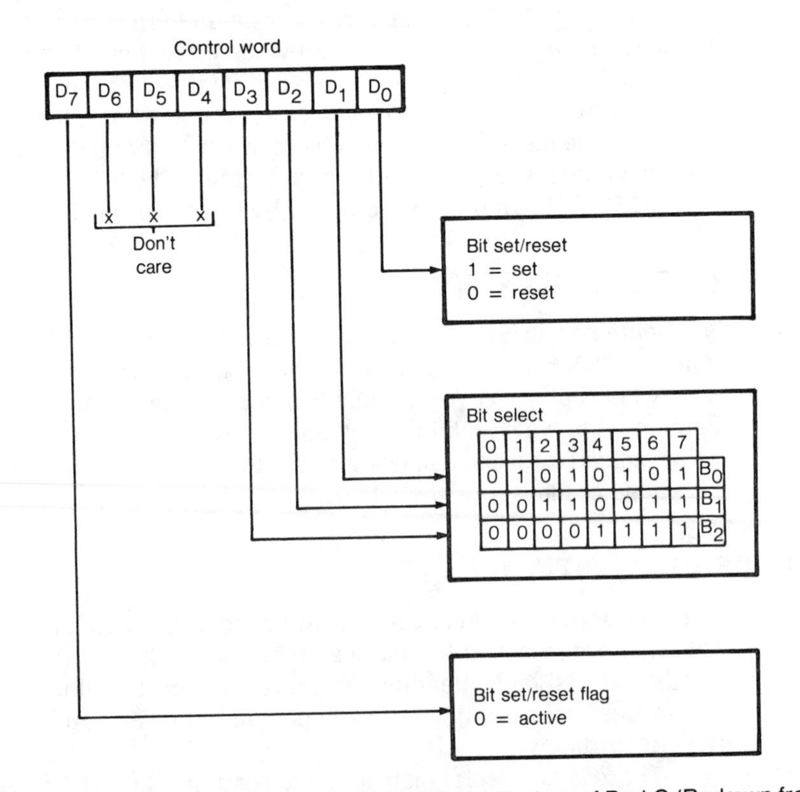

FIGURE 18–12 Control Word Format for Bit Set/Reset Feature of Port C (Redrawn from data sheet for 8255A PPI with permission. Intel Corporation, Santa Clara, CA)

the control register is cleared to the logic 0 state, then the single-bit set/reset feature of port C is activated.

If the user has connected the 8255A to the μP as an isolated I/O device, then an output instruction is used to send the control word. If the 8255A and the μP are connected in a memory-mapped I/O configuration, then the control word is sent by a MOV or STA instruction.

As shown in Figure 18–12, bit 7 of the control word is a logic 0. This tells the 8255A that the single-bit feature is being used. If this bit is a 1, the control word contains one of the mode selections. Therefore, this bit distinguishes the control word for mode selection or for single-bit selection. From Figure 18–12, we see that bits D_1, D_2, and D_3 determine which of the 8 bits of port C is being programmed. If the bit of port C is to be set, then $D_0 = 1$; or if the bit of port C is to be programmed as a logic 0, then $D_0 = 0$. Bits D_4, D_5, and D_6 of the control word can be either a logic 0 or a logic 1 because they are not used in this feature.

18.10 INTERRUPT CONTROLS

In previous sections, we saw that when the 8255A device is programmed in either mode 1 or mode 2, an interrupt signal can be sent to the μP using the INTR line. For this line to go "high," certain conditions have to be met. One of these conditions is that the INTE flip-flop within the 8255A has to be in the logic 1 state. This flip-flop is programmed using the single-bit set/reset feature described in Section 18.9. If the INTE flip-flop is programmed to a logic 0, then the interrupt line remains "low" and, therefore, no interrupt request signal is sent to the μP. We may want to send an interrupt request in some programs but not in others. Therefore, we either enable or disable the flip-flop accordingly. The mode of operation and whether the port is programmed as an input or an output port determine which bit of port C must be controlled. Table 18–7 lists the conditions and the bit that must be controlled.

TABLE 18–7 Control of Interrupt Enable Flip-Flop by Bit Set/Reset Feature

Mode 1 Operation			
Port	Direction of Port Lines	Flip-Flop	Controlled by Bit
A	Input	$INTE_A$	PC_4
	Output	$INTE_A$	PC_6
B	Input	$INTE_B$	PC_2
	Output	$INTE_B$	PC_2

Mode 2 Operation			
Port	Direction of Port Lines	Flip-Flop	Controlled by Bit
A	Input	$INTE_2$	PC_4
	Output	$INTE_1$	PC_6

18.11 KEYBOARD SCANNING APPLICATION

In many small μC systems, the μP is idle, waiting for something to do. In these systems, external events may occur slowly, and often the start of one operation is dependent on the finish of a previous event. Therefore, the μP can be programmed to scan an I/O port or ports on a regular basis. This technique is called *scanned I/O*. Many single-board computers (SBC) use this method to read a keyboard.

Figure 18–13 shows a hexadecimal keyboard. It consists of a matrix of conductor patterns with a switch at each junction. When a switch is closed, a row and column are shorted together. This is known as a *key closure*. The μP is

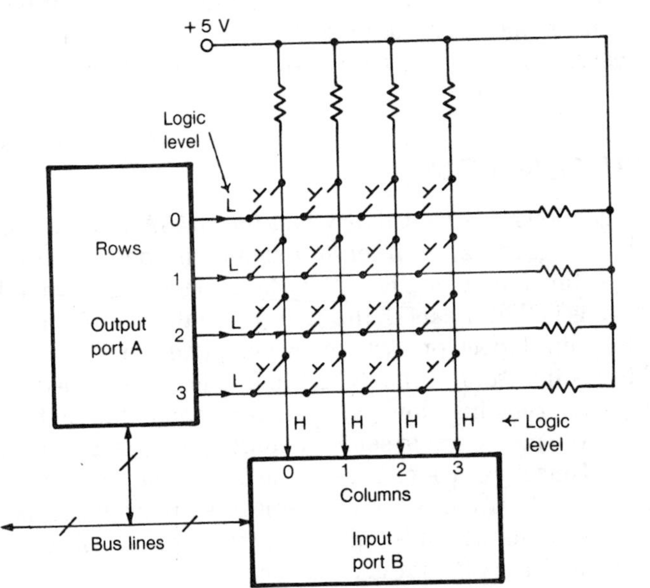

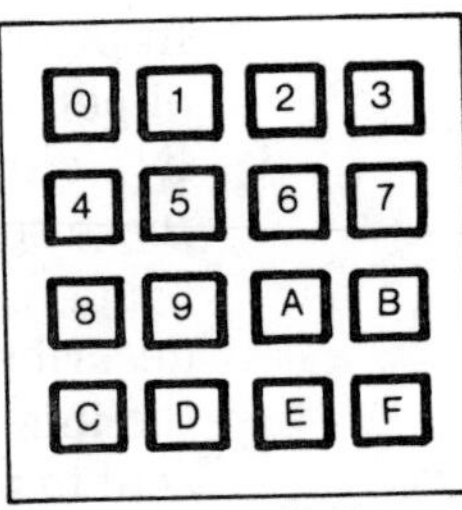

Key	Row Number	Column Position
0	00	0111
1	00	1011
2	00	1101
3	00	1110
4	01	0111
5	01	1011
6	01	1101
7	01	1110
8	10	0111
9	10	1011
A	10	1101
B	10	1110
C	11	0111
D	11	1011
E	11	1101
F	11	1110

FIGURE 18–13 Hexadecimal Keyboard and Key Position

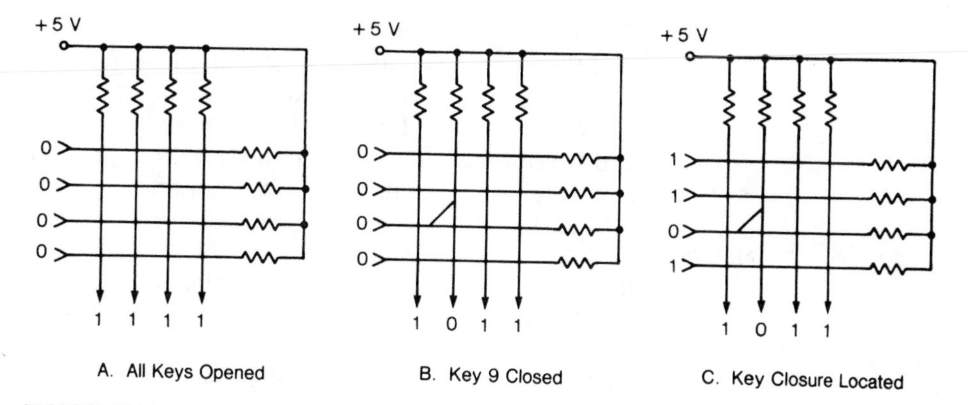

FIGURE 18–14 Key Closure Location

used to determine whether a switch is closed and if so, which one. Since any mechanical switch exhibits a phenomenon known as *switch or contact bounce*, the scanned I/O program must include a time delay subroutine (as shown later in Figure 18–15). Many keyboards have a switch bounce less than 10 ms.

Figure 18–13 shows that the rows are programmed as output lines and the columns are programmed as input lines. Each output row is programmed for a low logic level. When no key is closed, all the column input lines are at a high logic level. When a key is closed, one column line is forced low. The column lines are monitored constantly for a logic 0. If a switch closure is detected and a time delay has elapsed, then the closed key must be identified. This is done by placing a logic 0 on one row and logic 1s on all the others. The input columns are rechecked. If a column input line is 0, the key has been found; if not, the program moves to the next row. This process is repeated until the closed key is found. When the program is finished, the row number and column position are known, and the actual hex value can be found from a hex table. Figure 18–14 shows key closure locations; the hex table is in Figure 18–13.

EXAMPLE 18.1 Write a program for scanning a hexadecimal keyboard. Consider (a) port A is output port 20, (b) port B is input port 20, and (c) hex table begins at memory location 0500.

Solution In Chapter 7, we examined time delay programs for the 8080A μP. In the flowchart of Figure 18–15 and in the following program, the time delay program is referred to as a subroutine (CALL TDELAY). The program is as follows:

```
PUSH PSW      Save μP registers.
PUSH B
PUSH D
PUSH H
```

```
WAIT:    IN 20          Input port B.
         ANI 0F         Mask out column bits 4-7.
         CPI 0F         Compare input column data for a closure.
         JZ WAIT        If Z = 1, jump to WAIT.
         CALL TDELAY    Call time delay program (not listed here).
         MVI C, 03      Initialize row counter.
         MVI A, F7      Initialize accumulator.
NEXT:    OUT 20         Make one row low.
         RRC            Rotate accumulator.
         MOV B, A       Save accumulator for next test.
         IN 20          Input port B.
         ANI 0F         Mask out bits 4-7.
         CPI 0F         Test input column data for closure.
         JNZ KEYC       If Z = 0, jump to KEYC.
         DCR C          Decrement counter.
         JM ERROR       If N = 1, jump to ERROR.
         MOV A, B       Move B register to accumulator.
         JMP NEXT       Jump to NEXT row.
KEYC:    MOV D, A       Save accumulator.
         MOV A, C       Move C register to accumulator.
         RLC            Rotate count.
         RLC
         RLC
         RLC
         ORA D          Combine row and column number as in
                        Figure 18-13.
         LXI H, 0500    Initialize HL register pair.
         MOV C, 0F      Initialize counter.
KEYTST:  CMP M          Check table.
         JZ KEYFD       Found key.
         INX H          Increment HL register pair.
         DRC C          Decrement C register.
         JP KEYTST      If N = 0, jump to KEYTST.
ERROR:   MOV A, FF      Return to main program.
         RET
KEYFD:   MOV A, L       Hex value in accumulator.
         POP H          Return µP registers.
         POP D
         POP B
         POP PSW
         RET            Return to main program.
```

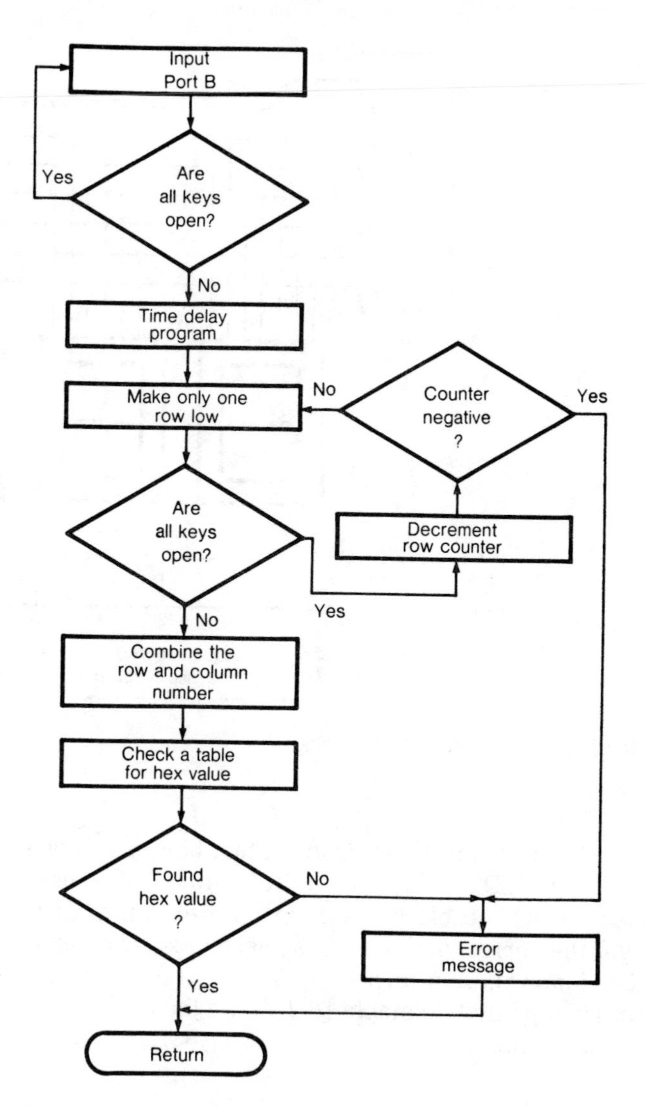

FIGURE 18–15 Flowchart for Key Scanning Routine

18.12 MULTIPLEXED I/O LINES

Figure 18–16 shows a three-digit display. Each display is a seven-segment unit. Additional transistor drivers may be required on each segment line. For our example, consider that only BCD numbers are to be displayed. If data is stored in memory as straight binary, then a binary-to-BCD conversion is needed, similar to that covered in Chapter 13. Figure 18–17 shows which segments are lit for each BCD value.

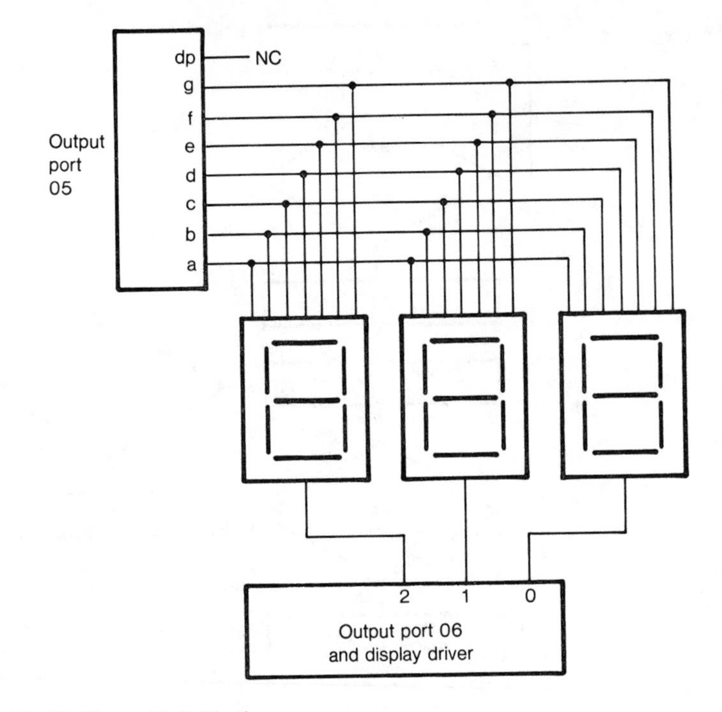

FIGURE 18–16 Three-Digit Display

When the program is executed, binary values stored in memory are converted to BCD numbers. Each BCD value is now used as a pointer to a table in memory. This table holds binary patterns that are sent to the output port to light the corresponding display segments. The display is turned on for a fixed time interval, then turned off. The next BCD number is retrieved and the process is repeated. Example 18.2 shows the programming steps needed to display a BCD number.

EXAMPLE 18.2 For the multiplexed display shown in Figure 18–16, write a program to display three BCD numbers. Consider (a) the BCD values are stored in memory beginning at location 0300 and (b) the look-up table for the seven-segment binary pattern is stored in memory beginning at location 0400.

Solution A flowchart for a seven-segment display routine is shown in Figure 18–18. The program is as follows:

```
PUSH PSW        Save μP registers.
PUSH C
PUSH H
LXI H, 0300     Initialize HL register pair.
MVI C, 02       Initialize C register.
```

a f b g e c dp d

Number	Display	Segments Lit
0	0	a, b, c, d, e, f
1	1	b, c
2	2	a, b, d, e, g
3	3	a, b, c, d, g
4	4	b, c, f, g
5	5	a, c, d, f, g
6	6	a, c, d, e, f, g
7	7	a, b, c
8	8	a, b, c, d, e, f, g
9	9	a, b, c, d, f, g
Decimal point	.	dp

FIGURE 18–17 Seven-Segment Display

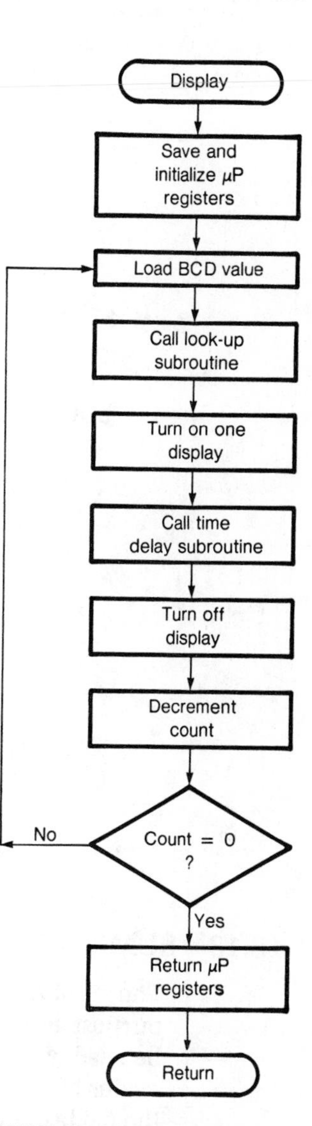

FIGURE 18–18 Flowchart for Seven-Segment Display Routine

```
REPEAT:  MOV A, M       Load accumulator with BCD value.
         CALL SEGMTS    Look up table.
         OUT 05         Output to port 05.
         MOV A, C       Move C register to accumulator.
         OUT 06         Turn on one display.
         CALL TDELAY    Call time delay subroutine (not listed here).
         MVI A, FF
```

```
         OUT 06        Turn off display.
         INX H
         DCR C
         JP REPEAT     If positive, jump to REPEAT.
         POP H         Return µP registers.
         POP C
         POP PSW
         RET           Return to main program.
SEGMTS:  PUSH B        Save µP registers.
         PUSH H
         MVI B, 09     Initialize B register as counter.
LOOP:    LXI 0400      Look up table.
         CMP M         Compare accumulator with memory.
         JZ EXIT       If Z = 1, jump to EXIT.
         INX H
         DCR B
         JM ERROR      Invalid BCD number found.
         JMP LOOP      Continue the look-up.
EXIT:    POP H         Return µP register.
         POP B
         RET           Return to multiplex program.
```

The time delay subroutine is similar to the subroutines presented in Chapter 8.

18.13 SUMMARY

The 8255A programmable peripheral interface device is Intel's general-purpose input/output IC. Although it is designed primarily for the 8080A, it can be used with other µPs. This chapter covered the 8255A's pin descriptions and modes of operation. The binary pattern stored in the control register programs the mode of operation. Therefore, the user selects how port A, port B, or port C is programmed. Depending on the mode of operation, port C lines may be I/O lines or control lines for port A and port B.

Sections 18.4, 18.5, and 18.6 show how the 8255A can be programmed for mode 0, 1, and 2 operations, respectively. Mode combinations exist when port A and port B are programmed in different modes, as discussed in Section 18.7. Section 18.8 shows how port C can be used to read peripheral status information. Another feature of port C is the single-bit set/reset feature. This allows the user to set (logic 1) or reset (logic 0) the individual bits even when port C is being used for another purpose. As with other peripheral devices, the 8255A can send an interrupt request signal to the µP. Sections 18.11 and 18.12 show two applications for the 8255A.

PROBLEMS

18-1 When the reset pin on the 8255A goes high, what are the predetermined logic states of its internal registers and its data bus lines?

18-2 Does the chip select pin have an active high or active low state?

18-3 Given the following logic levels, which port or register is selected?

	$\overline{CS}$	A_1	A_0
(a)	0	1	0
(b)	0	1	1

18-4 Given the following logic levels, which port or register is selected and which direction is the data flowing?

	$\overline{CS}$	A_1	A_0	$\overline{RD}$	$\overline{WR}$
(a)	0	1	1	1	0
(b)	0	0	1	0	1
(c)	1	1	0	0	0
(d)	0	0	0	1	0

18-5 Can all three ports of the 8255A be programmed as either input or output ports?

18-6 Can all three ports be programmed for mode 2 operation? If your answer is no, which port or ports can be?

18-7 What is the primary function of mode 2 operation?

18-8 Can port C be programmed separately for mode 0 operation?

18-9 What binary pattern must be sent to the control register so that the 8255A can be programmed for the following operations: (a) all ports programmed as output lines and mode operation; (b) all ports programmed for mode 1 input operation, (c) port A, mode 1 input and port B, mode 0 input operation; (d) port A, mode 2 input operation and port B, mode 1 output operation.

18-10 Is there handshaking capability when the 8255A is programmed for mode 0 operation?

18-11 In mode 0 operation, is the (a) output and (b) input data latched?

18-12 In mode 1 operation, what is the function of port C?

18-13 In mode 1 input operation, which lines of port C are output control lines?

18-14 Repeat Problem 18-13 for output operation.

18-15 When the 8255A is programmed for mode 1 input operation for both port A and port B, what are the I/O lines of port C?

18-16 Answer the following questions for mode 1 operation: (a) When is the data from the peripheral equipment latched? (b) What is the function of the IBF line? (c) What is the function of the $\overline{OBF}$ line? (d) What is the function of the $\overline{ACK}$ line?

18-17 How many mode 1 combinations are there?

18-18 When port A is programmed for mode 2 operation, are there handshaking signals?

18-19 If port A is programmed for mode 2 operation, what happens with lines PC_0, PC_1, and PC_2?

18-20 What must be the logic state of bit 7 of the control register to use the single-bit set/reset feature?

Peripheral Interface Adapter 6821

19.0 INTRODUCTION

The 6821 peripheral interface adapter (PIA) is a general-purpose programmable input/output chip housed in a 40-pin dual-in-line package, as shown in Figure 19–1. Although this interface chip has been designed by and for Motorola's μP products, it can be used with other μPs. For example, users of 6502 μPs often use this chip. The purpose of any I/O chip is to simplify the problem of connecting the μP to peripheral equipment. Peripheral equipment could be connected to the μP by using logic gates and combinational logic circuits. This technique usually requires a large number of components, however, thus defeating one of the major advantages of a μC system—a design requiring few ICs. Like other peripheral devices, the 6821 eliminates many individual components and it is programmable. It has 16 I/O lines in two groups, port A and port B.

The operation of the I/O lines of the 6821 differs significantly from the operation of the I/O lines of Intel's 8255A PPI. Remember that the 8255A has three ports—port A, port B, and port C. All of the lines of ports A and B are either programmed as input lines or output lines. They cannot be programmed independently. The user of the 6821 PIA has control over all 16 I/O lines. For example, the programmer may choose two lines of port A to be input lines and the remaining six lines of port A to be output lines. At the same time, any number of lines of port B may be programmed as input lines and the remaining

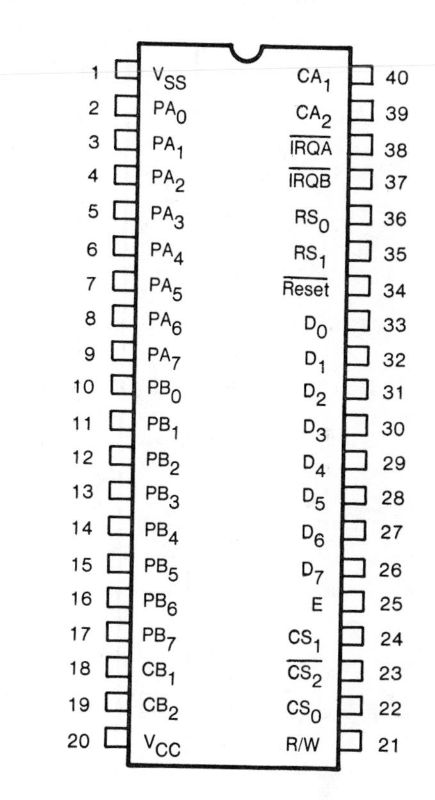

FIGURE 19–1 Pin Assignments for Peripheral Interface Adapter 6821 (Redrawn from data sheet for MC6821 PIA with permission. Motorola Incorporated, Phoenix, AZ)

lines as output lines. Therefore, one difference between these two interface devices is that the 6821 has fewer ports and thus fewer I/O lines, but each line can be programmed independently.

19.1 MICROPROCESSOR AND PIA CONNECTIONS

The μP and the PIA are interconnected by the data bus, address bus, and control bus, as shown in Figure 19–2. These connections include an 8-bit bidirectional data bus, three chip select lines, two register select lines, two interrupt lines, a read/write line, an enable line, and a reset line. Let's examine the function of each line or group of lines.

19.1.1 Data Bus

The eight bidirectional data lines (D_0–D_7) allow the transfer of data between the μP and the PIA. Each line has a three-state output driver. These devices remain in the high impedance (off) state except when the μP selects the PIA *and* the μP is reading (receiving) data from the PIA. For the μP to read data from the PIA, the R/W line must be in the read (high) state.

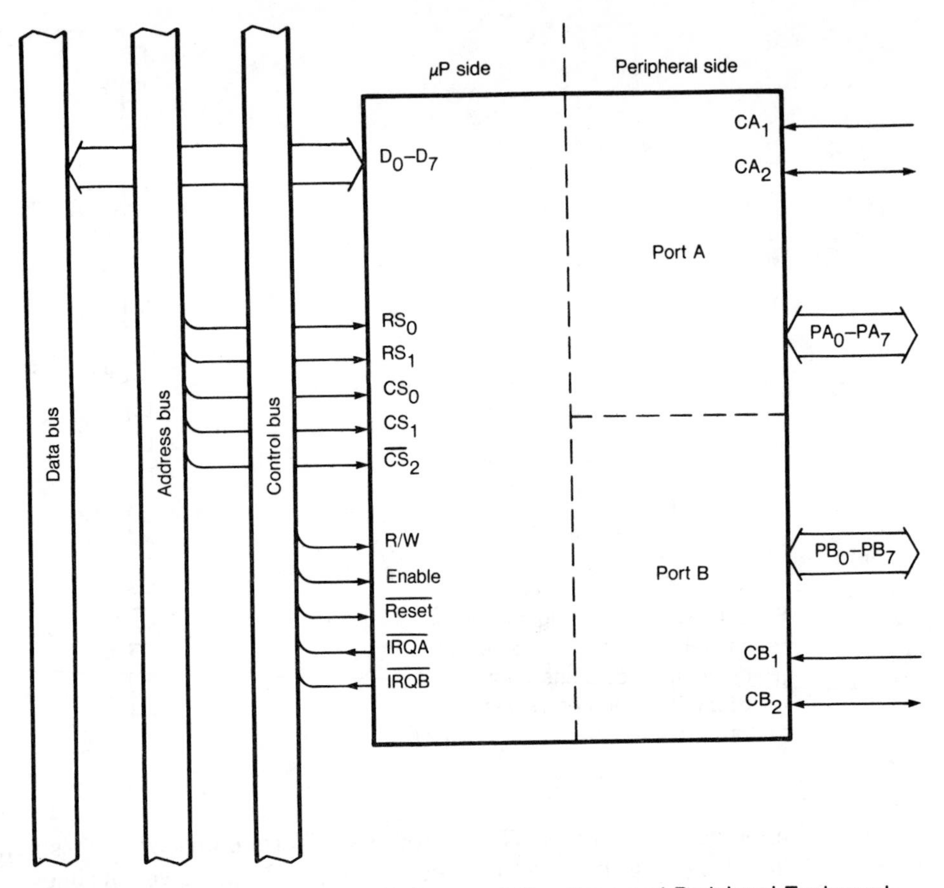

FIGURE 19–2 6821 PIA Connected between μP Bus Lines and Peripheral Equipment

19.1.2 Address Bus

The 6821 has five pins that are connected to the address bus lines. Although the user could choose any combination of the 16 address bus lines, we will look at one or two wiring diagrams that yield a good solution to most problems. The five pins on the PIA are grouped into chip select lines and register select lines.

Chip Select Pins (CS_0, CS_1, and $\overline{CS_2}$): These three pins are used by the μP to select the PIA. They may be connected directly to three address bus lines, or one pin may be wired to a decoder chip while the other pins are wired to their appropriate logic states, as shown in Figures 19–3A and 19–3B. In order for the device to be selected, both CS_0 and CS_1 must be high and $\overline{CS_2}$ must be low. The voltage levels on the chip select pins must be stable whenever the μP is reading or writing data to the PIA.

Register Select Pins (RS_0 and RS_1): The two register select pins should be connected to address bus lines A_0 and A_1, as shown in Figure 19–3C. The logic levels on these pins are used to select the various registers inside

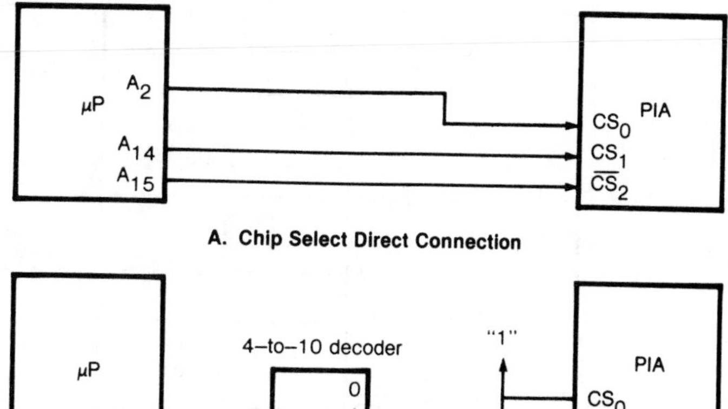

A. Chip Select Direct Connection

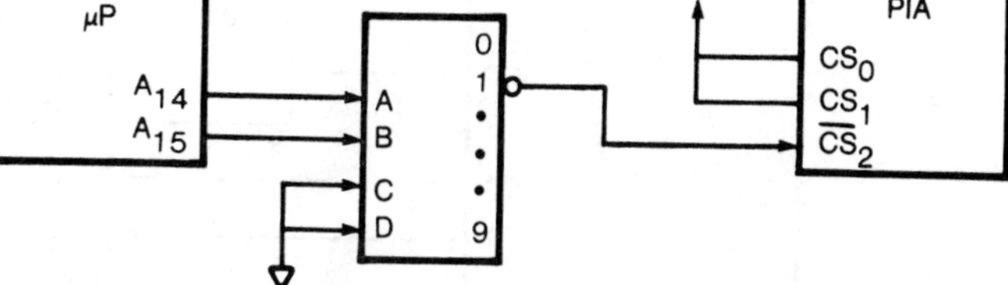

B. Chip Select Decoder Connection

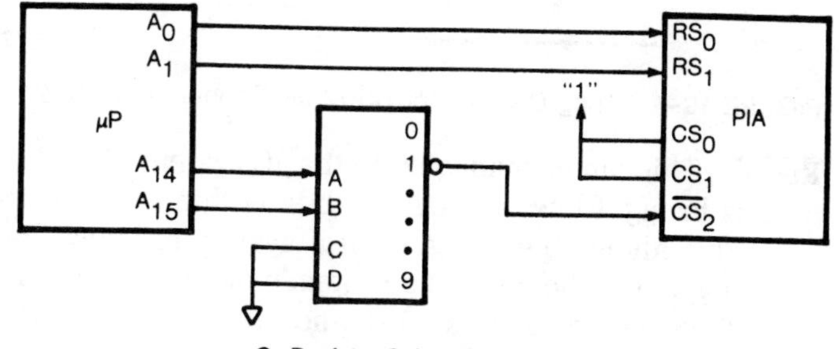

C. Register Select Connection

FIGURE 19–3 Wiring Diagrams for Chip Select Pins (CS_0, CS_1, and $\overline{CS_2}$) and Register Select Pins (RS_0 and RS_1)

the PIA. Like the chip select pins, the voltage levels on the register select pins must be stable whenever the μP is reading or writing data to the PIA. The reason that these pins are wired to address bus lines A_0 and A_1 is that the PIA's internal registers will be in four consecutive memory locations. For the connections shown in Figure 19–3B, the memory locations can be 4000, 4001, 4002, and 4003.

19.1.3 Control Bus

The 6821 has five pins that are connected to four control bus lines. The reason that five PIA pins need only four control lines is that two of the pins ($\overline{IRQA}$ and $\overline{IRQB}$) are wired together to one line, as shown in Figure 19–4. A brief description of each control line follows.

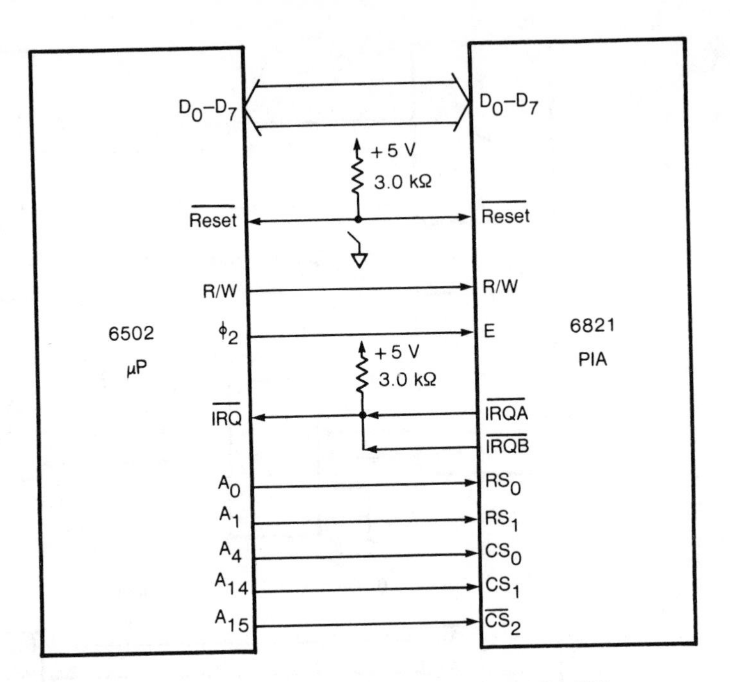

FIGURE 19–4 Wiring Diagram for 6502 μP Connected to 6821 PIA

$\overline{\text{Reset}}$: This pin is connected to the μC system's reset line. Whenever this line is brought low, all register bits within the PIA are cleared to a logic 0. This allows the designer of a system to know the logic state of the PIA registers whenever the system's master reset button is pressed. On the diagrams in Figures 19–1 and 19–4, the line over the word "reset" indicates that the active state of this pin is a logic 0.

Enable (E): The enable pin is the only pin on the PIA that receives a timing signal. The timing of all other signals and data transfers is controlled by either the leading or trailing edge of the enable pulse. If a 6821 is used with a 6502 μP, then the enable pin should be connected to the ϕ_2 clock signal line, as shown in Figure 19–4. If a 6821 PIA is used with a 6800 μP, then the ϕ_2 clock signal should be ANDed with the μP's VMA signal.

Interrupt Request ($\overline{\text{IRQA}}$ and $\overline{\text{IRQB}}$): The interrupt request lines ($\overline{\text{IRQA}}$ and $\overline{\text{IRQB}}$) are used to send an interrupt signal to the μP. The lines may be tied directly to the μP's $\overline{\text{IRQ}}$ pin, as shown in Figure 19–4. The $\overline{\text{IRQA}}$ and $\overline{\text{IRQB}}$ lines are "open drain" lines (there is no internal load device on the chip) and are capable of sinking 1.6 mA. The open connection permits all PIA interrupt request lines to be ORed together.

Each interrupt request line on the PIA has two flag bits that cause the line to go low. Each flag bit is associated with a peripheral control line. For port A, the peripheral control lines are labeled CA_1 and CA_2. For port B, the peripheral control lines are CB_1 and CB_2. A simplified drawing is shown in Figure 19–5. The 6821 can be programmed so that one or more of the peripheral control lines can be disabled.

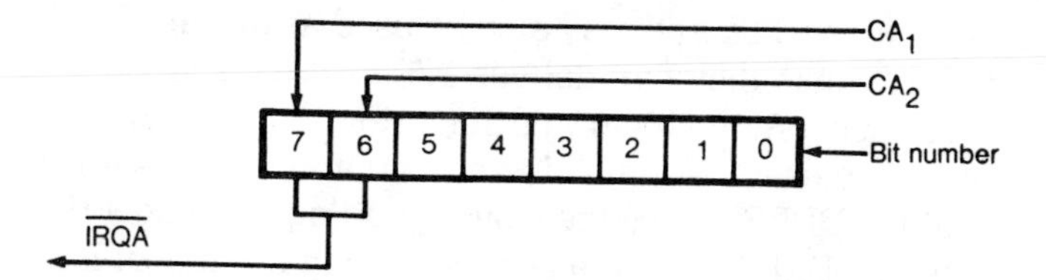

FIGURE 19–5 Status Information Bits (Bits 6 and 7) of Control Register

In Section 19.6, we will look at a program that allows the μP to read and test the PIA flag bits to determine which peripheral interrupt line is signaling the μP. These flag bits are cleared to a logic 0 when the μP reads the data from the correct port or when the $\overline{\text{Reset}}$ line goes low.

Control lines CA_2 and CB_2 have a dual function. Each can be programmed either as an input interrupt request line, as described above, or as an output line to control peripheral equipment.

19.2 PERIPHERAL INTERFACE LINES

The 6821 PIA has two ports, and each port has eight bidirectional I/O lines. Associated with each port are two interrupt/control lines. Although the port lines are described as bidirectional I/O lines, note that each line can be programmed as either an input line or an output line, but not both at the same time.

19.2.1 Port A

Each peripheral data line of port A can be programmed either as an input line or as an output line. This is accomplished by loading a binary pattern into a data direction register for port A (DDRA). This register is inside the PIA and can be addressed by the μP. If a logic 1 is loaded into a bit of the data direction register, the corresponding port line becomes an output line. If a logic 0 is loaded into a bit of the data direction register, the corresponding port line becomes an input line. This register and how to program it are covered in Section 19.4. When a line is programmed as an output line, it is capable of driving two TTL loads. When it is programmed as an input line, it is the equivalent of one TTL load.

19.2.2 Port B

Like port A, each peripheral data line of port B can be programmed either as an input line or as an output line. Unlike the output lines of port A, the output buffers of port B have three-state capability. Those of port A are only TTL compatible. When a peripheral data line of port B is programmed as an input line, the output buffer associated with that line enters its high impedance state. When a peripheral data line of port B is programmed as an output line, data on this line (or lines) can be read back to the μP correctly even if the voltage on a line drops below 2.0 V for a logic 1. As output lines, port B lines are compatible with standard TTL and may also be used as drivers for the base of a transistor switch because they can deliver 1.5 mA at 1.5 V.

Like port A, the binary pattern stored in the data direction register of port B (DDRB) determines which is an input and which is an output line. A logic 0 in a bit of the DDRB makes the corresponding bit in port B an input line. A logic 1 in a bit of DDRB makes the corresponding bit in port B an output line. Remember, the binary pattern in the data direction register only sets up the port lines as input or output lines; the pattern is not the data that is sent to or received by the port. The μP has to write or read the data to the port as a separate set of instructions.

19.2.3 Interrupt Lines (CA_1 and CB_1)

Lines CA_1 and CB_1 can be used only as input interrupt lines. These lines set the interrupt flag bit (bit 7) of the control register. The PIA can be programmed so that either a low-to-high or a high-to-low transition can be recognized on these peripheral lines.

19.2.4 Interrupt/Control Line (CA_2)

The peripheral interrupt/control line, CA_2, can be programmed either as an input line or as an output line. As an input line, CA_2 is used as an interrupt line. When programmed as an output line, CA_2 is used as a control or handshake signal line from the PIA to peripheral equipment. This line is TTL compatible.

19.2.5 Interrupt/Control Line (CB_2)

Like CA_2, peripheral line CB_2 can be programmed as an input interrupt line or as an output control line. As an output, it is compatible with TTL and may be used as a source of up to 1 mA and 1.5 V to drive a transistor.

19.3 INTERNAL OPERATION

Each 6821 PIA has two peripheral sides, side A and side B. Each side has a peripheral interface register (also called a port), a data direction register, and a control register. Therefore, there are a total of six registers within the 6821 that can be addressed by the μP: two peripheral interface registers (port A and port B), two data direction registers (DDRA and DDRB), and two control registers (CRA and CRB). Figure 19-6 shows the internal block diagram for the 6821 PIA.

Although there are six addressable registers, a 6821 chip requires only four memory locations. Two registers on each side—the port and the data direction register—have the same address. In this section, we will see how the μP distinguishes one register from another. In the next section, we will focus on how to program the 6821.

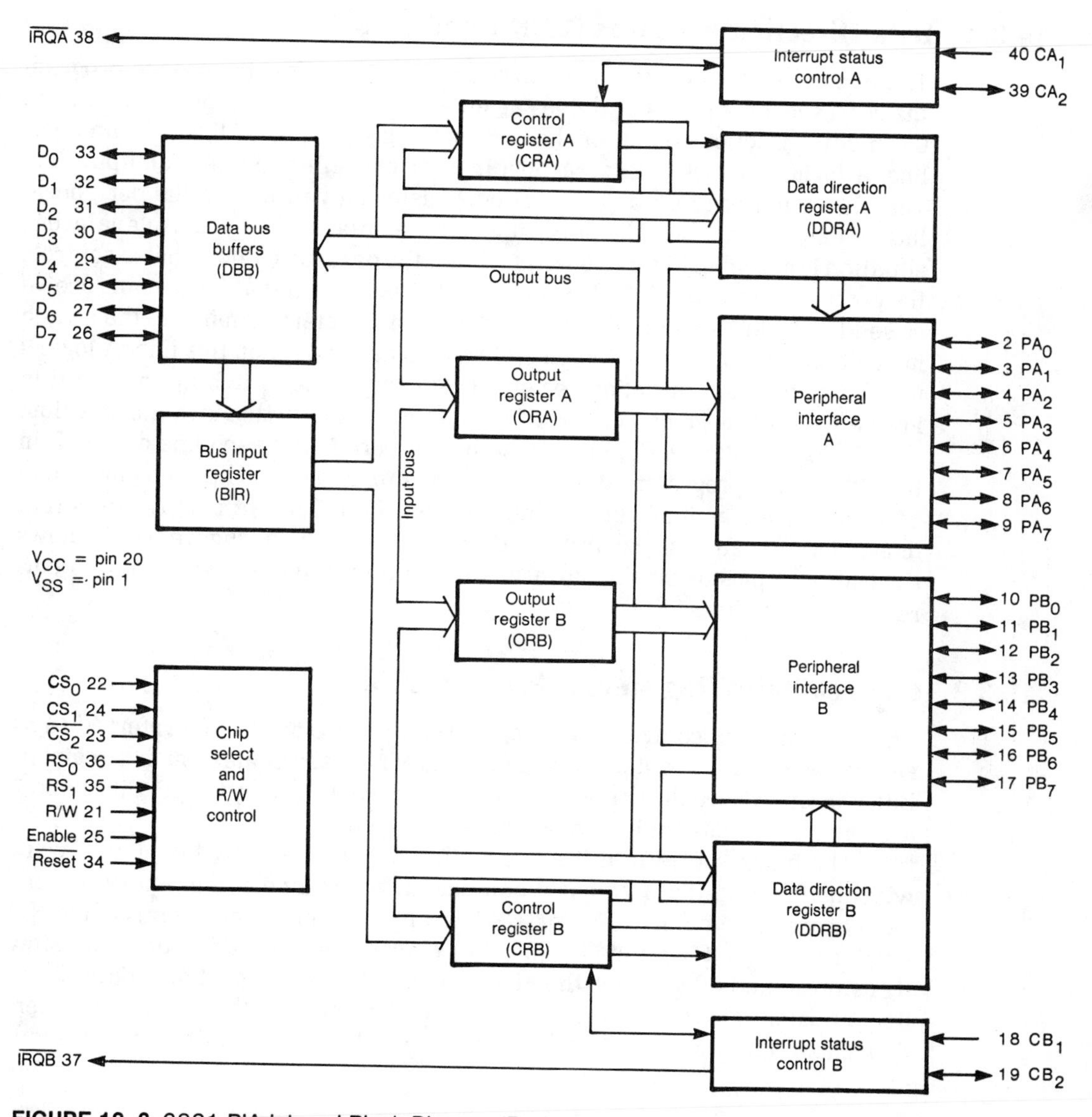

FIGURE 19–6 6821 PIA Internal Block Diagram (Redrawn from data sheet for MC6821 PIA with permission. Motorola Incorporated, Phoenix, AZ)

19.3.1 Peripheral Interface Registers

Inside the PIA, the peripheral interface register or port is the addressable register that allows the μP to send and receive data over the I/O lines. If the lines are programmed as input lines, the μP takes in the data by executing a load instruction at the port address. The μP sends data to a port and then to lines programmed as output lines by having the μP execute a store instruction. The port register, as with all the PIA registers, should be treated as any other memory location. Therefore, all the instructions that a μP contains to process data in a memory location can be used for the PIA registers.

19.3.2 Data Direction Registers (DDRA and DDRB)

The two data direction registers (DDRA and DDRB) allow the user to program the corresponding peripheral lines as either input lines or output lines. A logic 0 in a data direction bit causes the corresponding peripheral line to be an input line; a logic 1 causes the corresponding peripheral line to be an output line. The binary pattern in a data direction register only programs the peripheral lines as input or output; the pattern is not the data on the lines. An analogous situation is shown in Figure 19–7. The bit in the data direction register controls the position of the switch; it does not determine the data that the μP can receive or send. A logic 1 in a bit of the data direction register is similar to the switch in position A in Figure 19–7A. The μP can only send data on this line. A logic 0 in a bit of the data direction register is similar to the switch in position B in Figure 19–7B. The μP can only receive data when the switch is in this position.

Unlike the 8255A PPI chip, each line of port A and each line of port B in the 6821 PIA is programmed individually. For example, two lines on port A can be programmed as input lines while the remaining lines of port A are output lines. Port B can also be programmed in any fashion. Figure 19–8 shows several examples of binary patterns in a data direction register and the corresponding I/O lines.

19.3.3 Control/Status Registers (CRA and CRB)

The 6821 has two control/status registers. They are most often referred to as simply the control register. Both the A and B portions contain such a register. Bits 0 through 5 are the control bits and can be written to by the μP. Bits 6 and 7 are the status bits and can only be read by the μP.

The binary pattern in the control bits determines how the μP will work with the PIA and the peripheral equipment. For example, the binary pattern determines (1) whether CA_2 (or CB_2) is an input or output control line; (2) whether CA_1 (or CB_1) and CA_2 (or CB_2) respond to low-to-high or high-to-low transitions; and (3) whether the μP communicates with a port or a data direction register. Figure 19–9 shows the word format of the control register. Remember, the word format is a binary pattern that programs how the PIA will

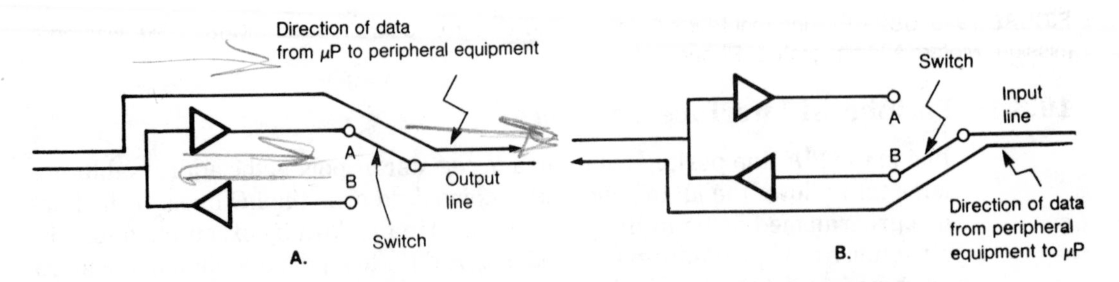

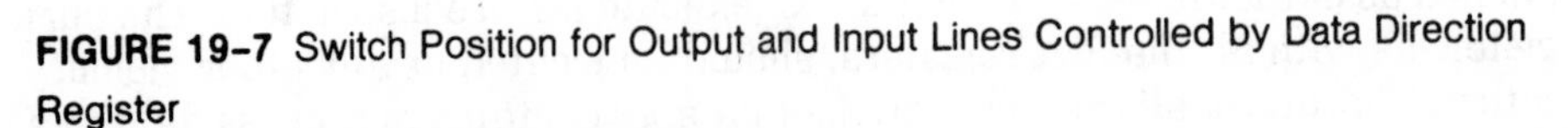
FIGURE 19–7 Switch Position for Output and Input Lines Controlled by Data Direction Register

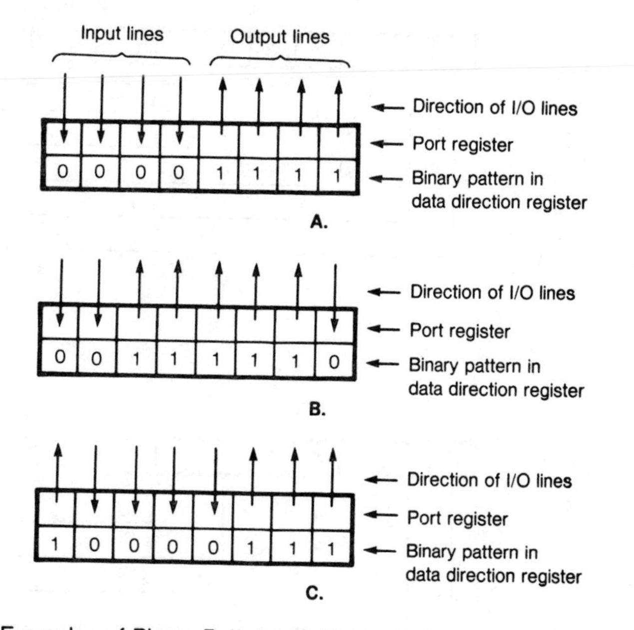

FIGURE 19–8 Examples of Binary Patterns in DDR and Corresponding I/O Lines

operate. Although the μP sends an 8-bit binary pattern, only bits 0 to 5 are loaded into the control register. Bits 6 and 7 are read-only locations and the data on lines 6 and 7 never reaches bits 6 and 7 of the control/status register. Let's examine the function of each control bit.

Control Bit 2

Bit 2 of the control/status register selects whether the μP addresses the data direction register or the port. This bit is needed because the port and the data direction register have the same memory address. If bit 2 of the control register is a logic 0, the μP is communicating with the data direction register. If bit 2 is a logic 1, the μP is communicating with the port. The memory addresses for the 6821 may be confusing to the first-time user. For both the A and B portions, the port and data direction register have the same address, while the control/status register has the next memory address. In most applications, however, the data direction register is addressed only once and that is during initialization. The advantage is that several 6821 chips can be connected to the system and be easily decoded, as we will see in Section 19.5. Remember, each 6821 gives the user 16 I/O lines and four peripheral control lines, and takes only four memory addresses. These memory addresses are wired to be four consecutive locations, such as the following:

4000 (port A and DDRA)
4001 (control/status register A)
4002 (port B and DDRB)
4003 (control/status register B)

Section 19.4 gives the programming steps needed to use a 6821 PIA.

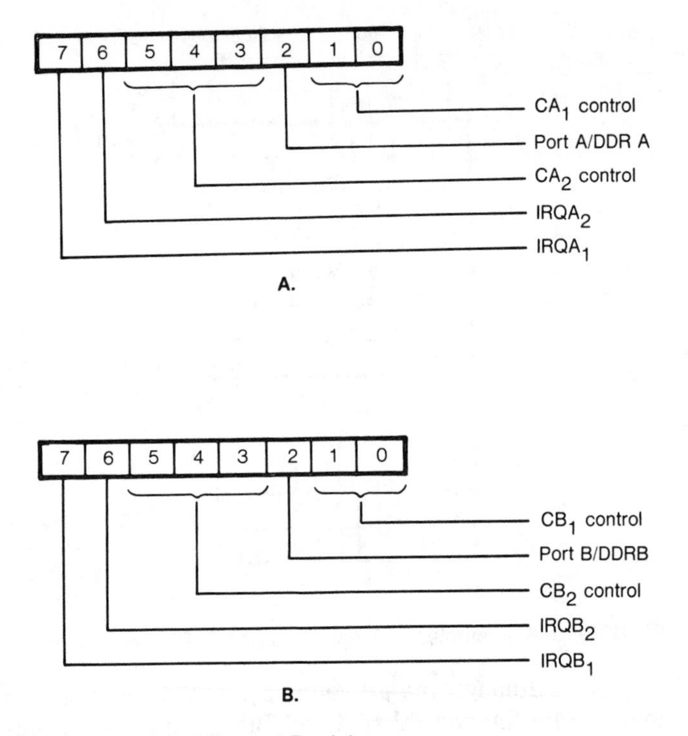

FIGURE 19–9 Word Format of Control Register

Control Bits 0 and 1

Bits 0 and 1 of both control registers determine how lines CA_1 and CB_1 are to operate. Bit 0 in control register A enables or disables the $\overline{IRQA}$ line. Bit 0 of control register B does the same for the $\overline{IRQB}$ line. Bit 1 of each register determines whether the PIA's CA_1 (or CB_1) line recognizes a high-to-low transition or a low-to-high transition. Table 19–1 summarizes the binary patterns for the first two control register bits.

Control Bits 3, 4, and 5

Bits 3, 4, and 5 of both control registers are used to program peripheral control lines CA_2 and CB_2. When bit 5 is a logic 0, the control line is programmed as an interrupt input line. When bit 5 is a logic 1, the line is programmed as an output control line. When programmed as output, control lines CA_2 and CB_2 have different characteristics. Tables 19–2, 19–3, and 19–4 summarize how the control bits 3, 4, and 5 control CA_2 and CB_2.

Status Bits

Bits 6 and 7 of the control register are the interrupt flag bits. Bit 7 indicates the status of the peripheral interrupt line CA_1 (or CB_1). This bit is set to a logic 1 when there is an active transition on the peripheral interrupt line. When line CA_2 (or CB_2) is programmed as an input line, then bit 6 of the control/status register is the interrupt flag bit for this line. These bits can only be read by the

TABLE 19–1 Control of Interrupt Inputs CA_1 and CB_1

CRA-1 (CRB-1)	CRA-0 (CRB-0)	Interrupt Input CA1 (CB1)	Interrupt Flag CRA-7 (CRB-7)	MPU Interrupt Request $\overline{IRQA}$ ($\overline{IRQB}$)
0	0	↓ Active	Set high on ↓ of CA1 (CB1)	Disabled — $\overline{IRQ}$ remains high
0	1	↓ Active	Set high on ↓ of CA1 (CB1)	Goes low when the interrupt flag bit CRA-7 (CRB-7) goes high
1	0	↑ Active	Set high on ↑ of CA1 (CB1)	Disabled — $\overline{IRQ}$ remains high
1	1	↑ Active	Set high on ↑ of CA1 (CB1)	Goes low when the interrupt flag bit CRA-7 (CRB-7) goes high

Notes: 1. ↑ indicates positive transition (low to high)
2. ↓ indicates negative transition (high to low)
3. The Interrupt flag bit CRA-7 is cleared by an MPU Read of the A Data Register, and CRB-7 is cleared by an MPU Read of the B Data Register.
4. If CRA-0 (CRB-0) is low when an interrupt occurs (Interrupt disabled) and is later brought high, $\overline{IRQA}$ ($\overline{IRQB}$) occurs after CRA-0 (CRB-0) is written to a "one".

Source: Reprinted with permission of Motorola Incorporated, Austin, TX.

TABLE 19–2 Control of CA_2 as CB_2 as Interrupt Inputs [CRA-5 (CRB-5) low]

CRA-5 (CRB-5)	CRA-4 (CRB-4)	CRA-3 (CRB-3)	Interrupt Input CA2 (CB2)	Interrupt Flag CRA-6 (CRB-6)	MPU Interrupt Request $\overline{IRQA}$ ($\overline{IRQB}$)
0	0	0	↓ Active	Set high on ↓ of CA2 (CB2)	Disabled — $\overline{IRQ}$ remains high
0	0	1	↓ Active	Set high on ↓ of CA2 (CB2)	Goes low when the interrupt flag bit CRA-6 (CRB-6) goes high
0	1	0	↑ Active	Set high on ↑ of CA2 (CB2)	Disabled — $\overline{IRQ}$ remains high
0	1	1	↑ Active	Set high on ↑ of CA2 (CB2)	Goes low when the interrupt flag bit CRA-6 (CRB-6) goes high

Notes: 1. ↑ indicates positive transition (low to high)
2. ↓ indicates negative transition (high to low)
3. The Interrupt flag bit CRA-6 is cleared by an MPU Read of the A Data Register and CRB-6 is cleared by an MPU Read of the B Data Register.
4. If CRA-3 (CRB-3) is low when an interrupt occurs (Interrupt disabled) and is later brought high, $\overline{IRQA}$ ($\overline{IRQB}$) occurs after CRA-3 (CRB-3) is written to a "one".

Source: Reprinted with permission of Motorola Incorporated, Austin, TX.

TABLE 19–3 Control of CB_2 as Output (CRB-5 high)

CRB-5	CRB-4	CRB-3	CB2 Cleared	CB2 Set
1	0	0	Low on the positive transition of the first E pulse following an MPU Write "B" Data Register operation.	High when the interrupt flag bit CRB-7 is set by an active transition of the CB1 signal.
1	0	1	Low on the positive transition of the first E pulse after an MPU Write "B" Data Register operation.	High on the positive edge of the first "E" pulse following an "E" pulse which occurred while the part was deselected.
1	1	0	Low when CRB-3 goes low as a result of an MPU Write in Control Register "B".	Always low as long as CRB-3 is low. Will go high on an MPU Write in Control Register "B" that changes CRB-3 to "one".
1	1	1	Always high as long as CRB-3 is high. Will be cleared when an MPU Write Control Register "B" results in clearing CRB-3 to "zero".	High when CRB-3 goes high as a result of an MPU Write into Control Register "B".

Source: Reprinted with permission of Motorola Incorporated, Austin, TX.

TABLE 19–4 Control of CA_2 as Output (CRA-5 is high)

CRA-5	CRA-4	CRA-3	CA2 Cleared	CA2 Set
1	0	0	Low on negative transition of E after an MPU Read "A" Data operation.	High when the interrupt flag bit CRA-7 is set by an active transition of the CA1 signal.
1	0	1	Low on negative transition of E after an MPU Read "A" Data operation.	High on the negative edge of the first "E" pulse which occurs during a deselect.
1	1	0	Low when CRA-3 goes low as a result of an MPU Write to Control Register "A".	Always low as long as CRA-3 is low. Will go high on an MPU Write to Control Register "A" that changes CRA-3 to "one".
1	1	1	Always high as long as CRA-3 is high. Will be cleared on an MPU Write to Control Register "A" that clears CRA-3 to a "zero".	High when CRA-3 goes high as a result of an MPU Write to Control Register "A".

Source: Reprinted with permission of Motorola Incorporated, Austin, TX.

μP. They are cleared to the logic 0 state when the μP reads the data from the port or when the reset line goes low.

Remember, the term *active transition* means that lines CA_1, CA_2, CB_1, and CB_2 can be programmed to recognize either a low-to-high transition or a high-to-low transition.

19.3.4 Reset Line

When the reset line goes low, it causes all I/O lines to become input lines and all bits of the other registers to be cleared to the logic 0 state. Peripheral lines CA_2 and CB_2 become input lines. Therefore, any time the reset line is activated (goes low), the PIA must be reprogrammed as the user wants it. Programming steps for the data direction registers and the control registers are given in the next section.

19.4 PROGRAMMING THE 6821 PIA

One of the first programming steps in any μC system is to initialize all the I/O ports when the power is applied. In most applications, once a line is programmed as either an input or output line, it is left in that state. Occasionally, however, the user may wish to reprogram one or more of the I/O lines or a control line. The following examples show the programming steps necessary to initialize the 6821 for different uses. Example 19.1 shows how to program both port A and port B. Example 19.2 shows how to program port A and its control lines.

EXAMPLE 19.1 Write the programming steps necessary to satisfy the following conditions:

1. All lines of port A are to be input lines.
2. All lines of port B are to be output lines.
3. Control lines are not used.
4. The PIA is wired at locations 4000–4003.

Solution The first two memory locations (4000 and 4001 in this example) always apply to the A side. The third and fourth locations (4002 and 4003 in this example) always apply to the B side. From Section 19.3.3, we have the following:

A side 4000 (port A and DDRA)
4001 (control register A)
B side 4002 (port B and DDRB)
4003 (control register B)

The programming steps must include the following functions:

1. Load bit 2 of each control register with a logic 0 so the μP communicates with the data direction registers.
2. Load DDRA with all logic 0s, making port A all input lines.
3. Load DDRB with all logic 1s, making port B all output lines.
4. Reload bit 2 of each control register with a logic 1, allowing the μP to communicate with the port at a future time.

The programming steps to satisfy the preceding conditions are as follows:

```
LDA #00      Clear bit 2 of each control register.
STA 4001
STA 4003
STA 4000     DDRA loaded with 0s.
LDA #FF      DDRB loaded with 1s.
STA 4002
STA 4001     Reset bit 2 of each control register.
STA 4003
```

The control lines in this example were not going to be used. Therefore, we are not concerned with the logic state of control bits 0, 1, 3, 4, and 5.

EXAMPLE 19.2 Write the programming steps necessary to initialize a 6821 PIA to meet the following conditions:

1. Port line A_0 is to be an output line and all other lines of port A are to be input lines.
2. Interrupt input line CA_1 is to be receiving a high-to-low transition signal and the PIA should be capable of sending an interrupt request signal to the μP.
3. Line CA_2 is to be an output control line and is to be able to send a low-to-high signal to peripheral equipment after the CA_1 signal is received.
4. Port B is not being used.
5. The PIA is wired at locations 8000–8003.

Solution Although port B is not being used, the device is connected as follows:

A side 8000 (port A and DDRA)
8001 (control register A)

B side 8002 (port B and DDRB)
8003 (control register B)

From Tables 19–1 and 19–4, we know that the final binary pattern that must be stored in control register A is as follows:

7 6	5 4 3	2 1 0
X X	1 0 0	1 0 1
Don't care	CA_2 from Table 19–4	CA_1 from Table 19–1

The following programming steps satisfy the preceding conditions:

```
LDA #00      Clear bit 2 and temporarily disable the IRQA line.
STA 8001
LDA #01      Port A0 is an output line; all other lines are input.
STA 8000
LDA #25      Control register is loaded with final binary pattern.
STA 8001
```

In this example, the "don't care" conditions are considered to be a logic 0. If logic 1s are to be sent on data lines 6 and 7, then the last two steps are as follows:

```
LDA #E5
STA 8001
```

Remember, the logic levels on data lines 6 and 7 never reach bits 6 and 7 because these bits are the status bits.

19.5 CONNECTING SEVERAL PIAS TO THE SYSTEM

Each PIA has six registers (two ports, two DDRs, and two control registers) that can communicate with the μP. However, the port and the data direction register have the same address. Therefore, four memory locations are needed to address one PIA completely. This use of the same address for the port and data direction register may seem confusing at first. The register with which the μP communicates depends on bit 2 of the control register. As the previous programming examples showed, the control register may have to be addressed twice. The first time is to clear bit 2 so the μP can load data into a DDR. The second time is to set bit 2 so the μP can read or write data to the port. What appears to be an awkward arrangement becomes an easy interface to the μP as more I/O ports are added.

Figure 19–3A showed how one PIA chip could be connected directly to a μP. However, when several PIAs are being used, decoder chips are needed. Using only four memory locations to identify a PIA makes maximum use of the decoder chips and thus creates an efficient system. Let's consider a μC system that is to have four PIAs wired between memory locations 4000 and 400F. This is the same memory allocation that was given to I/O in Chapter 16, as shown in Figure 16–9. As we will see, the decoder line, line 1 of Figure 16–9, will be wired to each PIA chip. A low on this line indicates that the μP wants to communicate with one of the PIAs. We still have to identify which PIA and which register within the PIA is to send or receive data. These two functions can be carried out by the lowest four address lines. Figure 19–10 shows all the binary combinations that can exist on four address lines. Thus, all memory locations between 4000 and 400F are included.

Figure 19–10 also shows how a 74LS42 decoder chip can be used to decode address lines A_2 and A_3. Address lines A_0 and A_1 are wired to all the PIAs. From Figure 19–10, we see that lines A_2 and A_3 remain at the same logic state for four counts (four memory locations). It is for this reason that the design of the 6821 PIA requires only four memory locations.

If more PIAs are to be connected to the system, address line A_4 would be wired to the C input on the 74LS42 chip. The D line would remain grounded. These connections would permit four more PIAs to be connected to the system. Hence, maximum use is made of each address line, creating a very efficient system.

Figure 19–11 shows the completed PIA circuitry. In Section 19.1.2, we saw that each 6821 PIA has three chip select pins. Each pin has to be at the

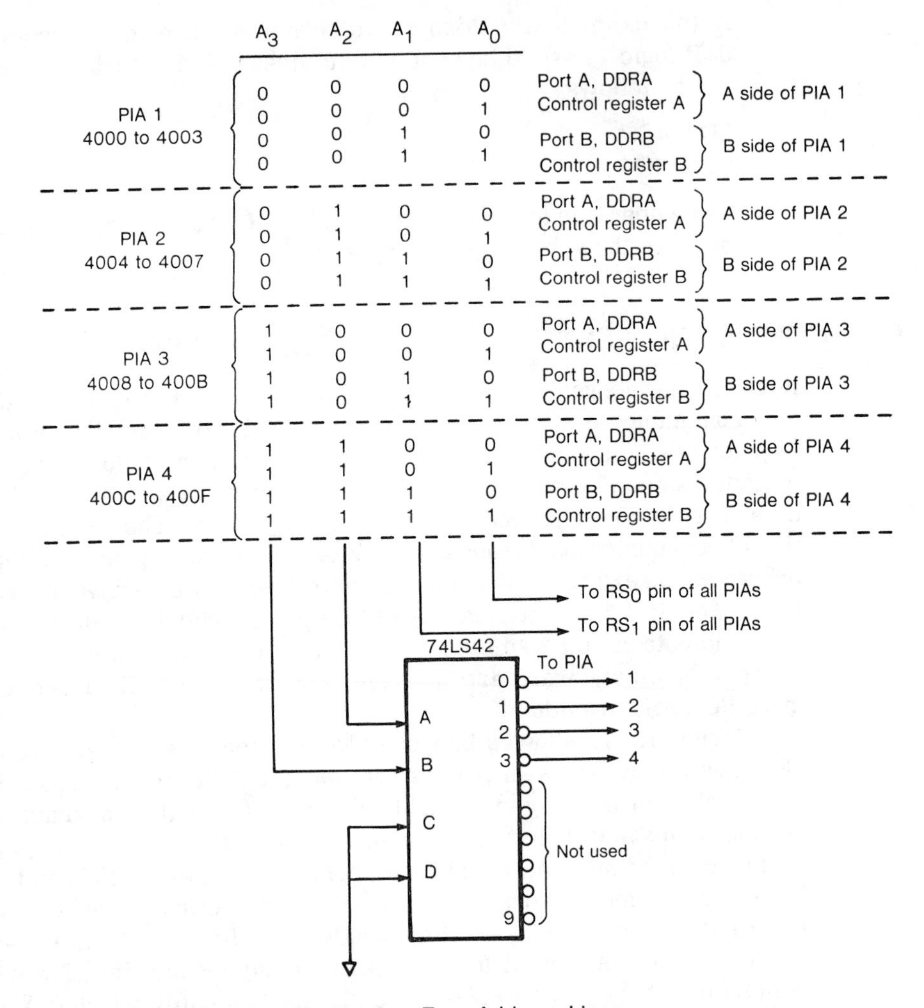

FIGURE 19–10 Binary Combinations on Four Address Lines

proper logic level (CS_0 and CS_1 high and $\overline{CS}_2$ low) for the PIA to communicate with the μP. When selected, the output line of a decoder goes low; therefore, the inverter on line 1 of the memory map decoder is needed. No inverters are needed on the PIA's $\overline{CS}_2$ pin because this pin is wired directly to the output line of a decoder chip. Remember, the output lines of decoder chips are an active low state. The CS_1 pin of each PIA is wired high because the chip select pins of any peripheral device should not be left floating.

19.6 A SOFTWARE POLLING TECHNIQUE

The 6800 and 6502 μPs have one interrupt request pin. It is designed to be an open-drain device so that several PIA interrupt request lines can be tied to it through a 3.0-kilohm pull-up resistor. However, when several PIA interrupt request lines are used in a system, the μP must be able to distinguish one inter-

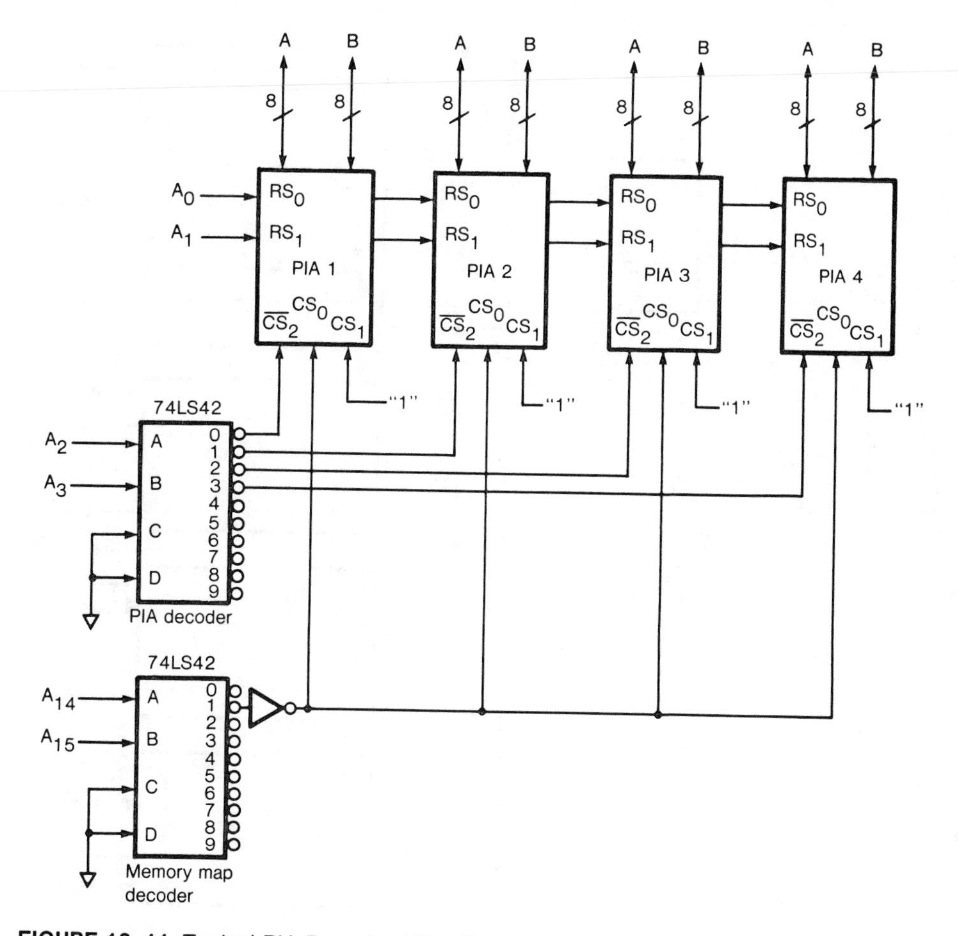

FIGURE 19–11 Typical PIA Decoding Circuit

rupt request signal from another. The schematic of Figure 19–12 shows how the interrupt request lines of the four PIAs of Figure 19–11 can be tied to a 6800 or 6502 μP. Each interrupt request line coming from the PIA represents two possible interrupt signals. (See either Figure 19–5 or PIA 1 of Figure 19–12.)

When the μP receives an interrupt request signal, it must determine which PIA and which peripheral interrupt line (CA_1, CA_2, CB_1, or CB_2) on the PIA needs servicing. If a program is used to do this, it is called a *software polling technique*. The programmer chooses the priority of servicing by determining which control register and which bit (either 7 or 6) is tested first. If the four PIAs are wired between locations 4000 to 400F, then Table 19–5 gives the address of each control register. Consider that the μP is the 6502. When the bit test instruction for the 6502 is executed, bits 7 and 6 are loaded immediately into the sign and overflow flags, respectively. This permits the bit test instruction to be followed by two branch instructions: check the sign bit and check the overflow bit. If either bit is a logic 1, then that indicates which line is requesting service. The following programming steps show how each control

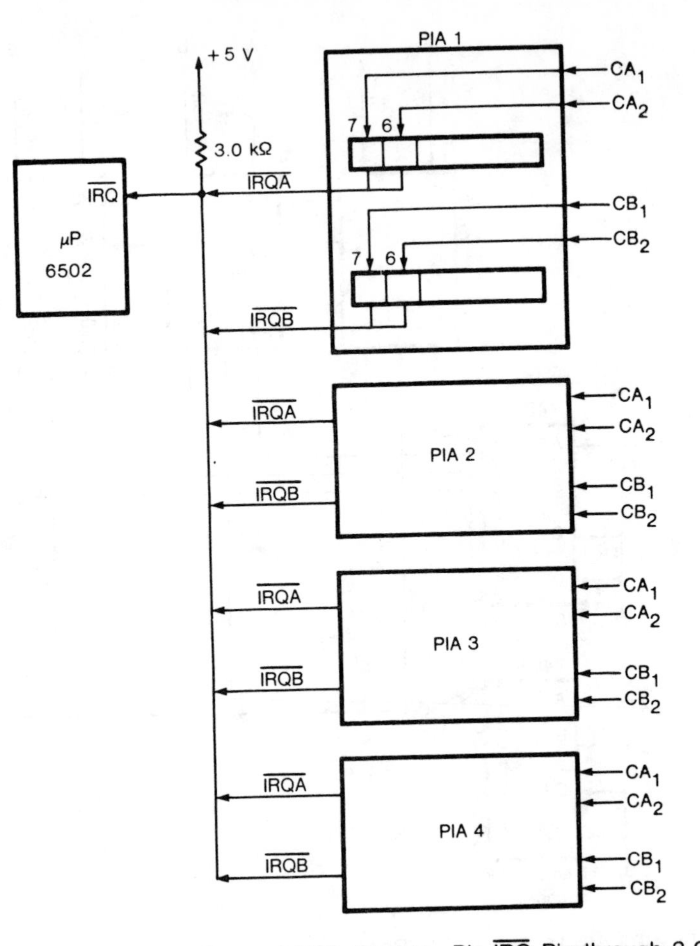

FIGURE 19-12 PIA Interrupt Request Lines Tied to μP's $\overline{IRQ}$ Pin through 3.0 KΩ Pull-up Resistor

register and each interrupt request bit can be checked. The offset (P_1, P_2, and so on) for each branch instruction would direct the μP to a program to service that particular interrupt. The software polling program is as follows:

BIT	4001	BVS	P_6	BMI	P_{11}
BMI	P_1	BIT	4007	BVS	P_{12}
BVS	P_2	BMI	P_7	BIT	400D
BIT	4003	BVS	P_8	BMI	P_{13}
BMI	P_3	BIT	4009	BVS	P_{14}
BVS	P_4	BMI	P_9	BIT	400F
BIT	4005	BVS	P_{10}	BMI	P_{15}
BMI	P_5	BIT	400B	BVS	P_{16}

TABLE 19-5 Address of Control Register

Control Register	PIA Number	Location
A	1	4001
B	1	4003
A	2	4005
B	2	4007
A	3	4009
B	3	400B
A	4	400D
B	4	400F

19.7 INTERFACING A PIA WITH AN ALPHANUMERIC PRINTER

As previously mentioned, the MC6821 is a general-purpose interface device. In this section, it is used as the link between the μP and an alphanumeric printer. This printer and interface circuit are used in the automatic test equipment (ATE) system covered in Chapter 20.

19.7.1 Printer Description

The printer used in the ATE system is a Gulton Model AP-20, a self-contained alphanumeric thermal printer. All its electronics, including a memory buffer RAM, a character generator ROM, a power supply, and control circuitry, are enclosed in the printer's case. The print format is 20 characters per line. Each character is a 5 × 7 dot matrix, as shown in Figure 19-13. The printer is designed to accept 64 ASCII characters. (Figure 3-3, columns 2, 3, 4, and 5, lists the most frequently used characters.)

Data is sent from the PIA to the printer one character at a time. The data is stored in a RAM buffer. When 20 characters have been stored, or when a carriage return code or an end-of-line code has been received, the printer begins printing the data. The print head contains 100 thermal print dots so that an entire row of character dots is printed at one time. The bottom row of dots is printed first, as shown in Figure 19-13. After one entire line is complete, the paper is automatically advanced one or more lines.

19.7.2 PIA-Printer Connections and Operation

The PIA of Figure 19-14 uses peripheral lines PB_0 to PB_6 to transmit a 7-bit ASCII character. Peripheral line PB_7 and control lines CB_1 and CB_2 are used for handshake signals.

Line CB_2 is used as a clock signal to the printer. The inverter gate on this line is needed because the printer's external clock line (pin 18 on the printer)

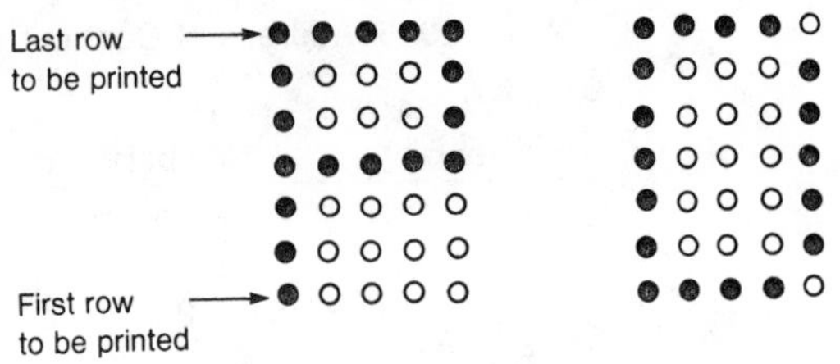

Last row to be printed

First row to be printed

FIGURE 19–13 5 × 7 Dot Matrix of Printer

requires a positive-going pulse. By using the CB_2 line in this fashion, the data sent to port B from the μP will have enough time to stabilize on the peripheral lines before it is clocked into the printer.

The printer also requires a positive pulse on its load data line (pin 19 on the printer). This pulse is sent by the μP through the port B_7 line (pin 17 on the PIA). The inverter gate is needed because the μP is sending a 7-bit ASCII character with a logic 0 on the eighth data bus line. In this system, the load data lines goes high on the first character and the data is transmitted when the external clock line goes high.

When the printer decodes a carriage return command or an end-of-line signal or when the 20-character RAM buffer is full, the $\overline{BUSY}$ line goes low. This signal is sent back to the PIA's CB_1 pin indicating that a line of data is being printed. When the $\overline{BUSY}$ line goes low, the PIA sends an interrupt request signal back to the μP on the $\overline{IRQB}$ line. The μP recognizes the interrupt request and jumps to an interrupt subroutine that is a time delay program. The printer then has enough time to print one line before the μP begins sending the printer the next line of data. Figure 19–15 shows how the CB_2 and $\overline{BUSY}$ handshake signals operate.

19.7.3 Programming the PIA

In order to satisfy the handshake signals, the B side of the PIA must meet the following criteria:

1. All peripheral lines of port B must be programmed as output lines.
2. Control line CB_1 must be programmed to send an interrupt request signal to the μP when it receives a high-to-low transition.
3. Control line CB_2 must be programmed as an output line and the line must go low when the μP writes data to port B.
4. After the μP initializes the data direction register of port B, the μP must always be able to communicate with the peripheral lines.

To meet these specifications, we need to use data in Tables 19–1 and 19–3. The final binary pattern stored in control register B is shown in Figure 19–16.

EXAMPLE 19.3 Consider the PIA to be wired at memory locations 8000, 8001, 8002, and 8003. After the $\overline{\text{reset}}$ line is activated and released, program the B side of the PIA to meet criteria 1–4.

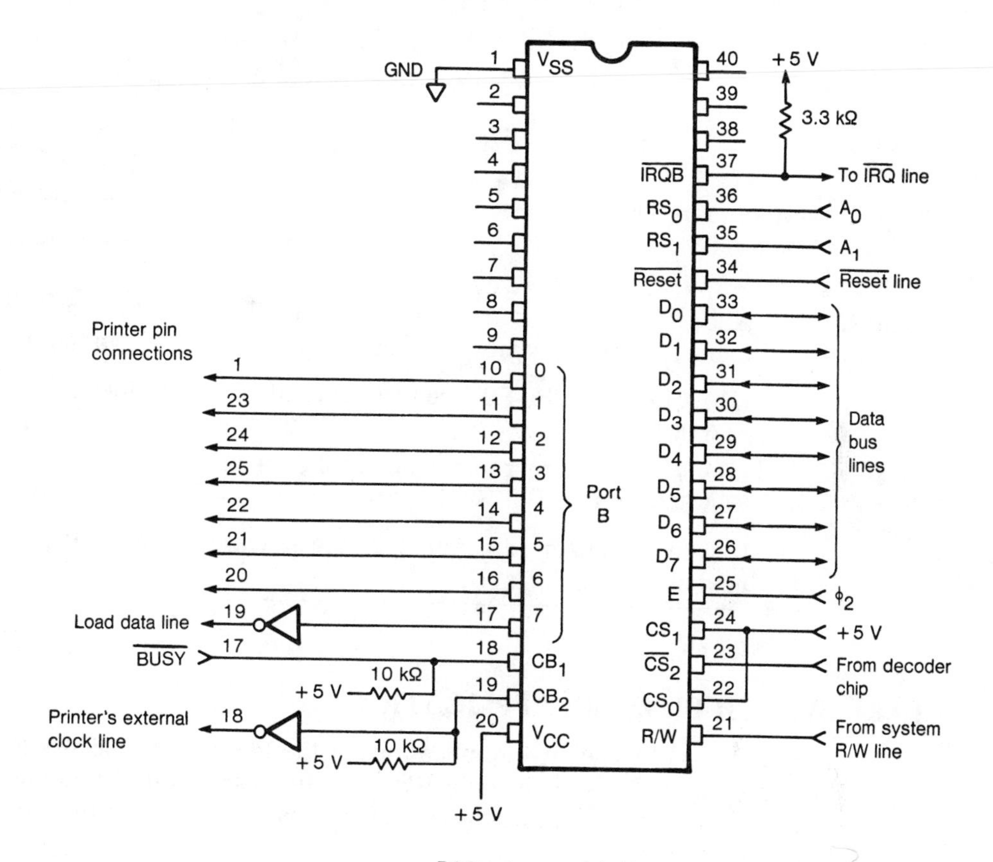

FIGURE 19–14 6821 Used as Interface Link between μP and Alphanumeric Printer

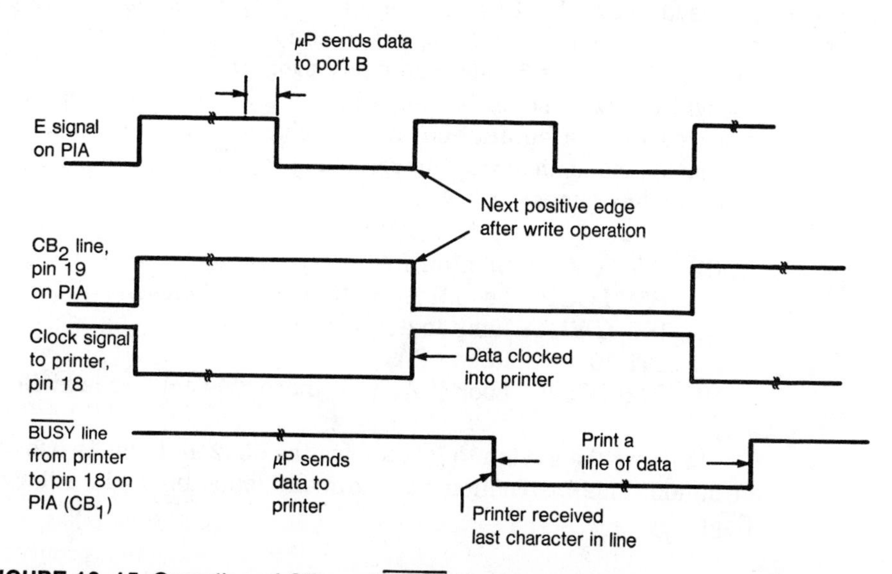

FIGURE 19–15 Operation of CB_2 and $\overline{BUSY}$ Handshake Signals

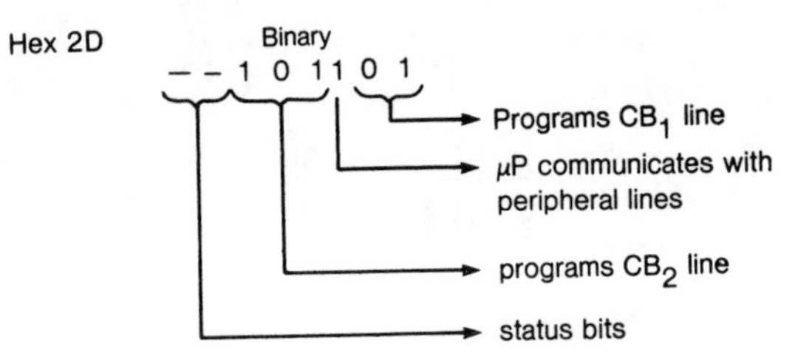

FIGURE 19–16 Binary Pattern Stored in Control Register B

Solution After $\overline{\text{Reset}}$, all lines are input lines and all register bits contain a logic 0. Using the 6502 assembly language mnemonics, we have the following:

```
LDA #FF      PB0-PB7 are programmed as output lines.
STA 8002
LDA #2D      Programming control register B.
STA 8003
```

Now any data stored at port B by the μP will be sent to the printer on the next clock signal.

19.8 SWITCH CLOSURE APPLICATION

Figure 19–17 shows two applications of the PIA, switch closure and vacuum pump control. These two applications use the A side of the PIA shown in Figure 19–14. This section covers the switch closure, while Section 19.9 deals with the vacuum pump.

A switch and a pull-up register are wired to PIA line A_7. Once the μP recognizes that this switch is closed, the μP jumps to another program and does not need to monitor PA_7 again until the program is finished. Figure 19–18 is a flowchart showing how the 6502 μP can monitor bit 7 (port line A_7) of memory location 8000. The 50 ms time delay program guarantees that the μP will not recognize any noise on the line or switch bounce. The time delay program is referred to as a subroutine in the following program. Using 6502 assembly language mnemonics, we can write the programming steps necessary to satisfy the flowchart steps:

```
LOOP: BIT 8000     Monitor PA7.
      BMI LOOP     Loop if A7 = 1 (switch not closed).
      JSR TDELAY   Jump to delay subroutine.
      BIT 8000     Retest PA7.
      BMI LOOP     Loop if A7 = 1 (there was not a true switch closure).
```

Wiring the switch to PA_7 allows the 6502 μP to make use of its bit test instruction. This instruction automatically loads bit A_7 into the sign flag bit (N flag).

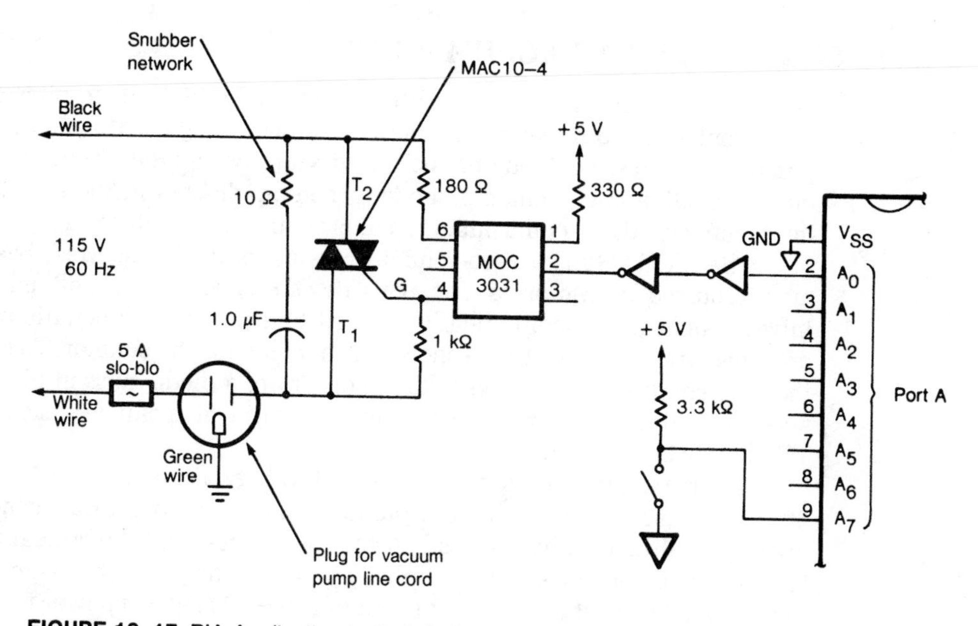

FIGURE 19–17 PIA Application in Switch Closure and Vacuum Pump Control

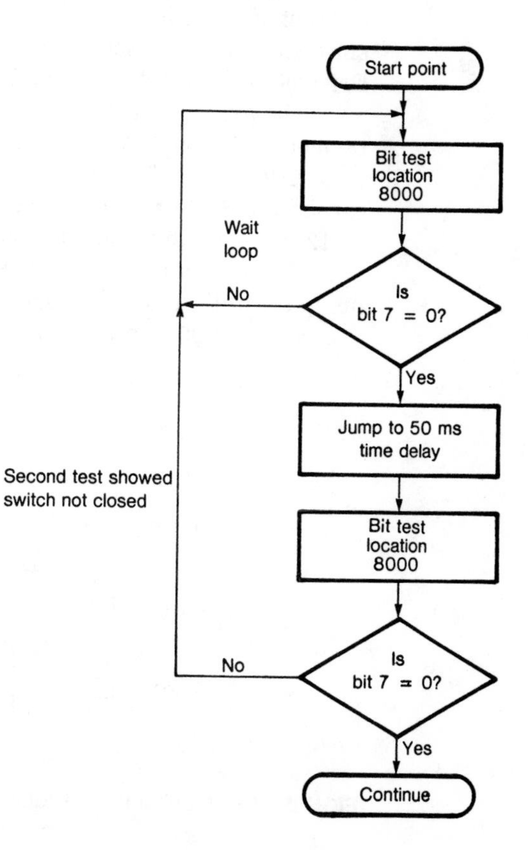

FIGURE 19–18 Flowchart for 6502 μP Monitoring Bit 7

19.9 CONTROLLING A VACUUM PUMP

One peripheral line and some additional external interface circuitry allow the μP to control a 1/6 hp vacuum pump, as shown in Figure 19–17. The vacuum pump is needed for a "bed-of-nails" test fixture. When the μP outputs a logic 0 on the PA_0 line, the vacuum pump is turned on. Since a PIA's output line is a latch network, the vacuum pump remains on until the μP stores a logic 1 at PA_0.

The MOC3031 is a zero-voltage-crossing, optically isolated, triac driver manufactured by Motorola, Inc. This device consists of a gallium arsenide infrared-emitting diode, optically coupled to a photo triac containing a zero-crossing circuit. Figure 19–19 shows a schematic for the coupler. To guarantee that the emitting diode triggers the photo triac, a diode current of 10–15 mA must flow. Since this current is greater than that which can be sinked by PA_0, a TTL buffer is needed.

The maximum rms current that can flow between pins 6 and 4 of the MOC 3031 is 100 mA. Since the vacuum pump draws several amps during normal operating conditions, a heat-sinked power triac is needed. The optically coupled triac turns on the power triac, applying power to the plug. The vacuum pump's line cord is inserted into this plug, and thus the μP controls power to the pump. The snubber network ensures that the power triac does not have a false turn-on. (For more information on optical couplers, power triacs, heat sinks, and snubber networks, see *Solid State Devices and Applications*, by Frederick F. Driscoll and Robert F. Coughlin, Prentice-Hall, Inc., Englewood, N.J., 1975.)

The arrangement shown in Figure 19–17 allows the interface circuitry to be mounted near the μP and the vacuum pump a short distance away.

After the switch described in Section 19.8 is closed, the vacuum pump is turned on. A 5 s delay is inserted to allow the pump to come up to pressure (~12 psi), and then the main program continues.

The following program initializes the A side of the PIA and keeps the pump off until it is to be turned on later in the main program. The A side addresses are 8000 and 8001. This program uses the 6502 μP mnemonics.

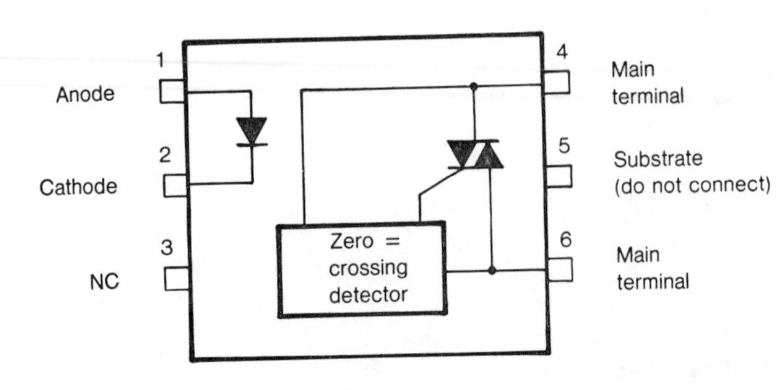

FIGURE 19–19 Schematic of MOC3031

LDA #01 STA 8000	Set only vacuum pump line PA_0 as an output line.
LDA #04 STA 8001	Set bit 2 of control register A.
LDA #01 STA 8000	Output line PA_0 is latched high to keep the pump off.

19.10 SUMMARY

The 6821 peripheral interface adapter is a general-purpose I/O device. Although this chip was designed primarily for the 6800 μP, it is often used with the 6502 μP. The 6821 has two ports, A and B. Each port has eight peripheral lines; each line can be programmed as either an input or an output line. In addition to these I/O lines, the 6821 has other peripheral lines for "handshaking." Like other peripheral devices, the 6821 is easily connected to the μP's address, data, and control buses. It is capable of sending an interrupt request signal back to the μP either from peripheral side A or peripheral side B.

Sections 19.3 and 19.4 show how to program the 6821's peripheral lines and control (handshake) lines. Section 19.5 shows how decoder chips are used to connect several PIAs to a μP. When a μP is capable of receiving an interrupt request from several PIAs, a software polling technique, as shown in Section 19.6, can be used to identify which PIA is requesting service. Sections 19.7, 19.8, and 19.9 show three applications of how the PIA is used as the interface device between the μP and peripheral equipment.

PROBLEMS

19-1 How many ports has the 6821?
19-2 Can the I/O lines be programmed independently?
19-3 How many pins on the 6821 are connected to the address bus?
19-4 What are the logic levels on the chip select pins?
19-5 Is the active state of the reset pin high or low?
19-6 What is the function of the enable pin?
19-7 What is the difference between the I/O lines of port A and the I/O lines of port B?
19-8 The binary pattern in what register determines whether an I/O line is programmed as input or output?
19-9 What lines are the peripheral interrupt lines?
19-10 Which two registers within the 6821 have the same address?
19-11 The following binary pattern is stored in data direction register A·

7	6	5	4	3	2	1	0	Bit number
1	1	1	0	0	1	1	0	DDRA

Which lines are programmed as input lines and which are output lines?
19-12 How many bits of the control register are used for status information?
19-13 What is the function of bit 2 of the control register?

19–14 When the reset line is activated, are the lines automatically programmed as input or output lines?

19–15 The following binary pattern is stored in control register A:

7	6	5	4	3	2	1	0	Bit number
X	X	1	0	0	1	0	0	Control register

(a) Will the μP communicate with the port or with the data direction register? (b) What is the active transition on the CA_1 line? (c) Is CA_2 programmed as an interrupt or a control line?

19–16 The PIA is wired at locations 4000–4003. Write the programming steps necessary to satisfy the following conditions: (a) All lines of port A are output lines; (b) All lines of port B are input lines; (c) CA_1 and CA_2 are not used; (d) CB_1 is an interrupt request line with high-to-low active transition; and (e) CB_2 is an output control line with low-to-high active transition when the CB_1 signal is received.

19–17 Refer to Figures 19–10 and 19–11. If two more PIAs have to be added to the system, how should they be decoded?

Automatic Testing System

20.0 INTRODUCTION

Today's designers are placing more and more complex circuitry on a single printed circuit board. In order to catch failures before a product is released, automatic test equipment (ATE) is required for all levels of quality control, from incoming inspection of components to final product testing. Incoming inspection is designed to weed out faulty components before they are used. This step may require static and dynamic testing as well as temperature cycling tests. The printed circuit board (PCB) must also be tested before any components are inserted and soldered. Manufacturers cannot rely solely on visual inspection to check for all PCB wiring errors. On some high-density boards, the conductor patterns may be only 0.005 inch thick (5 mils) and the board may contain thousands of mounting holes (donuts). Visual inspection can only be trusted to ensure cosmetic quality and to catch flagrant errors on low-density boards. There is no way to check multilayer boards visually. Therefore, electrical testing is required for the printed circuit board.

After all parts are checked, the final product requires additional testing before it is shipped. Manufacturers cannot leave the testing only for the last stage. This could prove economically disastrous because a considerable amount of time is required to track down even a single fault. Although automatic test equipment can be expensive, it can pay for itself by allowing a manufacturer to produce a quality product at a lower cost.

In this chapter, we will examine a μC system that has been designed by the author to test students' printed circuit boards. The PCB is used in a digital clock. After the test is completed, the student receives a printout indicating whether the board is okay or has errors. If there are errors, the location and type of each error is shown on the printout. Thus, the student can correct any wiring errors before components are mounted and soldered. The system has been designed to test a particular printed circuit board, so it is referred to as a dedicated PCB tester.

20.1 PRINTED CIRCUIT BARE BOARD TESTER

Figure 20–1 shows the complete system. It consists of three parts: (1) the μC, (2) the bed-of-nails, and (3) a vacuum pump. The μC uses the 6502 μP, which controls everything, even turning the vacuum pump on and off. There is one line cord from the back of the μC case to a wall outlet (115 V, 60 Hz). The vacuum pump's line cord is plugged into a socket mounted on the back panel of the μC's case. Power is applied to the vacuum pump under control of the μP and only when a PCB is being tested. Control of the vacuum pump was discussed in Section 19.9.

The μC is also connected to the bed-of-nails by a harness containing 192 wires. Although the PCB being checked contains only 160 test points, the μC can be used in the future to test boards with more donuts.

The vacuum pump is also connected to the bed-of-nails. When the vacuum pump is activated by the μC, the PCB is drawn down onto the test probes. Each test probe in the bed-of-nails is connected to an I/O pin on a peripheral interface adapter chip in the μC. Figure 20–2 shows a cross-sectional view of the bed-of-nails test fixture. Figure 20–2 also shows the relationship of the different parts when the vacuum pump is off. When the pump is on, it draws out the air between the flex board and the base support. Outside pressure forces the PCB down onto the test probes. The probes are cemented into the base support. Although the PCB and neoprene should form an airtight seal, in most bed-of-nails text fixtures they do not. The solution to this problem is to place a piece of surgical rubber over the PCB, creating an airtight seal when the pump is turned on. It takes about 5 s for the vacuum pump to come up to pressure. Therefore, a time delay is built into the main program before the μP makes any test.

20.2 BASIC TEST PROCEDURE

The system has been designed to be self-contained and even to provide instructions for a first-time user. When power is applied, the set of instructions shown in Figure 20–3 is printed out.

The master board is now placed on the bed-of-nails, and the test switch is pressed. The board is aligned correctly by two mounting pins. The μC activates the vacuum pump and a 5 s delay is included to allow the pump to come up to pressure (~ 12 psi).

During this test, the μP stores all of the possible combinations of test

FIGURE 20–1 Three Parts of PC Board ATE — μC System with Printer, Bed-of-Nails, and Vacuum Pump

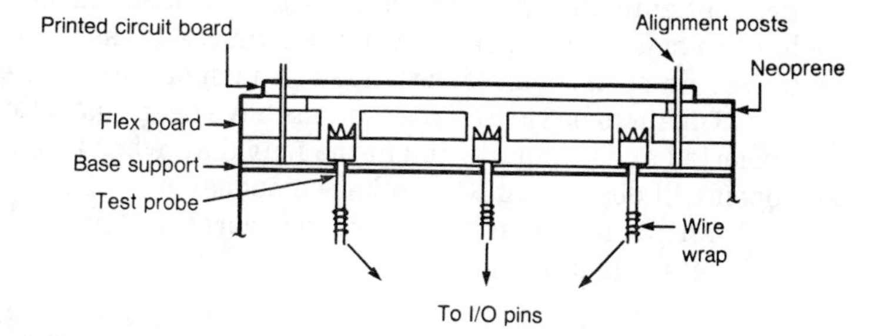

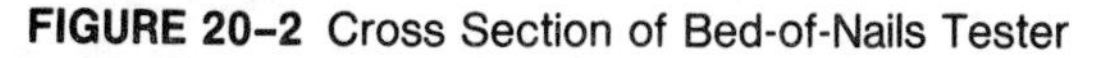

FIGURE 20–2 Cross Section of Bed-of-Nails Tester

```
  INSTRUCTIONS FOR
    LOADING DATA

THE MICROCOMPUTER
SYSTEM IS READY TO
LOAD DATA FROM THE
MASTER PC BOARD.

PLACE THE MASTER PC
BOARD ON THE BED OF
NAILS AND DEPRESS
THE "PRESS TO TEST"
SWITCH.

       M²VDC
```

FIGURE 20–3 Printout of Instructions for Loading Data

points into RAM. Since the μC can test 192 points and since each point is tested against itself and all the other points, there are 192 × 192 = 36,864 combinations. Each combination is stored as one bit in RAM; therefore, the total storage requires 36,864/8 = 4608 bytes.

After all of the data from the master board is loaded into memory, a second set of instructions is printed and the vacuum pump is turned off. The new instructions are shown in Figure 20-4.

The master board is removed, and the student's board can now be tested. As stated in the instructions, the master board does not have to be placed on the bed-of-nails unless the power to the μC is lost. Figure 20-5 shows examples of a printout that a student may receive. Figure 20-5A is a printout for a PCB with no errors; Figure 20-5B is an example of a PCB with six errors; and Figure 20-5C is a printout for a board that has more than 30 errors. Figure 20-5B shows that the printout contains a heading, the total number of errors, the drive pin, error point, and type of error. Each test point is numbered. A donut master with a correct wiring pattern is posted. Figures 20-6 and 20-7 show the donut master and master PC board, respectively. Each student receives an unnumbered copy. This guarantees that each donut will be aligned properly with a test probe on the bed-of-nails fixture. Therefore, a student who receives a printout with an error or errors checks the donut master and quickly knows where to make a correction. A short requires breaking a conductor pattern, whereas an open requires insertion of a jumper wire. The student now checks the PCB again to be sure all corrections have been made. Components may now be inserted and soldered without the fear that, when power is applied, a short or open will destroy an IC or other components.

With an understanding of how the overall system works, let's examine the individual parts of the μC.

```
INSTRUCTIONS FOR
 TESTING BOARDS

DATA FROM THE MASTER
PC BOARD HAS BEEN
LOADED INTO THE
COMPUTER'S MEMORY.

THE SYSTEM IS NOW
READY TO TEST A
STUDENT'S PC BOARD.
THERE IS NO NEED TO
REPLACE THE MASTER
PC BOARD UNLESS
THERE IS A POWER
FAILURE.

REMOVE THE MASTER PC
BOARD FROM THE BED
OF NAILS AND REPLACE
IT WITH A STUDENT'S
PC BOARD.  TEST THE
STUDENT'S BOARD BY
DEPRESSING THE
"PRESS TO TEST"
SWITCH.
```

FIGURE 20-4 Printout of Instructions for Testing Boards

```
WENTWORTH INSTITUTE
OF TECHNOLOGY

ELECTRONIC SHOP
BARE BOARD TESTER

THE PC BOARD NOW
BEING TESTED HAS
NO WIRING ERRORS.
JOB WELL DONE.
```

A. No Errors

```
WENTWORTH INSTITUTE
OF TECHNOLOGY

ELECTRONIC SHOP
BARE BOARD TESTER

6 WIRING ERRORS

DRIVE ERROR TYPE OF
PIN POINT ERROR

12--  13---SHORT
12--  59---SHORT
13--  39---SHORT
39--  59---SHORT
100-- 110---OPEN
106-- 110---OPEN
```

B. Six Errors

```
WENTWORTH INSTITUTE
OF TECHNOLOGY

ELECTRONIC SHOP
BARE BOARD TESTER

THE PC BOARD NOW
BEING TESTED HAS
MORE THAN 30 ERRORS.
YOU MAY HAVE TO MAKE
A NEW PC BOARD.
```

C. More Than 30 Errors

FIGURE 20-5 Computer Printouts Student May Receive

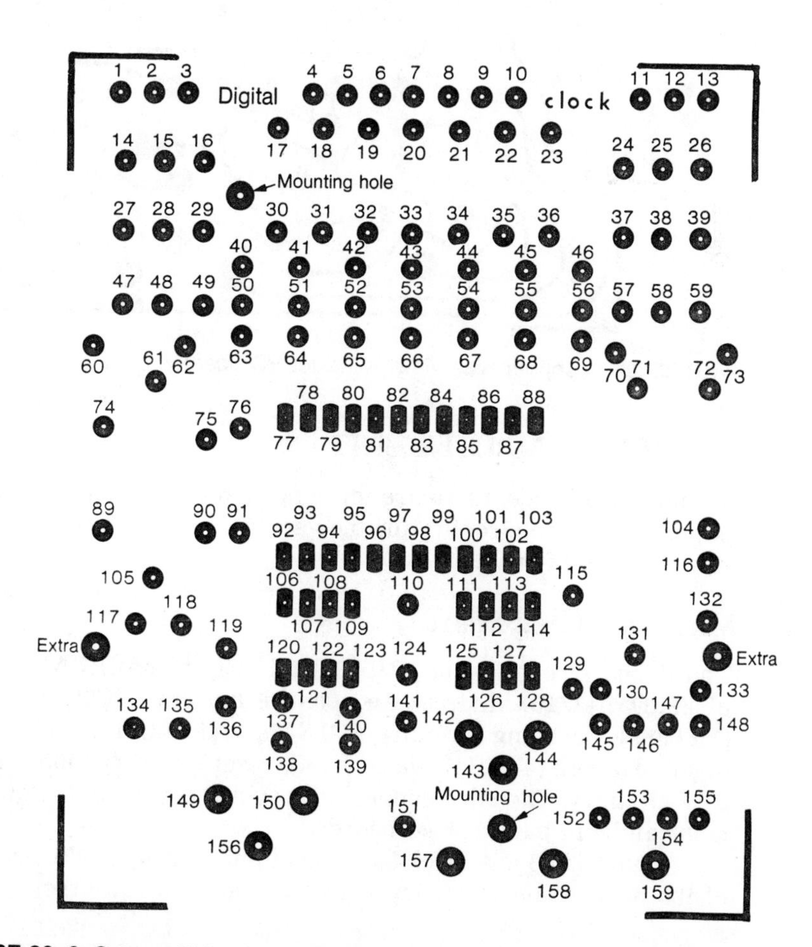

FIGURE 20-6 Copper Side View of Donut Master

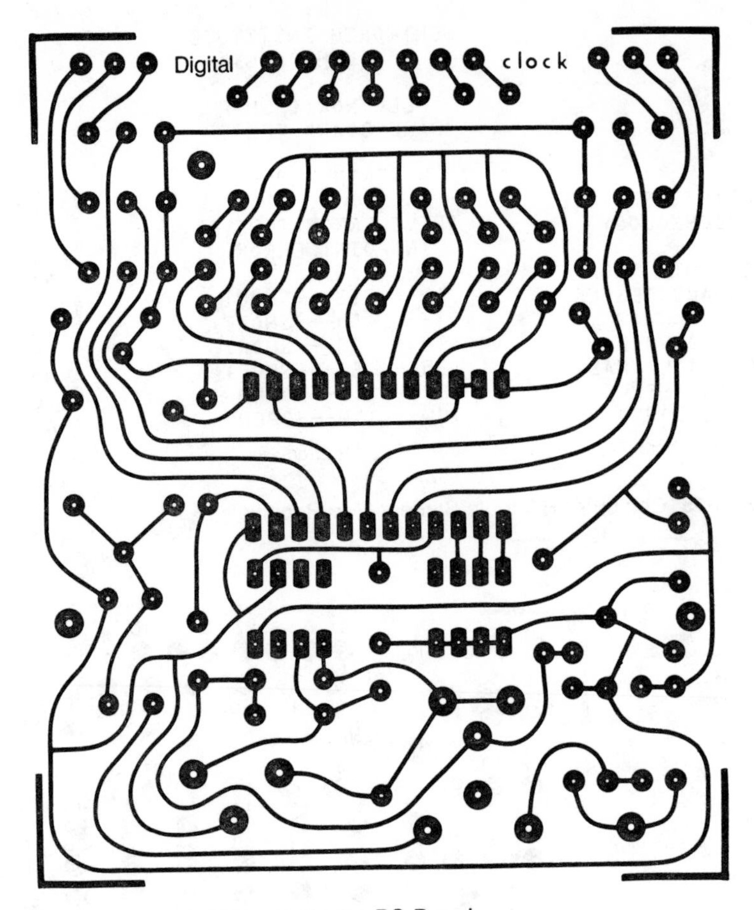

FIGURE 20-7 Copper Side View of Master PC Board

20.3 THE MICROCOMPUTER UNIT

Within the μC case, there are three printed circuit boards, a printer, a power supply, interface circuitry for the vacuum pump and printer, and cables that go to the bed-of-nails.

20.3.1 Microcomputer Board

The μC board contains the μP (6502); 6K bytes of static RAM (21L14s); 2K bytes of EPROM (2716); address and control buffers (MC6885); data bus buffers (MC6889); decoding circuitry (74LS42s and 74LS138); clock generator and divide network (4 MHz divided by 4); reset circuitry (555 timer); and system R/W circuitry. The edge connector provides power and allows the μP to communicate with the other μC boards.

Figure 20-8 is a block diagram of the μC board. We have examined most of the devices and circuitry shown in the figure in other parts of this text.

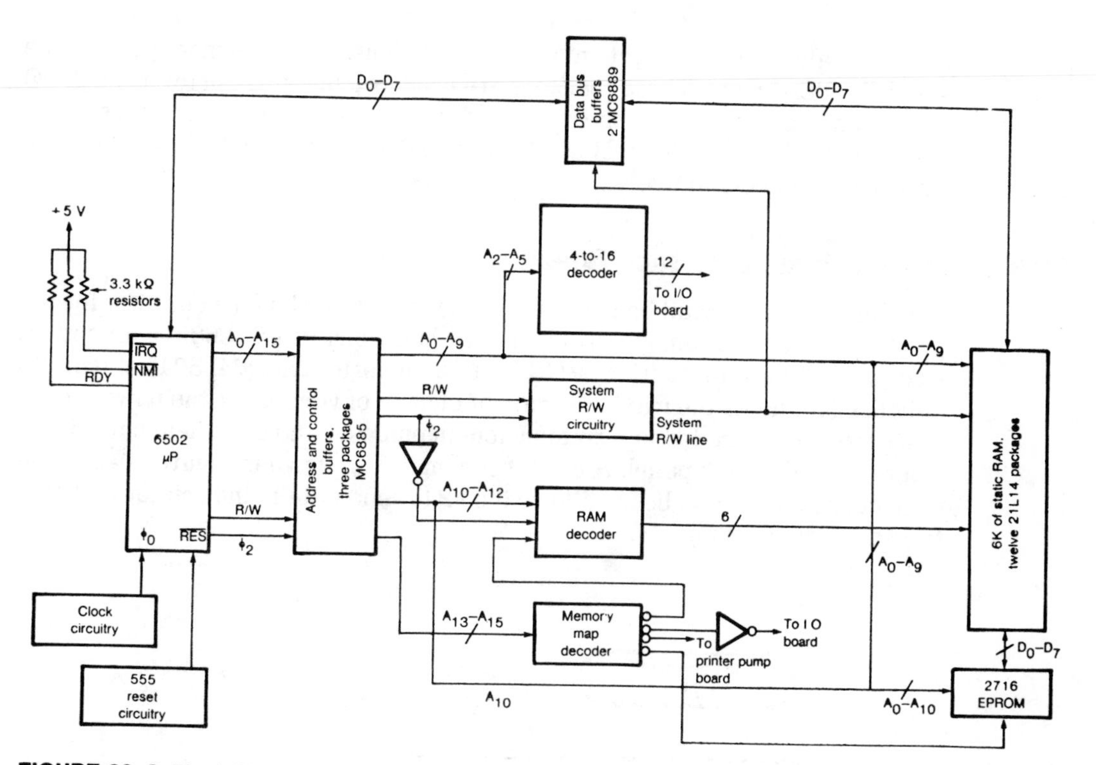

FIGURE 20–8 Block Diagram of μC Board

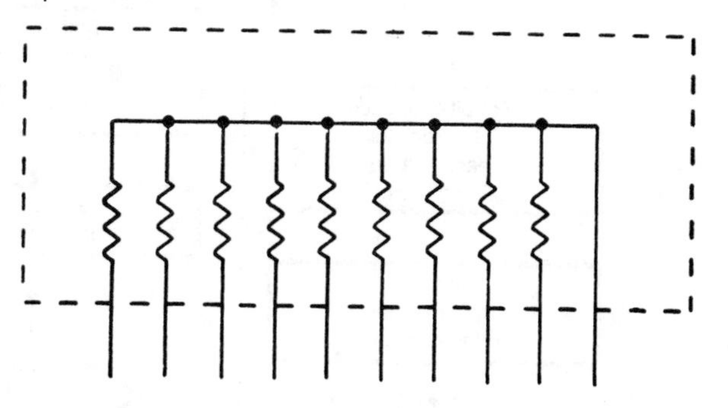
FIGURE 20–9 Single In-Line Resistor Package with Common Line

The block diagram shows how the individual parts are put together to make a system.

20.3.2 I/O Peripheral Interface Board

The I/O interface board to the bed-of-nails contains 12 peripheral interface adapter (PIA) chips (MC6821); 24 single-in-line resistor packages; and 192 wire wrap pins (mounted on the other side of the board). Each resistor package contains nine 220-kilohm resistors; however, only eight are used on each port. Figure 20–9 shows how the resistors are connected within the package; all resistor values in this system are 220 kilohms. The common power line simplifies PCB layout. These resistors are used as a pull-up resistor on each I/O line. Each line is a connection from an I/O pin on the PIA to a test probe in the bed-of-nails. The edge connector allows the μP to communicate with a PIA and thus with the bed-of-nails.

20.3.3 Printer/Pump Interface Board

The third printed circuit board in the μC contains the interface circuitry for the printer and the vacuum pump. The board holds one PIA (MC6821); an optical isolator with low-power triac (MOC3031); an inverter chip (74LS04); and an *RC* network that limits the maximum rate of change of voltage for the power triac. The power triac needed to turn the vacuum pump on and off is heat sinked and mounted on the back panel. A circuit schematic is shown in Figure 19–17. The edge connector on this board allows the μP to send data to the printer and control the vacuum pump.

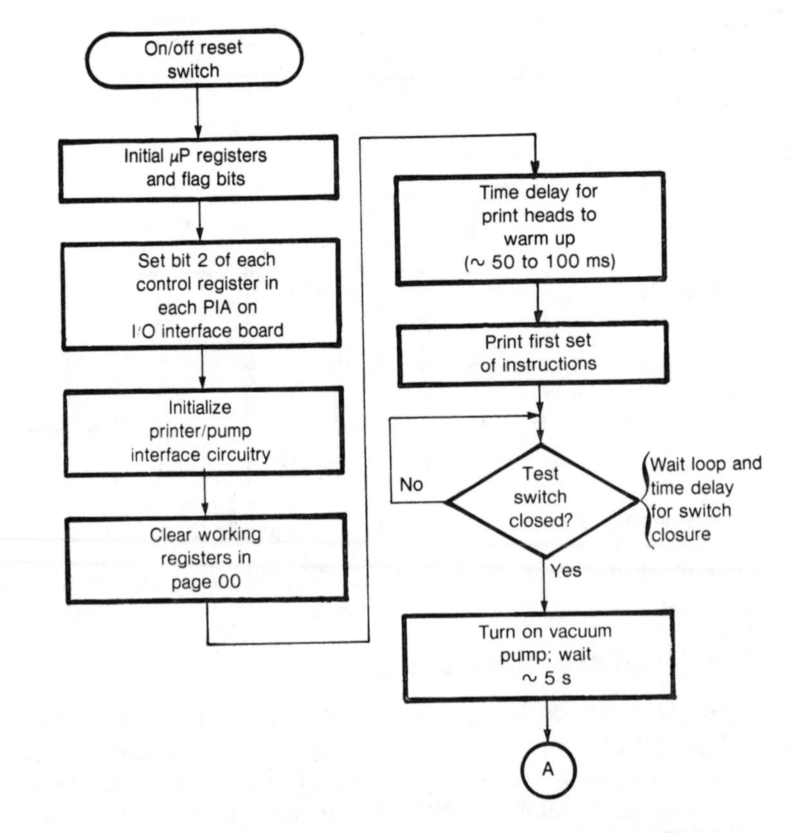

FIGURE 20–10 Operational Flowchart for Automatic Test Equipment System

20.4 OPERATIONAL FLOWCHART

The flowchart in Figure 20–10 shows the major blocks that were needed for this system's software. An algorithm then was written and tested for each block. The program was written in assembly language so it could be stored in 2048 bytes of read-only memory. The 2716 EPROM on the μC board contains the program, including the instructions.

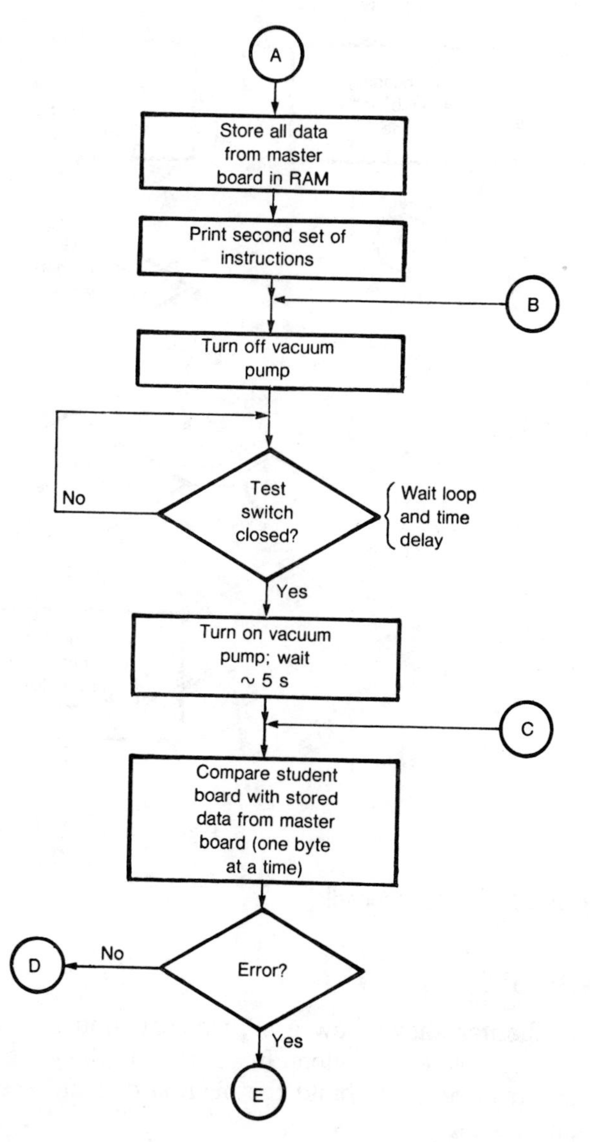

FIGURE 20–10 (Continued)

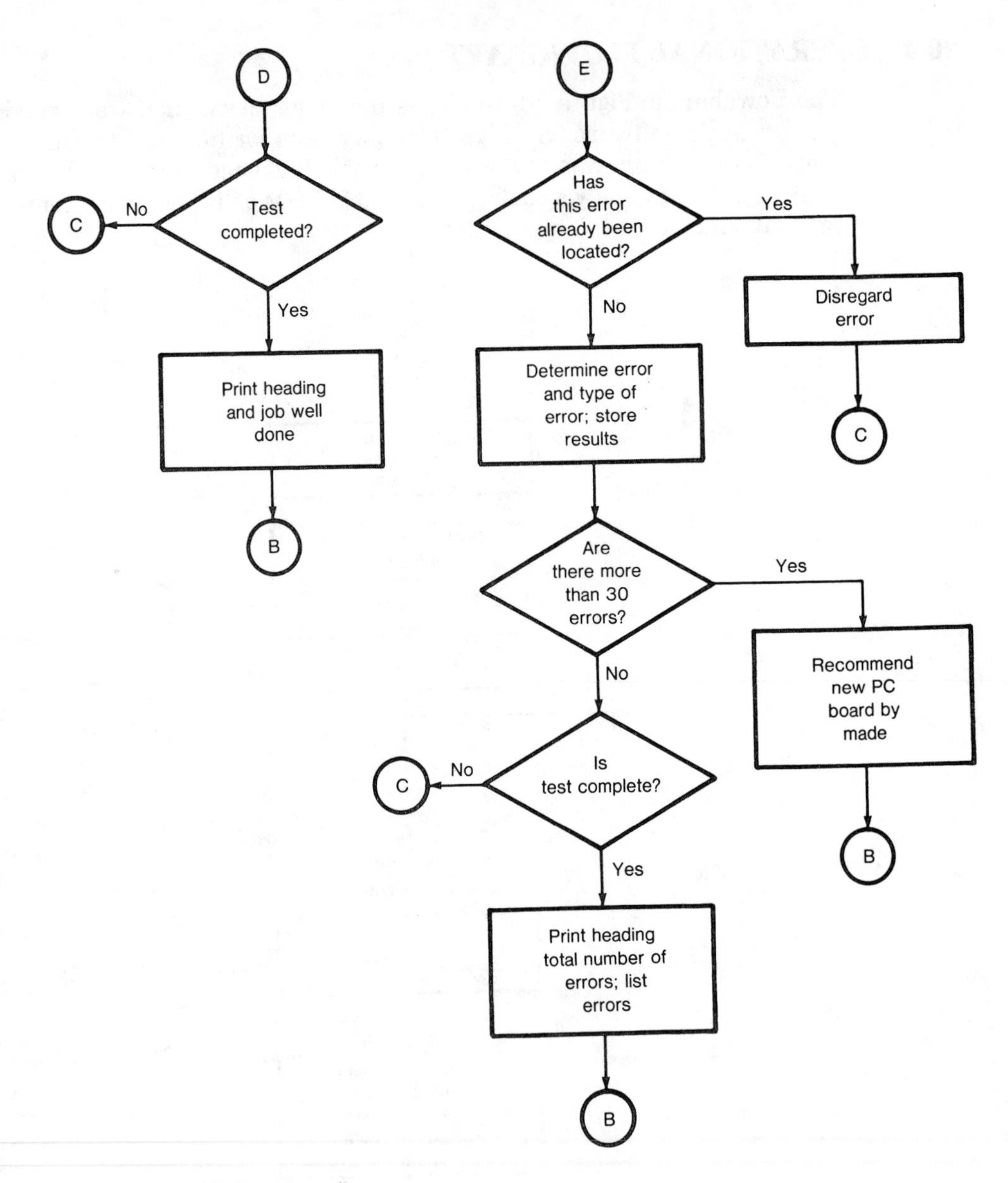

FIGURE 20–10 (Continued)

20.5 SUMMARY

This chapter shows how a μP, memory, and I/O chips are interconnected to form a complete μC system. In addition to the μC, a bed-of-nails and a vacuum pump are needed to build the printed circuit bare board tester as shown in Figure 20–1.

Section 20.2 describes how the automatic test system operates and shows examples of typical printouts. The μC system is designed and built on three PC boards. They are (1) the μC board, (2) the peripheral interface board, and (3) the printer/pump interface board.

Section 20.4 shows the operational flowchart that was used to write the system's software. The entire program was written in assembly language and loaded into a 2K EPROM.

Appendix A Binary Number System

A.0 INTRODUCTION

Digital computers use the binary system because electronic circuitry can easily be designed around it. The binary system is used by digital computers for all operations, regardless of whether the computer is handling data, instructions, numbers, words, punctuation, or special characters. We are all much more familiar with the decimal system and the English alphabet than with the binary system, so we have to learn a new "language" when we work with computers. In this appendix, we will review some of the basic concepts of the decimal number system, learn how the same concepts apply to the binary number system, and learn how to convert from one system to the other.

A.1 CHARACTERISTICS OF THE DECIMAL SYSTEM

A.1.1 Defining Numbers and Digits

People count and calculate using the decimal system, a system based on 10 digits. Many other number systems have been tried at one time or another in the course of history, and most have been discarded as being too cumbersome or inadequate for advanced calculations. Let's start at the beginning and review what we mean by "number."

A *number* represents the value of something. We are familiar with numbers like 12, 129, and 250, and we know that values can be expressed as whole numbers (also called *integers*) and fractions, like 3.5 or 2.14. The fundamental building block of a number system is the *digit*, and numbers are made up of a series of digits. The digit is the most important characteristic of a number system.

A.1.2 Base of a Number System

In the decimal system, 10 digits are used. They are 0, 1, 2, 3, 4, 5, 6, 7, 8, and 9. The total number of digits is so basic to each number system that it is called, appropriately, the *base*. The base of a number system describes the total number of digits in the system. In the decimal system, the base is 10.

A.1.3 Positional Value

Another important characteristic of a number system is the fact that the same digit can represent different values depending upon the position it occupies in the number. For example, the decimal number 444.4 has the same digit in each position. We automatically read this number as "four hundred forty-four and four-tenths," and we forget how we learned this reading process and what it means. When we begin to read a number, we look at each digit and its position with respect to the decimal point. If we did not do this, we could not distinguish between 444.4 and 4444.

The position of each digit carries a weight that is expressed as a power of 10 (the base of the decimal system). Figure A–1 shows the positional weights in the decimal system. We follow a sequence of mental steps as follows:

1. The third digit to the left of the decimal point means four hundred.
2. The second digit to the left of the decimal point means forty.
3. The first digit to the left of the decimal point means four.
4. The first digit to the right of the decimal point means four-tenths.

We read the sequence from 1 to 4 because we have been trained to read and write from left to right. We also know that the values of the digits are to be added. That is, we understand 444.4 as four hundred plus forty plus four plus four-tenths.

In summary, we read the weight of each digit and add the weights. This evaluation procedure can be modified to work in the binary system or in any other system.

A.1.4 Counting in the Decimal System

As we count, we go from 0 to 9. After reaching 9, the first position on the right goes back to 0 and the next digit position to the left is incremented by 1 (10, 11,

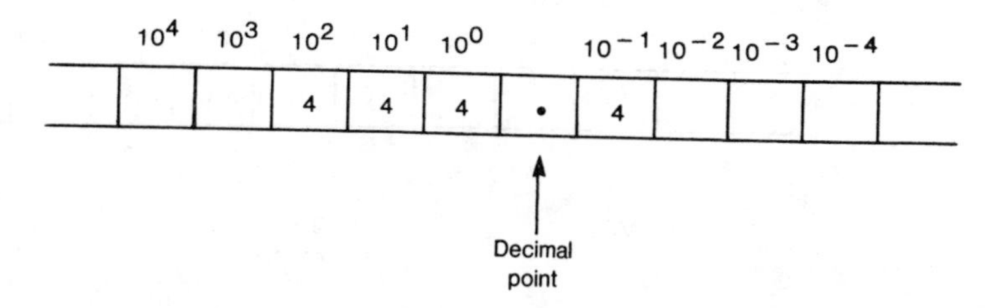

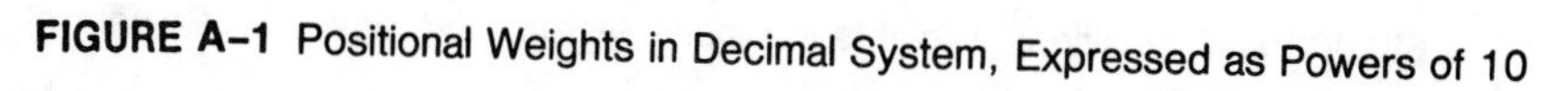

FIGURE A–1 Positional Weights in Decimal System, Expressed as Powers of 10

12, and so forth). When we reach 19, the first position goes back to 0 again and the next position is again incremented by 1, from 1 to 2 (20, 21, 22, and so forth).

A.2 THE BINARY NUMBER SYSTEM

A.2.1 Binary Digits and Base

The binary number system only has two digits, 0 and 1. Therefore, its base is 2. Electronic computers use the binary system because it is easy to distinguish between two possible electronic states. For example, a relay is either open or closed. If computers used the decimal system, there would have to be some way to distinguish 10 different electronic states. The practical problems of manufacturing devices to do this are too great. Although the relay is no longer used in building computers, it may still be used as an input or output device. The transistor, the basic building block of the computer, would have the same problems if it tried to distinguish between 10 different voltage levels. The binary system is more practical.

A.2.2 Positional Value

Like the decimal system, the binary number system also uses positional values. Each binary bit has its own value or weight depending on where it is relative to the *binary point*, the equivalent of the decimal point. The weights can be expressed as powers of 2, as shown in Figure A–2. In the figure, the decimal equivalent of each power of 2 is also given. This will be helpful when we convert from the binary to the decimal number system in Section A.4.

The binary 1 farthest to the left in a binary number is called the *most significant bit* (MSB), while the binary bit farthest to the right is called the *least significant bit* (LSB). These bits are identified in Figure A–2.

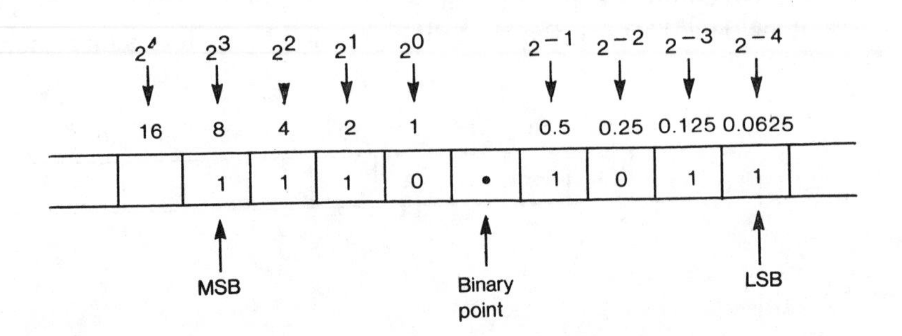

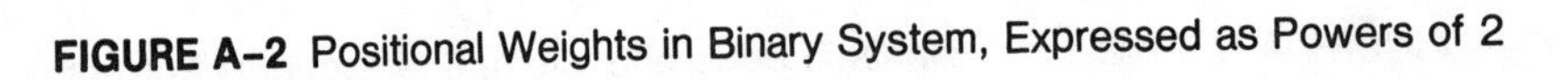

FIGURE A–2 Positional Weights in Binary System, Expressed as Powers of 2

0000
0001
0010
0011
0100
0101
0110
0111
1000
1001
1010
1011
1100
1101
1110
1111

FIGURE A–3 Binary count progresses from 0000 to 1111.

A.2.3 Counting in the Binary Number System

Counting in binary is based upon the same principles as counting in decimal. The count begins at 0 and the next count is 1. Because we have now exhausted all possible binary digits for the first position on the right, we place a 1 in the next position to the left and repeat the binary sequence 0, 1 (10, 11). When all possibilities have been used in the first two positions, we must add 1 in the third position to the left on the next count (100, 101, 110, 111). The sequence continues as shown in Figure A–3. Notice that the digit position column on the right alternates 0, 1, 0, 1. The second column alternates 0, 0, 1, 1, 0, 0, 1, 1. Each higher-position column has twice as many 0s or 1s in each alternate group as the column to its right. Once this pattern is recognized, it is easy to duplicate.

A.3 DECIMAL TO BINARY CONVERSION

A decimal number is made up of a whole number, or integer, and a fraction. The *integer* is the part of the number before (to the left of) the decimal point, and the *fraction* is the part of the number after (to the right of) the decimal point. In the decimal number 23.375, the integer is 23 and .375 is the fraction. The method used to convert an integer to binary is different from the method used to convert a fraction, so we will study decimal to binary conversion in two steps.

A.3.1 Integer Conversion

A decimal integer is converted to its binary-equivalent by repeatedly dividing the integer by 2 (the base of the binary system) and writing down the remainders after each division until a quotient of 0 is obtained. The first remainder will be the first digit to the left of the binary point. The binary number equals the remainders. To convert 23 to binary, the steps are as follows:

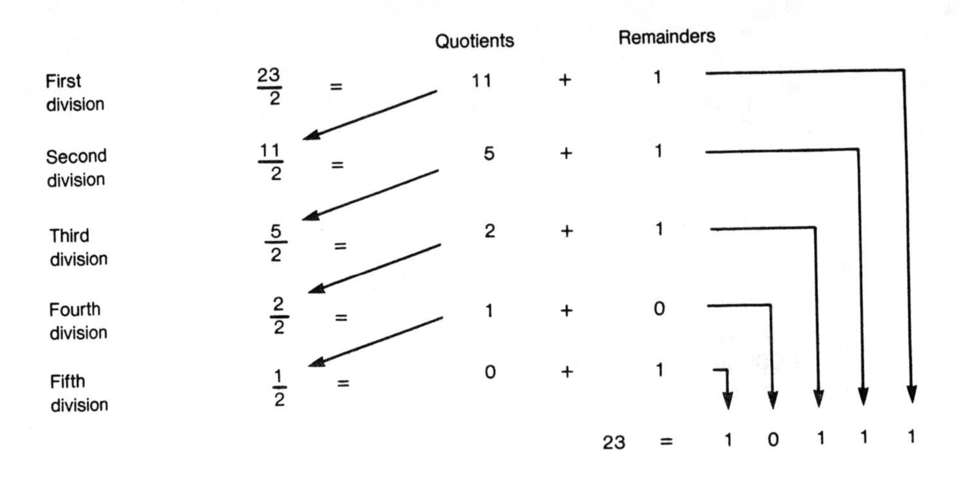

A.3.2 Fractional Conversion

A decimal fraction is converted to its binary equivalent number by repeatedly multiplying the fractional part by 2 and writing the integer carries after each multiplication. The first carry is the first digit to the right of the binary bit. This process is continued until a product of 1.0 is obtained. The following steps are involved in our example:

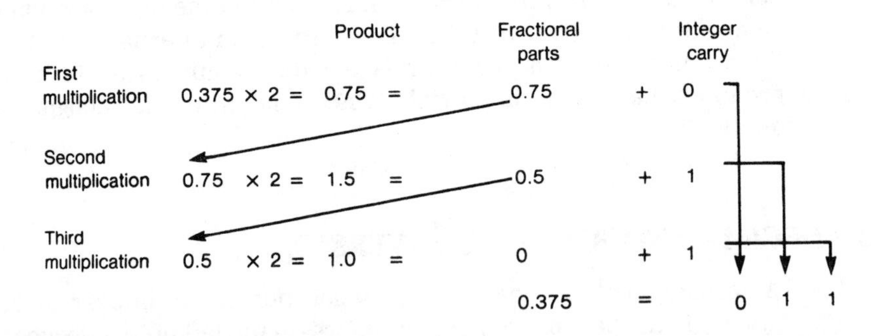

Note: It is not always possible to get a final product of 1.0. In these cases, the multiplication process is ended after a suitable number of steps. What a "suitable" number of steps is may depend on the programmer or the design of the computer itself. The final result then has what is known as a "rounding-off error."

The binary equivalent of the decimal number 23.375, then, is the combination of the integer part and the fractional part:

$$23.375_{10} = 10111.011_2$$

↑ Decimal point ↑ Binary point

The subscripts 10 and 2 are the conventional methods of avoiding confusion when more than one number system is used.

A.4 BINARY TO DECIMAL CONVERSION

In Section A.2.2, we saw that binary bits are weighted according to their location with respect to the binary point. A binary number is converted to a decimal number by adding the binary equivalent weights of the positions in which the digit is 1. Let's convert 1110 to decimal.

Binary number	1	1	1	0
Binary weights	$2^3 = 8$	$2^2 = 4$	$2^1 = 2$	$2^0 = 1$
Weights with a binary 1	$8 + 4 + 2 = 14$			

Therefore, $1110_2 = 14_{10}$.

Binary numbers that contain a fractional part are converted to decimal in the same way, using positional values. For example, to convert 1001.11 to decimal, we have:

Binary number	1	0	0	1	1	1
Binary weights	$2^3 = 8$	$2^2 = 4$	$2^1 = 2$	$2^0 = 1$.	$2^{-1} = 0.5$	$2^{-2} = 0.25$
Weights with a binary 1	$8 + 1 + 0.5 + 0.25 = 9.75$					

Therefore, $1001.11_2 = 9.75_{10}$.

Appendix B Conversion between Decimal and Hexadecimal

Most Significant Hex Digit	Least Significant Hex Digit															
	0	1	2	3	4	5	6	7	8	9	A	B	C	D	E	F
0	0	1	2	3	4	5	6	7	8	9	10	11	12	13	14	15
1	16	17	18	19	20	21	22	23	24	25	26	27	28	29	30	31
2	32	33	34	35	36	37	38	39	40	41	42	43	44	45	46	47
3	48	49	50	51	52	53	54	55	56	57	58	59	60	61	62	63
4	64	65	66	67	68	69	70	71	72	73	74	75	76	77	78	79
5	80	81	82	83	84	85	86	87	88	89	90	91	92	93	94	95
6	96	97	98	99	100	101	102	103	104	105	106	107	108	109	110	111
7	112	113	114	115	116	117	118	119	120	121	122	123	124	125	126	127
8	-128	-127	-126	-125	-124	-123	-122	-121	-120	-119	-118	-117	-116	-115	-114	-113
9	-112	-111	-110	-109	-108	-107	-106	-105	-104	-103	-102	-101	-100	-99	-98	-97
A	-96	-95	-94	-93	-92	-91	-90	-89	-88	-87	-86	-85	-84	-83	-82	-81
B	-80	-79	-78	-77	-76	-75	-74	-73	-72	-71	-70	-69	-68	-67	-66	-65
C	-64	-63	-62	-61	-60	-59	-58	-57	-56	-55	-54	-53	-52	-51	-50	-49
D	-48	-47	-46	-45	-44	-43	-42	-41	-40	-39	-38	-37	-36	-35	-34	-33
E	-32	-31	-30	-29	-28	-27	-26	-25	-24	-23	-22	-21	-20	-19	-18	-17
F	-16	-15	-14	-13	-12	-11	-10	-9	-8	-7	-6	-5	-4	-3	-2	-1

Appendix C
Data Sheets

8085A/8085A-2 Single Chip 8-Bit N-Channel Microprocessors

- **Single +5V Power Supply**
- **100% Software Compatible with 8080A**
- **1.3 μs Instruction Cycle (8085A); 0.8 μs (8085A-2)**
- **On-Chip Clock Generator (with External Crystal, LC or RC Network)**
- **On-Chip System Controller; Advanced Cycle Status Information Available for Large System Control**
- **Four Vectored Interrupt Inputs (One Is Non-Maskable) Plus an 8080A-Compatible Interrupt**
- **Serial In/Serial Out Port**
- **Decimal, Binary and Double Precision Arithmetic**
- **Direct Addressing Capability to 64k Bytes of Memory**

The Intel® 8085A is a complete 8 bit parallel Central Processing Unit (CPU). Its instruction set is 100% software compatible with the 8080A microprocessor, and it is designed to improve the present 8080A's performance by higher system speed. Its high level of system integration allows a minimum system of three IC's [8085A (CPU), 8156 (RAM/IO) and 8355/8755A (ROM/PROM/IO)] while maintaining total system expandability. The 8085A-2 is a faster version of the 8085A.

The 8085A incorporates all of the features that the 8224 (clock generator) and 8228 (system controller) provided for the 8080A, thereby offering a high level of system integration.

The 8085A uses a multiplexed data bus. The address is split between the 8 bit address bus and the 8 bit data bus. The on-chip address latches of 8155/8156/8355/8755A memory products allow a direct interface with the 8085A.

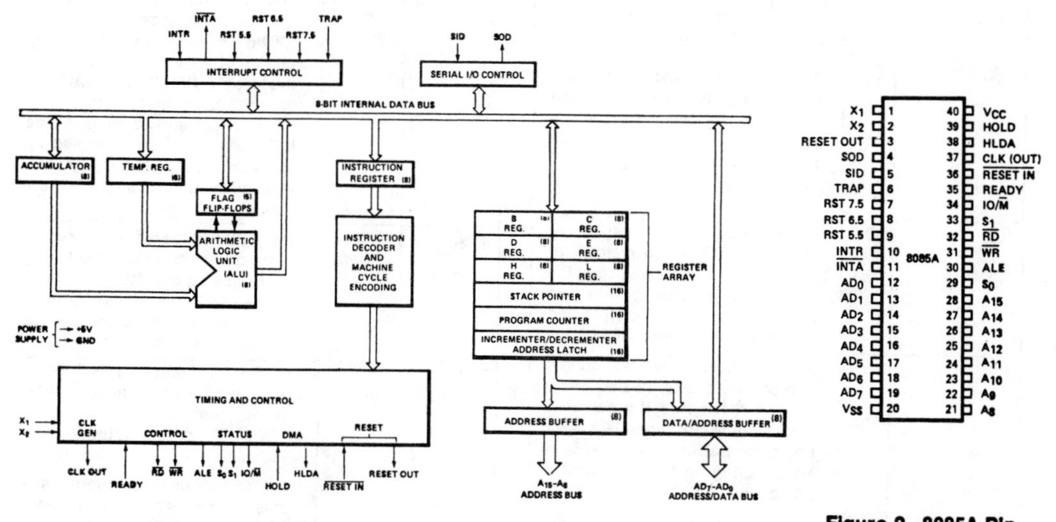

Figure 1. 8085A CPU Functional Block Diagram

Figure 2. 8085A Pin Configuration

8085A/8085A-2

Table 1. Pin Description

Symbol	Type	Name and Function
A_8–A_{15}	O	**Address Bus:** The most significant 8 bits of the memory address or the 8 bits of the I/O address, 3-stated during Hold and Halt modes and during RESET.
AD_{0-7}	I/O	**Multiplexed Address/Data Bus:** Lower 8 bits of the memory address (or I/O address) appear on the bus during the first clock cycle (T state) of a machine cycle. It then becomes the data bus during the second and third clock cycles.
ALE	O	**Address Latch Enable:** It occurs during the first clock state of a machine cycle and enables the address to get latched into the on-chip latch of peripherals. The falling edge of ALE is set to guarantee setup and hold times for the address information. The falling edge of ALE can also be used to strobe the status information. ALE is never 3-stated.
S_0, S_1, and IO/$\overline{M}$	O	**Machine Cycle Status:** **IO/$\overline{M}$ S_1 S_0 Status** 0 0 1 Memory write 0 1 0 Memory read 1 0 1 I/O write 1 1 0 I/O read 0 1 1 Opcode fetch 1 1 1 Opcode fetch 1 1 1 Interrupt Acknowledge * 0 0 Halt * X X Hold * X X Reset * = 3-state (high impedance) X = unspecified S_1 can be used as an advanced R/$\overline{W}$ status. IO/$\overline{M}$, S_0 and S_1 become valid at the beginning of a machine cycle and remain stable throughout the cycle. The falling edge of ALE may be used to latch the state of these lines.
$\overline{RD}$	O	**Read Control:** A low level on $\overline{RD}$ indicates the selected memory or I/O device is to be read and that the Data Bus is available for the data transfer, 3-stated during Hold and Halt modes and during RESET.
$\overline{WR}$	O	**Write Control:** A low level on $\overline{WR}$ indicates the data on the Data Bus is to be written into the selected memory or I/O location. Data is set up at the trailing edge of $\overline{WR}$. 3-stated during Hold and Halt modes and during RESET.
READY	I	**Ready:** If READY is high during a read or write cycle, it indicates that the memory or peripheral is ready to send or receive data. If READY is low, the cpu will wait an integral number of clock cycles for READY to go high before completing the read or write cycle. READY must conform to specified setup and hold times.
HOLD	I	**Hold:** Indicates that another master is requesting the use of the address and data buses. The cpu, upon receiving the hold request, will relinquish the use of the bus as soon as the completion of the current bus transfer. Internal processing can continue. The processor can regain the bus only after the HOLD is removed. When the HOLD is acknowledged, the Address, Data $\overline{RD}$, $\overline{WR}$, and IO/$\overline{M}$ lines are 3-stated.
HLDA	O	**Hold Acknowledge:** Indicates that the cpu has received the HOLD request and that it will relinquish the bus in the next clock cycle. HLDA goes low after the Hold request is removed. The cpu takes the bus one half clock cycle after HLDA goes low.
INTR	I	**Interrupt Request:** Is used as a general purpose interrupt. It is sampled only during the next to the last clock cycle of an instruction and during Hold and Halt states. If it is active, the Program Counter (PC) will be inhibited from incrementing and an $\overline{INTA}$ will be issued. During this cycle a RESTART or CALL instruction can be inserted to jump to the interrupt service routine. The INTR is enabled and disabled by software. It is disabled by Reset and immediately after an interrupt is accepted.
$\overline{INTA}$	O	**Interrupt Acknowledge:** Is used instead of (and has the same timing as) $\overline{RD}$ during the Instruction cycle after an INTR is accepted. It can be used to activate an 8259A Interrupt chip or some other interrupt port.
RST 5.5 RST 6.5 RST 7.5	I	**Restart Interrupts:** These three inputs have the same timing as INTR except they cause an internal RESTART to be automatically inserted. The priority of these interrupts is ordered as shown in Table 2. These interrupts have a higher priority than INTR. In addition, they may be individually masked out using the SIM instruction.

8085A/8085A-2

Table 1. Pin Description (Continued)

Symbol	Type	Name and Function
TRAP	I	**Trap:** Trap interrupt is a nonmaskable RESTART interrupt. It is recognized at the same time as INTR or RST 5.5-7.5. It is unaffected by any mask or Interrupt Enable. It has the highest priority of any interrupt. (See Table 2.)
$\overline{\text{RESET IN}}$	I	**Reset In:** Sets the Program Counter to zero and resets the Interrupt Enable and HLDA flip-flops. The data and address buses and the control lines are 3-stated during RESET and because of the asynchronous nature of RESET, the processor's internal registers and flags may be altered by RESET with unpredictable results. $\overline{\text{RESET IN}}$ is a Schmitt-triggered input, allowing connection to an R-C network for power-on RESET delay. The cpu is held in the reset condition as long as $\overline{\text{RESET IN}}$ is applied.
RESET OUT	O	**Reset Out:** Reset Out indicates cpu is being reset. Can be used as a system reset. The signal is synchronized to the processor clock and lasts an integral number of clock periods.
X_1, X_2	I	**X_1 and X_2:** Are connected to a crystal, LC, or RC network to drive the internal clock generator. X_1 can also be an external clock input from a logic gate. The input frequency is divided by 2 to give the processor's internal operating frequency.
CLK	O	**Clock:** Clock output for use as a system clock. The period of CLK is twice the X_1, X_2 input period.
SID	I	**Serial Input Data Line:** The data on this line is loaded into accumulator bit 7 whenever a RIM instruction is executed.
SOD	O	**Serial Output Data Line:** The output SOD is set or reset as specified by the SIM instruction.
V_{CC}		**Power:** +5 volt supply.
V_{SS}		**Ground:** Reference.

Table 2. Interrupt Priority, Restart Address, and Sensitivity

Name	Priority	Address Branched To (1) When Interrupt Occurs	Type Trigger
TRAP	1	24H	Rising edge AND high level until sampled.
RST 7.5	2	3CH	Rising edge (latched).
RST 6.5	3	34H	High level until sampled.
RST 5.5	4	2CH	High level until sampled.
INTR	5	See Note (2).	High level until sampled.

NOTES:

1. The processor pushes the PC on the stack before branching to the indicated address.
2. The address branched to depends on the instruction provided to the cpu when the interrupt is acknowledged.

8085A/8085A-2

FUNCTIONAL DESCRIPTION

The 8085A is a complete 8-bit parallel central processor. It is designed with N-channel depletion loads and requires a single +5 volt supply. Its basic clock speed is 3 MHz (8085A) or 5 MHz (8085A-2), thus improving on the present 8080A's performance with higher system speed. Also it is designed to fit into a minimum system of three IC's: The cpu (8085A), a RAM/IO (8156), and a ROM or EPROM/IO chip (8355 or 8755A).

The 8085A has twelve addressable 8-bit registers. Four of them can function only as two 16-bit register pairs. Six others can be used interchangeably as 8-bit registers or as 16-bit register pairs. The 8085A register set is as follows:

Mnemonic	Register	Contents
ACC or A	Accumulator	8 bits
PC	Program Counter	16-bit address
BC,DE,HL	General-Purpose Registers; data pointer (HL)	8 bits x 6 or 16 bits x 3
SP	Stack Pointer	16-bit address
Flags or F	Flag Register	5 flags (8-bit space)

The 8085A uses a multiplexed Data Bus. The address is split between the higher 8-bit Address Bus and the lower 8-bit Address/Data Bus. During the first T state (clock cycle) of a machine cycle the low order address is sent out on the Address/Data bus. These lower 8 bits may be latched externally by the Address Latch Enable signal (ALE). During the rest of the machine cycle the data bus is used for memory or I/O data.

The 8085A provides $\overline{RD}$, $\overline{WR}$, S_0, S_1, and IO/$\overline{M}$ signals for bus control. An Interrupt Acknowledge signal ($\overline{INTA}$) is also provided. HOLD and all Interrupts are synchronized with the processor's internal clock. The 8085A also provides Serial Input Data (SID) and Serial Output Data (SOD) lines for simple serial interface.

In addition to these features, the 8085A has three maskable, vector interrupt pins and one nonmaskable TRAP interrupt.

INTERRUPT AND SERIAL I/O

The 8085A has 5 interrupt inputs: INTR, RST 5.5, RST 6.5, RST 7.5, and TRAP. INTR is identical in function to the 8080A INT. Each of the three RESTART inputs, 5.5, 6.5, and 7.5, has a programmable mask. TRAP is also a RESTART interrupt but it is nonmaskable.

The three maskable interrupts cause the internal execution of RESTART (saving the program counter in the stack and branching to the RESTART address) if the interrupts are enabled and if the interrupt mask is not set. The non-maskable TRAP causes the internal execution of a RESTART vector independent of the state of the interrupt enable or masks. (See Table 2.)

There are two different types of inputs in the restart interrupts. RST 5.5 and RST 6.5 are *high level-sensitive* like INTR (and INT on the 8080) and are recognized with the same timing as INTR. RST 7.5 is *rising edge-sensitive.*

For RST 7.5, only a pulse is required to set an internal flip-flop which generates the internal interrupt request. (See Section 5.2.7.) The RST 7.5 request flip-flop remains set until the request is serviced. Then it is reset automatically. This flip-flop may also be reset by using the SIM instruction or by issuing a $\overline{\text{RESET IN}}$ to the 8085A. The RST 7.5 internal flip-flop will be set by a pulse on the RST 7.5 pin even when the RST 7.5 interrupt is masked out.

The status of the three RST interrupt masks can only be affected by the SIM instruction and $\overline{\text{RESET IN}}$. (See SIM, Chapter 5.

The interrupts are arranged in a fixed priority that determines which interrupt is to be recognized if more than one is pending as follows: TRAP — highest priority, RST 7.5, RST 6.5, RST 5.5, INTR — lowest priority. This priority scheme does not take into account the priority of a routine that was started by a higher priority interrupt. RST 5.5 can interrupt an RST 7.5 routine if the interrupts are re-enabled before the end of the RST 7.5 routine.

The TRAP interrupt is useful for catastrophic events such as power failure or bus error. The TRAP input is recognized just as any other interrupt but has the highest priority. It is not affected by any flag or mask. The TRAP input is both *edge and level sensitive.* The TRAP input must go high and remain high until it is acknowledged. It will not be recognized again until it goes low, then high again. This avoids any false triggering due to noise or logic glitches. Figure 3 illustrates the TRAP interrupt request circuitry within the 8085A. Note that the servicing of any interrupt (TRAP, RST 7.5, RST 6.5, RST 5.5, INTR) disables all future interrupts (except TRAPs) until an EI instruction is executed.

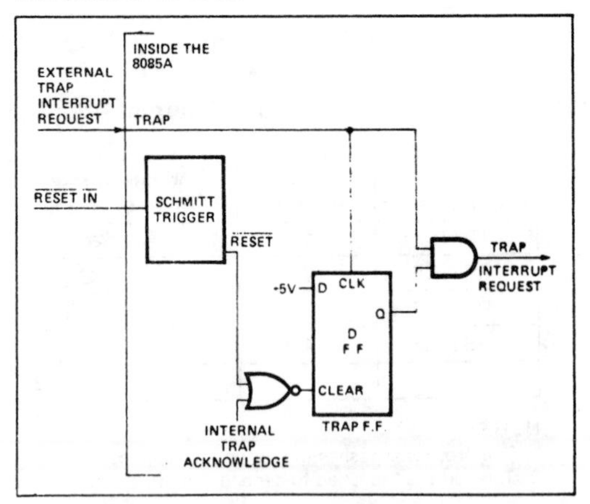

Figure 3. TRAP and RESET IN Circuit

The TRAP interrupt is special in that it disables interrupts, but preserves the previous interrupt enable status. Performing the first RIM instruction following a TRAP interrupt allows you to determine whether interrupts were enabled or disabled prior to the TRAP. All subsequent RIM instructions provide current interrupt enable status. Performing a RIM instruction following INTR, or RST 5.5–7.5 will provide current Interrupt Enable status, revealing that Interrupts are disabled. See the description of the RIM instruction in Chapter 5.

The serial I/O system is also controlled by the RIM and SIM instructions. SID is read by RIM, and SIM sets the SOD data.

8085A/8085A-2

DRIVING THE X_1 AND X_2 INPUTS

You may drive the clock inputs of the 8085A or 8085A-2 with a crystal, an LC tuned circuit, an RC network, or an external clock source. The driving frequency must be at least 1 MHz, and must be twice the desired internal clock frequency; hence, the 8085A is operated with a 6 MHz crystal (for 3 MHz clock), and the 8085A-2 can be operated with a 10 MHz crystal (for 5 MHz clock). If a crystal is used, it must have the following characteristics:

Parallel resonance at twice the clock frequency desired
C_L (load capacitance) $\leq$ 30 pf
C_s (shunt capacitance) $\leq$ 7 pf
R_s (equivalent shunt resistance) $\leq$ 75 Ohms
Drive level: 10 mW
Frequency tolerance: $\pm$.005% (suggested)

Note the use of the 20 pF capacitor between X_2 and ground. This capacitor is required with crystal frequencies below 4 MHz to assure oscillator startup at the correct frequency. A parallel-resonant LC circuit may be used as the frequency-determining network for the 8085A, providing that its frequency tolerance of approximately $\pm$10% is acceptable. The components are chosen from the formula:

$$f = \frac{1}{2\pi\sqrt{L(C_{ext} + C_{int})}}$$

To minimize variations in frequency, it is recommended that you choose a value for C_{ext} that is at least twice that of C_{int}, or 30 pF. The use of an LC circuit is not recommended for frequencies higher than approximately 5 MHz.

An RC circuit may be used as the frequency-determining network for the 8085A if maintaining a precise clock frequency is of no importance. Variations in the on-chip timing generation can cause a wide variation in frequency when using the RC mode. Its advantage is its low component cost. The driving frequency generated by the circuit shown is approximately 3 MHz. It is not recommended that frequencies greatly higher or lower than this be attempted.

Figure 4 shows the recommended clock driver circuits. Note in D and E that pullup resistors are required to assure that the high level voltage of the input is at least 4 V.

For driving frequencies up to and including 6 MHz you may supply the driving signal to X_1 and leave X_2 open-circuited (Figue 4D). If the driving frequency is from 6 MHz to 10 MHz, stability of the clock generator will be improved by driving both X_1 and X_2 with a push-pull source (Figure 4E). To prevent self-oscillation of the 8085A, be sure that X_2 is not coupled back to X_1 through the driving circuit.

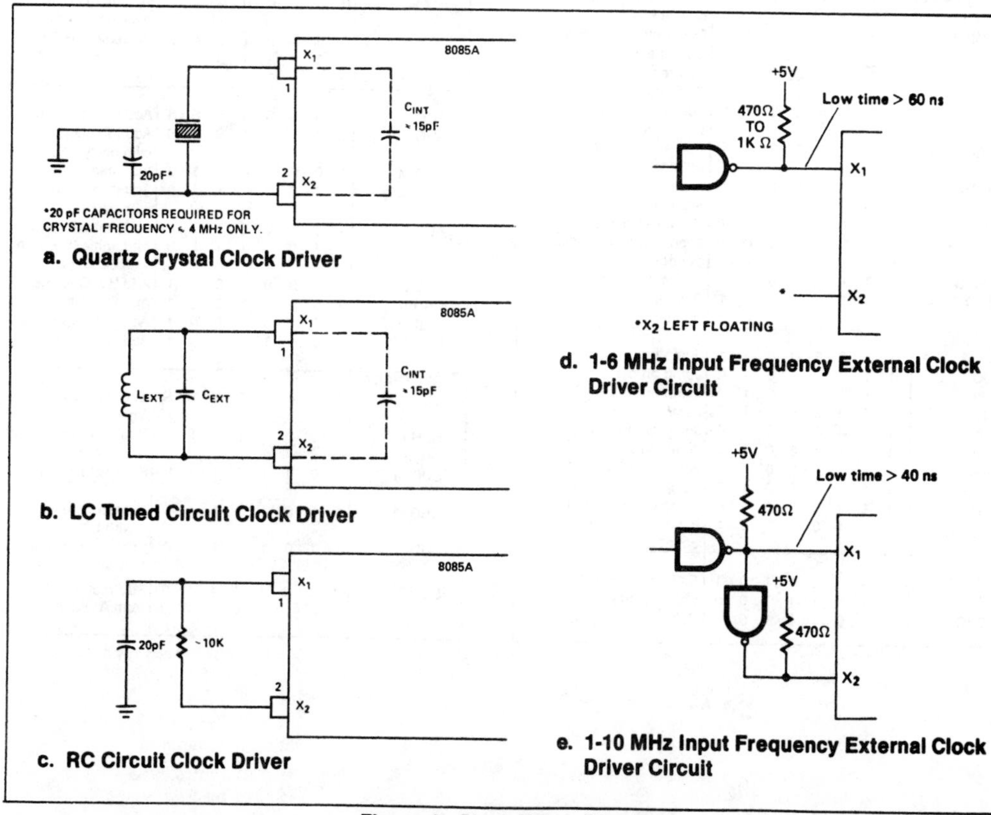

Figure 4. Clock Driver Circuits

8085A/8085A-2

Instruction Set Summary

Mnemonic	D_7	D_6	D_5	D_4	D_3	D_2	D_1	D_0	Operations Description
MOVE, LOAD, AND STORE									
MOVr1 r2	0	1	D	D	D	S	S	S	Move register to register
MOV M.r	0	1	1	1	0	S	S	S	Move register to memory
MOV r.M	0	1	D	D	D	1	1	0	Move memory to register
MVI r	0	0	D	D	D	1	1	0	Move immediate register
MVI M	0	0	1	1	0	1	1	0	Move immediate memory
LXI B	0	0	0	0	0	0	0	1	Load immediate register Pair B & C
LXI D	0	0	0	1	0	0	0	1	Load immediate register Pair D & E
LXI H	0	0	1	0	0	0	0	1	Load immediate register Pair H & L
STAX B	0	0	0	0	0	0	1	0	Store A indirect
STAX D	0	0	0	1	0	0	1	0	Store A indirect
LDAX B	0	0	0	0	1	0	1	0	Load A indirect
LDAX D	0	0	0	1	1	0	1	0	Load A indirect
STA	0	0	1	1	0	0	1	0	Store A direct
LDA	0	0	1	1	1	0	1	0	Load A direct
SHLD	0	0	1	0	0	0	1	0	Store H & L direct
LHLD	0	0	1	0	1	0	1	0	Load H & L direct
XCHG	1	1	1	0	1	0	1	1	Exchange D & E, H & L Registers
STACK OPS									
PUSH B	1	1	0	0	0	1	0	1	Push register Pair B & C on stack
PUSH D	1	1	0	1	0	1	0	1	Push register Pair D & E on stack
PUSH H	1	1	1	0	0	1	0	1	Push register Pair H & L on stack
PUSH PSW	1	1	1	1	0	1	0	1	Push A and Flags on stack
POP B	1	1	0	0	0	0	0	1	Pop register Pair B & C off stack
POP D	1	1	0	1	0	0	0	1	Pop register Pair D & E off stack
POP H	1	1	1	0	0	0	0	1	Pop register Pair H & L off stack
POP PSW	1	1	1	1	0	0	0	1	Pop A and Flags off stack
XTHL	1	1	1	0	0	0	1	1	Exchange top of stack, H & L
SPHL	1	1	1	1	1	0	0	1	H & L to stack pointer
LXI SP	0	0	1	1	0	0	0	1	Load immediate stack pointer
INX SP	0	0	1	1	0	0	1	1	Increment stack pointer
DCX SP	0	0	1	1	1	0	1	1	Decrement stack pointer
JUMP									
JMP	1	1	0	0	0	0	1	1	Jump unconditional
JC	1	1	0	1	1	0	1	0	Jump on carry
JNC	1	1	0	1	0	0	1	0	Jump on no carry
JZ	1	1	0	0	1	0	1	0	Jump on zero
JNZ	1	1	0	0	0	0	1	0	Jump on no zero
JP	1	1	1	1	0	0	1	0	Jump on positive
JM	1	1	1	1	1	0	1	0	Jump on minus
JPE	1	1	1	0	1	0	1	0	Jump on parity even
JPO	1	1	1	0	0	0	1	0	Jump on parity odd
PCHL	1	1	1	0	1	0	0	1	H & L to program counter
CALL									
CALL	1	1	0	0	1	1	0	1	Call unconditional
CC	1	1	0	1	1	1	0	0	Call on carry
CNC	1	1	0	1	0	1	0	0	Call on no carry

Mnemonic	D_7	D_6	D_5	D_4	D_3	D_2	D_1	D_0	Operations Description
CZ	1	1	0	0	1	1	0	0	Call on zero
CNZ	1	1	0	0	0	1	0	0	Call on no zero
CP	1	1	1	1	0	1	0	0	Call on positive
CM	1	1	1	1	1	1	0	0	Call on minus
CPE	1	1	1	0	1	1	0	0	Call on parity even
CPO	1	1	1	0	0	1	0	0	Call on parity odd
RETURN									
RET	1	1	0	0	1	0	0	1	Return
RC	1	1	0	1	1	0	0	0	Return on carry
RNC	1	1	0	1	0	0	0	0	Return on no carry
RZ	1	1	0	0	1	0	0	0	Return on zero
RNZ	1	1	0	0	0	0	0	0	Return on no zero
RP	1	1	1	1	0	0	0	0	Return on positive
RM	1	1	1	1	1	0	0	0	Return on minus
RPE	1	1	1	0	1	0	0	0	Return on parity even
RPO	1	1	1	0	0	0	0	0	Return on parity odd
RESTART									
RST	1	1	A	A	A	1	1	1	Restart
INPUT/OUTPUT									
IN	1	1	0	1	1	0	1	1	Input
OUT	1	1	0	1	0	0	1	1	Output
INCREMENT AND DECREMENT									
INR r	0	0	D	D	D	1	0	0	Increment register
DCR r	0	0	D	D	D	1	0	1	Decrement register
INR M	0	0	1	1	0	1	0	0	Increment memory
DCR M	0	0	1	1	0	1	0	1	Decrement memory
INX B	0	0	0	0	0	0	1	1	Increment B & C registers
INX D	0	0	0	1	0	0	1	1	Increment D & E registers
INX H	0	0	1	0	0	0	1	1	Increment H & L registers
DCX B	0	0	0	0	1	0	1	1	Decrement B & C
DCX D	0	0	0	1	1	0	1	1	Decrement D & E
DCX H	0	0	1	0	1	0	1	1	Decrement H & L
ADD									
ADD r	1	0	0	0	0	S	S	S	Add register to A
ADC r	1	0	0	0	1	S	S	S	Add register to A with carry
ADD M	1	0	C	0	0	1	1	0	Add memory to A
ADC M	1	0	0	0	1	1	1	0	Add memory to A with carry
ADI	1	1	0	0	0	1	1	0	Add immediate to A
ACI	1	1	0	0	1	1	1	0	Add immediate to A with carry
DAD B	0	0	0	0	1	0	0	1	Add B & C to H & L
DAD D	0	0	0	1	1	0	0	1	Add D & E to H & L
DAD H	0	0	1	0	1	0	0	1	Add H & L to H & L
DAD SP	0	0	1	1	1	0	0	1	Add stack pointer to H & L
SUBTRACT									
SUB r	1	0	0	1	0	S	S	S	Subtract register from A
SBB r	1	0	0	1	1	S	S	S	Subtract register from A with borrow
SUB M	1	0	0	1	0	1	1	0	Subtract memory from A
SBB M	1	0	0	1	1	1	1	0	Subtract memory from A with borrow
SUI	1	1	0	1	0	1	1	0	Subtract immediate from A
SBI	1	1	0	1	1	1	1	0	Subtract immediate from A with borrow

8085A/8085A-2 Instruction Set Summary (Cont'd)

Mnemonic	D7	D6	D5	D4	D3	D2	D1	D0	Operations Description
LOGICAL									
ANA r	1	0	1	0	0	S	S	S	And register with A
XRA r	1	0	1	0	1	S	S	S	Exclusive OR register with A
ORA r	1	0	1	1	0	S	S	S	OR register with A
CMP r	1	0	1	1	1	S	S	S	Compare register with A
ANA M	1	0	1	0	0	1	1	0	And memory with A
XRA M	1	0	1	0	1	1	1	0	Exclusive OR memory with A
ORA M	1	0	1	1	0	1	1	0	OR memory with A
CMP M	1	0	1	1	1	1	1	0	Compare memory with A
ANI	1	1	1	0	0	1	1	0	And immediate with A
XRI	1	1	1	0	1	1	1	0	Exclusive OR immediate with A
ORI	1	1	1	1	0	1	1	0	OR immediate with A
CPI	1	1	1	1	1	1	1	0	Compare immediate with A
ROTATE									
RLC	0	0	0	0	0	1	1	1	Rotate A left
RRC	0	0	0	0	1	1	1	1	Rotate A right
RAL	0	0	0	1	0	1	1	1	Rotate A left through carry
RAR	0	0	0	1	1	1	1	1	Rotate A right through carry

Mnemonic	D7	D6	D5	D4	D3	D2	D1	D0	Operations Description
SPECIALS									
CMA	0	0	1	0	1	1	1	1	Complement A
STC	0	0	1	1	0	1	1	1	Set carry
CMC	0	0	1	1	1	1	1	1	Complement carry
DAA	0	0	1	0	0	1	1	1	Decimal adjust A
CONTROL									
EI	1	1	1	1	1	0	1	1	Enable Interrupts
DI	1	1	1	1	0	0	1	1	Disable Interrupt
NOP	0	0	0	0	0	0	0	0	No-operation
HLT	0	1	1	1	0	1	1	0	Halt
NEW 8085A INSTRUCTIONS									
RIM	0	0	1	0	0	0	0	0	Read Interrupt Mask
SIM	0	0	1	1	0	0	0	0	Set Interrupt Mask

NOTES:

1. DDS or SSS: B 000, C 001, D 010, E011, H 100, L 101, Memory 110, A 111.
2. Two possible cycle times (6/12) indicate instruction cycles dependent on condition flags.

Appendix D
Tables

APPENDIX TABLE D-1 Summary of 8080A Microprocessor Instructions

Mnemonic	Description	Instruction Code[1] D_7	D_6	D_5	D_4	D_3	D_2	D_1	D_0	Clock[2] Cycles
$MOV_{r1,r2}$	Move register to register	0	1	D	D	D	S	S	S	5
MOV M, r	Move register to memory	0	1	1	1	0	S	S	S	7
MOV r, M	Move memory to register	0	1	D	D	D	1	1	0	7
HLT	Halt	0	1	1	1	0	1	1	0	7
MVI r	Move immediate register	0	0	D	D	D	1	1	0	7
MVI M	Move immediate memory	0	0	1	1	0	1	1	0	10
INR r	Increment register	0	0	D	D	D	1	0	0	5
DCR r	Decrement register	0	0	D	D	D	1	0	1	5
INR M	Increment memory	0	0	1	1	0	1	0	0	10
DCR M	Decrement memory	0	0	1	1	0	1	0	1	10
ADD r	Add register to A	1	0	0	0	0	S	S	S	4
ADC r	Add register to A with carry	1	0	0	0	1	S	S	S	4
SUB r	Subtract register from A	1	0	0	1	0	S	S	S	4
SBB r	Subtract register from A with borrow	1	0	0	1	1	S	S	S	4
ANA r	And register with A	1	0	1	0	0	S	S	S	4
XRA r	Exclusive Or register with A	1	0	1	0	1	S	S	S	4
ORA r	Or register with A	1	0	1	1	0	S	S	S	4
CMP r	Compare register with A	1	0	1	1	1	S	S	S	4
ADD M	Add memory to A	1	0	0	0	0	1	1	0	7
ADC M	Add memory to A with carry	1	0	0	0	1	1	1	0	7
SUB M	Subtract memory from A	1	0	0	1	0	1	1	0	7
SBB M	Subtract memory from A with borrow	1	0	0	1	1	1	1	0	7
ANA M	And memory with A	1	0	1	0	0	1	1	0	7
XRA M	Exclusive Or memory with A	1	0	1	0	1	1	1	0	7
ORA M	Or memory with A	1	0	1	1	0	1	1	0	7
CMP M	Compare memory with A	1	0	1	1	1	1	1	0	7
ADI	Add immediate to A	1	1	0	0	0	1	1	0	7
ACI	Add immediate to A with carry	1	1	0	0	1	1	1	0	7
SUI	Subtract immediate from A	1	1	0	1	0	1	1	0	7
SBI	Subtract immediate from A with borrow	1	1	0	1	1	1	1	0	7
ANI	And immediate with A	1	1	1	0	0	1	1	0	7
XRI.	Exclusive Or immediate with A	1	1	1	0	1	1	1	0	7
ORI	Or immediate with A	1	1	1	1	0	1	1	0	7
CPI	Compare immediate with A	1	1	1	1	1	1	1	0	7
RLC	Rotate A left	0	0	0	0	0	1	1	1	4
RRC	Rotate A right	0	0	0	0	1	1	1	1	4
RAL	Rotate A left through carry	0	0	0	1	0	1	1	1	4
RAR	Rotate A right through carry	0	0	0	1	1	1	1	1	4
JMP	Jump unconditional	1	1	0	0	0	0	1	1	10
JC	Jump on carry	1	1	0	1	1	0	1	0	10
JNC	Jump on no carry	1	1	0	1	0	0	1	0	10
JZ	Jump on zero	1	1	0	0	1	0	1	0	10
JNZ	Jump on no zero	1	1	0	0	0	0	1	0	10
JP	Jump on positive	1	1	1	1	0	0	1	0	10
JM	Jump on minus	1	1	1	1	1	0	1	0	10
JPE	Jump on parity even	1	1	1	0	1	0	1	0	10
JPO	Jump on parity odd	1	1	1	0	0	0	1	0	10
CALL	Call unconditional	1	1	0	0	1	1	0	1	17
CC	Call on carry	1	1	0	1	1	1	0	0	11/17
CNC	Call on no carry	1	1	0	1	0	1	0	0	11/17
CZ	Call on zero	1	1	0	0	1	1	0	0	11/17
CNZ	Call on no zero	1	1	0	0	0	1	0	0	11/17
CP	Call on positive	1	1	1	1	0	1	0	0	11/17
CM	Call on minus	1	1	1	1	1	1	0	0	11/17
CPE	Call on parity even	1	1	1	0	1	1	0	0	11/17
CPO	Call on parity odd	1	1	1	0	0	1	0	0	11/17
RET	Return	1	1	0	0	1	0	0	1	10
RC	Return on carry	1	1	0	1	1	0	0	0	5/11
RNC	Return on no carry	1	1	0	1	0	0	0	0	5/11
RZ	Return on zero	1	1	0	0	1	0	0	0	5/11
RNZ	Return on no zero	1	1	0	0	0	0	0	0	5/11
RP	Return on positive	1	1	1	1	0	0	0	0	5/11
RM	Return on minus	1	1	1	1	1	0	0	0	5/11
RPE	Return on parity even	1	1	1	0	1	0	0	0	5/11
RPO	Return on parity odd	1	1	1	0	0	0	0	0	5/11
RST	Restart	1	1	A	A	A	1	1	1	11
IN	Input	1	1	0	1	1	0	1	1	10
OUT	Output	1	1	0	1	0	0	1	1	10
LXI B	Load immediate register Pair B & C	0	0	0	0	0	0	0	1	10
LXI D	Load immediate register Pair D & E	0	0	0	1	0	0	0	1	10
LXI H	Load immediate register Pair H & L	0	0	1	0	0	0	0	1	10
LXI SP	Load immediate stack pointer	0	0	1	1	0	0	0	1	10
PUSH B	Push register Pair B & C on stack	1	1	0	0	0	1	0	1	11
PUSH D	Push register Pair D & E on stack	1	1	0	1	0	1	0	1	11
PUSH H	Push register Pair H & L on stack	1	1	1	0	0	1	0	1	11
PUSH PSW	Push A and Flags on stack	1	1	1	1	0	1	0	1	11
POP B	Pop register pair B & C off stack	1	1	0	0	0	0	0	1	10
POP D	Pop register pair D & E off stack	1	1	0	1	0	0	0	1	10
POP H	Pop register pair H & L off stack	1	1	1	0	0	0	0	1	10
POP PSW	Pop A and Flags off stack	1	1	1	1	0	0	0	1	10
STA	Store A direct	0	0	1	1	0	0	1	0	13
LDA	Load A direct	0	0	1	1	1	0	1	0	13
XCHG	Exchange D & E, H & L Registers	1	1	1	0	1	0	1	1	4
XTHL	Exchange top of stack, H & L	1	1	1	0	0	0	1	1	18
SPHL	H & L to stack pointer	1	1	1	1	1	0	0	1	5
PCHL	H & L to program counter	1	1	1	0	1	0	0	1	5
DAD B	Add B & C to H & L	0	0	0	0	1	0	0	1	10
DAD D	Add D & E to H & L	0	0	0	1	1	0	0	1	10
DAD H	Add H & L to H & L	0	0	1	0	1	0	0	1	10
DAD SP	Add stack pointer to H & L	0	0	1	1	1	0	0	1	10
STAX B	Store A indirect	0	0	0	0	0	0	1	0	7
STAX D	Store A indirect	0	0	0	1	0	0	1	0	7
LDAX B	Load A indirect	0	0	0	0	1	0	1	0	7
LDAX D	Load A indirect	0	0	0	1	1	0	1	0	7
INX B	Increment B & C registers	0	0	0	0	0	0	1	1	5
INX D	Increment D & E registers	0	0	0	1	0	0	1	1	5
INX H	Increment H & L registers	0	0	1	0	0	0	1	1	5
INX SP	Increment stack pointer	0	0	1	1	0	0	1	1	5
DCX B	Decrement B & C	0	0	0	0	1	0	1	1	5
DCX D	Decrement D & E	0	0	0	1	1	0	1	1	5
DCX H	Decrement H & L	0	0	1	0	1	0	1	1	5
DCX SP	Decrement stack pointer	0	0	1	1	1	0	1	1	5
CMA	Complement A	0	0	1	0	1	1	1	1	4
STC	Set carry	0	0	1	1	0	1	1	1	4
CMC	Complement carry	0	0	1	1	1	1	1	1	4
DAA	Decimal adjust A	0	0	1	0	0	1	1	1	4
SHLD	Store H & L direct	0	0	1	0	0	0	1	0	16
LHLD	Load H & L direct	0	0	1	0	1	0	1	0	16
EI	Enable Interrupts	1	1	1	1	1	0	1	1	4
DI	Disable interrupt	1	1	1	1	0	0	1	1	4
NOP	No-operation	0	0	0	0	0	0	0	0	4

NOTES: 1. DDD or SSS – 000 B – 001 C – 010 D – 011 E – 100 H – 101 L – 110 Memory – 111 A.
2. Two possible cycle times, (5/11) indicate instruction cycles dependent on condition flags.

Source: Reprinted from data sheet for 8080A microprocessor with permission. Intel Corporation, Santa Clara, CA

APPENDIX TABLE D-2 Summary of 8080A Microprocessor Cycles

MNEMONIC	OP CODE		M1[1]					M2		
	$D_7D_6D_5D_4$	$D_3D_2D_1D_0$	T1	T2[2]	T3	T4	T5	T1	T2[2]	T3
MOV r1, r2	0 1 D D	D S S S	PC OUT STATUS	PC = PC +1	INST→TMP/IR	(SSS)→TMP	(TMP)→DDD			
MOV r, M	0 1 D D	D 1 1 0				X[3]		HL OUT STATUS[6]	DATA →	DDD
MOV M, r	0 1 1 1	0 S S S				(SSS)→TMP		HL OUT STATUS[7]	(TMP) →	DATA BUS
SPHL	1 1 1 1	1 0 0 1				(HL) →	SP			
MVI r, data	0 0 D D	D 1 1 0				X		PC OUT STATUS[6]	B2 →	DDDD
MVI M, data	0 0 1 1	0 1 1 0				X			B2 →	TMP
LXI rp, data	0 0 R P	0 0 0 1				X			PC = PC + 1 B2 →	r1
LDA addr	0 0 1 1	1 0 1 0				X			PC = PC + 1 B2 →	Z
STA addr	0 0 1 1	0 0 1 0				X			PC = PC + 1 B2 →	Z
LHLD addr	0 0 1 0	1 0 1 0				X			PC = PC + 1 B2 →	Z
SHLD addr	0 0 1 0	0 0 1 0				X		PC OUT STATUS[6]	PC = PC + 1 B2 →	Z
LDAX rp[4]	0 0 R P	1 0 1 0				X		rp OUT STATUS[6]	DATA →	A
STAX rp[4]	0 0 R P	0 0 1 0				X		rp OUT STATUS[7]	(A) →	DATA BUS
XCHG	1 1 1 0	1 0 1 1				(HL)↔(DE)				
ADD r	1 0 0 0	0 S S S				(SSS)→TMP (A)→ACT		[9]	(ACT)+(TMP)→A	
ADD M	1 0 0 0	0 1 1 0				(A)→ACT		HL OUT STATUS[6]	DATA →	TMP
ADI data	1 1 0 0	0 1 1 0				(A)→ACT		PC OUT STATUS[6]	PC = PC + 1 B2 →	TMP
ADC r	1 0 0 0	1 S S S				(SSS)→TMP (A)→ACT		[9]	(ACT)+(TMP)+CY→A	
ADC M	1 0 0 0	1 1 1 0				(A)→ACT		HL OUT STATUS[6]	DATA →	TMP
ACI data	1 1 0 0	1 1 1 0				(A)→ACT		PC OUT STATUS[6]	PC = PC + 1 B2 →	TMP
SUB r	1 0 0 1	0 S S S				(SSS)→TMP (A)→ACT		[9]	(ACT)-(TMP)→A	
SUB M	1 0 0 1	0 1 1 0				(A)→ACT		HL OUT STATUS[6]	DATA →	TMP
SUI data	1 1 0 1	0 1 1 0				(A)→ACT		PC OUT STATUS[6]	PC = PC + 1 B2 →	TMP
SBB r	1 0 0 1	1 S S S				(SSS)→TMP (A)→ACT		[9]	(ACT)-(TMP)-CY→A	
SBB M	1 0 0 1	1 1 1 0				(A)→ACT		HL OUT STATUS[6]	DATA →	TMP
SBI data	1 1 0 1	1 1 1 0				(A)→ACT		PC OUT STATUS[6]	PC = PC + 1 B2 →	TMP
INR r	0 0 D D	D 1 0 0				(DDD)→TMP (TMP) + 1→ALU	ALU→DDD			
INR M	0 0 1 1	0 1 0 0				X		HL OUT STATUS[6]	DATA → (TMP)+1 →	TMP ALU
DCR r	0 0 D D	D 1 0 1				(DDD)→TMP (TMP)+1→ALU	ALU→DDD			
DCR M	0 0 1 1	0 1 0 1				X		HL OUT STATUS[6]	DATA → (TMP)-1 →	TMP ALU
INX rp	0 0 R P	0 0 1 1				(RP) + 1 →	RP			
DCX rp	0 0 R P	1 0 1 1				(RP) - 1 →	RP			
DAD rp[8]	0 0 R P	1 0 0 1				X		(ri)→ACT	(L)→TMP, (ACT)+(TMP)→ALU	ALU→L, CY
DAA	0 0 1 0	0 1 1 1				DAA→A, FLAGS[10]				
ANA r	1 0 1 0	0 S S S				(SSS)→TMP (A)→ACT		[9]	(ACT)+(TMP)→A	
ANA M	1 0 1 0	0 1 1 0	PC OUT STATUS	PC = PC + 1	INST→TMP/IR	(A)→ACT		HL OUT STATUS[6]	DATA →	TMP

Source: Reprinted from data sheet for 8080A microprocessor with permission. Intel Corporation, Santa Clara, CA

APPENDIX TABLE D-2 (continued)

M3			M4			M5				
T1	T2[2]	T3	T1	T2[2]	T3	T1	T2[2]	T3	T4	T5
HL OUT STATUS[7]	(TMP) →	DATA BUS								
PC OUT STATUS[6]	PC = PC + 1 B3 →	rh								
↑	PC = PC + 1 B3 →	W	WZ OUT STATUS[6]	DATA →	A					
	PC = PC + 1 B3 →	W	WZ OUT STATUS[7]	(A) →	DATA BUS					
↓	PC = PC + 1 B3 →	W	WZ OUT STATUS[6]	DATA → WZ = WZ + 1	L	WZ OUT STATUS[6]	DATA → H			
PC OUT STATUS[6]	PC = PC + 1 B3 →	W	WZ OUT STATUS[7]	(L) → WZ = WZ + 1	DATA BUS	WZ OUT STATUS[7]	(H) →	DATA BUS		
[9]	(ACT)+(TMP)→A									
[9]	(ACT)+(TMP)→A									
[9]	(ACT)+(TMP)+CY→A									
[9]	(ACT)+(TMP)+CY→A									
[9]	(ACT)-(TMP)→A									
[9]	(ACT)-(TMP)→A									
[9]	(ACT)-(TMP)-CY→A									
[9]	(ACT)-(TMP)-CY→A									
HL OUT STATUS[7]	ALU →	DATA BUS								
HL OUT STATUS[7]	ALU →	DATA BUS								
(rh)→ACT	(H)→TMP (ACT)+(TMP)+CY→ALU	ALU→H, CY								
[9]	(ACT)+(TMP)→A									

APPENDIX TABLE D-2 (continued)

MNEMONIC	OP CODE		M1[1]					M2		
	$D_7 D_6 D_5 D_4$	$D_3 D_2 D_1 D_0$	T1	T2[2]	T3	T4	T5	T1	T2[2]	T3
ANI data	1 1 1 0	0 1 1 0	PC OUT STATUS	PC = PC + 1	INST→TMP/IR	(A)→ACT		PC OUT STATUS[6]	PC = PC + 1 B2 →	TMP
XRA r	1 0 1 0	1 S S S				(A)→ACT (SSS)→TMP		[9]	(ACT)+(TPM)→A	
XRA M	1 0 1 0	1 1 1 0				(A)→ACT		HL OUT STATUS[6]	DATA →	TMP
XRI data	1 1 1 0	1 1 1 0				(A)→ACT		PC OUT STATUS[6]	PC = PC + 1 B2 →	TMP
ORA r	1 0 1 1	0 S S S				(A)→ACT (SSS)→TMP		[9]	(ACT)+(TMP)→A	
ORA M	1 0 1 1	0 1 1 0				(A)→ACT		HL OUT STATUS[6]	DATA →	TMP
ORI data	1 1 1 1	0 1 1 0				(A)→ACT		PC OUT STATUS[6]	PC = PC + 1 B2 →	TMP
CMP r	1 0 1 1	1 S S S				(A)→ACT (SSS)→TMP		[9]	(ACT)-(TMP), FLAGS	
CMP M	1 0 1 1	1 1 1 0				(A)→ACT		HL OUT STATUS[6]	DATA →	TMP
CPI data	1 1 1 1	1 1 1 0				(A)→ACT		PC OUT STATUS[6]	PC = PC + 1 B2 →	TMP
RLC	0 0 0 0	0 1 1 1				(A)→ALU ROTATE		[9]	ALU→A, CY	
RRC	0 0 0 0	1 1 1 1				(A)→ALU ROTATE		[9]	ALU→A, CY	
RAL	0 0 0 1	0 1 1 1				(A), CY→ALU ROTATE		[9]	ALU→A, CY	
RAR	0 0 0 1	1 1 1 1				(A), CY→ALU ROTATE		[9]	ALU→A, CY	
CMA	0 0 1 0	1 1 1 1				$(\overline{A})$→A				
CMC	0 0 1 1	1 1 1 1				$\overline{CY}$→CY				
STC	0 0 1 1	0 1 1 1				1→CY				
JMP addr	1 1 0 0	0 0 1 1				X		PC OUT STATUS[6]	PC = PC + 1 B2 →	Z
J cond addr[17]	1 1 C C	C 0 1 0				JUDGE CONDITION		PC OUT STATUS[6]	PC = PC + 1 B2 →	Z
CALL addr	1 1 0 0	1 1 0 1				SP = SP - 1		PC OUT STATUS[6]	PC = PC + 1 B2 →	Z
C cond addr[17]	1 1 C C	C 1 0 0				JUDGE CONDITION IF TRUE, SP = SP - 1		PC OUT STATUS[6]	PC = PC + 1 B2 →	Z
RET	1 1 0 0	1 0 0 1				X		SP OUT STATUS[15]	SP = SP + 1 DATA →	Z
R cond addr[17]	1 1 C C	C 0 0 0			INST→TMP/IR	JUDGE CONDITION[14]		SP OUT STATUS[15]	SP = SP + 1 DATA →	Z
RST n	1 1 N N	N 1 1 1			φ→W INST→TMP/IR	SP = SP - 1		SP OUT STATUS[16]	SP = SP - 1 (PCH) →	DATA BUS
PCHL	1 1 1 0	1 0 0 1			INST→TMP/IR	(HL) →	PC			
PUSH rp	1 1 R P	0 1 0 1				SP = SP - 1		SP OUT STATUS[16]	SP = SP - 1 (rh) →	DATA BUS
PUSH PSW	1 1 1 1	0 1 0 1				SP = SP - 1		SP OUT STATUS[16]	SP = SP - 1 (A) →	DATA BUS
POP rp	1 1 R P	0 0 0 1				X		SP OUT STATUS[15]	SP = SP + 1 DATA →	r1
POP PSW	1 1 1 1	0 0 0 1				X		SP OUT STATUS[15]	SP = SP + 1 DATA →	FLAGS
XTHL	1 1 1 0	0 0 1 1				X		SP OUT STATUS[15]	SP = SP + 1 DATA →	Z
IN port	1 1 0 1	1 0 1 1				X		PC OUT STATUS[6]	PC = PC + 1 B2 →	Z, W
OUT port	1 1 0 1	0 0 1 1				X		PC OUT STATUS[6]	PC = PC + 1 B2 →	Z, W
EI	1 1 1 1	1 0 1 1				SET INTE F/F				
DI	1 1 1 1	0 0 1 1				RESET INTE F/F				
HLT	0 1 1 1	0 1 1 0				X		PC OUT STATUS	HALT MODE[20]	
NOP	0 0 0 0	0 0 0 0	PC OUT STATUS	PC = PC + 1	INST→TMP/IR	X				

APPENDIX TABLE D-2 (continued)

M3			M4			M5						
T1	T2[2]	T3	T1	T2[2]	T3	T1	T2[2]	T3	T4	T5		
[9]	(ACT)+(TMP)→A											
[9]	(ACT)+(TMP)→A											
[9]	(ACT)+(TMP)→A											
[9]	(ACT)+(TMP)→A											
[9]	(ACT)+(TMP)→A											
[9]	(ACT)-(TMP); FLAGS											
[9]	(ACT)-(TMP); FLAGS											
PC OUT STATUS[6]	PC = PC + 1 B3 —→	W									WZ OUT STATUS[11]	(WZ) + 1 → PC
PC OUT STATUS[6]	PC = PC + 1 B3 —→	W									WZ OUT STATUS[11,12]	(WZ) + 1 → PC
PC OUT STATUS[6]	PC = PC + 1 B3 —→	W	SP OUT STATUS[16]	(PCH) —→ SP = SP − 1	DATA BUS	SP OUT STATUS[16]	(PCL) —→	DATA BUS			WZ OUT STATUS[11]	(WZ) + 1 → PC
PC OUT STATUS[6]	PC = PC + 1 B3 —→	W[13]	SP OUT STATUS[16]	(PCH) —→ SP = SP − 1	DATA BUS	SP OUT STATUS[16]	(PCL) —→	DATA BUS			WZ OUT STATUS[11,12]	(WZ) + 1 → PC
SP OUT STATUS[15]	SP = SP + 1 DATA —→	W									WZ OUT STATUS[11]	(WZ) + 1 → PC
SP OUT STATUS[15]	SP = SP + 1 DATA —→	W									WZ OUT STATUS[11,12]	(WZ) + 1 → PC
SP OUT STATUS[16]	(TMP = 00NNN000) —→ (PCL) —→	Z DATA BUS									WZ OUT STATUS[11]	(WZ) + 1 → PC
SP OUT STATUS[16]	(rl) —→	DATA BUS										
SP OUT STATUS[16]	FLAGS —→	DATA BUS										
SP OUT STATUS[15]	SP = SP + 1 DATA —→	rh										
SP OUT STATUS[15]	SP = SP + 1 DATA —→	A										
SP OUT STATUS[15]	DATA —→	W	SP OUT STATUS[16]	(H) —→	DATA BUS	SP OUT STATUS[16]	(L) —→	DATA BUS	(WZ) —→	HL		
WZ OUT STATUS[18]	DATA —→	A										
WZ OUT STATUS[18]	(A) —→	DATA BUS										

APPENDIX TABLE D–2 (continued)

NOTES:

1. The first memory cycle (M1) is always an instruction fetch; the first (or only) byte, containing the op code, is fetched during this cycle.

2. If the READY input from memory is not high during T2 of each memory cycle, the processor will enter a wait state (TW) until READY is sampled as high.

3. States T4 and T5 are present, as required, for operations which are completely internal to the CPU. The contents of the internal bus during T4 and T5 are available at the data bus; this is designed for testing purposes only. An "X" denotes that the state is present, but is only used for such internal operations as instruction decoding.

4. Only register pairs rp = B (registers B and C) or rp = D (registers D and E) may be specified.

5. These states are skipped.

6. Memory read sub-cycles; an instruction or data word will be read.

7. Memory write sub-cycle.

8. The READY signal is not required during the second and third sub-cycles (M2 and M3). The HOLD signal is accepted during M2 and M3. The SYNC signal is not generated during M2 and M3. During the execution of DAD, M2 and M3 are required for an internal register-pair add; memory is not referenced.

9. The results of these arithmetic, logical or rotate instructions are not moved into the accumulator (A) until state T2 of the next instruction cycle. That is, A is loaded while the next instruction is being fetched; this overlapping of operations allows for faster processing.

10. If the value of the least significant 4-bits of the accumulator is greater than 9 or if the auxiliary carry bit is set, 6 is added to the accumulator. If the value of the most significant 4-bits of the accumulator is now greater than 9, or if the carry bit is set, 6 is added to the most significant 4-bits of the accumulator.

11. This represents the first sub-cycle (the instruction fetch) of the next instruction cycle.

12. If the condition was met, the contents of the register pair WZ are output on the address lines ($A_{0\text{-}15}$) instead of the contents of the program counter (PC).

13. If the condition was not met, sub-cycles M4 and M5 are skipped; the processor instead proceeds immediately to the instruction fetch (M1) of the next instruction cycle.

14. If the condition was not met, sub-cycles M2 and M3 are skipped; the processor instead proceeds immediately to the instruction fetch (M1) of the next instruction cycle.

15. Stack read sub-cycle.

16. Stack write sub-cycle.

17.

CONDITION		CCC
NZ	– not zero (Z = 0)	000
Z	– zero (Z = 1)	001
NC	– no carry (CY = 0)	010
C	– carry (CY = 1)	011
PO	– parity odd (P = 0)	100
PE	– parity even (P = 1)	101
P	– plus (S = 0)	110
M	– minus (S = 1)	111

18. I/O sub-cycle: the I/O port's 8-bit select code is duplicated on address lines 0-7 ($A_{0\text{-}7}$) and 8-15 ($A_{8\text{-}15}$).

19. Output sub-cycle.

20. The processor will remain idle in the halt state until an interrupt, a reset or a hold is accepted. When a hold request is accepted, the CPU enters the hold mode; after the hold mode is terminated, the processor returns to the halt state. After a reset is accepted, the processor begins execution at memory location zero. After an interrupt is accepted, the processor executes the instruction forced onto the data bus (usually a restart instruction).

SSS or DDD	Value	rp	Value
A	111	B	00
B	000	D	01
C	001	H	10
D	010	SP	11
E	011		
H	100		
L	101		

APPENDIX TABLE D-3 6800 Microprocessor Instruction Set in Alphabetic Order

ABA	Add Accumulators	CLR	Clear	PUL	Pull Data
ADC	Add with Carry	CLV	Clear Overflow	ROL	Rotate Left
ADD	Add	CMP	Compare	ROR	Rotate Right
AND	Logical And	COM	Complement	RTI	Return from Interrupt
ASL	Arithmetic Shift Left	CPX	Compare Index Register	RTS	Return from Subroutine
ASR	Arithmetic Shift Right	DAA	Decimal Adjust	SBA	Subtract Accumulators
BCC	Branch if Carry Clear	DEC	Decrement	SBC	Subtract with Carry
BCS	Branch if Carry Set	DES	Decrement Stack Pointer	SEC	Set Carry
BEQ	Branch if Equal to Zero	DEX	Decrement Index Register	SEI	Set Interrupt Mask
BGE	Branch if Greater or Equal Zero	EOR	Exclusive OR	SEV	Set Overflow
BGT	Branch if Greater than Zero	INC	Increment	STA	Store Accumulator
BHI	Branch if Higher	INS	Increment Stack Pointer	STS	Store Stack Register
BIT	Bit Test	INX	Increment Index Register	STX	Store Index Register
BLE	Branch if Less or Equal	JMP	Jump	SUB	Subtract
BLS	Branch if Lower or Same	JSR	Jump to Subroutine	SWI	Software Interrupt
BLT	Branch if Less than Zero	LDA	Load Accumulator	TAB	Transfer Accumulators
BMI	Branch if Minus	LDS	Load Stack Pointer	TAP	Transfer Accumulators to Condition Code Reg.
BNE	Branch if Not Equal to Zero	LDX	Load Index Register	TBA	Transfer Accumulators
BPL	Branch if Plus	LSR	Logical Shift Right	TPA	Transfer Condition Code Reg. to Accumulator
BRA	Branch Always	NEG	Negate	TST	Test
BSR	Branch to Subroutine	NOP	No Operation	TSX	Transfer Stack Pointer to Index Register
BVC	Branch if Overflow Clear	ORA	Inclusive OR Accumulator	TXS	Transfer Index Register to Stack Pointer
BVS	Branch if Overflow Set	PSH	Push Data	WAI	Wait for Interrupt
CBA	Compare Accumulators				
CLC	Clear Carry				
CLI	Clear Interrupt Mask				

Source: Reprinted from data sheet for MC6800 microprocessor with permission. Motorola Incorporated, Phoenix, AZ

APPENDIX TABLE D-4 6800 Microprocessor Accumulator and Memory Operations

		ADDRESSING MODES															BOOLEAN/ARITHMETIC OPERATION	COND. CODE REG.					
		IMMED			DIRECT			INDEX			EXTND			IMPLIED			(All register labels refer to contents)	5	4	3	2	1	0
OPERATIONS	MNEMONIC	OP	~	#	OP	~	#	OP	~	#	OP	~	#	OP	~	#		H	I	N	Z	V	C
Add	ADDA	8B	2	2	9B	3	2	AB	5	2	BB	4	3				A + M → A	↕	●	↕	↕	↕	↕
	ADDB	CB	2	2	DB	3	2	EB	5	2	FB	4	3				B + M → B	↕	●	↕	↕	↕	↕
Add Acmltrs	ABA													1B	2	1	A + B → A	↕	●	↕	↕	↕	↕
Add with Carry	ADCA	89	2	2	99	3	2	A9	5	2	B9	4	3				A + M + C → A	↕	●	↕	↕	↕	↕
	ADCB	C9	2	2	D9	3	2	E9	5	2	F9	4	3				B + M + C → B	↕	●	↕	↕	↕	↕
And	ANDA	84	2	2	94	3	2	A4	5	2	B4	4	3				A · M → A	●	●	↕	↕	R	●
	ANDB	C4	2	2	D4	3	2	E4	5	2	F4	4	3				B · M → B	●	●	↕	↕	R	●
Bit Test	BITA	85	2	2	95	3	2	A5	5	2	B5	4	3				A · M	●	●	↕	↕	R	●
	BITB	C5	2	2	D5	3	2	E5	5	2	F5	4	3				B · M	●	●	↕	↕	R	●
Clear	CLR							6F	7	2	7F	6	3				00 → M	●	●	R	S	R	R
	CLRA													4F	2	1	00 → A	●	●	R	S	R	R
	CLRB													5F	2	1	00 → B	●	●	R	S	R	R
Compare	CMPA	81	2	2	91	3	2	A1	5	2	B1	4	3				A − M	●	●	↕	↕	↕	↕
	CMPB	C1	2	2	D1	3	2	E1	5	2	F1	4	3				B − M	●	●	↕	↕	↕	↕
Compare Acmltrs	CBA													11	2	1	A − B	●	●	↕	↕	↕	↕
Complement, 1's	COM							63	7	2	73	6	3				M̄ → M	●	●	↕	↕	R	S
	COMA													43	2	1	Ā → A	●	●	↕	↕	R	S
	COMB													53	2	1	B̄ → B	●	●	↕	↕	R	S
Complement, 2's (Negate)	NEG							60	7	2	70	6	3				00 − M → M	●	●	↕	↕	①	②
	NEGA													40	2	1	00 − A → A	●	●	↕	↕	①	②
	NEGB													50	2	1	00 − B → B	●	●	↕	↕	①	②
Decimal Adjust, A	DAA													19	2	1	Converts Binary Add. of BCD Characters into BCD Format	●	●	↕	↕	↕	③
Decrement	DEC							6A	7	2	7A	6	3				M − 1 → M	●	●	↕	↕	4	●
	DECA													4A	2	1	A − 1 → A	●	●	↕	↕	4	●
	DECB													5A	2	1	B − 1 → B	●	●	↕	↕	4	●
Exclusive OR	EORA	88	2	2	98	3	2	A8	5	2	B8	4	3				A⊕M → A	●	●	↕	↕	R	●
	EORB	C8	2	2	D8	3	2	E8	5	2	F8	4	3				B⊕M → B	●	●	↕	↕	R	●
Increment	INC							6C	7	2	7C	6	3				M + 1 → M	●	●	↕	↕	⑤	●
	INCA													4C	2	1	A + 1 → A	●	●	↕	↕	⑤	●
	INCB													5C	2	1	B + 1 → B	●	●	↕	↕	⑤	●
Load Acmltr	LDAA	86	2	2	96	3	2	A6	5	2	B6	4	3				M → A	●	●	↕	↕	R	●
	LDAB	C6	2	2	D6	3	2	E6	5	2	F6	4	3				M → B	●	●	↕	↕	R	●
Or, Inclusive	ORAA	8A	2	2	9A	3	2	AA	5	2	BA	4	3				A + M → A	●	●	↕	↕	R	●
	ORAB	CA	2	2	DA	3	2	EA	5	2	FA	4	3				B + M → B	●	●	↕	↕	R	●
Push Data	PSHA													36	4	1	A → M_{SP}, SP − 1 → SP	●	●	●	●	●	●
	PSHB													37	4	1	B → M_{SP}, SP − 1 → SP	●	●	●	●	●	●
Pull Data	PULA													32	4	1	SP + 1 → SP, M_{SP} → A	●	●	●	●	●	●
	PULB													33	4	1	SP + 1 → SP, M_{SP} → B	●	●	●	●	●	●
Rotate Left	ROL							69	7	2	79	6	3				M }	●	●	↕	↕	⑥	↕
	ROLA													49	2	1	A }	●	●	↕	↕	⑥	↕
	ROLB													59	2	1	B } C ← b7 ← b0	●	●	↕	↕	⑥	↕
Rotate Right	ROR							66	7	2	76	6	3				M }	●	●	↕	↕	⑥	↕
	RORA													46	2	1	A }	●	●	↕	↕	⑥	↕
	RORB													56	2	1	B } C b7 → b0	●	●	↕	↕	⑥	↕
Shift Left, Arithmetic	ASL							68	7	2	78	6	3				M }	●	●	↕	↕	⑥	↕
	ASLA													48	2	1	A } C ← b7 b0 ← 0	●	●	↕	↕	⑥	↕
	ASLB													58	2	1	B }	●	●	↕	↕	⑥	↕
Shift Right, Arithmetic	ASR							67	7	2	77	6	3				M }	●	●	↕	↕	⑥	↕
	ASRA													47	2	1	A } b7 b0 → C	●	●	↕	↕	⑥	↕
	ASRB													57	2	1	B }	●	●	↕	↕	⑥	↕
Shift Right, Logic	LSR							64	7	2	74	6	3				M }	●	●	R	↕	⑥	↕
	LSRA													44	2	1	A } 0 → b7 b0 → C	●	●	R	↕	⑥	↕
	LSRB													54	2	1	B }	●	●	R	↕	⑥	↕
Store Acmltr	STAA				97	4	2	A7	6	2	B7	5	3				A → M	●	●	↕	↕	R	●
	STAB				D7	4	2	E7	6	2	F7	5	3				B → M	●	●	↕	↕	R	●
Subtract	SUBA	80	2	2	90	3	2	A0	5	2	B0	4	3				A − M → A	●	●	↕	↕	↕	↕
	SUBB	C0	2	2	D0	3	2	E0	5	2	F0	4	3				B − M → B	●	●	↕	↕	↕	↕
Subtract Acmltrs	SBA													10	2	1	A − B → A	●	●	↕	↕	↕	↕
Subtr. with Carry	SBCA	82	2	2	92	3	2	A2	5	2	B2	4	3				A − M − C → A	●	●	↕	↕	↕	↕
	SBCB	C2	2	2	D2	3	2	E2	5	2	F2	4	3				B − M − C → B	●	●	↕	↕	↕	↕
Transfer Acmltrs	TAB													16	2	1	A → B	●	●	↕	↕	R	●
	TBA													17	2	1	B → A	●	●	↕	↕	R	●
Test, Zero or Minus	TST							6D	7	2	7D	6	3				M − 00	●	●	↕	↕	R	R
	TSTA													4D	2	1	A − 00	●	●	↕	↕	R	R
	TSTB													5D	2	1	B − 00	●	●	↕	↕	R	R
																		H	I	N	Z	V	C

LEGEND:

- OP Operation Code (Hexadecimal);
- ~ Number of MPU Cycles;
- # Number of Program Bytes;
- + Arithmetic Plus;
- − Arithmetic Minus;
- · Boolean AND;
- M_{SP} Contents of memory location pointed to be Stack Pointer;
- + Boolean Inclusive OR;
- ⊕ Boolean Exclusive OR;
- M̄ Complement of M;
- → Transfer Into;
- 0 Bit = Zero;
- 00 Byte = Zero;

CONDITION CODE SYMBOLS:

- H Half-carry from bit 3;
- I Interrupt mask
- N Negative (sign bit)
- Z Zero (byte)
- V Overflow, 2's complement
- C Carry from bit 7
- R Reset Always
- S Set Always
- ↕ Test and set if true, cleared otherwise
- ● Not Affected

CONDITION CODE REGISTER NOTES:

(Bit set if test is true and cleared otherwise)

1 (Bit V) Test: Result = 10000000?
2 (Bit C) Test: Result = 00000000?
3 (Bit C) Test: Decimal value of most significant BCD Character greater than nine? (Not cleared if previously set.)
4 (Bit V) Test: Operand = 10000000 prior to execution?
5 (Bit V) Test: Operand = 01111111 prior to execution?
6 (Bit V) Test: Set equal to result of N⊕C after shift has occurred.

Note – Accumulator addressing mode instructions are included in the column for IMPLIED addressing

Source: Reprinted from data sheet for MC6800 microprocessor with permission. Motorola Incorporated, Phoenix, AZ

APPENDIX TABLE D-5 6800 Microprocessor Index Register and Stack Pointer Operations

		IMMED			DIRECT			INDEX			EXTND			IMPLIED				COND. CODE REG. 5	4	3	2	1	0
POINTER OPERATIONS	MNEMONIC	OP	~	=	OP	~	=	OP	~	=	OP	~	=	OP	~	=	BOOLEAN/ARITHMETIC OPERATION	H	I	N	Z	V	C
Compare Index Reg	CPX	8C	3	3	9C	4	2	AC	6	2	BC	5	3				$X_H - M, X_L - (M+1)$	•	•	①	↕	②	•
Decrement Index Reg	DEX													09	4	1	$X - 1 \to X$	•	•	•	↕	•	•
Decrement Stack Pntr	DES													34	4	1	$SP - 1 \to SP$	•	•	•	•	•	•
Increment Index Reg	INX													08	4	1	$X + 1 \to X$	•	•	•	↕	•	•
Increment Stack Pntr	INS													31	4	1	$SP + 1 \to SP$	•	•	•	•	•	•
Load Index Reg	LDX	CE	3	3	DE	4	2	EE	6	2	FE	5	3				$M \to X_H, (M+1) \to X_L$	•	•	③	↕	R	•
Load Stack Pntr	LDS	8E	3	3	9E	4	2	AE	6	2	BE	5	3				$M \to SP_H, (M+1) \to SP_L$	•	•	③	↕	R	•
Store Index Reg	STX				DF	5	2	EF	7	2	FF	6	3				$X_H \to M, X_L \to (M+1)$	•	•	③	↕	R	•
Store Stack Pntr	STS				9F	5	2	AF	7	2	BF	6	3				$SP_H \to M, SP_L \to (M+1)$	•	•	③	↕	R	•
Indx Reg → Stack Pntr	TXS													35	4	1	$X - 1 \to SP$	•	•	•	•	•	•
Stack Pntr → Indx Reg	TSX													30	4	1	$SP + 1 \to X$	•	•	•	•	•	•

① (Bit N) Test: Sign bit of most significant (MS) byte of result = 1?
② (Bit V) Test: 2's complement overflow from subtraction of ms bytes?
③ (Bit N) Test: Result less than zero? (Bit 15 = 1)

Source: Reprinted from data sheet for MC6800 microprocessor with permission. Motorola Incorporated, Phoenix, AZ

APPENDIX TABLE D-6 6800 Microprocessor Jump and Branch Operations

		RELATIVE			INDEX			EXTND			IMPLIED				COND. CODE REG. 5	4	3	2	1	0
OPERATIONS	MNEMONIC	OP	~	#	OP	~	#	OP	~	#	OP	~	#	BRANCH TEST	H	I	N	Z	V	C
Branch Always	BRA	20	4	2										None	•	•	•	•	•	•
Branch If Carry Clear	BCC	24	4	2										C = 0	•	•	•	•	•	•
Branch If Carry Set	BCS	25	4	2										C = 1	•	•	•	•	•	•
Branch If = Zero	BEQ	27	4	2										Z = 1	•	•	•	•	•	•
Branch If ≥ Zero	BGE	2C	4	2										$N \oplus V = 0$	•	•	•	•	•	•
Branch If > Zero	BGT	2E	4	2										$Z + (N \oplus V) = 0$	•	•	•	•	•	•
Branch If Higher	BHI	22	4	2										C + Z = 0	•	•	•	•	•	•
Branch If ≤ Zero	BLE	2F	4	2										$Z + (N \oplus V) = 1$	•	•	•	•	•	•
Branch If Lower Or Same	BLS	23	4	2										C + Z = 1	•	•	•	•	•	•
Branch If < Zero	BLT	2D	4	2										$N \oplus V = 1$	•	•	•	•	•	•
Branch If Minus	BMI	2B	4	2										N = 1	•	•	•	•	•	•
Branch If Not Equal Zero	BNE	26	4	2										Z = 0	•	•	•	•	•	•
Branch If Overflow Clear	BVC	28	4	2										V = 0	•	•	•	•	•	•
Branch If Overflow Set	BVS	29	4	2										V = 1	•	•	•	•	•	•
Branch If Plus	BPL	2A	4	2										N = 0	•	•	•	•	•	•
Branch To Subroutine	BSR	8D	8	2										See Special Operations	•	•	•	•	•	•
Jump	JMP				6E	4	2	7E	3	3				See Special Operations	•	•	•	•	•	•
Jump To Subroutine	JSR				AD	8	2	BD	9	3				See Special Operations	•	•	•	•	•	•
No Operation	NOP										01	2	1	Advances Prog. Cntr. Only	•	•	•	•	•	•
Return From Interrupt	RTI										3B	10	1		①	①	①	①	①	①
Return From Subroutine	RTS										39	5	1	See Special Operations	•	•	•	•	•	•
Software Interrupt	SWI										3F	12	1	See Special Operations	•	•	•	•	•	•
Wait for Interrupt*	WAI										3E	9	1	See Special Operations	•	②	•	•	•	•

*WAI puts Address Bus, R/W, and Data Bus in the three-state mode while VMA is held low.

① (All) Load Condition Code Register from Stack. (See Special Operations)
② (Bit 1) Set when interrupt occurs. If previously set, a Non-Maskable Interrupt is required to exit the wait state.

Source: Reprinted from data sheet for MC6800 microprocessor with permission. Motorola Incorporated, Phoenix, AZ

APPENDIX TABLE D-7 6800 Microprocessor Special Operations

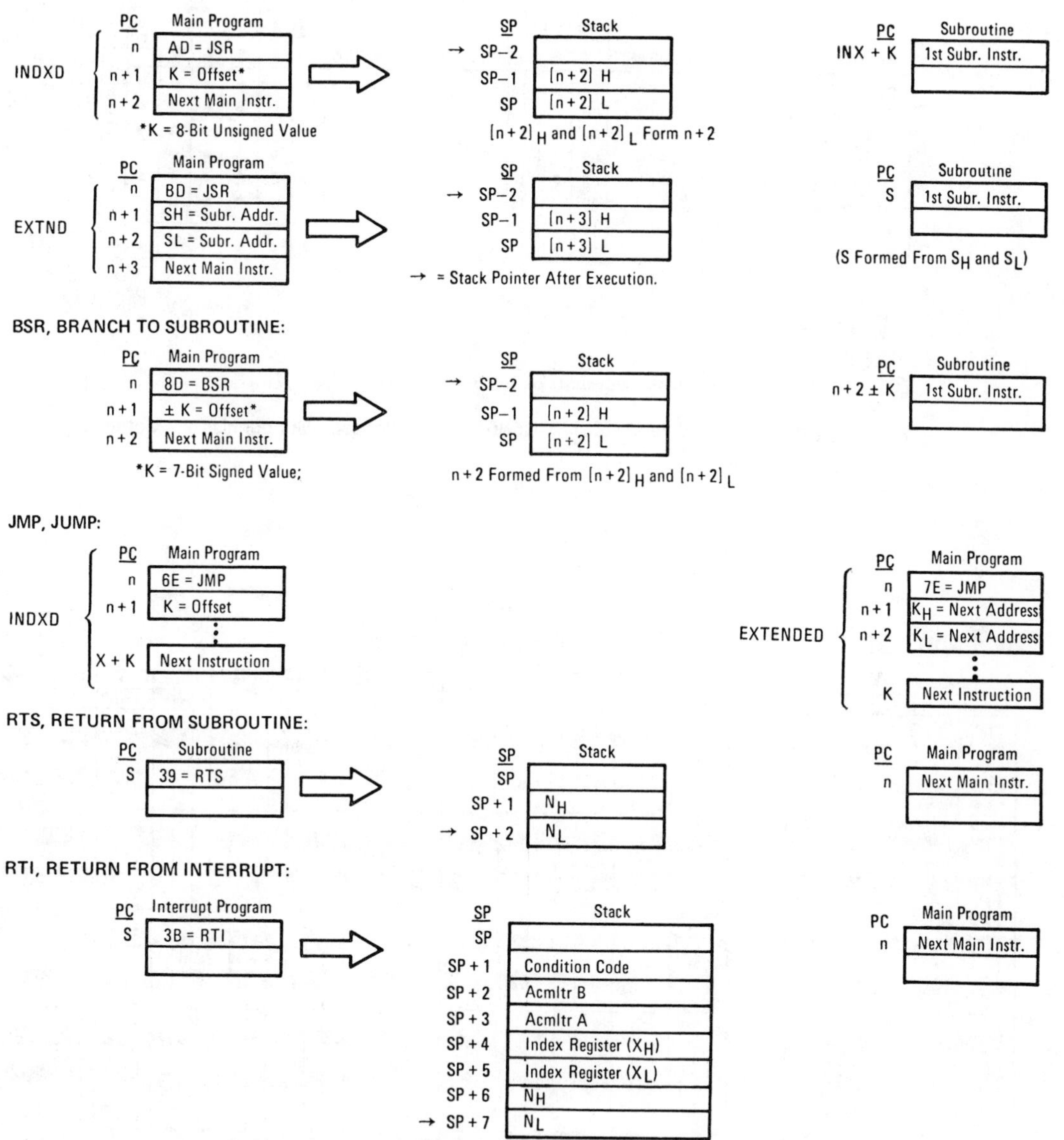

Source: Reprinted from data sheet for MC6800 microprocessor with permission. Motorola Incorporated, Phoenix, AZ

APPENDIX TABLE D-8 6800 Microprocessor Condition Code Register Operations

		IMPLIED				COND. CODE REG.					
						5	4	3	2	1	0
OPERATIONS	MNEMONIC	OP	~	=	BOOLEAN OPERATION	H	I	N	Z	V	C
Clear Carry	CLC	0C	2	1	0 → C	●	●	●	●	●	R
Clear Interrupt Mask	CLI	0E	2	1	0 → I	●	R	●	●	●	●
Clear Overflow	CLV	0A	2	1	0 → V	●	●	●	●	R	●
Set Carry	SEC	0D	2	1	1 → C	●	●	●	●	●	S
Set Interrupt Mask	SEI	0F	2	1	1 → I	●	S	●	●	●	●
Set Overflow	SEV	0B	2	1	1 → V	●	●	●	●	S	●
Acmltr A → CCR	TAP	06	2	1	A → CCR	①					
CCR → Acmltr A	TPA	07	2	1	CCR → A	●	●	●	●	●	●

R = Reset
S = Set
● = Not affected

① (ALL) Set according to the contents of Accumulator A.

Source: Reprinted from data sheet for MC6800 microprocessor with permission. Motorola Incorporated, Phoenix, AZ

APPENDIX TABLE D-9 Summary of 6502 Mircroprocessor Instructions

INSTRUCTIONS		IMMEDIATE			ABSOLUTE			ZERO PAGE			ACCUM.			IMPLIED			(IND,X)		
MNEMONIC	OPERATION	OP	N	#	OP	N	#	OP	N	#	OP	N	#	OP	N	#	OP	N	#
ADC	A+M+C → A (4) (1)	69	2	2	6D	4	3	65	3	2							61	6	2
AND	A∧M → A (1)	29	2	2	2D	4	3	25	3	2							21	6	2
ASL	C ← [7 … 0] ← 0				0E	6	3	06	5	2	0A	2	1						
BCC	BRANCH ON C=0 (2)																		
BCS	BRANCH ON C=1 (2)																		
BEQ	BRANCH ON Z=1 (2)																		
BIT	A∧M				2C	4	3	24	3	2									
BMI	BRANCH ON N=1 (2)																		
BNE	BRANCH ON Z=0 (2)																		
BPL	BRANCH ON N=0 (2)																		
BRK	(See Fig. 1)													00	7	1			
BVC	BRANCH ON V=0 (2)																		
BVS	BRANCH ON V=1 (2)																		
CLC	0 → C													18	2	1			
CLD	0 → D													D8	2	1			
CLI	0 → I													58	2	1			
CLV	0 → V													B8	2	1			
CMP	A−M (1)	C9	2	2	CD	4	3	C5	3	2							C1	6	2
CPX	X−M	E0	2	2	EC	4	3	E4	3	2									
CPY	Y−M	C0	2	2	CC	4	3	C4	3	2									
DEC	M−1 → M				CE	6	3	C6	5	2									
DEX	X−1 → X													CA	2	1			
DEY	Y−1 → Y													88	2	1			
EOR	A⊻M → A (1)	49	2	2	4D	4	3	45	3	2							41	6	2
INC	M+1 → M				EE	6	3	E6	5	2									
INX	X+1 → X													E8	2	1			
INY	Y+1 → Y													C8	2	1			
JMP	JUMP TO NEW LOC				4C	3	3												
JSR	(See Fig. 2) JUMP SUB				20	6	3												
LDA	M → A (1)	A9	2	2	AD	4	3	A5	3	2							A1	6	2

MNEMONIC	(IND),Y			Z,PAGE,X			ABS,X			ABS,Y			RELATIVE			INDIRECT			Z,PAGE,Y			CONDITION CODES					
	OP	N	#	OP	N	#	OP	N	#	OP	N	#	OP	N	#	OP	N	#	OP	N	#	N	Z	C	I	D	V
ADC	71	5	2	75	4	2	7D	4	3	79	4	3										✓	✓	✓	-	-	✓
AND	31	5	2	35	4	2	3D	4	3	39	4	3										✓	✓	-	-	-	-
ASL				16	6	2	1E	7	3													✓	✓	✓	-	-	-
BCC													90	2	2							-	-	-	-	-	-
BCS													B0	2	2							-	-	-	-	-	-
BEQ													F0	2	2							-	-	-	-	-	-
BIT																						M_7	✓	-	-	-	M_6
BMI													30	2	2							-	-	-	-	-	-
BNE													D0	2	2							-	-	-	-	-	-
BPL													10	2	2							-	-	-	-	-	-
BRK																						-	-	-	1	-	-
BVC													50	2	2							-	-	-	-	-	-
BVS													70	2	2							-	-	-	-	-	-
CLC																						-	-	0	-	-	-
CLD																						-	-	-	-	0	-
CLI																						-	-	-	0	-	-
CLV																						-	-	-	-	-	0
CMP	D1	5	2	D5	4	2	DD	4	3	D9	4	3										✓	✓	✓	-	-	-
CPX																						✓	✓	✓	-	-	-
CPY																						✓	✓	✓	-	-	-
DEC				D6	6	2	DE	7	3													✓	✓	-	-	-	-
DEX																						✓	✓	-	-	-	-
DEY																						✓	✓	-	-	-	-
EOR	51	5	2	55	4	2	5D	4	3	59	4	3										✓	✓	-	-	-	-
INC				F6	6	2	FE	7	3													✓	✓	-	-	-	-
INX																						✓	✓	-	-	-	-
INY																						✓	✓	-	-	-	-
JMP																6C	5	3				-	-	-	-	-	-
JSR																						-	-	-	-	-	-
LDA	B1	5	2	B5	4	2	BD	4	3	B9	4	3										✓	✓	-	-	-	-

Source: Reprinted from MCS6500 instruction set summary with permission. Commodore Business Machines, Inc., MOS Technology, Division, Norristown, PA.

APPENDIX TABLE D-9 (continued)

MNEMONIC	OPERATION	IMMEDIATE OP	N	#	ABSOLUTE OP	N	#	ZERO PAGE OP	N	#	ACCUM. OP	N	#	IMPLIED OP	N	#	(IND,X) OP	N	#
LDX	M → X (1)	A2	2	2	AE	4	3	A6	3	2									
LDY	M → Y (1)	A0	2	2	AC	4	3	A4	3	2									
LSR	0 → [7 … 0] → C				4E	6	3	46	5	2	4A	2	1						
NOP	NO OPERATION													EA	2	1			
ORA	A V M → A	09	2	2	0D	4	3	05	3	2							01	6	2
PHA	A → Ms S−1 → S													48	3	1			
PHP	P → Ms S−1 → S													08	3	1			
PLA	S+1 → S Ms → A													68	4	1			
PLP	S+1 → S Ms → P													28	4	1			
ROL	[7 … 0] ← [C] (rotate left)				2E	6	3	26	5	2	2A	2	1						
ROR	[C] → [7 … 0] (rotate right)				6E	6	3	66	5	2	6A	2	1						
RTI	(See Fig. 1) RTRN. INT.													40	6	1			
RTS	(See Fig. 2) RTRN SUB													60	6	1			
SBC	A−M−C̄ → A (1)	E9	2	2	ED	4	3	E5	3	2							E1	6	2
SEC	1 → C													38	2	1			
SED	1 → D													F8	2	1			
SEI	1 → I													78	2	1			
STA	A → M				8D	4	3	85	3	2							81	6	2
STX	X → M				8E	4	3	86	3	2									
STY	Y → M				8C	4	3	84	3	2									
TAX	A → X													AA	2	1			
TAY	A → Y													A8	2	1			
TSX	S → X													BA	2	1			
TXA	X → A													8A	2	1			
TXS	X → S													9A	2	1			
TYA	Y → A													98	2	1			

MNEMONIC	(IND),Y OP	N	#	Z, PAGE, X OP	N	#	ABS, X OP	N	#	ABS, Y OP	N	#	RELATIVE OP	N	#	INDIRECT OP	N	#	Z, PAGE, Y OP	N	#	N	Z	C	I	D	V
LDX										BE	4	3							B6	4	2	✓	✓	-	-	-	-
LDY				B4	4	2	BC	4	3													✓	✓	-	-	-	-
LSR				56	6	2	5E	7	3													0	✓	✓	-	-	-
NOP																						-	-	-	-	-	-
ORA	11	5	2	15	4	2	1D	4	3	19	4	3										✓	✓	-	-	-	-
PHA																						-	-	-	-	-	-
PHP																						-	-	-	-	-	-
PLA																						✓	✓	-	-	-	-
PLP																						(RESTORED)					
ROL				36	6	2	3E	7	3													✓	✓	✓	-	-	-
ROR				76	6	2	7E	7	3													✓	✓	✓	-	-	-
RTI																						(RESTORED)					
RTS																						-	-	-	-	-	-
SBC	F1	5	2	F5	4	2	FD	4	3	F9	4	3										✓	✓	(3)	-	-	✓
SEC																						-	-	1	-	-	-
SED																						-	-	-	-	1	-
SEI																						-	-	-	1	-	-
STA	91	6	2	95	4	2	9D	5	3	99	5	3										-	-	-			
STX																			96	4	2	-	-	-	-	-	-
STY				94	4	2																-	-	-	-	-	-
TAX																						✓	✓	-	-	-	-
TAY																						✓	✓	-	-	-	-
TSX																						✓	✓	-			
TXA																						✓	✓	-	-	-	-
TXS																						-	-	-	-		
TYA																						✓	✓	-	-	-	-

(1) ADD 1 TO "N" IF PAGE BOUNDRY IS CROSSED
(2) ADD 1 TO "N" IF BRANCH OCCURS TO SAME PAGE.
ADD 2 TO "N" IF BRANCH OCCURS TO DIFFERENT PAGE.
(3) CARRY NOT = BORROW.
(4) IF IN DECIMAL MODE Z FLAG IS INVALID.
ACCUMULATOR MUST BE CHECKED FOR ZERO RESULT.

X INDEX . X
Y INDEX Y
A ACCUMULATOR
M MEMORY PER EFFECTIVE ADDRESS
Ms MEMORY PER STACK POINTER

+ ADD
− SUBTRACT
∧ AND
V OR

⊻ EXCLUSIVE OR
✓ MODIFIED
- NOT MODIFIED
M_7 MEMORY BIT 7
M_6 MEMORY BIT 6

N NO. CYCLES
\# NO. BYTES

OP - CODE TABLE

MSD \ LSD	0	1	2	3	4	5	6	7	8	9	A	B	C	D	E	F	LSD / MSD
0	BRK	ORA-IND, X				ORA-Z, Page	ASL-Z,PAGE		PHP	ORA-IMM	ASL A			ORA ABS	ASL-ABS		0
1	BPL	ORA-IND, Y				ORA-Z, Page,X	ASL-Z,Page,X		CLC	ORA-ABS,Y				ORA ABS, X	ASL-ABS, X		1
2	JSR	AND-IND,X			BIT-Z,Page	AND-Z, Page	ROL-Z, Page		PLP	AND-IMM	ROL A		BIT ABS	AND ABS	ROL-ABS		2
3	BMI	AND-IND,Y				AND-Z,Page,X	ROL-Z,Page,X		SEC	AND-ABS,Y				AND ABS,X	ROL-ABS,X		3
4	RTI	EOR-IND,X				EOR Z, Page	LSR-Z,Page		PHA	EOR-IMM	LSR-A		JMP-ABS	EOR ABS	LSR ABS		4
5	BVC	EOR-IND,Y				EOR-Z,Page,X	LSR-Z,Page,X		CLI	EOR-ABS,Y				EOR ABS, X	LSR-ABS, X		5
6	RTS	ADC-IND, X				ADC-Z, Page			PLA	ADC-IMM			JMP IND	ADC-ABS			6
7	BVS	ADC-IND, Y				ADC-Z,Page,X			SEI	ADC-ABS,Y				ADC-ABS, X			7
8		STA-IND, X			STY-Z, Page	STA-Z, Page	STX-Z Page		DEY		TXA		STY-ABS	STA-ABS	STX-ABS		8
9	BCC	STA-IND, Y			STY-Z,Page,X	STA-Z,Page,X	STX-Z,Page,Y		TYA	STA-ABS, Y	TXS			STA-ABS, X			9
A	LDY-IMM	LDA-IND, X	LDX-IMM		LDY-Z,Page	LDA-Z, Page	LDX-Z, Page		TAY	LDA-IMM	TAX		LDY ABS	LDA ABS	LDX-ABS		A
B	BCS	LDA-IND, Y			LDY-Z,Page,X	LDA-Z,Page,X	LDX-Z, Page,Y		CLV	LDA-ABS, Y	TSX		LDY ABS, X	LDA-ABS, X	LDX-ABS, Y		B
C	CPY-IMM	CMP-IND, X			CPY-Z Page	CMP-Z, Page	DEC-Z Page		INY	CMP-IMM	DEX		CPY ABS	CMP ABS	DEC-ABS		C
D	BNE	CMP-IND, Y				CMP-Z,Page,X	DEC-Z,Page,X		CLD	CMP-ABS, Y				CMP ABS, X	DEC-ABS, X		D
E	CPX-IMM	SBC-IND, X			CPX-Z Page	SBC-Z, Page	INC-Z, Page		INX	SBC-IMM	NOP		CPX ABS	SBC ABS	INC-ABS		E
F	BEQ	SBC-IND, Y				SBC-Z,Page,X	INC-Z,Page,X		SED	SBC-ABS, Y				SBC ABS, X	INC-ABS, X		F

IMM - IMMEDIATE ADDRESSING – THE OPERAND IS CONTAINED IN THE SECOND BYTE OF THE INSTRUCTION.

ABS - ABSOLUTE ADDRESSING – THE SECOND BYTE OF THE INSTRUCTION CONTAINS THE 8 LOW ORDER BITS OF THE EFFECTIVE ADDRESS. THE THIRD BYTE CONTAINS THE 8 HIGH ORDER BITS OF THE EFFECTIVE ADDRESS.

Z. PAGE- ZERO PAGE ADDRESSING – SECOND BYTE CONTAINS THE 8 LOW ORDER BITS OF THE EFFECTIVE ADDRESS. THE 8 HIGH ORDER BITS ARE ZERO.

A. - ACCUMULATOR – ONE BYTE INSTRUCTION OPERATING ON THE ACCUMULATOR.

Z. PAGE,X - Z. PAGE,Y - ZERO PAGE INDEXED – THE SECOND BYTE OF THE INSTRUCTION IS ADDED TO THE INDEX (CARRY IS DROPPED) TO FORM THE LOW ORDER BYTE OF THE EA. THE HIGH ORDER BYTE OF THE EA IS ZEROS.

ABS,X ABS,Y ABSOLUTE INDEXED THE EFFECTIVE ADDRESS IS FORMED BY ADDING THE INDEX TO THE SECOND AND THIRD BYTE OF THE INSTRUCTION

(IND, X) - INDEXED INDIRECT – THE SECOND BYTE OF THE INSTRUCTION IS ADDED TO THE X-INDEX, DISCARDING THE CARRY. THE RESULTS POINTS TO A LOCATION ON PAGE ZERO WHICH CONTAINS THE 8 LOW ORDER BITS OF THE EA. THE NEXT BYTE CONTAINS THE 8 HIGH ORDER BITS

(IND),Y - INDIRECT INDEXED – THE SECOND BYTE OF THE INSTRUCTION POINTS TO A LOCATION IN PAGE ZERO. THE CONTENTS OF THIS MEMORY LOCATION IS ADDED TO THE Y INDEX, THE RESULT BEING THE LOW ORDER EIGHT BITS OF THE EA. THE CARRY FROM THIS OPERATION IS ADDED TO THE CONTENTS OF THE NEXT PAGE ZERO LOCATION, THE RESULT BEING THE 8 HIGH ORDER BITS OF THE EA.

Index